MEDIEVAL ARCHAEOLOGY

MEDIEVAL ARCHAEOLOGY
AN ENCYCLOPEDIA

EDITED BY
PAM J. CRABTREE
New York University

GARLAND PUBLISHING, INC.
NEW YORK & LONDON
2001

Published in 2001 by
Garland Publishing, Inc.
29 West 35th Street
New York, NY 10001

Garland is an imprint of the Taylor & Francis Group.

10   9   8   7   6   5   4   3   2   1

Library of Congress Cataloging-in-Publication Data

Medieval archaeology : an encyclopedia / edited by Pam J. Crabtree.
        p. cm.
    Includes bibliographical references and index.
    ISBN 0-8153-1286-5 (acid-free paper)
        1. Europe—Antiquities—Dictionaries.   2. Archaeology, Medieval—Dictionaries.
    3. Excavations (Archaeology)—Europe—Dictionaries.   I. Crabtree, Pam J.

D125 .M42 2000
936—dc21

                                                              00-056156

Printed on acid-free, 250-year-life paper
Manufactured in the United States of America

For Bernard Wailes
with thanks

CONTENTS

PREFACE

Medieval archaeology is one of the fastest-growing fields in archaeology today. Road construction and urban redevelopment have led to the discovery of new rural sites and to major programs of urban excavation in cities such as Winchester, York, Trondheim, and Lübeck. The rich medieval archaeological database has been used to address a range of important theoretical concerns in contemporary archaeology. Carefully collected faunal and floral data have been used to address problems of human economy and the natural environment in the Middle Ages. Data from medieval excavations, especially when combined with detailed documentary research, are especially well suited to addressing some of the important issues in post-processual archaeological theory, including questions of gender, agency, and power. In addition, the Medieval period in Europe witnesses the origin and growth of cities, the development of long-distance trade and craft specialization, and the formation of political states. These processes of cultural and economic change have been of interest to archaeologists since the days of V. Gordon Childe. As a result, medieval archaeology is playing an increasingly important role in archaeological thinking throughout the world.

While medieval archaeology plays an increasingly important role in contemporary archaeological debate, the discipline itself remains fragmented. Although some medieval archaeologists, especially in the United Kingdom and Scandinavia, are housed in stand-alone departments of archaeology or programs in medieval archaeology, many others find themselves in departments of history, anthropology, and classics. Medieval archaeologists also work in museums, and still others are part of ongoing archaeological units or research programs. In addition, medieval archaeologists are trained in a variety of ways. Many archaeologists who work in the Dark Ages (migration period) are trained as prehistorians, while archaeologists who specialize in the High Middle Ages are often trained as art historians or historians. One of the goals of this encyclopedia is to bring together in one volume the research of a diverse range of scholars who work on a wide variety of archaeological problems.

In order to accomplish this goal, medieval archaeology has been defined as broadly as possible. The Middle Ages begin with the collapse of the Western Roman Empire in the fifth century, and end with the dawn of the Modern Era, ca. A.D. 1500. Several entries also address the Iron Age background to medieval society and the collapse of the Roman Empire in the West. The geographical range is equally broad. This encyclopedia focuses primarily on the Latin west, stretching from Poland to Iceland and from southern Italy to northern Scandinavia. An entry on the important medieval excavations in Novgorod, Russia, has also been included. However, the encyclopedia excludes the archaeology of the Byzantine world and the Balkans.

This volume is designed to provide the interested reader with a guide to contemporary research in medieval archaeology. It includes country and regional surveys for many areas of Europe, entries that focus on major archaeological sites and research programs, and entries that deal with specific technologies and archaeological concepts. For example, the encyclopedia includes entries on dendrochronology and radiocarbon dating as well as entries on medieval cloth-making and jewelry. The entries are followed by detailed bibliographies that include suggestions for further readings. The encyclopedia includes a number of entries on sites and research programs in east-central

Europe. Archaeological research by Czech, Slovak, Polish, and Hungarian archaeologists has not been widely available in English until now. These entries should be of especial interest to both archaeological students and established scholars.

In consulting the entries in this encyclopedia, it is important to remember that archaeology is an ongoing process of excavation and analysis. New discoveries are made each year, and new techniques of analysis can be applied to materials that were excavated many years ago. The World Wide Web is an important source for information about new discoveries in medieval archaeology.

Pam J. Crabtree

ACKNOWLEDGMENTS

The preparation of an encyclopedia of medieval archaeology is a daunting task, especially for an American archaeologist. All of my colleagues conduct their archaeological research in Europe, and many also live and work in Europe. The Internet and the fax machine made this project possible. I would like to begin by thanking all my colleagues who so graciously agreed to contribute to this encyclopedia. Without their generosity and patience, this encyclopedia would never have been completed. I am especially grateful to my colleagues for sharing the details of their ongoing research and for providing the wonderful photographs and drawings that illustrate this encyclopedia.

My colleagues and students at New York University also made this project possible. I am particularly grateful to the students in my medieval archaeology courses in 1994, 1997, and 2000 who provided support and encouragement throughout the long development of this project. My current and past M.A. and Ph.D. students contributed to this project, and I would like to thank all of them. Special thanks go to Dr. Julie Zimmermann Holt, who translated several of the German entries, and to Maura Smale and Thalia Gray, who contributed entries. I am also grateful for the support of my friends and colleagues at the Anthropology Department at New York University.

I would like to thank Richard Steins of Garland Publishing for helping me see this project to completion. I would also like to thank my family—Doug, Mike, Tom, and Robby—for their support, help, and patience. And last, I will be forever grateful to Professor Bernard Wailes, my Ph.D. advisor at the University of Pennsylvania, who introduced me to medieval archaeology and who has supported me throughout my academic career.

Pam J. Crabtree

CONTRIBUTORS

Alcock, L.
Department of Archaeology
University of Glasgow

Ambrosiani, B.
Birka Excavations

Ammerman, A.
Department of Classics
Colgate University

Anderson, H.
Forhistorsk Museum
Moesgård

Ayres, B.
Norfolk Archaeological Unit

Baillie, M.G.L.
Queen's University
Belfast

Baker, E.
Bedfordshire County Archaeology Service

Baker, N.J.
School of Geography
University of Birmingham

Barford, P.M.
Institute of Archaeology
University of Warsaw

Barry, T.
Department of Medieval History
Trinity College
Dublin

Bartosiewicz, L.
Archaeological Institute
Hungarian Academy of Sciences

Batey, C.
Glasgow Museums

Blair, C.
Center for Ancient Studies
University of Minnesota

Bonet, C.
Archéologue Cantonal
Genève, Switzerland

Busch, R.
Director
Hamburg Museum of Archaeology and History

Butler, L.A.S.
Department of Archaeology
University of York

Carlsson, D.
Gotland University College

Carr, K.E.
Department of History
Portland State University

Carver, M.
Professor of Archaeology
University of York

Cejnková, D.
Museum of the City of Brno

Christie, N.
School of Archaeological Studies
University of Leicester

Clark, D.
Mucking Excavation Project

Crabtree, P.
Anthropology Department
New York University

Crumley, C.
Department of Anthropology
University of North Carolina–Chapel Hill

Daniels, R.
Archaeological Section
Cleveland County Council

Dix, B.
Northamptonshire Archaeology

Driscoll, S.
Glasgow University Archaeological Research Division

Egan, G.
Museum of London

Ellmers, D.
Director, Deutsches Schiffahrtmuseum

Fehring, G.
City of Lübeck Excavations

Filmer-Sankey, W.
Snape Historical Trust

Fisher, G.
Peabody Museum
Harvard University

Gardini, A.
Genova Excavations

Gelling, M.
Department of Ancient History and Archaeology
University of Birmingham

Gibson, B.
Dysert O'Dea Excavations

Godbold, S.
Westbury Press

Goodburn, M.
Museum of London

Gray, T.
Anthropology Department
New York University

Greene, J.P.
Museum of Science and Industry
Manchester

Gustin, I.
University of Lund

Haith, C.
London

Hall, A.
Environmental Archaeology Unit
University of York

Hall, D.
Department of Archaeology
University of Cambridge

Heckett, E.W.
Department of Archaeology
University College Cork

Heidinga, H.A.
IPP
University of Amsterdam

Highham, N.J.
Department of History
University of Manchester

Hill, D.
University of Manchester

Hills, C.
Department of Archaeology
University of Cambridge

Hindle, P.
Department of Geography
University of Salford

Hlavicová, J.
Academia Istropolitana

Hollinrake, C.
Glastonbury

Hollinrake, N.
Glastonbury

Huml, V.
Museum of the City of Prague

Janssen, W.
University of Würzburg

Jones, E.A.
Department of Anthropology
University of North Carolina–Chapel Hill

Jones, R.H.
Planning and Development Services
Bristol City Council

Klapste, J.
Institute of Archaeology
Prague

Klingelhofer, E.
Department of History
Mercer University

Knüsel, C.
Department of Archaeological Science
University of Bradford

Lane, A.
School of History and Archaeology
University of Wales

La Rocca, C.
Department of History
University of Padua

Legoux, R.
Nantes, France

Loskotivá, I.
Museum of the City of Brno

MacDonald, K.
Institute of Archaeology
University College
London

MacDonald, R. H.
Cambridge University

Malm, G.
Central Board of Antiquities
Sweden

McCormick, F.
Queen's University
Belfast

McGovern, T.H.
Hunter College, CUNY

McLees, C.
Norwegian Institute for Cultural Heritage Research

McNeill, T.
Queen's University
Belfast

Meduna, P.
Ustav Archeologické Panátkové Péce Severozápních Cech

Moreland, J.
Department of Archaeology and Prehistory
University of Sheffield

Morris, C.
Department of Archaeology
University of Glasgow

Murphy, P.
University of East Anglia

Muslow, R.
Kulturhistoriches Museum der Hansestadt Rostock

Mytum, H.
Department of Archaeology
University of York

Newman, J.
Archaeology Section
Suffolk County Planning Department

Nice, A.
Collège Jean Murmoz
Laon

O'Connor, T.
Department of Archaeology
University of York

Ottoway, P.
York Archaeological Trust

Parczewski, S.
Instytut Archeologii
Kraków

Perdikaris, S.
Department of Anthropology
CUNY Graduate Center

Plachá, V.
Mestské Múzeum
Bratislava

Qualmann, K.
Winchester Archaeological Unit

Racinet, P.
Université Paris-Nord

Rackham, O.
Corpus Christi College
Cambridge University

Redknap, M.
School of History and Archaeology
University of Wales

Renoux, A.
Université du Maine

Roberts, C.
Department of Archaeological Sciences
University of Bradford

Roesdahl, E.
Department of Medieval Archaeology
Aarhus

Rogerson, A.
Norfolk Landscape Archaeology

Rötting, H.
Neidersächsisches Landesverweltungsamt

Rybina, E.
Novgorod

Rynne, C.
Department of Archaeology
University College Cork

Sabo, K.
University of Lund

Scott, B.
Program in Ancient Studies
University of Minnesota

Smale, M.
Anthropology Department
New York University

Stahl, A.
University of Michigan

Stephan, H.G.
Seminar für Ur- und Frühgeschichte der Georg-August
Universität

Stopford, J.
Department of Archaeology
University of York

Sveinbjarnardottír, G.
London

Taavitsainen, J.-P.
National Board of Antiquities
Helsinki

Tabaczyński, S.
Institute of Archaeology and Ethnology
Polish Academy of Sciences

TeBrake, W.
Department of History
University of Maine

Thurston, T.
Department of Anthropology
University of Wisconsin-Madison

Van de Noort, R.
Humber Wetlands Project
University of Hull

Van Doornick, F.
Department of Anthropology
Texas A&M University

Verhoeven, A.
Instituut voor Prae- en Protohistoire
University of Amsterdam

Vermeulen, F.
Universiteit Gent

Vince, A.
City of Lincoln Archaeology Unit

Wade, K.
County Archaeologist
Suffolk

Ward, S.
Field Archaeological Officer
Chester Co. Council

Wells, P.S.
Department of Anthropology
University of Minnesota

Wicker, N.
Art Department
Minnesota State University, Mankato

Wollett, J.
Anthropology Department
CUNY Graduate Center

Worthington, M.
University of Manchester

Wrathmell, S.
Skipton, North Yorkshire

Yoon, D.
Anthropology Department
CUNY Graduate Center

Young, B.
History Department
Eastern Illinois University

SITE ENTRIES BY COUNTRY

Czech Republic
Brno
Prague

Denmark
Aggersborg
Danevirke
Fröjel Harbor
Fyrkat
Jelling
Nonnebakken
Ribe
Trelleborg

England
Boss Hall
Bristol
Cadbury Castle
Chester
Glastonbury
Grove Priory
Hamwic
Hartlepool
Hyde Abbey
Ipswich
London
Mucking
Norton Priory
Norwich
Offa's Dyke
Raunds Area Project
Shrewsbury

Snape
Spong Hill
Sutton Hoo
Sutton Hoo Regional Survey
Thetford
Tintagel
Warden Abbey
Wat's Dyke
West Stow
Wharram Percy
Winchester
Worcester
York

France
Bulles
Goudelancourt-les-Pierrepont
Herpes
Mont Dardon
Quentovic
Saint-Nicolas D'Acy

Germany
Brunswick
Corvey
Haithabu
Hamburg
Lübeck
Rostock

Hungary
Buda

SUBJECT GUIDE

Agriculture, Animal Husbandry, and Hunting
Animal Husbandry
Archaeozoology: Eastern Europe
Archaeozoology: Western Europe
Croft
Deserted Medieval Villages
Dye Plants
Farm Abandonment (Iceland)
Fishweirs
Forests
Hedges
Hunting
Messuage
Open Fields
Paleoethnobotany
Parks
Poultry
Toft
Woodland

Background to the Middle Ages
Collapse of the Roman Empire
Iron Age
Place Names
Pre-Viking Scandinavia

Castles and Fortified Sites
Cadbury Castle
Cashels
Castles
Crannógs
Danevirke

Devín Castle
Dinas Powys
Llangorse Crannóg
Messuage
Mont Dardon
Normandy: Castles and Fortified Residences
Offa's Dyke
Ostrów Lednicki
Prague
Raths
Trelleborg Fortresses
Wat's Dyke

Celtic and Germanic Tribes
Lombards
Picts
Visigoths

Cemeteries and Burials
Barrows
Boss Hall Cemetery
Bulles
Cemeteries and Burials
Goudelancourt
Herpes
Mont Dardon
Mucking
Skeletal Populations
Snape
Spong Hill
Sutton Hoo
Tintagel

A

Aggersborg
See Trelleborg Fortresses.

Alt Clut
See Scotland: Early Royal Sites.

Anglo-Saxons
See England.

Animal Husbandry

The period between A.D. 500 and 1500 encompasses many changes in animal husbandry in northwest Europe. The most important was probably the transition of agricultural produce from the context of a subsistence economy to that of a cash commodity, in which the production of a surplus and long-distance trade became its primary purpose. This change was not consistent either temporally or spatially, but it generally coincided with the advent of a widely based monetary economy in any given area.

Livestock husbandry during the Medieval period was characterized by underdevelopment and low productivity, with improvement, in most cases, beginning only during the postmedieval period. It has been estimated that, between the fourteenth and the nineteenth centuries, carcass weights of sheep and cattle trebled, fleece weights increased 2.5-fold, and milk yields increased fourfold. This increase was achieved by improved breeding and, more important, by improved feeding. It is estimated that the average live weight of medieval cattle was as low as c. 200 kg, of pigs 60 kg, and of sheep 30 kg. Medieval

livestock were also slow growing and took much longer to develop to full size than their modern counterparts.

The principal limiting factor for the rearing of all livestock during the Medieval period was the availability of feed, especially during the winter. Strategies for feeding livestock were generally underdeveloped, and this is reflected in the fact that, in English estates, the stocking densities during the medieval period tend to be consistently lower than in the same areas during the early postmedieval period.

Two approaches were taken to manage the availability of winter fodder during the Medieval period. In areas in which the winters were particularly severe, such as continental Europe and Scandinavia, the snow cover was regularly so deep and long lasting that livestock could not exploit any winter grazing that might be present. The only option was to keep the animals indoors during the winter and bring the fodder to them. The archaeological evidence for this consists of long stall houses with part of the building given over to human habitation and the remainder divided into stalls for animals. Viking sagas often refer to the saving of hay, and evidence for the practice of hay saving is provided by the presence of scythes on archaeological sites. The importance of hay is reflected in Frankish laws that deal with the cutting and stealing of hay from the meadows of others. Organic material in prehistoric longhouses has shown that, instead of hay, the winter fodder consisted of gathered leaves, and it seems likely that this practice continued into the Medieval period.

In the more temperate west, it was possible to leave the livestock outdoors throughout the year. The Venerable Bede, living in northern England, noted of Ireland that snow rarely lay on the ground for more than three days and that, consequently, the Irish did not need to save hay or stall animals. This implies that winters were more severe in England and that hay saving and overwintering in stalls was necessary. In Ireland, and other temperate areas, the absence of the practice of saving hay meant that an alternative strategy had to be undertaken to ensure that livestock would survive the winter. The Irish laws make it clear that certain areas of "preserved grass" were cordoned off during the summer and reserved for winter grazing, and the dead winter grass in these reserved areas served the same purpose as hay. All methods of managing fodder depended on adequate fencing and supervision of the herds by shepherds, and much early law is concerned with livestock breaking into the fields of others. The documentary sources testify to the use of hobbles and bells, as well as the branding of livestock, in order to control and monitor the grazing of livestock.

In the more extreme areas, such as the islands of Scotland, it is clear that the reproduction rate of livestock clearly outstripped the ability of the land to produce adequate fodder. A nineteenth-century Scottish Hebridean saying stated that it was "better to have one calf than two skins," and it was policy throughout much of postmedieval Scotland to kill every second calf. That this policy was also undertaken during the Medieval period is clearly evidenced by the presence of large quantities of very young calf bones on Scottish archaeological sites of the period.

One of the principal ways of preserving winter fodder, be it *in situ* preserved grass or utilizing grassland for the production of hay, was to move the livestock to temporary grazing grounds during the summer. The nature of these summer transhumance grounds depended on the topography of a given area. They were essentially marginal areas that were unsuitable for livestock during winter because they were too wet or too high and exposed. In general, they consisted of either mountain areas or bogs and marshlands into which the shepherds and their flocks would move during the summer months. In Ireland, evidence for these seasonal pastures can be found in the form of enclosures and small huts in upland areas in County Down that have been dated to the eighth century A.D. Documentary sources provide evidence for similar transhumance areas in northern England. The Venerable Bede, in his life of St. Cuthbert written c. A.D. 700, tells of the saint encountering some "shepherd's huts, very makeshift constructions, built for the summer, and deserted." Such exploitation of summer pastures was a continual feature of livestock rearing throughout the Medieval period. The summer pasturing of sheep in the French Alps is well documented during medieval times, and both the routes taken and the areas grazed were strictly regulated.

It must be stressed, however, that long-distance transhumance could be practiced only in areas where marginal land was readily available. The practice was alien to many farmers during the Medieval period. In the great expanses of rich arable land of southern England, the provision of fodder was firmly imbedded within the greater farming system of the production of cereals, and the grazing of livestock was undertaken over a much more limited geographical area. In seventh- and eighth-century Anglo-Saxon England, every village or group of two or three villages had an area of grazing commonage known as the *feld*. This was usually the poorest land in each particular area, and the herds were confined to this land while the hay and the grain were being grown in the better areas. After harvest, the livestock were moved onto the stubble to graze and, equally important, to fertilize the ground with their dung. Sheep provide the richest of all dungs, with higher levels of nitrogen, potassium, and phosphorus than that of cattle, for instance. Medieval farmers were acutely aware of this; during the period, there is a clear correlation between the importance of cereals in a given area and the number of sheep kept. Thus, large quantities of sheep are a feature of the great cereal areas of the south of England throughout the Medieval period. The importance of sheep dung is emphasized by continual litigation during the Norman period (eleventh–twelfth centuries) concerning the rights of having an estate's sheep grazing on an individual's stubble. The lords of many manors often ordained that their tenants' sheep had to graze on the stubble of the fields belonging to the lord, so leaving the tenants' own arable land bereft of fertilizer.

The seasonal availability of fodder often dictated the time of year at which some animals were slaughtered. The dearth of winter fodder often led to the killing and curing of excess livestock in autumn. The traditional date for this was around Martinmas, which falls on November 11. The accounts of a certain Alice de Bryene of Acton in Suffolk in 1418–1419 indicate that, of seventeen cattle slaughtered by the household in that year, ten were killed in October and November. Of eighty-one sheep killed in the same year, thirty-one were killed before June, while fifty were killed after shearing in the late summer and autumn.

The management of pigs differed greatly from other livestock. They lived on roots and tubers rather than grass, and their favored grazing areas were not the open fields but the forest, where their diet during the autumn was augmented by beech and oak mast (i.e., the fallen nuts of those trees). Anglo-Saxon and Irish documentary sources consistently associate the rearing of pigs with forest. The seventh-century Saxon laws of Ine make it clear that forest-mast pasturage was regulated, and a tenth-century Irish text notes that eight sacks of mast were collected under each tree during a particularly good year of mast growth. This implies that mast was collected like hay and could be brought to the stalled animals. Indeed, during the following century Irish sources record the selling of mast at market, indicating that it had been elevated to the status of a cash crop. The pre-A.D. 1000 Irish sources are more specific than either Anglo-Saxon or Frankish texts in describing the range of food consumed by pigs. Along with mast, it included the roots of ferns, hazelnuts, and kitchen waste; pigs were fattened for slaughter on grain and milk. To rear pigs efficiently, access to forested lands was necessary. Where such resources were unavailable, the effect on pig production is reflected in the faunal remains from archaeological sites. The windswept islands of Scotland had virtually no forest during medieval times, and, consequently, only small quantities of pig remains are found on sites of the period.

Pigs were principally, if not exclusively, meat-producing animals. Their ability to thrive on the late autumn and winter mast crops meant that their meat-producing cycle differed from other livestock, ensuring a more even distribution of meat throughout the year. Unlike other animals, they could also be reared within towns, where domestic waste would have constituted much of their diet. They were especially popular during the Viking period (c. A.D. 800–1050); faunal remains from urban areas throughout western Europe at that time often demonstrate that pigs outnumbered other animals.

While the documentary sources provide much information concerning the management of different species, one must turn to the archaeological evidence to determine the relative importance of the different species at any given place or time. Such data are often at odds with the contemporary documentary evidence and also show great regional and temporal variation. Anglo-Saxon laws have led one leading livestock historian to conclude that "the pig was almost certainly the hallmark of Saxon pastoral husbandry, far more so than the ox or sheep." Yet, this impression is not supported by the remains of animal bones from Anglo-Saxon settlements. Most have indicated that sheep were numerically the most important

species present, with pigs usually in third place behind cattle. This literary bias toward pigs is also noted in contemporary Irish sources, with a noted historian concluding that "there are no beef-eating heroes in Irish literature, the doughtiest Irish warriors relied on pig-meat for their protein"—a sentiment belied by the zooarchaeological evidence, which generally shows cattle to be the dominant animal present. Frankish laws, too, emphasize the importance of pig, but again this is contradicted by faunal evidence. It seems likely that this overemphasis simply reflects the dietary preferences of the aristocratic class, whose members both compiled the laws and produced the non-legal literature that has survived to the present. Pork was the preferred food of the aristocratic feast, while the other animals tended to be regarded as inferior species. Tastes, however, change, and, in the later Middle Ages, beef was regarded among the affluent classes as a superior meat to either pork or mutton.

It is extremely difficult, on the basis of faunal remains from archaeological sites, to ascertain the specific way in which animals were used. The exception was pig, which was regarded exclusively as a meat-producing species. Cattle and sheep could be exploited for a range of purposes, including meat, milk, traction, wool, and hides, and the emphasis on these different products varied greatly. The Irish documentary evidence suggests that, during the early Medieval period, cattle were kept primarily for their milk, but elsewhere in Europe their value as plow animals was considered of primary importance. In both instances, it appears that meat was regarded as a secondary product. Cattle are not the only producers of milk, and late Anglo-Saxon sources, including the *Domesday Book,* make it clear that sheep were the principal suppliers of this produce. The *Domesday Book* implies that meat and wool were regarded as being of secondary importance as far as sheep were concerned.

The *Domesday Book* includes a census of livestock in England in 1086 and, in many ways, demarcates the passing of the old order as far as livestock husbandry was concerned. Until then, livestock rearing could be regarded as an aspect of an enclosed farming economy. Essentially, animal produce, be it meat, milk, hides, or wool, provided the necessities of life for the farmer and his family with any excess constituting renders and tribute to the local lord or chief. Trade of livestock produce would have been very limited. The introduction of a monetary economy transformed this system, with the production of a cash surplus becoming the primary motivation for all levels of farming society. The lord no longer wanted his rent in

A

food tribute but instead demanded it in the form of cash. While livestock-rearing strategies had been organized in the past to service local needs, they were now generally dictated by regional and international markets. The more perishable goods, such as meat and dairy produce, were sold in local or regional markets, whereas wool and grain could be stored, transported, and traded internationally.

Wool, because of international demand, became the most profitable product of medieval western European farming. The development of massive sheep flocks to satisfy continental demand for wool, especially from Flanders and Italy, became a dominant feature of livestock farming in Britain and Ireland during the later Medieval period. Much of this was spearheaded by international monastic orders such as the Cistercians. In some cases, this was to the detriment of other aspects of the local farming. In southern Scotland, there are noted instances in which arable land was turned over to sheep grazing, leading to acute local and regional shortages of grain.

The market for livestock produce evolved and changed throughout the Medieval period, but, with the exception of peripheral areas, livestock farming continued to function within the context of a regional or international market system. The idea of it as a means of self-sufficiency became a thing of the past for most farmers. The permeation of the cash economy to even the lowest levels of society is illustrated by the fact that, in 1320–1325, an impecunious cobbler in the peasant French village of Montaillou recorded that he could not be paid for repairing shoes until after his customers had sold their poultry at Whitsuntide market. The predominance of the cash-driven economy throughout Britain at the end of the Medieval period is epitomized by the driving of cattle from peripheral and sparsely populated Scottish islands over hundreds of miles to the congested meat markets of the city of London.

While cattle, sheep, and pigs dominated medieval livestock farming, other species were also important. Goats seem to have been regarded as suitable only for the lowest peasants in medieval Ireland, and their similar status elsewhere is probably indicated by the paucity of documentary references to them in Anglo-Saxon and Frankish law. Their bones are usually encountered in only small quantities on archaeological sites, but they tend to become more numerous in urban contexts during the later Medieval period. It is possible that they were raised within towns for their milk-producing capabilities.

Horses could be used only for light traction until the introduction of the breast harness in the ninth century A.D. Prior to this, they were generally used for riding or light traction, such as harrowing and pulling carts. Plowing was undertaken by oxen, generally in groups of eight. Despite the widespread adoption of the improved harness allowing horses to pull heavier weights, oxen remained the preferred plowing animal throughout the Medieval period. Oxen were easier to feed, as they did not need the dietary supplement of costly grain that horses needed to be kept in good working condition.

In addition to mammalian livestock, most medieval farmyards would also have contained a range of fowl. Frankish laws mention not only the common species of chickens, ducks, and geese, but also more unusual types, such as tame swans and cranes. During the later Middle Ages, doves and peacocks became a common feature of many aristocratic farms. Such animals contributed variety rather than significant quantities of meat to the diet. This was especially the case during Lent and other times of fasting when the strictures forbidding the consumption of meat were generally interpreted as pertaining only to the flesh of quadrupeds, thus excluding fish and fowl. The chicken bones from medieval archaeological sites tend to be from mature birds, suggesting that they were kept as much for their eggs as their meat.

FURTHER READINGS

Astill, G., and A. Grant, eds. *The Countryside of Medieval England*. Oxford: Basil Blackwell, 1988.

Campbell, B.M.S. Commercial Dairy Production on Medieval English Demesnes: The Case for Norfolk. *Anthropozoologica* (1992) 16:107–118.

Dyer, C. *Standards of Living in the Later Middle Ages*. Cambridge: Cambridge University Press, 1989.

Finberg, H.P.R., ed. *The Agrarian History of England and Wales*. Cambridge: Cambridge University Press, 1972.

Le Roy Ladurie, E. *Montaillou*. Harmondsworth: Penguin, 1980.

Lucas, A.T. *Cattle in Ancient Ireland*. Kilkenny: Boethius, 1989.

Rivers, T.J. *Laws of the Salian and Ripurian Franks*. New York: AMS, 1986.

Ryder, M.L. *Sheep and Man*. London: Duckworth, 1983.

Trow-Smith, R. *A History of British Livestock to 1700*. London: Routledge and Kegan Paul, 1957.

Finbar McCormick

SEE ALSO

Archaeozoology: Eastern Europe; Archaeozoology: Western Europe; Poultry

Archaeology and History

Archaeology is the most recent discipline to achieve recognition as centrally relevant to the study of the Middle Ages and has therefore had greater difficulty than others in establishing a clearly defined and authoritative role and in taking its place alongside history, history of art and architecture, and literary criticism. As a self-confident, discrete area of practical and intellectual activity, medieval archaeology has matured only over the last quarter of the twentieth century or so, and its growth to maturity has been so sudden that many scholars in neighboring disciplines remain skeptical of, and thus resistant to, its contribution. This problem originates in part from the failure of many historians, for example, to acquaint themselves even in broad outline with archaeological methodologies, objectives, and types of information; they therefore resist a source of information that they do not understand and consequently feel unable to test. In part it is inherited from the numerous pre- and even postwar archaeologists who initially trained in one or other of the parent disciplines and then brought with them to the practice of archaeology a pronounced respect for the objectives, language, and methodologies of these other subjects. It was this generation that trained current medieval archaeologists. Intellectual dependency was a fundamental characteristic of archaeology throughout its adolescence as a discipline and is only now in belated retreat.

The dependency of archaeology was first challenged successfully not by medievalists but by prehistorians, who were better placed to carve out an independent intellectual niche, in that prehistoric societies had, by definition, produced no surviving literature or documentation and little fine art. Prehistorians were able to develop unique and defining methodologies, collect appropriate data, and address problems that stemmed from, and could only be answered by, archaeology. They were aided in this process by the development and subsequent refinement of absolute dating techniques such as radiocarbon age determination and dendrochronology. The new dating methods made prehistorians independent of those chronologies established by historians for ancient Egypt that initially underpinned the periodization of all European and Middle Eastern prehistory.

By contrast, medieval archaeologists were slow to emerge from the shadow cast by historians and to develop their own objectives, methodology, and language. Even where a paucity of written sources offered opportunities for those with access to alternative techniques—as in the migration period—archaeologists long remained little more than self-appointed "handmaidens" to historians. Archaeologists' input was expected to conform to "facts" already established in the literature. They borrowed (and still borrow) wholesale from, for example, the Venerable Bede's *Historia Ecclesiastica* (Ecclesiastical History of the English People) in establishing both a terminology and an explanation for the processes by which Anglo-Saxon England came into existence, adopting even such terms as *adventus* (Latin for "the arrival") from his text. Pottery and metalwork were characterized as "Saxon," "Anglian," or "Jutish" not primarily because they were similar to continental examples that were known by archaeological criteria to be "Saxon," etc., but because they were distinctive of regions of England that Bede (673–735), considered to have been peopled by "Saxons," etc. Such regional cultures were then related to putative migrations and origin myths culled from noncontemporary literary sources (such as the *Anglo-Saxon Chronicles*) on the assumption that history provided the basic narrative on which all else must hang. The earliest archaeological investigation of an Anglo-Saxon settlement (by E.T. Leeds [1947], near Sutton Courtenay in Berkshire) was therefore interpreted not in terms of the organization of the finds on site but with reference to an entirely unevidenced state of warfare between its inhabitants and the Britons, by whom the investigator envisaged it was ultimately "either exterminated or temporarily put out of action," thus explaining its abandonment (Leeds 1947:93). Most works on Anglo-Saxon archaeology produced in this period were characterized by a narrative style and subject matter better suited to history and obedient to a chronological framework that derived from the written word. Put simply, most Anglo-Saxon archaeologists felt obliged to write history.

Two publications, *The Archaeology of Anglo-Saxon England* (Wilson 1976) and *Anglo-Saxon Cemeteries 1979* (Rahtz et al. 1980), signaled the beginning of the end of this period of dependence among Anglo-Saxonists, although many archaeological works continued even thereafter to focus almost exclusively on what were fundamentally historical issues. Although earlier, smaller works had already appeared that pursued more specifically archaeological objectives, these two volumes were on such a scale and so central to the discipline that their message was unavoidable—that archaeological research should address issues better suited to the techniques and data that are available than the historical and pseudohistorical migrations that had hitherto attracted so much attention. At the same time, a new generation of archaeologists, who were trained not only by medieval archaeologists but also by prehistorians, turned their attention to the settlements and cemeteries of the early Middle Ages, with sufficient confidence in their own methologies to treat both as prehistoric and to interpret them accordingly. One consequence has been the recognition that only large-scale projects are capable of addressing many of the issues raised by the data. Recourse to now much improved radiocarbon dating methods and to dendrochronological dating has at last provided the necessary on-site dating techniques that liberate medieval archaeology from history. To date, only a very small number of such projects have been undertaken, and only the precocious example of Mucking is published in full. In contrast, archaeologists working in southern Scandinavia, Holland, and Germany have been less constrained by the views of historians and were prepared to extend the prehistoric period up to the central Middle Ages or even beyond. Consequently, they developed such techniques as field walking, phosphate analysis, and large-scale excavation of settlements, field systems, and cemeteries a generation earlier. A greater profusion of substantive publications of high quality is the consequence, and attention among Anglo-Saxonists is now diverting to this body of research in an attempt to interpret the rural settlements of early England.

One result is a tendency today for archaeology and history to become increasingly separate, as regards both personnel and output. Few scholars can now do what such figures as Leslie Alcock (1971) and J.N.L. Myres (1969) did a generation ago and claim acceptance both as archaeologists and as historians—indeed, both disciplines have become increasingly specialized internally with considerable consequences for the capacity of any single scholar to establish an overview. The objectives pursued by practitioners of each are increasingly distinctive, with historians focusing on persons and politics, social and military systems, dialectic, and religious ideas, and archaeologists on settlement form, function, and development, trade, manufacturing, material culture, diet, and microeconomics.

There are both strengths and weaknesses inherent in this divergence. On the one hand, each discipline is more inclined today to focus on those topics in which its own methodologies are the more effective and its products the more authoritative. On the other hand, there are numerous subjects of general interest to which both can contribute effectively and concerning which exponents of each discipline need to listen carefully to the voices of the other. The study of the landscape and settlement pattern of early England is just one example. Historians established an early hold on this area, but archaeologists

have taken it over almost exclusively. However, in many respects, the most informative excavation so far published is that of Yeavering, whose excavator, Brian Hope-Taylor, was able to take advantage of reference to the site in Bede's *Historia Ecclesiastica* to discuss both its history and its function with a confidence that would otherwise be quite misplaced (Hope-Taylor 1977). Few such sites are as adequately documented as Yeavering, yet literature surviving from the early eighth century (which is largely retrospective) contains far more information concerning the estates and settlements of the conversion period than has hitherto been recognized or utilized.

The wider availability of written sources for the central and late Middle Ages further delayed the acceptance of archaeology as a tool appropriate to research in these periods. Deserted medieval villages, for example, were recognized as a distinct class of site only in the 1950s. Fieldwork on the premiere research program—that at Wharram Percy—is only just complete, and publication is still underway at the present date. Numerous other sites have seen some excavation, but no English example has been excavated in its entirety (Raunds remains nearest to this ideal). The contrast with the large-scale interventions on abandoned, nucleated rural sites in continental Europe is marked.

The systematic investigation of towns by archaeologists had barely begun before the 1960s and 1970s, when the necessary funding and posts began to be put in place. Even then, medieval and postmedieval deposits were only gradually and episodically allowed a status equivalent to those of the Roman period. It was long believed by historians that so much information concerning towns was accessible via written sources and topographical research that excavation was unlikely to justify its extraordinary expense. Indeed, social and economic histories of the Middle Ages written as late as 1980 show almost no recognition of the potential input offered by archaeology.

Today there is much less excuse for such complacency since archaeology has attained a critical mass regarding the quantity and quality of both primary research and publication, with new works building on an ever-growing database and an ever-developing understanding of those data. What is more, the precise dating made available by the development of dendrochronology means that it has become possible to offer what amounts to a detailed narrative account of many important archaeological sites where waterlogged conditions prevail. London's waterfront, Carlisle, York, Dublin, and Hedeby (Haithabu) are apt examples. This plethora of precisely dated information has become central to the modern study of towns and town life and their origins—topics that are discussed in early literary sources only through short, idiosyncratic references to the foundation and destruction of towns and to towns as sites of events of unusual importance.

In contrast to the increasing disconnection between archaeologists and historians studying the period c. 400–700, the late 1980s and the 1990s tended to reinforce the interdependence between history and archaeology—and, for that matter, place-name studies, historical ecology, and historical geography—among those interested in the late Anglo-Saxon period and the High Middle Ages. This is in part because significant numbers of historians have had firsthand experience of archaeological work—and the role of Wharram Percy has been central to this process. Additionally, there are numerous projects in which the varying objectives of history and archaeology are seen as interdependent and capable of mutual integration, yet methodologically distinct. Examples include much of the work of the Royal Commission for Historical Monuments for England, Michael Aston's ongoing Shapwick project in Somerset, Christopher Dyer's study of Hanbury (Worcestershire), and N.J. Higham's work at Tatton, Cheshire (Dyer 1991; Higham 1995). In general, it may be argued that it is archaeologists who are today showing the greater capacity for interdisciplinary work; this may be a natural consequence of the much broader spectrum of research tools with which they are familiar compared to the narrower paleographic and critical skills of the historian. It is primarily archaeological publications that take note of historical thinking, rather than the reverse. Examples include the "Documentary Evidence" chapter of *The Countryside of Medieval England* (Astill and Grant 1988), which is essentially a book by archaeologists about archaeology and aimed at archaeologists, and the command of current historical debate evidenced by David A. Hinton's synthesis of the archaeology of medieval England, *Archaeology, Economy, and Society: England from the Fifth to the Fifteenth Century* (1990). Similarly, the "Feeding the City" project was initiated by archaeologists working in London but used a traditional, historical approach to those manuscript sources that were relevant to the estates of the medieval equivalent of Greater London for this particular project. (The project seeks to examine how and what medieval Londoners were fed.) In contrast, many of even the very best recent works of medieval history omit all reference to archaeology. This is in some instances entirely voluntary and may, of course, be justified by the parameters the author has established.

For example, in his excellent 1991 study, *Goths and Romans, 332–489,* Peter Heather specifically denies archaeological research any value for his primarily political concerns and elects to exclude it from discussion. Archaeology's absence from such works is more likely a weakness than a strength, not necessarily in regard to such specific and carefully circumscribed studies as Heather's—which deservedly received much critical acclaim—but more in regard to the richer research methodologies and objectives that might have been available were a more broadly based research program on, for example, the very same Goths, to be designed by experts from different parts of the intellectual spectrum.

For the future, it seems inevitable that the greater range of inquiry and the depth of understanding that are accessible to interdisciplinary research will divert more and more energy into projects that archaeologists, historians, and others have conceived cooperatively. These projects will respond to discussions that have identified objectives that are both more complex and more searching than those that can be mounted exclusively within a single discipline. Even where research remains the work of an individual, much work will be improved by scholars cross-referencing the methodologies, ideas, and insights of whichever related disciplines are applicable in a particular context. This does not require that archaeologists should practice history, or vice versa, but merely that their work is likely to benefit from cross-fertilization. One result will be a better understanding of the past; another will be a better mutual understanding by practitioners of the several disciplines involved. At present, however, it is arguably the world of historical scholarship that is more in need of this development than the world of medieval archaeology.

FURTHER READINGS

Alcock, L. *Arthur's Britain: History and Archaeology, A.D. 367–634.* London: Penguin, 1971.

Astill, G., and A. Grant, eds. *The Countryside of Medieval England.* Oxford: Basil Blackwell, 1988.

Bede. *Ecclesiastical History of the English People.* Ed. B. Colgrave and R.A.B. Mynors. Oxford: Oxford Medieval Texts, 1969.

Beresford, M., and J. Hurst. *Wharram Percy: Deserted Medieval Village.* London: Batsford/English Heritage, 1990.

Bolton, J.L. *The Medieval English Economy, 1150–1500.* London: Dent, 1980.

Campbell, B.M.S., J.A. Galloway, D. Keene, and M. Murphy. *A Medieval Capital and Its Grain Supply: Agrarian*

Production and Distribution in the London Region c. 1300. Lancaster: Institute of British Geographers, 1993.

Dyer, C. *Hanbury: Settlement and Society in a Woodland Landscape.* Department of English Local History Occasional Paper (4th Series) 4. Leicester: Leicester University Press, 1991.

Hamerow, H. *Mucking 2.* London: English Heritage, 1993.

———. Review Article: The Archaeology of Rural Settlement in Early Medieval Europe. *Early Medieval Europe* (1994) 3(2):167–179.

Heather, Peter. *Goths and Romans, 332–489.* Oxford: Oxford University Press, 1991.

Higham, N.J. *Tatton: The History and Prehistory of One Cheshire Township. Chester Archaeological Society Journal* (1995) 71.

Hinton, David A. *Archaeology, Economy, and Society: England from the Fifth to the Fifteenth Century.* London: Seaby, 1990.

Hope-Taylor, B. *Yeavering: An Anglo-British Centre of Early Northumbria.* London: HMSO, 1977.

Leeds, E.T. A Saxon Village Near Sutton Courtenay, Berks. *Archaeologia* (1947) 92:78–94.

Miller, E., and J. Hatcher. *Medieval England: Rural Society and Economic Change, 1086–1348.* Harlow: Longman, 1978.

Myres, J.N.L. *Anglo-Saxon Pottery and the Settlement of England.* Oxford: Oxford University Press, 1969.

Rahtz, P., T. Dickinson, and L. Watts, eds. *Anglo-Saxon Cemeteries 1979.* BAR British Series 82. Oxford: British Archaeological Reports, 1980.

Wilson, D.M., ed. *The Archaeology of Anglo-Saxon England.* Cambridge: Cambridge University Press, 1976.

N.J. Higham

SEE ALSO

Dendrochronology; Deserted Medieval Villages; Haithabu; Mucking; Radiocarbon Age Determination; Raunds Area Project; Wharram Percy

Archaeozoology: Eastern Europe (Carpathian Basin)

The geopolitical position of the Carpathian Basin largely corresponds to modern-day Hungary. It may be characterized as a historical fault line, where various waves of eastern migrations stormed the borders of the Roman, Frankish, and, subsequently, Hapsburg Empires. The Hungarians themselves arrived during the late ninth century as a migrating eastern people and settled in the area.

Since prehistoric times, intensive culture change has been concentrated in the corridor between the Eurasian region and central Europe. The archaeozoological aspects of these events were first investigated by Sándor Bökönyi (in Hungary and the former Yugoslavia) and János Matolcsi (in Hungary and the former Soviet Union) following World War II.

The analysis of faunal remains requires different approaches for the early and the late phases of the Middle Ages in this region. For the early, pre-Christian phase, a distinction must be drawn between faunal remains recovered from burials and those recovered from settlements. While remains of the first group (e.g., the graves of equestrian Avar warriors in Slovakia and Hungary) contain high-quality information on individual animals, food offerings in graves provide only a selected picture of animal exploitation. Kitchen refuse from settlements, on the other hand, offers low-quality information, since many of the eighth–tenth-century cultures of eastern Europe seem to have been, at best, semisedentary. The pastoral form of life or even a transition to sedentism required no monumental architecture, and periods of occupation were evidently short at many sites between the Danube River and the northern Pontic region.

The analysis of faunal remains from early medieval sites presents several methodological problems. Due to the rapid spread of pastoral populations, accurate dating of early medieval faunal assemblages is indispensable. Dating is usually based on historical sources and ceramic distributions rather than physical methods such as radiocarbon that may have large margins for error. Dendrochronology, an attractive alternative, has not been used in Hungarian archaeology because of the lack of a reference tree-ring sequence for the region. In estimating the relative importance of different animal species, percentages based on the number of identifiable bone specimens and the minimum numbers of individuals are often used indiscriminately in the literature relevant to the early Middle Ages in eastern Europe.

By the Middle Ages, wild animals evidently played a negligible role as suppliers of meat at most sites. Cattle were undoubtedly the most important sources of animal protein, even when the typically heavy fragmentation of their bones is taken into account. Their overwhelming dominance at rural, fortified, and later medieval urban settlements makes cattle remains more or less useless for cross-cultural comparisons, especially when only small and heterogeneous bone assemblages are available.

Bones of sheep and goats are often not distinguishable from each other and often occur together in faunal lists. In Hungary, the bones of sheep are usually more common than those of goats. The contribution of goat remains, however, is significant at some sites east of the Carpathian Basin (e.g., Saltovo-Majack culture, Khazar Khanate). Sheep and goats are most typical in the European steppe region, although they were important in the Carpathian Basin as well.

Pigs are comparable to sheep and goats in terms of individual meat output; however, their reproduction rate and kill-off intensity are even higher. This species is commonly associated with a relatively sedentary form of life. Pig bones dominate in the settlement assemblages of early medieval Slavic cultures both inside and east of the Carpathian Basin. At the end of the early Middle Ages in Hungary, the colonization of eastern Europe by noneastern Europeans started. The predominantly Germanic colonists, who were settled into Hungary by Christian kings from the eleventh century onward, may have contributed to the increasing importance of pig husbandry. The importance of pigs increased during the late Middle Ages until the sixteenth-century Ottoman occupation, when sheep and goats once again became important sources of meat.

Horses were undoubtedly one of the most important domestic animals in migration, especially in the pastoral cultures whose influence defined eastern Europe throughout the early medieval period. Aside from the eastern Saltovo-Majack culture, horse bones occur most frequently in the period of the Árpád dynasty (eleventh–thirteenth centuries) in the Carpathian Basin. High percentages of sheep and goat bones seem to correlate with high numbers of horse remains. These species are often referred to in the Hungarian archaeological literature as *steppe elements*.

Even before the Christian prohibition against eating horseflesh was imposed, it is unlikely that these slow-growing, highly valuable animals provided meat for the everyday diet. On the other hand, horses kept for secondary products, such as power or milk rather than meat, may be underrepresented in many faunal assemblages from settlements. It is of special interest that, while the consumption of horse meat was regarded as a sinful, pagan ritual in Hungary by the eleventh century, horse bones

with defleshing marks occur sporadically as late as the fifteenth century at the habitations of late arrivals in the Carpathian Basin, such as the Cumanians.

The mechanisms by which one domestic species gradually replaces another may become particularly apparent under the pressures of environmental change. Environmental changes were caused by both natural and cultural factors. The temperate, continental climate of the Carpathian Basin had a less visible impact than regional habitat differences and historical events on medieval domestic faunas. This is illustrated most clearly by the changing proportions of sheep and pigs in the Carpathian Basin. In addition to developing a sedentary way of life during the early Middle Ages, conquering Hungarian populations only gradually adopted pig husbandry from the local populations. Three centuries later, Islamic influence limited the late medieval exploitation of pigs and stimulated sheep and goat husbandry once again.

FURTHER READINGS

Bartosiewicz, L. Early Medieval Archaeozoology in Eastern Europe. In *Bioarchäologie und Frühgeschichtsforschung*. Ed. H. Friesinger, F. Daim, E. Kanelutti, and O. Cichocki. Archaeologia Austriaca Monograph 2. Wien: Institute für Ur- und Frühgeschichte der Universität Wien, 1993. pp. 123–131.

Bökönyi, S. Die Entwicklung der mittelalterlichen Haustierfauna Ungarns. *Zeitschrift für Tierzüchtung und Züchtungsbiologie* (1962) 77:8–9.

———. The Development and History of Domestic Animals in Hungary: The Neolithic through the Middle Ages. *American Anthropologist* (1971) 73:640–674.

———. *History of Domestic Animals in Central and Eastern Europe*. Budapest: Akadémiai Kiadó, 1974.

Matolcsi, J. *Állattartás Őseink Korában* (Animal Keeping in the Time of Our Ancestors). Budapest: Gondolat Kiadó, 1982.

László Bartosiewicz

SEE ALSO
Buda

Archaeozoology: Western Europe

Studies of animal bones from medieval sites in western Europe have been dominated by the very large quantities recovered from later medieval urban sites and have tended to be descriptive archives of data rather than topic

A

oriented. A few major projects are prominent in the literature, with less emphasis on synthesis of smaller sites and the formulation of explicit research questions.

The immediate post-Roman period is poorly represented in the literature, not least because much of the archaeology of the fifth–seventh centuries consists of burials rather than occupation sites. The burials themselves have produced zooarchaeological data, in the form of numerous examples in which one or more animals have been interred with the human corpse. Typically, the animal is a horse, nearly always an adult stallion, and examples extend from eastern England through the Netherlands and Germany into Poland, eastern Austria, and even northwestern Hungary (Oexle 1984). Burials of dogs with humans are also encountered through this region, and there is increasing evidence of the placement of cremated horses and other animals with human cremations in England and Germany (Bond 1994; Kühl 1984). Few occupation sites of this period have produced substantial bone assemblages. A notable exception is West Stow in England, where a small agrarian settlement seems to have relied principally on sheep as an animal resource, with pigs important in the earliest phases and perhaps some use of cattle for dairying (Crabtree 1990). Dairying is an important topic at this early date, and there are differences of opinion between those who see mortality profiles as evidence for it, as at West Stow, and those who interpret the evidence differently, as at some early Christian Irish sites (McCormick 1992).

The eighth through eleventh centuries saw the emergence of towns in western Europe, and it is from these sites that large animal bone assemblages have mostly been recovered. Around the North Sea and the Baltic, a number of sites have been identified as early trading centers, including Southampton and York (England), Dorestad (Netherlands), and Ribe and Hedeby (Denmark) (Bourdillon and Coy 1980; O'Connor 1992; Prummel 1983; Hatting 1991). The diversity of bone assemblages from these sites is low compared to assemblages from contemporary high-status or ecclesiastical sites, a contrast that is interpreted by some in terms of the trading sites having been provisioned, rather than directly procuring their meat supply. The social disruption of the migration period has little impact on the zooarchaeological record, the differences between assemblages from Saxon and Anglo-Scandinavian sites in eastern England, for example, being few and rather subtle. Some urban excavations have been extensive enough to allow questions to be posed about use of space within them. Parts of the Wood

Quay sites in Dublin (Ireland) were examined to see whether the spatial distribution of bones gave much information about refuse-disposal patterns. A distinct lack of system was noted, and many other early medieval towns in western Europe show the same dense and extensive scatters and accumulations of refuse, often with evidence of gnawing by dogs before burial. The increasingly common use of sieving for bone recovery has underlined this point, with frequent finds of bones of rodents and scavenging birds. Data from agricultural sites are scarce for this period, a notable exception being the very large assemblage from the settlement at Eketorp (Sweden), although this study concentrated on the acquisition of quantified data at the expense of archaeological interpretation. Farther south, the published data are few, though attention has recently turned to northern Italy and to questions of supply and demand in the hinterland of towns in that area.

From the twelfth century onward, large tracts of western Europe can be seen as the hinterland of urban centers, and it is still from excavations in towns that the majority of published material has come. In some instances, the sheer quantity of material has presented problems of selectivity, and the study of animal bones from a particular site has not always been well integrated with other studies of the same site. Oslo serves as a good example, the bones having been examined in isolation from the excellent studies of other biota from the same deposits (Schia 1988). Elsewhere, studies have concentrated on the deposition and taphonomic history of the deposits. At Calatrava la Vieja (Spain), for example, the presence of articulated skeletons and a high frequency of cat and dog bones were taken to represent mortality and deposition consequent upon abandonment of the settlement (Morales Muñiz et al. 1988). In this case, a careful consideration of the circumstances of deposition allowed information concerning the economy of the settlement to be separated from the consequences of particular social events.

Synthetic studies have been surprisingly few. Notable is F. Audoin-Rouzeau's (1992) overview of the relative contribution made to the diet by cattle, sheep, and pigs over 262 medieval and recent sites in western Europe. The general dominance of beef is underlined by this study, which also shows pork to have been important on the seigneurial estates but not in contemporary towns or among peasant communities. This distinction is interpreted in terms of productive surpluses and market forces. Pigs figure large in bone assemblages from the southern Baltic area as well, generally being the most abundant species in seventh–eleventh-century assemblages from southern Jutland east to the River Oder (Benecke 1988). This predominance is evident in sites of quite different social context and is probably of cultural or environmental, rather than economic, origin.

Castles and ecclesiastical sites present more of a problem than towns, as both often lack substantial bone assemblages, having had effective disposal systems. Castles and similar institutions typically produce bone assemblages that differ in some respects from those of contemporaneous urban sites, often having more pig and deer bones. The implication is that castles were tapped into a different source of supply, presumably their associated estates. Monastic sites are difficult to understand. Little correlation can be seen between the nature of bone assemblages and the food proscriptions of different orders. This is probably because most such houses had both monastic and lay residents, who may have differed in their diet, a difference that is no longer apparent in the mixed refuse that constitutes most bone assemblages.

The livestock themselves have been the subject of some synthetic study. Bones of cattle from medieval sites throughout western Europe show little size variation, though possible regional size trends across Europe have been postulated. It is only at the very end of the Medieval period that there is clear evidence of a general increase in carcass size, and that development appears to have been rather slow and sporadic. It is much the same story with sheep and pigs, neither of which show any convincing evidence of attempts to develop a larger carcass much before the sixteenth or seventeenth centuries. In the case of cattle and sheep, this is probably because they were multipurpose animals and the carcass was of less importance than milk, wool, traction power, and dung. In the case of pigs, their place as the household garbage disposal unit may have predisposed against selective breeding for body size.

Fish bones from medieval sites are increasingly recognized as representing an important resource, not merely in coastal sites. In northwestern Europe, the development of the historically important herring (*Clupea harengus* L.) fishery can be traced archaeologically, as can the increasing utilization of fishes of the cod family (Gadidae) from the twelfth century onward, with the implication that deeper waters were being exploited and a greater capital investment was being made in fishing.

From urban sites, in particular, bird bones constitute a mixture of domestic refuse, the remains of scavengers, incidental chance occurrences, and the prey of domestic cats and ferrets. Much of the work that has been under-

taken on medieval birds in Europe has focused on this question of classification—for example, the question of whether bones of white-tailed eagle *(Haliaeetus albicilla)* on ninth–eleventh-century sites throughout Germany represent a widespread scavenger or the trading of eagle wings to provide feathers to fletch arrows. Elsewhere, the occurrence of different species may have social significance; native Irish settlements have far fewer domestic bird bones than do contemporary Anglo-Norman settlements in Ireland, for example (McCormick 1991).

Bones of rodents and other small mammals are recovered in appreciable numbers only where sieving has been undertaken, though sufficient evidence is available to show the widespread occurrence of house mouse (*Mus* sp.) and ship rat *(Rattus rattus)* throughout western Europe in the Medieval period. Continuity with Roman populations of these species has yet to be convincingly demonstrated in some areas.

In all, medieval zooarchaeology in western Europe has passed through a stage of rather indiscriminate data collection and is now focusing on particular questions of resource and supply and the interpretation of bird and fish remains to a far greater extent than previously. There is almost an overabundance of data from urban sites from the ninth century onward, and very little from the earlier centuries or from small rural settlements, with the danger that livestock trade and exchange systems will be seen only at their "consumer" end.

FURTHER READINGS

Audoin-Rouzeau, F. Approche archéozoologique du commerce des viandes au moyen age. *Anthropozoologica* (1992) 16:83–92.

Barker, Graeme. *A Mediterranean Valley: Archaeology as Annales in the Biferno Valley.* London: Leicester University Press, 1995.

Benecke, N. *Archaeozoologische Untersuchungen an Tierknochen aus der frühmittelalterlichen Siedlung von Menzlin.* Materialhefte zur Ur- und Frügeschichte Mecklenburgs 3. Schwerin: Museum für Ur- und Frühgeschichte Schwerin, 1988.

Bond, J.M. Appendix I: The Cremated Animal Bone. In *The Anglo-Saxon Cemetery at Spong Hill, North Elmham. Part VIII: The Cremations,* by J. McKinley, East Anglian Archaeology 69. Ipswich: Suffolk County Planning Department, 1994, pp. 121–135.

Bourdillon, J., and J. Coy. The Animal Bones. In *Excavations at Melbourne Street Southampton, 1971–76,* by P. Holdsworth. London: Council for British

Archaeology, 1980, CBA Research Reports 33. pp. 79–121.

Crabtree, P.J. *West Stow: Early Anglo-Saxon Animal Husbandry.* East Anglian Archaeology 47. Ipswich: Suffolk County Planning Department, 1990.

Hatting, T. The Archaeozoology. In *Ribe Excavations, 1970–76.* Vol. 3. Ed. M. Bencard, C.B. Jorgensen, and H.B. Madsen. Esbjerg: Sydjysk Universitetsforlag, 1991, pp. 43–57.

Kühl, I. Animal Remains in Cremations from the Bronze Age to the Viking Period in Schleswig-Holstein, North Germany. In *Animals and Archaeology 4. Husbandry in Europe.* Ed. C. Grigson and J. Clutton-Brock. BAR International Series 227. Oxford: British Archaeological Reports, 1984, pp. 209–220.

McCormick, F. The Effect of the Anglo-Norman Settlement on Ireland's Wild and Domesticated Fauna. In *Animal Use and Culture Change.* Ed. P.J. Crabtree and K. Ryan. MASCA Research Papers, Supplement to Vol. 8. Philadelphia: University Museum, University of Pennsylvania, 1991, pp. 40–52.

———. Early Faunal Evidence for Dairying. *Oxford Journal of Archaeology* (1992) 11:201–209.

Morales Muñiz, A., R. Moreno Nuño, and M.A.C. Pecharroman. Calvatara la Vieja: primer informe sobre la fauna de vertebrados recuper en el yacimiento almohade. Primera pare: mamiferos. *Boletin de Arqueologia Medieval* (1988) 2:7–48.

O'Connor, T.P. *Bones from 46–54 Fishergate.* The Archaeology of York 15(4). London: Council for British Archaeology, 1992.

Oexle, J. Merowingerzeitliche Pferdebestattungen: Opfer oder Beigaben? *Frühmittelalterliche Studie* (1984) 18:122–172.

Prummel, W. *Early Medieval Dorestad: An Archaeozoological Study.* Nederlandse Oudheden 11. Amersfoort: Rijksdienst voor het Oudheidkundig Bodemonderzoek, 1983.

Schia, E., ed. *De arkeologiske utgravninger i Gamlebyen, Oslo.* Vol. 5. Oslo: Alvheim & Eide, 1988.

T.P. O'Connor

SEE ALSO
Animal Husbandry

B

Barrows

The construction of barrows, or burial mounds, must be regarded as a peculiar form of mortuary practice in the early Middle Ages, and only several hundred barrows are known for the period for the whole of Europe. Extensive archaeological research on barrows, of both prehistoric and medieval date, took place in the nineteenth and the early twentieth centuries. The poor quality of these early excavations has put severe limitations on current interpretations and understanding of the distribution, age, and significance of the early medieval barrow, and only a minority can be securely dated. Recent reexcavations of barrows that were originally investigated by antiquarians often turn out to be part of larger cemeteries rather than isolated mounds or small barrow cemeteries, as was once thought (e.g., Moos-Burgstall in Germany and Basel-Bernerring in Switzerland).

Although barrows of early medieval date have been identified from as far afield as Cornwall in England in the west, Žuran near Brünn in the east, Vestlandet in Norway in the north, and Lazio in Italy in the south, four regions can be recognized in which the construction of barrows were of particular significance. In Scandinavia, barrows were constructed from the later Roman Iron Age until the tenth century. Most common are barrow cemeteries such as Högem and Gamla Uppsala, both in Sweden. The sites consist of several very large barrows (60–70 m in diameter and 10–12 m in height at Gamla Uppsala) with a larger number of small barrows nearby. Both inhumed and cremated bodies had been interred beneath the mounds, some of these accompanied by wealthy grave goods and some within a timber burial chamber. Other important barrow cemeteries in this region are known from Bert-

nem, Borre, and from the area of Vestlandet, all in Norway, and the two tenth-century barrows on either side of the engraved stone and church at Jelling in Denmark. In England, the vast majority of barrows are dated between A.D. 550 and 750, and the mounds occur particularly in the east, with a concentration of barrow cemeteries or burial mounds within flat-grave cemeteries in the southeast. Although a number of early seventh-century barrows and barrow cemeteries include graves or burial chambers with extremely wealthy grave goods (e.g., Taplow, Sutton Hoo, and Benty Grange), the vast majority of barrows do not display such wealth. In the areas of barrow construction, the intensive reuse of prehistoric barrows can be observed (e.g., Wigber Low). In the Rhine and Upper Danube region, barrows are also dated between A.D. 550 and 750, and, as in England, the majority of barrows do not include graves with wealthy grave goods, although exceptions are known (e.g., Oberflingen in Germany and Dondelange in Luxembourg). Recent research indicates that the majority of early medieval burial mounds are components of larger flat-grave cemeteries. In this region, secondary interments of early medieval date in prehistoric barrows are common. To the east of the Elbe, very large barrow cemeteries have been identified and dated to the later eighth, ninth, and tenth centuries (e.g., Ralswiek in Germany); these cemeteries consist exclusively of small mounds (1–2 m in diameter) over inhumed bodies.

Burial mounds are generally considered to indicate a relatively high status of the deceased thus commemorated. This can, for example, be argued from the relative energy expanded on mound construction. While the largest barrows in Scandinavia have been assigned to the elite, or elite dynasties, thereby supported by the high

B

correlation between the size of the mounds and the wealth of the grave goods, such a clear sociopolitical attribution cannot be made for the barrows in the other regions. With the aforementioned exemptions of Taplow, Sutton Hoo, Oberiflingen, and Dondelange, the large majority of barrows in England and the Rhine/Upper Danube region must be assigned to a local elite, while the barrows in the area east of the Elbe are not indicative of status.

The early medieval barrow, in much the same way as its Bronze Age counterparts, was constructed in Scandinavia, England, and the Rhine/Upper Danube regions to stress ownership of newly acquired land and as a physical monument to reinforce that claim by the successors of the deceased. The distribution of barrows in England and the Rhine/Upper Danube area, and the geographically and temporally associated secondary use of prehistoric barrows, is significant in this respect. Barrows were constructed and reused in areas where Germanic people were politically and militarily dominant in previously Romanized lands, with the notable exception of the core of the Merovingian Empire. In these areas, the barrows are usually associated with Angles, Saxons, Jutes, Bavarians, Alamanns, and Austrasian Franks. The barrows in the area east of the Elbe, on the other hand, are always considered to be of Slavs.

The religious connotation of barrows has received much discussion. In Scandinavia, the burial mound is considered an inherent and integrated part of the dominant ideology in the pre-Christian era. The barrows in England and the Rhine/Upper Danube region can also be linked to the non-Christian-warrior ideology. The use of the burial mound as a lasting monument is linked in time and space to the occurrence of churches as grave monuments. The construction of the barrow cemeteries by the Slavs to the east of the Elbe is, paradoxically, linked to the change from cremation to inhumation as the dominant funerary behavior, an innovation that is part of the Christianization of this area.

FURTHER READINGS

Carver, M.O.H. Sutton Hoo in Context. *Settimane di studio del Centro Italiano di Studi sull'Alto Medioevo* (1986) 32:77-117.

Müller-Wille, M. Monumentale Grabhügel der Völkerwanderungszeit in Mittel- und Nordeuropa: Bestand und Deutung. In *Mare Balticum: Beiträge zur Geschichte des Ostseeraums in Mittelalter und Neuzeit. Festschift zum 65. Geburtstag von Erich Hoffmann.*
Ed. W. Paravicini, Sigmaringen: Jan Thorbecke Verlag, 1992, pp. 1–20.

Van de Noort, R. The Context of Early Medieval Barrows in Western Europe. *Antiquity* 67:66–73.

Robert Van de Noort

SEE ALSO
Sutton Hoo

Birka

One of Sweden's best-known complexes of ancient monuments lies on the island of Björkö, c. 30 km west of Stockholm. It comprises the site of the Viking Age town of Birka: 6–7 ha of soot-black occupation layers surrounded by defenses—a rampart, a fortress, and an underwater palisade. The urban area is also surrounded by cemeteries with at least two thousand cremations under mounds and at least one thousand other graves, mainly inhumations without surface markings. The whole complex dates from the Viking Age (800–1050).

Lake Mälaren is now an inland lake c. 110 × 60 km in size, but in the Viking Age it was an inlet of the Baltic Sea. (Land elevation at the rate of c. 0.5 m per century has changed its original topography.) The lake is split into a number of small fjords and sounds between islands and peninsulas. The whole area is, and was, connected by waterways.

The island of Björkö flanks the island of Adelsö, on which there was an early medieval royal estate, and Björkö seems to have formed part of its demesne. One of the most important fairways northward from the Baltic Sea to the central settlement region of the Svea Kingdom centered on Uppsala ran through the strait between the two islands. It was mainly traversed by small vessels, as the route involved two portages: 15 km south and 25 km north of Björkö. The Baltic could also be reached through the easterly sound, where Stockholm stands today; this was the usual route to Finland and Russia.

Björkö lies within an area that was densely populated in the Viking Age, when there were hundreds of farmsteads along the shores of Lake Mälaren. The farmsteads are characterized by cemeteries of cremations covered by mounds, often containing grave goods manufactured by, or brought from, Björkö merchants.

From c. 800 onward, the Scandinavians began to dominate western Europe, thanks to their naval superiority. The Viking raids became increasingly widespread throughout this period, and, finally, the Frankish emperor attempted to counteract them by sending missionaries to the north.

The best known of these missionaries was Ansgar. He began his missionary work in Denmark but was later sent to a place in the Svea Kingdom called Birka, which he visited in 829–830 and 851–852. During the time between his two visits, he was elevated to the see of Hamburg, subsequently to be amalgamated with Bremen, so he became the archbishop of Hamburg-Bremen. In c. 870, his successor, Rimbert, wrote his biography, *Vita Anskarii,* in which he included descriptions of Birka, its people, customs, and the events that took place there. These were reiterated by Adam of Bremen in the *Bremen Chronicles* of the 1070s, which also mentioned Bremen's later contacts with Birka and Scandinavia.

Ansgar's Birka is the first recognizable place in Scandinavia to be mentioned by name. Late medieval sources equate Birka with Björkö in Lake Mälaren—the only place where Viking Age occupation layers and graves are dense enough to indicate a town.

Antiquarian interest in Birka dates from an early period. Swedish medieval town law is called *Bjärköarätt* and so seemed to have been a law originally associated with Birka. In 1687, State Antiquary Johan Hadorf published an edition of the *Bjärköarätt,* and during the course of his work he visited Björkö and made some modest excavations, the finds from which are still in Historiska Museet, Stockholm. He also commissioned a map of the island that recorded most of the place-names (Korshhamn, Kugghamn, Bystaden—Black Earth), which are still used today when describing the area of the early town.

The next two hundred years saw sporadic excavations on Björkö, but it was only through the work of Hjalmar Stolpe (1871–1882) that the topography, monuments, and finds from the site became commonly known. Stolpe excavated c. 4,500 m² of the settlement (Black Earth) and eleven hundred graves. He recorded the graves in great detail, drawing them on graph paper and describing them in excavation diaries. Even though they were not published until the 1940s by Holger Arbman and were not given scientific publication until the 1980s by Arwidsson, they became the standard for the typology and chronology of the Viking Age (Arbman and Arwidsson 1939–1989).

In contrast, Stolpe's finds from the Black Earth have not yet been researched and, apart from some exceptional cases, remain unpublished. His documentation of these excavations was far from complete, as he, like other people of his generation, had little experience in urban

excavations. Thus, the stratigraphy and the chronology of his excavated sites are unclear.

At the beginning of the 1930s, Arbman excavated some small areas around the fortress. There were no further archaeological excavations until 1969–1971, when there was an excavation beside the shoreline of the Viking Age town; this revealed a stone jetty from the mid-tenth century, the final phase of the occupation of the town of Birka.

Since then there have been a few small excavations on parts of the island, including one beside the rampart that revealed a number of buildings.

Excavations in the years 1990–1995 opened up an area in the Black Earth on the landward side of the jetty discovered in 1969–1971. The stratigraphic deposits, c. 2 m in depth, of great complexity, and containing many finds, will lead to much new work in Viking Age studies. The excavated area includes the shoreline immediately outside the area of earliest settlement whose property boundaries, consisting of ditches, run into the excavated area. A stone jetty from Birka's earliest period lay on the shoreline; it was probably extended out into the water with a wooden deck carried on trestles. Occupation refuse was dumped around the jetty. When the land dried out through land elevation, new buildings and building plots were constructed toward the new shoreline. The jetties were also moved farther forward.

A bronze-casting workshop was built on the newly won ground; it produced the bronze jewelry and tools found in graves around the Mälaren Valley and in Birka. The workshop dates from A.D. 750–850.

Stolpe's finds from the excavated Birka cemeteries were attributed to the traditional date of the Viking Age; thus, Birka has been assumed to have been founded c. A.D. 800 and abandoned in the 970s. Recent finds such as the jetty area mentioned above, objects discovered at Staraja Lagoda near St. Petersburg in Russia and dated to A.D. 760 onward, and objects from the second half of the eighth century at Ribe in southwest Denmark all indicate that the date of the beginning of the Viking Age must be revised, based on cultural criteria, to A.D. 800.

The cemeteries with at least three thousand graves are significant for the understanding of Birka. The burials at Birka are of two main types. The first type comprises mounds over cremations, concentrated in the area outside the fortifications. They must represent an indigenous east Swedish population who moved to Birka from the hamlets and farmsteads in its surroundings. The size of the mounds shows that the town dwellers were of the same or slightly higher status than the country folk, and the number of graves (including the inhumations mentioned below) suggests a population of five hundred to one thousand individuals at any one time in Birka.

The second type of burial lays between the mound cemeteries and the settlement—that is, beside and inside the fortifications. There are large numbers of coffin and chamber graves containing inhumations and the most magnificent grave goods: weapons, jewelry, textiles, and imported luxuries of glass and bronze. Some of the graves appear to be Christian (e.g., those with small silver pendant crosses), but most do not show signs of this religion. These inhumations are probably graves of foreign merchants and craftsmen and their families. This difference in burial customs may also be reflected in the buildings in the settlement. Those found near the rampart were of indigenous type, whereas those by the jetties seem to have been built according to foreign traditions, with timber framing on sills rather than the native longhouse.

The graves from the tenth century, in particular, display pronounced eastern characteristics, with imports from the lands of the Rus in Kiev, the Khazars, and the Arabs. Such eastern connections have also been found in the upper layers of the Black Earth. In contrast, the ninth-century graves and the earliest layers in the Black Earth were influenced from the southwest: Hedeby and Ribe in Denmark and Dorestad in the Rhineland.

It is still difficult to date when contacts changed from southwest to east, but it must have happened sometime at the end of the ninth century. The eastern connection continued for a hundred years after Birka was abandoned; the finds from its successor, Sigtuna, still show eastern influence until the middle of the eleventh century.

The beginning of the easterly orientation in Birka seems to have coincided with the late-ninth-century foundation of a grand duchy in Novgorod and Kiev that was strongly influenced by the Svear.

Birka was founded before the middle of the eighth century, probably according to a defined plan such as that of Ribe at the beginning of the eighth century or Sigtuna at the end of the tenth century. The connection with the royal estate of Adelsö suggests that a Svea king founded the town in order to concentrate trade and manufacture in a place close to the coast but by the fairway leading to the center of his kingdom. As with most other Viking Age trading centers, this happened long before the traditional beginning of the Viking Age, c. 800. Contacts with the rest of Europe had begun long before the beginning of the Viking raids.

In the eighth century, an extensive network of small trading centers/prototowns grew up around the coast of the Baltic Sea. They specialized in trade and manufacture, either making consumer products, such as bronze jewelry, glass beads, and antler combs, for the local market or assembling raw materials (furs and iron at Birka, for example) for redistribution elsewhere. Natives and foreigners cooperated in this activity, and the king both supported and protected it.

The greater part of Björkö, including the monuments of Birka, belongs to the Swedish state, and in 1993 it and the remains of the royal estate of Adelsö were included in UNESCO's World Heritage List.

FURTHER READINGS

Adam of Bremen. *History of the Archbishops of Hamburg-Bremen.* Trans. with Introduction and Notes Francis J. Tschan. Records of Civilization Sources and Studies 53. New York: Columbia University Press, 1959.

Ambrosiani, B., and H. Clarke, eds. *Early Investigations and Future Plans.* Birka Studies 1: Investigations in the Black Earth. Stockholm: RAÅ-SHMM, 1992.

Arbman, H., and G. Arwidsson, eds. *Birka I–V.* Stockholm: KVHAA, 1939–1989.

Clarke, H., and B. Ambrosiani. *Towns in the Viking Age.* Leicester: Leicester University Press, 1991.

Björn Ambrosiani, translated by Helen Clarke

SEE ALSO
Haithabu; Novgorod

Birsay

The Brough of Birsay, a tidal island, is one of the best-known archaeological sites in Orkney, projecting out into the Atlantic at the northwest corner of Birsay Bay and separated by the 238-m-wide Brough Sound from the Point of Buckquoy. Its name derives from Old Norse *borg* (fortress or stronghold), which can refer to either a broch (a fortified dwelling), or, as is more likely in this case, the natural defensive qualities of an island difficult of access.

The earliest archaeological work on this site appears to have been by Sir Henry Dryden in 1870, who cleared out the chapel. The site came into the care of the secretary of state for Scotland in 1934, and considerable clearance and excavation took place to prepare the site for the general public. This work was curtailed with the outbreak of World War II, but the finds from the excavations have been published by C.L. Curle, along with the finds from the later campaigns of C.A.R. Radford and S.H. Cruden in the 1950s and 1960s. Interim accounts of aspects of the later work have been published. Earlier structural elements uncovered below the chapel have generally been associated with the pre-Norse church. However, these earlier structural elements no longer need to be associated with the so-called Celtic church but, by analogy with the Brough of Deerness and Brattahlið in Greenland, may be dated to the Norse period.

Work was resumed on a small scale in 1973; in the area to the east of the chapel, Room 5 was excavated. Essentially, four major periods were distinguished. From analysis of the associated finds, together with some radiocarbon C-14 (ninth century or later) dating, the first may be assigned to the pre-Norse (Pictish) phase (pre-800) and the later three to the Norse. Only the last phase relates to the laid-out, standing building. Following this work, a renewed large-scale series of excavations was begun by J.R. Hunter and C.D. Morris in 1974 and continued until 1982. There is now clear evidence from the Brough of Birsay for many buildings (far more, across a wider area, than originally envisaged) dating to the Norse and Pictish periods. There is also clear evidence here for multiphase activity, with the replacement of buildings and often their complete reorientation in relation to the local topography.

There has been much discussion of the significance of the entries in the *Orkneyinga Saga* concerning the "minster dedicated to Christ" at Birsay established by Earl Thorfinn the Mighty. Both Radford and Cruden take the view that the buildings mentioned in the *Saga* can be identified with structures excavated on the brough. Others (e.g., the Royal Commission on the Ancient and Historical Monuments of Scotland; R.G. Lamb) see these structures as twelfth century (rather than eleventh) and monastic in character and favor a location for the "minster" in the village area. In 1982, excavations took place under the direction of Barber in advance of restoration of the parish church of St. Magnus. Structural elements uncovered below the present church have been accorded a probable twelfth-century date, and it is suggested that the present building was preceded by a pre-Reformation church of some sophistication. However, the dating accorded to the remains does not enable firm associations with the historical data, and so it cannot yet be claimed that the "minster" was originally located in the village.

Norse Christianity clearly focused upon Birsay, but once the cathedral was built in Kirkwall, the focus of secular and ecclesiastical power shifted away. Little is known of events here between the twelfth and the sixteenth centuries. However, by the sixteenth century, much of Birsay had been transferred from the hands of the earl of Orkney to the bishops of Orkney, and in that century it is clear that the bishops used a palace hereabouts. In the sixteenth century, an otherwise unknown writer, "Jo Ben," described Birsay as having "an excellent palace"; according to local tradition, the presence of walls and other features in the area to the south of the parish church may relate to this palace.

The significance of Birsay in the sixteenth century is reinforced by the building of an imposing Earl's Palace to the north of the Burn of Boardhouse. This was constructed with ranges of buildings around a courtyard with projecting rectangular towers at three corners, perhaps dated to 1574. It is probable that, in the construction of the Earl's Palace, stones from the older Bishop's Palace were reused. However, the regained significance of Birsay was short lived, and P.D. Anderson (1983) has suggested that deterioration of the Earl's Palace is recorded from as early as 1653. The gaunt ruins of the palace are perhaps visible reminders of what has been described as the "dark period" of Orkney's history under the Stewart earls.

There are clear indications that buildings from the Viking and late Norse periods remain to be discovered in the area to the south of the village. The place-name Tuftaback, bank or slope of house sites, might well be equated with the area to the south of the Burn of Boardhouse. Here, buildings and middens of some complexity have been uncovered on top of a mound site composed of archaeological deposits presumably going back into prehistory. A second such mound site almost certainly exists below an adjacent modern building and extends down to the riverbank.

Beyond the village to the south are the Links, at the southern end of which is Saevar Howe, another multiperiod mound site, which was examined in the nineteenth century by Farrer and more recently by J.W. Hedges. Pictish buildings here were apparently built on top of a prehistoric site and were themselves superseded by Viking Age dwellings. On top of these were the remains of a Christian Norse cemetery—although not recognized as such in the nineteenth century.

Cemeteries from both the Roman Iron Age/Pictish and the Viking periods have also been recognized from the area between the village and the brough to the north. The earlier burials are marked by cist graves below mounds of sand and stone cairns, without accompanying grave goods. The later burials were either in cists or simply dug

B

into the contemporary ground surface, but they were accompanied by grave goods recognizably Viking in form and date. Radiocarbon determinations have confirmed these chronological attributions. Even earlier, the area was clearly of significance in the earlier Iron Age (structural evidence) and the Bronze Age (midden deposits). Fragmentary traces of settlement remains of the Viking period have also been excavated in this area, with accompanying rich midden deposits, and a characteristic figure-eight-shaped dwelling from the late Pictish period. This series of excavations directed by Morris between the village and the brough has received full publication. Of particular interest and significance was the nearby site at Buckquoy excavated by A. Ritchie. Here, a Pictish farmstead was uncovered, of two major periods, succeeded by a Norse farmstead. It has also been suggested that the evidence points to some degree of coexistence by the two groups.

Extensive archaeological research supports the conclusion, derived from written sources, that Birsay was a center of political and ecclesiastical power during the Viking and late Norse periods. In addition, there is also evidence to support Birsay's importance in the preceding Pictish period, together with its imperfectly understood role in prehistoric Orkney.

FURTHER READINGS

Anderson, Peter D. Birsay in the Sixteenth Century. *Orkney Heritage* (1983) 2:82–96.

Cruden, Stewart H. Earl Thorfinn the Mighty and the Brough of Birsay. In *Third Viking Congress, Reyjavik, 1956.* Ed. Kristján Eldjárn. Reykjavik: Thjóðminjasafn Íslands, 1958, pp. 156–162.

———. Excavations at Birsay, Orkney. In *Fourth Viking Congress, York, 1961.* Ed. Alan Small. London: Oliver & Boud, 1965, pp. 22–31.

Curle, Cecil L. *The Pictish and Norse Finds from the Brough of Birsay, 1934–74.* Edinburgh: Monograph Series 1. Society of Antiquaries of Scotland, 1982.

Hedges, John W. Trial Excavations on Pictish and Viking Settlements at Saevar Howe, Birsay, Orkney. *Glasgow Archaeological Journal* (1983) 10:73–124 (and microfiche 40–102).

Hunter, John R. Recent Excavations on the Brough of Birsay. *Orkney Heritage* (1983) 2:152–170.

———. *Rescue Excavations on the Brough of Birsay, 1974–82.* Monograph Series 4. Edinburgh: Society of Antiquaries of Scotland, 1986.

Hunter, John R., and Christopher D. Morris. Recent Excavations at the Brough of Birsay, Orkney. In *Proceedings of the Eighth Viking Congress, Aarhus, 1977.* Ed. Hans Bekker-Nielsen, Peter G. Foote, and Olaf Olsen. Odense: Odense University Press, 1981, pp. 245–258.

———. Appendix: Excavation of Room 5, Brough of Birsay, Clifftop Settlement, 1973–74. In *The Pictish and Norse Finds from the Brough of Birsay 1934–74,* by Cecil L. Curle. Monograph Series 1. Edinburgh: Society of Antiquaries of Scotland, 1982, pp. 124–38.

Lamb, Raymond G. The Cathedral of Christchurch and the Monastery of Birsay. *Proceedings of the Society of Antiquaries of Scotland* (1974) 105:206–235.

———. The Cathedral and the Monastery. *Orkney Heritage* (1983) 2:36–45.

Morris, Christopher D. Excavations around the Bay of Birsay. *Orkney Heritage* (1983) 2:142–147.

———. *The Birsay Bay Project.* Vol. 1. Department of Archaeology Monograph Series 1. Durham: University of Durham, 1989.

———. *Church and Monastery in the Far North: An Archaeological Evaluation.* Jarrow Lecture 1989. Jarrow: St. Paul's Church, 1990.

———. The Birsay Bay Project: A Résumé. In *The Viking Age in Caithness, Orkney, and the North Atlantic.* Select Papers from the *Proceedings of the Eleventh Viking Congress, Thurso and Kirkwall, 1989.* Ed. Colleen E. Batey, Judith Jesch, and Christopher D. Morris. Edinburgh: Edinburgh University Press, 1993, pp. 285–307.

Radford, C.A. Ralegh. *The Early Christian and Norse Settlements at Birsay.* Official Guide. Edinburgh: HMSO, 1959.

———. The Celtic Monastery in Britain. *Archaeologia Cambrensis* (1962) 111:1–24.

———. Birsay and the Spread of Christianity to the North. *Orkney Heritage* (1983) 2:13–35.

Ritchie, Anna. Pict and Norsemen in Northern Scotland. *Scottish Archaeological Forum* (1974) 6:23–36.

———. Excavation of Pictish and Viking-Age Farmsteads at Buckquoy, Orkney. *Proceedings of the Society of Antiquaries of Scotland* (1977) 105:174–212.

———. Birsay around A.D. 800. *Orkney Heritage* (1983) 2:46–66.

Christopher D. Morris

SEE ALSO

Northern Isles; Scotland, Dark Age

Boatbuilding: Small Boats from Northwest Europe

Boats are often distinguished from ships by size. Vessels up to c. 10 m in length can be considered boats; those above that, ships. Archaeological evidence for boats in northwest Europe takes four main forms: boat burials, wrecks or abandoned vessels, finds of reused timbers in waterside excavations, and images on artifacts. The ever-growing corpus of material suggests that six broad types of construction were commonly used:

1. Hollowing large logs to make a variety of basic dugout boats (or "logboats"), such as the late tenth-century Clapton boat from London.
2. Adding planks to a dugout base to make an "extended dugout," such as the Kentmere 1 boat of c. A.D. 1300 from northwest England.
3. Expanding thin-hulled dugouts, such as the pre-Viking Slusegard vessels from eastern Denmark.
4. Combining all three previous methods, especially in the Low Countries, where such a system was also used for ships, such as the c. eleventh-century Velsen boat from central Netherlands.
5. Clinker-planked ("lapstrake") construction, in which boats were built of a shell of overlapping planks to which the frame timbers were then fitted. This system was used for both ships and boats. Examples of boats built using this system include the late medieval Kalmar 3 boat and the tenth-century small boats found with the Gokstad ship in southern Norway. For most of the Medieval period, the planking was split out, but sawn planks were slowly adopted in many areas from the fourteenth century. The overlaps could be fastened with iron rivets, wedged wooden pegs ("treenails"), or fiber lashings.
6. Skin-covered, wood-framed construction. This technique is thought to have been used in the west, where there is still a surviving tradition of building such craft. They are said to be shown often on memorial stones.

The building of basic dugout boats was by far the most common system until c. 1300; most of these craft were restricted to inland or water use. They were relatively small: from c. 2.5 m to c. 6 m. They could be built with few tools, mainly axes and adzes, which would have been part of the equipment of most large rural households. It is likely that many peasants built their own, since variations in shape are sometimes confined to particular river systems. They were always built out of local trees.

FURTHER READINGS

Greenhill, B. *The Archaeology of the Boat.* London: Adam and Charles Black, 1976.

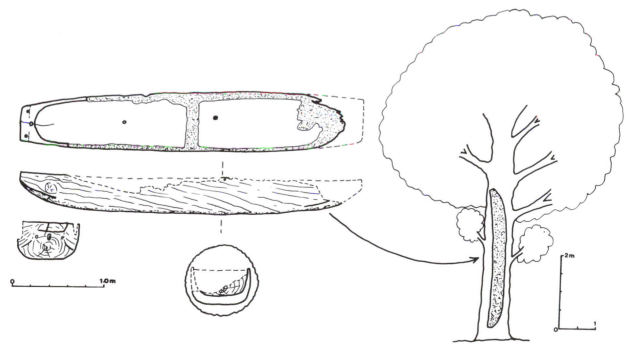

The tenth-century Clapton dugout boat and the reconstructed "parent tree" from which the hull was hewn.

B

Goodburn, D. New Light on Ship and Boat Building in the London Area. In *Waterfront Archaeology*. Ed. G. Good, R. Jones, and M. Ponsford. Research Report 74. London: Council for British Archaeology, CBA, 1991.

McGrail, S. *Rafts, Boats, and Ships*. London: HMSO, 1981.

D.M. Goodburn

SEE ALSO
Shipbuilding

Bohemia: Early Medieval Villages

The chronological division of the early Middle Ages in Bohemia, based on the interpretation of development of the country's socioeconomic and political systems, includes the early Slavic period (sixth–seventh centuries), followed by the old (seventh–eighth centuries), middle (c. 800–950), late (950–twelfth century) and final Slavic periods (twelfth century–1250). From the sociopolitical viewpoint, the first of these three periods constitutes an age characterized by the preponderance of autonomous regional units, while the centralization activities resulting from the efforts of the central Bohemian Přemysl lineage characterize the third period. The Přemyslids gradually rose to sovereignty over all Bohemia, first as tribute-collecting overlords and then as direct rulers, in the fourth period. The fifth period shows the growth of discord among the individual components of the system, leading ultimately, in the course of the thirteenth century, to the emergence of the fully fledged medieval state of Bohemia with all its distinctive attributes.

Studies of early medieval settlement in Bohemia follow several basic problem orientations, differing in the geographical, chronological, and thematic extent of the investigations. In archaeology, there has been a shift away from broadly conceived settlement-pattern studies comprising all Bohemia based on partial regional studies and toward a closer focus on minor landscape units. Changes are also perceptible in research on early medieval hillforts; in addition to the fortified areas themselves, more and more authors take the satellite agglomerations and broader hinterland areas into consideration (Bubeník 1991; Gojda 1992; Klápště 1993; Meduna and Černá 1991; Richter and Smetánka 1991; Sláma 1967).

All of the early Medieval period is characterized by the movement from areas with optimum natural conditions into less favorable zones, regardless of whether the differences are sought in geomorphological, pedological, hydrological, climatic, or other definable factors of the environment. In general, the idea of an incessant cyclical interaction between population and the carrying capacity of a given territory in terms of selection of an appropriate economic strategy seems justified, subject to social and political influences.

The emergence of settlement patterns in the "classic" zones cultivated intensely as early as the prehistoric period may be documented for the early Slavic period, when settlements playing the role of the so-called primary cores of the settlement patterns became stabilized. Ever since the initial stages, landscape morphology determined the basic types of settlement forms—compact, dispersed, and cellular. Throughout the earliest periods, settlement advances assumed mostly "natural" forms, affected mainly by population growth and, to a certain extent, by the increasing control of natural resources by the chiefly elites. In the centralization period at the close of the middle Slavic period, the first example of a deliberate, military colonization, linked with gradual expansion of the Přemyslid power, may be documented. The military groups were settled especially on strategic communications segments.

A greater intensity of settlement processes may be observed in the late and the final Slavic periods. As a consequence of earlier ducal activities, the eleventh century, in particular, saw a number of migrations when the Přemyslids settled groups of people mainly in the vicinity of the newly built second-order centers, both outside and inside the basic settlement patterns. The selection of assarted (newly colonized) areas was dominated by considerations of intensification of natural-resource use (mostly iron) and of specialized agricultural (vines) and animal-husbandry production. The following century ushered in the phenomenon of private assarts by a growing number of temporal and spiritual overlords. The property titles to these assarts were nonetheless still regulated by the interests of the sovereign. In these estates, settlement advances beyond the basic settlement patterns assume the form of smaller segments, emerging especially by the extension of settlement lines. The rising intensity of the assarting process is, in part, compensated for by the contrast between the extent of the newly settled regions and the sizes and forms of individual settlements. The productive capacity in adverse conditions allows hardly more than dispersed and cellular settlements. In addition to settlement growth, the basic settlement patterns show condensation due to the emergence of settlement complexes in primary-core areas and to the birth of secondary cores as a manifestation of *microcolonization*. Transformations of the internal structures of settlements take particularly remarkable forms in the development of compact settlements, in which the desertion of primary-core consumption areas and transition toward dispersed forms may be observed. This may have been caused by the growth of estate-holding by spiritual and temporal overlords, which is visible in two variant forms. In the first, the social capacity of the settlements was overloaded, leading to the separation of the minor landed gentry. In the second, the estates of individual landowners were distinguished within a single settlement.

It was in the course of the late and the final Slavic periods that these complex interconnections gained momentum through changes in both basic parameters: population and territorial capacity. To a certain extent, this situation can be described by catastrophe theory. The system, which had undergone a series of partial failures and exhausted all suitable interaction strategies, fell back to its own initial state. The discord between the rising socioeconomic demands and the diminished potential of the assarting strategy led to only one possible alternative strategy (the only one acceptable in terms of preservation of the local populations): increasing the carrying capacity of the settlement area while preserving its spatial extent through a transformation of the economic system. This change in rural settlement resulted in a completely different design of the internal structure of settlement areas, represented by settlement concentration and the rigid articulation of production, consumption, and residential areas that is seen in the course of the thirteenth century.

FURTHER READINGS

Bubeník, J. The Archaeology of the Early Middle Ages (Sixth–Twelfth Centuries): On the Present State of Early Medieval Archaeology in Bohemia. In *Archaeology in Bohemia, 1986–1990*. Prague: Institute of Archaeology, 1991, pp. 27–34.

Gojda, M. Early Medieval Settlement Study in Bohemia: Tradition and Perspectives. *Památky Archeologické* (1992) 83:174–180.

Klápště, J. Změna: Stredověká transformace a její předpoklady (Změna: The Medieval Transformation and Its Previous Conditions). *Památky Archeologické* (1993) 2:59–60.

Meduna, P., and E. Černá. Settlement Structure of the Early Middle Ages in Northwest Bohemia: Investigations of the Pětipsy Basin Area. *Antiquity* (1991) 65:388–395.

Neustupný, E. Sídelní areály pravěkých zemědělců (Settlement Areas of Prehistoric Farmers). *Památky Archeologické* (1986) 67:226–234.

Richter, M., and Z. Smetánka. Medieval Archaeology, 1986–1990: Traditions and Perspective. In *Archaeology in Bohemia, 1986–1990*. Prague: Institute of Archaeology, 1991, pp. 44–55.

Sláma, J. Příspěvek kvnitrní kolonizaci raně středověkých Čech (Contribution on the Native Sites of Early Medieval Bohemia). *Archeologické rozhledy* (1967) 19:433–445.

Smetánka, Z. Únětice and Levý Hradec in the Twelfth Century: The Results of Recent Fieldwork. *Archeologické rozhledy* (1992) 44:231–242.

Petr Meduna

SEE ALSO
Bohemia and Moravia: High Medieval Settlement

Bohemia and Moravia: High Medieval Settlement

In the Czech lands of Bohemia and Moravia (52,000 km^2 and 22,000 km^2, respectively), the High Medieval period refers to the thirteenth and fourteenth centuries. The thirteenth century, in particular, saw a fundamental change in the character of settlement, reflecting new social and economic needs. Changing settlement patterns and the appearance of new types of settlements laid the foundation for subsequent development and have shaped the present-day landscape in the Czech lands. As in a number of other European countries, the High Medieval settlement transformation involved several processes, including the extension of settlement into previously unoccupied lands, changes in the settlement structure of existing villages, the development of towns, and the appearance of feudal residences.

The Extension of the Settlement Network

Archaeological evidence indicates that gradual long-term settlement growth took place during the early Medieval period. Between the sixth century and the early thirteenth, those parts of the Czech lands that were essential for agriculture were settled, leaving only the less attractive areas for thirteenth- and fourteenth-century colonization. Owing to the diverse geographical conditions, the patches that had been left unoccupied occurred both around the edges of, and inside, Bohemia and Moravia, often close to the areas of early settlement.

The Drahany Highlands in central Moravia, close to the city of Brno, provide an example of a well-studied area that was not colonized until the High Middle Ages

B

(Černý 1992). The landscape, situated 400–700 m above sea level, remained wooded until the thirteenth century. In the thirteenth and the early fourteenth centuries, more than a hundred villages and several lesser towns and castles were established through the colonization of an area of 650 km². In the wake of the wave of desertion that affected the Drahany Highlands in the fifteenth century, 50 percent of the villages and most of their fields were abandoned. The depopulation and forest regeneration created ideal conditions for the preservation of unique archaeological remains that were studied by archaeological survey. Short double-row forest field villages, whose lengths ranged from 115 m to 450 m, make up the highest proportion of deserted villages. Surface remains show that these villages generally comprised eight to sixteen homesteads. The field patterns were identified with the help of existing traces of balks (small, unexcavated areas between excavation units) and beds. Some field patterns were belt-type backyards, usually with additional side sections. The area of the smallest deserted-field pattern is 49 ha; the largest, 399 ha. Homesteads had 3–23 ha of arable land. A conspicuous feature is apparent in the development of the Drahany Highlands: the postmedieval settlement is composed of settlements established in the thirteenth century. The complex political and economic conditions following the colonization of the Drahany Highlands did not necessitate a change in the settlement type itself; its structure was flexible enough to adapt to the new conditions.

A basically different type of thirteenth-century colonization can be seen in the Kostelec-nad-Černými-lesy region near Prague (Smetánka and Klápště 1981). This area, which is 300–400 m above sea level, had also remained wooded until the beginning of the High Medieval period, due to its unfavorable natural environment. Following the thirteenth-century colonization of the area, the wave of desertion associated with forest regeneration started as early as the late thirteenth century and continued until the late fifteenth century. The site-surface survey was focused on an area of c. 60 km², within which five deserted villages containing well-preserved surface remains were studied. The ground-plan analysis suggests that the villages were not large, comprising five to eight homesteads. It was only during the wave of desertion that settlement became concentrated into the larger and more regular villages that have survived in the area to the present day.

Structural Changes Affecting Villages in Earlier Settlement Areas

Since only a very small proportion of the Czech lands were unoccupied at the beginning of the thirteenth century, the High Medieval transformation was concerned primarily with areas of earlier medieval settlement. Larger villages emerged, showing a more stable layout of homesteads and a more unified economic hinterland. The woodland had also receded in these areas, and the sharp division between fields and wooded areas, which stands out so clearly today, gradually began to stabilize. New colonization also occured.

Archaeology plays a key role in providing evidence for, and an appreciation of, the changes affecting the regions of earlier settlement. Systematic archaeological research leaves no doubt about the general significance of these changes. At present, there is no evidence available of any village that did not undergo major changes in either the earlier or the later part of the High Medieval period (cf. Klápště 1991). An example is the town of Most in northwestern Bohemia. Long-term rescue activity in the region, brought about primarily by open-cast coal mining, offers a representative set of examples attesting to the tranformation process. Early medieval habitation areas can be recognized; they were abandoned in virtually one time horizon, datable to the mid-thirteenth century (Klápště 1994). A similar phenomenon has been recorded archaeologically in the environs of Prague (Klápště et al. 1983).

The High Medieval transformation involved a new approach to dealing with space. Early medieval settlement consisted of a fairly flexible pattern of settlement areas that allowed movement within the layout of both the homesteads and the agricultural hinterland. In the High Medieval period, the homestead had become a basic economic unit and included a more or less firmly marked-out piece of land. This spatial delineation was also the basis for rent assessment. Space stabilization affected the character of the homesteads, which began to be built to last, and stone was commonly used as a bulding material for the first time. Its use, however, always depended upon the availability of material resources and, therefore, varied greatly by region.

The process of medieval transformation unified a substantial part of Europe; in this context, the changes affecting the Czech village were relatively delayed. It is likely that this contributed to the conspicuously regular village-core and homestead layouts recorded in some Bohemian and Moravian localities. The lost village of Svídna near Slaný, central Bohemia, datable to the thirteenth—

fifteenth centuries, provides an example of a regular site. Evidence from surface survey and testing through excavation indicate that the village occupied an area of 245 × 175 m; the village green, 156 × 38 m in area, was surrounded by thirteen homesteads and a manorial farm. The homestead cores were three-part houses formed of three basic rooms: living room, hall, and storage room (Smetánka 1994). A similar type of house is known from the lost village of Pfaffenschlag in southwestern Moravia. This short, double-row forest field village, datable to the thirteenth–fifteenth centuries, was subjected to an extensive excavation, which has provided valuable information about High Medieval homesteads (Nekuda 1975).

The Beginnings of High Medieval Towns

Beginning in the 1220s and 1230s, a qualitatively new chapter of urbanization commenced. Its basis was a town with privileges ensuring it a special legal position and controlling its region by means of the market. The network of these smaller and larger towns grew step by step, depending upon, among other things, the stages of development of different parts of the Czech lands. A number of the localities of this new type were based, of course, on a previous settlement structure, which already in the early Medieval period had some urban functions. Prague represents a distinctive example of this category of town, having been the most extensive and well-developed early medieval settlement agglomeration in the Czech lands. Historical analysis of its development and legislation has been supplemented by archaeological evidence attesting to major changes that took place in the life of the Prague agglomeration during the thirteenth century. A change that stands out in the fairly stable pattern of the town's plots and commons concerns waste disposal. The growth of extensive stratified layers with a high proportion of organic matter, characteristic of the early Middle Ages, ended in the thirteenth century. The levels of deposits began to stabilize, and deliberate fills were used to level the surface (Hrdlička 1984).

The network of High Medieval urbanization in the Czech lands relied on major royal towns; in many regions, however, very modest urban bases served the purpose (Richter and Velímský 1993). An example of this type of lesser town is the monastic town near the community of Hradištko south of Prague. The settlement was set up in the thirteenth century (c. 1240); its forced abandonment in the same century (1278/1283) resulted in very good preservation of the archaeological remains from the initial phase of the life of a small urban settlement. The core of the site consisted of a trapezoidal central space of more than 1.0 ha in size. Some fifty to sixty fairly small plots, c. 10 × 30 m, were attached to it around the perimeter. A sunken-featured house (Grubenhaus) was generally located at the front of the plot, serving as a makeshift dwelling on the site where an actual burgher house was to be built. Characteristic urban features can also be seen in the simplicity of the initial stage of development and are reflected both in the spatial arrangement and the small finds. The sunken-featured houses served as makeshift dwellings in major Bohemian and Moravian towns, too, presumably also featuring in the frequently complex development leading to the compact burgher house (Richter and Smetánka 1987).

The Emergence of High Medieval Feudal Residences

During the thirteenth century, a principal change can be seen in the residences of sovereigns, prelates, and the higher and lower nobility. The preceding period saw, on the one hand, fairly extensive hillfort settlements and, on the other, small residences with only simple fortifications. New conditions prompted the establishment of royal castles built of stone (Durdík 1994a, 1994b). In the thirteenth century, stone castles were also erected in the domains of leading families of the nobility, who mostly preferred the Bergfried (great tower) type. The lower social ranks opted for the motte-and-bailey type, while the lowest-ranked nobility continued to reside in manors. From the mid-twelfth century, landed nobility started to emerge in the Czech lands, deriving their power from ownership of land and residing in provincial seats. This social framework offered favorable conditions for the reception of the High Medieval changes. The emergence of stone castles also provides examples of asynchronous development, represented by castles newly profiting from their strategic positions but constructed using persisting archaic building techniques.

FURTHER READINGS

Černý, E. Výsledky výzkumu zaniklých středovkých osad a jejich plužin (Historicko-geografická studie v regionu Drahanské vrchoviny). (Deserted Medieval Villages and Field Patterns in Drahany Highlands). Brno: Muzejní a vlastivědná společnost v Brně, 1992.

Durdík, T. Anfänge der hochmittelalterlichen Burgen in Böhmen. Château Gaillard (1994a) 16:143–153.

———. Kastellburgen des 13. Jahrhunderts in Mitteleuropa. Praha: Academia, 1994b.

B

Hrdlička, L. Outline of Development of the Landscape of the Prague Historical Core in the Middle Ages. *Archeologické rozhledy* (1984) 36:638–652.

Klápště, J. Studies of Structural Change in Medieval Settlement in Bohemia. *Antiquity* (1991) 65:396–405.

———. *Paměť krajiny středověkého Mostecka* (Memory Recorded within the Landscape of the Medieval Most Region). Most: Archeologický ústar AVČR, 1994.

Klápště, J., Z. Smetánka, and Zv. Dragoun. Příspěvek ke studiu zemědělského zázemí středověké Prahy (A Contribution to the Study of Rural Hinterland of the Medieval City of Prague). *Archeologické rozhledy* (1983) 35:387–426.

Nekuda, V. *Pfaffenschlag: Zaniklá středověká ves u Slavonic* (Pfaffenschlag: Deserted Medieval Village near Slavonica). Brno: Blok, 1975.

Richter, M. *Hradištko u Davle, městeko ostrovského kláštera* (Hradištko Near Davle, a Small Town of Ostrover Cloister). Praha: Academia, 1982.

Richter, M., and Z. Smetánka. Archäologische Untersuchungen zum städtischen Wohnhaus des Mittelalters in Böhmen, unter besonderer Berücksichtigung von Prag. *Siedlungsforschung Archäologie-Geschichte-Geographie* (1987) 5:67–95.

Richter, M., and T. Velímský. Die archäologische Erforschung von Stadtwüstungen des 13. Jahrhunderts in Böhmen. *Siedlungsforschung Archäologie-Geschichte-Geographie* (1993) 11:83–110.

Smetánka, Z. *Život středověké vesnice: Zaniklá Svídna* (The Life of a Medieval Village: Deserted Village Svídna). Praha: Academia, 1988.

———. K problematice trojdílného domu v Čechách a na Moravě v období vrcholného a pozdního středověku (A Discussion of Problems Associated with the Three-Part House in Bohemia and Moravia during the Period of the High and Late Middle Ages). *Památky Archeologické* (1994) 2:S117–138.

Smetánka, Z., and J. Klápště. Geodeticko-topografický průzkum zaniklých středověkých vsí na Černokostelecku (Geodetical-Topographical Survey of Deserted Medieval Villages in the Kostelec-nad-Černými-lesy Region). *Památky Archeologické* (1981) 72:416–458.

Jan Klápště

SEE ALSO

Bohemia: Early Medieval Villages; Brno; Castles; Prague

Boss Hall Cemetery

During a routine visit to inspect a building site on the Boss Hall Industrial Estate on the western edge of Ipswich (England) in May 1990, a mixed inhumation and cremation cemetery of early Anglo-Saxon date was discovered. In all, twenty-two inhumation graves and five cremations were located and rapidly excavated over an area of 350 m². While the acidic nature of the underlying sand and gravel deposits precluded the survival of any skeletal material in the inhumation graves, it was possible to record fully and recover grave goods from the nineteen furnished burials. The excavated part of the site represents a significant but unknown proportion of a cemetery of which only the western edge appears to have been defined. The Boss Hall Cemetery site is close to the River Gipping, one of the main waterways in southeast Suffolk. While the site now lies well within the administrative district covered by Ipswich, at one time it lay in the parish of Sproughton close to its boundary with the Bramford parish. The cemetery site is just under 3 km northwest of the center of middle Saxon Ipswich.

For the most part, the Boss Hall Cemetery is a typical Anglian burial ground of sixth- and early seventh-century date. Of the nineteen furnished graves on the site, nine can be identified as female burials on the evidence of the grave goods, while seven appear to be male, and three are not sexable. The assemblages from eight of the female graves can be considered standard Anglian examples for this period, containing small/long, annular, and cruciform brooches, including one florid type. Other female grave goods include a pair of stamped silver bracelets, girdle hangers, and beads. The seven burials with male grave goods include four with a spearhead and shield boss, one with only a shield boss, and one with only a spearhead.

The seventh male grave was a more complex example, with three spearheads, a shield boss, and various small items, including evidence for a leather bag associated with a purse fastener/strike-a-light. The male grave containing this relatively large assemblage is also of note as it appears to have been contained within a large, timber-lined chamber. It may also be inferred that a small mound or barrow originally covered the chamber as four of the cremation urns recovered from this site formed a semicircular arc around this burial. Evidence for small barrows within early Anglo-Saxon cemeteries is becoming increasingly common in East Anglia (as at Spong Hill and Snape), and it is probable that all cemeteries contained complex grave structures and markers that can be located using modern excavation techniques but were not recorded during earlier cemetery excavations.

One female grave proved to be somewhat later in date and to contain an exceptionally rich assemblage of grave goods. This grave contained a group of objects that was apparently deposited in a bag in the chest area of the burial. The only other objects in the grave were an iron knife and a glass bead. The main complex of objects was lifted in a small soil block and excavated under laboratory conditions, which greatly facilitated the recovery of evidence for organic materials associated with the burial.

The contents of this bag included a composite brooch set with numerous small garnets, four disc-shaped gold pendants, and two cabochon garnet and gold pendants. A cabochon is a gem that is cut in a convex form and highly polished but not faceted. The bag also contained a regal solidus of Sigebert III (A.D. 634–656) set as a pendant, a primary series B sceat (c. A.D. 690), fragments of silver spacer beads, glass beads, and a silver cosmetic set. The high status of this assemblage is clear from the objects present and is supported by the preserved organic remains, which include traces of silk. This rich burial can be closely dated by the presence of the series B sceat to c. A.D. 700. It would, therefore, appear that some reuse was being made of an old cemetery site well into what is generally accepted as the Christian Era of the middle Saxon (c. A.D. 650–850) period.

Finally it should be noted that documentary evidence indicates that the Boss Hall area may have contained an important estate center in the Anglo-Saxon period. This is indicated by the large royal and ecclesiastical estates in Bramford parish listed in the *Domesday Book* and by evidence for a church dedicated to St. Aethelbeorht (king of East Anglia, d. 794) close to the Boss Hall area.

FURTHER READINGS

Newman, J. The Anglo-Saxon Cemetery at Boss Hall, Ipswich. *Bulletin of the Sutton Hoo Research Committee* (1993) 8:33–36.

Shearman, F. Excavation, Examination, and Conservation of Anglo-Saxon Jewellery from Boss Hall, Ipswich. *Conservator* (1993) 17:26–31.

Webster, L., and J. Backhouse. *The Making of England (Anglo-Saxon Art and Culture, 600–900)*. London: British Museum Press, 1991.

John Newman

SEE ALSO

Ipswich; Snape; Spong Hill; Sutton Hoo

B

Bratislava

Bratislava, the capital of the Slovak Republic, is situated in the heart of Europe at the border of Hungary and Austria. Its advantageous natural and strategic position at the foot of the Small Carpathians, on the banks of the River Danube, stimulated the continuous settlement of this area from earliest times to the present. Results of archaeological research convincingly confirm this fact. The beginnings of Bratislava (Pressburg, Pozsony) as a town go back to the last century before Christ, when an important administrative and economic center was fortified and developed here. It covered an area of more than 50 ha.

In the fifth and sixth centuries, the territory of present Slovakia began to be settled by the Slavs, who founded their first state—the Great Moravian Empire—in the ninth century. On the hill next to the River Danube, a settlement appeared that was protected by a huge fortification built of earth and wooden beams. Through archaeological research, the foundation and part of the walls of a stone palace were discovered. The most important find is the remains of a sacral building: the three-nave basilica decorated inside with paintings. There was a cemetery in its surroundings, with the oldest graves dating to the ninth century. The graves contained jewels, some metal dress accessories, and spurs used by the upper class of the society. Bratislava's castle hill can be considered an important Great Moravian fortress and the church and secular center for the larger area. There was a residence for a prince's entourage and probably also for church dignitaries. Surrounding the fortress were several settlements.

The oldest written reference to Bratislava attesting to its important position appeared in the *Annals of Salzburg,* in which it was called Brezalauspurc, one of three known names in the Great Moravian area. The author of the annals briefly mentioned a battle between Magyar and Bavarian troops on July 4, 907. The battle, which ended with the defeat of the Bavarians, at whose side the Moravians fought, opened the way to the West for the Magyars. Because of this, the fortress temporarily lost its role.

Around A.D. 1000, a multinational Hungarian Kingdom arose, and the territory of Transdanubia and present southwest Slovakia became its central part. Brezalauspurc played an important role in this process, as it was already under the governance of the first Hungarian king, Stephan (1000–1038). Coins with his name, "STEPHANUS REX," on the obverse and the inscription "RESLAVVA CIV" on the reverse were probably struck here. The new landlords refortified the former Slav fortress and

B

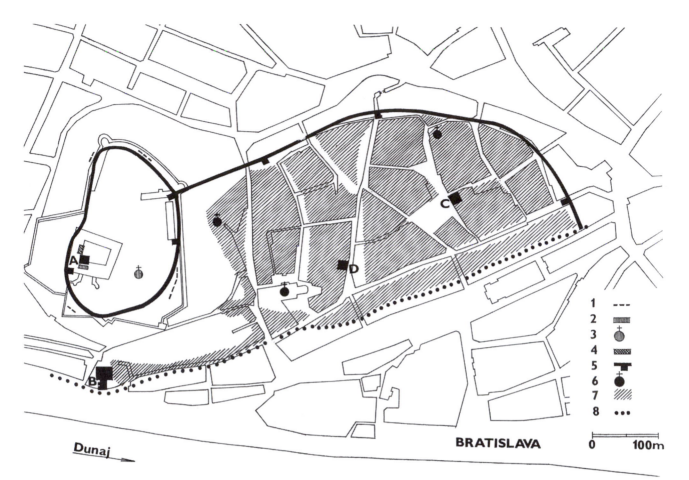

Medieval Bratislava

1. Timber structure and earthwork fortification, ninth century.
2. Basilica, ninth century.
3. Palace, ninth century.
4. Palace, twelfth century.
5. Urban area, thirteenth century.
6. Fortification, thirteenth century.

7. The original bank of the River Danube:
    A. castle and its fortification, thirteenth century;
    B. piers of the bridge and remains of the tower in the port;
    C. town hall;
    D. Academia Istropolitana.
8. Sacral buildings, thirteenth century.

erected a central castle for the county, which served as the administrative center. This castle, together with a system of watch stations, protected the northwest border of the Hungarian Kingdom.

The settlement below the castle further developed around the marketplace. The area already had at least two churches surrounded by cemeteries. Archaeological research discovered a fortified port on the left bank of the River Danube from this period. Several piers from its bridgehead have been preserved.

In the second half of the twelfth century, significant changes occurred in the residential structure and the social composition of the inhabitants. According to archaeological research, the inhabitants now lived in one-

or two-room dwellings, some of them built on a base of stone. A new palace building appeared on the castle hill. Its fortification was gradually strengthened, so that the castle was considered one of the most solid in the whole Hungarian Kingdom.

In the first half of the thirteenth century, the Tartars interfered with the growth of the settlement below the castle. They plundered the powerless country from the beginning of the year 1242. After their withdrawal, the Hungarian King Bela IV began a revival of the destroyed country. In this period, a Gothic town (with a concentration of buildings) arose. The castle and the settlement below it received a common fortification. The unification of both settlements within the same fortification created a large fortress on the country's border. In place of the earlier castle palace, a huge rectangular keep, fortified by several defensive towers, was erected. The settlement below the castle was protected by a new stone wall with prismatic towers and with three city gates. Civic architecture existed as two-room, two-story stone houses and houses with towers. One such building was later rebuilt as a town hall.

Parochial and monastic churches, monasteries and nunneries, chapels, a chapter house, and the residence of a provost represented the sacral architecture of the town below the castle. The parish churches were connected with schools. These facts indicate that the settlement below the castle became a town, although it had a long wait before it was awarded town privileges. The charter of Andrew III, given on December 2, 1291, simply represents the legal confirmation of the older independence of the town.

Throughout the fourteenth and fifteenth centuries, the town grew. Sigismund of Luxembourg, the emperor and king, decided to establish the residence of Hungarian kings here in the beginning of the fifteenth century. As part of this effort, a new palace was built on the castle hill, and the castle fortification was improved. In 1465, King Matthew Corvinus obtained Pope Paul II's permission for the foundation of the first university in the town. The university received a statute from the Bologna University and became known as Academia Istropolitana.

The economic life of the inhabitants was represented primarily by the developing craft industries. Despite a lack of written information, archaeological finds indicate a high standard of craft production. In the town were workshops of blacksmiths, glassworkers, butchers, tanners, winemakers, carpenters, bakers, tailors, fishermen, furriers, shoemakers, goldsmiths, hatters, glovers, and others.

The initial archaeological information on the town's history was gained in the late nineteenth and early twentieth centuries. At first, there were only collections of casual finds. It was not until the 1960s that systematic archaeological research began. Among those who participated in this research were P. Baxa, B. Egyházy-Jurovská, A. Fiala, V. Ferus, S. Holcík, K. Klincoková, B. Lesák, M. Musilová, A. Piffl, V. Plachá, B. Polla, D. Rexa, L. Snopko, T. Stefanovicová, and A. Vallasek. Their research produced many finds, including pottery in a large variety of shapes and functions (pitchers, pots, cups, bowls, basins, funnels, strainers, chandeliers, and the like), tools, and weapons. Among the most impressive discoveries were of glass, including glasses, bottles of various shapes, and fragments of windowpanes. Bone chessmen and little earthen sculptures are unique finds. The existence of a medieval mint is demonstrated not only by the discovery of coins, but also by the recovery of items for their production.

The archaeological finds demonstrate that Bratislava was one of the most important central European towns in the Middle Ages. Its development continued in the centuries that followed.

Veronika Plachá and Jana Hlavicová

Bristol

The medieval city and port of Bristol lay at the confluence of the Frome and Avon Rivers on a rocky outcrop of Triassic marls and sandstones, c. 10 km inland from the Severn Estuary, where the modern Port of Bristol is situated. The River Severn and its tributary, the Avon, have one of the highest tidal ranges in the world; the problems to seamen of the rapid ebb and flow of the tide, combined with the twisting course of the River Avon, must have made the choice of site at first unattractive. However, Bristol had several notable advantages: it was far enough inland to be protected from the prevailing westerly winds by the limestone gorge on its western side; the original settlement was located on a well-drained site defended on three sides by water; and, with skillful handling, the fast-flowing river was used to advantage by mariners, who could reach the port and discharge their cargo well in advance of competitors in rival ports.

Origins

The precise date of the origin of the town is uncertain. It was certainly in existence by the reign of Cnut (A.D. 1016–1035), when silver pennies were being minted there. It is likely that coins were first minted in the town in the reign of Aethelred II (978–1016), probably in the early years of the eleventh century (Grinsell et al. 1973; Grinsell 1987). It was founded primarily as a port, probably c. A.D. 950, to take advantage of the lucrative trade with Ireland, stimulated by the Norse settlements on Ireland's east coast, and to act as a distribution center for the increasingly prosperous markets of the west of England and south Wales (Lobel and Carus-Wilson 1975:3).

The earliest settlement probably extended over all the promontory between the Frome and the Avon Rivers. Excavations at Mary-le-Port Street, roughly central to the promontory (Watts and Rahtz 1985), produced evidence for occupation of pre-Conquest date (1066) in the form of timber buildings alongside a road of tenth–eleventh-century date, together with evidence for metalworking, leather working, and spinning. Substantial Saxon occupation deposits have been found in the eastern part of the promontory on the site of the castle. Saxon pottery has been found in pits in the western part of the town close to Broad Street, and evidence for occupation was found at St. Bartholomew's Hospital on the north bank of the River Frome (Price 1979a). It is not certain when a gridded system of streets was laid out, although it is likely that the streets were laid out shortly after the foundation of the town.

Medieval Development

Shortly after the Norman Conquest, and certainly by 1088, a castle was founded at the eastern end of the promontory, effectively defending the settlement from attack from the east. The excavator thought that the castle was initially built in the form of a ringwork, revetted with a mortared stone wall. It was quickly modified, however, with the addition of a large motte (mound). Before 1147, the motte was replaced by a massive stone keep, built by Robert, earl of Gloucester and bastard son of Henry I. It measured c. 27 m square and had a forebuilding on its eastern side (Ponsford 1979).

At about the same time, a stone wall was erected around the old town, fragments of which have been excavated at various times (e.g., Rahtz 1960; Price 1979b; Boore 1982). Within the walled area, there would have been intense demand for space, with the houses of wealthy merchants occupying the prime positions close to

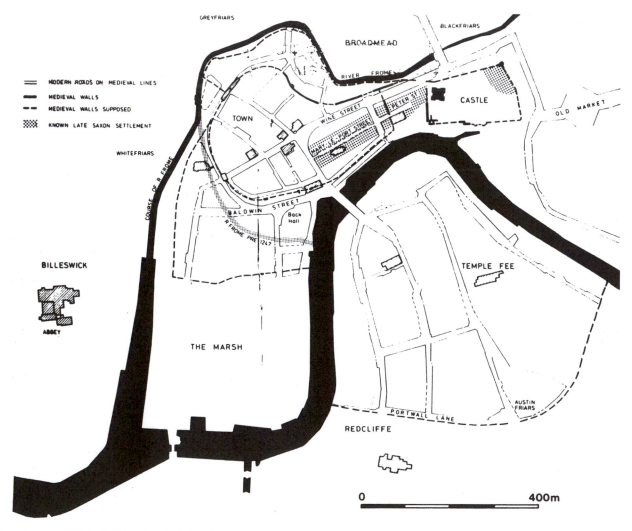

Plan of medieval Bristol (after Ponsford 1987).

the commercial heart of the town. At Tower Lane, in the northwestern part of the walled town, a substantial first-floor hall of the early twelfth century was excavated. It was constructed entirely of stone, with walls more than 1 m thick, and may have belonged to Robert Fitzharding, the future lord of Berkeley (Boore 1984). On a neighboring site, a building of similar pretension and date was excavated in 1990.

Outside the town wall, by contrast, there would have been much open land. To the south, the area was largely unreclaimed marsh before the twelfth century. On the north bank of the River Frome, on high ground overlooking his stone castle, Robert of Gloucester endowed the Benedictine Priory of St. James before 1147. Recent excavations here have uncovered part of the priory burial ground and suggested the possibility of pre-twelfth-century occupation of the site (Jones 1989). To the west, an Abbey of Augustinian Canons was founded between 1140 and 1148 in the suburb of Billeswick, where there may already have been pre-Conquest occupation.

In the thirteenth century, Bristol underwent a transformation, as new land was reclaimed, particularly on its south side. From a relatively small town of c. 8 ha, it became one of the largest towns in the country, with c. 53 ha contained within the walled area. The new land was walled during the second quarter of the thirteenth century. At the same time, a massive engineering project was undertaken involving the diversion of the River Frome from its former course to the south of the old town to a new course cut through the large tract of marsh on the southwest side of the town. The available port facilities were more than doubled, and henceforward the new Frome channel became the main focus of port activity, forming the "town quay," where the largest vessels would have docked. The old quays on the opposite side of the peninsula became known as the Backs or Welsh Back, where Welsh and other coastal vessels would have berthed.

In Redcliffe and Temple, low-lying land to the south of a loop in the River Avon, occupation had begun in the mid-twelfth century. This area was under separate jurisdiction from Bristol, and, during the twelfth and thirteenth centuries, Bristol and Redcliffe were great rivals for economic supremacy. This rivalry was not fully resolved until Bristol was created a county by Edward III in 1373. A series of quays was built along the western side of Redcliffe. Excavations along this waterfront have uncovered remains of these quays and associated slipways, which were a common feature of the Bristol waterfront. Timbers associated with the earliest of these quays have been dated dendrochronologically to the mid-twelfth century (Nicholson and Hillam 1987). These excavations showed that the original river-bank lay close to the present line of Redcliffe Street and that, in parts of the waterfront, more than 60 m of land had been reclaimed from the river in the period c. 1150–1450 (Williams 1982; Jones 1986; Good 1990). Redcliffe and Temple formed the center of Bristol's flourishing cloth industry, and workers in several crafts associated with cloth finishing, such as dyers, fullers, and weavers, were established here. Archaeological evidence for these industries has been found in excavation, such as the stone bases for dyers' vats (Williams 1981) and the remains of dye-plant seeds and colored fibers in the waterlogged deposits adjacent to the River Avon (Jones and Watson 1987).

By the fourteenth century, Bristol had become one of the foremost cities in the country outside London and the predominant exporter of finished wool cloth. It had lucrative trading links with southwest France and the Iberian Peninsula, as well as with Ireland and the rest of Britain. It had a wealthy burgess class who lived within the city and endowed many of the fine buildings that were to be found there. One of these was Richard le Spicer, who built for himself a great house in Welsh Back, which was partly excavated in 1958 (Barton 1960).

During the fifteenth century, Bristol remained preeminent. Its most notable citizen was the younger William Canynges, who possessed a large fleet and who lived in a great house in Redcliffe beside the Avon (Jones 1986). No major expansion of the city took place until the late seventeenth century. By this time, the city was becoming overcrowded and disease ridden. Its wealthier citizens sought escape from the overcrowding of the walled area. New development took place on the hills overlooking the city, and Bristol rapidly began to take on the urban form that is still recognizable in modern times. Devastating air raids in 1940, however, decimated the heart of medieval Bristol so that relatively little still survives above ground of the fabric of the medieval town.

FURTHER READINGS

Aston, M., and R. Iles, eds. *The Archaeology of Avon.* Avon: Avon County Council, 1987.

Barton, K.J. Excavations Near Back Hall, Bristol, 1958. *Transactions of the Bristol and Gloucestershire Archaeological Society* (1960) 79:251–286.

Boore, E.J. Excavations at Peter Street, Bristol, 1975–6. *Bristol and Avon Archaeology* (1982) 1:7–11.

———. *Excavations at Tower Lane, Bristol.* Bristol: City of Bristol Museum and Art Gallery, 1984.

Good, G.L. The Excavation of Two Docks at Narrow Quay, Bristol, 1978–9. *Post-Medieval Archaeology* (1987) 21:25–126.

———. Some Aspects of the Development of the Redcliffe Waterfront in the Light of Excavation at Dundas Wharf. *Bristol and Avon Archaeology* (1990) 9:29–42.

Good, G.L., R.H. Jones, and M.W. Ponsford, eds. *Waterfront Archaeology.* CBA Research Report 74. London: Council for British Archaeology, 1991.

Grinsell, L.V. The Mints of Bath and Bristol. In *The Archaeology of Avon.* Ed. M. Aston and R. Iles. Avon: Avon County Council, 1987, pp. 173–175.

Grinsell, L.V., C.E. Blunt, and M. Dolley. *Sylloge of Coins of the British Isles.* Bristol: Bristol and Gloucester Museums, 1973.

Jones, J., and N. Watson. The Early Medieval Waterfront at Redcliffe, Bristol: A Study of Environment and Economy. In *Studies in Palaeoeconomy and Environment in South-West England.* Ed. N.D. Balaam, B. Levitan, and V. Straker. BAR British Series 181. Oxford: British Archaeological Reports, 1987, pp. 135–162.

Jones, R.H. *Excavations in Redcliffe, 1983–5.* Bristol: City of Bristol Museum and Art Gallery, 1986.

———. Excavations at St. James' Priory, Bristol, 1988–9. *Bristol and Avon Archaeology* (1989) 8:2–7.

Lobel, M.D., and E.M. Carus-Wilson. *Historic Towns Atlas: Bristol.* London: Historic Towns Trust, 1975.

Nicholson, R.A., and J. Hillam. A Dendrochronological Analysis of Oak Timbers from the Early Medieval Site at Dundas Wharf, Bristol. *Transactions of the Bristol and Gloucestershire Archaeological Society* (1987) 105:133–145.

Ponsford, M.W. Bristol Castle: Archaeology and the History of a Royal Fortress. M.Litt. thesis, University of Bristol, 1979.

———. Bristol. In *The Archaeology of Avon.* Ed. M. Aston and R. Iles. Avon: Avon County Council, 1987, pp. 145–159.

Price, R.H. *Excavations at St. Bartholomew's Hospital, Bristol.* Bristol: City of Bristol Museum and Art Gallery, 1979a.

———. Excavations at the Town Wall, 65 Baldwin Street, Bristol. In *Rescue Archaeology in the Bristol Area.* Vol. 1. Ed. N. Thomas. Bristol: City of Bristol Museum and Art Gallery, 1979b, pp. 15–28.

Rahtz, P.A. Excavations by the Town Wall, Baldwin Street, Bristol, 1957. *Transactions of the Bristol and Gloucestershire Archaeological Society* (1960) 79:221–250.

Watts, L., and P.A. Rahtz. *Mary-le-Port, Bristol: Excavations 1962–3.* Monograph 7. Bristol: City of Bristol Museum and Art Gallery, 1985.

Williams, B. *Excavations in the Medieval Suburb of Redcliffe, Bristol, 1980.* Bristol: City of Bristol Museum and Art Gallery, 1981.

———. Excavations at Bristol Bridge, 1981. *Bristol and Avon Archaeology* (1982) 1:12–15.

———. Excavation of Medieval and Post-Medieval Tenements at 94–102 Temple Street, Bristol, 1975. *Transactions of the Bristol and Gloucestershire Archaeological Society* (1988) 106:107–168.

Robert H. Jones

Brno

The town of Brno is located in the Brno Valley in Moravia in the present-day Czech Republic at the confluence of the Svitava and Svratka Rivers. The name Brno is derived from the Old Slavic term for mud. In the sixth century, Slavs continued to occupy a rich settlement in this area (Brno-Pisárky) that was originally established in prehistoric times. At the end of the eighth century and during the ninth, the Brno Valley was a part of the Great Moravian Empire. At this time, the fortified settlement of Staré Zámky near Lisen was a tribal and economic center. The extensive area behind the fortification was built on earlier settlements. This fortified settlement was the site of systematic archaeological research in the 1950s and 1960s. Within the 11-ha site, a fortification with a gate, a magnate farmstead, underground living rooms, supply pits, and a furnace had been built, and some destroyed stone buildings were found. A burial site was established in the extramural settlement. Sometime at the end of the ninth century and the beginning of the tenth century, the fortified settlement was violently destroyed. This area was settled again in a reduced form in the eleventh century. The Great Moravian horizon in the Brno Valley is represented by thirty burial sites and settlements (including Brno-Stary Lískovec, Medlánky, Obrany, Malomerice, and Zidenice). Another concentration of settlements developed at the same time in the Old Town of Brno (Fig. 1, *1*) near a ford over the Svratka River. These settlements became more important after the destruction of the fortification at Staré Zámky at the end of tenth century.

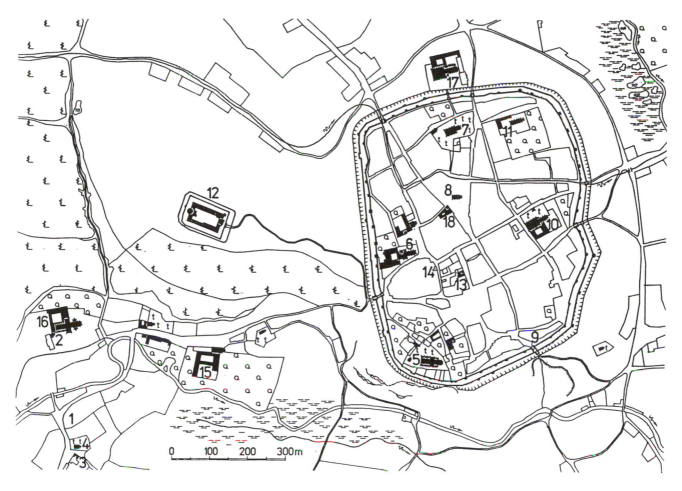

FIG. 1. Plan of Brno in the Middle Ages, showing the location of the sites mentioned in the text.

In the beginning of the eleventh century, an early Romanesque rotunda was built in the Old Town (Fig. 1, *2*, excavated 1976–1982). The remains of a fortification discovered by archaeological research (Fig. 1, *3*, Old Brno-Modry Lev, excavated in 1985) also belong to this time period. The St. Prokop and St. Václav Chapels were established at this time, and a new market parish was formed. According to written documents, in the beginning of the eleventh century the first castle in Brno was founded by Prince Bretislav I as the center of his princely kingdom. Its location is unknown.

Between the late twelfth and the early thirteenth centuries, the settlement moved from Old Brno to the modern town center. The conditions of Old Brno were not appropriate for urban development. Written sources and archaeological evidence document the formation of parishes in new areas. Czech parishes, including the

Church of St. Petr and Pavel (Fig. 1, *5*) and the Church of St. Michal (Fig. 1, *6*), were established in the areas of Josefská Street, Dominikánská Street, Orlí Street, and the Old Town Hall. Colonial parishes made up of settlers from Germany and the Holy Roman Empire are documented in the areas of Kozí Street, Ceská Street, and around the Churches of St. Jakub (Fig. 1, *7*) and St. Mikulás (Fig. 1, *8*, archaeological research conducted in the 1960s). The Jewish quarter near the Jewish gate (Fig. 1, *9*), which is mentioned in a written source of 1454 and is documented by finds from Frantiskánská Street (archaeological research conducted in the 1990s), is still not well known. Archaeological research in the 1990s uncovered underground living rooms, economic objects of various kinds, the remains of a forge and bread furnaces, and the historical foundations of stone houses, including the Old Town Hall and the coin master's house.

B

On a hill overlooking the town, the main Church of St. Petr and Pavel was built. The original Romanesque three-aisled basilica with a double tower from the end of the twelfth century was probably built by the Moravian Prince Konrád Ota (based on the most recent archaeological research in the 1990s). Many cloisters in Brno also originated at this time. They include the Benedictine monastery "Na luhu" dating to the end of the twelfth century (Brno-Komárov, archaeological research in 1970s), the Premonstratian monastery (Brno-Zábrdovice) founded in 1209, the Dominican monastery of 1228 (Fig 1, 6), the Minorite monastery built before 1239 (Fig. 1, 10, archaeological research in the 1980s), and the Augustinian convent called Herburs after Abbess Herburga (Fig. 1, 11).

The development of this settlement ended with the construction of walls around the town. The town of Brno was legally recognized in 1243, when the Czech King Václav I published so-called foundation documents. Around the middle of the thirteenth century, the Přemysl King Otakar II built a new royal castle on Spilberk Hill to protect the town (Fig. 1, 12). Archaeological research (1985–1994) documented the existence of an extensive Gothic castle with a built-up area around it, a cylindrical and prismatic tower, and a palace.

The 36.4-ha town was encircled with walls in the form of an irregular oval with defensive towers and five gates. Two main streets led from each gate to the marketplaces. The town was divided into four residential quarters, as was the suburb, which covered an area of 105 ha. Management of the town was centered in the town hall (Fig. 1, 13). Houses originally made of wood and mud were replaced by stone buildings. In 1365, according to tax rolls, 519 premises and many economic buildings were located inside the walls. The main occupations were handicrafts and trade. Production was concentrated in small workshops using simple equipment. In the period before the Hussites, 147 different kinds of crafts and trades were practiced here. The most popular crafts were garment making, food production, metalworking, and textiles. The Old Town Hall produced evidence of metal-, leather, and bone working; Josefská yielded evidence for the making of food products.

Brno was a crossroads of a long-distance trade (archaeologically documented by finds including foreign coinage, ceramics from North Moravia, stoneware from an area along the Rhein River, and blown glass).

A mint operated throughout most of the Middle Ages (Fig. 1, 14). The building that housed the mint before the Hussite period was located close to the Dominican Cloister (Brno-Mecová Street, archaeological research in the 1990s). Many coins from Brno were found in wells and waste pits. In 1312, Queen Eliska Přemyslovna founded the Dominican convent at St. Anna (Fig. 1, 15) in Old Brno; the Dowager Queen Eliska Rejcka founded a Cistercian convent nearby in 1323 (Fig. 1, 16, archaeological research of 1976–1982). Outside the town walls, the Moravian margrave Jan Jindrich, brother of Emperor Karel IV, founded a monastery for Augustinian recluses in 1350 (Fig. 1, 17), which included a family vault of Moravian margraves from the Lucemburc dynasty. The same margrave founded a monastery for courtesans in Brno-Královo Pole in 1375 (archaeological research at the end of the 1970s). The period of the Lucemburc margaves, the second half of the fourteenth century until 1411, represents the greatest level of development of Brno in the Middle Ages. The first half of the fifteenth century, the period of Hussite wars, brought a general stagnation. The Hussites twice unsuccessfully besieged Brno, as is sporadically documented by archaeological evidence from the suburbs (Brno-Komárov, Benedictine monastery).

During the second half of the fifteenth century, Brno was affected by battles between the Czech King Jiríz Podebrad and the Hungarian King Matyás Korvín and came under Hungarian domination for many years. The strong influence of Hungarian culture is already apparent by the middle of the fifteenth century. This influence is reflected in finds of tiles from the Knight's Stove in Spilberk and in the King's House (Fig. 1, 18) in the town. They include a heraldic tile with a motif of the dragon order from Spilberk.

The first archeological evidence for medieval Brno comes from a nineteenth-century source. At this time, the town wall was pulled down, and the extensive reconstruction of the medieval core of the town was begun. Large collections of medieval ceramics were made at the time, and the collections continue to increase as archaeological research continues.

Dana Cejnková and Irena Loskotová

Brunswick

Brunswick, in Lower Saxony in northwestern Germany, is the oldest medieval group town consisting of five parts (Pentapolis) in Europe. Situated on both sides of the River Oker, it was composed of the separate towns of the Altstadt (Old Town), the Neustadt (New Town), the

Hagen, the Alte Wiek, and the Sack, each developing from functionally and temporally different roots.

In contrast to towns like Cologne, Brunswick did not derive from Roman times, and it was neither an imperial town *(Reichsstadt)* like Nuremburg nor a bishop's city *(Bischofsstadt)* like Hildesheim. As archaeological evidence shows, Altstadt, which developed gradually from the ninth century onward, had its roots in the agricultural settlement of Dankwarderobe (Thoncguarderoth) on the west bank of the River Oker. The settlement consisted of pithouses *(Grubenhäuser)*. Weaving and the production of iron took place here. The village gave its name to the castle of the Brunonian counts, which was erected on a nearby peninsula of the Oker before the end of the tenth century. Under the influence of the Dankwarderobe castle, this settlement expanded inland in the direction of area C/D (Fig. 1). In area A, a church was founded and a churchyard laid out. The name Brunswick, which was

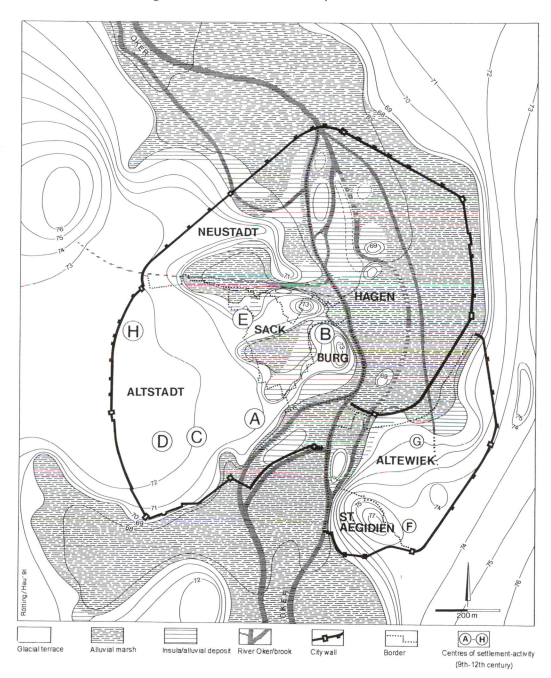

FIG. 1. Settlement activity, ninth–twelfth centuries.

later used for the group town, was transformed from *villa brunesguik,* later the Alte Wiek, on the east side of the river.

The oldest document concerning the later town dates from 1031. There are a few other scattered documents of the eleventh and twelfth centuries, but historical sources do not become more frequent before the middle of the thirteenth century. A Common Council made up of the three largest towns—the Altstadt, the Neustadt, and the Hagen—was established in 1269. The Alte Wiek and the Sack participated in the council shortly after 1300. Brunswick was a "free town," under its own authority, with about twenty thousand inhabitants during the late Middle Ages and early modern times, but it became subject to Duke Rudolf August of Brunswick and Luneburg in 1671.

An interdisciplinary archaeological team of the Institute of Monument-Conservation has been working on urban development since 1976. The main goals of the research are to clarify the topography of the plots, the construction of houses, and the material culture. The archaeological material—c. 1.2 million medieval finds—derives from about three hundred plots and nine thousand layers and sections. More than one hundred excavations have taken place, opening up about 10 percent of the urban area.

The Altstadt, already surrounded by a rampart and ditch by c. 1100, exemplifies the development of a castle town during the eleventh and twelfth centuries. This development took place in an area that bore the imprint of mining in the region of the Harz Mountains and that was a favored region for royal residences (Königslandschaft, Pfalzen) of the Ottonians and the succeeding Salians.

A series of thirty-six dendrochronologically dated, timber-built wells and the stratigraphic relationship of the layers demonstrate that, from the year 1065 onward, the scattered settlement of pithouses found in area C/D was replaced by a well-planned settlement and by new house types. A market settlement, first documented by historical records in the late eleventh century, developed and led to the group town under the progressive rule of the Saxon Duke Henry the Lion during the twelfth century. Henry supported Brunswick (as well as Munich, Lübeck, and Stade, or Schwerin) and made it a prosperous center of production and commerce, favorably situated with regard to transport facilities.

Brunswick was now a territorial center with space comparable to a royal residence. The surface of more than 50 percent of the town area (at least 1.0 km²) was reclaimed from the Oker Valley. Its level was raised, beginning on a large scale in the second half of the twelfth century, by means of drainage, layers of logs, and heaps of sand that amounted to more than 2 million m³.

The marketplace and early town were, above all, characterized by the presence of merchants, craftsmen, and members of the nobility. The archaeological evidence shows significant differences from rural settlements in the way houses and stores were built, in the use of imported goods, and in the standard of everyday goods, which were of high technical quality and had specialized functions.

In addition to posthouses and timber-built houses, stone-built dwelling houses existed from the eleventh century onward. Two-part types predominate, and there is a correspondence between their functions and their locations on the plots.

The first type (Fig. 2, *1*; Fig. 2, *2*), which dates from the eleventh to the late thirteenth centuries, consisted of a detached stone cellar on the back of the plot with a timber-framed upper floor and a ramp *(Kellerhals)* leading into the cellar. This storehouse was connected to a separate timber-framed hall; later, it was also connected to a stone dwelling house situated on the street side of the plot, with its eaves turned toward the street.

In the second type (Fig. 2, *3*), which dates from the thirteenth century onward, the cellar with its timber-framed upper floor was transformed into a *Kemenate,* built entirely of stone, with a cellar and two upper floors. The *Kemenate* was integrated into another house, built of stone or timber, which was situated on the street side of the plot, with its gable turned toward the street.

In the thirteenth century, both types located on the back side of plots were used together as storehouses and as dwelling houses *(Kamin).*

The size of the narrow rectangular-to-square plots varied from the beginning. During the twelfth century, each plot occupied an area of c. 600–1,000 m². During the following centuries, some remained the same size, but others became smaller.

From prehistoric times onward, the traditional materials used for the production of household utensils and tools were natural ones, such as wood and bone. These natural materials continued to predominate throughout the Middle Ages, although new, specialized materials, including tin-lead alloys, leaded glass, and hard-fired stoneware, were added and played a progressively more important role.

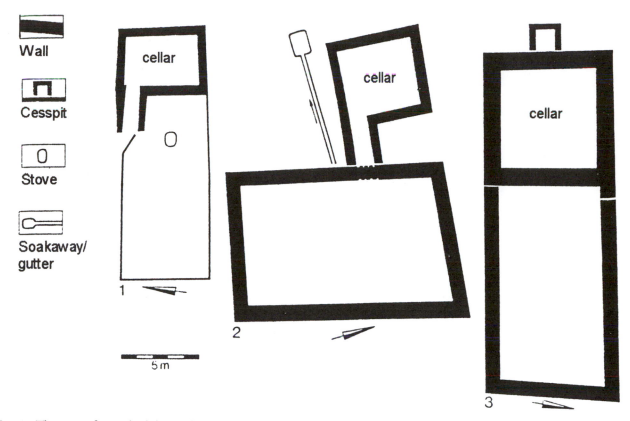

Wall

Cesspit

Stove

Soakaway/
gutter

cellar

cellar

cellar

1

2

3

5 m

FIG. 2. The types of stone-built house during the central Middle Ages. *1–2, Kellerhals,* stone-built cellar with timber-framed upper floor and a ramp leading into the cellar on the back side of the plot: *1,* connected to a separate timber-framed hall with its gable turned toward the street, c. 1100; *2,* connected to a stone-built dwelling house with its eaves turned toward the street, c. 1200. *3,* Cellar and two upper floors built entirely of stone on the back side of the plot *(Kemenate),* integrated into a house built of stone or timber situated on the street side of the plot with its gable turned toward the street, c. 1230.

Before A.D. 1200, ceramic pots, jugs, and bowls, which were used in the kitchen, in the cellar, or at the table, were available in limited patterns and a very few sizes. From c. 1200 onward, a wide variety of sizes and specialized types of pottery for different purposes appeared. Stoneware emerged, and standardized kitchenware was produced, which differed in its form and method of manufacture (Fig. 3).

In general, household items were locally produced and consumed. From the fourteenth century onward, increasing numbers of mass-produced items, both local and imported, were consumed.

Especially during the twelfth and thirteenth centuries, the material culture of a small upper class consisting of merchants and members of the Town Council differed markedly from the standard of living of the lower classes. The upper class made use of imported luxury goods, which are found in most important central European towns by c. 1300, such as Islamic and Venetian enamel-painted glass beakers, leaded-glass objects termed *Bleiglas,* and decorated caskets called *Minnekästchen.*

FURTHER READINGS

Fehring, Günter P. *The Archaeology of Medieval Germany.* London: Routledge, 1991.

Ottaway, Patrick. *Archaeology in British Towns.* London: Routledge, 1992.

Rötting, Hartmut. *Stadtarchäologie in Braunschweig.* Forschung der Denkmalpflege in Niedersachen 3. Hameln: C.W. Niemeyer, 1985.

SEE ALSO

Stoneware

Hartmut Rötting

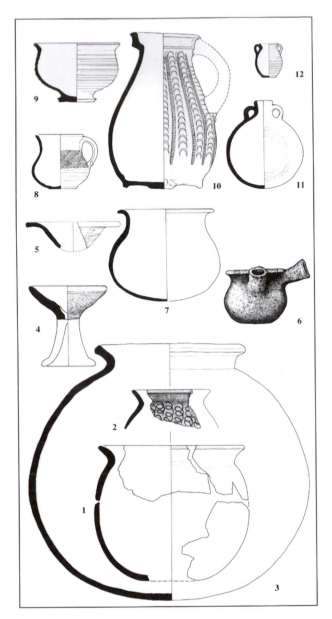

Fig. 3. Specialized types of earthenware pottery. Pots with a vaulted bottom *(Kugeltöpfe): 1,* tenth century; *2,* end of the eleventh century; *3,* first half of the twelfth century; *7,* first half of the thirteenth century. Pot with a vaulted bottom, spout, and handle: *6,* second half of the twelfth century. Other items: *4,* table lamp, eleventh century; *5,* droplight, second half of the twelfth century; *8, 10,* jugs; *9,* bowl; *11,* water bottle; *12,* miniature vessel. Scale 1:5.

Buda

The present town of Budapest, the capital of Hungary, is composed of three parts, which were united in 1873. Of these, Óbuda is built on the ruins of Aquincum, the capital of the Roman province of Pannonia (first–fourth centuries A.D.) on the right bank of the River Danube. The early medieval rural settlement of Pest was located on the alluvial plain of the left bank. The elongated Castle Hill of Buda emerges south of Óbuda and west of Pest across the river. Its present settlement covers c. 40 ha.

Castle Hill is chiefly composed of marl and karstic limestone deposited by hot springs. The lowermost archaeological stratum of ancient humus contained pottery sherds from the middle Bronze Age Vatya Culture (1700–1650 B.C.). Remains of middle Bronze Age rural settlement occurred at many points on the hill. Following this prehistoric occupation, Castle Hill was scarcely inhabited until the early Middle Ages, despite its proximity to Roman Aquincum.

The first Christian king of Hungary, István I (Stephen I in English), c. 975–1038, was crowned in A.D. 1000. His royal seat was in Székesfehérvár, a town 67 km west of Buda. At this time, Pest served as a commercial center. Its mixed population included a contingent of Volga Bulgarian Islamic people, who were forcibly replaced by Austrian and Saxon settlers *(hospes)* invited by King Béla IV (1235–1270) in 1235. The hinterlands of Pest included Buda, which was only a modest rural settlement at the time.

In 1242, the invading Tartar army of Batu Khan crossed the frozen River Danube and destroyed the right-bank settlements as well. Evidence of early rebuilding was sporadically recorded at the Buda rural settlement. In 1247, King Béla IV started large-scale constructions at Buda and moved the royal seat to this well-protected site. The town's layout, with its longitudinal streets and small squares, was similar to the plans of contemporary western towns. Two gothic churches were also erected, dedicated to Holy Our Lady and Mary Magdalene, respectively. The charter of privileges granted to Pest in 1244 was expanded to include Buda as well. Buda has been the nation's capital ever since.

Coeval stratigraphy revealed that the oldest fortified walls of the Buda castle had been built directly on the ruins of rural houses and cellars. Fearful of a new Tartar invasion, the population of the surrounding settlements, including the Germanic inhabitants of Pest, were moved within the fortified area. People from as far away as Székesfehérvár, Esztergom, and even Zagreb were brought in, sometimes by force, to strengthen the new capital. Jews, who were granted privileges as Servants of the Royal Chamber in 1251, started populating Buda as well.

Hungarians lived mostly on the northern section of the hill around Mary Magdalene Church. Holy Our Lady Church, located in the central part of the town, was used mostly by Germans. Coins found during excavation of the adjacent deeply stratified cemetery indicate that it was abandoned by the early fifteenth century. After this time, people were buried outside the city walls. The Jewish quarter was first located in the southwestern part of the Castle Hill. Later, it was moved to the northern section, where excavations revealed the remains of two Gothic synagogues. Other important churches and churchyards investigated in the civil town included the Dominican St. Nicholas Church and a Franciscan monastery. The ruins of this monastery were buried under the Pasha's Palace, which was built during the sixteenth century when the town fell under Ottoman Turkish rule. In addition to these buildings, a number of smaller churches as well as secular institutions and private houses were identified. The systems of lots and civilian housing were also mapped, and remains of thirteenth–fifteenth-century schools and commercial centers located. By the end of the Middle Ages (c. 1500), at least 285 wells and numerous cisterns supplied water to more than three hundred houses of this town. Waterworks that were developed during the fourteenth and fifteenth centuries increasingly utilized water from the Danube as well.

The Hungarian Árpád dynasty died out in 1301, and the throne was taken over by the Anjou dynasty of Naples. After 1310, construction of a separate fortification started on the southern rock tip of the hill, which subsequently became the site of the Royal Palace. This area lay c. 15 m below the highest, central part of Castle Hill. Its water supplies had to be drawn entirely from cisterns. C. 1410, a foot-powered pump was built to provide additional water from the Danube. Excavation has also revealed a system of walls that linked this fortified section to the northern civil town.

Excavation plans show that when the palace area was extended by c. 200 m to the north, thirty houses were torn down in the construction zone. By the end of the Anjou period, in the fourteenth century, the city was densely populated. When the city had to be fortified to withstand enemy artillery, the new walls were built on the outer slopes of the hills. Gaps between the new walls and the original fortifications were either filled with earth or turned into cellars under the defenses along the inner side. The expanded plateau was a welcome addition to the city's area. Despite its dwindling status and peripheral position, Pest still remained an important bridgehead and fortified buffer zone across the River Danube.

Excavations at the fourteenth–fifteenth-century Royal Palace revealed traces of a luxurious lifestyle. They include sixty-two Gothic statues of great art historical significance,

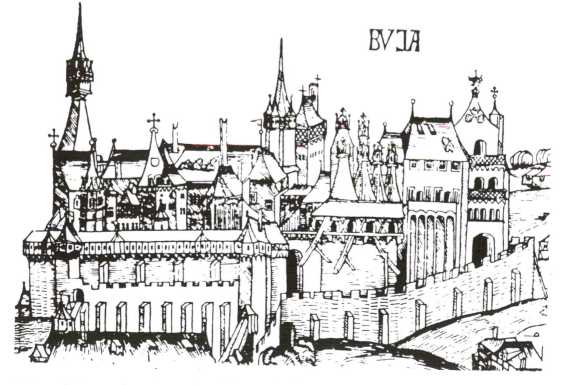

The Royal Palace of Buda, seen from the east. (Detail of a woodcut by Master Wolgemuth, 1493.)

B

as well as high-quality artifacts, including many imports, which were used in day-to-day life.

By the fifteenth century, Buda's suburbs also flourished. The reign of King Mátyás (1458–1490), the outstanding personality of the Hungarian Renaissance, brought unprecedented development. An improved water system channeled fresh water from the higher neighboring hills. Mátyás modernized the fortification system and also established important institutions, such as the famous library, the Bibliotheca Corviniana. Monks in a monastery nearby were in charge of copying manuscripts, but a printing house operated within the town's walls as well. The cosmopolitan court of Mátyás employed Italian architects and poets and musicians from all over Europe. Archaeologically, a variety of imported wares and remains of sophisticated marble carvings bear witness to this prosperous period. Following the death of Mátyás, however, development halted.

Hungary fell to the Ottoman Turkish expansion in 1526. This date conventionally marks the end of the Middle Ages in Hungary. Although this new wave of eastern influence produced an interaction between civilizations that could serve as a model for culture change, the 150 years of subsequent Turkish rule fall outside the scope of archaeological research in a strict sense.

FURTHER READINGS

Gerevich, László. *The Art of Buda and Pest in the Middle Ages.* Budapest: Akadémiai Kiadó, 1971.

———. *Towns in Medieval Hungary.* Budapest: Akadémiai Kiadó, 1990.

Holl, Irme. *Mittelalterliche Funde aus einem Brunnen von Buda.* Budapest: Akadémiai Kiadó, 1966.

Takáks, Sarolta. *Urban Architecture in Budapest.* Budapest: Officina Nova, 1991.

Zolnay, László. *A Budai Vár* (The Buda Castle). Budapest: Gondolat Zsebkönyvek, 1981.

László Bartosiewicz

Bulles

Bulles is a small village located 20 km from Beauvais in the center of Oise, France. Its Merovingian cemetery was discovered in 1963, 1.8 km north of the village. In the vicinity are the springs of Saine-Fontaine. Exhaustive investigation of this important site was completed in 1984. It contains 832 graves, which, due to reuse, correspond to nearly a thousand burials between the mid-fifth century and the beginning of the eighth century A.D. This is the most important site in Picardy investigated during the last few decades.

The earliest graves, c. A.D. 450–460, contain grave goods in the Gallo-Roman tradition. In the central area, northern and eastern orientations coexist with the Germanic rite of cremation until the beginning of the sixth century. In the burials dating to the Childeric/Clovis transition in 481, various influences appear, including the presence of Saxon brooches, Hunnish arrowheads and small male earrings, Visigothic belt-buckle plates, and Alemannic pottery, indicating numerous contacts between populations.

In the fifth and sixth centuries, wooden burial cases (sometimes double) and coffins were used. Some children were buried in hollowed tree trunks. The first stone sarcophagi appear in the second half of the sixth century. They are made of two parts, carved out of limestone blocks recovered from Gallo-Roman monuments. In the seventh century, monolithic sarcophagi were used, as well as the traditional wooden burial cases.

The custom of burial with grave goods persisted for a long time. Men were buried with their weaponry, such as spears, axes, and scramasaxes (single-edged short swords), and women were buried with jewelry, including bead necklaces. Pottery vessels or glassware are found in many graves, which perpetuate the principle of the food offerings, even though these vessels are empty. Certain of the largest graves belong to the "chiefs" and their wives, sometimes surrounded by children. Chiefs' graves are characterized by the presence of a two-edged long sword and a shield, of which only the boss and grip remain. In the women's graves, the jewelry is often made of gold-plated silver, and the pottery is sometimes replaced by a bronze bowl. The cemetery contains ten chiefs' graves dating from the middle of the fifth century to the end of the sixth century, at which time they disappear from the cemetery. After the sixth century, as a result of Christianization, the chiefs were buried in churches, followed progressively by the rest of the population.

The oldest weapons are mainly spears with split socket heads and profiled throwing axes called *francisque.* The bow was also in use, but all organic material has vanished. Only arrowheads, generally in groups of three and often of different types, can be found. In the second half of the sixth century, weaponry evolved. Axes became more massive, and spears with closed socket heads appeared, as did the straight-backed scramasax. A change in women's fashions is also seen during this period. The first fibulae (clasps) were small (bird-shaped, s-shaped, round, three-armed), followed by five-armed fibulae of larger size. The most

Animal-style decoration from pottery vessel in Grave 732, Merovingian Cemetery at Bulles, Oise, France.

commonly used gemstone was a flattened garnet set in cloisonné. In the seventh century, round fibulae have gemstones mounted on raised settings. Bronze or iron symmetrical-bow fibulae are found in the latest graves.

Earrings also changed through time. The first ones, often of silver, were small rings with a small cubic pendant. The size of the earrings then increased, and large cubic pendant earrings faced with garnets prevailed in the sixth century. In the seventh century, the earrings were very large and made of bronze with hollow spherical or conical pendants of iron plate. Collars and bracelets of beadwork are found at the beginning of the sixth century. The beads are very small and made of glass paste. Through time, opaque multicolored decorative beads of progressively larger sizes appear on these collars. Amber was also used.

Several items, such as knives, bone combs, and small instruments, are often suspended by a leather string or a small chain from a belt on a woman's left side. In the seventh century, a large chatelaine plate is inserted between the belt and these items.

Buckles and buckle plates also changed through time. In the second half of the fifth century, buckle plates related to those of late Roman type are found. Solid bronze models, more or less triangular in shape, characterized the mid-fifth century, but late in the fifth century round buckle plates of either bronze or iron appeared. Some iron plates were decorated with either silver or brass wire inlay (damascening). The first decorations were monochrome and included beehive motifs and imitations of cloisonné. The buckle plates became progressively trapezoidal with the presence of counterplates and back plates. The decoration changed first to a geometric (basketry, interlace) and then to a zoomorphic (serpentine monsters) style in two-color damascening, sometimes with silverplating. The use of this damascening is a resurgence of a technique used in the late fifth century on rectangular and kidney-shaped buckles and buckle plates that were decorated with concentric circles and spirals.

Pottery is a major element of the cemetery. Nearly 430 vessels have been discovered, of which 205 are decorated (some with stamped decoration, most with roulettes—a toothed wheel or disk). The design inventory is rich and varied. Complex geometric and zoomorphic designs characteristic of the Paris Basin and Picardy were found. A large comparative study determined that identical designs are found in a 180-×-90 km area from south of Paris to north of Amiens, demonstrating the existence of regional workshops (Legoux 1992).

Toward the end of the seventh century (A.D. 680–690), the custom of burial with grave goods disappears from the cemetery. The new graves are either shallow or on top of earlier ones. Unusual body positions can be observed, including flexed burials, burials with the arms crossed over the chest, and burials facing the ground.

In the last peripheral group, the orientation of the graves changes: the graves point southward. A demographic study of the population dates the abandonment of the site to c. A.D. 720–730. This cemetery is a key site for Picardy. Its study served as the basis for the development of a regional chronology using the automatic matrix permutation method. This method finds correlations between all the grave goods in order to determine their relative chronological phases. These phases are then given absolute dates through comparisons to other Merovingian graves that have been dated by coins. These processes are carried out using a computer. This method has been used successfully at numerous cemeteries, and the results have laid the groundwork for a unified chronology for a large part of France.

FURTHER READINGS

Legoux, René. La nécropole mérovingienne de Bulles (Oise): Caractères généraux et particularismes. *Revue archéologique de Picardie* (1988), 314: 81–88.

———. L'art animalier et la symbolique d'origine chrétienne dans les décors de céramiques du VIème siècle après J.C. au nord du bassin parisien. *Revue archéologique de Picardie* (1992), 1/2: 111–142.

Perin, Patrick, with a contribution by R. Legoux. *La datation des tombes mérovingiennes, historique, méthodes, applications.* Genève: Editions DROZ, 1980.

Young, Bailey. Paganismes, christianisation et rites funéraires mérovingiens. *Archéologie médiévale* (1977) 7:5–81.

René Legoux

SEE ALSO
France

Burghal Hidage

There exists a document in Old English known since the close of the nineteenth century as the *Burghal Hidage.* It comprises, in its various forms, a list of thirty-three fortified places in southern England under the control of the kings of Wessex. Because it contains Oxford (taken by Edward the Elder in 911) and Buckingham (built in 914), it is usually dated to c. 919. The *Burghal Hidage* assigns tax assessments in *Hides* (units of land) to the thirty-three places. An appendix allows the assessment to be converted into lengths of defended wall. The document, therefore, enables the state of the defenses of Wessex to be charted and the extent of the defended area of individual towns to be assessed at one fixed point in time. Individual studies have been conducted on various sites. Some have been extensively studied (e.g., Winchester), while others have only recently been defined (e.g., Sashes in Berkshire) and are being actively investigated, and still others are not yet clearly defined (e.g., *Eorpeburnan*).

The ramifications of this document have yet to be completely investigated, but it should be remembered that it is the sole survivor of a whole class of administrative vernacular documents that are signaled in the works of Alfred the Great (849–899). It has clear mathematics and shows detailed control over a wide area, emendation, and storage.

FURTHER READINGS

Hill, D., and A. Rumble. *The Defence of Wessex.* Manchester: Manchester University Press, 1996.

David Hill

Burials

See Cemeteries and Burials.

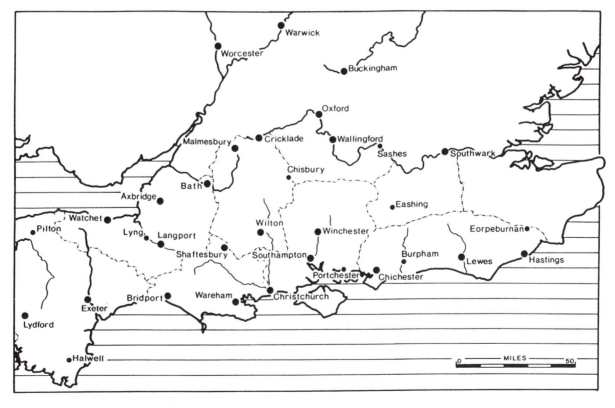

Location of sites identified in the *Burghal Hidage.*

C

Cadbury Castle

Cadbury Castle, Somerset, England (NGR ST 6225), is a major Iron Age hillfort, excavated 1966–1970. This revealed that it had been the setting for two episodes of early medieval fortification and occupation: Cadbury 11, c. A.D. 475–550, and Cadbury 12, c. A.D. 1010–1020. While sharing both the wider locational significance and the immediate topographical advantages of the Cadbury hillfort with their Iron Age predecessor, these later phases received no legacy from it other than a ready-made, albeit decayed, defensive system.

The site stands athwart the spine of the southwest peninsula of Britain. There is no military significance in this, but the site enjoyed communications with southwest, southeast, and northeast England. Some routes were merely long-distance trackways, but others, such as the Fosse Way, were consolidated during the Roman occupation. Moreover, river access from the Bristol Channel was possible for small boats.

The hill is an isolated knoll, rising steeply from the surrounding lowlands to a gentle whaleback of 7-ha area, thus combining the defensive advantage of steepness with a suitable area for occupation. In the Iron Age, five tiers of ramparts enclosed the hill. Even in decay, these ramparts were considerable obstacles; more important, their appearance is still extremely formidable. By c. A.D. 450, Cadbury was just one of many derelict hillforts. It had, however, the unusual advantage of a ready water supply within the outer lines of defense.

At a time of political upheaval between the emergent Celtic kingdoms and Anglo-Saxon settlers, the derelict Cadbury fort was refortified. This phase, Cadbury 11, is dated c. A.D. 475–550 by pottery imported from the Mediterranean and stratified in the defenses. There are also glass sherds, two datable Anglo-Saxon trinkets, and iron objects, especially knives, which are typical of this period.

The new defenses were built upon the Iron Age inner rampart, in a deliberate policy of creating a fort that is one of only four or five exceptionally large forts of this date. Moreover, it surpasses all the others in the structural complexity and work effort involved in building the rampart. In the southwest entrance, a timber gate tower was also erected.

In a commanding position on the summit ridge, the plan of a timber hall was uncovered. At 19 × 10 m (i.e., 190 m² in floor area), it had slightly bowed sides and rounded gables. It is identified as a noble feasting hall, partly because of the plan, partly because of a concentration of sherds from Mediterranean wine jars and fine tableware, as well as glass beakers, in and around it. It was divided internally in the proportions 2:1, suggesting a hall for feasting and a smaller private chamber.

It is possible that the hall succeeded a large round building with a floor area of c. 200 m², which had also been the scene of feasting and drinking. Such round buildings are known on high-status sites throughout Britain at this period.

Comparing the quantity of imported pottery from the major excavated sites of Cadbury, Congresbury, and Tintagel, it appears that Cadbury was not a major trading center. On the other hand, it is quite certain that the work effort involved in building the Cadbury 11 rampart greatly exceeded that at either Tintagel or Congresbury.

C

Clearly, a strong political authority was needed to enforce and organize the necessary labor services. Toward A.D. 500, such authority would have been exercised by a king, immediate forerunner of the kings known from historical sources in western Britain by c. A.D. 550.

With Cadbury 12 we move from speculation to historical certainty. The hilltop was refortified by Æthelred II (968–1016) to protect a mint that began coining in A.D. 1009–1010. This is demonstrated by coins of the last issue of Æthelred, bearing mint marks such as CAD-ABYR. These were followed by coins of his successor, Cnut's (c. 995–1035), first issue, minted A.D. 1017–1020. This coin-based chronology establishes the political circumstances of Cadbury 12: the collapse of the rule of Æthelred and his son Edmund in the face of Viking ravaging and ultimate conquest by Cnut. In archaeological terms, it provides a firm dating bracket for the late Saxon artifacts of Cadbury, from major structures to pottery and ironwork.

The built structures of Cadbury 12 comprised a perimeter bank faced with a masonry wall, and gates with monumental arches. Such late Saxon defenses were already known at Wareham and Cricklade, but at Cadbury the defenses are both better preserved and securely dated. Moreover, on the summit ridge, the foundation trench for a church had been dug, but the work had been abandoned on Æthelred's death. The plan was for a cruciform church, with all four arms of equal length (i.e., a Greek-cross plan) and with the crossing projecting beyond the four arms, thus creating a large central space. This unusual plan may have been intended for a royal chapel.

Iron keys and many nails indicate that there were substantial timber buildings in Cadbury 12, but no plans have been established among a rash of postholes. Under Cnut, the site was abandoned to agriculture, with quantities of pottery, iron objects, and even ornamental panels from a casket being tidied away into pits.

In the past, it was asserted that the Cadbury hilltop was an unsuitable location for a permanent town and that, therefore, Æthelred's intention was merely to found an emergency mint and a temporary *burh* (fortified place). This interpretation, however, overlooks the ready water supply beside the northeast gate and was made in ignorance of the substantial masonry *burh* wall and gates and the projected church. The results of excavation demonstrate that Æthelred II intended a substantial and permanent town—an intention thwarted by his death and the succession of Cnut.

FURTHER READINGS

Alcock, L. *"By South Cadbury is that Camelot . . .": The Excavation of Cadbury Castle, 1966–1970.* London: Thames and Hudson, 1972.

———. *Cadbury Castle, Somerset: The Early Medieval Archaeology.* Cardiff: University of Wales Press, 1994.

Leslie Alcock

SEE ALSO
Tintagel

Cahercommaun

See Cashels.

Cahercommaun Project

See Survey.

Carbon-14 Dating

See Radiocarbon Age Determination.

Cashels

The cashel is a type of fortified settlement known from early Christian Ireland (A.D. 500–1200). A cashel is basically a ringfort (a circular living area surrounded by an earthen bank and ditch) in which the bank surrounding the settlement is a stone wall; often, cashels did not have a surrounding ditch. The stone wall of a cashel was dry built, or built without mortar, and the buildings inside the cashel were also usually made of stone. Cashels are most often found in areas where stone is readily available, such as the Burren, County Clare, a limestone plateau in the west of Ireland. When the surrounding wall has collapsed and become overgrown with soil and plants, cashels can often initially resemble raths (a type of early medieval single-family farm settlement surrounded by an earthen bank and ditch) and may be properly identified only after excavation.

Cashels are often equated almost completely with raths. They have an average diameter of 30 m, as do raths, and the univallate (single-walled) cashels probably were quite similar to univallate raths in function. They served as single-family farmsteads, surrounded by land on which the inhabitants probably raised their crops and grazed their livestock. There are also examples known of multivallate cashels that were probably the higher-status residences, such as Cahercommaun, County Clare, which has been identified as the home of a chieftain in the ninth century A.D. (Hencken 1938). There are fewer cashels than raths in Ireland, and cashels are more geographically restricted than are raths. Since cashels were built of stone rather than earth, they were usually restricted to the stonier areas of Ireland.

FURTHER READINGS

Edwards, Nancy. *The Archaeology of Early Medieval Ireland.* Philadelphia: University of Pennsylvania Press, 1990.

Flanagan, Laurence. *A Dictionary of Irish Archaeology.* Dublin: Gill and Macmillan, 1992.

Hamlin, Ann, and C.J. Lynn, eds. *Pieces of the Past: Archaeological Excavations by the Department of the Environment for Northern Ireland.* Belfast: HMSO, 1988.

Hencken, Hugh O'Neill. *Cahercommaun: A Stone Fort in Co. Clare.* Dublin: The Royal Society of Antiquaries of Ireland, 1938.

O'Kelly, Michael J. *Early Ireland.* Cambridge: Cambridge University Press, 1989.

O'Ríordáin, Seán P. *Antiquities of the Irish Countryside.* 5th ed. London and New York: Routledge, 1991.

Maura Smale

SEE ALSO
Raths

Castles

Castles were meant to be, as they still remain, the overwhelming physical symbol of the medieval aristocracy's power. From the start, they were built for a number of overlapping purposes: to house the lord and his household, to act as a center for the administration of his power, and to defend the center in the case of armed attack. Each of these functions might be stressed more or less according to the circumstances at the time of building a castle, and each saw a separate line of development. This means that one of the first problems, and fascinations, of castles is that there is no single yardstick by which to measure any one example. Because display and originality were also important to the builders of castles, there could never be such a thing as a typical castle.

In France, the origin of castles lies with the origins of the new aristocracy who rose to power in the aftermath of the collapse of the Western Carolingian Empire. Because this was not a sudden event, it is impossible to identify the first structures associated with the new castellans, the men who built them. There will have been no idea of a standard castle that we might recognize physically. An idea of the sort of thing that these new centers were was provided by the excavations at Doué-la-Fontaine; there a ground-floor stone hall was converted to a first-floor one, like the standing remains at Langeais, presumably to make it more defensible. This was dated to some time after a fire in the mid-tenth century. The hall at Doué was buried in an earth mound, or motte, during the mid-eleventh century. In the Rhineland of Germany, at the Husterknupp and elsewhere, excavation has shown that sites could become castles, mottes, by a process of piling up earth on the site. In an evolutionary process such as this, it is impossible to put a finger on the moment when a site becomes a castle. The new builders of castles were the aristocrats who developed feudal power and the link between power and the detailed control of land; castles clearly played a significant part in this control. The same problem has been experienced in England, where there have been attempts to find castles dating from before the Norman Conquest of 1066. Neither the structures put up as castles after 1066 nor those discovered from before are sufficiently uniform to allow us to identify a castle, in the sense of an instrument of feudal lordship, from the physical remains alone.

If the building of castles had its origin in the development of the new aristocratic framework of the modern France and Germany, the practice spread well beyond that area. Perhaps the most famous example of this is that of the castles of the Crusader states of Palestine and Syria, but also in Spain and Italy. The Crusades in northeast Europe took castles to the Baltic, while the growth of the kingdoms of the east and north also produced castles. They were not confined to feudal societies; structures that must be considered castles were to be found in the Byzantine Empire or in the kin-based societies of "Celtic" Wales, Scotland, and Ireland. Islamic castles are also to be found.

As men appreciated the usefulness of castles, they were increasingly built by lesser lords, so that the building of castles expanded not only geographically with time, but also across class boundaries. In the story of this expansion, earthwork castles were crucial; they could be erected

C

quickly, if political or military circumstances demanded, and without much skilled labor. Mottes, high round mounds of earth surmounted by a palisade and a tower or other buildings, became the most widespread form of earthwork castles, particularly in the period 1050–1150. Unfortunately, attempts have been made to extend this to the idea that discovering the origin of mottes might somehow discover the origin of castles as a whole. Castles involve a range of types, changing with time, region, and class.

The pace was naturally set by the castles built for the kings and major aristocracy. From the first, these tended to be of stone, but from the middle of the twelfth century they were overwhelmingly so. Below them in the social scale within the feudal hierarchy of medieval Europe were others that graded from being simply smaller to developing different varieties of buildings, which are still in some way castles. At the top of society, and increasingly toward the later Middle Ages, castles merged with luxurious, undefended country houses and were linked to the moated enclosure that became a common feature of the countryside from the twelfth century on. Castles notoriously fade off at the lower end of the social scale. During the thirteenth century, in Scotland and Ireland in particular, there appeared simple hall houses—buildings of stone with first-floor halls taking up the entire space at that level. In contrast physically to these were the tower houses, built normally in areas that saw a breakdown in central authority during the fourteenth century and later. These accommodated lesser lords and their immediate households in towers that gave a level of protection against raids and low-level military action; they were particularly popular in parts of France affected by the Hundred Years' War (1337–1453), in Scotland and northern England after the Scottish war of independence (early fourteenth century), and in Ireland.

If we consider the role of castles in war, we find that their main aim was defensive and to buy time. It is very difficult to find examples of the successful building of castles as part of the actual fact of attack or conquest of land; castles follow the initial success on the battlefield, to hold the gains made there. England after 1066 is a good case: the numbers of castles are quite small, too few to hold the country against any real internal rebellion. The new Norman lords built them primarily to serve the lordships established by the seizing of English estates. If a country was faced by invasion or civil war, castles provided strong military bases for counterattack. To the attackers, they represented places that must be taken, if their grip on the

land was to be made permanent or if small parties of their troops were to be able to move freely without the fear of ambush. To besiege a castle, however, cost them the advantage of their initial initiative and success. This applied to all forces, from the full-scale army of a king to a raiding party crossing a border. The means to counter such varied attacks were not equal, however. A castle was only as strong as the men paying for it thought it needed to be in their estimate of the danger it was likely to have to face. The castle of Bodiam has been denigrated because it may have been too weak to face a full-scale siege by a contemporary (late fourteenth century) army. It was, however, designed to counter small, mobile raiding forces of French landing from the English Channel and was perfectly adequate to cope with the sort of attack that they might mount.

The basic problem in defending a castle was choosing whether to build a strong point, typically a tower, which could be defended by a small number of men but would have to withstand all the concentrated attack of the enemy, or to spread the defense to an enclosure, which could accommodate more buildings and would diffuse the attack but needed a greater number of men to defend it and might well have weak points. The motte of earth, with a palisade and tower on top, was a classic form of strongpoint defense. It was normally linked to a subsidiary courtyard, or bailey, which provided space for living and working but was less well defended. This is especially so, as many mottes were erected for men who cannot have commanded large garrisons or households; defending the motte would have been their limit. In stone, the strongpoint was, again, a tower. In England and northern France, these could be massive square buildings (since the sixteenth century known as keeps) that attempted to accommodate all the essential parts of the castle under the one roof. These culminated in the great towers of Henry II of England's castles, such as Dover. In Germany, the tower was more often a simple tower of refuge, the *Bergfried,* attached to the main living accommodation of the castle.

During the twelfth century, methods of attacking castles and other fortifications were developed in several ways. The armies, with an increasingly mercenary foot-soldier element, became more skilled, especially at undermining walls and towers. The widespread use of crossbows made defense from battlements on the wall top increasingly dangerous if it meant leaning out or showing oneself. The development of the *trebuchet,* a catapult powered by a counterbalancing weight that was more powerful and accurate than its predecessors, gave the attackers better artillery. All these made strongpoints vulnerable.

The dominant tower was not abandoned in castles from the late twelfth century, but it ceased to be the principal means of defense of the whole. During the thirteenth century, the emphasis of the major castles moved to the defense of the perimeter, the curtain wall. This defense was built around two principles: to deny an enemy access to the base of the wall and to fortify the gate strongly. The first was accomplished by providing a deep (preferably water-filled) ditch outside the wall and by equipping the wall with towers, which projected to the field and provided archers a field of fire along the face of the wall. The gate was defended by placing it between two towers, which were bound together into a single structure or gate house, encompassing the towers and the gate passage between them. The latter might be protected by a sequence of gates and portcullises (iron gratings) across the passage, holes in the roof above, and arrow loops on either side. The King's Gate at Caernarvon Castle of the 1290s, with five gates and six portcullises along the gate passage, was a most elaborate example. During the fourteenth and fifteenth centuries, the height of walls was emphasized, and the tops of walls and towers were equipped with overhanging machicolation (a gallery or parapet containing openings from which missiles could be discharged). At the same time, loops might be redesigned for use with handguns rather than bows.

The expansion of the major magnates' castles was as much about providing room for ever-increasing households as it was about the defense of the whole. In the eleventh century, castles provided a single chamber for the lord, while members of his household were accommodated in the hall like earlier Germanic warriors. Neither side of this equation remained satisfied. From the late twelfth century, lords retreated steadily from the public life of the hall. In France, King Philip Augustus built a number of fine round towers to provide private accommodation at castles from Gisors to Villeneuve-sur-Yonne, towers that did not contain a hall or public rooms. The private accommodation for the lord, marked out by its fine carving, windows with seats in the embrasures, fireplaces, and access to private single latrines, steadily increased to suites of two rooms (outer and inner chambers) or more with the addition of a presence chamber (sitting room). The tendency for the lord's suite to be placed in a dominant tower was a constant theme up to the sixteenth century. From the early thirteenth century

onward, the more important members of the households were accommodated in individual rooms (occasionally in double ones), often located in the mural towers (wall towers). The fourteenth-century reconstruction of Windsor Castle saw an early example of a full range of such lodgings down one side of a courtyard.

The lower members of the castle community and the less important visitors met the inner household in the great hall. From the thirteenth century onward, the great hall saw the formalization of service space in a pair (buttery and pantry) of rooms at one end with a passage between, leading to the kitchen. By the end of the century, the hall is the pivotal centerpiece of the domestic layout, with the service elements dependent on the lower end, which also had the main door. At the other end, linked to the presence of the dais and the high table, was access to the lord's rooms and the principal household suites. This provided the key for truly formal overall design of the castle as a whole, from the regular plans of French royal castles of the early thirteenth century, through symmetrical show façades of the fourteenth century, to the creation of Renaissance houses. Within the walls the courtyard was the obvious unit for the arranging of space. Raglan Castle, in Wales, is an example of the systematic ordering of the community and space in a fifteenth-century magnate's castle. There are two courtyards, joined (or divided) by the great hall: the outer one, with the kitchen, stores, and services; and the inner one, with ranges of better-class lodgings for the inner household. From the inner courtyard, through the state apartments, lay the way to the lord's detached chamber tower, dominating the whole complex.

Developments along these lines, which are often presented as those of castles as a whole, do not apply universally. Defensively, Mediterranean castles, whether of the Crusading Orders, Byzantine, or Islamic states, tended to rely much more on manning the battlements than on archery from the flanking towers. Castles like the Mediterranean ones and many of those in northeast Europe that were built more to house a garrison than a large feudal household put much less emphasis on providing a multiplicity of lodgings.

Many of the key parts of major stone castles were to be found at upper-floor levels. Excavation is, therefore, of little use in studying these. Much excavation in the past concentrated on uncovering the ground plans of elements, such as the defensive line of curtain walls and towers, which may not be the most effective use of archaeological techniques. One clear role for excavation is the

C

study of timber structures. Excavation of these involves usually either the outer, service areas of the castle or its earlier phases, both of which often have been destroyed by later activity. A second role has been to uncover artifacts and environmental evidence. Pottery sequences, for example, may be tied down chronologically by the excavation of well-dated contexts in castles. While studies of animal bones have been undertaken, they may be hampered by the difficulty of understanding their origin in a castle that had a large household of very mixed social class. The use of the wet deposits in moats for the study of the local environment through pollen and microfauna has scarcely been started.

FURTHER READINGS

Brown, R.A. *English Castles*. London: Batsford, 1976.

Higham, R.A., and P. Barker. *Timber Castles*. London: Batsford, 1992.

Kenyon, J.R. *Medieval Fortifications*. Leicester: Leicester University Press, 1990.

King, D.J.C. *The Castle in England and Wales*. London: Croom Helm, 1988.

McNeill, T.E. *Castles*. London: Batsford/English Heritage, 1992.

Platt, C. *The Castle in Medieval England and Wales*. London: Secker and Warburg, 1982.

Pounds, N.J.G. *The Medieval Castle in England and Wales*. Cambridge: Cambridge University Press, 1990.

Thompson, M.W. *The Decline of the Castle*. Cambridge: Cambridge University Press, 1987.

———. *The Rise of the Castle*. Cambridge: Cambridge University Press, 1991.

T.E. McNeill

Cemeteries and Burials

Cemeteries contain a variety of evidence for the study of medieval life. At the most fundamental level are the dead themselves. From skeletal remains, one may deduce such basic parameters as age, sex, diet, disease, and biological relationships. At a somewhat less elementary level are the grave goods that, as components of costume or as grave furnishings, accompany the dead. The kind, number, and location of these objects differ from burial to burial. The grave itself—its construction and its relationship to other burials within the cemetery—may also be considered. Finally, the position of the cemetery within the landscape may refer to larger questions of sociopolitical development.

In the earlier centuries of the Medieval period, before burial custom came to be regulated by the Christian Church, the community dictated those funerary customs acceptable for use in the local cemetery (James 1979). For this reason, it is difficult to detail any but the most simplistic commonalities of burial practice to which an exception from some corner of medieval Europe cannot be identified.

Historical Background

Despite the opening of elite burials at St.-Germain-des-Prés (France) in 1645, the discovery in Tournai (Belgium) of the grave of the Frankish King Childeric (d. 481/482) in 1653, and the meditation by Sir Thomas Browne on "sad sepulchral Pitchers" from Walshingham (England) in 1658, the scholarly study of early medieval cemeteries did not flourish until the late eighteenth and nineteenth centuries. Later medieval graves in churches and churchyards, likewise, were opened by enthusiastic nineteenth-century antiquarians and clerics. Church burials of illustrious clerics and royal personages were generally reclosed, often after removing personal items from the grave. Those anonymous individuals interred in churchyards or in unsanctified ground received less respect: the grave goods, rather than the skeletal remains of the individuals who accompanied them, were generally salvaged, recorded, and turned over to newly formed museums and historical societies.

Components of Cemetery Data

Human Remains. Although skeletal remains allow for the identification of age and sex of the deceased, poor preservation and inadequate record keeping continue to lead some archaeologists to assign these traits on the basis of grave goods or grave size alone. In order to construct an accurate demographic profile, a burial sample of the living community must be obtained. For most of the medieval period, infants are, through cultural practice and/or preferential destruction due to skeletal fragility, underrepresented in cemetery populations. Life expectancy in the early medieval period, as represented by Spong Hill (England), was thirty–forty years (McKinley 1989:242). Childbearing, with its attendant dangers, carried a costly price for women, as is reflected in higher adult male sex ratios. The containment of the infirm in leper hospitals and the variety of physical ailments identified as leprosy provide evidence about the history of medical care and disease.

Grave Furnishings. From the fifth century, in most of Europe, the dead were often furnished with grave goods, frequently related to feasting, and dressed in clothing rather than shrouds. These garments often carried an array of jewelery and dress fittings. Men often carried weapons into the afterlife; women were occasionally buried with weaving paraphernalia, chatelaines, or amulets. These grave goods form much of the basis of the chronological schemes that have structured our understanding of the medieval past.

From the early eighth century, the number of unfurnished or poorly furnished graves increased, and the burial of weapons decreased dramatically. Rather than being dressed for burial in their clothing, the dead were generally wrapped in shrouds. Yet, despite suppression by the Christian Church of pagan burial practice, elite and even holy individuals continued to be interred with precious goods throughout the medieval period. The bodies of priests, dressed in their vestments, were often accompanied by the communion vessels, the paten and chalice. The ring, mitre, and crozier symbolic of the episcopal office sometimes were interred with their bishop (Finucane 1981:44).

In violation of the sancity of the cemetery and punative laws, the wealth lavished on the dead sometimes returned, through grave robbing, to the living, as with the disturbed burials at St. Denis (France) (Werner 1964) and Sutton Hoo (England) (Bruce-Mitford 1975, 1978, 1983). During the translation of the dead to a holier burial site or the honorific opening of a royal grave, physical relics or personal furnishings were sometimes removed.

Burial Practices: The Grave. In late Roman Europe, by the third century A.D., inhumation was the prevailing burial practice. This treatment, in which the body was deposited directly into a grave dug into the ground, continued into the early Medieval period. Occasionally, the burial pit was lined with wood or stone packing. Although wood-coffined inhumations continued in some areas through the Medieval period, other graves incorporated stone sarcophagi and slabs in their construction. Carriage bodies were substituted for coffins in the elite female graves of Viking Age Denmark.

In the areas of northern Germany occupied by the continental Saxons and in eastern Anglo-Saxon England, cremation burial, in which the dressed body was burned and a selection of bones interred in a ceramic, hide, cloth, or metal container or simply deposited into the ground, was the prevailing rite. Funeral pyres on which the dead

were cremated have been identified at Liebenau (Germany) (Cosack 1982) and, possibly, at Snape (England) (Carnegie and Filmer-Sankey 1993). Both cremation and inhumation rites were practiced at the same time and sometimes in the same cemeteries. However, from the fourth century, the practice of cremation waned in northern Europe and, by the eleventh century, even Scandinavia, like the inhuming regions to the south and west, abandoned cremation (Randsborg 1980).

Boat burials, in which the body was interred within a sailing ship, were a uniquely Anglo-Scandinavian phenomenon (Müller-Wille 1968–1969). Developing from Roman Iron Age boat graves at Bornholm (Denmark), this practice spread across Norway and Sweden by the sixth century to reach eastern England by the late sixth or early seventh centuries. Although only briefly popular in England, boat burial continued in Scandinavia, as witnessed by examples from the tenth century at Hedeby and Ladby, Fyn (Denmark) and the eleventh century at Vendel (Sweden).

While the majority of the dead were interred without aboveground markers, the existence of postholes, ring ditches, or barrows indicates a limited popularity of this practice. At some early medieval sites, a mixed ritual was practiced: mounds were erected over a portion of the graves at Finglesham (England), Sutton Hoo (England), Spong Hill (England), Basel-Bernerning (Switzerland), Dittigheim (Germany), and Moos-Burgstall (Germany). In the seventh century, separate elite cemeteries, composed of mound burials, characterize the Upper Rhine and Upper Danube regions (Van de Noort 1993). Burial near or underneath mounds, considered to be a pagan practice, was forbidden by Charlemagne in the late eighth century. Outside of the Merovingian and Carolingian sphere, as in the eighth–tenth-century cemeteries at Ralswick (Rügen), barrows were erected over all graves in the cemetery.

Burial Practices: The Cemetery. The early Medieval period is characterized by large cemeteries, sometimes containing several thousand interments. In northern France, Belgium, southern and western Germany, and Switzerland, these sixth–seventh-century inhumation burials are aligned in rows (Reihengräber). Equally large cremation cemeteries, some continuing in use on the Continent into the tenth century, have been identified in Anglian England and northern Germany.

During the preceding Roman period (first to fourth centuries), cemeteries were, by legal mandate, sited

C

outside city limits. Early medieval cemeteries were generally located in the countryside, where they served newly settled communities, as in Anglo-Saxon England and Merovingian Gaul, or continued the tradition of extramural burial. Until recently, pagan Anglo-Saxon cemeteries were thought to have been sited at some distance from settlements (Arnold 1977; Hawkes 1973:186), but the discovery of settlements adjacent to contemporary cemeteries indicates that the dead and the living existed in close proximity. Early medieval cemeteries were sometimes located near earthworks of prehistoric and Roman date, suggesting that this landscape still carried importance in the collective memory of the community (Van de Noort 1993).

From the fourth century, Christian Frankish cemeteries were often sited near Roman graveyards containing burials of saints and martyrs. Following the Merovingian King Clovis (d. 511), a preference for burial within the church was enjoyed by the elite (Périn 1987). The wealthy graves found under the Cologne Cathedral (Germany) date to the second quarter of the sixth century, and the burial associated with Arnegund (the woman who was the consort of King Chlotar I but who may not be the person interred) at the Royal Abbey of St. Denis (France) is attributed to the late sixth or, more likely, early seventh century (James 1988). Indeed, the monastery of Sts. Peter and Paul in Canterbury (England) served as a dynastic mausoleum for the Kentish royal families. Church burial spread to less elite groups from the eighth century (Van de Noort 1993). Even in the late Medieval period, a hierarchy of burial location sought proximity to the altar (Finucane 1981:43–44; Harding 1992). The ineffectiveness of prohibitions, dating from the sixth century, against burial within the church was recognized by the accommodation in the ninth century of church burial for important clerics and laymen (Finucane 1981:43). The continuing practice of interring the political and sacred elite within and adjacent to churches may be associated not only with spiritual values, but also with the increasing power held in the hands of those individuals and the institutions they supported.

To accommodate the increasing popularity of churchyard burial, new cemeteries were established. In some instances, churches with their churchyards were established outside the walls of preexisting Roman towns, as at Sts. Peter and Paul, Canterbury (England), and Saint-Victor, near Marseilles (France). Less often, because of prohibitions against the consecration of a church in an unsanctified cemetery, was a church built within a preexisting cemetery.

The practice of churchyard burial, often in cemeteries still active today, restricts accessibility to many medieval graves. At heavily used cemeteries, the remains of previous interments were often exhumed during the course of grave digging. Around the fourteenth century, space limitations came to be addressed by the practice of disinterring and moving the remains of previous burials to charnels or ossuaries to accommodate new dead (Ariès 1981:54–56).

With the increasing frequency of churchyard burial, urban cemeteries came to be established within, rather than outside, the towns they served (Bullough 1983). By the twelfth century, urban mother-churches in Germany and parts of England controlled burial practices within their cemeteries. The siting of smaller urban parish churches suggests that these structures were erected in conjunction with establishment of their cemeteries. Access to these town church cemeteries was restricted to those who could provide mortuary fees. In most of Europe by the end of the eleventh century, members of rural communities were buried in their parish churchyards or, less frequently, in the graveyard of a field church or chapel subordinate to the parish church.

Outside the walls or within marginal intramural communities were buried such socially excluded groups as lepers, Jews, excommunicates, and unbaptized infants (Barrow 1992:94; Finucane 1981:54–56). In times of epidemic, grave pits for mass burial were often excavated to accommodate the victims.

Medieval cemeteries occasionally united the sacred and profane worlds in obvious ways. At Bonn (Germany) and Xanten (Germany), medieval towns developed around cemetery churches (Bassett et al. 1992). On the Continent during the eleventh century, cemeteries, immune from secular jurisdiction, were the sites of trading (Barrow 1992:93).

Reconstructing the Past: Social Structure

Cemeteries provide an understanding of how the medieval world accommodated, honored, and reified its dead. In some instances, the graves of historically known personages, such as the Frankish King Childeric, not only provide chronologically informative grave goods, but also indicate the standards for elite burial.

Social complexity may be structured vertically or horizontally. The vertical dimension refers to rank or status grading in the society. Structural components that are equal at each hierarchical level, such as ethnic groupings, constitute the horizontal dimension.

Vertical Differentiation: Wealth and Status. Recognizing from historical sources that medieval Europe was a hierarchical society, some archaeologists have sought to correlate social rank with grave goods (Christlein 1979; Stein 1967). Drawing from the early laws, it has been suggested that the cemeteries present an index to society. Attempts to correlate legally encoded social roles with specific burials have been criticized for their failure to accommodate spatial and temporal variability; their conflation of economic and social status; and their obscuration of differences such as age, gender, religious beliefs, manner of death, morals, occupation, wealth, ethnicity, personal relationships, or status of the deceased, that cut across status groupings. However, graves furnished with luxury goods or graves that are large, that incorporate structural elements, that are located under barrows, or are uniquely oriented, or isolated from other burials, or located within the church, or sited in close proximity to other elite burials indicate that these dead enjoyed special privileges.

Despite the ascribed status signaled by the adult-size weapons and putative sceptre buried c. 537 with the six-year-old boy beneath the Cologne Cathedral (Germany), the graves of children are overwhelmingly among the most poorly constructed and poorly furnished within their cemeteries. The rare outfitting of a child's burial with lavish grave goods may best be seen as an expression of the social concerns not of the deceased but of the surviving parents or guardians.

Cemetery evidence of social ranking can support an explanatory model for political development. In the region around Metz (Germany/Austria), a change from grave goods that, in the sixth century, marked social differentiation on the basis of sex and gender to, in the seventh century, those that distinguished class or rank has been associated with the consolidation of power among the Merovingian aristocracy (Halsall 1992). Likewise, in Anglo-Saxon England from the sixth to the seventh centuries, an increasing amount of wealth in a decreasing number of graves, an increase in the wealth of male graves relative to female graves, an increase in the quantity of luxury goods, and the appearance of burials singled out for interment under mounds or within churches—all are seen as documenting the consolidation of power in the hands of a few local leaders (Arnold 1982).

Horizontal Variability: Ethnicity. In a context of mixing populations, archaeologists have sought to map the meeting of native and immigrant. Using cemetery evidence, such as skeletal material, grave goods, grave orientation, and body position, archaeologists have attempted to identify the ethnic origins of the dead. The appearance of a new dress style or burial ritual, rather than of a single element, may reflect the arrival of a new population. At Herpes in southwest France, for instance, graves similar in grave goods and burial treatment to those from *Reihengräber* in the north may represent Frankish settlement (James 1988:111–114). Burial custom may be a more sensitive indicator of ethnic or regional custom than are grave goods (Fisher 1988).

Reconstructing the Past: Religious Practices

The historically documented transition from paganism to Christianity has served as a conceptual backdrop against which some archaeologists have interpreted changes in early medieval burial practices. However, the documentary and archaeological records of the conversion do not mesh well (Bullough 1983). Despite the popularity of Christian belief from the fourth and fifth centuries onward, burial practices continued to be determined by local social custom, rather than simply by theological doctrine (Young 1977). The Anglo-Saxon missions, such as Augustine's to the Kentish Court (597) and Paulinius's to Edwin of Northumbria (627), have often been associated with the seventh-century appearance of new artifact types, a general decrease in the quantity of grave goods, and a preference for west-east grave orientation (Hyslop 1963; Meaney and Hawkes 1970:53). Yet, none of these attributes can be identified as an exclusively Christian practice. In both England and Gaul, it was the elite who first adopted the new religion and buried their families at ecclesiastical sites while occasionally supplying the dead with elaborate grave goods. Even among the devout, other concerns sometimes dictated burial practice; the late Saxon burials at York Minster, for example, followed the alignment of nearby Roman buildings rather than typical Christian east-west orientation (Bullough 1983:190, note 34). Morever, the continued burial of amulets, in violation of seventh–eighth-century Church law (Geake 1992:90), the construction of mound burials (Van de Noort 1993), and the practices of cremation under mound, ship burial, and human sacrifice at Sutton Hoo (England) (Carver 1992: 365–366) may represent acts of defiant paganism.

C

FURTHER READINGS

Ariès, P. *The Hour of Our Death*. New York: Knopf, 1981.

Arnold, C.J. Early Anglo-Saxon Settlement Patterns in Southern England. *Journal of Historical Geography* (1977) 3:309–315.

———. Stress as a Stimulus to Socioeconomic Change: England in the Seventh Century. In *Ranking, Resource, and Exchange*. Ed. C. Renfrew and S. Shennan. Cambridge: Cambridge University Press, 1982.

Barrow, J. Urban Cemetery Location in the High Middle Ages. In *Death in Towns: Urban Responses to the Dying and the Dead, 100–1600*. Ed. S. Bassett. Leicester: Leicester University Press, 1992.

Bassett, S., C. Dyer, and R. Holt. Introduction. In *Death in Towns: Urban Responses to the Dying and the Dead, 100–1600*. Ed. S. Bassett. Leicester: Leicester University Press, 1992, pp. 1–7.

Browne, Sir Thomas. Hydriotaphia or Urne Buriall. In *The Works of Sir Thomas Browne*. Vol. 1. Ed. G. Keynes. London: Faber and Faber, 1964, 1658, pp. 131–172.

Bruce-Mitford, R.L.S. *The Sutton Hoo Ship Burial*. Vol. 1. London: British Museum, 1975.

———. *The Sutton Hoo Ship Burial*. Vol. 2. London: British Museum, 1978.

———. *The Sutton Hoo Ship Burial*. Vol. 3. London: British Museum, 1983.

Bullough, D.A. Burial, Community, and Belief in the Early Medieval West. In *Ideal and Reality in Frankish and Anglo-Saxon Society*. Ed. P. Wormald. Oxford: Basil Blackwell, 1983, pp. 177–201.

Carnegie, S., and W. Filmer-Sankey. A Saxon "Cremation Pyre" from the Snape Anglo-Saxon Cemetery, Suffolk. *Anglo-Saxon Studies in History and Archaeology* (1993) 6:107–111.

Carver, M. The Anglo-Saxon Cemetery at Sutton Hoo: An Interim Report. In *The Age of Sutton Hoo: The Seventh Century in North-Western Europe*. Ed. M. Carver. Woodbridge: Boydell, 1992, pp. 343–371.

Christlein, R. *Die Alamennen*. Stuttgart: Aalen, 1979.

Cosack, E. *Das sächsiche Gräberfeld bei Liebenau, Kr. Nienburg (Weser)*. Teil 1. Berlin: Mann, 1982.

Finucane, R.C. Sacred Corpse, Profane Carrion: Social Ideals and Death Rituals in the Later Middle Ages. In *Mirrors of Mortality: Studies in the Social History of Death*. Ed. J. Whaley. New York: St. Martin's Press, 1981, pp. 40–60.

Fisher, G. Style and Sociopolitical Organization: A Preliminary Study from Early Anglo-Saxon England. In *Power and Politics in Early Medieval Britain and Ireland*. Ed. S.T. Driscoll and M. R. Nieke. Edinburgh: University of Edinburgh Press, 1988, pp. 128–144.

Geake, H. Burial Practice in Seventh- and Eighth-Century England. In *The Age of Sutton Hoo: The Seventh Century in North-Western Europe*. Ed. M. Carver. Woodbridge: Boydell, 1992, pp. 83–94.

Halsall, G. Social Change Around A.D. 600: An Austrasian Perspective. In *The Age of Sutton Hoo: The Seventh Century in North-Western Europe*. Ed. M. Carver. Woodbridge: Boydell, 1992, pp. 265–278.

Harding, V. Burial Choice and Burial Location in Later Medieval London. In *Death in Towns: Urban Responses to the Dying and the Dead, 100–1600*. Ed. S. Bassett. Leicester: Leicester University Press, 1992, pp. 117–135.

Hawkes, S.C. The Dating and Social Significance of the Burials in the Polhill Cemetery. In *Excavations in West Kent, 1960–1970*. Ed. B. Philp. Dover: Kent Archaeological Society, 1973, pp. 186–201.

Hyslop, M. Two Anglo-Saxon Cemeteries at Chamberlains Barn, Leighton Buzzard, Bedfordshire. *Archaeological Journal* (1963) 120:161–200.

James, E. Cemeteries and the Problem of Frankish Settlement in Gaul. In *Names, Words, and Graves: Early Medieval Settlement*. Ed. P.H. Sawyer. Leeds: University of Leeds Press, 1979, pp. 55–89.

———. *The Franks*. Oxford: Basil Blackwell, 1988.

McKinley, J. Spong Hill: Anglo-Saxon Cemetery. In *Burial Archaeology: Current Research, Methods, and Development*. Ed. C.A. Roberts, F. Lee, and J. Bintliff. BAR British Series 211. Oxford: British Archaeological Reports, 1989, pp. 241–248.

Meaney, A.L., and S.C. Hawkes. *Two Anglo-Saxon Cemeteries at Winnall, Winchester, Hampshire*. Monograph Series 4. London: Society for Medieval Archaeology, 1970.

Müller-Wille, M. Bestattung im Boot. *Offa* (1968–1969) 25–26: whole volume.

Périn, P. Des nécropoles romaines tardives aux nécropoles de haut moyen âge: Remarques sur la topographie funéraire en Gaul mérovingiennes et à sa périphérie. *Cahiers archólogiques* (1987) 35:9–30.

Randsborg, K. *The Viking Age in Denmark: The Formation of a State*. London: Duckworth, 1980.

Stein, F. *Adelgräber des 8.Jahrhunderts in Deutschland*. Serie A, Band 9. Bern: Germanische Denkmäler der Völkerwanderungszeit, 1967.

Van de Noort, R. The Context of Early Medieval Barrows in Western Europe. *Antiquity* (1993) 64:66–73.

Werner, J. Frankish Royal Tombs in the Cathdrals of Cologne and St. Denis. *Antiquity* (1964) 38:201–216.

Young, B.K. Paganisme, christianisation et rites funéraires mérovingiens. *Archéologie médiévale* (1977) 7:5–81.

Genevieve Fisher

SEE ALSO

Barrows; Herpes; Skeletal Populations; Snape; Spong Hill; Sutton Hoo

Ceramic Floor Tiles

See Tiles.

Ceramics (Netherlands)

The estuaries of the Rhine and Meuse Rivers in the Low Countries have formed a cultural border from prehistoric times onward. In the Roman period (the first four centuries A.D.), the imperial frontier was situated along the Rhine River, and the territories south of the border were incorporated into the Roman Empire. These events had a profound effect on the inhabitants of these regions and on their material culture. In the southern part of the country, which was integrated into the Roman Empire, handmade Iron Age pottery was replaced by mass-produced, wheel-thrown Roman pottery in the first century A.D. North of the Rhine River, pottery continued to be made in an Iron Age tradition. Imports of Roman pottery into this free Germanic world were scarce and probably limited to the higher echelons of society.

Invasions of Germanic tribes shattered the Dutch part of the Roman frontier in the late third and the fourth centuries A.D. and destroyed the imperial economic system. The incoming Germanic peoples introduced their own pottery, as demonstrated by excavations of such migration period settlements as Gennep. Because the shape of the Germanic vessels is closely related to Iron Age forms, it is often difficult to differentiate migration period vessels from earlier ones. This is especially the case in those parts of the country that were never part of the Roman Empire and in which there is no sharp transition between an early medieval and an Iron Age pottery tradition. During the fifth century, most pottery was generally made by hand within the confines of the settlement. Small amounts of pottery were brought in from outside the region, especially from the Mayen area near the present-day town of Koblenz (Germany). Mayen was already an important supplier of mass-produced, wheel-thrown pottery in the

Roman period, and it continued to be so until the ninth century.

In the Merovingian period (A.D. 500–700), two cultural zones became apparent in the Low Countries: a zone north of the Rhine River in which locally produced, handmade pottery predominated, and a zone south of the Rhine River in which most pots were wheel thrown and not made in settlements. This division already existed in the Roman period, but then it could be ascribed to the presence of the political, economic, and military frontier between the Roman Empire and the "free" Germanic world. In later periods, no such clear border was present to account for the differences in material culture. In the north, only a few wheel-turned vessels seem to have reached the inhabitants during the early Medieval period. Elsewhere, Mayen and smaller workshops in the central and southern parts of the Netherlands supplied wheel-thrown pottery to the settlements, and few if any pots were made by the villagers themselves. Several of these workshops have been found in the Netherlands (e.g., in Maastricht).

Only a few vessel types were used in the fifth–seventh centuries. Handmade pottery often consisted of neckless bowls of a coarse fabric. Wheel-thrown pottery occurred in a coarse and in a fine fabric. Steep-walled, bucket-shaped pots and jugs were the main forms of the coarse ware, while the fine wares consisted of so-called biconical pots and bowls with a burnished surface. These pots were often decorated. Vessels of both coarse and fine fabrics were used in domestic contexts and served as grave goods for the dead.

The expansion of trading networks in the Carolingian period (A.D. 700–900) contributed to the success of the Rhineland pottery. A second large-scale production center, Badorf, developed in the eighth century in the Vorgebirge near Cologne. Vessels from Badorf and Mayen are found in virtually every settlement of the eighth and ninth centuries in the Low Countries and Germany. They occur in large numbers in the newly created trading places of the Carolingian Empire like Dorestad and Medemblik. Some researchers state that these trading places played an important role in the distribution of pottery from the Rhineland to the hinterland. Settlements of the Veluwe (Kootwijk), situated c. 40 km from Dorestad, however, display a dramatic drop in the percentage of Rhineland pottery when compared to Dorestad itself. It therefore does not seem justified to attribute a retail function to these trading places.

From the Merovingian to the Carolingian period, a change took place in the vessel types produced. A small

C

cooking pot was the main type produced in Mayen; spouted jugs and large storage vessels were the dominant forms produced in the kilns near Cologne. A significant typological development in the local, handmade pottery in the eighth century was the creation of a new vessel type that would dominate the household pottery in the northern Netherlands and Germany west of the Elbe River for the next six centuries. The newly created vessel type was a simple globular pot without any addition of handles, spouts, or feet. These vessels were made without the use of a fast wheel. The earliest examples of this globular pottery (German *Kugeltopf,* Dutch *kogelpot*) are found in the Dutch coastal area in the beginning of the eighth century. Inland regions adopted the globular pottery more slowly, and it persisted longer there, until the fourteenth or even the fifteenth century. In the first half of the twentieth century, there was some debate about the reason for the appearance of this globular pottery. Most archaeologists believed that there was a relationship between the expansion of Saxon or Frisian peoples and the expansion of globular pottery. Now it is generally believed that such explanations are untenable. The connection between ethnic groups known from written sources and pottery is a very loose one. Political divisions are often not discernable in the distribution of either ceramics or ceramic types. Developments in the local, handmade wares of the Netherlands and Germany show little influence from political events such as the integration of these regions into the Carolingian Empire.

After the death of Charlemagne in 814, his empire fell prey to political chaos and economic instability. This is reflected in the disappearance of Mayen and Badorf products from Dutch settlements. The economic stagnation is perhaps more clearly visible in the southern Netherlands and northern Belgium. For the first time in centuries, the inhabitants of these regions were forced to make their own pottery, because the supply of pottery from the Rhineland was much reduced. When the economic situation recovered in the eleventh century, domestic production of pottery ceased.

During the High Middle Ages (A.D. 1000–1300), most pottery in the northern Netherlands consisted of globular vessels that were produced on a small scale within the settlements. Not more than one out of ten vessels was not of local origin. Wheel-thrown pottery was brought in from Pingsdorf, situated only a few km from Badorf. Ceramics from Pingsdorf were widely distributed across most of northwest Europe and were especially popular in the Low Countries. Near Cologne, a second pot-

tery industry developed in the village of Paffrath in the tenth century. The distribution of this ware followed that of Pingsdorf pottery into the Netherlands, Belgium, Germany, England, Denmark, and southern Sweden. This situation changed when the region along the Meuse River between Liège and Namur in Belgium developed a powerful economy. The economic prosperity of this region is reflected in the success of its pottery industry in places such as Andenne, Huy, and Wierde. In the tenth century, the wheel-thrown, partly glazed vessels from the Meuse region reached northern Belgium and the southern Netherlands. During the twelfth century, the distribution reached its peak, extending over the western and central Netherlands and Flanders as well. Later, in the thirteenth century, the economy of the Meuse Valley stagnated, and the export of pottery was markedly reduced.

The only village industry that developed in the Netherlands itself was situated in the south of the country in the province of Limburg along the Meuse River. Several kiln sites have been found there, and the pottery has been subject to extensive typological and technological investigation. All this makes the Limburg pottery the best-studied production center in the Low Countries. None of the kiln sites near Cologne has been studied in such detail, despite their importance for European medieval archaeology. The Limburg pottery existed from the eleventh century to the fourteenth and distributed its products in the southern parts of the Netherlands.

During the early and High Middle Ages, markets were of only minor importance for the exchange of objects such as ceramics. Most large production sites were situated near early urban centers, like Cologne and Liège, which could generate a constant demand. Outside these towns, the population, as well as the demand for goods, was low. A market system had yet to evolve. These regions of the Low Countries were probably supplied with Rhineland pottery by itinerant traders or peddlers. Apart from peddlers, the manorial system played an important role in the distribution of ceramics. Cologne and Liège were both seats of bishoprics, and in both places numerous monasteries were established. These feudal elites controlled some of the village industries and the exchange of their products. At the same time, they were in possession of large estates in the Low Countries; the manorial system guaranteed a regular provisioning of food for these elites, which was transported to them by the rural peasantry. It is likely that pottery was part of the return cargo of the peasants who delivered goods to their lord.

A period of major change in the economic and demographic development of northwest Europe occurred in the thirteenth century. Everywhere, new towns were created or grew out of old settlements. In the next centuries, most of these urban settlements had their own pottery workshops that supplied the local market. Two characteristic phenomena of the previous period had disappeared by the middle of the fourteenth century: imports from large village industries and the production of handmade globular pottery. Urban workshops produced new types of wheel-thrown vessels, first in a gray and later in a red fabric. Kilns from the period have been found near Utrecht, Haarlem, Leiden, and other towns. The development from handmade gray wares to wheel-thrown red wares has been well documented by excavations of late thirteenth- to fourteenth-century pottery workshops near Utrecht. The newly created urban workshops produced a wide range of products for specific functions, such as skillets, tripod cooking pots, bowls, colanders, fire covers, storage jars, and oil lamps.

Jugs and beakers were usually brought in from the Rhineland. To produce a vitrified product with a low porosity, Rhenish potters of the thirteenth and fourteenth centuries increased the firing temperatures of their kilns. In the beginning of the thirteenth century, a hard-fired protostoneware was produced. By the end of the thirteenth century, the first stonewares were introduced, fired at temperatures of 1,200–1,350°C. Local Dutch clays cannot be fired at such high temperatures because they are of a younger geological age than those used in Germany. During the fourteenth and fifteenth centuries, the most important supplier of stoneware to the Netherlands was situated near Cologne in Siegburg. Other suppliers were Langerwehe near Aachen and the Limburg kilns in their final stage of existence. Stoneware production took place on a nearly industrial scale.

Imports other than German stonewares are rare in Dutch settlements. Small amounts of thirteenth-century highly decorated pottery originating in Flanders, France, or England are sometimes found in the coastal areas. Soon thereafter these vessels, mostly jugs, were copied by local potters (e.g., in Haarlem).

During the late Middle Ages and early modern times, a competitive market developed for ceramics. The market was supplied, on the one hand, by local producers and, on the other, by the Rhenish stoneware industries that specialized in vessels for drinking and pouring.

FURTHER READINGS

Bruijn, A. Die mittelalterliche keramische Industrie in Südlimburg. *Berichten van de Rijksdienst voor het Oudheidkundig Bodemonderzoek* (1962–1963) 12–13:357–459.

———. *Pottersvuren langs de Vecht, aardewerk rond 1400 uit Utrecht.* Rotterdam Papers 3, 1979.

Brongers, J.A. Ceramological Investigations into Medieval Pottery Produced at Schinveld. *Berichten van de Rijksdienst voor het Oudheidkundig Bodemonderzoek* (1983) 33:375–418.

Es, W.A. van, and W.J.H. Verwers. *Excavations at Dorestad.* Vol. 1: *The Harbour: Hoogstraat I.* Nederlanse Oudheden 9. Amersfoort: RoB, 1980.

Janssen, H.L. Later Medieval Pottery Production in the Netherlands. In *Ceramics and Trade: The Production and Distribution of Later Medieval Pottery in North-West Europe.* Ed. R. Hodges and P. Davey. Sheffield: Sheffield University Press, 1983, pp. 121–186.

Verhoeven, A.A.A. Ceramics and Economics in the Low Countries, A.D. 1000–1300. In *Medieval Archaeology in the Netherlands: Studies Presented to H.H. van Regteren Altena.* Ed. J.C. Besteman, J.M. Bos, and H.A. Heidinga. Assen/Maastricht: Van Gorcum, 1990, pp. 265–281.

Arno A.A. Verhoeven

SEE ALSO
Stoneware

Chester

Chester was originally founded as a Roman legionary fortress and owes its site and basic street plan to the Romans. It lies on a low sandstone ridge north of the River Dee, near the head of its estuary, which provided a site for harbor facilities and a bridging point.

By the eighth century A.D., Chester was part of the Saxon kingdom of Mercia. The church of St. John the Baptist, which lies outside the Roman walls, was reputedly founded in A.D. 689. Fragments of cross shafts from this period have been found at St. Johns, but no structural elements have been identified. Archaeological evidence for settlements of this period is also elusive. Perhaps the middle Saxon settlement lay around St. Johns, outside the ruined Roman settlement.

In A.D. 907, Aethelfleda, daughter of King Alfred the Great (d. 918), founded a *burh* (fortified settlement) at

C

Chester, extending the old Roman walls down to the river. Chester prospered during the ninth and tenth centuries, as the city benefited from the Norse trade in the Irish Sea area. During this period, three or four more churches were founded. In general, soil conditions in Chester do not allow the survival of wood, so timber buildings are traceable only as negative soil impressions. Remains of timber structures have been found on many archaeological sites. The sizes and designs of these buildings vary, and some had sunken areas or basements. Common finds on sites of this period include Chester ware pottery, a fine wheel-thrown pottery of this period, and metalwork. The finds indicate that Chester had a mixed Saxon and Scandinavian culture. The city also had a major mint. Coins occur in large numbers in hoards but are rarely found individually in archaeological contexts.

While Chester was only a small city in the later eleventh century, it was the major urban center in northwest England, and the Norman Conquest (1066) had a major impact on the city's form. King William (1028–1087) built a motte-and-bailey castle in the southern corner of the city in 1070. Motte-and-bailey castles are characterized by an artificial mound of earth and stones (the motte), topped by a wooden palisade and surrounded by an enclosure (the bailey). Through the twelfth century, the castle, including the tower on the motte and the inner ward, was rebuilt in stone. An outer ward, initially of earth and timber, was also added. The circuit of the city walls was completed with the river frontages.

William the Conquerer also established the earldom of Chester. The Norman earls founded the major medieval institutions in the city. In 1093, a large Benedictine abbey was founded at St. Werburgh's Church. St. Johns was rebuilt and served for a period as a cathedral. A Benedictine nunnery was founded c. 1150 just north of the castle. Plentiful and impressive evidence for these Norman structures still survives. Interestingly, however, there is very little evidence for domestic structures or artifacts for two centuries following the Norman Conquest. Presumably, this period saw a shift of occupation to the street frontages. The buildings were probably timber, and the evidence for them has been destroyed by later occupation.

In 1237, the earldom was annexed by the Crown. The later thirteenth century was another period of prosperity. Chester served as the headquarters of Henry III (1207–1272) and Edward I's (1239–1307) conquest of north Wales (1282–1283). All the forces and supplies for the construction of the Edwardian castles in north Wales

passed through Chester. This prosperity is evidenced in the remarkable series of surviving townhouses of the period, incorporating rows. The rows are continuous public galleries running through the street fronts at first-floor level. The upper floors overhang them, thus forming a covered way. They formerly existed on all four of the main streets, although some are now lost. At street level, there was an undercroft, frequently of fine masonry and sometimes arcaded or vaulted in stone. The upper levels could be built of either timber framing or masonry. The main hall lay at row level, and the front of the hall was frequently partitioned off to form a shop. Row level corresponds with ground level to the rear, where the yards were located. Other chambers were built over the row.

The rear yards contained rubbish and cesspits, often a rich source of artifacts and environmental remains, including pottery and wooden and leather artifacts. The pottery included imports from southwestern and northern France, an offshoot of the wine trade. Leather working was an important industry in Chester, using, in part, skins imported from Ireland. Bones, seeds, and plant remains have provided evidence for medieval diet. The pits also contained insect and parasite remains, showing how unsanitary conditions could become. In the back areas, there remained extensive plots of open land given over to agriculture.

In the thirteenth century, three friaries were established. They acquired large precincts, and, by the mid-fourteenth century, more than 20 percent of the walled area was occupied by religious houses. Excavations on the site of the Dominican (Black) Friary church revealed a complex building sequence. The church grew from a simple chapel into a large aisled building with a crossing tower. Numerous burials lay beneath the floor. Unlike the extensively excavated Dominican Friary, the Franciscan and Carmelite Friaries are known from only casual discoveries. St. Werburgh's Abbey was rebuilt in a long building campaign starting in the mid-thirteenth century and continuing until the sixteenth. The abbey survives today as one of the most complete monastic complexes in Britain, with a large church, cloister ranges, and outer court.

The later Middle Ages was a period of economic decline for Chester. In particular, the harbor silted and became harder to use. Although there was still much open land within the walls, there was a significant growth of suburbs, particularly outside the Eastgate along Foregate Street. The Middle Ages closed with the dissolution of the religious houses by Henry VIII (1491–1547). The friaries

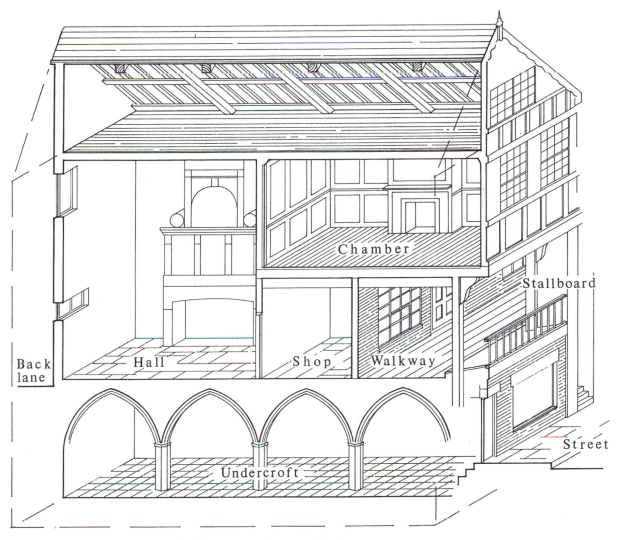

A section through a typical Chester row building. (Drawn by P.H. Alebon).

were surrendered in 1538; the abbey and nunnery, in 1540. The abbey was refounded as a cathedral, which it remains to this day.

FURTHER READINGS

Carrington, P. *The English Heritage Book of Chester.* London: Batsford, 1994.

Mason, D.J.P. *Excavations at Chester, 26–42 Lower Bridge Street: The Dark Age and Saxon Periods.* Grosvenor Museum Archaeological Report 3. Chester: Chester City Council, 1985.

Matthews, K.J. *Excavations at Chester, the Evolution of the Heart of the City: Investigations at 3–15 Eastgate Street 1990/1.* Grosvenor Museum Archaeological Report 8. Chester: Chester City Council, 1995.

Ward, S.W. *Excavations at Chester, 10–12 Watergate Street 1985: Roman Headquarters Building to Medieval Row.* Chester: Grosvenor Museum Archaeological Report 5. Chester: Chester City Council, 1988.

———. *Excavations at Chester, the Lesser Medieval Religious Houses: Sites Investigated 1964–83.* Grosvenor Museum Archaeological Report 6. Chester: Chester City Council, 1990.

———. *Excavations at Chester, Saxon Occupation within the Roman Fortress: Sites Excavated 1971–81.* Grosvenor Museum Archaeological Report 7. Chester: Chester City Council, 1990.

S.W. Ward

C

Church Archaeology

Throughout medieval Europe, the archaeology of religion is essentially the record of Christianity. There were still parts of the eastern Baltic and northern Scandinavia that were pagan until A.D. 1200, and Livonia (the Baltic region that includes nothern Latvia and southern Estonia) was not converted until 1400. Part of Mediterranean Europe was under the political control of Islamic rulers. In the Iberian Peninsula, mosques, minarets, and rabats were built; cemeteries were extended beyond their Visigothic Christian limits; and nonfigural art developed until the reconquest of Spain from the Muslims was completed in 1492. Farther east, the fall of Constantinople in 1453 brought Greece and the Balkans totally under the control of the Ottoman Turks; in 1529, the Ottomans were repulsed from the gates of Vienna, but Catholic Hungary was under threat throughout the sixteenth century. Orthodox Serbia, Wallachia, and Moldavia became tributary to the Turks, and Catholic Poland lost its coastal territory on the Black Sea. It is against this background that the archaeology of Catholic Christian Europe must be assessed. The course of the Protestant Reformation in Britain, Germany, the Netherlands, and Scandinavia closed down monastic and religious institutions, famous shrines, and wayside chapels. Indirectly, the Reformation conditioned attitudes of the state in the protection and presentation of medieval religious antiquities.

The archaeology of the church was a study with deep roots in the mid-nineteenth-century conservation movements. To restore religious buildings accurately, architects had to understand their styles, the sequence of their development, and the methods of construction. The Oxford movement in England sought to restore worship in an authentic setting. Archaeology (meaning the study of the ecclesiastical past) used both excavation and building restoration to provide information that supported this study of churches. Accurate restoration was the aim of Sir Gilbert Scott in England and Viollet-le-Duc in France, and the completion of Cologne Cathedral followed similar authentic Gothic models. The archaeological approach was applied equally to great cathedrals and minor parish churches. Yet, it was initially used to serve architectural restoration rather than to provide scholarly analysis. This attitude was predominant until 1950 with few church excavations: Waterperry (Oxon.) in 1848 and Lead (West Yorks.) in 1934 were two exceptions. Far more attention was paid to the clearance of ruined abbeys and to the architectural history of cathedrals. The main change in Britain came with the study and excavation of churches at deserted medieval settlements, such as Wharram Percy (East Yorks.) in the years 1952–1990 (Thorn 1987). However, there was a parallel concern with the excavation of churches in war-damaged cities, as in London (Grimes 1968: 182–209) and Bristol (Watts and Rahtz 1986), and with the impending demolition of "redundant" churches as approved by ecclesiastical courts (Binney and Burman 1977:157–191; Butler in Hinton 1983). There were parallel developments in Germany, the Netherlands, and Denmark, where many of the same problems and academic studies were present (Addyman and Morris 1976: 15–17; Fehring 1991). Indeed, the frequent exchange of ideas has benefited the archaeology of the Christian Church. The four most useful recent studies have been W. Rodwell (1989), Sundner in H. Andersson and J. Wienberg (1993), J. Oexle (1994), and W.J. Blair and C.A. Pyrah (1996).

Construction

Archaeology can not only best answer questions about the construction of a church, including the practical details of foundations, wall thicknesses, openings, mortars, and repairs, it can also postulate structures that no longer exist: bell-founding pits indicate bells within towers, postholes or sill beams indicate vertical timbers. In some parts of Europe, especially Scandinavia, Champagne, and the Ukraine, timber construction was normal for all or part of the church. More detailed studies concentrate directly upon the development of constructional techniques, the quarry sources for stone, and the recycling of earlier squared masonry, or indirectly upon the travels of individual master masons and the identification of stonemasons' tools. The examination may be augmented by scientific dating techniques, such as the use of radiocarbon (C-14) for charcoal in mortars or dendrochronology for roof timbers (Foot et al. 1986). These studies may be period based, emphasizing a single century or a particular architectural style; they may be area based, looking at a political or geographical entity; or they may be material based, examining stave-built churches or timber belfries (Gem 1995). One particular problem may be isolated, such as innovative technology in designing a distinctive type of roof vault or window tracery (Heyman 1968; Morris 1978–1979). In this sense, church archaeology expands from a dependence on material culture into an exploration of mentalities.

Adornment

The second area of archaeological inquiry has examined the adornment of the structure and the artifacts of religious use. The decorative treatments of plastered internal wall surfaces with figurative or symbolic painting has had a long history of antiquarian interest (the more obscure the saint's life cycle, the greater was the antiquarian challenge!), but the survival of major schemes of external painting in Romania and Transylvania has produced increased problems of preservation and conservation (Buxton 1981; Weatherhead 1993). The use of decorative floor tiles as a "hard-wearing carpet" has also led to a fuller study of design skills, kiln processes, transportation, and floor laying, as well as repair or replacement after burial disturbance. Even when paving or earth floors have been altered, previous patterns of wear indicating ritual pathways may still be recoverable (Biddle 1975:312, 318–320).

Adornment by sculpture and statuary has more often been the exclusive concern of art historians, but archaeological techniques can discern early repairs, recutting, and the grime shadow of lost sculpture. Excavation can discover statues buried in times of iconoclasm, often hidden close to their original locations. Similarly, the physical imprint of altars and fonts can survive after their stone or metal originals have been removed. Window glass may survive in its intended location and arrangement but has more usually been subject to loss and disarray during repair. Archaeological work can identify the phases of repair and the inserted pieces; it may discover early windows walled up in later alterations or stained glass panels fallen onto the ground and intentionally buried, as at Bradwell, Bucks (Croft and Mynard 1986).

Ritual Use

One major concern in church archaeology is the definition of ritual space and a better understanding of how the division between clergy and laity changed over the centuries (Graves 1989; Morris 1989:293–295). This third area of discussion highlights zones of increasing sanctity as the worshiper passed from the churchyard into the church, from the rood arch into the chancel, and from the chancel into the sanctuary or altar space. The zones may be defined by doors or screens; they may also be emphasized by the quality of the paving and by the treatment of the roof decoration. In archaeology, the physical barriers and the changes to their positions can be identified, even though the spiritual barriers can only be assumed from the documented or painted record. The paving may be carved to indicate ceremonial stations; it may show wax stains of candle positions or the cavities for the disposal of "holy dust" (Parsons in Butler and Morris 1986). Chancels

and chantries were often enclosed by wooden screens, of which the sill beams (or the slots dug into the floor to receive them) may survive; sometimes the vertical members may leave traces in the adjacent walls, either where moldings have been cut through or where wall plaster has been interrupted by their location. Other evidence of ritual may be the position of holy-water bowls (piscinae), of which the drain channels still survive, cupboards (aumbries), and squints, whose blocking walls can still be identified by removal of plaster or by heat-sensitive photography (Brooke in Butler and Morris 1986). Except in substantially complete churches and chapels, it is less easy to observe the position of windows, situated to throw light on the focal points of religious ceremonies, especially the dramatic Elevation of the Host in the Mass, and to emphasize the reader of the epistle and the gospel. The enlargements to windows and the changes in their position are often most informative of ritual enhancement (Morris 1989:296–301). For such changes, it is necessary to undertake structural analysis of the total building (Taylor 1972) or what in Italy is called *unita stratigrafica muraria*—unifying the belowground and the aboveground evidence to give a coherent understanding of a church's development and whether it shows expansion or contraction.

Burial

Another area of ritual use, and one for which churches are a predominant source, is Christian burial. This could take place within the church or in the ground outside (Oexle and Schneider 1988:469–493). Burial inside the church indicates patronage and high status (social or spiritual), and it may denote a commitment to maintain a chantry. The identity of a person commemorated by a tomb effigy, brass figure, or floor slab is frequently known and, if these are excavated, they can give information about diet, age, and cause of death. This examination applies equally to parish churches, cathedrals, hospital chapels, friary naves, and to those parts of monastic houses where burial of the laity was permitted or purchased. Study of the monuments is another active branch of church archaeology. In the churchyard (unless the period of religious life was brief), there would be extensive reuse of the ground, with the skeletons lifted and the bones deposited in burial pits or charnel houses. The undisturbed burials may show changes in grave orientation influenced by adjacent structures, pathways, or boundary banks. These burials may also be studied for evidence of life expectancy and pathological changes. During the Christian centuries, there is

C

little evidence for goods accompanying graves. Royalty were buried in fine clothing; bishops were clothed in vestments with gloves, sandals, miter, crozier, and finger ring; priests were buried with chalice and paten (plate) in silver or lead; a pilgrim might have his staff, sandals, hat badges, and scallop shells (Oexle and Schneider 1988:463; Lubin 1990).

The burial ground might have additional structures, such as lych-gates, priests' houses, church guildhalls, and devotional crosses; evidence of these has been recovered by excavation. The area might be used for secular purposes, such as markets or archery practice, and artifactual evidence often survives. In Denmark, finds of coinage are particularly numerous, both outside and inside churches.

The Wider Scene

The final aspect to stress is that the church structure may be a testimony of individual benevolence or of communal enterprise. The construction may mark a single action or a process extending over many centuries (Anglert 1995). It is not only a cumulative document of faith but a narrative chronicle of the society that supported it and worshiped within it over the centuries. Its appearance and location are part of the landscape, influenced by a variety of social and economic factors. The challenge to archaeology is to identify those factors and to read the landscape setting. In this way, the church no longer is regarded in isolation as the antiquarian collection of disarticulated phenomena but is a mirror of its society and a key to a fuller understanding of that society that created and used the church.

FURTHER READINGS

Addyman, P., and R. Morris. *The Archaeological Study of Churches.* CBA Research Report 13. London: Council for British Archaeology, 1976.

Andersson, H., and J. Wienberg. *The Study of Medieval Archaeology.* Stockholm: Almqvist and Wikseil, 1993.

Anglert, M. *Kyrkor och herravälde.* Lund: Lund University Press, 1995.

Biddle, M. Excavations at Winchester 1971: Tenth and Final Interim Report. Part II. *Antiquaries Journal* (1975) 55:295–337.

Binney, M., and P. Burman. *Change and Decay: The Future of Our Churches.* London: Studio Vista, 1977.

Blair, W.J., and C.A. Pyrah. *Church Archaeology: Research Directions for the Future.* CBA Research Report 104. London: Council for British Archaeology, 1996.

Butler, L.A.S., and R. Morris. *The Anglo-Saxon Church.* CBA Research Report 60. London: Council for British Archaeology, 1986.

Buxton, D. *The Wooden Churches of Eastern Europe: An Introductory Survey.* Cambridge: Cambridge University Press, 1981.

Croft, R.A., and D.C. Mynard. A Late Thirteenth–Century Grisaille Window Panel from Bradwell Abbey, Milton Keynes, Bucks. *Medieval Archaeology* (1986) 30:106–112.

Fehring, G. *The Archaeology of Medieval Germany.* London: Routledge, 1991.

Foot, N., C.D. Litton, and W.G. Simpson. The High Roofs of the East End of Lincoln Cathedral. *Medieval Art and Architecture at Lincoln Cathedral. British Archaeological Association Conference Transactions* (1986) 8:47–74.

Gem, R. Staged Timber Spires in Carolingian North-East France and Late Anglo-Saxon England. *Journal of the British Archaeological Association* (1995) 148:29–54.

Graves, C.P. Social Space in the English Medieval Parish Church. *Economy and Society* (1989) 18:297–322.

Grimes, W.F. *The Excavation of Roman and Medieval London.* London: Routledge, 1968.

Heyman, J. On the Rubber Vaults of the Middle Ages. *Gazette des Beaux Arts* (1968) 40:177–188.

Hinton, D.A. *Twenty-Five Years of Medieval Archaeology.* Sheffield: University of Sheffield, 1983.

Lubin, H. *The Worcester Pilgrim.* Worcester: West Mercian Archaeological Consultants, 1990.

Morris, R.K. The Development of Later Gothic Mouldings in England c. 1250–1400. *Architectural History* (1978–1979) 21:18–57; 22:1–48.

———. *Churches in the Landscape.* London: Dent, 1989.

Oexle, J. *Frühe Kirchen in Sachsen.* Stuttgart: Konrad Theiss, 1994.

Oexle, J., and J.E. Schneider. *Stadtluft, Hirsebrei und Bettelmönch: die stadt um 1300.* Stuttgart and Zurich: Konrad Theiss, 1988.

Rodwell, W. *Church Archaeology.* London: Batsford, 1989.

Taylor, H.M. Structural Criticism. *Anglo-Saxon England* (1972) 1:259–272.

Thorn, J. *Wharram: A Study in Settlement on the Yorkshire Wolds.* III: *Wharram Percy, the Church of St. Martin.* Monograph 11. London: Society for Medieval Archaeology, 1987.

Watts, L., and P. Rahtz. *Mary-le-Port, Bristol: Excavations 1962–3.* Research Monograph 7. Bristol: City Museum, 1986.

Weatherhead, F. Wooden Churches and Their Paintings in the Maramures Region of Romania. *Antiquity* (1993) 67:369–377.

L.A.S. Butler

Cloth

During the medieval period, cloth had many uses, both domestic and industrial. Clothing is the obvious one; the importance of cloth and dress was much greater then for marking status and prestige than today. Clothing often formed part of people's wages and was passed from generation to generation in their wills. The difficulties of production and of procuring luxury items meant that the possession of good-quality cloth was highly prized. In some places, such as Iceland and Frisia, cloth was accepted as a unit of currency and produced to a legally determined size. Silk scarves were used as a means of payment in Prague, Bohemia, in the Viking period (A.D. 800–1050).

In a culture in which paper and cardboard were largely unknown, cloth was used as packaging. It was needed for sacks and for baling goods. Marine transport for trade between countries was dependent on cloth to provide sails and sail power to move people and goods. In subsistence economies (as many parts of medieval Europe were then), the ability to stay alive through cold winters could have depended on warm cloth to provide cloaks and blankets. From such considerations, it can be seen that cloth played an important part in medieval society—far greater than it does in modern culture, in which there are so many more materials and sources of energy and a multitude of other ways to display conspicuous consumption.

Because of changes in technology, medieval cloth in Europe is usefully considered by dividing the period in two: A.D. 400–1200 and A.D. 1200–1500. Also, the cultural influences in the south and southeast were different from those in the north and northwest. In the earlier period, the structures of the Roman Empire were still important in the south. There were cross-cultural links among the European Mediterranean regions, the Near East, and the North African Mediterranean areas. For example, the rise of the Eastern Roman Empire in Byzantium led to the development of a sophisticated textile industry unparalleled in other areas of Europe. There the silk industry flourished from the sixth century onward, so that valuable silks were dispersed in trade and as diplomatic gifts into barbarian Europe. In Italy, however, it was not until the thirteenth century that silk manufacturing

was established. In Spain, the Arab diffusion from the Near East influenced material culture. After the Arab conquest in the eighth century, Islamic Spain became a center for the specialized production of sophisticated silk-and-wool cloth *(tiraz),* very different from cloth produced elsewhere in Europe.

Textile remains are generally found either in anaerobic conditions in damp soil deposits, as mineralized remains on metal objects very often in graves, in permafrost conditions, or in dry climates with unchanging temperatures. In medieval Europe, remains are almost all of wool, linen, and silk. Excavations in the old quarters of towns and cities have yielded textiles preserved in such places as house floors, refuse and cesspits, and abandoned wells. Wool, being a protein fiber, survives well in northern European anaerobic conditions where flax (the vegetable fiber from which linen is produced) rarely does. However, finds of flax plants, written references to flax and linen, and some carbonized remains of textiles show that linen was also in common use. From Switzerland southward, because of different climatic conditions, more linen and fewer wool remains are found. In both the north and the south, silk is found more rarely, being a valuable import from lands to the east as far away as China. A large number of Anglo-Saxon grave finds of mineralized textiles on items such as brooches, rings, and weapons have been analyzed. The princely ship burial of Sutton Hoo (England) provides some interesting examples. There are many finds from Germany, the Low Countries, and Scandinavia.

In the period A.D. 400–1200, cloth was largely produced in the home. People lived in villages and small settlements, and the raw materials for cloth were mostly produced locally and made up domestically. There were probably some specialist producers making luxury cloth for high-born people, and this was also traded from place to place.

From the late twelfth century onward, the cloth-making industry developed swiftly in quality and variety of textiles produced and in complexity of organization. New technology was introduced. Specialization in many areas developed so that, for example, England and then Spain became major sources of raw materials for the wool trade, while the Low Countries concentrated on the weaving industry. By the fifteenth century, the wool-weaving industry in England had become highly developed, and English broadcloth became a prestige export item. Flax, however, was grown in large quantities in the Low Countries. The silk-manufacturing industry, set up in Italy in

C

the thirteenth century, soon produced beautiful complex velvets and brocades. Lucca (Italy) was particularly noted for its expertise. Italian merchants spread throughout Europe to sell the eagerly sought-after products of the silk industry.

The development of towns and the organization of cloth making by the new trade guilds marked a radical change from precapitalist toward capitalist economies. The growth in population of the thirteenth century in the new towns provided a market for the extra production. New technology began to lead cloth makers toward capitalist structures, in which fashion became important, and merchants and merchandizing dominated the market.

FURTHER READINGS

Bender Jorgensen, L. *North European Textiles until A.D. 1000.* Copenhagen: Aarhus University Press, 1991.

Crowfoot, E. Textiles. In *The Sutton Hoo Ship Burial.* Vol. 3. Ed. R. Bruce-Mitford. London: British Museum, 1976, pp. 409–479.

———. Textiles. In *Object and Economy in Medieval Winchester.* Ed. Martin Biddle. Winchester Studies 7(2). Oxford: Clarendon, 1990, pp. 467–494.

Crowfoot, E., F. Pritchard, and K. Staniland. *Textiles and Clothing c. 1150–1450.* Medieval Finds from Excavations in London 4. London: HMSO, 1992.

Harte, N., and K. Ponting, eds. *Cloth and Clothing in Medieval Europe.* London: Heinmann, 1983.

Walton, P. *Textiles, Cordage, and Raw Fibre from 16–22 Coppergate.* The Archaeology of York 17(5). London: Council for British Archaeology, 1989.

Since 1981, a triennial Northern European Symposium for Archaeological Textiles (NESAT) has been held, with the proceedings published in book form. A part of each is devoted to recent research in medieval textiles (English and German texts).

Bender Jorgensen, L., and K. Tidow, eds. *Textilsymposium Neumunster.* Proceedings of the First NESAT, Neumunster, 1981. Neumunster: Textilmuseum Neumunster, 1982.

Bender Jorgensen, L., B. Magnus, and E. Munksgaard, eds. *Archaeological Textiles.* Proceedings of the Second NESAT, Bergen, 1984. Copenhagen: Arkeologisk Institut, Copenhagen University, 1988.

Bender Jorgensen, L., and E. Munksgaard, eds. *Archaeological Textiles in Northern Europe.* Proceedings of the Fourth NESAT, Copenhagen, 1990. Tidens Tamd 5. Copenhagen: Konservatorskolem Det Kongelige Kunstakademi, 1992.

Walton, P., and J.-P. Wild, eds. *Textiles in Northern Archaeology.* Proceedings of the Third NESAT, York, 1987. London: Archetype, 1990.

The journal *Textile History* is published semiannually by Pasold Research Fund, London School of Economics, Houghton Street, London WC2A 2AE, England. Although not mainly directed to the medieval period, valuable articles in this field occur regularly. For example, Vol. 20(2), Autumn 1989, *Ancient and Medieval Textile Studies,* was largely devoted to medieval Europe. An index to the series is available. The *Archaeological Textiles Newsletter* first appeared in 1985 and is published semiannually. The publication (almost entirely in English) presents current finds and reports of work in progress, bibliographies, and related matters. The contact address is G.M. Vogelsang-Eastwood, Textile Research Centre, National Museum of Ethnologie, Postbox 212, 2300 AE Leiden, Netherlands.

Elizabeth Wincott Heckett

SEE ALSO
Cloth Making; Sutton Hoo

Cloth Making
Spinning and Preparation of Yarn
The main fibers produced in Europe that were used for making yarn for cloth were wool and flax (from which linen comes). Silk was known but was a precious import from the Middle and Far East, coming originally from China. Although cotton was used throughout the Middle Ages in India, few traces of it seem to have come to Europe. A very little has been found from the later Medieval period in Poland, probably imported along an eastern trade route.

In the period A.D. 400–c. 1200, yarn was spun by hand with a spindle and whorl and distaff. By the thirteenth century, the spinning wheel came into use, although hand spinning also continued. At first, fibers were prepared for spinning by combing; later, hand carders were used. Combing produces smooth yarn (after the thirteenth century known as *worsted*) with the fibers lying parallel. The cloth woven with this yarn has a smooth, shiny finish that shows off clearly both pattern and weave. Carding makes a woollier yarn, since the fibers are mixed together irregularly and at angles. This yarn is better adapted to cloth that will undergo further finishing (*fulling*) processes that produce a soft, woolly surface. In the later part of the period, both combed and carded wool yarn was used.

Linen yarn was produced by a complex process of breaking down the stems of flax plants and then cleaning and softening the fibers to prepare them for spinning.

Yarn may be spun either in a lefthand or a righthand direction (known as *Z-* and *S-spinning*). Choice of spin may change for either cultural or technical reasons.

Weaves

Cloth was made in many different weaves and qualities using a variety of techniques. Plain *(tabby)* and twill weaves were known. In tabby weave, one thread system (the *weft*) is woven over one and under one thread of the other system (the *warp*). In a *twill* weave, the weft thread is woven over one or more and under two or more warp threads. In following or succeeding rows of the weft, the sequence is shifted by one place, making a cloth with a pronounced diagonal rib. Some Viking period (A.D. 800–1050) textiles favored the combed yarn that made up the well-defined shiny weave already described. Viking period cloth makers often chose Z-spun yarn for warp and weft, since this further added to the definition of weave and pattern. Imported silk was woven in both plain and complex weaves, including satin and damask, in which several weft threads were allowed to float over the warp threads so that the cloth had a shining, lustrous appearance. Both spinning and weaving involved making reasoned choices to produce exactly the effect desired.

Looms

The upright warp-weighted loom and the upright two-beam loom seem to have been the preferred means of production before the twelfth–thirteenth centuries. At this time, cloth was probably produced mainly in the home by women. Perhaps there were also specialized units of production attached to wealthy secular households or church institutions.

Then ways of making cloth began to change. By the end of the twelfth century, new technology, probably from the East, influenced the choice of weaves. Spinning wheels, fulling mills, and the horizontal loom using treadles were introduced. Far longer bolts of cloth could be produced more quickly. Much more yarn was needed to keep up with these new looms; spinning wheels could produce perhaps nine times as much as the hand spindle and distaff. The power to turn the wheels of the fulling mills came from rivers and streams; this gave greater productivity than hand or foot cloth processing in troughs of water. Fulling (cloth processing) after weaving gave a woollier appearance to the cloth, and so pattern became less

important, except for some luxury cloth. English broadcloth was an example of a high-quality cloth produced by the new methods; it was fulled, napped, and shorn, sometimes four times over, to produce a soft, smooth surface.

Production was centered in the newly expanding towns in the hands of men organized into trade guilds. Spinning remained a female occupation. Town sites that have yielded important groups of finds include Hedeby, Denmark (Viking period); Lübeck, Germany (twelfth–fifteenth centuries); Amsterdam, the Netherlands (eleventh–sixteenth centuries); Lund, Sweden (tenth–sixteenth centuries); York, England (tenth–fifteenth centuries); Winchester, England (tenth–thirteenth centuries); Dublin, Ireland (tenth–thirteenth centuries); and Novgorod, Russia (tenth–fifteenth centuries).

Besides the cloth woven on large looms, many items were woven on narrow looms, including tablet (or *card weaving*) looms. The level of skill and artistic achievement in tablet weaving is impressive. Fine examples are the girdles and bands found in clerics' tombs and the braids and ribbons in rich secular graves. Examples include the tomb of St. Cuthbert, Durham Cathedral, England (tenth century) and the graves at Birka, Sweden (Viking period).

Dyeing

Vegetable dyes from plants and extracts from insects and shellfish were used to color cloth. The plants of madder *(Rubia tinctorum)* dyed red, weld *(Reseda luteola)* yellow, woad *(Isatis tinctoria)* blue, and a variety of nuts, oak galls, and barks gave browns and blacks. Expensive and valued dyes of scarlet came from the eggs of the beetle living on the holm oak that grows in the Mediterranean region. This was known as *kermes* and was collected by women scraping down the oak bark with their fingernails to gather the eggs. When dried, the eggs, known as grain or *grana,* provided a deep, glowing red. Lichen dyes collected from rocks *(Ochrolechia tartarea, Rocella tinctoria)* gave a purple color; these lichens were widely available. In the Mediterranean, the sea whelk *(Murex brandea)* yielded the coveted and expensive imperial purple. Blue and red seem to have become popular colors for wool cloth. Silk has been found dyed with lichen purples and *kermes,* while other silk seems to have been left the natural yellow of the yarn. Bright reds and blues from expensive dyes were a mark of high status. The use of mordants (chemicals that fix dyes by combining with them to form insoluble compounds), such as alum, was widespread. Dyeing was a highly skilled craft, with practitioners using combinations of dyestuffs to produce richly colored effects.

C

FURTHER READINGS

Ponting, K. *A Dictionary of Dyes and Dyeing.* London: Bell and Hyman, 1981.

An annual symposium on *Dyes in History and Archaeology* is held in England, and the proceedings have been published annually since 1982. Information and back issues are available from P. Walton Rogers, ed., *Dyes in History and Archaeology*, Textile Research Associates, 12 Bootham Terrace, York YO3 7DH, England.

Elizabeth Wincott Heckett

SEE ALSO

Cloth; Hedeby; Lübeck; Novgorod

Coinage

Medieval coins differ from most other artifacts in their origin, their distribution, and their recovery. They also differ from the coinages of other eras chiefly in the difficulty of assigning precise dates to many specimens and in their sparseness in excavation at many sites.

Coins are the products of governmental manufacture and distribution, unlike most other artifacts, which were made domestically or by private artisans. In the Middle Ages, coinage, like political power, was often on a very local level; various counts, dukes, communes, monasteries, and bishoprics with coinage rights could mint very near to each other. Their coins might intermix competitively or be limited to the territory of the issuer. In general, the higher the denomination a coin was, the farther it would travel, with coins that were mainly of copper staying close to the mint, those of fine silver traveling throughout a region, and those of gold often going great distances.

Coin Losses and Finds

Coins usually enter the archaeological context as the result of one of three distinct processes: accompaniment to a burial, casual loss, and unretrieved concealment. Only counterfeit coins are subject to the intentional disposal typical of broken pottery and food remains. Especially in the early Middle Ages, coins are a frequent attribute of furnished burials; they continued to be put in graves long after Christian practices had eliminated other kinds of burial goods, such as weapons and pottery.

Unintentionally lost coins are usually of the lowest circulating denominations; coins of greater worth would have been searched for extensively and also tend to be of the bright metals that would have caught the eye of a subsequent passerby. Medieval excavation finds of lost coins tend to be mostly from periods when a copper-based coinage was in common circulation and to consist primarily of such coins.

Coins intentionally buried in the Middle Ages provide the richest source of medieval numismatic finds. In the period before deposit banking, which developed in Italy in the thirteenth century, people usually kept much of their wealth in their homes. If the home was to be left unguarded, the valuables would often be concealed in the walls or the floor of the building, in the yard, or in a field. Coins were usually buried in a container, such as a ceramic pot or a leather purse. The location of the deposit would be known only to the owner and possibly a few other trusted individuals. If for some reason (including, but not limited to, war and plague) none of these individuals retrieved the concealed coins, these became a hoard, to be discovered later either in archaeological excavation or (more often) as a result of agricultural or construction digging. Such hoards tend to represent the highest denominations in circulation, as these would usually have been the pieces sought for saving.

Coins for Dating

Coins are often of most interest to the archaeologist in that they offer the best evidence for dating a level or feature. The chronology and circulation of any coinage must be understood before such inferences can be valid, and this is especially true for medieval coins. Few medieval sites produce the thousands of coins that are typical of Roman excavations, so the number of specimens associated with any one feature can become uncomfortably small.

There are many problems associated with the dating of coins found on medieval sites. Many medieval coins were immobilized—that is, a given issue was continued for decades and even centuries with only insignificant changes, if any at all. An example of an immobilized issue are the twelfth-century coins from the major mint of Melle in France, which are virtually indistinguishable from those of the ninth century. Many coinages were subject to imitation and counterfeiting, which extended their apparent minting period. For example, long after the death of the Venetian doge Andrea Dandolo in 1354, ducats with his name were produced in Greece and Turkey. Coins sometimes circulated for many years before being lost; medieval hoards often contain a few coins minted much earlier than the most recent ones, and coins found on sites may have been lost decades after their issue.

C

The Migration Period: The Age of Gold

The coinage of medieval Europe can be conveniently divided into three periods on the basis of the metals and denominations in common circulation. The archaeological interpretation of numismatic finds of these eras is distinct, as is the precision with which invididual specimens can be dated.

The coinage of Europe in the fifth–seventh centuries consisted almost entirely of gold issues, modeled after late Roman denominations, chiefly the *solidus* (c. 4.54 grams) and its third, the *tremissis.* At first, these issues carried the name of a current or recent Roman or Byzantine emperor; such pseudoimperial issues have been assigned to various Germanic rulers on the basis of find spots, occasional monograms, and similarities to subsequent, signed issues. Series of pseudoimperial solidi and tremisses have been assigned to the Ostrogoths and the Lombards in Italy, the Visigoths in Gaul and Iberia, the Suevi in Iberia, the Burgundians and the Merovingians in Gaul, and the Alamanni in Germany (Fig. 1).

In the late sixth century, European rulers began to put their own names on their coins, limited almost entirely to the gold tremissis, with only exceptional larger solidi or even rarer silver issues. Royal Visigothic coins were issued from as many as three dozen mints throughout Iberia in the seventh century (Fig. 2). Merovingian coins identify hundreds of mints in France, though most of the seventh-century tremisses have a minter's name rather than that of a king, rendering their chronology problematic. Frisian issues resemble those of the Merovingian Kingdoms in appearance, and England had an apparently brief period of minting of gold *thrymsas* (tremisses), also on the Frankish model, in the seventh century. Even in the seventh century, Lombard coins rarely have legible royal names, making their attribution to specific reigns and mints difficult. The Lombard Duchy of Benevento in southern Italy was the last minter of gold coinage in the early Middle Ages, with regular issues of solidi and tremisses well into the ninth century.

FIG. 1. Pseudoimperial gold tremissis attributed to the Visigoths, sixth century.

FIG. 2. Visigothic royal gold tremissis.

Other than these gold issues, there was apparently a residual circulation of earlier coins, chiefly the bronze issues of the fourth century, the last Roman coins to circulate widely in Europe. The lack of more recent coins on habitation sites of this period is not necessarily a sign of abandonment or decline, as new issues were all of gold and, hence, too valuable to occur commonly as stray losses.

The Central Middle Ages: The Period of the Silver Penny

By the beginning of the eighth century, most of Europe had stopped minting gold coins and begun the issue of silver. At first, these were mainly small, thick pieces with simple, abstracted designs. Those of the Merovingian Kingdom tend mainly to have simple letters and monograms, while the coinage produced on both sides of the English Channel, known to numismatists as *sceattas,* has a variety of animal and geometric forms (Fig. 3).

At the end of the eighth century, Charlemagne regularized the coinage throughout the Frankish Kingdom, following a reform of his father, Pepin, several decades earlier. From then on, there was to be a single denomination, the silver penny (Latin: *denarius,* French: *denier*) of simple geometric imagery (with occasional portraits) and the name of the king (later emperor) and that of the mint. Half-pennies (called *oboles* and *mailles*) were also occasionally issued. The simple, uniform penny coinage of Charlemagne was followed in the areas under Carolingian influence in Italy (Benevento and Venice) and in England, beginning with the reforms of Offa of Mercia, which quickly followed those of Pepin and Charlemagne (Fig. 4).

For the next four centuries, the silver penny (and its occasional half) would be virtually the only coin produced

FIG. 3. Anglo-Saxon silver sceatta, eighth century.

C

FIG. 4. Silver penny of Charlemagne, c. A.D. 800.

FIG. 5. English silver penny of Æthelred.

in Latin Europe. The *libra* (pound) and the *solidus* (shilling) that appear in documents were simply counting terms for 240 and 12 pennies, respectively, and were not actual coins.

As the Carolingian hegemony broke down, so did the uniformity of the penny issues. In the French regions, various dynasties of dukes and counts took over the coinage of the mints in their realms, often continuing or abstracting the Carolingian imagery. The coinage of seigneurial France from the tenth through the twelfth centuries is usually immobilized, and most specimens can only be dated within a few decades. By the end of the twelfth century, many of these silver pennies had become so debased with copper in their alloys (making them *billon*) that they lost much of their intrinsic value and, hence, appear more commonly in site finds than those of earlier periods.

In Germany, mints proliferated to an even greater extent, with ecclesiastical institutions as well as lay magnates producing issues of *denars* on their own standards and of distinctive appearance. Less often immobilized than their French counterparts, German pennies are frequently difficult to attribute because they often lack a legible issuer's name; moreover, the literature on the various issues is extremely widespread. In Italy, the minting became mainly communal, with each city-state eventually issuing its own *denaro*. These usually bore only the name of the city and either that of the patron saint or the emperor who had originally granted the minting privilege, so these coins are usually very difficult to date precisely.

English pennies are much more unified in issue than those of the Continent and, moreover, circulated according to a system of periodic recoinages, apparently accompanied by the demonetization of old issues, so not only the production date but also the circulation period of a given coin found in England can often be known to within a few years (Fig. 5). This is not the case for the plentiful Scandinavian finds of English coins, where frequent imitation and the lack of demonetization make the date of deposition of any single coin much less certain.

In the North Sea area, the importation of coins in this period is a major archaeological phenomenon, comprising silver Islamic and Byzantine issues in the ninth and tenth centuries, shifting to German and English sources in the tenth and eleventh. By the twelfth century, the silver penny had become the base of indigenous royal coinages in regions beyond the scope of earlier minting, in Scandinavia, Bohemia, Hungary, Poland, and Russia.

In the Mediterranean world, the European tradition of silver pennies was often combined with issues based on Byzantine and Islamic coinages. In Barcelona and Castile, imitation Arabic gold dinars were issued along with pennies. In the eleventh century, Amalfi and Salerno issued imitations of Islamic gold quarter dinars (*tari*), as well as bronze coins modeled after those of Byzantium; both issues were continued by the Normans and extended to their possessions in Sicily. In the Crusader states of the Levant, base silver pennies were issued, along with imitations of fine silver and gold Islamic denominations.

The Later Middle Ages: The Multiplicity of Denominations

By the thirteenth century, most of Europe was experiencing a need for new denominations beyond the simple silver penny, which had been heavily debased by most minters. The expansion of issues went in both directions, with more valuable issues of heavy, fine silver or of gold meeting the needs of long-term commerce and finance, and small coins with a preponderance of copper used in the increasingly monetized local market economy.

The higher denominations were often of a well-maintained recognized standard, so they could circulate widely geographically and for a long period of time. The exceptions were mainly England and France, where the efforts to maintain a constant ratio between gold and silver coinages led to a frequent change in the standards of both. In France, moreover, the later Middle Ages witnessed a series of radical debasements and devaluations of all denominations, though not always a demonetization of

FIG. 6. Gold florin of Florence.

FIG. 8. Billon piccolo of Florence. All coins are in the collection of the American Numismatic Society, New York, and reproduced with their permission.

old issues. The large, well-struck higher denominations of this period are usually relatively easy to date in terms of issue, but their period of active use is much harder to ascertain (Fig. 6). The development of banking and letters of exchange contributed to a dearth of hoard finds from this period in some regions, most notably in northern Italy.

The lower denominations were, in most places, affected by frequent debasements and devaluations, leading to a multiplicity of issues that, when fully studied and well published, can often result in fairly precise dates for the minting of pieces found in archaeological contexts (Fig. 7). The increasing baseness of the lowest denominations also adds to their likely presence as stray losses on a site. However, the lowest-denomination coins often have little writing on them and are poorly struck, and their base metal is most subject to corrosion in the soil, so individual specimens may be difficult to attribute (Fig. 8). Copper-based coins are not likely to be subject to the clipping and culling for melting and export that afflicts coins of silver or gold, and many of them appear to have circulated for long periods. The generally low profitability of such issues led minters to issue them only sporadically, adding to the likelihood of long periods of circulation before loss.

In general, the total amount of coinage in most of Europe increased steadily throughout the Middle Ages, with the possible exception of the period c. 1400, when there appears to have been a bullion famine. The general growth in the coin pool, added to the increased production of "losable" low-denomination coins as the Middle Ages wore on, leads to a heavy preponderance of late coins on most medieval sites, even those whose population and economic activity were constant or even declining in the later Middle Ages.

FURTHER READINGS

Casey, John, and Richard Reece, eds. *Coins and the Archaeologist.* 2nd ed. London: Seaby, 1988.

Clain-Stefanelli, Elvira. *Numismatic Bibliography.* Munich: Battenberg, 1985.

Grierson, Philip. *Bibliographie numismatique.* 2nd ed. Brussels: Cercle d'Etudes Numismatiques, 1979.

———. *The Coins of Medieval Europe.* London: Seaby, 1991. This volume provides the best general history of medieval coinage.

———. Numismatics. In *Medieval Studies: An Introduction.* 2nd ed. Ed. James M. Powell. Syracuse: Syracuse University Press, 1993, pp. 114–161.

Grierson, Philip, and Mark Blackburn. *Medieval European Coinage.* Vol. 1: *The Early Middle Ages (Fifth–Tenth Centuries).* Cambridge: Cambridge University Press, 1986. This is the first volume in a proposed thirteen-volume series on medieval coinage.

Stahl, Alan M. Numismatics and Medieval Archaeology. In *Medieval Archaeology.* Ed. Charles R. Redman. Medieval and Rennaissance Texts and Studies. Binghamton: 1989, pp. 119–126.

Alan M. Stahl

Collapse of the Roman Empire

See Roman Empire, Collapse of.

Cooperage

Cooperage, or barrel making, is the art of making stave-built vessels ranging from small cups to large hogsheads or vats. In medieval Europe, coopers were important craftsmen, since many goods, such as beer and salted meats, in addition to wine, were transported in casks. Medieval stave-built vessels are found on waterlogged archaeological

FIG. 7. Silver grosso of Florence.

C

sites in a number of contexts; they were most commonly reused as well linings. Such vessels were also used as vats sunk into the ground, and they were sometimes dismantled so that the timber could be reused. By the end of the medieval period, some specialization in cooperage work had developed. Some coopers concentrated on making the most demanding barrel-shaped, water-tight casks, while others made open-topped, tub-shaped vessels, such as milking pails.

The making of stave-built vessels was a conservative craft, and many medieval tools and techniques survived up to modern times. For example, in England and in France, medieval styles of broad axe were still used by coopers until recently, although these tools had long been abandoned by craftsmen practicing other trades. Most medieval stave-built vessels were made of oak, some of pine, and others of silver fir or beech. All the timber was split out of straight-grained trees and shaped mainly with axes, although shaving tools and adzes were also used. The edges of the staves were planed for a water-tight fit. Generally only high-status drinking vessels and some buckets had metal hoops. The other containers had hoops of small split ash, hazel, willow, and other woods. The making of the hoops was a specialized craft using specially managed coppice woodland (trees are cut near the base to produce new shoots). Most of the stave timber came from large, old trees growing in seminatural high forest. For example, oak-stave timber was traded from the remnant Polish wildwoods to parts of western Europe by the Hanseatic merchants.

FURTHER READINGS

Earwood, C. *Domestic Wooden Artefacts in Britain and Ireland from Neolithic to Viking Times.* Exeter: Exeter University Press, 1993.

Goodburn, D. Some Unfamiliar Aspects of Early Woodworking Revealed by Recent Rescue Excavations in London. In *Proceedings of the International Council of Museums, Wet Organic Archaeological Materials Group Conference.* Ed. P. Hoffman. Bremerhaven: International Council of Museums, 1991, pp. 143–155.

D.M. Goodburn

SEE ALSO
Forests

Corvey

Corvey was founded in A.D. 822 as the first Benedictine monastery in Saxony by Adalhard, abbot of Corbie in northeastern France, and his brother Wala. The unusual transfer of the name of the Frankish motherhouse, (new) Corbeia, reflects their intention to establish an exemplary center of monastic life and Frankish imperial culture in northern Germany.

Corvey soon became the most important monastery in northern Germany. It was the starting point for the mission of Ansgar, bishop of Hamburg, to Scandinavia to convert the Swedes, and it seems also to have played an important role in the early Church history of Bohemia during the Ottonian Era. In the imperial confirmation record of 823, the place of the foundation is said to belong to the *villa regia hucxori* (royal villa of Höxter).

There has been much dispute about the location of the Carolingian settlement and its probable elements, such as a seigneurial and/or imperial manor. Today there is plenty of archaeological evidence indicating that parts of the old town center of Höxter were occupied c. 800, if not earlier in the sixth–seventh centuries, and that in the course of the Carolingian period a complex settlement of extraordinary size was established.

This settlement was oriented on three branches of the Westphalian Hellweg (the most important central European east-west route at that time), a north-south route (Frankfort-Bremen), and the River Weser. The early medieval settlement was situated on dry ground and possessed a natural water resource provided by two small rivers and the Weser with a ford. The oldest parish church of the *pagus Auga* (Auga region), St. Kilian, and the court of justice were situated nearby. Part of the market was probably also located nearby, while the main market may have been farther northwest at the junction of all three branches of the Hellweg at Bremer Straße.

The early medieval center of the preurban settlement seems to have had a rather irregular street plan. It must be stressed that, as a result of later disturbance, it has not been possible to uncover more than small parts of what are believed to be building lines and street surfaces or water flows along roads. Still, the widespread pattern of *Grubenhäuser* (sunken-featured buildings) and pottery shows that the density of settlement was rather high from the ninth century onward. The settlement was composed of a central area of c. 400 × 300 m (12 ha), plus rows of plots of up to 1,500 m oriented east-west on the Rodewiek and the Grube Rivers. The Grube was a channel 5 km long, accompanied by a road built in the late

Carolingian period to provide the monastery with fresh water and a new, straighter access to the Hellweg.

The date and the character of the Church of St. Peter in the west are not precisely known. The earliest excavated structure may date to c. 1000, but it may also be ninth century. The Church of St. Nicholas in the north may be younger, but it may have been previously dedicated to St. Denis. It is the parish church of an early settlement agglomeration, so it may also be ninth or tenth century in date.

The settlement structure in the monastery of Corvey itself and its immediate surroundings were not as well known until recently. The core was the abbey precinct. Until the late twentieth century, only the main church has been the subject of thorough research. The first church seems to have been modest in dimensions but well outfitted and may reflect the ideals of the monastic reform movement at that time. In the mid-ninth century, the church was much elongated to the east. The famous surviving Westwerk (873–885) and a long atrium in the classical tradition were added soon thereafter, so that the whole complex was much more than 100 m long.

In addition to the plan of St. Gall (826–829), the statutes of Adalhard, the abbot of Corbie, for Corbie (822), which sought to reorganize the framework of monastic life, are a most important source of knowledge of early medieval monasteries. Given the favorable historical and topographical situation, it seems likely that Corvey was laid out to the highest standards of the time. The cloisters were situated north of the abbey church. The south branch of the cloisters was excavated recently. Additionally, some elements of a highly sophisticated heating system attached to the east wing were detected during excavation. In the course of rescue work and prospection, the first insights were provided into the inner function and building structure of the precinct. A number of stone buildings were situated west of the cloisters.

A unique sequence of large hearths was recorded immediately north of the cloisters. These seem to have formed a part of the bakery and brewery of the ninth–eleventh centuries. Other massive, timber-framed buildings of uncertain date and function lay farther to the north up to the outer wall. The area to the southwest of the abbey church seems to have been much less densely and elaborately built up. There seems to have been more free space, and the area was primarily devoted to functions such as agricultural buildings and cattle byres. On the other hand, the area immediately to the south and east of the atrium and the church was reserved for a huge cemetery. The area

adjoining the abbey church was the monks' burial place; to the west were the burials of the laymen, along with the chapel of St. Martin. The cemetery probably included more chapels and a specific architectural layout. It played a leading role in the life of the monastic community, whose prominent members were sometimes buried there near the saint's relics. The location of a number of main buildings can as yet be only roughly identified using later written sources. Examples include the St. Gertrudis Hospital south of the main church, the palace of the emperor somewhere nearby, and the abbot's palace at the west end of the atrium. The possible locations of some monastic functions, including the monks' hospital and the novitiate, can be identified only through analogies to other monasteries.

Workshops make up another important part of monastic life, although these are rarely located and investigated. They may have included temporary workshops for construction purposes, such as a lime kiln or the remains of bell casting in the atrium. Additional glass and metal workshops have been found northwest and, particularly, northeast of the cloisters. As these have not yet been systematically excavated, it is not certain whether they represent longer-lasting activities or not. A bit more can be said about a larger industrial area in the northeast corner of the precinct. A small part of this area could be investigated through excavation. At this locality during the ninth century, stone was prepared by masons; lime was burnt and mixed; and glass, iron, and nonferrous metals were smelted and worked. This appears to be a complex workshop area at the periphery of the big monastic building site during the Carolingian Era. It was situated on a landing place for ships at the shore of the Weser, and it was abandoned at the end of the first building phase when the adjoining riverbank was filled up. Material for botanical research was recovered from the bottom of the river bed. This botanical research offers detailed insights in the early medieval vegetation. The most surprising find was a peach pit that shows that the inscription on the plan of St. Gall and the recommendation in Charlemagne's *capitulare de villis* were not mere theory.

The abbey precinct, which included c. 7 ha, seems to have been one of the largest and most impressive architectural ensembles in north Germany during the early Middle Ages.

In the course of the foundation of the monastery, some lay settlements also developed immediately outside the precinct. They were located near the river ford and along

C

the Hellweg to the south of it. Another nucleus of occupation can be identified 400 m west of the abbey. Its dimensions are not yet clear. There may be further scattered settlements to the east and south, where the nunnery or collegiate Church of St. Paul, dedicated in 863, was situated. Nothing can be said about early medieval occupation north of the precinct, as there have been insufficient opportunities for exploration. The development was no doubt favored by the prosperity of the abbey in the Carolingian period and by the privileges granted to the abbey by Charlemagne's son, Louis the Pious (778–840). As is stated in a record of 833, they include the right to mint coins and to create a trading place and collect tolls there. Nevertheless, the site of the market church has not yet yielded evidence of a ninth- or tenth-century foundation. The choir of a large Romanesque basilica (c. 40–60 m long) and small parts of the main burgess church of the town in the twelfth and thirteenth centuries were excavated.

The early medieval occupation around the abbey is known only through test excavations, mostly on fields in agrarian use. Because of erosion, accumulation, and destruction by later building, our present knowledge is insufficient. Nevertheless, it seems that much of the occupation was situated farther to the west in the later town of Höxter or that it was oriented in and around the pre-Carolingian village with its ford across the Weser. The foundation of Corvey brought a new dimension into the settlement pattern. It was the basis for an unusually quick and important development, but it did not radically dislocate or change the center of commercial life.

In this short survey, the early structures have been emphasized. It must not be forgotten, however, that the peak of the settlement history was in the twelfth and thirteenth centuries, as is clearly reflected by the bulk of the archaeological finds. At c. A.D. 1100, a large area west of the abbey was settled, as shown by a cobbled north-south road and widespread finds, some of which reflect metal-working and crafts based on bone preparation. At c. 1150–1200, the economic center of the town shifted to the south of the abbey. There an elaborately built new branch of the Hellweg, the new large market church, and a bridge over the River Weser were laid out as the most important elements of a new urban type that then spread rapidly in central Europe. For the first time, the whole town (c. 55 ha) was protected by a fortification consisting of a wall and a ditch. Together with the twin town of Höxter, Corvey covered nearly 100 ha. Corvey provides a splendid opportunity for detailed studies of the early

development of true towns in Germany, as large parts are preserved without later disturbances. Since there have been so few systematic excavations, it can only be said that there must have been more cobbled streets and presumably larger plots than those that are known from later medieval towns. The rows of houses seem not to have formed complete building fronts. Instead, a building and functional structure not completely unlike that of a rural site should be envisioned. On the other hand, it is obvious that the main street had a lot of small Romanesque stone buildings, the most representative of which would have looked like a tower. The town of Corvey was destroyed in 1265 and soon thereafter lost its former importance. After 1348, it was only a village, and the last buildings were demolished shortly after 1500. The abandonment reflects the rapid decline of the abbey in the later Middle Ages; the inhabitants mostly went to Höxter.

The above summary provides a very simplified picture of some main results of interdisciplinary archaeological and historical work in and about Corvey and Höxter. During years of intensive research and excavations starting in the 1960s, there has been a continuous interrelationship between the interpretation of finds, structures, and written sources. In addition, much valuable information has been gained through contacts with colleagues in the sciences.

FURTHER READINGS

Stephan, H.-G. *Studien zur Siedlungsentwicklung und Struktur von Stadtwüstung und Kloster Corvey (ca. 800–1680).* Bonn: Denkmalpflege und Forschung in Westfalen-Lippe, 1995.

Hans-Georg Stephan

Crannógs

Crannógs are a type of rural settlement known from early Christian Ireland (A.D. 500–1200). They are best described as simply raths or cashels surrounded by water. Crannógs are artificial islands built in small lakes or marshy areas. They were usually constructed of layers of timber, peat, and brush piled on top of each other and surrounded by a sturdy wooden fence, termed a *palisade.* Crannógs are wonderfully rich sites for archaeologists, as they are frequently found in peat bogs or other waterlogged areas, and, consequently, organic remains such as leather, wood, and cloth are often preserved. The excellent preservation of many crannóg sites provides another advantage for archaeologists. When wood is well preserved, dendrochronological dates can be obtained from the wood samples. Dendrochronology consists of studying the growth rings found in tree trunks and comparing them to a sample of known age. This dating method can be much more accurate than the radiocarbon (C-14) dating method that is usually used for early Christian sites in Ireland.

Crannógs probably held no more than a few wooden buildings, and, like raths and cashels, crannógs were probably single-family homes. The crannóg inhabitants probably owned the land on the shore near their home, which they used for farming and grazing their livestock. The evidence from crannóg excavations includes many rich and luxurious objects, particularly jewelry and other metal, especially bronze, objects. Crannógs are less numerous in Ireland than raths and cashels and required considerably more effort to build than these other settlement types. In addition, early Irish historical sources, the annals, suggest that Lagore crannóg, in County Meath, was the seat of local kings in the period A.D. 785–969 (Hencken 1950). All of this evidence seems to indicate that crannógs were the homes of the wealthy in early Christian Ireland, who were, in many cases, the rulers over the rath and cashel dwellers.

FURTHER READINGS

Edwards, Nancy. *The Archaeology of Early Medieval Ireland.* Philadelphia: University of Pennsylvania Press, 1990.

Flanagan, Laurence. *A Dictionary of Irish Archaeology.* Dublin: Gill and Macmillan, 1992.

Hamlin, Ann, and C.J. Lynn, eds. *Pieces of the Past: Archaeological Excavations by the Department of the Environment for Northern Ireland.* Belfast: HMSO, 1988.

Hencken, Hugh O'Neill. Lagore Crannóg: An Irish Royal Residence of the Seventh to Tenth Centuries A.D. *Proceeding of the Royal Irish Academy* (1950) 53C:1–247.

O'Kelly, Michael J. *Early Ireland.* Cambridge: Cambridge University Press, 1989.

O'Ríordáin, Seán P. *Antiquities of the Irish Countryside.* 5th ed. London and New York: Routledge, 1991.

Maura Smale

SEE ALSO

Cashels; Dendrochronology; Raths

Croft

The term *croft* is Old English in origin, meaning "a small enclosed field." It occurs occasionally in pre-Conquest charters and far more commonly thereafter. Latin equivalents are *praediolum,* which was used in the classical period for an entire farm, and *agellu(lu)us septus,* literally "little enclosed field," *agellus* being the diminutive of *ager* (field). *Agellus* occurs from the seventh century onward. The cognate terms *agellarius* (husbandman) and *agularius* (hayward) occur in the post-Conquest period and should probably be associated with the use to which crofts were put.

Croft occurs commonly in medieval field names, wherein it appears to be applied to comparatively small, enclosed fields without respect to their use. Some were certainly held and cultivated in strips, but most were held in severalty and either cultivated or pastured as individual landowners or tenants saw fit. The term was, therefore, one that was defined primarily by the physical fact of enclosure rather than by function. The means of enclosure vary from region to region, including walls, banks, hedges, ditches, and fences of various kinds, often in combination.

In an archaeological context, the term is regularly applied to the close of land that was often, but not invariably, attached to the building plot on which a peasant farm was constructed. Such crofts were a common feature of medieval villages, often serving to separate the houses and attendant farmyards from the open fields of the township. Such crofts were often roughly rectangular in shape and of any size up to an acre (0.4 hectares) or even more, but they could be any shape and significantly smaller. In the more regular or planned villages (as at Goltho, Upton, Appleton-le-Moors, or Laxton), occupation occurred along one or more central roads, with crofts behind but separated by a back lane from the open fields. Elsewhere, the layout was often more agglomerate in plan, with crofts arranged as if enclosed severally and successively over a long period. The degree to which crofts were divided from building plots, or *tofts,* tends to vary both regionally and topographically, but some of this variation may be an artificial product of the varying clarity of the surface remains of medieval settlements and their immediate environs. Crofts also sometimes occur in association with hamlets and dispersed farms.

The use to which crofts were put seems to have varied and may often have changed from time to time, depending on the needs of the proprietor or tenant. The surface evidence on many crofts of broad ridge-and-furrow indicates that plowing has occurred, perhaps on a regular basis

C

and in the Middle Ages, so grain production (or similar) was necessarily an option where crofts were large enough to accommodate a plow. Other crofts, as at Wharram Percy, seem never to have been cultivated and may have served as permanent pasture, particularly for the family's horse or milch cow, or may have been mown for hay (as the use of the term *agularius* may imply). The important characteristics of such small enclosed pastures may well have been their proximity to the farmstead and the monopoly of use enjoyed by the occupier. At some sites (such as Houndtor), crofts were so small that they are generally referred to as gardens and seem to have been cultivated by hand. Gardening is a possible use in many instances.

FURTHER READINGS

Astill, G., and A. Grant, eds. *The Countryside of Medieval England.* Oxford: Basil Blackwell, 1988, pp. 48–51.

N.J. Higham

SEE ALSO

Deserted Medieval Villages; Toft; Wharram Percy

D

Danevirke

Danevirke (from the Middle Danish *Danæwirchi,* "Dyke of the Danes") is the biggest medieval monument in northern Europe. This complex of fortifications near the town of Schleswig marked the southern frontier of the oldest Danish realm. It functioned as a border fortification from the seventh to the thirteenth century and again in the middle of the nineteenth century.

Danevirke has always played an important role in the consciousness of the Danish people, and it was undoubtedly important in the development of a Danish national identity. Local place-names indicate that Danish settlement was dominant from the borderline northward, while Slavs and Saxons lived south of Danevirke. In the Middle Ages, Danevirke also served as a defense against attacks from early European powers, such as the Frankish and German Empires and the territorial states of the German princes.

Militarily, the long ramparts of the Danevirke established a frontal defense that required naval support. Only a centralized military organization could meet such a demand. Danevirke has an unusually long and complicated building history, which makes it an archaeological challenge. Excavations of Danewirke began in the middle of the nineteenth century, but old maps and descriptions existed before that.

As the building activity took place before written Danish history, contemporary historical sources are sparse. The historical importance of Danevirke lies in the fact that it indicates the existence of an early Danish state in a period without written sources. We have, however, a unique collection of Danish legends from the twelfth century dealing with the period, some of which are known

also from Old English poetry. Frankish sources such as Gregory of Tours (538–594), Alcuin (735–804), and the *Annals of the Frankish Empire* also occasionally refer to early Danish kings, namely Chochilaicus (sixth century), Ongendus (eighth century) and Sigfred (eighth century). From c. A.D. 800 onward, the Danish kings are quite well known, and whenever Danevirke is mentioned the king is identified as its builder.

The total length of Danevirke's ramparts is c. 30 km (Fig. 1). It is composed of two major defensive lines, Danevirke and Kovirke. The Danevirke line is the result of successive building efforts, but the Main Rampart always formed the center of the line. Kovirke is a separate line with only one building phase. The ramparts defended a lowland passage between the Firth of Schlei to the east and the River Treene to the west. The Military Road of Jutland—the connection between Denmark and the Continent—passed through both Kovirke and Danevirke. A third line, the East Rampart, protected the peninsula of Schwansen.

Kovirke was laid out as a completely straight line across a flat plain. It is an earthwork, 8 m wide and 2 m high, with a frontal palisade and a triangular ditch. The palisade was constructed of a triple row of posts made of one vertical central post and two supporting oblique beams. A similar construction technique was used in Aggersborg, one of four circular Danish strongholds from c. A.D. 980. Radiocarbon (C-14) dates, however, suggest that Kovirke may be older than that, and the question of dating this line remains unanswered.

The important line was Danevirke. The initial rampart of Danevirke consisted of a simple earthwork 7 m wide and 2 m high, with a low ditch at the front. Today we

D

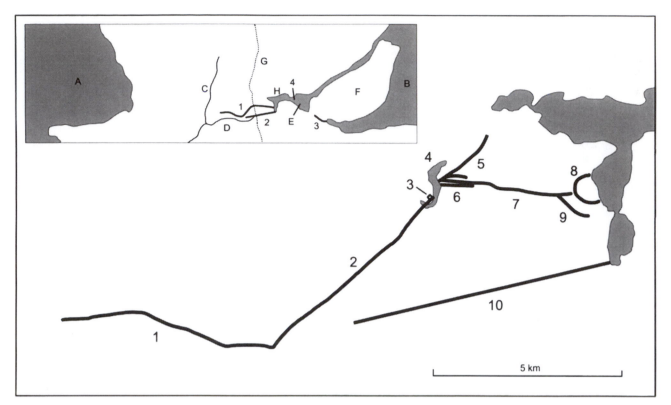

FIG. 1. Danevirke (main map and inset). Inset shows the southern part of the peninsula of Jutland: *A,* the North Sea; *B,* the Baltic; *C,* the River Treene; *D,* the River Rheide; *E,* the Firth of Schlei; *F,* the peninsula of Schwansen; *G,* the Military Road of Jutland; *H,* the town of Schleswig: *1,* Danevirke; *2,* Kovirke; *3,* East Rampart; *4,* Sea barrage (A.D. 737). Main map shows the ramparts: *1,* Curved Rampart (along the valley of the River Rheide); *2,* Main Rampart (across plain, lowland passage); *3,* Thyraborg (medieval stronghold, c. A.D. 1200); *4,* Lake Danevirke (now dried up); *5,* North Rampart (on the morain in the eastern part of Jutland, older wing); *6,* Double Rampart and Bowed Rampart (triple defense line—the Iron Gate); *7,* Connection Rampart (on the morain in the eastern part of Jutland, younger wing); *8,* Semicircular Rampart (around Hedeby, the predecessor of Schleswig); *9,* Forewall (late fortification of 8); *10,* Kovirke (across plain, lowland passage).

know that this insignificant building constitutes the nucleus of both the Main Rampart and the Curved Rampart. The initial rampart has been C-14 dated, yielding a range of dates for the line. The lower limits of the radiocarbon date are c. A.D. 650, and the initial rampart is unlikely to be much younger than this. A state of unrest among the southern peoples, caused by the migration of the Slavs, may have provoked the building of this first fortification. It was soon reinforced by a minor earthwork; later, by a considerable additional earthwork (Fig. 2).

In A.D. 737, Danevirke was reinforced with a strong oak palisade, 2 m high, and a sea barrage was placed in the Firth of Schlei. Evidence for this palisade has been found on the Main Rampart, the North Rampart, and the East Rampart. These building efforts have been dated through dendrochronology. Later on, the palisade of the Main Rampart was replaced by a stone wall, 3 m high and 3 m

wide, with a wooden revetment and a ditch. This wall incorporated the still-standing vertical posts from the 737 Palisade. This means that the wall cannot be much younger than the palisade.

In the eighth century, the Franks represented an increasing threat to their neighbors; at the beginning of the ninth century, the Danes and the Franks were in a state of war. In A.D. 808, Danevirke appears in a written source for the first time. The *Annals of the Frankish Empire* indicate that a Danish king, Godfred (d. 810), ordered a rampart to be built. This rampart has not, as yet, been identified with certainty.

In the middle of the tenth century, Danevirke was "revived" after a long break in building activity. Denmark was then under pressure from the German Empire, and in 934, 974, and 983 open war broke out. An admittedly late *Annal* calls the Danish King Harold Blacktooth

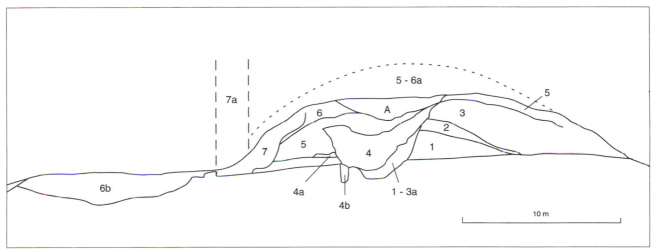

FIG. 2. *Top,* section through the Main Rampart, 30 m long and 4.5 m high, SE left, illustrating the intricate stratigraphy of this central line. The section shows seven building phases, the top of the initial phase touching the center of the excavation step; this insignificant rampart was then covered by the subsequent reinforcements. In front of the craterlike formation, above the ditch of the first phase, the burnt remnants of the collapsed 737 Palisade are seen as a horizontal black stratum of charcoal. The spotted dark layer, to the left above the excavation step, represents the sloping turf front of a later building phase. The remnants of Waldemar's Wall are seen to the left of the section—the wall has been almost totally plundered. (Excavation 1993. Photograph by H. Möller, Archälogisches Landesmuseum, Schloss Gottorf). *Bottom,* seven building phases: *1–3a,* sunken frontal parts of the ramparts 1–3, now filling the initial ditch; *4a,* the collapsed burnt palisade from 737; *4b,* 737 posthole; *5–6a,* later removed parts of the phases 5–6 (the continuation of the phases 5–6 can be traced in the little mound on top of the rampart as seen on the photograph); *6b,* a late ditch, presumably belonging to phase 6; *7a,* Waldemar's Wall; *A,* modern intrusion. The stone wall mentioned in the text was not built at this place.

(c. 960–c. 985) the "innovator" of Danevirke. He added a new east wing—the Connection Rampart. This connected the already existing Semicircular Rampart around Hedeby with the Main Rampart, which, as far as we know, was also reinforced on this occasion. Harold's Con-

nection Rampart is an earthwork, 14 m wide and 3.5 m high, with a sloping turf front and a wooden breastwork on the top; this rampart had no ditch. Special fortifications were later added to the western part of the rampart to protect a road passage. This part of the rampart was

D

popularly known as the Iron Gate. In spite of Harold's efforts, the German Emperor Otto II (955–983) took Danevirke by storm in 974. But the fortunes of war had changed by 983, and a few decades later the Danish King Canute the Great (c. 995–1035), the ruler of Denmark and England, was able to secure peace with the German Empire.

Continued troubles with the Slavs and the Germans made new reinforcements of Danevirke necessary in the eleventh and twelfth centuries, and now the ramparts reached a height of c. 6 m and a width of 20–30 m. These earthworks always had sloping turf fronts, and a ditch was now added as well. In A.D. 1134, this rather formidable "obstacle" stopped an attack by the German Emperor Lothar III. The final building on the rampart took place at the end of the twelfth century. Aggressive German princes, such as the Saxon Duke Henry the Lion (1129–1195) and the Holstein counts of Schauenburg, threatened the security of Denmark. King Waldemar the Great (1157–1182) therefore decided to fortify the most exposed part of the Danevirke—the Main Rampart—with a 7-m-high regular brick wall accompanied by a 10-m-wide berm, a 15-m-wide ditch, and a forewall. The depth of the defense line was almost 100 m. Such a wall was unique in these regions, bricks being a novelty as a building material. But new techniques of warfare meant that Waldemar's Wall, despite its "modern" concept, was already outdated by the following century.

An attempt to modernize the old rampart in the middle of the nineteenth century, during the wars between Denmark and Germany in 1848–1850 and 1864, proved useless. Danevirke was abandoned in 1864, and Denmark lost the territory.

This brief description of Danevirke includes results from the latest excavations (1990–1993). It thus precedes a publication in preparation, in which all previous works will be revised on the basis of our present knowledge of Danevirke.

FURTHER READINGS

Hellmuth Andersen, Henning. *Danevirke og Kovirke/ Danewerk und der Kograben,* (working title), in preparation.

Hellmuth Andersen, Henning, Hans Jørgen Madsen, and Olfert Voss. *Danevirke.* Copenhagen: Jysk Arlæologisk Selskab, 1976.

Jankuhn, Herbert. *Die Wehranlagen der Wikingerzeit zwischen Schlei und Treene.* Neumünster: Karl Wachholtz Verlag, 1937.

Müller, Sophus, and Carl Neergaard. *Danevirke.* Copenhagen: Det Kgl. Nordiske Oldskriftselskab, 1903.

H. Hellmuth Andersen

SEE ALSO
Haithabu; Trelleborg Fortresses

Dendrochronology

Dendrochronology is the dating of timbers by the measurement and analysis of their growth rings. In practice, species-specific, regional, master chronologies are constructed by overlapping the ring patterns of successively older timbers from living trees to historic timbers to archaeological timbers. Individual ring patterns of the same species from the same area can then be dated by comparison of the sample ring pattern with the established master tree-ring chronology. When successful, the method supplies dates of absolute calendrical accuracy for every ring in the sample ring pattern. In the case of samples complete to the underbark surface, the method allows the establishment of the date of the exact year in which the tree last grew. Thus, from the point of view of archaeologists studying the Medieval period, the method can provide dates fully compatible with written history. The synchronization is so exact that in some cases, where the final underbark ring is incompletely formed, it is possible to attribute felling to a range of about two months.

While outside the United States until the 1960s the only long chronologies were in Germany, the last quarter of the twentieth century saw the blossoming of regional chronologies. There is now extensive coverage from most countries in northern Europe, with many local chronologies within individual countries. Chronologies have also been constructed for the dating of buildings and archaeological remains from Greece and Turkey.

So, dendrochronology supplies dates for buildings and archaeological timbers of appropriate species. More than that, its accumulated evidence supplies a wider context for human constuctional activity. Since the master chronologies are continuous annual records, the method provides a parallel backdrop to written history at annual resolution; for any year in the Medieval period, it is now possible to see from their ring patterns what trees recorded about their growth conditions. This means that, through dendrochronology, we can look at the "history" of a parallel biological system. Dendrochronology is, therefore, more wide ranging than other dating methods in that it dates and provides context simultaneously.

Types of Information Derived from Dendrochronology

Dendrochronology can date buildings, sites, and objects, provided that the timber samples are of the correct species, are long lived (because sample ring patterns are required to be long for unique cross-dating), are complete or nearly complete, and come from an area compatible with available master chronologies. If we define the Medieval period as A.D. 400 to 1500, then we can point to the absolute dating of thousands of individual timbers in the U.S. Southwest and something of the same order of magnitude in Europe.

Dates have been produced for every type of context in which timbers survive: houses, mills, chateaux, churches, cathedrals, castles, crannógs (artificial islands), mills, wells, and even coffins. Thus, precise dates are being sprinkled throughout the archaeological record, helping refine the overall picture of the archaeological past. Concerted dating in a small region can trace detailed histories of building development from Amerindian pueblos to whole German valleys. While such datings are highly useful to individual researchers, the real power of dendrochronology may lie in the information that is beginning to appear from the accumulation of dates and from environmental reconstruction. Because all classic dendrochronology aims at the establishment of absolute calendrical dates, resulting dating patterns can be compared both temporally and geographically.

Accumulated Dates

As soon as workers, in any given tree-ring area, begin to date individual timbers in large numbers, patterns begin to emerge at several levels. It becomes apparent that timbers are not equally distributed through time but may exhibit distinct periods of abundance and depletion that may reflect changing human or environmental influences. Studies on oak across northern Europe show a notable depletion in timber availability c. A.D. 800, while the Black Death shows up clearly as a notable building pause, from Germany to Greece, in the fourteenth century. Studying the dates when trees started to grow (by concentrating on the dates of inner growth rings, as opposed to the felling dates) allows the reconstruction of periods of regeneration that may reflect reduction in human pressure on forest resources. There is a clear example of this from Ireland, where it proved difficult to obtain timbers that grew *across* the fourteenth century. So, accumulated dates are providing a backdrop against which written history must be viewed.

Environmental Information from Tree Rings

Dendrochronology works because trees of the same species share common environmental forcing and their ring patterns cross-match. It is, therefore, obvious that tree-ring patterns must contain environmental information. It has proved possible, in areas in which growth is largely controlled by a single factor, to reconstruct detailed environmental records. For example, temperature has been reconstructed for Fennoscandia back to A.D. 500. Unfortunately, reconstruction is less easy in temperate regions, where many factors control growth; however, even here it is possible to make some deductions on the severity of growth conditions that may have had implications for past human populations. For example, it is becoming apparent that there was a widespread environmental downturn c. A.D. 540, which can be traced in tree-ring chronologies around the Northern Hemisphere. This information ties in extremely well with historical evidence for a dry-fog event in A.D. 536, assumed to be volcanic in origin, with widespread famines from China to Ireland in the years after 536, and with the outbreak of the Justinian plague in A.D. 542. Accumulated dendrochronological evidence in both Europe and the United States shows a rapid increase in the number of dates after A.D. 550. This example serves to demonstrate how dendrochronology, in its widest sense, is capable of adding dramatically to the historical record. Even these preliminary dendrochronological interpretations suggest that environmental determinism may have to be reconsidered as a factor in human affairs.

FURTHER READINGS

Baillie, M.G.L. *Tree-Ring Dating and Archaeology.* London: Croom-Helm, 1982.

———. *Chronology and Environment.* London: Batsford, 1985.

Bartholin, T.S., B.E. Berglund, D. Eckstein, and F.H. Schweingruber, eds. *Tree-Rings and Environment.* Proceedings of the International Dendrochronological Symposium, Ystad, South Sweden, September 3–9, 1990. Lundqua 34. 1992.

Cook, E.R., and L.A. Kairiukstis, eds. *Methods of Dendrochronology: Applications in the Environmental Sciences.* Dordrecht: Kluwer, 1990.

Hollstein, E. *Mitteleuropaische Eichenchronologie.* Mainz am Rhein: Phillip von Zabern, 1980.

Kuniholm, P.I., and C.L. Striker. Dendrochronological Investigations in the Aegean and Neighboring Regions. *Journal of Field Archaeology* (1987) 14:385–398.

D

Robinson, W.R., and C.M. Cameron. *A Directory of Tree-Ring Dated Sites in the American Southwest.* Tucson: University of Arizona Press, 1991.

Schweingruber, F.H. *Tree-Rings: Basics and Applications of Dendrochronology.* Dordrecht: Kluwer, 1989.

M.G.L. Baillie

Deserted Medieval Villages

A deserted medieval village (commonly and hereafter shortened to DMV) is the remains of an abandoned, nucleated, rural settlement, usually defined as of six or more economic units. These units would normally have been farms, but abandoned fishing settlements might occasionally be included. Seigneurial settlements (such as castles, palaces, manor houses, or hunting lodges) and religious sites are excluded from the definition in instances in which no agglomeration of peasant settlement can be identified, as are settlements that are primarily focused on manufacturing or commerce. Smaller abandoned settlements are normally termed deserted hamlets or farms. Many DMVs today have at least one modern farm on or near the settlement remains, but this pattern can be distinguished from shrunken villages, in which a significant part of the early settlement has continued in occupation.

In England, the term DMV is normally used only for settlements occupied and abandoned between the ninth century (at the earliest) and the eighteenth century, when numerous sites, such as Tatton in Cheshire, were deserted owing to emparkment. Abandoned settlements of the earlier Anglo-Saxon period, such as Mucking or West Stow, are not normally included, although this is a matter of ongoing debate. DMVs also occur in Germany, southern parts of Scandinavia, northern France, Holland, parts of eastern Europe, and Italy, but only in upland areas are there generally upstanding remains comparable to those frequently found in England. On the Continent, the distinction between the early and later Middle Ages is far less a factor in the use of terminology. This entry focuses on English examples.

DMVs are most visible where they occur as upstanding earthworks with underlying stone walls, as at Wharram Percy. Deserted villages in lowland areas devoid of stone (generally on clay land) normally leave much less obvious traces, and sites that have been plowed may be identifiable only through soil or crop marks or scatters of pottery and settlement debris. The distribution of DMVs is uneven across Britain, with notable voids in Scotland and parts of Wales and the southwest peninsula. The majority are con-centrated in a broad band from the Isle of Wight and Hampshire in the south, through the central and eastern Midlands and Yorkshire, to Northumberland. Examples are rare in areas of medieval woodland or forest. This distribution mirrors the distribution of villages that survived into the modern period and contrasts with neighboring areas where settlement was less nucleated or entirely dispersed, even during the Middle Ages. Around 2,800 examples are known in England.

DMVs were first recognized as a distinct class of field monument by M.W. Beresford and W.G. Hoskins in the 1940s. The first systematic excavation occurred at Wharram Percy between 1952 and 1992, around which the Medieval Village Research Group was formed. Important excavations have also occurred at Gomeldon, Upton, Goltho, Barton Blount, Hound Tor, Thrislington, Cosmeston (in Wales), Raunds, and Tatton, but most sites have been the subject of nondestructive research based on field walking, the mapping of aerial photographs, or the plotting of surface features. Details of most examples are held in national and regional (or county) sites and monuments records, and many are legally protected to some extent through scheduling as historic monuments.

DMVs vary enormously in size from c. 1 ha to 15 ha. The appearance of any particular example can owe much to the vagaries of postabandonment land use, but the more complete instances are normally based on rows or agglomerations of individual farm units. Many are very regular and appear to have been as systematically planned as were many urban developments of the same period, while others are highly irregular and may have developed without significant planning or control.

Many, particularly of the more regular type, were contained within a perimeter wall or hedge bank and ditch. Roadways generally form one of the most easily identified features, passing centrally through the settlement, where junctions often occur, but with secondary routeways serving as back lanes to provide access to the rear of farm units. These farm units often survive as earthwork enclosures of varying sizes laid out in a regular and rectilinear pattern between the roads. They are often referred to as *messuages* or *tofts* and *crofts* (particularly in northern England), the latter being small fields the use of which might vary but was specific to that farm. Within the messuage or croft are concentrated the buildings and open areas that composed the farmyard, including peasant houses, barns, and, less frequently, granaries, sheepcotes and byres, stables, sties, kitchens, bake houses, and lesser buildings for storage. Interspersed were fenced enclosures for livestock, crew yards for cattle, threshing floors, middens, pits, wells, kilns, ovens, and areas used for various rural crafts.

Peasant houses and laborers' cottages were the standard habitations in any village, of which the former are much better represented in the archaeological record than the latter. Up to the thirteenth century, peasant houses were timber-framed buildings supported by earth-fast timbers set in individual postholes, construction trenches, or beam slots. Thereafter, the use of earth-fast timbers gave way to the use of stone foundations or padstones but only where suitable stone was easily available. Elsewhere, the use of earth-fast timbers prevailed until cruck construction and bricks became available in the late Medieval and postmedieval periods. In the fourteenth century, peasant housing took on a new sophistication, with the advent of locks and keys, for example.

Although the presence of the earthworks of roads, enclosures, and peasant housing is alone sufficient to justify the classification of a site as a DMV, many also have a variety of other features. Manor houses or aristocratic residences (even castles) are common features, many of which have extensive remains comprising ancillary structures and large, well-marked enclosures, often moated. Churches, chapels, and graveyards can also occur. Some are in an abandoned condition, as at Wharram Percy, while some remain in use but isolated from the focus of modern settlement. Many sites additionally are associated with ponds, drains, water mills, their dams or leets, or postmills, while high-status residents often had the use of fishponds.

The upstanding remains of a DMV can be confused with similar nucleated settlements of the Roman period, but their medieval provenance can be established by the identification of pottery, by field walking or excavation, by objective dating techniques, or by documentary research. Very few substantial DMVs are entirely undocumented in surviving medieval sources. On purely morphological grounds, it can be more difficult to distinguish a DMV from a failed medieval town, but these are comparatively well documented, although some overlap between minor planted towns and large villages with markets is inevitable.

Medieval villages came into existence over several centuries, beginning in the ninth century, as at Raunds, and continuing as late as the thirteenth century. In many areas, this process seems to have made little progress until the twelfth century. Their inception was clearly part of the major reorganization of the countryside that brought into existence open-field agriculture. It is probably also significant that their emergence was contemporary with the revival of urbanism, which in England is closely associated with Kings Alfred (849–899) and Edward the Elder (reigned 899–924), but which is, in fact, a broadly contemporary, Europe-wide phenomenon. The reorganization of settlement and land use may have been initially stimulated, in part, by the increasing centralization of society and rising demands on the part of landowners and governments for a greater share of production, as much as by changes in farming practice or technology, but this remains a major area of debate.

Desertion was an equally lengthy process, with marginal settlements, such as Hound Tor on the edge of Dartmoor, being abandoned in the early fourteenth century, while many sites shrank during the late fourteenth and the fifteenth centuries as a consequence of population decline, falling grain prices, and the migration of farmers to better holdings elsewhere. Many settlements that had become demographically or economically weakened by these processes were lost to sheep pasture during the fifteenth and sixteenth centuries, as landowners sought to reverse declining revenues from their estates. At many sites, shrinkage occurred only gradually, leading to total or near-total desertion only in the modern period. The proliferation of stately homes with deer parks in the eighteenth and nineteenth centuries brought a second, if minor, wave of casualties.

Many DMVs provide evidence of major reorganization during the period of occupation, with the addition of new rows or groups of tenements, the insertion into the plan of a green, the addition of a high-status holding, or the conversion of a high-status holding to peasant farms. In most instances, the recoverable plan should be taken as that of the settlement in the final stages of its development rather than during its inception. Notwithstanding, some settlements—particularly those providing strong evidence of initial planning—appear to have existed virtually unchanged throughout their period of occupation.

Today, DMVs remain a very active area of research, particularly among members of the Medieval Settlement Research Group (which replaced the Medieval Village Research Group and the Moated Sites Research Group in 1986). Their *Annual Report* provides an excellent starting point for anyone developing a new interest. It is generally now recognized that DMVs are best examined as just one element in a wider landscape that encompasses other types of settlement, field systems, route and trading patterns, and social, seigneurial, and governmental interactions. Their size is such that no example in England has

D

yet been subjected to excavation of more than about 5 percent of the total area. Partly for this reason, interpretation has tended to become increasingly multidisciplinary, with several new insights derived from textual research allied to field walking and surveying.

FURTHER READINGS

Astill, G., and A. Grant, eds. *The Countryside of Medieval England.* Oxford: Basil Blackwell, 1988.

Aston, M., D. Austin, and C. Dyer, eds. *The Rural Settlements of Medieval England.* Oxford: Basil Blackwell, 1989.

Austin, D. *The Deserted Medieval Village of Thrislington, Co. Durham: Excavations, 1973–4.* Monograph 12. Lincoln: Society for Medieval Archaeology, 1989.

Beresford, G. *The Medieval Clay-Land Village: Excavations at Goltho and Barton Blount.* Monograph 6. London: Society for Medieval Archaeology, 1975.

————. Three Deserted Medieval Settlements on Dartmoor: A Report of the Late E. Marie Minter's Excavations. *Medieval Archaeology* (1979) 23:98–158.

Beresford, M.W., and J.G. Hurst, eds. *Deserted Medieval Villages.* Guildford and London: Lutterworth, 1971.

————. *Wharram Percy: Deserted Medieval Village.* London: Batsford/English Heritage, 1990.

Cadman, G. Raunds, 1977–1983: An Excavation Summary. *Medieval Archaeology* (1983) 27:107–122.

Chapelot, J., and R. Fossier. *The Village and House in the Middle Ages.* London: Batsford, 1985.

Dyer, C. Deserted Medieval Villages in the West Midlands. *Economic History Review,* 2nd ser. (1982) 35:19–34.

Higham, N.J. Tatton: The History and Prehistory of One Cheshire Township. *Chester Archaeological Society Journal* (1995) 71 (entire volume).

Hilton, R.H., and P.A. Rahtz. Upton, Gloucestershire, 1959–1964. *Transactions of the Bristol and Gloucestershire Archaeological Society* (1966) 85:70–146 (see also vol. 88:74–126).

Hooke, D., ed. *Medieval Villages.* Monograph 5. Oxford: Oxford University Committee for Archaeology, 1985.

Hurst, J.G. *Wharram: A Study of Development on the Yorkshire Wolds.* Monograph 8. London: Society for Medieval Archaeology, 1979.

Roberts, B.K. *The Making of the English Village.* London: Longman, 1987.

Taylor, C.C. *Village and Farmstead.* London: George Philip, 1983.

Vyner, B.E., ed. *Medieval Rural Settlement in North-East England.* Research Report 2. Durham: Architectural and Archaeological Society of Durham and Northumberland, 1990.

Wade-Martins, P. *Fieldwork and Excavation on Village Sites in Launditch Hundred, Norfolk.* East Anglian Archaeology 10. Dereham, 1980.

Wrathmell, S. Medieval England: Perspectives and Perceptions. In *Building on the Past: Papers Celebrating 150 Years of the Royal Anthropological Institute.* London: Royal Anthropological Institute, 1994, pp. 178–194.

See also *Annual Reports* of the Medieval Settlement Research Group, available from R. Glasscock, School of Geography, University of Cambridge, Cambridge CB2 3EH, England.

N.J. Higham

SEE ALSO
Croft; Messuage; Mucking; Raunds Area Project; Toft; West Stowe; Wharram Percy

Devín Castle

Devín Castle is one of the most important historical monuments in Slovakia. It is situated at the confluence of the Danube and the Morava Rivers on the Austrian-Slovak border c. 10 km west of the center of the Slovak capital, Bratislava. It was erected where ancient fords crossed the River Danube, and Adriatic trade routes connected the Devín area with the whole known world from early times, thus creating the possibility of cultural influences from both western and eastern European civilizations. This was confirmed by intensive archeological research, which uncovered evidence of settlement from the Neolithic period (5000 B.C.) to the present. The place was intensively settled by the Celts between the first century B.C. and the first century A.D. From the first to the fourth century A.D., Devín was one of the Roman watch points on the northern bank of the River Danube. The origins of Devín as a medieval stronghold begin in the ninth century and coincide with the rise of the so-called Great Moravian Empire, which represents the first Slavic state in central Europe. The Moravian Duke Rastislav built a walled settlement on the site in the ninth century, which was part of a wide fortification system protecting the western border of his dukedom against the Franks. The advantageous location of this settlement, which was situated on a sheer cliff, surrounded by rivers, and strengthened by mounds of earth, palisades, and a moat, provided an impregnable defense. Besides indications of dwellings, the foundations of a Christian church with the remains of a cemetery were also found in the area of the settlement. The discovery of fragments of interior plaster in the nave of the church testifies to the original colorful wall decoration. Sacral buildings of this type were rather rare in the ninth century and were found only in remarkable locations such as Devín.

After the decline of the Moravian Kingdom (at the beginning of the tenth century), the importance of this place declined, but its settlement continued. The territory of Devín became a part of the Hungarian Kingdom. Archeological research confirms a continuation of the settlement. Rastislav's stronghold was replaced by a smaller settlement whose inhabitants used the original Moravian fortification. Research has uncovered remains of walls of both single- and double-roomed dwellings. The single-roomed huts averaged 7 × 5 m; the double-roomed ones, 9 × 6 m. They were built mainly of stone held together by clay mortar. Some of the houses were timber built on

stone foundations. The layout of the dwellings indicates that they were situated along a street. The cemetery on the hill above the settlement, with c. 700 graves, also belonged to this settlement. There also was a chapel on a circular foundation, which has survived to the present time. Archeological finds from the dwellings and the objects from the graves date the whole complex to the eleventh–twelfth centuries. The most convincing finds are coins from this historical period (Ladislaus, Andreas I, Bela I—Hungarian kings of the eleventh and twelfth centuries).

In the thirteenth century, the settlement in the former stronghold decayed, and a new settlement appeared outside the fortification.

The advantageous strategic position of this place was later used for building a king's boundary castle that consisted of a tower with a small courtyard at the top of the rock and several spaces carved directly into the rock. The only entrance, from the east side, was protected by a deep moat. The most intensive building activity occurred during the fifteenth century, when the castle became the property of the important aristocratic family Garay. The

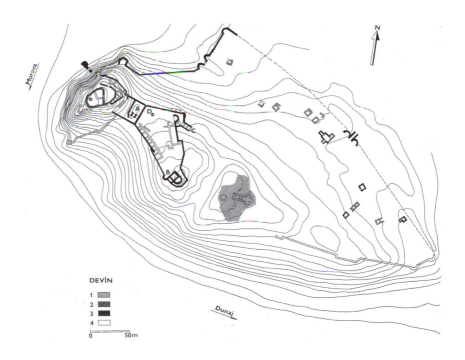

Medieval Devín
1. ninth to twelfth centuries
2. thirteenth to fourteenth centuries
3. fifteenth century
4. sixteenth to eighteenth centuries

A. deep moat
B. Garay palace
C. entrance to the courtyard
D. well

D

new owners modified the original building on the top of the rock and significantly increased the area of the castle. They built a new three-story palace on the southeast edge of the central part of the castle and fortified the entire new space by a new wall. The entrance to the courtyard was protected by a huge shield wall with a semicircular tower at the north end. There was a gate in front of the tower with a moat and a drawbridge. From the east side, the fortification was strengthened by another moat. In the courtyard, there was a well 55 m deep. Ashlar blocks covering the well were marked by 775 markings from the 22 types of medieval masons. In the following decades, the fortification was perfected and widened.

Only ruins survive from the original Gothic castle. Its appearance after Renaissance and Baroque modifications is shown in several Romantic paintings. The most faithful of them is a picture by Bernard Belloto (who was called Canaletto) from 1759–1760.

The research on the castle produced many archaeological finds that vividly illustrate the life of the inhabitants in the Middle Ages. Large amounts of various artifact types were found, especially fragments of gray pottery (such as pots, bowls, pitchers, and foot bowls), weapons (including shot for rifles), tools, broken glass from vessels and windows, and coins.

In the following centuries, the owners of the castle changed several times. They rebuilt various parts of it during the Renaissance and the Baroque periods. In 1809, the castle was destroyed by the army of the French Emperor Napoleon.

FURTHER READINGS

Pieta, K., Plachá, V., and J. Hlavicová. Devín v dobe laténskeja rímskej. In *Najstaršie dejiny, Bratislavy*. Ed. T. Stefanovicová. Bratislava: Vyd. Elán, 1993, pp. 89–102.

Plachá, V., and J. Hlavicová. Osidlenie Devína v 10–12. storoči. *Archeologia Historica* (1978) 3:231–237.

Plachá, V., J. Hlavocová, and I. Keller. *Slovanský Devín*. Bratislava. 1990.

Plachá, V. and K. Pieta. Romerzeitliche Besiedlung von Bratislava-Devín. *Archeologický rozlety* (1986) 38(4–5): 339–357.

Veronika Plachá and Jana Hlavicová

SEE ALSO
Bratislava

Dinas Powys

Dinas Powys, Glamorgan, Wales (NGR ST 1671), occupies a naturally defensible position at the northern tip of a whaleback hill c. 5.6 km from the Bristol Channel near Cardiff. There are two medieval phases: in the late fifth–eighth centuries A.D. and in the late eleventh–twelfth centuries. In the first, the spur tip was cut off by a ditch and an earthen bank c. 6 m. wide overall, enclosing an area c. 60×45 m. Within this, in an initial subphase, was a rectangular timber building, not fully excavated; in a later subphase, the plans of two buildings with parallel sides and rounded ends were demarcated by external drainage gullies. It is not certain whether these buildings were of wood or drystone. The external dimensions of the larger were c. 16×7.5 m.

This insignificant enclosure yielded an extraordinarily rich collection of artifacts, evidence of the social status, economy, and industrial activities of the inhabitants. The most common finds were sherds of imported pottery, representing two major sources and two chronological phases. The earlier, datable to the later fifth and sixth centuries, included amphorae and red-slipped tableware from the east Mediterranean and North Africa, evidence for continuing romanized—and especially Byzantine—contacts, as well as for a trade in Mediterranean wine and olive oil. In the later phase, in the seventh–eighth centuries, tablewares were imported from western Gaul, probably accompanied by a trade in wine in cask from the Bordeaux region.

Another import was fine glassware from unidentified Germanic sources on the Continent and in southeast England, and possibly also from Celtic British sources. In the past, it was thought that such glass came to western Britain as scrap for recycling as ornaments and inlays for jewelry, but now it seems likely that some, at least, reached the West as drinking vessels. These imports of wine, tableware, and glass vessels all mark Dinas Powys as a place of high social status, though it would be wrong to attempt to define this closely.

On-site activities included the working of local ores to make a range of iron objects; the casting of bronze jewelry in late Celtic style; the working of bone and antler to make pins, combs, and other objects; and the preparation of leather from the hides of locally raised cattle. Leather and raw hides were probably among the natural products that helped pay for imports of wine, tableware, and glass vessels.

The main evidence for the basic economy comes from great quantities of bones of cattle, pigs, and sheep, probably brought as tribute or food rents to the lord of Dinas Powys. It should be stressed, however, that the former belief that the economy of the early Welsh was entirely pastoral and nomadic has been discarded. The cultivation of grain crops was at least as important and is witnessed at Dinas Powys by the occurrence of a rotary quern (a grinding stone) of advanced type, as well as bakestones for bread.

After an abandonment in the eighth century lasting several centuries, the hilltop was briefly refortified in the Norman period (eleventh and twelfth centuries). This later medieval fort comprised a bank c. 8 m wide and more than 1.5 m high, enclosing an oval area 35 × 25 m. The bank was built of rubble from a rock-cut ditch more than 5 m wide by 1.5 m deep. Upright timbers in the core of this bank probably supported a wooden fighting platform on the crest of the rampart. Apparently in a second phase, two further large banks, with an intervening ditch, were raised outside the inner bank, but there is no firm evidence for the date of these.

The main bank, with its surrounding ditch and internal timberwork supporting a fighting platform, is an example of a type of fortification classed as *castle-ringworks*. These are considered to be Norman in origin and late eleventh–twelfth century in date. They are especially common in south Wales, where they outnumber the more usual Norman type of motte castle, but they are also widely distributed throughout England and Wales. At Dinas Powys, only a few potsherds were found consistent with this date. There was no trace of building within the defenses, and it seems that the ringwork was shortly replaced by a masonry castle c. 700 m distant.

FURTHER READINGS

Alcock, L. *Dinas Powys*. Cardiff: University of Wales Press, 1963.

———. *Economy, Society, and Warfare among the Britons and Saxons*. Cardiff: University of Wales Press, 1987.

King, D.J.C., and L. Alcock. Ringworks of England and Wales. In *Chateau Gaillard*. European Castle Studies 3. Ed. A.J. Taylor. London and Chichester: Phillimore, 1969, pp. 90–127.

Royal Commission on Ancient and Historical Monuments in Wales. *Glamorgan* III. 1a. *The Early Castles*. London: HMSO, 1991.

Leslie Alcock

SEE ALSO

Castles

D

Dorestad

See Emporia.

Dress Accessories

Dress accessories are common finds on most medieval sites. They have been recovered in recent years from closely dated deposits in sufficiently large numbers to give a fresh perspective on changing fashions in buckles, strap mounts, strap-end chapes, and other accessories in base metals for comparison with the precious-metal survivals in collections.

Iron and copper alloy was used for belt accessories throughout the Medieval period, with cheaper tin or lead/tin-alloy versions coming onto the mass market around the middle of the fourteenth century and apparently dominating some categories with their great popularity (in urban centers at least) in the next century. This rise of the lead/tin accessories was, from written records, resisted by the makers of those of iron and copper alloy, who wished to protect their established trade. Although some of the lead/tin buckles were prone to breakage, justifying to some extent the rival manufacturers' claims that the metals were inferior, many of the accessories of these materials seem to have served adequately for years of wearing.

In the Norman period (eleventh and twelfth centuries), ornate copper-alloy and plainer iron-strap accessories were available, buckles of the former often having openwork, tooling, and outlines of an elaborateness that was generally not matched in the predominant, cheap fashions in the later Medieval period. The majority of earlier copper-alloy buckles were probably gilded, but, by the late fourteenth century, this was unusual, and those that were coated had a wash of tin. In the thirteenth–fourteenth centuries, a new range of mass-produced buckles, with a limited number of basic shapes for the frames, became widely available across much of western Europe, with essentially the same styles from the south of France to Scandinavia. Tooling and different numbers and combinations of knops and ridges gave variety. There is evidence for the manufacture of these buckles in Lund, Sweden, and Toulouse, France, as well as in London, where clay molds have been found in association with what appears to have been a foundry furnace. The molds show that production was in groups of tens, if not hundreds, in one casting. Unfinished buckles from another London workshop, some still joined together from the mold, show some of this range of forms that gained a large share of the

D

market across such a wide area. It is likely that these accessories were produced in most large towns.

A category of buckle that appears to be particularly English is a composite form, with two separate sheets set on a two-pronged spacer (integral with the oval frame) to make a sleeved plate into which the strap fitted—this seems to represent the best quality among mass-produced buckles in the late fourteenth–fifteenth centuries.

A later assemblage of manufacturers' waste from the late fifteenth century to the early sixteenth in London illustrates an extension of the use of copper-alloy sheeting beyond strap-end chapes and buckle plates to the frame itself, made sufficiently robust by ingenious folding and bending. A more labor-intensive approach was needed in this branch of the industry, although a fixed workplace with plant and fuel for heating was not necessary. Similar items to those from the London workshop, made there or by others using similar templates elsewhere, have been found in the east and west of England and on the Isle of Man. Metallurgical analyses are needed to characterize the alloys used by different workers to gauge the extent of trade or localized production against the emerging widespread fashions.

Mounts of sheet and cast copper alloy and tin-coated sheet iron were used as decorative embellishments, riveted onto many straps. Large numbers, sometimes more than a hundred mounts of one or two shapes on a single belt, were used together for overall effect. Among the earlier mounts, the majority are of plain outline with relatively simple motifs or naturalistic devices, though, by the late fourteenth century, a much wider range of elaborate motifs was available in sheet mounts of the two traditional metals and also cast in lead/tin. Plain, narrow rectangles or rods ("bar" mounts) and simple flowerlike foliate mounts remained popular throughout the whole period. As with buckles, the transfer of mounts from an old belt to a new one is sometimes revealed by rough riveting or by rivets of a different metal or alloy from the main accessory.

Strap ends, small chapes set on the hanging ends of waist belts and on other straps, gave added robustness and were sometimes elaborately decorated. The majority of finds are, however, relatively plain, sometimes with simple tooling. The terminals occasionally feature an acorn or some other form of knop. Rare survivals among the cheaper accessories of strap ends and buckles together suggest that they were sometimes marketed in matching pairs.

Brooches, pinned at the front of the neck to fasten upper garments, were popular throughout the Medieval period, and many provided an opportunity across the social spectrum for eye-catching decoration. The roughest brooches are of remarkably crude workmanship, but, in the majority (including most of those of lead/tin), some effort was made to make them more attractive.

Perhaps the majority of excavated brooches are plain or very simply decorated rings, which are nevertheless well finished. The range of shapes and methods of embellishment known on the excavated finds is extremely wide. "Jeweled" brooches range from precious-metal versions with natural stones, through base-metal ones with glass stones, to those of very cheap lead/tin alloys, which, in the earlier part of the period, are occasionally set with glass. However, this kind of decoration on the cheapest kinds of brooch more often consists of false stones cast together with the frame in the same metal and probably originally painted.

Recent finds show that, in the Saxo-Norman period (eleventh–twelfth centuries), there was a series of brooches of lead/tin, cast with integral pins, in the form of birds and animals, crosses, and occasionally more abstract motifs. There appears to have been a break in the manufacture of this form of brooch (apart from the special instance of pilgrim badges) until the late fourteenth century, when cheap favors for political and other causes extended their popularity once more into the secular sphere. Brooches made of copper-alloy wire twisted into multiple loops, which look very complicated (though they were quick and easy to produce), were first made in the Medieval period. They lasted at least until the sixteenth century. Many medieval brooches have mottos on the frame; circular brooches in silver with the motto "Jesus Nazarenus" (Jesus of Nazareth) and in lead/tin or copper alloy with "Ave Maria gracia plena" (Hail, Mary, full of grace) seem to have been particularly widespread in the fourteenth century.

Several of the fashions evident in brooches also appear in finger rings, which were widely worn during the Medieval period. Attention has, in the past, tended to be concentrated on the more spectacular, large, precious-metal rings. Recent excavations that have produced base-metal rings in some numbers are showing just how exceptional the expensive rings were. As with brooches, there was a ready market for mass-produced, cheap versions of lead/tin, the roughest of which are very unsophisticated—some of the smallest may well have been for children. A number of twelfth- and thirteenth-century rings, like brooches of the same date, have the visible surface entirely covered with a dense decoration of simple motifs, such as circle-and-dot and cross hatching, often in combination.

Copper-alloy rings, both plain and quite elaborate forms, sometimes with glass stones, were also popular. There seem to have been relatively few in silver, but the finger ring of gold is the one accessory of the noblest metal that is found with any regularity during major programs of urban excavation (though numbers are inevitably very small in comparison with examples in the base metals). The reason for this greater emphasis on gold was its symbolic value, with its property of resisting tarnishing, as a visible token of marriage—if only one accessory of gold was affordable in a lifetime, this was the one to choose. The amount of metal used in most finds of this category is very small, though even the thinnest gold rings usually feature one or (again for the symbolism) two natural stones. Many gems were believed to have specific magical properties, such as the power to guard against specific diseases or drunkenness.

Wire frames to support textile headdresses worn by women are sometimes recognized among excavated material. Most are of copper alloy, though silver wire with pieces of silk attached may be related or may be from some other kind of accessory. The headdresses and false hair pieces (of which an example found in London is a rare survival) were held in place by pins, mainly of copper alloy and very plain, though sometimes with a tin or silver coating or a decorative form of head.

Beads seem to have been mainly for rosaries, to judge from excavated finds. They turn up in a wider range of materials than any other dress accessories. Bone beads were apparently the cheapest (the waste from manufacturing these is commonly encountered in urban excavations), and there are also versions in wood, tin, glass, jet, rock crystal, and especially amber (imported as raw material from the Baltic to other parts of Europe).

Purses were (like brooches) regularly worn by both men and women, hanging from the waist. Textile and leather examples, both plain and elaborate, are sometimes found in an identifiable state. Metal suspenders of various forms to hang purses from belts have been recognized probably in greater numbers than the accessories themselves, indicating how widespread the fashion for wearing them was.

FURTHER READINGS

Alexander, J., and P. Binski, eds. *The Age of Chivalry.* Exhibition catalog. London: Royal Academy of Arts, 1987.

Egan, G., and F. Pritchard. *Dress Accessories.* Medieval Finds from London Excavations 3. London: HMSO, 1991.

Evans, J. *Magical Jewels.* Oxford: Oxford University Press, 1922.

Hinton, D.A. *Medieval Jewellery: from the Eleventh to the Fifteenth Century.* Shire Archaeology, no. 21. Aylesbury: Shire Publications, 1982.

Murdoch, T., et al. *Treasures and Trinkets.* London: Museum of London, 1991.

Zarnecki, G., Holt, J., and T. Holland, eds. *English Romanesque Art, 1066–1200.* Exhibition catalog. London: Arts Council of Great Britain, 1984. See chapter on metalwork.

Geoff Egan

SEE ALSO
Jewelry

Dundurn
See Scotland: Early Royal Sites.

Dunnothar Castle and Bowduns
See Scotland: Early Royal Sites.

Dunollie
See Scotland: Early Royal Sites.

Dye Plants

Before the advent of synthetic dyestuffs in the middle of the nineteenth century, most dyeing of textiles relied on vegetable dyes from wild or cultivated plants. Dyes from animal sources were also often used (e.g., Tyrian purple and other dyes from Mediterranean molluscs of the families Muricidae and Thaididae, and kermes and cochineal from various scale insects [Hemiptera]). These were generally much more expensive and reserved for textiles worn by those of highest status.

Archaeological evidence for the use of dye plants in the Medieval period comes from two sources: from dyestuffs preserved on textiles and from remains of the plants themselves. Spectroscopic methods of examining dyes on textile fibers have been used by, for example, G.W. Taylor (1983), who identified extracts from ninth–eleventh-century Anglo-Scandinavian textiles from occupation deposits at 16–22 Coppergate, in the heart of York, England (see also Walton 1989). From these analyses, the use of madder (*Rubia tinctorum* L.) for reds, woad or indigo (*Isatis tinctoria* L. or *Indigofera* spp.) for blue, and lichens for purples has been established.

D

Examination of the remains of plants preserved by anoxic "waterlogging" in the same deposits from Coppergate revealed an abundance in many layers of remains of some of the actual dyeplants used. Their identification is discussed by P. Tomlinson (1985), and the evidence is put in archaeological context by H.K. Kenward and A.R. Hall (1995). The plants concerned were madder, woad, and dyer's greenweed (*Genista tinctoria* L., a good source of yellow). In addition, there were many records of a clubmoss, some, at least, being identified as *Diphasiastrum complanatum* (L.) J. Holub. The clubmoss was probably imported from Scandinavia for use as a mordant—a source of aluminum to "fix" certain dyes (in this case, madder and greenweed) to textile fibers. The use of clubmosses in dyeing continued in Scandinavia until the twentieth century.

There have also been records of madder, greenweed, dyer's rocket (or weld, *Reseda luteola* L.), and perhaps also woad from fourteenth-century riverside deposits in Bristol, England; more recently, remains of some of these plants have been recovered from excavations of other ninth–fourteenth-century sites in York and Beverley in England (reviewed by A.R. Hall, forthcoming).

Many other plant remains recovered from medieval archaeological deposits may represent materials that served in dyeing—almost any vascular plant will furnish some kind of dye, given a suitable mordant. The colors obtainable from plants will not always reflect their color in life; for example, many red and purple berries do not give good, fast dyes of these colors. Most ironically, very few green plants will give a good green dye—greens were typically obtained by dyeing with blue and top-dyeing with yellow (or vice versa). The use of one dye after another meant that a wide range of colors was available to the medieval dyer.

In the case of the plants mentioned here, various parts were used:

1. MADDER. The root, which contains alizarin, purpurin, and pseudopurpurin, gives a range of colors, from red and orange to brown, depending mainly on the mordant used.
2. DYER'S GREENWEED AND DYER'S ROCKET. Whole plants, fresh or dry (dyer's rocket was traditionally harvested just before seed set), were used. Both plants give rich yellows, from flavones (genistein and luteolin) enhanced by aluminum as a mordant.
3. WOAD. First-year leaves were harvested, crushed, and fermented (see Hurry 1930) to produce a soluble, colorless form of indigotin that oxidizes to the familiar blue color on exposure of dyed yarn or textile to air upon extraction from the dye vat. No mordant is necessary. (The fermentation necessary to obtain the dye from woad means that very little of the plant is likely to survive in the ground; some residues of strongly digested vascular plant tissue thought to come from woad have been recorded at Coppergate and elsewhere, but these are accompanied by remains of the characteristic winged seed pods.)

Undoubtedly, more evidence for dye plants will emerge through analyses of occupation deposits with good preservation by anoxic waterlogging, and it may eventually be possible to find sites where dye-plant waste can be linked directly to artifactual or structural evidence for dyeing other than that from textile fragments.

FURTHER READINGS

Brunello, F. *The Art of Dyeing in the History of Mankind.* Vicenza: Neri Pozza Editore, 1973.

Cardon, D., and G. du Chatenet. *Guide des teintures naturelles.* Paris: Delachaux et Niestlé, 1990.

Hall, A.R. *A Review of the Archaeological Evidence for Dyeplants in Medieval Britain.* Festschrift for Prof. R.G. West (forthcoming).

Hurry, J.B. *The Woad Plant and Its Dye.* London: Oxford University Press, 1930. Reprinted, Clifton, N.J.: Augustus M. Kelley, 1973.

Kenward, H.K., and A.R. Hall. *Biological Evidence from Anglo-Scandinavian Deposits at 16–22 Coppergate.* The Archaeology of York 14(7). York: Council for British Archaeology, 1995.

Taylor, G.W. Detection and Identification of Dyes on Anglo-Scandinavian Textiles. *Studies in Conservation* (1983) 28:153–160.

Tomlinson, P. Use of Vegetative Remains in the Identification of Dyeplants from Waterlogged Ninth–Tenth-Century A.D. Deposits at York. *Journal of Archaeological Science* (1985) 12:269–283.

Walton, P. *Textiles, Cordage, and Raw Fibre.* The Archaeology of York 17(5). London: Council for British Archaeology, 1989.

Allan R. Hall

SEE ALSO
Cloth; Cloth Making

E

Early Polish State

See Polish State, Early.

Early Slav Culture

In the sixth–seventh centuries A.D., a substantial part of Europe from the Don to the Elbe Rivers and from the Baltic to the Aegean Seas found itself within the reach of the early Slav culture (ESC). The archaeological data and historical sources show that the early Slav population lived in nonfortified settlements composed of small concentrations of buildings located along the banks of the river valleys. The homesteads were dug out on a square base with ovens made of stone or clay (Fig. 1, on p. 86). Agriculture was the basis of the economy, primarily the cultivation of millet and wheat. Cattle breeding played the most important role in the farming economy. There were no well-developed handicrafts. Simple forms of harnessing natural resources predominated and guaranteed absolute self-sufficiency to the inhabitants of the rural settlements, but with a relatively low standard of living. The dead were buried in flat cremation cemeteries or hollow burials that were poorly provided for. The most typical group of artifacts are plain, nonornamented, handmade clay pots with indistinct edges (Fig. 2).

The Polish area is crucial for clarifying the extremely unclear origins of the Slav ethnic group and the circumstances of its expansion around the middle of the first millennium A.D. The basic question is: are these people autochthonous to the Vistula and Odra River areas, or did they come from other areas?

Relics of sixth–seventh-century material culture tend to be extremely scant and defy precise dating. Therefore, the reconstruction of ESC origins in eastern and central Europe has to rely on the much more well-dated fourth–fifth-century cultural material.

Thorough analysis of archaeological finds from the late Roman (third–fourth centuries) and migration periods (fifth–sixth centuries) in central and eastern Europe (Godłowski 1970, 1983) and of written sources indicates that, at the close of the first half of the first millennium A.D., this area experienced a rapid collapse and the

FIG. 2. Typical early Slav pot (Bachórz, province of Przemyśl).

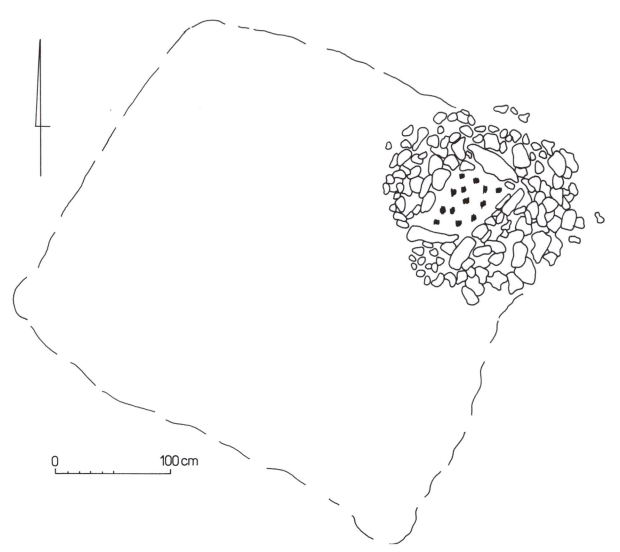

FIG. 1. Schematic plan of the dugout house (Bachórz, province of Przemyśl).

disintegration of the cultural and settlement pattern that, during the previous centuries, had formed a common province spanning barbarian lands from the Gothic territories on the Black Sea and the Sea of Azov to the various Germanic tribes of the Elbe Basin. Existing structures disintegrated and went into decline successively in the Ukraine and Moldova (fourth–fifth centuries); southeastern, southern, and, in part, western Poland (first half of the fifth century); central Poland (late fifth or even early sixth century); and Pomerania (first quarter of the sixth century), reaching the Elbe-Saale line in the late sixth century. This territory gradually saw the emergence of early Slav assemblages; the earliest known are from the Ukraine. They represent a cultural model entirely distinct from the one that earlier dominated the area. These facts may be

interpreted as the replacement of the earlier population by the Slavs.

The heartland of the ESC was in the east. So far, there are few assemblages reliably dated to the fifth century in the Ukraine from the Middle Dniester and the Upper Prut to the Middle Dnieper; they are linked with both the Prague and the Penkovka cultures (Fig. 3). While reconstructing a still earlier stage of the above-mentioned model, special attention must be paid to the so-called Kiev culture, which developed in the forest zone of the Upper and part of the Middle Dnieper Basin in the third–fifth centuries.

To appreciate the rate of settlement in Poland at the onset of the Middle Ages, it is necessary to examine the situation in the area in a number of successive time intervals every few decades. However, the nature of the archae-

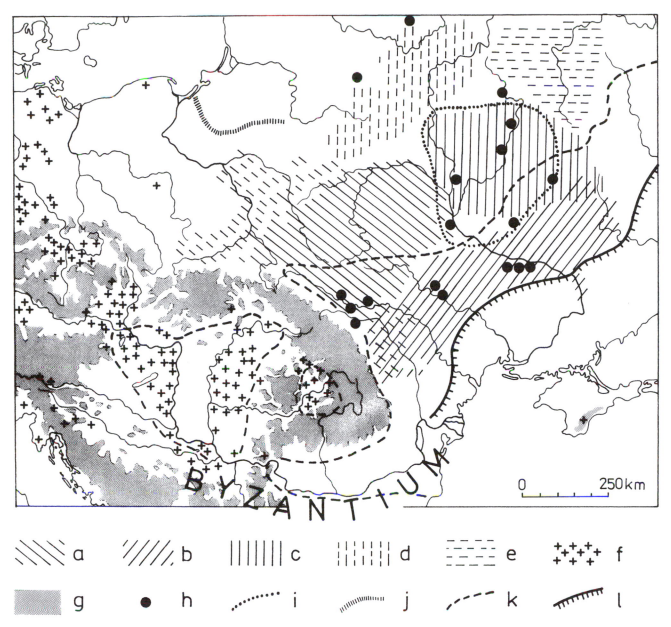

FIG. 3. Distribution of archaeological cultures in central and eastern Europe at the beginning of the sixth century: *a,* Prague culture; *b,* Penkovka culture; *c,* Kolochin culture; *d,* Bantserovshchina-Tushemla culture; *e,* Moshchiny culture; *f,* Merovingian ranked cemeteries and other contemporary inhumations; *g,* land more than 500 m above sea level; *h,* archaeological sites securely dated to the fifth century belonging to the early Slav culture; *i,* extent of Kiev culture in the fourth century; *j,* southwestern extent of the Balt cultures; *k,* boundary of the forest-steppe zone, *l,* northern border of the steppe zone.

ological sources currently available does not fully substantiate such a procedure. Nevertheless, an outline of the settlement situation in Poland in the early sixth century and the seventh century can be suggested. Obviously, comparisons with contemporaneous Byzantine and west European sources and the developments in other Slav lands can be very helpful.

There is growing evidence that the first Slav settlement (end of the fifth century–first half of the sixth century) occurred in the Upper and, in part, the Middle Vistula Basin (Fig. 4). These traces can be unequivocally identified with the Prague culture, with possible external infiltrations from the northeast affecting the mid-Vistula region (see Fig. 3).

E

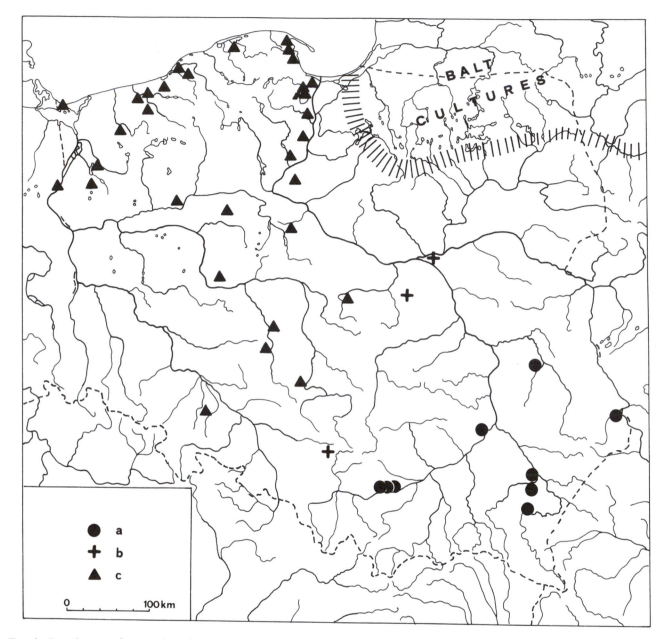

FIG. 4. Distribution of sites with probably the oldest early Slav assemblages (from the end of the fifth century to the first half of the sixth century) from the oldest stage of the early Slav culture in Poland: *a,* settlements; *b,* flat cremation burial grounds; *c,* non-Slavic sites, dated with no doubt to the latter half of the fifth century and the beginning of the sixth century (after Godłowski), 1970.

Mentions by the historians Jordanes and Procopius provide a picture, albeit fragmentary, of Slav settlements in Polish territory in the first decades of the sixth century (Fig. 5). The seats of the Sclaveni extended from the Lower Danube along the Carpathian ridge to the Vistula (Jordanes, *Getica* V. 34–35). The basin of the Upper Vistula, therefore, clearly delimited the northwestern extent of the expansion of the Sclaveni, who were one of the two or three components of the larger Venethi people, often

identified with the Slavs. The sources are silent on the remaining parts of Poland. They note, however, the Vidivarii (a Germanic name), a conglomerate of various tribal splinters at the mouth of the Vistula, and mention their Baltic neighbors, the Aesti. The settlement situation to the west and northwest of Little Poland (southeastern Poland) is illuminated by a single, significant piece of information on the migration of the Germanic Heruli, who moved c. A.D. 512 from the shores of the Middle

Danube, the area populated by all the Sclaveni tribes, and, after crossing a large desolate area, entered the land of the Germanic Varni (Procopius, *De bello Gothico* [The Gothic War] II.15). While scholars differ in their interpretation of the first stage, they generally agree that the later route ran through the Upper Vistula Basin, along the River Odra down to the mid-Elbe, the home of the Varni (see Fig. 5). The desolate area is probably Silesia (southwestern Poland).

The course of the Avar expedition against the Frankish state, which crossed southern Poland in 566–567 and was described by Gregory of Tours in his history of the Franks (*Historia Francorum* IV.29), also suggests the absence of population in the Odra Basin.

Archaeological finds correlate surprisingly well with the written sources. The earliest assemblages of the Prague culture discovered in Poland to date do not extend beyond the Upper Vistula Basin (see Fig. 4). This suggests that this area may be identified with the peripheral Sclaveni lands and corroborates Jordanes's credibility. Certainly, it is too early to pass judgment on the possible Sclavenian affiliation of the Mazovia archaeological assemblages from the Middle Vistula Basin whose closest links are probably with the Prague Culture Circle.

No early Slav finds dating to c. A.D. 600 are known from Upper Silesia and the eastern reaches of Lower Silesia. The absence of finds does not necessarily indicate a vacuum, yet it is evidence of the lack of mass settlement.

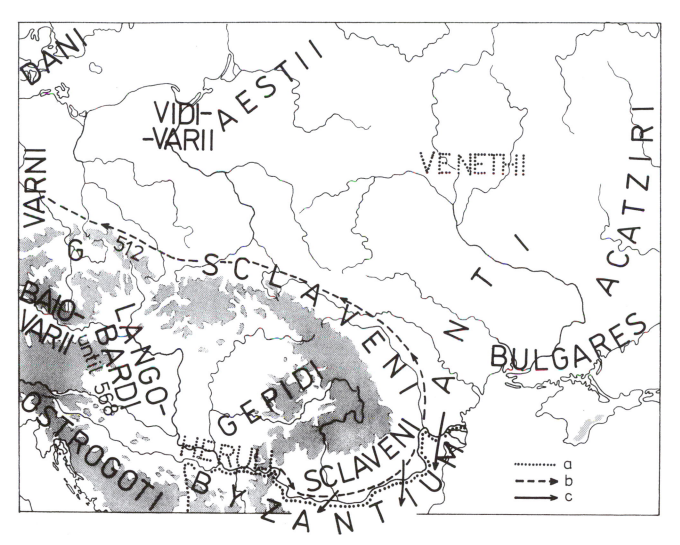

FIG. 5. Ethnic map of Europe in the first half of the sixth century in light of written sources: *a,* northern limits of the Byzantine Empire; *b,* presumed route of the Heruli; *c,* direction of Sclaveni and Anti invasions of the Byzantine Empire; *G,* Germanic people of unknown name in Bohemia.

E

It would hardly be correct to date the beginnings of more intensive occupation in the region and adjacent areas to the first decades of the sixth century. It may be that this process began only after the march of the Heruli, or even the Avars, through Silesia.

Probably as early as the mid-sixth century A.D., certain groups of Slavs from the Prague Culture Circle gradually moved into some of the western and, presumably, central regions of Poland (Kuyavia), where they developed their own variant (with possible, as yet undefined, influences from the northeast). This variant is usually referred to in the literature as the Sukow-Dziedzice group (Fig. 6). The difference between the Sukow-Dziedzice group and other early Slav cultures is that its population preferred surface or only partly sunken houses, and the dead were buried in a way that is imperceptible to archaeologists.

The only other historical datum for reconstructing the extent of Slav settlement in Polish territory in the sixth century A.D. is provided by Theophylactus Simocatla, who describes the capture of three Sclaveni in the 590s,

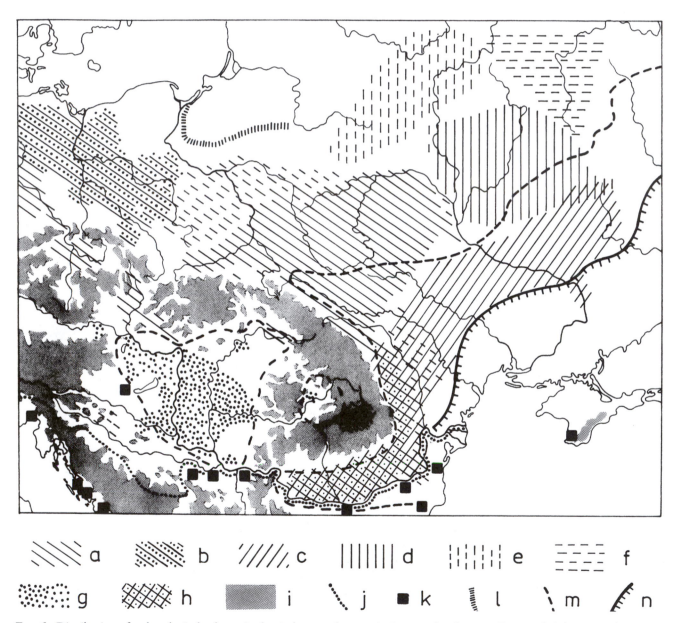

FIG. 6. Distribution of archaeological cultures in the sixth–seventh centuries in central and eastern Europe: *b,* Sukow-Dziedzice group; *g,* extent of early Avar burial grounds; *h,* early Slav culture in Romania; *j,* northern limit of the Byzantine Empire; *k,* major post-Roman and early Byzantine centers; remaining symbols as in Fig. 3.

probably the inhabitants of the Baltic coast (Fig. 7). Thus, at this time we can assume that Sclaveni (of the Sukow-Dziedzice group) populated northwestern Poland and, possibly, lands farther to the west (see Fig. 6).

Much more is known about the Balt lands in northeast Poland where both culture change and demographic movements have been noted. In the sixth–seventh centuries A.D., the Balts expanded to the west and southwest, reaching the Lower Vistula line and the Olsztyn Lakeland (see Fig. 6; Fig. 7). The Olsztyn group evolved during the fifth–sixth centuries A.D. and enjoyed lively, far-flung contacts with western Europe, Scandinavia, and the Danube and Dnieper areas, as shown by the wealth of artifacts (mainly metal) of foreign origin. The Olsztyn

group may have comprised, in addition to its Balt core (the Galindi), certain Germanic groups and possibly Slav ones as well. In the sixth century A.D., the links with other cultural centers must have at least in part traversed Slav territories, although no clear traces are available. The influence of the western Balts on the earliest stage of the early Slav culture is yet to be identified; much more is known about their interaction after the sixth–seventh centuries.

The advent of the Slavs in Poland was a protracted process that was still incomplete in the sixth century A.D. Eastern Pomerania was settled last, in the seventh century A.D., along with Upper Silesia and the eastern reaches of Lower Silesia.

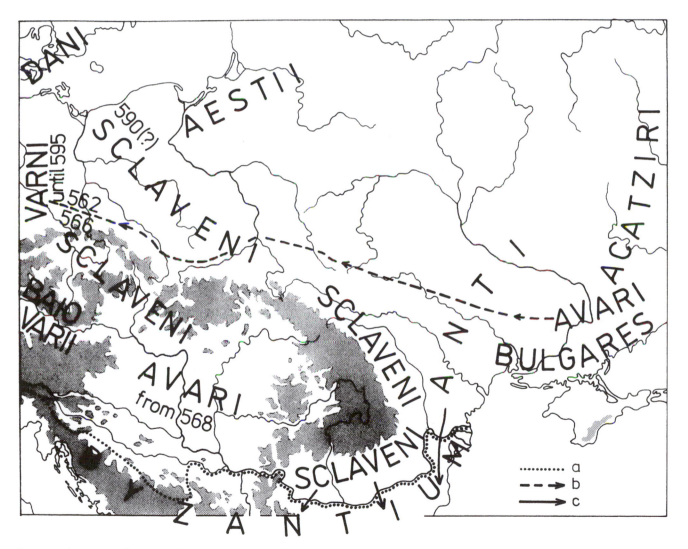

FIG. 7. Ethnic map of central and eastern Europe in the second half of the sixth century in light of the written sources: *a,* northern limit of the Byzantine Empire; *b,* presumed route of the 562 and 566–567 Avar expedition against the Franks; *c,* direction of the Sclaveni and Anti invasions of the Byzantine Empire.

E

Where did these waves of people originate, and how intense were they? From the sixth century onward, settlement over vast tracts of eastern and central Europe underwent destabilization due to the almost unhampered freedom of movement of human groups of various sizes. The attraction of the areas of urban civilization meant that the Slavs concentrated primarily on a southerly Danube-oriented expansion. This is confirmed by the enormous accumulation of early Slav culture relics with the Carpathian Arc and extending into the Dniester and Lower Danube regions. Similar finds are much less numerous in the Upper and Middle Vistula Basins, which documents the lesser importance of the westward trans-Vistula and Odra Basin expansion.

Concentrations of the Prague culture, larger than the ones in Poland, are recorded for Bohemia and the Middle Elbe, even though the beginnings of Slav settlement there date to the second half (and, in the case of eastern Germany, the end) of the sixth century A.D. These settlements theoretically antedate by up to a century the Little Poland-Mazovia group, whose evolution took much longer, despite its closer proximity to the early Slav culture heartland.

Areas along the Middle Danube and the Upper and Middle Elbe, contrary to the belief held until recently by Polish scholars, were most probably not directly settled from the north and east. It seems more probable that settlers moved into Bohemia from the southeast—from Moravia and southwestern Slovakia. The Middle Elbe Basin would have been the next stage in this colonization. Here, slow settlement could presumably have come from northern areas of the Carpathian Basin, which were already free from Germanic presence by the fifth–sixth centuries A.D.

The ancestors of the Prague culture group occupying the Vistula Basin arrived from the east and southeast as part of the spread of the Sclaveni. Without doubt, the internal ties unifying the Sclaveni in the sixth century A.D. were still strong, as testified by Jordanes and by certain shared elements of material culture that are recognizable over large areas from the Lower Danube to the Vistula.

FURTHER READINGS

Godłowski, K. The Chronology of the Late Roman and Early Migration Periods in Central Europe. *Zeszyty Naukowe UJ, Prace Archeologiczne* 11. Kraków, 1970.

———. Zur Frage der Slawensitze vor der grossen Slawenwanderung im 6. Jahrhundert. *Settimane di studio del Centro italiano di studi sull'alto medioevo* (1983) 30:257–284.

Gregory, Saint, Bishop of Tours. *The History of the Franks.* Translated from the Latin by Lewis Thorp. Harmondsworth: Penguin, 1974.

Parczewski, M. Origins of Early Slav Culture in Poland. *Antiquity* (1991) 65:676–683.

———. *Die Anfänge der frühslawischen Kultur in Polen.* (Österreichischen Gesellschaft für Ur- und Frühgeschichte.) Wien, 1993.

Michał Parczewski

Emporia

The standard picture of the early medieval European economy, until recently, was one of autarky, or economic self-sufficiency. The collapse of the political and military superstructures of the Roman state supposedly had an economic counterpart in the collapse of complex long-distance production and distribution systems. In the last twenty years of the twentieth century, archaeologists challenged this picture. Excavations of cemeteries and settlement sites across Europe have uncovered objects that were clearly of foreign provenance. Excavations at a series of coastal sites, dating from the late seventh to the ninth century, have suggested an increase in the volume of material being moved long distances across Europe. To understand the changing nature and significance of this phenomenon, archaeologists turned to models drawn from anthropology and geography. The works of K. Polanyi (1957) and M. Mauss (1967) on the forms of exchange that preceded capitalism were of particular significance, as was the study of "gateway communities" by geographers. Archaeologists borrowed the terms *gateway community* and *emporium* from anthropology and geography and used them to describe these coastal trading settlements.

Excavations since World War II along the coasts of Britain and northwest Europe have revealed a whole series of sites that bear all the hallmarks of emporia. These are sites situated on ethnic, political, and physical boundaries through which trade is mediated. They exist

> *at passage points into and out of a distinct natural or cultural region and link this region to external trade routes. . . . [They] tend to be located along natural corridors of communication, often at critical points between areas of high mineral, agricultural or craft productivity (Hodges 1988:43).*

The study of the material from such sites and the increasingly sophisticated application of anthropological

E

and geographical models have resulted in a transformation of our understanding of the early medieval European economy (see Smith 1976). Instead of an image of autarky, we are presented with a picture of long-distance exchange systems, mediated through emporia and the kings who controlled them, spanning the whole of Europe and linking Europe with northern Scandinavia and the Middle and Far East (see Hodges and Whitehouse 1983).

However, long-distance trade may have been overemphasized as an economic phenomenon of early medieval Europe and as the basis for the power of its elites, to the detriment of local and regional production and exchange systems. Final publication of the material from many of the European emporia has shown that exotic material represents only a fraction of the archaeological assemblages, which tend to be dominated by the products of local and regional production. To build on the work of those who destroyed the myth of "Dark Age" self-sufficiency, archaeologists must now seek to understand how the much vaunted long-distance exchange systems articulated with local and regional systems. That work has hardly begun, but some attempt can be made by turning once again to the evidence from the emporia and their regions.

Typology
Emporia obviously are not unique to the early Medieval period in Europe. They are widely known anthropologically, especially in the context of colonial contact with present-day Third World countries, and there is evidence for their existence in the Iron Age and Roman northern Europe (Cunliffe 1988). R. Hodges introduced discussion of emporia into early medieval archaeology in his book *Dark Age Economics: The Origins of Towns and Trade, A.D. 600–1000* (1982). In this work, he argues that such sites could be fitted into a three-part typology.

Type A Emporia. Hodges argues that the earliest and most ephemeral gateway communities in early medieval Europe resembled the fairs that are documented in historical sources such as the *Icelandic Sagas*. Type A emporia were probably visited only periodically and seasonally by foreign traders. British sites such as Bantham in Devon and Ipswich in Suffolk, as well as Dalkey Island in Ireland, may be examples of such Type A emporia.

Type B Emporia. Hodges argues that Type B emporia should be seen as an attempt "to maximise this hitherto periodic long-distance trade. This class is characterised by planned streets and dwellings which overlay the earlier clusters of structures. . . . These structures were housing

not only increased numbers of alien traders but also a considerable native work force to provide for the mercantile community" (Hodges 1982:52). Numerous examples of this type of emporium have been found, some of which are discussed in more detail below.

Type C Emporia. With changes in the social and political structures of the societies concerned, the trajectories of the emporia could take one of two directions. They could either totally disappear as a result of their "incompatibility" with the new social structures, or they could function, in an altered form, within a regionalized production and distribution system.

This entry focuses on what Hodges calls the Type B emporia, since these appear to represent the fluorescence of the associated production and exchange system. The archaeological evidence can be used to explore the significance of such sites for the development of complex social and political systems in the eighth and ninth centuries. The sites of Ribe (Denmark), Dorestad (Holland), and Hamwic (England) are used as exemplars. Among the other emporia of early medieval Europe are London, Ipswich, York (England), Hedeby (Denmark), Birka (Sweden), and Quentovic (France). (For brief descriptions, see Hodges 1982:66–86; Clarke and Ambrosiani 1991.)

Ribe
Ribe lies on the west coast of Denmark, and the historical sources have long been used to argue that it is one of the oldest, if not the oldest, town in that country (Bencard and Jorgensen 1990:576). Excavations have shown that a small village existed there in the late seventh and early eighth centuries (Frandsen 1989:37). This was all to change by the second decade of the eighth century.

Excavations in several parts of the town have produced evidence for a series of parallel ditches that probably divided the settlement into a series of equal plots: "the ditches were dividing lines between a row of plots, which marked the founding of a market-place" (Bencard and Jorgensen 1990:578). The ordering of these plots bespeaks planning and suggests that a centralized authority may have been implicated in the development of the site. The date of this planned settlement is provided by dendrochronology (tree-ring dating).

Soon after the settlement was laid out, a well, constructed from barrels, was sunk through the site. Dendrochronological studies of the wood show that it must have been felled c. A.D. 707. Other fragments of wood found on the site have been dated to A.D. 719, while

E

additional wood fragments were recovered from the wattle fences that were found in parts of early medieval Ribe. These have been dated to the middle of the eighth century. These dates indicate that Ribe was laid out as a planned settlement sometime c. A.D. 710.

Ribe is situated at the point where "north-south traffic on the land crosses a water route, the Ribe River, directly connected to the tidal sea" (Frandsen and Jensen 1987: 187). The finds from the site bear out the geographical potential of the location. Glass beakers, pottery, and basalt lava quern stones came from the Rhineland. It is probable that raw material for the production of jewelry, bead making, and bronze artifacts came from the same area (Frandsen and Jensen 1987:188). The most diagnostic of the imported pottery is known as Badorf Ware from the middle Rhineland and dates from c. A.D. 780–880 (Frandsen 1989:40).

More than one hundred *sceattas* (small, silver coinlike objects) have been recovered from Ribe, and it has been suggested that they were produced there (Bencard and Jorgensen 1990:582). In European terms, it is generally agreed that the types found at Ribe must have been produced between 720 and 755. These objects are commonly thought to have been used in long-distance exchange because of their association with emporia. However, if these objects were actually made at Ribe, they also point to craft production on the site.

In fact, there is a great deal of evidence for craft production on this site, and the fact that there was such large-scale production on one site immediately suggests that there must have been contact with a much wider area of consumption and, therefore, that there was trade of some sort. The archaeological evidence demonstrates the production of glass and amber beads, bronze jewels, gaming pieces, combs, and iron objects (Frandsen and Jensen 1987:187).

It is interesting to note that the craft producers at Ribe seem to have made their wares for the local and not the long-distance market. The bronze molds show that demonstrably Scandinavian types were being produced, and the beads are certainly north European in form.

In summary, Ribe is a site with good evidence for long-distance trade and craft production that was occupied throughout the eighth century. There are periods of abandonment on the site, and it is possible that activity here was seasonal. Most significant, all the evidence points to the planned and controlled nature of this site. The laying out of the site in plots suggests that "the purpose was to rent them and/or to tax them. From them we can deduce that the initiative was that of a Danish overlord or king" (Bencard and Jorgensen 1990:582). The dendrochronological dates for the laying out of the site might allow it to be associated with a king named Ongendus. The association between emporia and powerful kings is one that will be returned to later.

Dorestad

Dorestad is one of the most important archaeological sites discovered in western Europe. Archaeological investigations began before the middle of the nineteenth century, but our detailed knowledge of the site is the product of uninterrupted excavation between 1967 and 1977, which exposed c. 30 ha of the early medieval emporium.

Dorestad is situated at the point where, in the eighth and ninth centuries, the Kromme Rijn, the Lower Rhine, and the Lek diverged. As such, it was, like Ribe, located at the focal point of a major communications system (van Es 1990:153). The excavations show that the early medieval emporium ran for c. 3,000 m along the old course of the Kromme Rijn. The harbor area of the settlement can be divided into three zones: the actual harbor along the banks of the Rhine; the trading settlement *(vicus)* inland from this on the left bank of the Rhine; and another zone of more scattered buildings beyond this.

The harbor area is typified by a series of causeways, c. 8 m wide, running from the riverbank into the Rhine. These wooden structures should probably be seen as a series of landing bays projecting into the river and providing the first indicator of trade at Dorestad. The regular distribution of these piers along the banks of the Rhine suggests that the harbor area may have been divided into a series of parcels c. 20 m wide, and it is possible that they continued into the *vicus* to the east (van Es 1990:157). Rows of rectangular wooden houses stood on these parcels with their short ends toward the river. It seems clear that "the *vicus* and the harbour together show a systematic layout which makes it likely that there must have been a certain measure of central and regulating authority behind it" (van Es 1990:157).

In the third zone of the emporium, the buildings (large wooden boat-shaped houses situated on enclosed rectangular plots) were less densely distributed than on the *vicus* area. The houses were also bigger than those on the *vicus,* "and since some of them had granaries as outbuildings they are interpreted as farms" (van Es 1990:158).

Archaeological, historical, dendrochronological, and numismatic evidence has been used to date the main period of activity in the harbor area. The riverbank must have first been used c. 675, with a major change of use taking place between 700 and 725. The end of the site can be dated by the same means to between 850 and 875 (van Es 1990:163).

What does the archaeological evidence reveal about the function of the site? The extent of the harbor area at Dorestad points to trade. Given the number of barrels found (reused as well shafts), it appears that there was a fairly sizable wine trade with regions to the south and east, while the many fragments of lava quern stones point to the export of millstones from the quarries in the Eifel Mountains near Mayen. The imported pottery came from production centers near Mayen and from the Vorgebirge between Bonn and Cologne in present-day Germany.

Beyond this, little is known about the long-distance trade contacts that were mediated through Dorestad, and this leads to an important problem that has rarely been addressed by archaeologists—the nature of the site as an emporium means that one is unlikely to find any evidence there for most of the objects that passed through it. Thus, weapons and precious ornaments of glass and metal may well have been shipped through Dorestad but are more likely to be found on the sites to which they were directed than at the emporium itself. As a result, very little is known about the extent and nature of long-distance trade through Dorestad, and the same can be said of the other sites discussed here. One can only assume that "[l]uxury goods which were small in size such as jewellery, weapons, textiles, glasses and stimulants—a few casks of wine, some sacks of subtropical(?) fruit, spices(?) would have been the main [long-distance trade] products in the eighth and ninth centuries. . . ." (van Es 1990:169).

At Dorestad, as at Ribe, there is abundant evidence for craft production. It is clear that Dorestad was one of the preeminent settlements in its own region, and it was from that region that many of the materials used in craft production were drawn. Wood for the construction of houses, ships, and landing bays would have been available in the immediately surrounding region, as would the animal products necessary for many of the crafts carried out at Dorestad. Wool for weaving was especially important. Large numbers of baked-clay loom weights have been found. In addition, objects such as bone combs, skates, awls, needles, playing counters, and amulets, made from the bones of cattle and horses and the antlers of red deer and the occasional elk, have been recovered. The demand for these materials by the inhabitants of Dorestad must have resulted in the creation of a series of social and economic relationships with the farmers of the surrounding region, giving us our first direct connection between local and regional production and exchange.

Metalworking is demonstrated by finds of iron slag, crucibles, and a few tuyeres. (A tuyere is the nozzle that delivers a blast of air to a furnace.) Iron was not smelted on the site, and it may have been imported in bars to be worked into finished artifacts. This also points to relationships with the inhabitants of the wider region (Heidinga 1987). The objects made from these iron bars included craft and agricultural tools, boat hooks, nails, chest fittings, keys, and knives. It is also possible that Frankish swords—one of the most prestigious artifacts of the early Medieval period—were also made at Dorestad, since some of them were found there.

The common assumption of self-sufficiency in the early Middle Ages was thought to be particularly true of large-bulk, low-value goods like cereals. However, recent study of the cereals from Dorestad may force a reconsideration of even that assumption. Many of the cereal samples recovered contain weed species that demonstrate a foreign origin for the cereals themselves. Most of these weed seeds suggest that the cereals probably came from southwest Germany. The author of the report reaches the startling conclusion that "foreign import of corn in medieval Dorestad may be considered proven and local cereal cultivation very likely" (van Zeist 1990:347).

There is no doubt that Dorestad was an important link in the long-distance trade network that scholars like R. Hodges and D. Whitehouse (1983) see as so important to the political and social development of early medieval Europe. What is now becoming clear is that it, and many other emporia, were also important regional centers, and that control over regional production should be considered as essential to their functioning, and to elite power, as control over long-distance trade.

Hamwic

Excavations in the area of early medieval Southampton (Hamwic) have been going on since the nineteenth century, in the context of the extraction of brickearth. Most of the scientific excavations, however, have taken place since World War II. About 4 percent of Hamwic has been excavated and shows that, in the late seventh century, c. 45 ha of land were enclosed by a deep ditch. In terms of area, it was about twenty times larger than any other site in Wessex; in demographic terms, about forty to eighty times larger (Hodges 1989:86). Within this enclosure, a gridded street system was laid out consisting of three north-south streets and at least six interconnecting

E

east-west streets (Hodges 1989:80). At Hamwic, as at Dorestad and Ribe, therefore, there is evidence for the planned layout of the site and the intervention of some authority. All the evidence seems to point to King Ine of Wessex (688–726).

Hamwic has always been presented as a prime example of an emporium dealing in long-distance trade between the elites of Anglo-Saxon England and the Continent. There is evidence for such trade. Imported pottery came mostly from sources in northern France. Imported glassware, metalwork, ivory, bone work, quern stones, and hones are also found (Hodges 1989:84). Analysis of some pottery sherds shows that they formerly contained a mixture of meat and olive oil, pointing to the importation of the latter (Evans 1988:123). But one should also remember the point made about Dorestad—that one should not always expect to find the objects of long-distance trade in the emporia themselves.

The role of the emporia in long-distance trade has recently been downplayed. At Hamwic, for example, local pottery constitutes about 82 percent of the excavated assemblage (Timby 1988:73). As at Dorestad and Ribe, there is much more evidence for local ceramic production.

In addition to pottery manufacture, iron, copper alloy, lead, gold, bone and antler, wool, textiles, leather, glass, and wood were worked at Hamwic (Brisbane 1988:104). Further evidence for craft production, and perhaps its relationship with long-distance exchange, comes in the form of the numerous *sceattas* found, and known to have been made, on the site (Metcalf 1988:18–19).

As with Dorestad, the evidence for craft production on the site presupposes relationships with the region around Hamwic. Animals must have been supplied to make some of the craft products and also for subsistence needs:

> the animals represented [in the bone assemblage] were those that served other needs as well, and the patterns of age at their slaughter give good grounds for suggesting that they were valued for the contribution made in their lifetime as well as for their meat, and for those products such as horn and hide which would come once and for all after death (Bourdillon 1988:180).

A study of the cereals show that most were processed outside the settlement and then brought into the town (Hodges 1989:84). As J. Bourdillon suggests of Hamwic, "one has a sense of *considerable integration,* of animals that have been reared and used in the countryside coming to the end of their lives in the town" (Bourdillon 1988:184,

emphasis added). As with Dorestad and Ribe, we should no longer see Hamwic simply as one node in a panregional, long-distance trading system. It had considerable impact on the economy, and, therefore, on the people, of the region.

Conclusion

It has become clear that, in their reaction to the spurious orthodoxy of an autarkic, self-sufficient, and barbarian early Middle Ages, archaeologists have come close to producing another equally spurious orthodoxy. The emphasis on long-distance exchange, on the importance of prestige goods and gift giving, as the essential basis for the structuring of social relationships in early medieval Europe (i.e., as the basis for power) ignores the fact that, in such societies, most economic exchanges take place at the local level. Until recently, it has blinded many archaeologists to the fact that the control of local and regional production and distribution were equally, if not more, important (but see Astill 1985). The detailed analysis of the artifactual, faunal, and botanical material from the emporia has resulted in a change in that balance, a change that does not seek to ignore long-distance trade but rather to place it within the context of regional developments.

It is possible that the "belt and Hunnish sword" that the Carolingian Emperor Charlemagne (742–814) sent to King Offa of Mercia (d. 796), and referred to in a letter (Whitelock 1979:no. 197), passed through emporia like those discussed previously and that they exemplify the type of prestige-goods exchange once thought to typify the "economy of power" of the early Middle Ages. In light of the above discussion, however, it is likely that the wool cloaks and quern stones referred to by Charlemagne in the same letter were equally significant. Again, the faunal remains from Hamwic are significant since they show that

> Hamwic was not just a production centre for a few elitist gifts. In particular, the bone remains give an indication of the importance of wool and cloth and of the manufacture of pins, needles, and of combs, some indeed decorated with traces of refinement but many of them robustly shaped to serve a sound practical use and surely ideal for the various processes involved in the making of cloth (Bourdillon 1988:192).

What this, and the information from the other emporia considered here, reveals is not only that trade across regional and "national" boundaries did exist, that the emporia were important elements in this trade, and that kings were likely to have been heavily involved in this trade, but also that this trade was dominated by the craft products of the emporia and their regions (like the cloth from Hamwic) and may have included products like cereals and wine (see the previoius discussion of Dorestad). What this reassessment of the archaeology of early medieval emporia has done is to demonstrate once again the fallacy of notions of "Dark Age" autarky and to show that the economics of the period were even more complex than was proposed by those who believed in primacy of the long-distance exchange of prestige goods.

FURTHER READINGS

Astill, G. Archaeology, Economics, and Early Medieval Europe. *Oxford Journal of Archaeology* (1985) 4(2): 215–231.

Bencard, M., and L. Jorgensen. The Foundation of Ribe. *Antiquity* (1990) 64:576–583.

Bourdillon, J. Countryside and Town: The Animal Resources of Saxon Southampton. In *Anglo-Saxon Settlements*. Ed. Della Hooke. Oxford: Blackwell, 1988, pp. 176–196.

Brisbane, M. Hamwic (Saxon Southampton): An Eighth Century Port and Production Centre. In *The Rebirth of Towns in the West, A.D. 700–1050*. Ed. R. Hodges and B. Hobley. London: Council for British Archaeology, 1988, pp. 101–108.

Clarke, H., and B. Ambrosiani. *Towns in the Viking Age.* Leicester: Leicester University Press, 1991.

Cunliffe, B. *Greeks, Romans, and Barbarians: Spheres of Interaction.* London: Guild, 1988.

Evans, J. Report on the Organic Residues on Two Vessels from Sou 31. In *Southampton Finds*. Vol. 1: *The Coins and Pottery from Hamwic*. Ed. P. Andrews. Southampton: Southampton City Museums, 1988, p. 123.

Frandsen, L. Trade, Coins, and Foreign Influences during Pre-Viking and Viking-Age Ribe. In *Coins and Archaeology*. Ed. by H. Clarke and E. Schia. BAR International Series 556. London: British Archaeological Reports, 1989, pp. 37–42.

Frandsen, L., and S. Jensen. Pre-Viking and Early Viking Ribe: Excavations at Nicolajgade 8, 1985–86. *Journal of Danish Archaeology* (1987) 6:175–89.

Heidinga, H. *Medieval Settlement and Economy North of the Lower Rhine: Archaeology and History of Kootwijk and the Veluwe (the Netherlands)*. Cingula 9. Assen: Van Gorcum, 1987.

Hodges, R. *Dark Age Economics: The Origins of Towns and Trade, A.D. 600–1000*. London: Duckworth, 1982.

———. *Primitive and Peasant Markets*. Oxford: Blackwell, 1988.

———. *The Anglo-Saxon Achievement*. London: Duckworth, 1989.

Hodges, R., and D. Whitehouse. *Mohammed, Charlemagne, and the Origins of Europe*. London: Duckworth, 1983.

Mauss, M. *The Gift: Forms and Functions of Exchange in Archaic Societies*. New York: Norton, 1967.

Metcalf, D. The Coins. In *Southampton Finds*. Vol. 1: *The Coins and Pottery from Hamwic*. Ed. P. Andrews. Southampton: Southampton City Museums, 1988, pp. 17–59.

Polanyi, K. The Economy as Instituted Process. In *Trade and Markets in Early Empires*. Ed. K. Polanyi, C. Arensberg, and H. Pearson. New York: Free Press, 1957, pp. 243–269.

Smith, C. Exchange Systems and the Spatial Distribution of Elites: The Organisation of Stratification in Agrarian Societies. In *Regional Analysis*. Vol. 2. Ed. C. Smith. London: Academic, 1976, pp. 309–374.

Timby, J. The Middle Saxon Pottery. In *Southampton Finds*. Vol. 1: *The Coins and Pottery from Hamwic*. Ed. P. Andrews. Southampton: Southampton City Museums, 1988, pp. 73–122.

van Es, W. Dorestad Centred. In *Medieval Archaeology in the Netherlands*. Ed. J.C. Besteman, J.M. Bos, and H.A. Heidinga. Assen: Van Gorcum, 1990, pp. 151–182.

van Zeist, W. The Palaeobotany of Early Medieval Dorestad: Evidence of Grain Trade. *Proceedings of the Section of Sciences of the Koninklijke Akademie van Wetenschappen* (1990) 93 (3):335–348.

Whitelock, D., ed. *English Historical Documents*. Vol. 1. 2nd ed. London: Eyre Methuen, 1979.

John Moreland

SEE ALSO

Birka; Dendrochronology; England; Haithabu; Ipswich; London; Markets; Quentovic

England

In England, as in other areas of Europe, the modern discipline of medieval archaeology was born in the ashes of World War II. While pagan Anglo-Saxon burials and other medieval antiquities were examined by pioneering antiquaries as early as the seventeenth century, the systematic study of medieval sites using modern archaeological

E

techniques developed only in the last half of the twentieth century. Bomb damage in London and other major cities provided unprecedented opportunities to explore buried remains of medieval towns and cities. In addition, programs of urban redevelopment and highway construction have led to the discovery and exploration of medieval sites in both urban and rural areas.

Winchester Excavations

The excavations at Winchester, a cathedral town in south-central Britain that briefly served as the capital of England, played an important role in the development of medieval archaeology in the British Isles in the 1960s. A major program of excavation was carried out in Winchester between 1962 and 1971 in advance of urban redevelopment. The excavation program was directed by Professor Martin Biddle, now of Oxford University. Major research excavations were conducted at several locations in Winchester, including the Brook Street (Tanner Street) site, the Cathedral Green, the Bishop's Palace, and the castle. Smaller excavations were carried out at a number of other locations within the town. In addition, rescue excavations have continued in and around Winchester since the conclusion of the main research program in 1971.

The Winchester excavations were important to the history of medieval archaeology in England for several reasons. First, the Winchester project was the first large-scale program of archaeological research to have been conducted in a medieval city in England. The program employed hundreds of student volunteers from the British Isles and North America and served as an archaeological training ground for an entire generation of excavators. Second, in 1962 most archaeologists and historians believed that Winchester maintained its original Roman street plan. Excavations throughout Winchester showed clearly that the city had been replanned in the later ninth century and that the existing street plan is, in fact, late Saxon in date. Finally, large-scale, open-area excavations at the Brook Street site revealed many details of day-to-day life in medieval Winchester.

Although the Winchester excavation program was certainly innovative and productive, the project was not an unqualified success. Excavation must be followed by timely publication in order for archaeological data and conclusions to reach a wide audience. While Biddle and his colleagues regularly published interim reports on the Winchester excavations in the *Antiquaries Journal,* the final results of the medieval archaeological projects did not appear in book form until 1990 (Biddle 1990b). During that time, standards for archaeological recovery changed. For example, in the 1960s the animal bones at Winchester were hand collected without fine screening; by 1990 most excavators used fine screening to recover small bones of fish and birds. The lesson to be learned from the Winchester excavations is that the plan for an archaeological project must include plans for the rapid analysis of the materials excavated and timely publication of the results.

York Excavations

The other major large-scale urban excavation project that has been carried out in England since the 1970s is centered in York. York is located at the confluence of the Ouse and the Fosse Rivers in northeastern England. The city was founded by the Roman ninth legion in A.D. 71, and it was one of England's most important cities in both Roman and medieval times. The York Archaeological Trust, directed by Peter V. Addyman, was founded in 1972 as a response to accelerated development that threatened the city's archaeological heritage. Major excavations began in York in 1973, and excavation and research continue to the present day.

The founders of the York Archaeological Trust were in an excellent position to learn from Biddle's experiences at Winchester. Addyman and his colleagues were concerned about the timely publication of the results of urban excavations. They developed a modular publication series, The Archaeology of York, to disseminate the results of their excavations (Addyman, ed. 1976–1999). Through 1999, fifty-three titles were available in the series, and more are published each year. As a result of this innovative publication process, the York excavations have had a much greater impact on international medieval archaeology than the Winchester excavations had.

The excavations at York have revealed intimate details of life in this important medieval city. While there is little evidence for fifth- and sixth-century settlement in York, excavations at the Fishergate site near the River Fosse have revealed a seventh- to ninth-century trading settlement, or wic, similar to the emporia known from Hamwic, London, and Ipswich. It is likely that this trading center was established to serve the needs of York's ecclesiastical and royal center. The excavations at the Fishergate site revealed the remains of ninth-century timber buildings and evidence for a number of crafts, including metalworking, the preparation of furs, the manufacture of bone and antler combs, textile production, and leather- and woodworking.

The excavation of Viking Age sites in York have produced some of the most spectacular discoveries (Hall 1984). Historical sources indicate that the Vikings captured York in 866, and archaeological research has shown that this was followed by a tremendous boom in urban development. Beginning in the early 1970s, excavations at the Pavement site and later at the Coppergate site have revealed information on day-to-day life in Viking times, including houses and workshops, trade, and intensive craft production. The unique soil conditions of the Coppergate site, in particular, allowed for the preservation of organic artifacts such as wood, leather, textiles, and plant remains.

Excavations at the Coppergate site indicate that parts of the Viking city of York, Yorvik, were organized into long, narrow tenement plots that included both houses and workshops. The tenth-century oak houses have yielded large quantities of domestic items, ranging from frying pans to gaming pieces. The Viking period inhabitants of Yorvik engaged in a number of crafts, including jewelry making, metalworking, the production of antler combs, and leather working. After the major excavations at Coppergate were concluded, the Yorvik Viking Center was erected on top of the site. This center allows visitors to experience the sights and sounds of tenth-century Viking York.

The York excavations have also provided significant new information about the High Medieval city. The two castles that were erected by William the Conqueror (1028–1087) have been examined through excavation, and archaeologists have also excavated the Benedictine Abbey of St. Mary's, the old Jewish burial ground, a leper colony, and a number of parish churches.

The York excavations are important not only for the contribution that they have made to medieval archaeology in England, but also for their broader contribution to the public's understanding of archaeology and the role that archaeology can play in the study of medieval cities. Members of the York Archaeological Trust research team are involved in excavation, conservation, research, publication, and exhibition. Public education has always played an important role in the trust's mission. In addition to the popular Yorvik Viking Center, the York Archaeological Research Center has educated thousands of people, from schoolchildren to old-age pensioners, about the methods and techniques used in archaeological research.

Wharram Percy and the Deserted Medieval Village Research Project

While the Winchester and York excavation projects changed the nature of urban medieval archaeology in England, the forty years of archaeological research at Wharram Percy transformed the archaeology of medieval rural villages in the United Kingdom. Wharram Percy is located in rural Yorkshire, and it is one of c. three thousand deserted medieval villages known in Britain. When excavation began at Wharram Percy in the early 1950s, most historians thought that these villages were deserted as a result of the Black Death in 1349. Research at Wharram Percy and other deserted medieval villages has shown conclusively, however, that they were depopulated as a result of economic changes in the fifteenth century.

While the initial excavations at Wharram Percy were designed to identify the date of depopulation, the research strategy, under the leadership of Maurice Beresford and John Hurst (1990), quickly changed to one that focused on a study of peasant lifeways and material culture and on the development of the village during the Middle Ages. Excavations at Wharram provided unparalleled data on the structure of peasant farms and village layout in the Middle Ages, yielding information that was unavailable from historical records. Although the excavations at Wharram Percy concluded in 1991 after forty seasons, the site has been preserved as a historical monument and is accessible to visitors.

While Winchester, York, and Wharram Percy were landmark excavation projects in British medieval archaeology, our understanding of the archaeology of the English Middle Ages has been built up from a variety of excavation and research projects, both large and small. The following sections provide an overview of the state of contemporary medieval archaeology in England, including both the Anglo-Saxon and the High Medieval periods.

Anglo-Saxon Archaeology

Roman historical sources indicate that the imperial legions were withdrawn from Britain in the early part of the fifth century and that the citizens of Roman Britain were advised to see to their own defenses. Anglo-Saxon sources, such as the Venerable Bede's *History of the English Church and People,* describe the *Adventus Saxonum* (the

E

arrival of the Anglo-Saxons) in Britain in the early post-Roman period (fifth–sixth centuries A.D.). The Anglo-Saxons were speakers of a Germanic language whose original homelands were located in a broad belt from western Denmark to northern Germany and the Netherlands. Historical sources, however, provide almost no information about the day-to-day life, economy, and social and political organization of early Anglo-Saxon England. Most of what scholars know about life then is the result of archaeological research.

Archaeological research at Winchester, York, and a number of other Roman towns in Britain has shown that urban life did not survive long into the fifth century. While both Winchester and York apparently continued to function as important places, after c. A.D. 400 they were no longer home to dense urban populations and large numbers of nonagricultural workers. By the early fifth century, Roman towns in Britain had ceased to function as cities; early Anglo-Saxon England took on a decidedly rural character.

Only a small number of early Anglo-Saxon rural villages have been extensively excavated. The best known of these is undoubtedly the village of West Stow in Suffolk, where half a dozen small timber dwellings are surrounded by sunken-featured buildings that may have served as outbuildings and workshops. Although the excavation of the West Stow village yielded unprecedented information on day-to-day life in early Anglo-Saxon times, the West Stow cemetery was unscientifically excavated in the nineteenth century. It is now not possible to associate specific groups of artifacts with individual burials, so very little is known about burial rituals and social organization at West Stow. Since the 1980s, an extensive program of excavation was carried out at the early Anglo-Saxon village and cemetery at West Heslerton in Yorkshire. Both the village and the cemetery have been excavated using modern techniques, and the results of this excavation will undoubtedly shed new light on Dark Age life in England.

The vast majority of early Anglo-Saxon archaeological sites that have been excavated are cemeteries and burials. Well more than twenty-five thousand early Anglo-Saxon burials are known from England, and more are being discovered each year. Both inhumation and cremation were practiced by the early Saxons. There is a great variety in the quality and the quantity of grave goods associated with individual burials, suggesting that early Anglo-Saxon society was characterized by significant differences in social status, political power, and material wealth. While the wealthiest fifth- and sixth-century graves are usually found within communal cemeteries, by the seventh century they are often spatially isolated. Many of the richest seventh-century burials are associated with royal sites (Arnold 1984). Sutton Hoo, for example, appears to be associated with the East Anglian capital at Rendlesham. This may reflect the emergence of a small number of more powerful Anglo-Saxon kingdoms in the seventh century (see Arnold 1996).

Changing burial practices are just one of a number of social and economic transformations that took place in England in the seventh century. Many of the early Anglo-Saxon villages, including West Stow, were abandoned in the early to mid-seventh century, and a number of new settlements were established at that time. During the seventh and eighth centuries, emporia were established at Hamwic (Southampton), Ipswich, London, and York. Intensive archaeological research indicates that these settlements specialized in craft production and long-distance and regional trade. The emporia also appear to be closely associated with centers of political and ecclesiastical power.

Many Anglo-Saxon towns grew rapidly in the ninth, tenth, and eleventh centuries, and it was during the late ninth century that Winchester received its modern layout. Winchester's street plan includes four main elements: a main east-west axis street, a series of north-south streets running perpendicular to the axis street, smaller back streets behind the axis street, and an intramural road. Biddle (1990a) has suggested that the replanning of Winchester was a conscious reaction by King Alfred (849–899) to the threat posed to the Anglo-Saxon Kingdom of Wessex by the Vikings and that Winchester is one of many late Saxon planned towns that were established at this time. This replanning not only served to strengthen the defenses of Wessex, but also seems to have facilitated the growth of trade and commerce in Winchester and elsewhere in southern England.

The Norman Conquest (1066) forever altered the English political landscape, and it also left its mark on the architectural landscape. Motte-and-bailey castles were established by the Normans to control many of England's towns and cities. A number of these castles have been explored archaeologically, including the two that were built by the Normans in the city of York. Many cathedrals were rebuilt during the early years of Norman rule, including Winchester Cathedral and the great Minster at York. The impact of the Norman Conquest was far less marked on day-to-day life in medieval England. Domestic architecture, ceramics, metalwork, and patterns of agriculture and animal husbandry remained essentially changed throughout most of the eleventh century.

The High Middle Ages in England

The archaeology of this High Medieval period in England differs from earlier medieval archaeology in two important ways. First, there are simply far more historical sources available for the later Middle Ages. While the fifth and sixth centuries can be treated almost as a prehistoric period because the historical sources are so few, archaeologists working on later medieval sites have access to a wide range of documentary records. These historical records can be used in conjunction with archaeological data to produce a more nuanced and well-rounded picture of day-to-day life in the High Middle Ages. Second, archaeologists have explored a much wider range of High Medieval sites. While more early medieval excavations in England have focused on rural settlements, towns and trading settlements, churches, and cemeteries, archaeologists working in the later Middle Ages have also examined castles, hunting lodges, hospitals, and especially monastic foundations.

The 1971–1983 research program at Norton Priory is a classic example of the kind of multidisciplinary research that can be carried out on monastic sites in England (Greene 1989). Documentary sources provided some information on the history of the priory; archaeological fieldwork allowed the layout of the monastic buildings to be reconstructed; and the scientific study of human skeletons and food remains allowed the diet and health of the cannons to be reconstructed. The project also examined the history of the property after King Henry VIII's (1491–1547) dissolution of the monasteries in the early sixteenth century.

Nevertheless, most of what we know about the archaeology of the High Middle Ages in England is a result of urban excavations. In addition to the long-term archaeological research projects at Winchester and York, programs of archaeological research and conservation have been established in many other medieval towns and cities.

These programs are critical for archaeology's future since many important archaeological sites within towns and cities are threatened by urban growth and redevelopment. If steps are not taken to conserve medieval sites, many will disappear within a generation. This is one of the main challenges facing medieval archaeology in England and elsewhere in Europe today.

FURTHER READINGS

Addyman, Peter V., gen. ed. The Archaeology of York (series). London: Council for British Archaeology, 1976–1999.

Arnold, Chris. Social Evolution in Post-Roman Western Europe. In *European Social Evolution: Archaeological Perspectives*. Ed. John Bintliff. Bradford: University of Bradford, 1984, pp. 277–294.

———. *An Archaeology of the Anglo-Saxon Kingdoms*. 2nd ed. London: Routledge, 1996.

Beresford, Maurice, and John Hurst. *Wharram Percy: Deserted Medieval Village*. London: Batsford/English Heritage, 1990. Additional information is available from a Web site entitled The Lost Village: The Story of Wharram at http://loki.stockton.edu/~ken/wharram/wharram.htm.

Biddle, Martin. Albert Ricket Archaeological Trust Lecture: The Study of Winchester: Archaeology and History in a British Town, 1961–1983. In *British Academy Papers on Anglo-Saxon England*. Ed. E.G. Stanley. Oxford University Press, 1990a, pp. 299–341.

———. *Object and Economy in Medieval Winchester*. New York: Oxford University Press, 1990b.

Greene, J. Patrick. *Norton Priory*. Cambridge: Cambridge University Press, 1989.

Hall, Richard. *The Excavations at York: The Viking Dig*. London: Bodley Head, 1984.

Pam J. Crabtree

SEE ALSO

Burghal Hidage; Castles; Deserted Medieval Villages; Emporia; Ipswich; London; Norton Priory; Sutton Hoo; Urban Archaeology; West Stow; Wharram Percy

F

Farm Abandonment (Iceland)

The first settlers in Iceland, generally thought to have settled there permanently in the ninth century, were farmers; keeping sheep and cattle was the main basis of their livelihood. The location of farms, therefore, depended on access to good haymaking and grazing land.

The appearance of abandoned farm sites in the Icelandic landscape, many in out-of-the-way, sometimes badly eroded inland valleys, has been noticed for a long time. Until recently, the abandonment of such valleys was blamed exclusively on the big epidemic of 1402–1404 *(Plágan mikla),* an epidemic known to have caused many deaths and hardship. Abandoned sites are already mentioned in *Landnámabók* (The Book of Settlements), an account of the first settlement of Iceland. The earliest surviving version dates to the late thirteenth century, but it is thought to have been compiled originally perhaps as early as c. 1100. Initial speculations on the causes of farm abandonment, which were based on general observations and began appearing in print in the eighteenth century, blamed abandonment on diseases, worsening climate, and natural disasters; later, more thorough area studies took into account other factors as well. Some studies, for example, have shown that farm abandonment had already begun before the 1402–1404 epidemic.

A number of area studies, largely based on documentary sources, were undertaken in the 1950s, 1960s, and 1970s. All showed extensive farm abandonment during the fifteenth century and cited epidemics as a decisive factor in the decline in settlement. The notable exception was a coastal fishing community in western Iceland where increased trade in fish caused an expansion in the population. There were two big epidemics during the fifteenth century: The first one, in 1402–1404, which later sources wrongly termed Black Death *(Svarti daudi),* temporarily caused drastic devastation. Most of the abandoned farms were, however, later reinhabited. The later epidemic, in 1495–1496, seems to have had a more permanent effect in some areas.

Reliance on documentary sources for the study of early farm abandonment in Iceland is problematic. Sources are scarce and incomplete until c. 1700, and many sites that were abandoned early are not mentioned in the few available sources. A method that has been successfully applied to the study of farm abandonment in the early period is tephrochronology (dating by means of volcanic-ash layers). The method combines a survey of building remains with the excavation of trial trenches in an attempt to date the occupation on the basis of identifiable and datable volcanic ash layers situated within, or in the vicinity of, the structures. Sometimes ash layers are found in the turf used as building material, providing a date after which the structure was built; sometimes ash layers are found sealing a structure after it had gone out of use.

Ash layers have been extensively studied by geologists in Iceland. They are identified in the field by stratigraphic relationships, by color (which also indicates chemical composition), and by grain size, and in the laboratory by their mineralogical, chemical, and physical characteristics. Some ash layers have been dated by radiocarbon (C-14) dating of peat or wood chips lying directly above or below them, but most are dated by stratigraphic relationships and by written records, mostly annals, which are of differing reliability. Although tephrochronology can be criticized and is not 100 percent reliable, it is among the better dating methods available.

F

Studies of farm abandonment, dated largely by this method, have been undertaken in different parts of the country. All have revealed settlements, which were occupied and abandoned early, located far inland, often in areas that today would be regarded as uninhabitable. It is clear that settlement extended farther inland during the first centuries of habitation.

Most farms today lie less than 200 m above sea level. A common factor among the abandoned inland sites is a location above that altitude. This high altitude is bound to have had some effect on their viability. Average temperature is estimated to fall by 0.6–0.7°C for every 100 m above sea level. In cases of drastic deterioration in climate, such a drop could be a decisive element for farm viability.

Evidence from both environmental studies and documentary accounts indicates that Iceland has suffered considerable erosion since the time of settlement, apparently as a result of human impact upon the environment: there is a strong correlation between the initial settlement of Iceland in the ninth century and the escalation in erosion. Some of the abandoned sites are now badly eroded, and it has been possible to demonstrate that these areas (Thórsmörk, Einhyrningsflatir in the south) already suffered severe erosion during the Medieval period. Erosion, therefore, seems likely to have contributed to the abandonment of these sites.

Volcanic activity is a likely contributor to abandonment in other areas (Thjórsárdalur, Hrunamannaafréttur in the south, Austur- and Vesturdalur in the north). In these places, volcanic ash has been found on the floors of dwelling houses. Volcanic eruptions have been shown to affect settlement in areas that suffer a heavy fall of pumice. The effect is particularly severe if the pumice fall takes place during the growing season or before the hay is harvested in the autumn. In many cases, the effect would have been only temporary, whereas other areas were eventually devastated, perhaps by repeated ash falls combined with other factors.

It is possible that would-be settlers made a wrong decision when choosing the location of some of the earliest sites. This may, for example, have been the fate of c. 150 sites mentioned in *Landnámabók* that are no longer occupied. At Hraunthúfuklaustur in Vesturdalur, there is very little lowland for haymaking. The pumice fall from Hekla in 1104/1106 may have been the last straw for the site. Natural disasters that changed the local environment may also have caused farm abandonment. Several sites on the south coast were abandoned for safer locations farther inland because of the encroachment of the sea. A change in the course of a river, which cut the farm buildings off from the haymaking area, may have contributed to the demise of Broddaskáli in the east.

Other possible reasons for farm abandonment, including social or economic causes, such as changes in land ownership resulting in possible changes in land use, are more difficult to establish because of the lack of written records. Such reasons are unlikely to be detected through archaeological methods, except perhaps for the economic ones. We know that the bishopric at Hólar in the north became a large landowner, not least in the Skagafjördur area, where the inland valleys of Austur- and Vesturdalur are located, as early as the fourteenth century. This may have affected the land use to some extent. Similarly, areas like Thórsmörk in the south, where several farm sites are thought to have been abandoned by the twelfth century, became communal grazing areas at some point. A detailed study of the documentary sources may reveal when this happened and whether it affected the area's initial abandonment. From the fourteenth century on, when fish became an important export item, migration to the seashore may also account for some of the inland abandonment.

There are no simple or monocausal explanations for settlement fluctuations in Iceland; a number of factors must have played a part. Some trends, however, are apparent. In most cases, marginal land was abandoned. Despite drastic farm abandonment for economic and social reasons during the fourteenth century, the best farming land, located in the lowland, is still farmed. The earliest abandoned sites seem largely to have been the far-inland ones, often located at high altitudes. The delicate highland vegetation was often ill-prepared for the activities of humans and grazing animals, rendering the land unusable for farming through erosion. Climatic fluctuations also played a part. Falling temperatures reduce hayyields, forcing more reliance on grazing, and thus contributing to the erosion. Epidemics certainly caused at least temporary farm abandonment. Last but not least, there are the social and economic factors, which are often not as easily detectable as the environmental ones. The increased emphasis on fish as a trade item is bound to have affected the farming community, causing people to migrate to the seashore. Access to fish no doubt also saved the farming communities from total extinction in times of hardship. The Norse colonies in Greenland had no such access and suffered extinction, probably in the late fifteenth century.

FURTHER READINGS

Gissel, S., Jutikkala, Eino; Österberg, Eva; Sandnes, Jørn; and Teitson, Björn, eds. *Desertion and Land Colonization in the Nordic Countries c. 1300–1600.* Stockholm: Almquist and Wiksell International, 1981.

Jóhannesson, Jón. *A History of the Old Icelandic Commonwealth: Íslendinga Saga.* Trans. Haraldur Bessason. Winnipeg: University of Manitoba Press, 1974.

Maizels, J.K., and C. Caseldine, eds. *Environmental Change in Iceland: Past and Present.* Dordrecht: Kluwer Academic, 1991.

Sveinbjarnardóttir, Guthrún. *Farm Abandonment in Medieval and Post-Medieval Iceland: An Interdisciplinary Study.* Oxbow Monograph 17. Oxford, 1992.

Sveinbjarnardóttir, Guthrún, P.C. Buckland, and J. Gerrard. Landscape Change in Eyjafjallasveit, Southern Iceland. *Norsk geografisk Tidskrift* (1982) 36:75–88.

Thórarinsson, Sigurdur. Tephrochronology and Medieval Iceland. In *Scientific Methods in Medieval Archaeology.* Ed. R. Berger. Berkeley and Los Angeles: University of California Press, 1970, pp. 295–328.

Guthrún Sveinbjarnardóttir

SEE ALSO

Deserted Medieval Villages; Radiocarbon Age Determination

Finland

In 1843 the Finnish author Zachris Topelius, subsequently professor of history at Helsinki University, asked a question that may have relevance even today: "Is there a history to the Finnish people?" His answer was negative. Although later idealistic-national historiography has tried to present a different view, the history of the Finnish state as such did not begin until 1809. At that time, Finland was granted its own central administration as a Grand Duchy of the Russian Empire. Previously, what was to become the territory of Finland was part of Sweden. In the Middle Ages, some parts of Finland—though not the whole area—were also part of the state of Novgorod or under its economic sphere of influence, and areas in the north were under the influence of Denmark-Norway.

Topelius's question concerned the political history of the Finnish people and Finland as a subject of history. Finland, however, already had its own cultural history before the period of autonomy—that is, the history of internal development and of the people. The methods of medieval archaeology help to unravel the spread of settlement, the means of livelihood, and economic relationships. The stages of social and political organization, which can be discussed with reference to churches and castles, can also be regarded as cultural history.

To write an entry on Finland from the perspective of medieval archaeology is difficult; medieval archaeology is unorganized, and little basic research has been done. One reason for this is that the historical period is seen as beginning with the appearance of written sources and with the first Crusade in the 1150s, which started the Crusades from Sweden. The National Board of Antiquities, the central antiquarian administrative agency that also directs research, has used this boundary in its practical work. The subsequent period was not the domain of archaeologists but of historians, cultural historians, ethnologists and, above all, art historians, who mostly concentrated on the architectural monuments and the restoration of medieval castles and churches. Fieldwork and publications concerning other medieval phenomena and research by other institutions, with the exception of the City Museum of Turku, were sporadic. A clear change in attitudes began in the 1970s, but so far this change has not had an effect on the organization and is not reflected in any essential increase in published research.

A total of 66 original medieval documents and 223 copies of documents have been preserved in Finnish archives. In comparison, the medieval collections of Sweden comprise more than 20,000 documents. The chronological distribution of these sources reveals the small number of written sources especially for the earlier Medieval period. They are also geographically unrepresentative and do not cover different areas of life equally. The documents concentrate on the activities of the church and state, urban culture, and trade. In fact, the limited and unrepresentative nature of the Finnish historical sources entitles us to use the German term *Frühgeschichte* (protohistory) for almost all the medieval period in Finland. In central Europe, the protohistoric period has traditionally been the subject of intensive archaeological research. The very limited number of documents concerning medieval Finland should not have justified such a limited interest in medieval archaeology.

If the number of documents is regarded as a criterion, the Middle Ages or, in fact, prehistory does not end for the whole country at the generally accepted date of c. 1530, the time of Gustavus I Vasa (king 1523–1560), the executor of the Reformation and a proponent of the

F

centralized state system. In northern Finland, prehistory continued to as late as the eighteenth century. This entry, however, deals with Finland up to the traditional closing date of the Middle Ages (c. 1530) and uses its 1939 geographical borders.

There are a few sporadic and taciturn documents from the latest prehistoric period, called the Crusade period (c. 1025–1150/1300) in Finland. The permanently settled area covered Finland proper, Satakunta, and southern Häme. In eastern Finland, there was permanent settlement at places in Savo, and settlements had also "conquered" the northwestern coast of Lake Ladoga. Cemeteries indicating permanent settlement have not yet been found far into northern Finland or in the areas along the coast of the Gulf of Finland. The problem of the abandonment of the Åland Islands at that time and the question of agricultural settlement at river mouths and along the river valleys of Lapland and northern Ostrobothnia are currently being discussed.

On the basis of material culture, the earlier, materially uniform area of permanently settled Finland was divided in the Crusade period into the western (primarily comprising Finland proper and Satakunta) and eastern (Savo-Karelian) cultural spheres. Häme, a zone of both western and eastern artifacts, was between these areas. There is no clear picture of settlement outside these three areas. Archaeological finds hint at the possibility that these other areas were under economic utilization from different directions. The archaeologically poorly visible Lapps, the hunter-fishers of the Finnish interior, probably lived in these regions.

The extent of rural settlement was decisively conditioned by the way these communities were able to utilize the soils of the plowable layer. The geographic distribution of permanent settlement was closely linked to available farming technology. These settlements were concentrated in areas of light postglacial Litorina clays. The lack of suitable technology prevented the spread of settlement based on field cultivation outside this area.

A phenomenon called *eränkäynti* (wilderness resource utilization) was closely linked to the farming culture, especially in Satakunta, Häme, and eastern Finland. This phenomenon implies the economic utilization of demarcated hunting and fishing territories by farmers in wilderness areas in the coastal regions of Finland as well as inland. Because of Finland's numerous lakes and long water routes, wilderness areas that were up to a few hundred kilometers from the home regions could be used for hunting and fishing, long-distance slash-and-burn farming, and trading with Lapps.

Eränkäynti acted as a support for subsistence strategies, but it also produced a surplus through which Finland was connected to the international commercial networks of the period. It was, above all, a fur-procurement economy serving foreign trade. This required places of exchange for commodities. Scholars have attempted to prove the existence of such sites mainly on the basis of vague place-name studies. The urban or townlike settlement of Varikkoniemi, dated to the end of the Iron Age and early Middle Ages, appears from time to time in the literature. It is a multiperiod settlement site, whose interpretation as a townlike settlement is based on the misinterpretation and manipulative use of archaeological observations and badly mixed finds.

Finland did not form a political entity at the end of the Iron Age. The regional names Finland, Häme, and Karelia, and tribal names based on them, are mentioned in the earliest documents. They correspond to some degree with cultural areas. Politically organized historical provinces have not, however, been conclusively demonstrated. For example, hillforts have had a marked role in organizational speculations, but the small amount of labor required to build them as well as their accidental and often peripheral location do not point to any large degree of organizational power. A parish system, however, was probably known.

By the Middle Ages, competition between east and west is reflected in the emergence of different cultural areas oriented in different directions. The same situation characterizes the Middle Ages as a whole and even the later history of Finland. The Scandinavian kingdoms began their eastern—and Novgorod its western—expansion. At the same time, the territory of Finland came between the spheres of influence of the Roman Catholic and the Greek Orthodox Churches.

In the Middle Ages proper, from the second half of the twelfth century, the spread of settlement continued as an internal, mainly spontaneous colonization. The development of agricultural techniques and especially of plows, on the basis of both western (ard) and eastern (forked plow) influences, made possible the cultivation of the heavy clay soils of southwestern and southern Finland and the consolidation of settlement. This area developed into the core of the field-cultivation region of Finland. Settlement consolidated in southern Savo and on the Karelian Isthmus. The settlers came mainly from Ladoga Karelia. The river mouths of southern Ostrobothnia were colonized mostly from Häme and Satakunta. Even the northernmost river mouths, the valleys of the Tornionjoki and Kemijoki Rivers, tempted colonists practicing animal husbandry, salmon fishing, and *eränkäynti* from as far as Karelia.

External colonization, the Swedish *landnam,* was directed toward the coasts of Uusimaa and southern and middle Ostrobothnia, where animal husbandry initially played a prominent role, although these areas gradually developed into field-cultivation areas. The greater part of inner and northern Finland was, however, without permanent settlement, and the wilderness resources of these areas were still used, especially by farmers from Satakunta, Häme, and Savo-Karelia. Their activities also included long-distance slash-and-burn cultivation. Lapps, of course, lived in these areas.

It is generally maintained that the use of wilderness resources and the formation of permanent settlement are linked. *Eränkäynti* served as a trailblazer for colonization and settlement. It made the unsettled backwoods familiar and led to the establishment of fishing saunas and wilderness bases, which gradually grew into new expanding settlements. Thus, the border between the farmer and the hunter-fisher gradually moved farther north. The spread of permanent settlement was no simple conquest or invasion but rather a complex process in which activities connected with farming gradually displaced the traditional sources of food of the hunter-fishers and made them adopt new ways of life or move to virgin areas in the north. From the point of view of the utilization of wilderness resources, colonization was devastating. The procurement of furs, the main article of trade, could not withstand large-scale colonization. Therefore, colonization was regulated, which explains its intermittent spread in certain areas.

The competition over the wilderness areas and Karelia led to the Treaty of Schlüsselburg (Sw. Nöteborg, Finn. Pähkinänsaari) in 1323. In this treaty, Sweden and Novgorod agreed to divide Karelia between them. The course and nature of the border is problematic. According to the latest interpretation, northern Finland remained an area of mutual utilization. The border did not, however, prevent a wave of slash-and-burn colonization from Savo beginning at the end of the fifteenth century and continuing to the end of the sixteenth century. This expansion was probably based on a productive variety of cereal, swidden rye, and a slash-and-burn technique called *huuhta.*

They were suited to the morainic landscapes and spruce forests of the interior Finland. Colonization was partly spontaneous, continuing beyond the political borders.

Thus, soil and other prerequisites of livelihood determined the economy, which, in turn, had its effects on social organization, settlement, customs, and material culture. At the end of the Middle Ages (c. 1500), Finland was divided into roughly two cultural spheres: the western arable cultivation area and the eastern slash-and-burn cultivation area.

By the fourteenth century, some of the established coastal trading sites began to develop into towns. Shore displacement characteristic of the northern areas of the Baltic greatly affected the location and abandonment of the towns. At the end of the Middle Ages, there were six towns in Finland: Turku (Sw. Åbo), Viipuri (Sw. Viborg), Porvoo (Sw. Borgå), Ulvila (Sw. Ulfsby), Rauma (Sw. Raumo), and Naantali (Sw. Nådendal). Rauma and Naantali developed around monasteries. The proportion of the population that was urban never grew large; as late as the eighteenth century it was only 5 percent. The inner organization and the prototypes of the plans of the towns came from Hanseatic towns. On the basis of archaeological finds, the material culture of the towns was like that of other Baltic towns. German influence was felt by the burghers of the towns, but there was also German settlement in the countryside.

Towns, above all, exported furs and fish, wooden vessels, and products of animal husbandry in exchange for cloth, salt, grain, and various luxury products. Markets had a prominent role in the local exchange of commodities.

In southwestern Finland, the infrastructure was composed of roads between towns, castles, and the most important centers of population. Chains of lakes and rivers were the main routes of communication in the interior and in northern Finland. Ice prevented communication over the sea in the winter, but in the inland snow made it possible to transport heavy goods by sledges, often following routes, such as bogs, that were obstacles to traffic in other seasons.

The farming economy was mostly self-supporting, but barter and monetization began to reach Finland as well as other peripheries of the Swedish realm in the fifteenth century. Coin finds also help outline development of commercial relations and different economic areas. Trade with Gotland is strongly reflected in the thirteenth century. From the fourteenth century onward, Swedish coins dominate except on the coast of Uusimaa and parts

F

of Häme, where the connections to Livonia, to the south of the Gulf of Finland, are reflected in the find material. This is probably a relic of peasant maritime trade that bypassed the towns. Commercial relations can also be seen in the preserved ecclesiastical material.

The first Christian influences came through commercial contacts. The connection between trade and Christianity is clearly demonstrated by crucifix pendants dated to the eleventh century. They have been found in wealthy male graves, unlike at Birka, a site of missionary activity, where they are found in female graves. The explanation is probably a phenomenon called *primum signum.* The reason for adopting the first sign of the cross was not always religious but more or less practical and economic; it made contacts with Christian merchants possible. It was certainly useful for the Church to favor "half-Christians" because it created better conditions for missionary activity.

In light of primsignation, the claims that the first wooden churches and chapels were built at trading places are reasonable. Sanctuaries may have been erected not only by foreign merchants, but also by local merchants and chiefs with their families, who were gradually adopting Christianity, for their own use and for that of their trading partners.

According to general opinion, the Church was the earliest organizer of society. The diocese of Turku comprised the whole of Finland. It was the youngest of the six dioceses in the archdiocese of Uppsala. The organization of ecclesiastical administration in Finland did not come into being until the thirteenth century, which was later than in the central areas of the Swedish realm. The same time lag can be seen in the building of the country's 101 medieval stone churches—which compare to 1,150 stone churches in Sweden, 271 in Norway, 100 in Estonia, and 2,650 in Denmark.

The churches of Ahvenanmaa form the oldest group, some probably dating as early as the thirteenth century but most to the fourteenth century. The Cathedral of Turku was contemporaneous, but otherwise the building of churches on the Finnish continent began in the fifteenth century. There were two church-building periods, c. 1420/1430–1490 and c. 1480–1550, which were centered in different regions of the country.

The churches of Åland should be considered as an eastern branch of the Swedish churches. The churches of the mainland Finland have a special position in the history of European architecture. Because they were built late, they do not have direct parallels, although masters from both the southern coast of the Baltic and Sweden certainly participated in the building of them. In the area east of the border of the Treaty of Schlüsselburg, parishes with village churches and village cemeteries were organized following the principles of the Eastern Church.

The early organizing process of the Church bears evidence of a behavior well suited to the diffusion of Church doctrine and influence. To attain influence, it was expedient to acquire as many and varied bases as possible; churches erected by merchants, private chapels owned by chieftains, and villages with their own churches were adequate for this purpose. Once there were enough bases, a consolidation of influence and power was required so that the small churches with their varied types of ownership and potential problems could be entrusted to the Church. Maintenance and improvement of the activities of the Church, now in a dominant position, demanded means. A private Church was not the best possible solution for tax collection. The time had now come for founding parishes. Some churches and chapels may have been changed into parish churches; some were perhaps necessarily left as village churches; others may have been totally abandoned. Economic booms were exploited, and churches were built as symbols dominating the landscape. Later population growth and the consequent new settlement that was also promoted by the Church expanded the populated area. This, again, made it necessary to establish new chapels and to divide parishes in order to maintain the Church's influence. Thus, the development of Church organization is a function not only of a pursuit of power and influence, but also of demographic development.

The state followed in the footsteps of the Church. At the end of the thirteenth century and the beginning of the fourteenth, the castles of Turku, Häme, and Viipuri were founded in the support of the Swedish "conquest." Until that time, ancient hillforts were in use. Castle provinces and civil administration developed around the central castles of the state. More castles were founded in the fourteenth century. Especially at the end of the fourteenth century, small castles were built. This was probably connected with the spread of feudal ideas to Finland. The Crown also reacted to the population movements by founding, as late as A.D. 1475, the castle of St. Olaf to safeguard the colonization of Savo. The town wall of the border town of Viipuri, the only fortified town in Finland, is from the same period.

Europe after the 1350s was plagued by a regression of population, but in Finland, on the European periphery, the Middle Ages were characterized by the spread, intensification, and growth of population. The grip of the Church and the state became stronger as settlement intensified. The contest between the east and the west over the inland regions and northern Finland was settled in favor of the west, in the most eastern and northern parts only after the end of the Middle Ages. Finnish society was integrated into the cultural sphere of western Europe.

FURTHER READINGS

Hiekkanen, Markus. *The Stone Churches of the Medieval Diocese of Turku: A Systematic Classification and Chronology.* Helsinki: *Suomen Muinaismuistoyhdistyksen Aikakauskirja* 101 (1994).

Jutikkala, Eino, and Kauko Pirinen. *A History of Finland.* 4th rev. ed. Espov: Wailin and Göös, 1984.

Klackenberg, Henrik. *Moneta nostra: Monetarisering i medeltidens Sverige* (Monetization in Medieval Sweden; with English summary). *Lund Studies in Medieval Archaeology* 10 Lund, Sweden: Lund University Press, 1992.

Nordman, C.A. *Finlands medeltida konsthantverk* (Arts and Crafts in Medieval Finland; with English summary). Helsingfors: Museiverket, 1980.

Orrman, Eljas. Geographical Factors in the Spread of Permanent Settlement in Parts of Finland and Sweden from the End of the Iron Age to the Beginning of Modern Times. *Fennoscandia archaeologica* (1991) 8:3–21.

Taavitsainen, J.-P. *Ancient Hillforts of Finland: Problems of Analysis, Chronology and Interpretation with Special Reference to the Hillfort of Kuhmoinen.* Helsinki: *Suomen Muinaismuistoyhdistyksen Aikakauskirja* 94 (1990).

Vahtola, Jouko. *Tornionjoki-ja Kemijokilaakson asutuksen synty: Nimistötieteellinen ja historiallinen tutkimus* (The Origins of Settlement in the Tornio and Kemi River Valleys: An Onomastic and Historical Study; with English summary). Oulu, Finland: *Studia historica septentrionalia* 3 (1980).

See also the following volumes:

Historiallisen ajan arkeologia Suomessa (Archaeology of Historical Period in Finland) (all articles in both Finnish and Swedish). *Turun maakuntamuseo, Raportteja* 6 (1984).

Historisk Tidskrift för Finland 4, 1977 (Special Issue on History and Archaeology).

Historisk Tidskrift för Finland 3 or 4, 1994 (Special Issue on History and Archaeology).

Kulturhistoriskt lexikon för nordisk medeltid från vikingatid till reformationstid 1–22 (1956–1978).

Suomen antropologi 4, 1987 (Special Issue on Swidden Cultivation, in English).

J.-P. Taavitsainen

SEE ALSO
Animal Husbandry; Birka; Novgorod; Sweden

Fishweirs

A fishweir is a man-made obstruction erected across the flow of water in rivers or coastal estuaries, behind which fish are either left stranded by the falling tide or diverted into a trap or a net. The word *weir* comes from the old Saxon word *wera,* meaning a structure for trapping fish (Seebohm 1890:152). In the British Isles, fishweirs were constructed of fences of interwoven timber hurdles supported by wooden posts, or walls built of stone. They were usually erected to form two rows of fences converging to form a V-shape in plan or, less commonly, were curved or semicircular in shape. They were normally positioned near the low-water mark, often with one arm of the weir linked to the upper foreshore. The wide opening of the weir usually faced upstream or toward the foreshore so as to channel the fish within the arms of the structure on the ebb tide. There was often a net or a basket trap at the apex, or "eye," of the weir, where fish were trapped. Other types of weir consisted of rows or basket traps. This type was used exclusively on the River Severn, where lines of large conical-shaped basket traps known as *putts,* each 4.2 m long and 1.8 m wide at the mouth, were anchored to the bed of the river in rows up to 120 strong (Jenkins 1974:45). Smaller baskets, 1.5 m in length, called *putchers* are still in use on this river, where they are erected in tiered rows several hundred in number.

The use of timber weirs and fishtraps is known from prehistoric times. Fishtraps dated to the Mesolithic period have been recovered from a former channel of the River Seine at Noyen-sur-Seine in northern France (Mordant and Mordant 1992). Evidence from the British Isles comes from Seaton Carew, near Hartlepool, Cleveland, England, where a timber hurdle, interpreted as part of a fishweir, was discovered under a layer of peat on the foreshore and dated by stratigraphic means to the late Neolithic/early Bronze Age (information supplied by Richard Annis). Evidence also comes from New Ferry, Lough Beg, Northern Ireland, where an eelweir structure

F

of stakes and wattling was found in an ancient riverbed and dated to before 1000 B.C. (Mitchel 1965).

For the Medieval period, there is a wealth of documentary evidence to show the widespread use of fishweirs, mainly under the ownership of the great religious houses and manorial estates. Such evidence is available in the form of charters, monastic chronicles, monastic and manorial rolls, and the *Domesday Survey of 1086*. Indeed, weirs are mentioned in pre-Conquest charters dating back nominally to the eighth century A.D. (Hooke 1981).

Although few medieval fishweirs have been excavated, there has been a growing body of positive archaeological evidence in recent years to support the documentary evidence.

In England, structures interpreted as the remains of fishweirs have been located in a gravel pit at Shepperton adjacent to the River Thames, where a row of wattled stakes was radiocarbon (C-14) dated to the fifth century A.D., and lengths of wattle fencing from the silts of the River Witham at Lincoln have been variously dated from the second century to the tenth century A.D.

In recent years, two large excavations have added to our knowledge of medieval fishweirs. One of these was at Colwick, Nottinghamshire, England, the other in south Wales. At Colwick, the remains of a Saxon weir were discovered beneath 5 m of gravel deposits on the floodplain of the River Trent. The weir was formed of a double row of roundwood posts between which was a series of wattle panels. About 1.0 km upstream, a large V-shaped weir was found buried under 4–5 m of floodplain deposits. This structure consisted of a double row of posts, one 100 m long and the other 30.8 m long, supporting wattled hurdling. Parts of this weir were still upstanding, and it was radiocarbon dated to A.D. 1050–1245. Farther upstream, at Hemmington Fields, Castle Donington, the remains of a further five medieval weirs and a possible prehistoric structure were found in an old river channel (Losco-Bradley and Salisbury 1988; Salisbury 1991).

In south Wales in the county of Gwent, a 1991 archaeological survey of 50 ha of the intertidal zone in the River Severn in advance of the construction of the new Second Severn Bridge recorded and excavated a whole series of fishweirs dated from the ninth century A.D. to the early post-Medieval period. These included three fourteenth-century weirs, each consisting of a complex of V-shaped post alignments arranged side by side, the mouth of each V facing upstream. They were 2–5 m long and 1.5–2.5 m wide across their openings. These were the framework of weirs that once held putt-type basketwork fishtraps. Also discovered was a large semicircular weir, 30 m long, formed of a double row of posts. A post from this structure gave a tree-ring felling date of A.D. 1203 or 1204. The remains of two hurdle weirs were also found, dated to the ninth and tenth centuries, respectively. Two putt fishtraps were also located at the mouth of a diverted stream that had formerly flowed into the River Severn, including one of ninth-century date, the oldest of its type so far discovered (Godbold and Turner 1993). From the same area, a small fourteenth-century fish basket was recovered and has been conserved.

Further evidence comes from Essex, England, where a whole complex of Saxon fishweirs was discovered in the estuary of the River Blackwater (*British Archaeological News,* January 1993). This complex consists of parallel rows of timber posts, some forming broad V-shapes, together with the remains of wattling. This is the largest medieval site of its type so far found in the British Isles and is estimated to contain more than thirteen thousand posts, with some post alignments extending up to 1.05 km in length.

Archaeological evidence has also come from the Fergus Estuary, County Clare, Republic of Ireland, where a line of roundwood posts with rods woven horizontally between them was discovered forming a barrier on the shore diagonal to the current (O'Sullivan 1994). This structure was radiocarbon dated to A.D. 534–646.

FURTHER READINGS

Gilmour, B.J. Brayford Wharf East, Archaeology in Lincoln, 1981–82. *Tenth Annual Report of the Lincoln Archaeological Trust* (1982): 20–24.

Godbold, S., and R.C. Turner. *Second Severn Crossing, Archaeological Response. Phase 1: The Intertidal Zone in Wales. Final Report.* Cardiff: CADW-Welsh Historic Monuments, 1993.

Hooke, D. *Anglo-Saxon Landscapes of the West Midlands: The Charter Evidence.* BAR British Series 95. Oxford: British Archaeological Reports, 1981.

Jenkins, J.G. *Nets and Coracles.* Newton Abbott: David and Charles, 1974.

Losco-Bradley, P.M., and C.R. Salisbury. A Saxon and Norman Fishweir at Colwick, Nottinghamshire. In *Medieval Fish, Fisheries, and Fishponds in England.* Ed. M. Aston. BAR British Series 182 (ii). Oxford: British Archaeological Reports, 1988, pp. 329–351.

Mitchel, N.C. The Lower Bann Fisheries. *Ulster Folklife* (1965) 11:1–32.

Mordant, D., and C. Mordant. Noyen-sur-Seine: A Mesolithic Waterside Settlement. In *The Wetland Rev-*

olution in Prehistory. Ed. B. Coles. WARP Occasional Paper 6. Exeter: University of Exeter, 1992, pp. 55–64.

O'Sullivan, A. Harvesting the Waters. *Archaeology Ireland* (1994) 8(1):10–12.

Salisbury, C.R. Primitive British Fishweirs. In *Waterfront Archaeology.* Ed. G.L. Good, R.H. Jones, and M.W. Ponsford. CBA Research Report 74. London: Council for British Archaeology, 1991, pp. 76–87.

Seebohm, F. *The English Village Community.* 4th ed. London: n.p., 1890.

von Brandt, A. *Fish Catching Methods of the World.* 3rd ed. Oxford: Fishing News Books, 1984.

S. Godbold

Flanders

See Sandy Flanders: Early Medieval Settlement.

Fonteviot

See Scotland: Early Royal Sites.

Forests

In certain countries, there was the idea that the king had special rights over unoccupied land, including rights to game animals and sometimes to trees, and then the right to make regulations to protect the king's interest. Such land was called *forest;* this is the original meaning of the word *forest* over much of Europe. The idea of forests and their special laws may have originated in Merovingian France. It spread to other countries, reaching England, for example, with the Norman Conquest (1066). Great nobles, as well as kings, could hold forests. Forestal rights did not necessarily give the king the ownership of the land, however.

The forest idea developed differently in different countries. In France and Spain, the king expected to hunt native game animals on major ceremonial occasions. For Spain, there is a fourteenth-century list of hundreds of "mountains" or "forests"—the word is not differentiated—and of whether each contained deer, bear, or wild boar. In England, where there was no unoccupied land, the king's rights were added to whatever else was going on. English forests were not closely linked to woodland. They functioned as a kind of informal deer farm. If a forest was declared in an area having no deer, they might have to be introduced; such animals were often fallow deer, originally from Asia. The biggest numbers of forests were in Wales and Scotland, and here, too, they were not connected to woodland. Forests were a status symbol of the king and those who aspired to near-royal rank. Besides venison, they produced money from fines for breaking the forestal regulations and opportunities to reward loyal henchmen with sinecures in the forest bureaucracy.

Forests commonly had a complex, straggling shape. They have left little specific archaeological record, apart from occasional buildings or observation towers called *standings.* The most complex archaeology is probably in Hatfield Forest, Essex, England. This small medieval forest survives almost complete with its woods and earthworks round them, ancient trees, a lodge, and a rabbit warren, as well as earthworks from earlier periods.

FURTHER READINGS

Cummins, J. *The Hound and the Hawk: The Art of Medieval Hunting.* London: Weidenfeld and Nicholson, 1988.

Rackham, O. *The History of the [British and Irish] Countryside.* London: Dent, 1986.

Oliver Rackham

SEE ALSO
Hunting

France

Medieval archaeology first developed in France as an independent field of knowledge in the mid-nineteenth century and soon diverged into two distinct streams: monumental and Merovingian archaeology. After World War II, the far-reaching changes in the ways history is studied, and even in how it is defined, combined with the unprecedented transformations of the landscape (these entailed, somewhat paradoxically, both the outright destruction of much of the archaeological record and also an enormous expansion of excavation—nearly always under salvage conditions), led to a rebirth of medieval archaeology that continues today. The character of archaeology and its practitioners has changed dramatically. Until the 1970s, most archaeologists were amateurs who, in the best of cases, studied and published the results of their work themselves; today, most excavations are directed by professionals (often young), and the study of artifacts and the publication of results are collaborative works involving specialists from a variety of disciplines.

F

Origins

Medieval archaeology in France was born of two emotions that crystallized during the Romantic Era. The first was nostalgia inspired by visible medieval monuments, threatened by "progress" in the form of political and economic revolutions. "Everywhere one is confronted by the ruins of churches and monasteries recently demolished," wrote the Vicomte de Chateaubriand in *La génie du christianisme* (1802), launching a passionate appeal to salvage the values as well as the vestiges of the medieval past, an appeal soon taken up by popular writers and scholars like Victor Hugo and Jules Michelet. The second was a fascination with the mysteries of the thousands of buried tombs that were coming to light as a result of deliberate research or, more often, of development, whose pace picked up rapidly as France's ancient, long-stable landscapes began to be transformed by the early phases of the Industrial Revolution. A concern for both standing monuments and remains hidden away in the earth, awaiting discovery, was expressed by some of the earliest pioneers of this new historical consciousness, such as Alexander Lenoir, who created the first national archaeological museum in Paris around 1800 (the Musée des Monuments Français, housed in a former Augustinian cloister) from works of art confiscated during the French Revolution. Lenoir also urged the creation of a national register of historical monuments, including ancient burial sites. These concerns became incorporated into public policy, beginning with a decree of the minister of the interior in 1810 instructing prefects to survey all "ancient monuments, abbeys and chateaux" in their districts and leading to the creation of the Inspectorate of Historical Monuments (Monoments) in 1830 (from which Historiques has evolved a corps of historical architects responsible for the upkeep of France's historical monuments). Further, in 1837, a national committee of leading scholars was created from which the prestigious Académie des Inscriptions et des Belles Lettres is descended; its role in regard to historical and archaeological research is analogous to that of the Académie Française in regard to literature. At the same time, a number of initiatives at the local and regional levels led to the formation of learned societies to encourage and sponsor research, including the Académie Celtique, which after 1814 became the Société des Antiquaires de France (modeled on the older Society of Antiquaries of London); the Société des Antiquaires de Normandie (1824); and the Société Archéologique du Midi de la France (Toulouse, 1831). Among the many scholarly pioneers of this formative phase, one figure stands

out: Arcisse de Caumont, who published, at the age of twenty-two, an *Essai sur l'architecture réligieuse du moyen âge,* which laid the basis for the chronological classification of medieval monuments, and began teaching a regular Cours d'antiquités monumentales at Caen. His publication of these courses in six volumes between 1830 and 1841 provided a standard theoretical reference work on the development of medieval art, classified into regional schools, and distinguishing between the two great phases: "Romanesque" and "ogival" (in fact, Gothic). Republished many times under the title *Abécédaire ou rudiment d'archéologie,* it became the basis for instruction in a new academic discipline, known as Christian archaeology (as opposed to classical, or prehistoric), whose content filtered down from seminaries and universities into the textbooks used in secondary and primary schools. Arcisse de Caumont also founded in 1834 the Société française d'Archéologie, whose annual congresses and *Bulletin monumental* continue to play a leading role in medieval scholarship from a predominantly art-historical perspective.

By this time, medieval archaeology in France was developing two distinct traditions, which, for more than a century, were to have very little to do with each other. The predominant tradition, soon to be enshrined in the universities and government offices, was centered on the study and preservation of standing monuments and works of art associated with them. Jules Quicherat, professor at the Ecole des Chartes, emphasized the need to combine accurate and precise description of monuments (improving on the more intuitive stylistic criteria of Caumont) with an attentive study of historical documents relating to them, thus creating the basis for art-historical scholarship. Meanwhile, the state-sponsored Historical Monuments Commission, which published the first list of fifty-nine protected medieval monuments in 1840, launched an ambitious program of restorations under Viollet-le-Duc in the period 1854–1879. The art historian Jean Hubert calls him "the most gifted, the most illustrious, and the most damaging *(néfaste)*" of architects, quoting his own definition of the term *restoration:* "To restore an edifice does not mean to maintain it, to repair or to remake it, it means to re-establish it in a complete state which may never have existed at any particular moment" (Hubert 1961:278). This doctrine led Viollet-le-Duc himself and disciples like Paul Abadie to rebuild such monuments as the abbey church at Vézelay, the castle of Pierrefonds, and the Cathedral of Saint-Front at Périgueux not as they might have been but as they thought they ought to look. This doctrine inspired the creation of numerous false medieval monuments, until a reaction set in at the end of the nineteenth century.

Early Christian and Monumental Religious Archaeology

The study of Christian origins can be traced as far back as the ninth-century Carolingian Renaissance, and medieval pilgrimages were the ancestors of archaeological voyages of discovery: the twelfth-century *Pilgrim's Guide* recommends a tour of the early Christian cemetery of the Alyscamps in Arles, still visited by thousands of tourists today. In the thirteenth century, the discovery of a late Roman burial vault *(hypogée)* with decorated Christian sarcophagi at Sainte-Baume in Provence created a new pilgrimage site, for one sarcophagus was attributed to St. Mary Magdalene. During the seventeenth and eighteenth centuries, as the techniques of historical criticism were developed at the Abbey of Saint-Maur by Benedictine scholars like Dom Mabillon (*De re diplomatica,* 1681), scholars and antiquaries also published illustrated studies of ancient and medieval monuments and artifacts (*Gallia christiana,* 1656; *Monasticon gallicanum,* 1697; Comte de Caylus, *Recueil des antiquités . . . ,* 1752), thus forging a set of scholarly tools that remain indispensable. An interest in excavation developed in France during the nineteenth century, as news of Battisa De Rossi's explorations of early Christian Rome became available in French translations (from 1865). Edmond Le Blant was inspired to begin a systematic collection of the *Christian Inscriptions of Gaul* (first volume published in 1865), a survey then extended to sarcophagi (1878 and 1886); these volumes were carefully illustrated with accurate facsimile renditions of the inscriptions and drawings and photographs of the sarcophagi. However, little excavation was done in France itself, where almost no early Christian buildings were known (in French North Africa, early Christian structures abounded and many studies were launched, including the excavations at Thamugadi and Tipasa in Algeria, where the French School of Rome played a leading role). Jules Formigé, an architect with Monuments Historiques, did undertake extensive restoration campaigns on the early Christian baptisteries surviving within the medieval cathedral at Aix-en-Provence (from 1914) and at Fréjus (1925–1932). But as recently as 1952, the early Christian baptistry of Marseille, with a splendid set of mosaics, was destroyed to make way for a rebuilding of the cathedral.

The meeting of the fifth International Congress of Christian Archaeology at Aix-en-Provence in 1954 renewed research perspectives in this field. The work of art historians Jean Hubert (*L'art preroman,* 1938) and André Grabar (*Martyrium,* 1946) pointed to a new understanding of the complexity and the originality of the early Christian monuments in their predominantly urban context and led to new projects, like the systematic survey of pre-Romanesque figurative monuments still underway in France. The predominant influence was that of the great historian Henri-Irénée Marrou, who showed that the era from the fourth to the eighth centuries should be seen rather as an era of dynamic creativity (the Age of late Antiquity) than one of decline and that the entire society, with its distinct culture, should be the object of a study in which all possible sources—literary texts and inscriptions, iconography and figurative art, excavation of cemeteries and religious monuments, whether partly still visible in elevation or totally demolished—would be brought into play. When this congress met again in France in 1986, the extraordinary results of years of excavation in Lyons and Vienne (by Jean-François Reynaud), in Grenoble (by Renée Colardelle), in Aosta (by Rinaldo Perinetti and Charles Bonnet) and in Geneva (by Charles Bonnet and his highly professional team) were becoming accessible not only to scholars, but to the general public, who could visit the carefully restored archaeological sites. Work on late antique sites continued to grow and to diversify after 1986, aided by a systematic survey of the written and archaeological sources *civitas* by *civitas* prepared by a team of scholars (Gauthier and Picard 1986) and by preparation of an atlas of early Christian monuments in France published by the Ministry of Culture (*Naissance des arts chrétiens,* 1991; another volume, in the form of a gazetteer, *Les premiers monuments Chrétiens de La France,* 1995–98).

The most ambitious excavations of medieval religious monuments in the earlier twentieth century were led by American professors: James Conant of Harvard University worked on the vast abbey church of Cluny in the 1920s and 1930s, while, after World War II, Sumner Crosby of Yale University studied the abbey of Saint-Denis, most famous for its rebuilding under Abbé Suger (1081–1151). Monastic archaeology in a broader sense, concerned with complex interrelations within the community and linking it to the larger milieu, has only recently been undertaken; a survey has been published by Clark Maines and Sheila Bonde, who have been directing a project focusing on the former abbey of Saint-Jean-les Vignes in Soissons. Many major and lesser medieval churches have seen excavation on some scale in recent years; one

F

can cite the work of Gabrielle Demains d'Archimbaud on the cathedral of Digne, Jacques Le Maho's ongoing study of the cathedral area in Rouen and of the site of Saint-Georges-de Borscheville, the excavations of the Rhone-Alpes group (Jean-François Reynaud in Lyons, Vienne, and Meysse; Michel and Renée Colardelle in Saint Julien en Genevois, Viuz-Faverges, and Grenoble), and the studies and the work of the BURGONDIE group under Christian Sapin, including funerary churches in Autun and Macon and the abbey church of Saint-Germain in Auxerre. The most impressive large-scale coordinated work in any single area is no doubt that of Charles Bonnet and his team in the canton of Geneva, work that includes the total excavation of the cathedral of Saint-Pierre (see the catalog of the 1982 exhibition *Saint-Pierre, Cathedrale de Genève: Un Monument, Une Exposition* at the Musée Rath Genève) and its environment, as well as thorough excavation of a number of other churches within the canton.

Merovingian Archaeology

In 1841, Arcisse de Caumont focused his celebrated archaeological seminar at Caen around the question of cemeteries rich in grave goods: were they Gallo-Roman? were they Merovingian? what criteria could be established to answer the fundamental questions of chronology and to interpret the cultural significance of such customs? Such questions had been asked with increasing frequency since the eighteenth century by antiquarians and excavators in England and the German states as well as in France, especially as agriculture, roadwork, and more recently railway building brought more and more graves to light. The questions also reflected a growing public fascination with the national origins of the major western European countries, stimulated by such literary works as Edward Gibbon's *Decline and Fall of the Roman Empire* and, in France, Augustin Thierry's *Récits des temps mérovingiens,* as well as by the Romantic nationalism then in fashion. Even as Caumont spoke, the first generation of professional excavators was providing answers to his questions, answers that created the field of Merovingian archaeology in France (in effect, a subfield of migration period archaeology in western and central Europe). The well-illustrated publication of the site in Selzen (1848), meticulously excavated by the Lindenschmidt brothers in the Rhineland, offered convincing reasons to attribute this necropolis to the Franks and to identify a "Frankish" material culture (Lindenschmidt and Lindenschmidt, 1969). In Normandy itself, a great pioneer was at work,

the Abbé Cochet, whose numerous excavations were quickly published in a remarkable series of books: *La Normandie souterraine* (1855), *Sépultures . . .* (1856), and *Le tombeau de Childeric Ier* (1859). Writing with verve and passionate conviction that make them still very readable today, he not only fit the archaeological facts neatly into the narrative framework provided by the written sources, he also made a passionate apology for archaeology as a new science that allows one to reconstruct the lives of the ordinary people seldom, if ever, mentioned in those same sources. Thus was established the interpretative paradigm that was to dominate Merovingian archaeology for well over a century and still has its proponents today. This assumes that the various barbarian peoples cited in the sources as invaders of the Roman Empire brought with them an elaborate set of funerary customs that must reflect, to some degree, their ancestral religious beliefs and perhaps their social structure as well. Since the historical sources are so few in number and so selective in their concerns, funerary archaeology could fill in many gaps, measuring, for example, how many barbarians actually settled in Gaul and how they interacted with the conquered Gallo-Roman population.

In the background of such questions lurked a highly polarized historical debate over the long-term significance of the "barbarian invasions." One side viewed the Germans as a healthy, if brutal, young society that revitalized the decadent Roman world, while the other stressed the superior cultural values of Roman civilization over the violent primitives considered to have "assassinated" it.

The rest of the nineteenth century and the beginning of the twentieth (up to the outbreak of World War I in 1914) saw an enormous amount of excavation, much of it conducted under the aegis of regional antiquarian societies and local notables: landowners, doctors, and a good many priests. A retired general named Frederic Moreau began his career at age 75 in 1873 and over the next two decades opened more than twelve thousand graves in the Aisne River Valley. He considered himself a serious researcher, took daily notes, and published more than twenty-four volumes, lavishly illustrated at his own expense. Nevertheless, the descriptions and the illustrations are highly selective, and the general would make a present of interesting artifacts to distinguished visitors. The value, intrinsic or pedagogic, of grave goods was a principal motive for excavation. The Emperor Napoleon III, a great promoter of archaeology in a nationalist perspective, encouraged the excavation of Merovingian cemeteries and assembled a personal collection of artifacts with the grave assemblages carefully noted; this was intended to go to the new Museum of National Antiquities at Saint-Germain-en-Laye, created in 1866. Some excavators, like the notorious Lelaurain, were, in fact, grave robbers, intent on furnishing the growing and lucrative market of collectors. Surveying the vast and badly plundered cemetery of Marchélepot in Picardy, Camille Boulanger lamented that we shall never know even approximately how many graves it once contained (thousands), let alone the variety of objects within them. Other excavators deserve to be counted among the fathers of modern scientific archaeology. Jules Pilloy carefully excavated hundreds of Roman and post-Roman graves, publishing a grave-by-grave description and appending many carefully drawn plates to his three-volume *Etudes sur d'anciens lieux de sépulture dans l'Aisne* (1880–1899). His paper to the Charleroi Congress (1891) used grave-assemblage data carefully to build a relative chronology of artifacts within the Merovingian period. Ferdinand Scheurer and Anatole Labloiter published the 291 graves of Bourogne (1914) in tabular

form, with a number referring each object to the sixty plates of colored drawings; they complemented this with photographs within the text and detailed *in situ* drawings of five important graves.

The assumption that ethnic and religious values dictated funerary practice continued to govern the interpretation of this material. In 1860, Henri Baudot brought out a lavishly illustrated book seeking to identify the barbarian Burgundians who ruled a kingdom extending from Burgundy east into the Alps and south into Provence from c. 460 to 536 (Fig. 1). C. Barrière-Flavy studied the graves in southwestern France for vestiges of the Visigoths, who had a kingdom there from 418 until they were driven out by the Franks in 507. The rhythm of excavation was seriously disrupted by World War I and the economic crises that followed. Virtually the only major figure still in the field was Edouard Salin, an industrialist from Lorraine who published his first excavation in 1912 and capped his career with the four-volume *La civilisation mérovingienne* (1950–1959). This enshrines

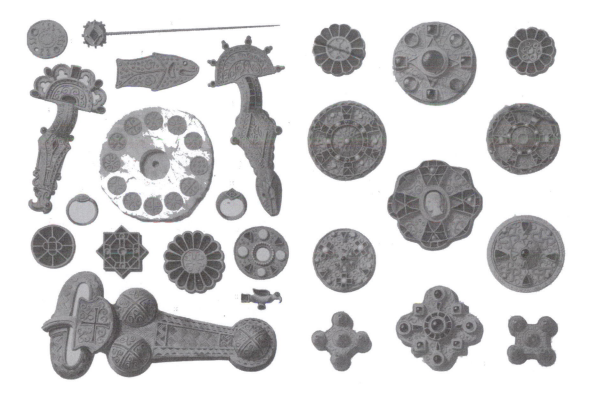

Fig. 1. Objects from graves found under the medieval church of Sainte-Sabine (Coté d'Or) in Burgundy in the mid-nineteenth century and published by Henri Baudot in 1860. Most are items of female ornament, including disc brooches in the cloisonné style (sixth century) and a triangular plate buckle from the seventh century with a prominent Christian cross on the buckle plate. These objects and the funerary practices they embody are no longer thought to derive from the Burgundians, who ruled this area as an independent kingdom c. A.D. 460–536, but to represent a regional variant of the burial fashions of the Frankish elite.

F

the ethnicoreligious paradigm and sometimes displays a tendency to overdramatize what are taken to be bizarre pagan barbarian burial rites. However, Salin also deserves credit for pioneering the use of laboratory analysis of artifacts, founding—along with Albert France-Lanord—the Musée du Fer in Nancy, for many years the only major laboratory in France where technical studies of metalwork could be done.

Merovingian archaeology stagnated for some years after Salin, who seemed to have dictated the answers to all the fundamental questions. Limited excavation, generally restricted to parts of cemeteries and often taking account only of object-laden graves, was carried out by amateur groups, like the Touring Club de France, on a weekend and vacation basis. The introduction of a stricter methodology (inspired by prehistorians like André Leroí Gourhan) and the creation of professional research structures were promoted by Dean Michel de Bouard of the University of Caen, who created a Center for Medieval Archaeological Research and started the review *Archéologie médiévale* in 1970. Results were spectacular. In the Caen region, previously thought to be barren of Merovingian cemeteries, site after site was discovered, meticulously excavated, and published, with technical studies of the various types of artifacts done in laboratories linked to the university and the CNRS (National Science Research Center). The necropolis of Frénouville was the first cemetery to be totally excavated and published in France; the study, which was published in 1975, was also the first to include a full-scale analysis of the skeletal material by a professional physical anthropologist, Luc Buchet. Fresh approaches to early medieval cemeteries were undertaken elsewhere. Some excavators continued to derive from the old tradition of dedicated amateurs, like Dr. René Legoux, a physicist who applied his skills in computer modeling as well as his scientific training to study the complex development of Bulles, a rural necropolis near Beauvais in the Oise. Others were full-time archaeologists attached to the CNRS or a university, like the team assembled by Gabrielle Demains d'Archimbaud at the University of Provence-Aix (known as the Laboratoire d'Archéologie Médiévale Mediterrenéene, or LAMM). Some were based in museums, like Claude Seillier of Boulogne and Pierre Demolon of Douai. Michel Colardelle began his career as a junior curator in the museum of ethnography in Grenoble but succeeded in creating an independent CNRS-based research team that has studied a wide variety of sites in the French Alps. Much of this work went into his general study (Colardelle 1983), the most thorough and innovative regional survey yet done in France, which develops methods of dating and interpreting burials with few or no grave goods. In the same region, but just over the border in the Swiss canton of Geneva, Beatrice Privati's exemplary excavation and publication *La nécropole de Sézegnin* (1983) was among the first to reveal the importance of wooden posthole structures within the cemetery that can be found only if all the area around the graves is as carefully examined as the graves themselves. She argues persuasively that what an old-fashioned excavator of the Salin school would have taken to be a typical rural pagan cemetery was articulated around three graves that, if undistinguished by artifacts, were nonetheless privileged because they were set off by a wooden structure interpreted as a Christian *memoria* (shrine). At Tournai, in Belgium, where Merovingian archaeology had begun back in 1654 with the chance discovery of the tomb of King Childeric I (d. 481), Raymond Brulet revolutionized our understanding of the generative phases of Frankish culture by revealing that the Childeric grave, once thought to be isolated, belonged to a rich funerary context, including a spectacular series of horse burials (see Fig. 1).

The renewal of Merovingian archaeology led to the creation, in 1979, of the Association Française d'Archéologie Mérovingienne (AFAM) under the leadership of Patrick Périn, who began his career as an excavator in the Ardennes and whose publications include a fundamental analysis of Merovingian chronological systems along with a history of Merovingian archaeology (Périn 1980). His seminar, formerly at the Ecole Pratique des Hautes Etudes (IVe Section) and now at the University of Paris I, has been the place for advanced students to obtain an overview of the field. AFAM holds a yearly congress whose papers are summarized in a *Bulletin;* it has sponsored a number of other publications, monographs, and collections of papers, as well as a bibliography of Merovingian archaeology by Michel Kazanski. Although the funerary evidence remains fundamental for this period, it is no longer regarded as a straightforward reflection of religion and ethnic identity; new interpretations seek to integrate it with the widest possible variety of data, for an enhanced understanding of political, social, technological, and economic, as well as cultural, history. New excavation programs are designed to take us beyond the fossilized cities of the dead *(necropolis)* and to recover more information about the living realities of early medieval society and their impact on future developments in medieval culture (Fig. 2).

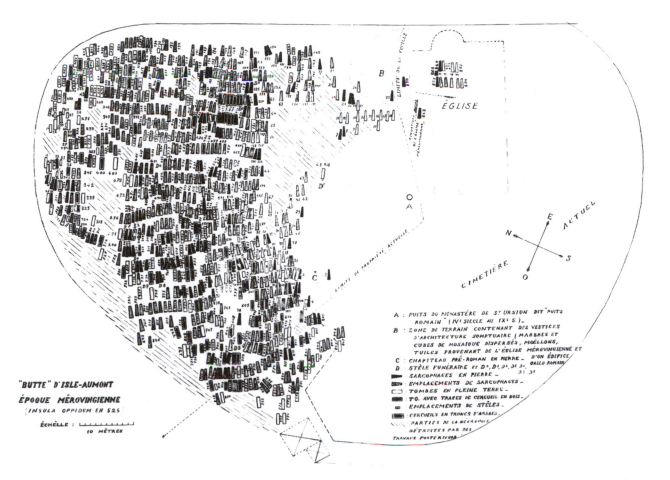

FIG. 2. Plan of the Merovingian cemetery of Isle-Aumont, near Troyes in Champagne. More than six hundred graves, many of them fine stone sarcophagi, were excavated by a local doctor, M. Jean Scapula, beside and under the medieval church and published by him in 1975.

Rural Settlement and Landscape

The archaeology of early medieval settlements is a very recent development in France. In 1950 Edouard Salin could sum up the subject in a dozen pages of Volume 1 of *La civilisation mérovingienne* (more than 1,500 pages), much of this based on literary sources or on excavations in Germany. The first Merovingian village in France to be excavated and published was Brebières, near Douai, in 1972. This was presented as a straggle of sunken-floor huts of modest dimensions. Much work has been done since then, usually directed by professionals working under pressure of salvage deadlines, although full-scale publications are still few in number. For the late antique period, one can now turn to the published thesis of Paul Van Ossel (1992), based on an analysis of more than a thousand sites between the Rhine and the Loire. On a more ambitious scale, Jean Chapelot and Robert Fossier (1985) attempted to fit the data into a larger interpreta-

tive framework enriched by parallels from European countries where more settlement archaeology had been done (Great Britain, Germany, Holland, and Scandinavia). They argued that, between the breakup of the Roman order in the fifth century and the creation of a new feudal order c. A.D. 1000, rural settlements were unstable, characterized by material poverty and primitive technology. Elisabeth Zadora-Rio, summing up the evidence in the 1989 general exhibition of recent French archaeology (see the exhibition catalog, *Archéologie de la France: 30 ans de découverts*), emphasized dispersion and instability as the most striking features of the early medieval landscape. Settlements, she argued, consisted of isolated farmsteads, poorly built in flimsy materials, often lasting only a few dozen years before shifting to a new location. An abandoned Gallo-Roman villa, perhaps reused as a necropolis, might serve as a territorial anchor; if there was a church of some sort (perhaps a funerary

F

chapel or a private oratory belonging to the major landowner), it was also isolated from settlement. Fossier/ Chapelot and Zadora-Rio would agree that less land was now cultivated than in Roman times, with forests taking over abandoned fields, and no evidence of new colonization. This interpretation of the available data, which echoes the traditional view of the earlier Middle Ages as a "Dark Age," has been challenged by Patrick Périn. He has argued that a society that could afford to alienate as much moveable wealth, including jewelry of intricate craftsmanship and fine, pattern-welded weapons, in graves as did the Merovingians can hardly be characterized as poor, and that the apparent instability of settlement is a false impression deriving from such factors as inadequate excavation and the likelihood that many of the sites that have been accessible to study were peripheral ones, readily abandoned. During the Merovingian period (fifth–seventh centuries), in his view, a stable village network was established (with at least some continuity with the earlier Gallo-Roman settlement pattern) in many regions of France that has persisted down to the present, with the consequence that such sites are not normally accessible to excavation.

There is some evidence of long-term continuity in settlement emerging from an exceptional site like St. Martin-de-Mondeville, near Caen, where occupation from the late Bronze Age to the fifteenth century has been documented. It will no doubt be some time before the immense body of data generated by excavations in the last quarter of the twentieth century can be properly analyzed, criticized, and confronted with fresh research; meanwhile, opinions are likely to remain divergent. But it is already clear that more allowance has to be made for regional differences as well as for the striking social and cultural differences that are clear in the written sources. No royal residence or well-appointed villa of a bishop or of the lay aristocracy comparable to those known for Gallo-Roman times has so far been identified and excavated in France. The site of Larina, at Hières-sur-Amby (Isère), overlooking the River Rhone, does provide an example (unique, for the moment) of a stone-built Merovingian "villa" intended for a family of the magnate class.

Excavation of later medieval settlements was originally stimulated by the Deserted Medieval Village project initiated in England in the 1950s; a group under Jean-Marie Pesez based at the Ecole Pratique des Hautes-Etudes en Sciences Sociales undertook a series of excavations of sites abandoned c. 1350–1450, with the first results published in *Archéologie du village déserté* (1970). These have pro-

vided a wealth of information about daily life and the technologies underlying it that differs significantly from, and complements, what can be extracted on these subjects from the written sources. Another series of excavations centering on Provence was undertaken by the Laboratoire d'Archéologie Médiévale Méditerranéenne (LAMM) under Gabrielle Demains d'Archimbaud, whose thorough excavations of the perched village of Rougiers (Var), occupied in the twelfth–fifteenth centuries, became available in a full-scale publication in 1980. Recent work by Patrice Beck in Burgundy has focused on *l'habitat intercalaire,* marginal settlements that developed on the borders of, and in relation to, the older villages as a result of the demographic surge of the High Middle Ages. An overall consensus seems to be emerging that the basic structures, technological and social, of the traditional European preindustrial village were already in place by the later Middle Ages: houses were solidly built and articulated around a hearth with its stone chimney, and the organization of space within and around the village had assumed the distinctive forms, varying from region to region, still visible to modern travelers.

Further research into settlement history from Carolingian to High Medieval times, between the eighth and twelfth centuries, will be needed to settle the current discussion on whether the medieval village, typically regrouping dwellings and workshops, church and cemetery, fields, pastures and woodland, and defenses, was "born" in the period c. 970–1050, when the written sources show power crystallizing in the hands of a new castle-building seigneurial class, or owes more to previous patterns than this thesis would allow. The case of Charavines, built on the shore of Lake Paladru near Grenoble in the French Alps, shows how much can be learned from a well-conducted excavation (begun in 1972) studied precisely in its regional context (see Colardelle and Verdel 1993). Most of the site is now underwater, allowing an exceptional recovery of organic matters and artifacts comparable to York in England. Agricultural implements are here associated with horse gear and military equipment, as well as objects like chess pieces, musical instruments, and silver coins, proving that the community sheltered behind wooden palisades here for only one generation (c. 1015/ 1025–c. 1040) was not merely peasant. The excavator, Michel Colardelle, argues convincingly that this new settlement of previously undeveloped land on the borders of Savoy and the Dauphiné reflects the twin phenomena of demographic upsurge and feudalization underway c. A.D. 1000. The rapid desertion of this lakeside site, vulnerable to attack, is explained by the construction of better-defended hilltop fortresses nearby (Le Châtelard, at Chirens). Dracy, an upland Burgundian hamlet in the hills west of Beaune, illustrates overpopulation and demographic collapse in the middle and later Middle Ages. The score of stone-built houses excavated by Jean-Marie Pesez between 1964 and 1979 (and restored as a historical site for visitors) reflect occupation mostly in the thirteenth–fourteenth centuries: with two ground-floor rooms, a loft, a fireplace, and a solid stone roof, they provided solid (if smoke-filled) shelter for the poor peasant families for whom there was no space in the other three nearby hamlets in the parish. But these, sited on better land, have survived to this day, while the ravages of war and plague had emptied Dracy by 1420. Similar studies on the microregional scale *(terroir)* will greatly enhance understanding of the complexities of rural history in the years to come.

Fortification

Although the Middle Ages is associated in the popular mind with stone castles, and Viollet-le-Duc did some castle "restoration" in the nineteenth century, it is only recently that archaeologists have treated fortification as a distinct research theme. Currently, archaeologists distinguish between an earlier phase of collective fortification and the High Medieval era of extensive private fortresses. The point of departure for the earlier phase was the aftermath of the third-century invasions, when stone ramparts were built to protect the *civitas* capitals of Gaul; these urban defenses were maintained throughout the first part of the Middle Ages. Some new types of fortification—around monasteries and the residences of bishops and counts—appeared during the Carolingian period (if not earlier), and there is some evidence of the reuse of Iron Age hillforts as refuges in exceptional circumstances. The impact of the Viking invasions in stimulating new fortification has only begun to be studied. But recent research has stressed the originality of the "castral revolution," which transformed the countryside between c. 980 and c. 1060. Private residences were surrounded by circular wooden defenses, and mottes—ranging from c. 20 to c. 100 m in diameter and rising 5–10 m in height—appeared in many regions, spreading outward from the Loire and Rhine Valleys. Jacques Le Maho's careful excavation of the motte of Mirville (20 m in diameter) showed the stages of development of a small seigneurial residence: a wooden building dating to the late eleventh century, first surrounded by a wooden palisade and ditch and then buried in the motte, which was constructed and

enlarged twice during the next century, before its abandonment. At Villejoubert (Charente), Andre Debord, working in a region with a strong tradition of construction in stone, has shown how an abandoned *castrum* (fort) in Iron Age and Roman times was refortified c. 950 by the count of Angoulême, who repaired the stone ramparts, added a deep ditch, and built both stone and wooden buildings within. Between 1020 and 1028, his successor abandoned this site in favor of a new motte-and-bailey castle better situated in regard to the road and river crossing. This example, like that of the castral motte of Chirens-Le Châtelard (Isère), cited previously, which replaced the lakeside settlement of Charavines, illustrates how profoundly the countryside was transformed as the feudal system developed.

The earlier generations of wooden fortifications, revealed by recent excavation, were replaced by the more familiar stone castles during the High Middle Ages. The expansion due to demographic and economic growth led many towns to replace their old Roman fortifications with new circuit walls, as Paris did under Philip Augustus (1165–1223) (one of the massive circular towers dating to this phase has been recently excavated under the Cour Carré of the Louvre, and its well-preserved foundations can now be visited within the remodeled museum), and later under Charles V (1338–1380). Jean Chapelot stresses the increasing professionalization of warfare as responsible for the development of a new generation of royal castles, in which the military function took precedence over the residential, like Richard the Lionheart's (1157–1199) Chateau-Gaillard in Normandy, or Vincennes beside Paris, where Chapelot launched a major archaeological program in 1989. Seigneurial, communal, and other types of private fortification continued to proliferate through the fifteenth century, however, particularly with the stimulus of the Hundred Years' War (1337–1453). Essertines (Loire) was a seigneurial residence of the Dukes Bourbon dominating a dependant village; Françoise Piponnier's recent study emphasizes how fieldwork can correct false impressions conveyed by a contemporary pictorial source. Didier Bayard's work at Hargicourt (Aisne) illustrates the other end of the scale: La Cologne began as a wooden seigneurial barn in the thirteenth century; later, a square wooden tower *(donjon)* was built on the farm, and a ditch and circuit wall were added, with entry by a drawbridge. In the later fourteenth century, the site was burned and the wall taken down, but the *donjon* was refortified and continued to serve as refuge and residence throughout the troubled years of the early fifteenth century.

F

Urban Archaeology and the Medieval Town

Archaeology in French towns is not new; during the nineteenth century many valuable observations were made during the extensive urban remodeling that took place. But these were piecemeal and haphazard, due to the absence of either research structures adapted to the urban environment or scholars with the training and vision necessary to interpret them in context. Paris was the exception and the pioneer in this respect; there the city engineer Theodore Vacquer was employed as the prototypical municipal archaeologist, surveying the various work sites for forty years (1848–1898) and conducting excavations whose results have been shown to be useful and accurate by later researchers. F.-G. de Pachtere, a talented young historian trained at the prestigious French School in Rome, published an excellent study (*Paris a l'epoque gallo-romaine,* 1912) based on Vacquer's notes and drawings that remains essential today. After 1898, the Commission du Vieux Paris was set up to coordinate archival and other research into the city's past; under the direction of Michel Fleury it has been active in recent years, developing new archaeological sites for visitors under the Parvis-Notre-Dame and the Cour-Carré du Louvre and supervising salvage operations. From the 1970s to the 1990s, there was a boom in excavation in Paris as the DRAH (Direction Régionale des Antiquités Historiques) played a more aggressive role and the Grand Louvre Project was undertaken.

Destruction during World War II and reconstruction during the 1950s and 1960s provided an opportunity for some archaeological observation and limited research in French towns, but many vestiges were simply destroyed. It was only in the 1970s that the city came to be viewed as an integrated subject of research in itself, under the influence of developments in England. In Tours, Henri Galinié, a veteran of the Winchester excavations, organized the Laboratoire d'Archéologie Urbaine, which in 1979 produced an archaeological resource assessment for the town and proceeded to develop excavations that integrated salvage and research considerations. In 1978, a national center for urban archaeology was created at Tours, associated with the CNRS, under Galinié's direction. In 1973, an urban archaeology unit was set up under Olivier Meyer and Nicole Meyer-Rodrigues in Saint-Denis, a major medieval manufacturing and trading center today in the suburbs of Paris, where major urban redevelopment was underway; costs for excavation (which was continuous until 1990) and postexcavation work were shared by the municipality and the developers. The results were to be put on permanent display in the town museum of history and archaeology, which expanded and relocated in a completely renovated historic building, the former Carmelite cloister where the sister of Louis XVI had once lived. A permanent Municipal Archaeology Office was subsequently established in Saint-Denis and in a number of other French towns as well. In Douai, Pierre Demolon made the municipal history museum, which had to rebuild its collections after disastrous losses during the war, into the center of coherent program of research into the origins and growth of one of the key "new" medieval towns of Flanders. Long-term excavation on the site of the demolished medieval castle showed how urbanization began with the decision of Count Arnold of Flanders (c. 945/946) to erect a wooden tower, defended by a ditch and palisade, where a riverside farm had stood. By the 1980s, excavations in many French towns, made possible by funds for rescue archaeology administered by the Sous-Direction d'Archéologie (a branch of the Ministry of Culture), were generating enormous quantities of new data whose analysis and historical interpretation has barely begun.

The most spectacular urban excavations in the 1980s were those connected with the renovation of the Louvre Museum in Paris, a project given high national priority by decision of President François Mitterand. The Cour Carré was dug up to expose one of the massive defensive towers of the new circuit wall built c. 1200 under Philip Augustus (project directed by Michel Fleury and Vensclas Kruta); thus, an important new medieval monument was added to France's architectural heritage, as the tower vestiges have been incorporated into the galleries of the Louvre. Directly to the west, under the Cour Napoléon (where the new entrance to the Louvre, a glass pyramid designed by I.M. Pei, stands today) and under the Carrousel Gardens, more than 3 ha of urban and peri-urban landscape were systematically excavated between 1984 and 1990 by professional teams under Jean-Pierre Trombetta and Paul Van Ossel. These teams were directly responsible to the Sous-Direction d'Archeologie, the branch of the Ministry of Culture that was granted increased powers in the late 1970s to set research agendas, oversee standards, and determine funding. The results reveal a complete vision (including paleoenvironmental studies) of the history of settlement from Neolithic times and allow one to follow in detail the development of a later medieval and modern urban quarter associated with the royal palace.

What has archaeology revealed about the medieval town? The first problem is to distinguish the older generation of towns from those that developed between A.D. 1000 and 1500. Hitherto, the dynamic achievements of the latter, still apparent in townscapes today, have almost totally obscured the reality of the former, which only careful excavation and analysis can hope to recapture. The Romans created a hierarchical network of *civitas* capitals with administrative functions and monumental public architecture—in some cases, on sites that had already seen some urban or more likely protourban development (Marseille, Vienne, Poitiers, Paris); in other cases, on new sites (Amiens, Lyons, Autun). After the first barbarian incursions, the core areas were enclosed in stone ramparts. During the fourth and fifth centuries, these were gradually transformed into Christian citadels, as the authority of the bishops balanced or replaced that of the secular officials, and Christian cemeteries, associating churches and burials in churchyards, transformed the landscape *extra muros* (outside the walls). Monumental building and decoration programs in the late antique tradition, as defined by H.-I. Marrou and his disciples, created a new type of town with powerful liturgical and administrative functions. Jean-François Reynaud in Lyons and Vienne, Renée Colardelle, and Jacques Le Maho in Rouen have worked on major monuments dating to this period, but nowhere can the transformation be better appreciated than in Geneva, as a result of Charles Bonnet's study of the cathedral group (the vestiges can now be visited in a specially designed and clearly explained crypt under the present cathedral) as well as on other sites in and around the city. Did these cities subsequently decay and urban life become reduced to a bare minimum as the "Dark Ages" took hold? Archaeological studies indicate that the network of more than a hundred Christianized *civitas* capitals survived, with very few changes, into the Middle Ages and down to the present day. Of the structure of these towns, and the vicissitudes they endured as a result of political events (dynastic wars, invasions of Vikings, and others) and economic and demographic trends (plague and famine, greater self-sufficiency of rural estates), little is now reliably known, but the work at Tours has provided us with one plausible model, indicating bipolar development. The older authorities (bishop, count) continued to hold sway within the late antique citadel while, at some distance, a dynamic new settlement grew up around a monastery (at Tours, Saint-Martin). At Saint-Denis and at Arras, too, wealthy monasteries stimu-

lated the development of trade- and craft-based settlements that, by the Carolingian period if not earlier, were expanding the earlier urban network. As recently as 1984, excavations in France had not revealed an independent early medieval trading emporium of the type explored in England at Hamwic and in Holland at Dorstad, though the site of Quentovic is known from written sources and from coins struck there. Recent excavations by a team from the University of Manchester have uncovered what appears to be the site of Quentovic near the hamlet of Visemarest along the former course of the River Canche. The site covers an area of more than 45 ha and appears comparable to other North Sea emporium sites. As more work is done on Carolingian and post-Carolingian phases of towns like Rouen, it is likely that more will be learned about *portus*-type (trading) quarters associated with the older towns.

The second great town network added—between c. 1000 and c. 1500—about two hundred new urban centers to the older one inherited from Roman times. Pierre Demolon has shown how Douai evolved from a marshy Merovingian farmstead into a thriving riverside administrative and commercial center after Count Arnold I of Flanders built a residence there in 945–946. This was subsequently enlarged as a wooden tower set on a motte and protected by a deep ditch; in the twelfth century, a stone *donjon* resembling the one still standing in Ghent replaced it. Outside the fortress, the mercantile town grew up as the flood-prone River Scarpe was brought under better control, and a circuit was built. The growth of Saint-Denis was driven more by religion and trade than by politics. This little *vicus* (small town), located at a crossroads on the plain just north of Paris, was the burial place of Dionysios (Denis), Paris's founding bishop martyr, around whose grave a monastic community developed that attracted royal favor (and burials) under both the Merovingian and the Carolingian dynasties. King Dagobert (d. 639) granted exemption from tolls, creating the conditions for the growth of a major periodic trade fair on the lands outside the abbey compound; Emperor Charles the Bald (d. 877) added new privileges and a new wall enclosing the trading town with a moat fed by a new water-management system, including an aqueduct. Urban excavations since 1973 have revealed much about the medieval industries that flourished there (ceramics and leather- and metalworking, and the manufacture of objects—like buttons—in bone, still a specialty there in the eighteenth century), as well as about wide-ranging trade connections and urban living conditions.

F

Daily Life and the Economy: Craft, Industry, and Trade

Archaeology, sometimes defined as *material culture,* provides an enormous body of information concerning the production of material goods, their exchange, and their function in daily life—all aspects of the economic life of the past. In the case of medieval France, some of this complements what can be learned from written sources alone, but most of it diverges, by its very nature, from the realities that writings tend to reveal. In many instances, indeed, archaeology provides the only significant documentation for important themes in the development of medieval civilization. The history of technology, for example, today a growing field, would be impossible without the material provided by excavation, laboratory analysis, and experimentation.

Regarded in this light, the archaeological evidence for the earlier Middle Ages suggests that the notion of catastrophic invasions and dramatic economic and technical regression accompanying the "fall" of the Roman Empire in the west is not accurate for France. There were many changes and, over half a millennium, some technological decline, with an economic shift toward self-sufficiency in basic matters at the local or regional level. The end of the tri-metallic Imperial coinage after c. 400 and its replacement by "barbarian" issues, mostly in gold, during the sixth and seventh centuries is one indication of economic regression. The eclipse of the glass industry in western Europe for centuries may be another, though luxury glass continued to appear in elite burial contexts. But the considerable research done on ceramics in recent years warns against drawing oversimple conclusions from the data. It shows the maintenance of ancient production types in many areas as late as the seventh century (like the DSP—or *dérivés de sigillée paléochrétienne,* early Christian derivatives of *[terra] sigillata,* a type of Roman pottery—common on sites in the south, and recipients made in workshops in the Argonne in the northeast), with the presence of imports from Roman Africa or the eastern Mediterrenean, notably in Provence and Languedoc (Marseille was clearly a major point of entry down into the seventh century, as the excavations of the Vieux Port there demonstrate). These are usually associated on the same sites with "common wares" of more local and/or regional origin, which are harder to date and to provenance precisely. But the series of decorated vases (some with Christian motifs) of good quality recovered intact from graves in Frankish regions has allowed some progress to be made in establishing regional distribution networks, implying trade contacts. The development of new trading ties with the North Sea region is also attested by the wide distribution of the Pingsdorf and Bardorf wares produced in the Rhineland from the seventh century. Handmade pottery that can be safely dated to the early Middle Ages is extremely rare in France; wheel-made wares remain the rule. In the area of metalwork, notions of decline are manifestly wrong. The quantity and the quality of weaponry in Frankish Gaul, reflected in written sources, are amply confirmed by excavation and by technological studies, which have succeeded in reconstructing the complex and delicate process, called pattern welding, required to produce a high-quality sword. Thanks to the popularity of dressed-burial customs in many regions from c. 350 to c. 660/700, quite a bit is known about brooches, belt fittings, hairpins, earrings, and other items of personal adornment during that period.

These vary greatly in value and craftsmanship. Items like the gold-and-garnet cloisonné jewelry found in the graves of King Childeric and other early chiefs and their wives or the gold filigree work that graces many later graves of elite Merovingian women (for example, the plate buckle of the late sixth-century lady identified by her ring as Queen Aregonde at Saint-Denis) are unique pieces showing superb technical finesse, but most graves include buckles and brooches in bronze or iron that were made in series. Regional production patterns can be demonstrated from a study of their distribution. Thus, c. 600, bronze plate buckles with a rectangular buckle plate decorated with vegetal, geometric, or animal motifs and a profusion of rivet heads, mostly nonfunctional, were in fashion in Aquitaine (southwest France); while in the mid-Seine region around Paris, a much smaller item—composed of a round bronze buckle plate decorated with concentric zig-zag, line, dot motifs, and a central human mask—was more often preferred. Before long, new fashions, like that for silver-inlay plate buckles, replaced these items, assuring their value to us for dating grave groups. The abandonment of furnished burial means a sharp drop in the datable artifacts after 700, for high-quality items are rarely found on settlement sites. Some potters' kilns have been excavated in recent years, and at Huy (Belgium) a site with vestiges of pottery, metalworking, and bone working has been explored. Graves furnished with a wide array of tools (like the one dating to c. 550 at Hérouvillette, near Caen) indicate the importance of itinerant smiths in the early medieval economy;

in the northern and eastern areas of Gaul, many of these also carried scales for weighing coins.

Excavation of late antique churches and related structures provides more confirmation that ancient craft skills survived and that industries connected with architecture in stone and its decoration (mosaics, wall painting) thrived at least into the seventh century. The handsome pavement mosaic of the sixth-century bishops of Geneva may now be seen by visitors of the archaeological crypt under the cathedral, and more and more examples of the survival of this craft are being identified as the notion that mosaics must be Roman in date yields to careful stratigraphic and stylistic analysis. Gold-backed tesserae from wall mosaics like those in Ravenna, previously attested only in literary sources for Gaul, have been found in relation to a sixth-century funerary church recently excavated in Macon (St. Clement). Renée Colardelle's excavations at Saint-Laurent in Grenoble reveal a sixth-century funerary church with an astonishingly sophisticated cruciform plan finished off by eleven elegantly rounded apsidal chapels radiating from the nave and transept arms. At the same time, evidence is turning up of timber building on an impressive scale, evidence that the Merovingian milieu could adapt non-Roman traditions as well—there was a timber phase to the fifth-century cathedral of Geneva. Beatrice Privati offered evidence in 1984 that a timber-built memorial structure was a major organizing feature in a rural necropolis near Geneva for two centuries. By the end of the 1990s, more evidence of timber and mixed stone-and-timber churches during the early Middle Ages was appearing, but little was as yet published.

Earlier in the twentieth century, Henri Pirenne aroused controversy by arguing that the fifth-century invasions did not create a drastic economic rupture between west and east; archaeology bears him out on this point, although discussion continues as to the nature of the contacts implied by particular items. Take the high-quality bronze vessels (whether Coptic, as once claimed, or more generally of Mediterrenean manufacture) that turn up in elite graves: were they objects of trade? or a kind of diplomatic gift? There is, however, no question that the thousands of late antique amphorae found at sites like the Vieux Port in Marseille, where quantities of ceramics made in North Africa or the eastern Mediterrenean also occur, are evidence of regular trading at least up to the first quarter or so of the seventh century, when this port was allowed to silt up. Off the coast of Fos-sur-Mer, where the written sources attest a royal customs station,

the first Merovingian wreck was explored in 1978, with an unglamorous cargo of wheat and pitch (written sources tend to note luxury goods, like spices or fine textiles). Even more surprising, the construction of this ship differs from ancient traditions in that the framework was built before the strakes—this was to become the dominant medieval technology. If Pirenne was right in placing a break in east-west Mediterrenean contacts in the seventh rather than the fifth century, archaeology now suggests that a new dynamic northern trade zone was developing at about this time, much earlier than he had thought. The spectacular growth of the Frisian port of Dorstad parallels that of Hamwic in England, in the later seventh century, but, as Stéphane Lebecq (1983) has emphasized, its greatest growth occurred in the next century, when it came within the sphere of Frankish power. Trade, and Christian missionary work, Lebecq argues, become linked to an expansionist political program under the Carolingian dynasty.

The balance between archaeological and written sources changes significantly as one moves beyond the twelfth century, when the latter become far more common and provide, for the first time, extensive and detailed information on economic matters. But, as Jean Chapelot points out, the two types of sources often diverge as to the reality they reflect. Archaeology alone would never have suggested the predominance of textiles as the great international medieval growth industry, for this has left behind few measurable material traces. The contrary is true of ceramics, whose very ubiquity has promoted many studies, including that of kiln sites in an urban context (Saint-Denis) and in rural milieux. Jacques Thiriot of the Aix-en-Provence laboratory (LAMM) has studied a number of production centers in the Lower Rhone Valley, notably a complex twelfth-century workshop at Saint-Victor-des-Oules, including seven kilns and the potter's house. The spectacular rebirth of the glass industry from the eleventh or twelfth century has been documented by recent research such as that of Danièle Foy (LAMM); this was the subject of a major exhibition at the Musée des Antiquités in Rouen in 1989, where the scholarly catalog can be obtained (*à travers Le Verre du moyen âge à la Renaissance*).

Excavation also provides an enormous quantitative mass of data on such vital everyday matters as nourishment, demographics, and pathology, thanks to the systematic study of human and animal bones, the most ubiquitous artifact of all. Only since the 1970s, or in some cases even later, have these data been reliably and

F

systematically collected in France, and it is not yet possible to push generalizations too far. Comparative studies of Norman cemeteries do suggest, however, that the basic physical type in this region changed very little from the late Bronze Age to modern times, despite cultural, religious, and political transformations. Since 1981, the physical anthropology laboratory of the national Centre des Recherches Archéologiques (CRA) at Valbonne, directed by Luc Buchet, has stimulated research and improved methodologies, holding regular colloquia and publishing them. The study of animal bones and of paleobotanic vestiges is at last becoming a normal research parameter on major sites like the Louvre in Paris and Saint-Denis, although few results are yet available in print. One case that is now available in full-scale publication is the underwater Colletiere site at Charavines, which includes many specialist reports (forty-two authors contributed).

Conclusion

Long the domain of amateur excavators of cemeteries and art historians concerned with particular monuments in isolation, medieval archaeology has greatly expanded and matured since 1970. Today it is taught in graduate-level seminars in universities in Paris, Caen, Aix-en-Provence, Lyons, Strasbourg, and elsewhere; a variety of research projects are underway under the aegis of the Centre National de la Recherche Scientifique in conjunction with local, regional, and national authorities; and data on the medieval period are continually being recovered from salvage operations carried out by professionals paid by the Association pour les Fouilles Archeologiques Nationales (AFAN) and working for the regional Direction des Antiquités Historiques (branches of the Sous-Direction d'Archéologie, which is part of the Ministry of Culture in Paris). Museum displays throughout France, from the Louvre in Paris to provincial and local museums, have been updated to present the new material and new historical viewpoints generated by research; special exhibits devoted to medieval archaeology have been organized (see Further Readings for some available catalogs); and new site museums and medieval historical monuments are open to the public. There is also more interaction between medievalists and other archaeologists to create long-range diachronic projects focused on particular sites, such as Mont-Beuvray in the Morvan, where research begun by coordinated international teams in 1984 has shown that this Celtic oppidum had an important medieval occupation. A diachronic, multidisciplinary project carried out by U.S. researchers from the anthropological tradition in the 1970s and early 1980s offers another example of promising new approaches, discovering major medieval reoccupation of an important prehistoric and Gallo-Roman site (Crumley and Marquardt 1987). The impact of the new conceptions deriving from the confrontation of archaeological with written sources and expanded dialogue among scholars from different horizons is just beginning to be felt at the level of textbook history, and there is no doubt that in the years to come archaeology will continue to stimulate a reevaluation of all our notions of the Middle Ages.

FURTHER READINGS

Barral i Altet, X., ed. *Artistes, artisans, et production artistique au moyen âge: Colloque internationale.* The Acts of an Interdisciplinary Colloquium at the University of Rennes. Paris: Picard, 1986.

Bouärd, Michel de. *Manuel d'archéologie médiévale.* Paris: SEDES, 1975.

Chapelot, J., and P. Benoit. *Pierre et metal dans le batiment au moyen âge.* Paris: Editions de l'École des Hautes Études en Sciences Sociales, 1985.

Chapelot, J., and Robert Fossier. *The Village and the House in the Middle Ages.* Berkeley and Los Angeles: University of California Press, 1985.

Chapelot, J., H. Galinié, and J. Pilet-Lemiere. *La céramique: Fabrication, commercialisation, utilisation. Actes du premier congrès international d'archéologie médiévale, Paris, 1985.* Caen: Société d'Archéologie Medievale, 1987.

Colardelle, M. *Sépulture et traditions funéraires dans les Alpes françaises du nord.* Grenoble, 1983.

Colardelle, Michel, and Eric Verdel, eds. *Les habitats du lac de Paladru (Isère) dans leur environnement: La formation d'un terroir au XIe siècle.* Documents d'Archéologie Française 40. Paris: 1993.

Crumley, C.L., and W.H. Marquardt, eds. *Regional Dynamics: Burgundian Landscapes in Historical Perspective.* San Diego: Academic, 1987.

Demains d'Archimbaud, Gabrielle. *Les Fouilles de Rougiers: Contribution a l'archéologie de l'habitat rural médiévale en pays méditerranéen.* Paris: CNRS, 1980.

Demolon, P., and E. Louis. *Douai: Une ville face à son passé.* Douai: Société Archéologique de Douai.

Duby, G., and A. Wallon, eds. *Histoire de la France rurale.* Vol. 1. Paris: Seuil, 1975.

———. *Histoire de la France urbaine.* Vol. 1. Paris: Seuil, 1980.

Duval, Noel, ed. *Naissance des arts chrétiens.* Paris: Imprimerie Nationale, 1991. A general introduction for late antique and early Christian archaeology. A second volume, in the form of a gazetteer entitled *Les premiers monuments chrétien de la France* (1995–1998) was published by Picard in Paris.

Fino, J.-F. *Fortresses de la France médiévale.* Paris: Picard, 1967.

———. Les fortifications de terre en Europe occidentale du Xe au XIIe siècle. *Archéologie médiévale* (1981) 11:5–123.

———. *La maison forte au moyen âge.* Paris: CNRS, 1986.

Galinié, H. *Les archives du sol à Tours et avenir de l'archéologie de la ville.* Tours: Laboratoire d'Archéologie Urbaine, 1979.

Gauthier, Nancy, and Jean-Charles Picard. *La topographie chrétienne des cités de la Gaule.* Paris: De Boccard, 1986.

Hubert, Jean. Archéologie médiévale. In *L'histoire et ses méthodes: Encyclopédie de la Pléiade.* Ed. Charles Samaran. Paris: Gallimard, 1961, pp. 275–328 and 1760ff.

Laming-Emperaire, A. *Origines de l'archéologie préhistorique en France: Des superstitions médiévales à la découverte de l'homme fossile.* Paris: Picard, 1964.

Lebecq, Stéphane. *Marchands et navigateurs frisons du haut moyen âge.* Lille: Presses universitaires de Lille, 1983.

Le grand atlas universalis de l'archéologie. Paris: Encyclopaedia Universalis, 1985. This volume offers a series of short articles by leading scholars on the major themes and periods, with excellent illustrations.

Le grand atlas de l'art. 2 vols. Paris: Encyclopedia Universalis, 1993. These volumes offer sections on the Early Medieval World, the Romanesque World, and the Gothic World.

Lindenschmidt, Wilhelm, and Ludwid Lindenschmidt. *Das germanische Todtenlager bei Selzen. Mainz am Rhein:* P. von Habern (reprint of Mainz 1848 edition), 1969.

Lorren, Claude and Patrick Périn, eds. *L'habitat rural du haut moyen âge: Acts des XIVe journées internationales d'archéologie mérovingienne, Guiry-en-Vexin et Paris, 1993.* Association Française d'Archéologie 6. Rouen: Musée des antiquités de la Seine-Marne, 1995.

Périn, Patrick. *La datation des tombes mérovingiennes: Historique, méthodes, applications.* Geneva: Droz, 1980.

Pesez, Jean-Marie. *Archéologie du village déserté.* Paris: Colin, 1970.

Privati, Beatrice. *La nécropole de Sézegnin.* Geneva: A. Julien, 1983.

Salin, Edouard. *La civilisation mérovingienne.* 4 vols. Paris: Picard, 1950–1959. This classic work must now be consulted with caution.

Trombetta, P.J. *Sous la pyramide du Louvre.* Monaco: Le Rocher, 1987.

Van Ossel, Paul. *Etablissements ruraux de l'antiquité tardive dans le nord de la Gaule.* Paris: CNRS, 1992.

Velay, Philippe. *De Lutece à Paris: L'ile et les deux rives.* Paris: Caisse Nationale des Monuments Historiques et des Sites et Presses du CNRS, 1992. A good introduction to Paris as an archaeological site and to the story of archaeology in Paris.

Young, Bailey. Text Aided or Text Misled? Reflections on the Uses of Archaeology in Medieval History. In *Text-Aided Archaeology.* Ed. Barbara J. Little. Orlando: CRC, 1992, pp. 135–147.

Periodicals

Archéologie médiévale, published annually since 1970 by the Centre des Recherches Archéologiques Médiévales (CRAM) at Caen, publishes articles covering the whole period and a thematically organized chronicle of ongoing excavations in any given year. *Archéologie du midi médiéval,* published by the Centre d'Archéologie Médiévale du Languedoc in Carcassonne since 1983, covers southern France. *Gallia* covers late Antique and Merovingian archaeology as well as all earlier periods, and publishes a brief annual chronicle of all excavations and finds reported by the Regional Directors of Antiquities. There are a number of regional publications as well. The articles in the popular glossy magazines *Archaeologia* and *Les dossiers d'archéologie* (Editions Faton S.A., BP 90, 21803 Quetigny Cedex) are usually written by serious scholars to inform a wide audience of ongoing projects, and provide bibliography. New work can be followed in the annual *Bulletin de l'association française d'archéologie mérovingienne* (AFAM) (198 rue Beauvoisine, 76000 Rouen); AFAM also publishes a monograph series, including a bibliography of works published between 1980 and 1988 by Michel Kazanski.

Exhibition Catalogs

A major resource is the catalog of the first national exhibition of archaeology in France, covering all periods paleolithic to modern, with articles by leading scholars and bibliography: *Archéologie de la France: 30 ans de découvertes,* Grand Palais (Paris: Editions de la Réunion des Musées Nationaux, 1989). Other exhibition catalogs of special interest for medieval archaeology

F

include *Des Burgondes à Bayard: 1000 ans de moyen âge,* (Grenoble: Centre d'Archéologie et d'Histoire des Musées de Grenoble et de l'Isère, 1981); *Aujourd'hui le moyen âge: Archéologie et vie quotidienne: 1981–1983* (Aix-en-Provence: Laboratoire d'archéologie médiévale méditerranéenne, 1981); *La Bourgogne médiévale, la mémoire du sol: 20 ans de recherches archéologiques,* (Dijon, 1987); *La Neustrie* (Rouen: Musée des Antiquités, 1985); *Premiers temps chrétiens en Gaule méridionale, antiquité tardive et haut moyen âge, IIIe-VIIIe siècles* (Lyon: Musée de la Civilisation Gallo-Romaine, 1986); *Dix ans de recherches archéologiques en Midi-Pyrennes* (Toulouse: Musée Saint-Raymond, 1987); *Un village aux temps de Charlemagne: Moines et paysans de l'abbaye de Saint-Denis du VIIe siècle a l'an mil* (Paris: Musée des Arts et Traditions Populaires, 1988); *Chateaux et villages du moyen âge: Forez, Bourgogne, Provence* (Montbrison, 1986).

Bailey Young

SEE ALSO

Bulles; Castles; Coinage; Deserted Medieval Villages; Emporia; Geneva; Mont Dardon; Normandy Castles and Fortified Residences; Quentovic

Freswick Links

Located in the extreme northeast corner of mainland Scotland, the coastal site of Freswick Links at Caithness has long attracted the attention of antiquarians in the area. In more recent years, scientific archaeological excavation has proceeded, and the true significance of the site is now more fully understood. Although there are remains on the site of prehistoric activity as well as an Iron Age broch tower which was excavated at the turn of the last century, it is the remains of the late Viking settlement (c. eleventh–fourteenth centuries) which have attracted recent investigation.

Caithness formed an integral part of the northern earldom of the earls of Orkney, geographically spreading northward from Orkney to include Shetland and southward to encompass much of northeast Caithness. The saga source, *Orkneyinga Saga,* probably written in Iceland in the late twelfth or thirteenth century, makes several references to activities in the area. There were frequent links across the Pentland Firth, which today separates the Orkney Islands from mainland Scotland but which united

these same lands for the Scandinavians who formed the late Viking or late Norse population into the mid-fourteenth century.

Apart from a rich place-name record, there remains only limited evidence of Viking and late Viking activity in this part of mainland Scotland: the settlements of Huna and Robert's Haven on the north coast and Freswick on the east; a handful of pagan Viking graves, including, for example, those at Reay and Castletown; and a small hoard of silver ring-money (a fixed unit of currency common in the tenth century). Until the recent excavations of Robert's Haven by J.H. Barrett, Freswick had been the focus of archaeological attention, with investigations by C.E. Batey, C.D. Morris, O. Rackham, and A.K.G. Jones concentrating on the rich environmental potential of the site.

The late Viking settlement of Freswick, suggested as the home of Svein Asleifsson (a medieval Norseman mentioned in the *Orkney inga saga*) in the saga sources, was originally investigated by A.O. Curle and V.G. Childe in the 1930s and the early 1940s, and a series of dry-built stone buildings was revealed. In many cases, the buildup of settlement was complex, with stones reused from one building in another at a later stage. Curle distinguished seven structures ranging from dwellings to storage structures, and Childe, working later at the cliff edge to the east of Curle's houses, added probably a further one or two structures to the total known. These excavators noted the presence of rich middens, or rubbish dumps, in the vicinity of the buildings, and Curle also noted a few of the animal species represented.

Today the eroding seaward edge of the site is revealing the remains of buildings, associated middens, and traces of agricultural activity in the form of cultivated areas. Excavations in the late 1970s and the 1980s were undertaken by Batey and Morris and their colleagues, concentrating primarily on the rich eroding banks of midden material, in an attempt to understand the nature and significance of this unparalleled amount of material—stretching c. 0.8 km north-south by c. 0.4 km east-west and fast eroding. A series of trenches placed behind the cliff edge enabled detailed analysis of the middens, with many hundreds of tons of materials being excavated and subsequently wet sieved on site. The deposits were commonly sieved through 1.0-mm mesh, and 500-micron mesh was used in selected cases. This evidence, now fully analyzed, shows that late Viking settlers at the site were catching substantial amounts of large fish—cod, ling, and saithe predominantly—and probably processing most of it on site in discrete areas. It is possible that this was an operation on a commercial scale and is currently unparalleled for the period (c. fifth–eighth centuries) in a late Viking context. In addition, animals were kept, including cattle and sheep.

Both barley and oats were grown at the site. Pollen analysis and impressions of cereal seeds in the coarse, handmade pottery from the site support the evidence of the charred seeds recovered in the samples. Fragmentary remains of striations in the sand, cultivation marks, suggest that the crops were grown adjacent to the settlements examined by Curle and Childe and more recently by Batey and Jesch et al. Detailed stratigraphical study shows that cultivation was also taking place in the pre-Viking, Pictish, period at the site. This is the first clear evidence recorded at this site for such pre-Viking occupation and, more significant, the first such cultivation traces from Picts anywhere in Scotland.

FURTHER READINGS

Batey, C.E. Recent Work at Freswick Links, Caithness, Northern Scotland. *HIKUIN* (1989) 15:223–230.

Batey, C.E., J. Jesch, and C.D. Morris, eds. *The Viking Age in Caithness, Orkney, and the North Atlantic.* Edinburgh: Edinburgh University Press, 1993. Papers and references therein.

Colleen Batey

SEE ALSO
Northern Isles; Picts

Fröjel

In spite of intensive study of the Viking period (800–1050), knowledge of the harbors and trading places of that period, as well as the extent of trade and the ways in which it was organized, is very limited. The best examples of early trading centers are such sites as Birka in Sweden, Hedeby (Haithabu) in Schleswig-Holstein, Grobin in the eastern Baltic, Wolin in Poland, and Paviken on the island of Gotland. The majority of investigations of Viking period trading places have focused on sites that are known from written sources, and archaeologists assumed that trade took place mainly between these well-documented places.

Until the mid-1980s, the only trading place that was known on the island of Gotland was the Viking Age harbor at Paviken. Archaeological investigations that have taken place since then have changed this picture dramatically. Today, approximately sixty places with evidence for Viking Age activities have been identified along the Gotlandic coast. Some of these sites are small fishing hamlets, but about six or seven can be classified as trading places or early towns.

One of the most important of these trading places is Fröjel, located in the western part of Gotland close to the ancient coastline. Fröjel is well sheltered from strong winds by a small island, and the site seethed with activity for a period of four hundred years. Excavations at the site have revealed at least three different cemeteries, including a Christian cemetery, an enormous settlement area, a medieval viceroy, and traces of the actual harbor.

A cluster of buildings surrounded the harbor with its jetties. In these small houses, craftsmen produced their wares. Gotlandish men and women could pick and choose among a large number of products. There were imported goods, such as wine and salt from southern Europe, precious metals from Arabia, and amber from Poland and the Baltic states. In the craftsmen's shops, one could buy typical Gotlandic jewelry, and those who were wealthy enough could order a gold-plated brooch. It is estimated that the site may have had a population of three hundred to four hundred persons in the summertime, although the population would have been less in winter.

The archaeological excavations that have been carried out at Fröjel are among the most extensive that have been conducted on any Viking harbor and trading place. Large areas of settlement and approximately fifty graves have been investigated. The remains from this trading place are both rich and varied. In all, about fourteen thousand artifacts have been found.

The results of the excavation clearly indicate that the harbor at Fröjel was established during the sixth–seventh centuries as a small fishing community and that the site was in use continuously until the early Middle Ages. The main period of activity is the eleventh century, as shown by the silver coins from the late tenth and early eleventh centuries. At that time, the settlement covered an area of c. 60,000 m². After the twelfth century, activities ceased, and the harbor was deserted, probably because the bay had become too shallow for the new, deep-drawing ships.

The harbor was later moved to the present coast. Written sources indicate that goods were shipped out from Fröjel from the sixteenth century onward. The new harbor

F

was located on the outside of the north part of the former island, and ships had to anchor along stone chests that were placed in the water. These stone chests are still visible today.

Dan Carlsson

SEE ALSO
Birka; Haithabu; Vikings

Fyrcat
See Trelleborg Fortresses.

G

Gender

Gender is a term used more and more widely within research in the humanities and social sciences. The fundamental principle underlying studies of gender is that the social and cultural conditions that shape differences in roles, expectations, and definitions of men and women and the concepts of *masculine* and *feminine* are defined socially not biologically.

Every academic subject has its own tradition regarding the use of the concept of *gender,* depending upon how and by whom it was introduced. In the field of prehistoric archaeology, gender was introduced in the 1980s. About ten years later, the first articles on gender started to appear in medieval archaeology.

The debate about women and how to make them visible in the historical record can be traced back to the 1970s. Archaeological research, primarily in the Scandinavian countries, Great Britain, and North America, was soon influenced by that question. An important step for research on women in the archaeological record was taken in Norway during the Norwegian archaeological meeting (Norske Arkaeologmoete, or NAM) in 1978, when questions were raised that initiated a seminar called "Were They All Men?" During the seminar, people discussed how a feminist approach could facilitate the discovery of individuals behind some of the standard analytical vocabulary of archaeology. Publication of the lectures given during the seminar was delayed on the ground that the topic was too narrow. Thus, it was not until 1987 that *Were They All Men? An Examination of Sex Roles in Prehistoric Society* appeared.

Often, accounts of women's lives have been appendices to traditional history. A need was felt to go further than just make women visible and instead to point out the connection between women's roles and society. In the United States, where archaeology is part of the field of anthropology, an article titled "Archaeology and the Study of Gender" by M.W. Conkey and J. Spector was published in 1984. The authors showed how androcentrism (male as norm) influences archaeological research and how a gendered perspective could pave the way for a viewpoint that sees each society's sexual roles as socially and not biologically predetermined.

Postprocessual theoretical influences have increasingly opened archaeological research to new perspectives. At the end of the 1980s and the beginning of the 1990s, more and more conferences on archaeology and gender were held. They resulted in publications like *Engendering Archaeology: Women and Prehistory* (1991), edited by J.M. Gero and Spector, and *The Archaeology of Gender: Proceedings of the Twenty-Second Annual Chacmool Conference* (1991), edited by D. Walde and N.D. Willows. Several archaeological journals have also had special issues focusing on gender questions.

Within medieval archaeology, little work has been done applying a gendered perspective to data. *Gender and Material Culture: The Archaeology of Religious Women* by R. Gilchrist was published in 1994. The book is based on her doctoral thesis, in which she used gender as an analytic category to study medieval English nunneries. Gilchrist takes a comparative approach and sees a series of similarities and differences between male and female monastic settlements, arguing that their location in the landscape, their approaches to estate management, and their roles in economic production and consumption are gender defined. She pays special attention to the organization of monastic

G

space. Through gender-related questions, Gilchrist raises the status of nunneries as she manages to extract new data from the archaeological record.

Gender Studies

Gender studies aim to make the relationship between women and men visible and to show how it has changed over time. It is possible to use gender in this sense, purely to focus on the lives of women and men in the past. However, it is also possible to work with gender studies in a more critical sense, looking for explanations as to why and how behavior and ideas were formed. This leads to questions about how archaeology is created and written. In this sense, gender studies build an awareness of the mechanisms that lie behind the production of historical texts. It is, therefore, also necessary to work beyond the traditional borders of academic subjects. Questions concerning education, presentation, the use of language, power, and attitudes are as relevant to archaeology as are chronology or typology.

The study of gender asymmetry, the unequal balance of power between different genders in a society, can be seen as a form of feminist research (feminist gender studies). "A feminist approach put forward an explicit theory of gender, to combat interpretations which accepted modern-day stereotypes as timeless, objective and 'natural'" (Gilchrist 1991:498). Feminist theory has contributed to the development of gender studies, especially concerning perception of the past. The feminist perspective is not homogeneous. How one looks at and defines the reasons for an unequal power balance vary, as do the solutions and the demands on today's society for change (see Tong 1989).

Gender system, a structuralist term first introduced in U.S. anthropological research in the 1970s, can be used to describe the pattern by which gender as well as social, economic, and political circumstances are arranged. In Western society, two main principles of order can be discerned. The first is the principle of hierarchy: men constitute the norm, and women are defined as the *other.* The second is the principle of dichotomy, or separation: that which is defined as male should not be mingled with what is defined as female.

The *gender system* concept has been criticized because it presupposes generalizations and thus does not take individual differences into account. This can be seen in the totally different ways women are described. Sometimes they are portrayed as strong and independent, and sometimes as victims of oppression.

Categories such as age, class, position, and ethnicity can be included in a gender system, as well as sex. This complexity makes *gender* a very broad concept, and it can easily be seen as too wide a concept to be useful as an analytical category. A solution is to define gender every time it is used in a new context to clarify the aspects that are to be addressed.

The invisibility of women in history is a serious symptom of social powers working to the disadvantage of women. The shaping of written history shows clearly that history is, and is used, as an ideology. As such, it is also power, as the knowledge of history affects contemporary society and gives us the tools to achieve a perspective upon our lives.

Western scientific knowledge is produced within accepted paradigms (i.e., models for the solution of problems and questions that are generally accepted). According to these models, scientists aim for objectivity and facts that are uninfluenced by prejudices. That gender can influence scientists in the production of knowledge has had little acknowledgement thus far.

FURTHER READINGS

Bertelsen, R., A. Lillehammer, and J. Naess, eds. *Were They All Men? An Examination of Sex Roles in Prehistoric Society.* Varia 17. Stravanger: Arkeologisk Museum i Stavanger, 1987.

Conkey, M.W., and J.M. Gero, eds. *Engendering Archaeology: Women and Prehistory.* Oxford: Basil Blackwell, 1991.

Conkey, M.W., and J. Spector. Archaeology and the Study of Gender. In *Advances in Archaeological Method and Theory.* Vol. 7. Ed. M.B. Schiffer. New York: Academic, 1984, pp. 1–38.

Gilchrist, R. Women's Archaeology? Political Feminism, Gender Theory, and Historical Revision. *Antiquity* (1991) 65:495–501.

———. *Gender and Material Culture: The Archaeology of Religious Women.* London: Routledge, 1994.

———. *Gender and Archaeology: Contesting the Past.* London: Routledge, 1999.

Tong, R. *Feminist Thought: A Comprehensive Introduction.* London: Unwin Hyman, 1989.

Walde, D., and N.D. Willows, eds. *The Archaeology of Gender: Proceedings of the Twenty-Second Annual Chacmool Conference.* Calgary: Archaeological Association of the University of Calgary, 1991.

In addition to the above references, the following journal issues are devoted to the topic of gender and archaeology: *Archaeological Review from Cambridge* (Spring

1998) 7(1); *Norwegian Archaeological Review* (1992) 25(1).

Ingrid Gustin and Katalin Sabo

Geneva

Around and beneath the cathedral of Geneva, Switzerland, a vast archaeological site is open to visitors. This site allows visitors to follow the development of the upper town and to understand the evolution of the episcopal complex.

The first occupation of the hilltop that was to become the old town of Geneva was established after the romanization of Allobrogian territory and dates from c. 80 B.C. In 122 B.C., however, a port with a bridge over the River Rhône and a settlement at Carouge only 1 km away were already established.

Julius Caesar fortified the town of Genua at the beginning of the Gallic Wars. Traces of large ditches indicate that the spur of land between the River Arve and Lake Geneva became the central core of the Roman *vicus* (town). The settlement of this period is made up of houses of earth and wood. An important artisans' quarter was located to the northeast of the hilltop. During the peaceful period of the early Roman Empire, the predominantly masonry buildings followed the outlines of earlier building lots. The city expanded, extending over the Plateau des Tranchées to the southeast and along the banks of the lake in the form of large villas.

The Germanic migrations at the end of the third century caused a remodeling of the urban center. A fortified enclosure soon protected the hilltop and the port area. After that, terraces were laid out, allowing new buildings to be erected. In one residence, apparently belonging to one of the city authorities, a group of buildings was erected, providing evidence for Christianity.

C. A.D. 350, a notable construction was begun in the eastern part of the city. A well-proportioned church was built in *opus africanum.* This technique, quite rare in Europe, employed vertical bonding made up of alternately vertical and horizontal large stones and appeared first in North African masonry construction. Linked to the choir with its polygonal apse, two annexes were attached to this episcopal complex. The rectangular annex was furnished with a baptismal font, placed laterally in relation to the axis of the room. A portico gave access to these areas. Along the western facade of the church, a second portico led to a series of heated cellules (small cells) placed against the lateral wall of the nave. They served as

lodging for clerics, who could thus easily enter the sanctuary. The residence of the bishop was built at approximately the same time in the immediate vicinity at the foot of the walls.

This cluster of buildings built between 350 and 375 formed a religious center upon which a part of the regional economy depended. Dwellings showing a certain degree of luxury were also constructed in a reduced walled city on the left bank of the Rhône near the port.

In A.D. 400, the episcopal compound grew in size to cover a vast area. To the south of a courtyard of porticoes (an atrium), a second cathedral permitted the catechumens to prepare for baptism. On the west side, the baptistery was moved to occupy the center of this architectural grouping. Numerous reception and meeting rooms were used by the community of clerics brought together by the bishop. The bishop himself made use of a private church close to his residence.

The wars of the Burgundian kings brought about important construction works at the beginning of the sixth century. The choir of the principal cathedral was reconstructed with an apse of exceptional proportions. The liturgical areas were elongated and raised; the space reserved for the clerics appears also to have extended into the transept. The baptistery, with its font and a canopy that covered it, was completely transformed. Remarkable decorations of stucco and mural paintings decorated the blind arcades, bays, and walls.

The relics could have been placed in a rotunda at the side of the bishop's church. This unusual building was later attached to a new two-story episcopal residence; two staircases were attached to its street facade. Later, at the expense of part of this building, a third cathedral was founded. Nearly square in plan, the church was bounded on the east side by three apses. In the central nave, a barrier of tuffa blocks was constructed and covered up with Greek decoration in stucco. This construction took place in two stages; later, the tomb of an important person was placed along the axis of the church.

Gradually, the third cathedral became the only sanctuary used by all the faithful; the other two cathedrals were abandoned and transformed. C. A.D. 1000, a crypt raised the *presbyterium,* and the high altar was placed 4.5 m higher than the floor of the nave. This monumentality was accentuated by the flights of stairs that obstructed the central nave and by a vaulted choir.

In 1160, Bishop Arducius de Faucigny undertook the construction of the cathedral that remains today. It was not until the thirteenth century that the nave and the

G

towers were completed. The bishop's palace, a cloister, and the cannons' houses, like the neighboring church of Notre-Dame-la Neuve, formed a remarkable medieval ensemble that has seen many transformations.

FURTHER READINGS

Bonnet, Charles. *Geneva in Early Christian Times.* Geneva: Fondation des Clefs de Saint-Pierre, 1986.
————. *Les fouilles de l'ancien groupe épiscopal de Gèneve (1976–1993).* Cahier d'archéologie genevoise 1. Geneva: Fondation des Clefs de Saint-Pierre, 1993.

Charles Bonnet

Gennep

Near Gennep, a small town in the Dutch province of Limburg on the east bank of the River Meuse, part of a large Germanic settlement from the migration period (fifth century) was excavated by the University of Amsterdam in the years 1989–1991 (Fig. 1). In 1994, a cemetery was found c. 175 m to the southeast of it. In this cemetery, a cremation-phase contemporary to the settlement was followed by inhumations from the sixth–seventh centuries, indicating continuity of habitation in this area after the fifth century.

In contrast to cemeteries (like the large one at Krefeld-Gellep on the Rhine not far from Gennep), very few settlements from the transition period between the Roman period and the Middle Ages are known from formerly Roman territory in western Europe. In the Dutch and Belgian Meuse area, a few small settlements from the late fourth–early fifth centuries have been discovered near former or still-existing Roman villas (e.g., Voerendaal, Neerharen-Rekem), inhabited by Germanic (i.e., Frankish) immigrants in Roman service who maintained the agrarian and metal production and possibly performed military tasks if necessary. (Northern Gaul became highly germanized in this period by these guest workers, mercenaries, and allies from Free Germany.)

The Gennep settlement was founded (c. A.D. 390) at a time when the Meuse-Lower Rhine area still formed the northern bridgehead of the Roman Empire. To the north, on the west bank of the River Meuse, the late Roman *castellum* (fort) of Cuijk (with a bridge across the river), was to be found; to the east, on the River Niers, which flows into the Meuse at Gennep, the contemporary fortress of Asperden (Germany). Close at hand, at Gennep, a (deserted?) villa and possibly a small fortress existed. In its initial phase, this settlement had much in common with the flimsy settlements mentioned above, which mainly consisted of sunken huts. However, instead of being deserted after the collapse of the Roman Empire, it grew into a large, well-structured settlement also containing large longhouses like the settlements known from Free Germany.

Only part (34,000 m²) of the settlement was excavated. Here, 127 sunken huts (rebuilding phase included), 8 large houses (which presumably are underrepresented because of the unfavorable disposition of the subsoil), 13 barns and other annexes, 19 four-post granaries, c. 110 oven pits (most of them probably used for food production), 4 wells, and a cemetery of 19 inhumation graves (without any recognizable human remains or any ritual deposits, however) were found (Fig. 2).

After the initial phase—a cluster of sunken huts around a well (and probably a small cemetery)—the whole area was built upon in the second quarter of the fifth century, including a row of four halls with their annexes, such as sunken huts, granaries, and some barns. In the second half of the fifth century, the settlement shrank, at least within the excavated area. At the end of this period, or not much later, the settlement was abandoned or, most likely, replaced.

All sunken huts belong to the six-post type. Their size ranges from 2 × 1.7 m to 4 × 3.3 m. Presumably, they had different functions: storage (e.g., food, tool chests for blacksmiths and bronze workers), workshops (textile working), and even dwellings (especially in the first phase of the settlement). Most of them were secondarily used as rubbish pits. The large buildings are related to the three-aisled types that are known from Free Germany to the northeast of the River Rhine (northern Netherlands, northern Germany). The average length ranges from 23 m to 32 m (apart from two connected houses forming a complex more than 60 m in length). Possibly these were assembly halls instead of traditional farmhouses inhabited by a family and its cattle. If any animals were kept in them, then these would have been mainly horses.

Apart from horse rearing, the inhabitants were hardly involved in food production themselves, as the paleobotanical and archaeozoological data suggest. Most cereals, cattle, pigs, and whatever else was needed were obtained from elsewhere. In the field of production, only blacksmithing and bronze, silver, and gold smelting played a considerable role, as was shown by the amounts of slag, crucibles, molds, and the like. The available data indicate that feasting and drinking (witnessed by large quantities of broken glass vessels), hunting (20 percent of the

FIG. 1. The location of Gennep on the River Meuse (the Netherlands).

analyzed bone material is from deer), and probably warfare were important occupations in this consumer community.

Strong relations existed with the Romans as well as with the barbaric world. Although the influx of small Roman currency stopped c. A.D. 405 (350 coins were found), the majority of the pottery (60 percent) and all of the glass (tableware and drinking vessels) were obtained from still-functioning Roman production centers (e.g., Mayen, Argonnen) during the entire fifth century. Apart from the mass of typical Frankish adornment, some brooches, mountings, and the like must be ascribed to

G

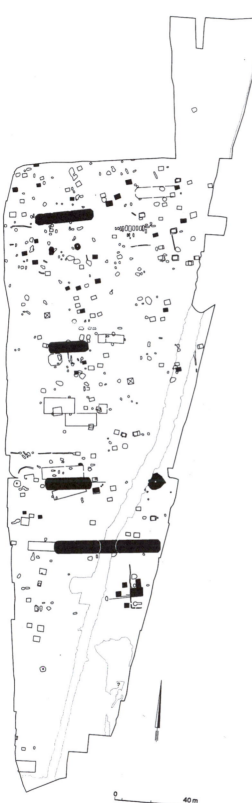

FIG. 2. The Frankish settlement at Gennep c. A.D. 450. Indicated in black are the longhouses, sunken huts, other outhouses, and wells from that period.

northwest France, the Alamannic realm, Anglo-Saxon England, and southeast Europe, indicating direct or indirect contacts with barbaric groups all over Europe. The domestic pottery and the building types suggest that the roots of these people should be sought in the northern Netherlands or Lower Saxony. Wherever they came from—they were probably an ethnically mixed group—in the perception of the Romans and probably of themselves they belonged to the Franks.

The population of this settlement appears to represent the retinue of a Frankish war leader. These people started as mercenaries or allies in Roman service and ended up as an elite group in the Rhenish-Frankish Kingdom centered on Cologne, which was annexed by Clovis (c. 466–511) in A.D. 507. Perhaps this date marks the replacement of the settlement and the start of the Middle Ages at Gennep.

FURTHER READINGS

Heidinga, H.A. Frankish Settlement at Gennep: A Migration Period Centre in the Dutch Meuse Area. In *The Archaeology of Gudme and Lundeborg: Papers Presented at a Conference at Svendborg, October 1991.* Ed. P.O. Nielsen, K. Randsborg, and H. Thrane. Copenhagen: Akademisk Forlag Universitetsforlaget i Køberhaven, 1994, pp. 202–208.

Heidinga, H.A., and G.A.M. Offenberg. *Op zoek naar de vijfde eeuw: De Franken tussen Rijn en Maas.* Amsterdam: De Bataafeche Leeuw, 1992.

H.A. Heidinga

SEE ALSO
Netherlands

Genoa

The first archaeological evidence found in the city of Genoa dates to pre-Roman (fifth–third centuries B.C.) and Roman (second century B.C.—fifth century A.D.) times. During the Medieval period, Genoa developed along a natural inlet situated between the Castello hill and the Cape of the Lighthouse. It is in this inlet that the port developed over the centuries, playing an important role in the history of the city.

It is difficult to say what the urban development of the city was like before A.D. 1000. The dense urbanization that characterized the late Middle Ages (eleventh–fifteenth centuries) is partly preserved in the actual historic center.

After the many vicissitudes connected with the crisis of the Roman Empire, Genoa was captured by the Byzantines in A.D. 537. It remained part of the Byzantine Empire until 641, when the Langobard occupation took place. Toward the end of the Langobard Kingdom in the 770s, the city became part of the Carolingian Empire. During the early Middle Ages beginning in the seventh century, the city developed within the limits of the Roman and the Byzantine city. Archaeological discoveries have helped compensate for the lack of information from written sources relating to this period.

In different parts of the city, remains of residential buildings with dry-stone and wooden walls and dirt floors have been found, especially around the primitive San Lorenzo Cathedral and in the area surrounding the old port. Early medieval houses, somewhat poor in general, are thought to have been rectangular. In addition, a series of individual tombs and burial grounds dating from the early Middle Ages were identified all along the Roman road axis, near the preexisting late antique necropolis, where large amphorae of North African manufacture were used to mark burial places. Further burial grounds have been discovered near San Lorenzo Cathedral and on top of the Castello hill. Small nuclei of tombs, probably belonging to a single family, have been found inside the buildings.

Regarding the origin of the Genoese church, the first written reference to the presence of the Genoese episcopacy was made in A.D. 381. On the basis of archaeological finds and documents, it is assumed that the primitive cathedral of the city of Genoa was situated in the area where the actual cathedral stands. The centers of religious power were concentrated here during the early Middle Ages (i.e., on the rise of San Lorenzo with the ancient cathedral and on the neighboring hill of Santa Andrea). Here there is documentary evidence for the Church of Sant'Ambrogio and the so-called Broglio area, where the refugees from Milan who had escaped the Langobards took shelter. Most of the archaeological relics from the early medieval city have been found in this area, including remains of houses, relevant stratigraphy, and burial grounds. In addition to the San Lorenzo Cathedral and the Church of Sant'Ambrogio, the Church of Santa Maria di Castello, probably built during the early Middle Ages, should also be mentioned. In addition, a series of extra-urban churches, such as San Stefano, San Siro, Santa Sabina, and San Fede, have been identified along the main-road axis on the basis of historical and archaeological sources.

On top of the Castello hill, where the most significant remains of the wall of the pre-Roman oppidum are preserved, the Bishop's Castle-Palace developed from the ninth and tenth centuries. The bishop, who also exercised civil powers until the eleventh century, used the building as a refuge during dangerous times and also as a summer residence. The Bishop's Castle had a defensive wall (ninth century–first half of the tenth century), to which a pentagonal tower, a quadrangular keep, and a square tower were later added. Some houses and the primitive Church of San Silvestro (first mentioned in 1160), with its annexed burial ground, stand inside the castle and in the surrounding area.

After A.D. 1000, Genoa became a free city-state and an important maritime city that controlled numerous strategic commercial points in the Mediterranean and the caravan routes coming from the Far East.

Research on the medieval city from the eleventh century onward has been possible due to its good preservation. Archaeological sources have been supplemented with an accurate study of the existing urban and building structures and the considerable quantity of local historical records.

During the eleventh century, the city started to expand beyond the limits of the first city wall (dating to A.D. 864). The new urban perimeter was confirmed by the new city walls (1155–1161) built with large square blocks from which three monumental gates stood out. The first harbor facilities were also built during this century, as demonstrated by archaeological research. On the so-called Old Mole Peninsula, a medieval mole built of large bossed stones has been found, which is thought to have delimited an internal dock used as a refuge for ships. (A mole is a massive work of masonry or large stones that are laid in the sea, often serving as a breakwater.) During the thirteenth century, the sea area encompassed by the mole was filled with earth for building purposes. Then, in an area of c. 1,000 m to the west of the Old Mole, a series of wharfs and slipways were built, originally in wood and later in masonry, where ships arrived or sailed toward the Mediterranean ports with which the Genoese merchants traded. From the thirteenth to the fifteenth century, the port acquired its modern appearance with the construction of the naval dockyard and the wet dock in the area, as well as the construction of masonry wharfs for ships. There is extensive archaeological documentation regarding the modifications and building techniques used in the construction of medieval moles.

G

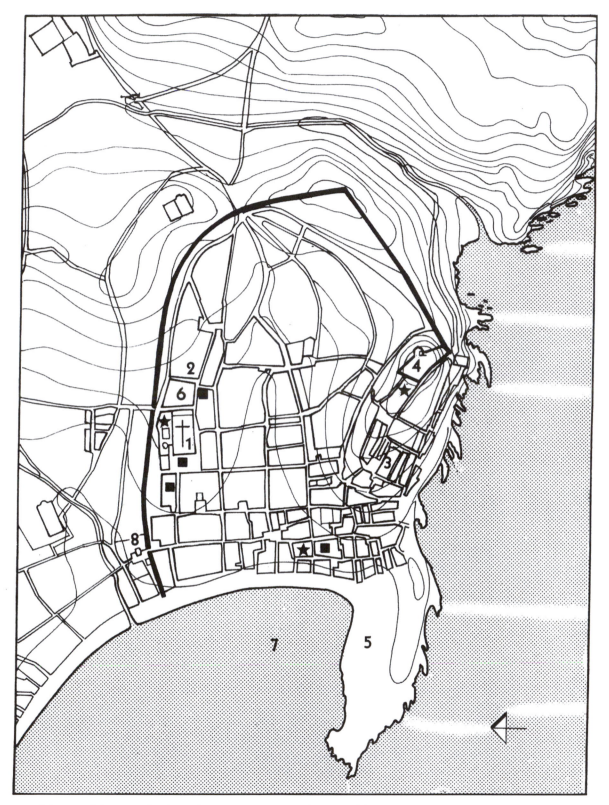

Planimetry of the city of Genoa in the eleventh century: continuous line with full stroke: ninth-century city walls; star: early medieval necropolis; square: remains of early medieval houses; numbers: *1*, San Lorenzo Cathedral; *2*, Church of Sant'Ambrogio; *3*, Church of Santa Maria di Castello; *4*, Bishop's Castle and Church of San Silvestro; *5*, Peninsula of the Old Mole; *6*, area near Palazzo Ducale; *7*, Old Port; *8*, Gate of San Pietro.

The excavation of deeply stratified areas has greatly aided the understanding of certain aspects of the development of the medieval city. In the west end of the city, for example, it has been possible to study the organization of the Ospedale dei Cavalieri di San Giovanni di Gerusalemme (Hospital of the Knights of Saint John of Jerusalem), which lodged the pilgrims leaving for the Holy Land. Wells, remains of houses, and roads have been excavated in different parts of the city. Traces of the craftsmen's neighborhoods have been found, as in the case of the metalwork scrap recovered near the cathedral where metallurgists had their workshops. A big four-sided tower (each side c. 20 m in length) has been found in the area where the Government Palace (also called the Doge's Palace) of the Republic of Genoa was built in the sixteenth century. The tower, dated between the end of the twelfth and the first half of the thirteenth century, is thought to have been built by order of a bishop. In fact, the bishopric was quite near the tower, whose characteristics are similar to those of the quadrangular *donjons* of northwest France rather than those of the narrow towers of the city of Genoa.

Another important aspect revealed through in-depth archaeological research is the flow of imported pottery that started in the twelfth century. These imported ceramics bear witness to the traffic and relationships Genoa had with various areas of the Mediterranean, including Sicily, Syria, Palestine, Egypt, Byzantine Greece, Provence, Spain, and Mediterranean Africa.

FURTHER READINGS

Andrews, D., and R.D. Pringle. Excavations in Medieval Genoa, 1971–1976: The Palace and Convent of San Silvestor with a Note on the Animal Bones by J. Cartledge. In *Papers in Italian Archaeology I, Part ii.* Ed. H. McK. Blake, T.W. Potter, and D.B. Whitehouse. BAR Supplementary Series 41. Oxford: British Archaeological Reports, 1978, pp. 339–372.

Christie, N. Byzantine Liguria: An Imperial Province against the Langobards, A.D. 568–643. *Papers of the British School at Rome* (1990) 58:229–271.

Grossi Bianchi, L., and E. Poleggi. *Una città portuale del medioevo: Genova nei secoli X–XVI.* Genova: Sagep Editrice, 1987.

Instituto per la Storia della Cultura Materiale. *Genova: Archeologia della città: Palazzo Ducale.* Ed. A. Boato and F. Varaldo Grottin. Genova: Sagep Editrice, 1992.

Mannoni, T., and E. Poleggi. *Archaeology and the City of Genoa: A Review of the Present State of Knowledge and Opportunities.* Lancaster: Lancaster University, Department of Classics and Archaeology, 1976.

Poleggi, E., ed. *Ripa: Porta di Genova.* Genova: Sagep Editrice, 1993.

Alexandre Gardini

SEE ALSO
Italy

German Stoneware
See Stoneware.

Germany

The archaeology of the Middle Ages in Germany can be understood as a historical science in terms of its goals and objectives. It is, however, an archaeological discipline, because its data are generally buried in the ground and because of its methodology.

The historic roots of the interest in German national history lie in the early nineteenth century. At that time, the admiration of classical antiquities, Romanticism, and the nationalist movement, which followed in the wake of the Napoleonic Wars (1796–1815), resulted in the rediscovery of the German Middle Ages.

Within the study of antiquities, a distinction was made between pagan prehistory and the Christian Middle Ages. Fundamentally, a disciplinary and organizational distinction was drawn between pre- and protohistory on the one hand and art and architectural history on the other. Accordingly, in 1852 two national museums were founded: the Römisch-Germanischen Zentralmuseum in Mainz for the prehistoric and Roman periods and the Germanisches Nationalmuseum in Nuremberg for the Christian-German periods. This resulted in a separation of the disciplines not only in museums, but also in historic preservation and in the universities. By the turn of the twentieth century, antiquarian studies had developed into two separate fields, increasingly distant from each other. These were prehistoric and early historic archaeology, focusing on the excavation of archaeological sites, and architectural and art history, focusing on the preservation of historic buildings.

A change in direction occurred between the world wars and intensified after World War II. Protohistoric archaeology turned increasingly toward the High Middle Ages, and, at the same time, architectural and art historians working with archaeological materials took note of the

G

methods and theories of prehistoric and protohistoric archaeology. In this way, the archaeology of the Middle Ages, as we understand it today, replaced the long-abandoned antiquarian studies.

Three main research areas—and roots—can be distinguished in German medieval archaeology: (1) cemeteries, churches, and churchyards; (2) defense works: castles and palaces; and (3) rural and urban settlements.

Cemeteries, Churches, and Churchyards

Until recently, early medieval cemeteries were primarily the concern of prehistoric and protohistoric archaeology rather than medieval archaeology. Despite the important graves located in the region of Slavic settlement and in northwest Germany, research centered on the southern and western German areas, in the central region of the Reihengräber civilization. Earlier efforts focused on typology and the classification of evidence from the early Middle Ages. J. Werner's 1935 work, *Münzdatierte austrasische Grabfunde* (Coin-Dating of Austrasian Grave Finds), aimed to provide a universal system of chronology. K. Böhner's 1958 work, *Die fränkischen Altertümer des Trierer Landes* (The Frankish Antiquities of the Trier Region), provided important refinements of the chronology. U. Koch used the cemetery from Schretzheim to demonstrate the possibilities of horizontal stratigraphy for a relative chronology, while dendrochronological (tree-ring dating) investigations of wood coffins from Hüfingen and Oberflacht contributed to an absolute chronology for the early Medieval period.

Cemeteries were initially used to answer far-reaching questions about settlement history and especially about social history. Eventually, the connection to written sources was also recognized, and this generated an extensive literature. Examples include the works of R. Christlein, *Die Alamannen* (The Alamanni) (1978), and of H. Steur, *Frühgeschichtliche Sozialstrukturen in Mitteleuropa* (Protohistoric Social Structure in Central Europe) (1982). Questions about ethnicity, about the history of production and commerce, and about Christianization were finally the subject of debate.

Churches and churchyards, long a subject of interest in architectural and art history as well as in Christian archaeology, constitute one of the three roots of the archaeology of the Middle Ages in Germany. In the context of preserving historical monuments and inventorying architectural and art-historical monuments, architects and art historians investigated the exposed walls of sacred buildings. In so doing, the proper historical relationships between buildings were established through typological comparisons and/or through connections with the written sources. Between the world wars, prehistorians with their more highly developed excavation techniques also contributed to this research through excavation. Examples include the works of F. Fremersdorf in Cologne, those of F. Behn in the Central and Upper Rhein, and all the research in Lorsch. Additional examples include the excavations of H. Lehner and W. Bader in Bonner Münster between 1928 and 1930 and those of W. Bader in the collegiate church at Xanten between 1933 and 1934. These excavations helped establish modern medieval archaeology by combining the methods and theories of prehistoric archaeology with those of Christian archaeology, territorial history, and art history.

After World War II, medieval archaeology came into its own with the Rhenish church excavations. These excavations were connected with the names of W. Bader and W. Zimmermann, H. Borger, G. Binding, and, above all, O. Doppelfeld and T. Kempf in the cities of Cologne and Trier. W. Rave, F. Esterhues, H. Thümmler, H. Claussen, and U. Lobbedey deserve mention for their work in Westphalia at such places as Münster, Paderborn, and Corvey. For south Germany, the names of A. Tschira, V. Milojcic, G.P. Fehring, W. Erdmann, K. Schwarz, and W. Sage should be noted for their excavations in Schwarzach and Solnhofen, Eßlingen, Unterregenbach and Reichenau, Regensburg and Bamberg, Eichstätt, Passau, and Augsburg. F. Bellmann and B. Leopold deserve recognition for their work in central Germany. The rich results of this research are summarized in *Vorromanische Kirchenbauten* (Preromanesque Church Construction), published in 1966–1971 and 1991.

The nature of missions and churches, including the problem of continuity from antiquity to the Middle Ages, and of settlement and social history, were also studied, as were culture history and the history of fine arts. The stratigraphic method of excavation became as important as the uncovering of large excavation areas. Dating became increasingly secure through stratigraphically controlled small finds. As a result of the adoption of a problem-oriented approach, publications presented increasingly comprehensive models and interpretations utilizing a variety of scientific approaches. Although churchyards are of great interest to medieval archaeologists, the goals of many investigations are still limited in nature. Many questions, both anthropological and archaeological, remain only partly answered.

Defense Works: Castles and Palaces

The study of castles and palaces provides the second root of the archaeology of the Middle Ages in Germany. Regardless of their date, ruined castles of earthen bank-and-ditch construction were generally studied by proto-historic archaeologists, while masonry castles and their surrounding ruins were studied by architectural and art historians. The beginnings of this research lie in the first half of the nineteenth century. The first excavations in the palace at Ingelheim date from 1852 to 1853. After the foundation of the German Empire in 1871, two German medieval research projects originated. First, the architectural and art-historical investigation of the imperial palaces initiated by P. Clemen led to the publication of their layout by Goslar, Eger, and Wimpfen. Second, C. Schuchhardt's investigation of castles in the Westphalian-Lower Saxon area established the connection between historical questions and archaeological excavations and led to the publication of the *Atlas vorgeschichtlicher Befestigungen in Niedersachsen* (Atlas of Prehistoric Fortifications in Lower Saxony), begun in 1883. Schuchhardt's *Burg in Wandel der Weltgeschichte* (The Castle in World History) (1931) provides an overview for all periods. The architectural and art-historical investigation of central and late medieval Adelsburg also led to a synthetic interpretation in *Burgenkunde* (The Science of Castles), by O. Piper, published in 1896.

After World War I, archaeological research into castles was expanded to the beginnings of the modern period, distinguished in eastern and northern Germany by W. Unverzagt, who worked in collaboration with historians and addressed their questions. After World War II, work continued systematically and successfully in East Germany through excavations by, for example, J. Herrmann in Tornow and by E. Schuldt in Mecklenburg. In the same tradition, G. Schwantes and especially H. Jankuhn have investigated the most important Saxon and Slavic castles in Schleswig-Holstein since 1930, attempting to clarify their relationship to settlement regions, trade routes, and economic areas.

A revival in the 1930s, which intensified after World War II, led to the investigation of Saxon circular ramparts and to the discovery of the Ottonian castles—most important, Werla and Tilleda, but also Pöhlde and Grona. The complete investigation and publication of Tilleda by P. Grimm is particularly significant. The postwar excavations of the imperial castles at Frankfurt am Main and at Magdeburg, Paderborn, and Ingelheim are noted here.

Historical questions about the inclusion of Hesse in the Frankish Kingdom, in connection with questions of settlement history concerning the inclusion of smaller castles and deserted settlements in the kingdom, led to systematic excavations on the large Frankish castle complexes at Christenberg and Büraberg. Similar questions motivated the work of K. Schwarz on the early medieval expansion of settlement in northeast Bavaria and the role of the castles there in relationship to settlement areas and communication routes.

H. Dannenbauer's thesis that the castle became the basis of the nobility's power led to one of the most successful castle excavations in south Germany, which took place at Runder Berg near Urach and was directed by V. Milojcic and R. Christlein. Excavations carried out since the 1950s in the Rheinland and in northwestern Europe on the origins of the motte (fortifications based on earthwork mounds) were connected with similar questions about the development of feudalism.

Rural and Urban Settlements

Settlement archaeology, a field of study that is borrowed from prehistory, forms the third root of the archaeology of the Middle Ages in Germany. P. Grimm's 1935–1937 excavations at Hohenrode, a tenth–fourteenth-century settlement in the Südharz, constitute a beginning and a milestone in the archaeology of the Middle Ages. The same is true of his 1939 publication, which in exemplary fashion consulted written and pictorial sources as well as scientific analyses and which presented interpretations of settlement patterns, trade, house construction and culture history, economic history, and social history. A parallel to this in early urban archaeology were the excavations at Haithabu near Schleswig, which were directed by H. Jankuhn from 1930 onward. The focus of these excavations ranged from questions of settlement and house construction to questions of economic and social history. Excavations in the area of Slavic settlement, for example at Wollin and Oppeln, have been just as systematic. In western and southern Germany, on the other hand, only salvage excavations, like those in the early medieval settlements at Gladbach (Kreis Neuwied) and Merdingen (Kreis Freiburg), had been undertaken before World War II.

The period after World War II brought further developments in excavation at Haithabu under the direction of H. Jankuhn and K. Schietzel. Additional work was conducted at the Slavic coastal settlements and at the fortified castle *(Burgwall)* settlements in the region of the former

G

East Germany. In western and southern Germany, only salvage excavations were conducted, among which those of W. Winkelmann have long stood out. Through these excavations, Winkelmann examined the Saxon settlement at Warendorf in Westphalia, using the rich archaeological record to answer questions about house and farmstead forms and their connection with the written records. The work of W. Janssen between 1960 and 1962 at the deserted settlement of Königshagen in southwest Harzvorland, occupied from the twelfth century through the fifteenth, represents a further development because of its inclusion of the village fields and because of its use of geographical techniques.

General questions about settlement and economic and social history led to differing research projects in coastal areas. Examples include the wurt excavations of A. Bantelmann at Wurt Elisenhof, as well as those of W. Haarnagel at Emden. Wurts are rural settlements on artificial mounds located in the marshlands along the North Sea coast. Additional examples include the excavations led by K. Brandt on the High-to-late medieval trading centers between Ems and Wesermündung and the excavations led by D. Zoller on the Oldenburger Geest. P. Schmid and H.W. Zimmermann introduced a historical-developmental approach to the excavations of the settlement at Flögeln in Kreis Wesermünde. This excavation project is particularly important because it integrated research from prehistory to the present, including the entire Middle Ages and the modern era, employing scientific, historical, and geographical techniques.

The archaeological projects that were undertaken by the University of Kiel in the years 1968–1983 had as their objective a paradigmatic examination of rural settlement, castles, and cities from the ninth through the fifteenth centuries in the contact zone between Scandinavians, Slavs, and Germans. The examination of the settlements of Bosau and Futterkamp by H. Hinz was designed to answer questions of rural settlement, while the excavations led by K.W. Struwe aimed at studying the Slavic fortified settlements at Scharstorf, Warder, and especially Oldenburg in Holstein. The excavations under the direction of V. Vogel in Schleswig and of G.P. Fehring in Lübeck investigated stages of urban development.

The destruction resulting from World War II presented unique opportunities to investigate the origins and early development of the medieval cities. Examples include the church excavations in Rhenish cities and the town-center excavations by R. Schindler in Hamburg, by H. Plath in Hannover, by W. Winkelmann in Paderborn and Münster, by U. Fischer and O. Stamm in Frankfurt am Main, and by W. Unverzagt and E. Nickel in Magdeburg. Additional questions, such as the structure of land plots and building development or the economic and social structure of these cities in later centuries, were only occasionally raised. Examples of such research include the work of W. Neugebauer and later G.P. Fehring at Lübeck. Some relevant publications also exist for cities in the former East Germany. These include the works of E. Nickel for Magdeburg, H.W. Mechelk for Dresden, K. Käus for Leipzig, and, above all, of E.W. Hath for Frankfurt on the Oder. During the 1980s, emphasis was placed on taking stock and on the conflict between urban renovation and archaeological preservation of historic monuments. Examples include the works of G. Isenberg in Westphalia, J. Oexle in Konstanz and Ulm, and S. Schütte in Göttingen. Still, there is no comprehensive program for archaeological research in urban areas of Germany.

Objectives of the Archaeology of the Middle Ages

Medieval archaeology differs from prehistoric archaeology in that medieval archaeology is only one of numerous disciplines that make their contribution to the study of the Middle Ages. Radically different statements about environmental and settlement history, trade and population history, economic and social history, culture and architectural history, church and political history, and occasionally even legal and constitutional history are possible from archaeology, which fundamentally is supported by scientific data. In this way, the data used by the different disciplines reflect entirely different sides of past reality. Only by working collaboratively can the historical sciences do justice to the many-faceted reality of the Middle Ages. Medieval archaeology requires an integrated, interdisciplinary collaboration in individual research projects and a close and constant communication among the disciplines. This is feasible only if the participants have a detailed knowledge of the methodological possibilities not only of their own discipline, but also of related disciplines, and if they make use of collaborative methods.

Organization of the Archaeology of the Middle Ages in Germany

Universities. Only in 1981 did Bamberg establish a professorship for the archaeology of the Middle Ages and the modern era. This chair is currently occupied by W. Sage. Protohistoric archaeologists such as W. Janssen at Würzberg and H. Steuer at Freiburg also commonly cover the later Middle Ages. Architectural historians such as G. Binding at Cologne also use archaeological methods. At some universities, the archaeology of the Middle Ages is represented, but only incidentally, through faculty members in new departments or in neighboring disciplines (e.g., G.P. Fehring at Hamburg, D. Lutz at Heidelberg, or B. Scholkmann at Tübingen).

Research Institutions. The Römisch-Germanisches Zentralmuseum in Mainz, the Kommissionen zur Erforschung des Spätrömischen Rätien at the Bayerische Akademie der Wissenschaften in Munich, and that for Alemannische Altertumskunde at the Heidelberg Akademie der Wissenschaften limit their research focus to the end of the Merovingian or Viking periods. In contrast, the Römisch-Germanische Kommission des Deutschen Archäologischen Instituts in Frankfurt am Main includes the archaeology of the Middle Ages within its area of research. In addition, the Niedersächsisches Institut für Historische Küstenforschung in Wilhelmshaven and the Arbeitsgruppe Küstenarchäologie im Forschungs- und Technologiezentrum of the University of Kiel in Büsum cover the entire period, including the High Middle Ages and modern times, as a result of interdisciplinary interests and increasingly broad chronological questions.

Museums and the Preservation of Historic Monuments. In museums, the historic separation between prehistoric and early historic archaeology, on the one hand, and art and culture history, on the other hand, have resulted in the High Middle Ages not being presented from an archaeological point of view. The Rheinisch Landesmuseum in Bonn was the first of the large museums to devote a separate section to the archaeology of the Middle Ages. From the traditional pre- and protohistoric archaeological perspective, the preservation of historic monuments of the High and late Middle Ages was usually neglected or, at best, looked after in passing. Still, in some states—Bavaria, Baden-Württemberg, Niedersachsen, and Westphalia—there are or were for a number of years separate departments for the archaeology of the Middle Ages within the framework of the preservation of archaeological monuments. The laws protecting historic monuments of individual states provide the basis for this work.

Organizations and Associations. The numerous historic and antiquarian organizations (mostly founded in the nineteenth century), museums, universities, and institutions for the preservation of historic monuments are joined in three umbrella organizations: the west and south German (founded in 1900), the northern German (founded in 1905), and the middle and east German (founded in 1991) Verband für Altertumsforschung. An association for the archaeology of the Middle Ages and the modern era has existed in these organizations since 1976.

FURTHER READINGS
Fehring, Günter P. *The Archaeology of Medieval Germany: An Introduction.* London and New York: Routledge, 1991.
———. *Einführung in die Archäologie des Mittelalters.* Darmstadt: Wissenschaftliche Buchgesellschaft, 1992.
The periodical *Zeitschrift für Archäologie des Mittelalter* has been in print since 1973.

Günter P. Fehring

SEE ALSO
Dendrochronology; Haithabu; Lübeck

Glastonbury

Introduction

The parish of Glastonbury in England is centered upon the Tor, a steep hill 158 m high whose prominence is emphasized by its situation within low-lying marshland that was reclaimed from the Medieval period onward. The River Brue formerly (before c. A.D. 1250) lapped the southern and western sides of the parish and provided communication and transport with the Bristol Channel via the River Axe. Although often referred to as an island, there has always been a dry-land approach to Glastonbury from the east, and it is actually a peninsula surrounded by marsh and moor rather than the sea. It is along this eastern clay ridge guarded by an earthwork of uncertain date, Ponters Ball, that access was available to the Roman Fosse Way, the lead mines on the Mendip Hills to the north, and the heartland of Wessex.

In the Dark Ages Glastonbury was on the eastern fringe of what has been called the Irish Sea Province comprising Cornwall, the Severn Sea (also called the Bristol Channel), Wales, Ireland, and Scotland (Bowen 1970). Excavation has produced Mediterranean imported pottery of the fifth and sixth centuries in two locations: the Mount (Carr 1985) and the Tor (Rahtz 1970).

The Mount (sometimes known as the Mound) was a small area of raised ground, now destroyed through development, adjacent to the original course of the River Brue and southwest of the abbey and town, which contained

G

occupation evidence from the prehistoric period until the twelfth century. In the tenth–twelfth centuries, the site was used for iron smelting, probably in connection with construction within the abbey. The assumption is that the Mount was a landing point for river traffic from the north and the Severn estuary.

The summit of the Tor was excavated in the years 1964–1966. The earliest finds were prehistoric flints and sherds of Roman pottery and tile, but any features of these periods that may once have existed were destroyed by successive building constructions from the Dark Ages onward (although two fragmentary north-south burials, presumably pagan [and ?Roman] were recorded). The Dark Age phase consisted of timber-built structures with rock-cut cavities, a bronze-working hearth, and quantities of food bones dated by Mediterranean pottery to the late fifth and the sixth centuries. Later occupation in the mid- and late Saxon periods was connected with a small monastic site attached to the abbey, and the ruined tower on the summit is a relic of a chapel that served pilgrims in the twelfth–sixteenth centuries. While the Mount is indisputably a late Saxon industrial site, there is no consensus about the interpretation of the Dark Age phase on the Tor, although the excavator believes that it may have been the site of the earliest monastery. No Mediterranean imported pottery has been recovered from the abbey precinct, and there is no other positive dating evidence to confirm that the abbey site was occupied between the fourth and the seventh centuries. The Dark Age religious center in Glastonbury still awaits positive identification.

Glastonbury Abbey

The *Anglo-Saxon Chronicle* has an entry for the year 688 that states: "In this year Ine succeeded to the kingdom of Wessex and ruled for 37 years: he built the monastery at Glastonbury" (Garmonsway 1972). In the late seventh and the early eighth centuries, King Ine endowed the monastery with large tracts of land in Somerset, and these estates formed the nucleus of Glastonbury's wealth and power for the following 850 years. Prior to Ine's donations, however, kings of Wessex from the 670s onward had granted land to Glastonbury, mostly of small or medium-size estates. The earliest grants suggest confirmation of small estates held by an existing religious foundation of Celtic type, one of many in southwest England founded in the later sixth or the early seventh century. Most of these small foundations were subsumed by the Saxon minsters and monasteries established in the sev-

enth–eighth centuries, leaving little or no trace of their existence.

In A.D. 940, when regular monastic life seems to have been virtually extinguished in southern England after the first Viking Wars (see Stevenson 1904), Dunstan was installed by King Edmund as abbot of Glastonbury. Born locally c. 910 and related to the Wessex royal family, he had been educated at the monastery by Irish teachers (Robinson 1923). There are no indications that Glastonbury had ever ceased to be a religious house prior to Dunstan's time (see Dumville 1992:36), although in the early tenth century the abbey may have been in the king's hands without formal conventual life. Land grants did continue through the ninth century, although the type of rule practiced by the early tenth century, if any, would seem to have been heavily influenced by the Irish (Finberg 1969). Glastonbury claimed many Celtic saints as patrons, including David, Gildas, Bridget, and Patrick. When this Celtic, predominantly Irish thread was first woven into Glastonbury's history is uncertain, although the ninth century, a period of widespread Irish travel in Britain and Europe, might be favored. There is no direct evidence for Irish contacts with Glastonbury before the ninth century, although this can never be ruled out, and it might be relevant to recall that (Saint) Aldhelm, bishop of southwest England under King Ine, was previously the first English abbot at Malmesbury, a monastery apparently founded by an Irishman, Maeldubh, in the seventh century, and Aldhelm's see, created in 705, was based at Sherborne, which was itself the successor of a Celtic foundation, Lanprobi, dedicated to the Cornish St. Probus.

That the monastery at Glastonbury survived the first Viking Wars of the ninth century with its buildings and endowments intact is evidenced by the survival of the wooden Old Chirche, the monastic relics and tombs, and the abbey records. A land book was written in the late tenth century containing all the charters that the abbey had received, and William of Malmesbury, who wrote a history of the abbey in the early twelfth century, was able to study original documents and monuments dating to the seventh century (Scott 1981).

Abbot Dunstan, in conjunction with King Edmund, carried out extensive rebuilding and reformed the monastery on Benedictine lines, training a new generation of monks, who spread out from Glastonbury to refound monasteries throughout southern England. He eventually became archbishop of Canterbury and was influential in forging strong bonds between the sovereign and the monastic houses. English kings throughout the second half of the tenth century returned many alienated estates to the abbey and donated so many new ones that, by the Norman Conquest (1066) Glastonbury was the wealthiest monastery in England (see Hill 1981). It is really to this period, the four decades following Dunstan's installation as abbot, rather than the preceding centuries that Glastonbury's medieval wealth and influence belong.

A disastrous fire in 1184 destroyed the new Norman monastery, together with the relics and tombs of saints accumulated over the previous five hundred years. The subsequent need to raise funds for rebuilding after the death of its patron, Henry II (1133–1189), and the parsimony of his successor, Richard I (1157–1199), who spent all his revenues on the Crusades, prompted the abbey to claim a bogus relationship with King Arthur, whose legends had become immensely popular after the publication c. 1138 of Geoffrey of Monmouth's *History of the Kings of Britain*. The Arthurian stories, and the later claims of a foundation by Joseph of Arimathea, ensured that Glastonbury attracted the pilgrims and royal patrons who guaranteed its wealth through to the dissolution of the monastery in A.D. 1539.

The earliest and most important building in the abbey was immediately west of King Ine's church and was known from an early date as the Old Church. This small wooden building stood until the fire of 1184 and was replaced immediately in stone, deliberately using the same ground plan, and survives today as the Lady Chapel.

The veneration shown to the original Old Church by the later Saxon and Norman abbots is striking and, given the complete disregard normally shown to earlier structures by Norman builders, possibly unique. Whether it was originally built as the earliest West Saxon church in the mid-seventh century or derived from the pre-Saxon period will probably never be known due to the excavation of a crypt dedicated to St. Joseph below the floor of the Lady Chapel by Abbot Richard Bere c. A.D.1500. The Saxon monastic churches respected the orientation of the Old Church. King Ine's church dedicated to St. Peter and St. Paul was built east of the wooden church and incorporated one or more stone mausoleums. Dunstan lengthened King Ine's church and built a small chapel immediately west of the Old Church. The Chapel of St. Benignus is on this same alignment and may have succeeded an older foundation, possibly a market chapel, as a triangle of land (built over in the Medieval period) between the monastery and St. Benignus has been proposed as a pre-Norman marketplace. If this alignment of churches is extended eastward, it runs through the modern street called Dod Lane and from there past the base of Glastonbury Tor. Extending this road eastward once more, it links with a recently discovered Roman settlement and road, visible on air photographs, at East Street, 3.5 km east of the abbey.

Glastonbury Abbey, like many Dark Age and early Saxon religious sites in Somerset, was built on or adjacent to the site of a Roman settlement, possibly a villa or other type of high-status establishment. Excavations in Silver Street, immediately north of the abbey precinct, recovered Roman pottery and, significantly, building materials, including hypocaust fragments and vessel glass (see Ellis 1982). Silver Street was formerly within the bounds of the medieval abbey, and Roman pottery and coins have also been found in the area of the monastic church, during nineteenth-century renovation work (Warner 1826) and in many twentieth-century archaeological excavations.

Excavations took place in the abbey precinct from the early 1900s to the 1960s. The walls of King Ine's church were uncovered between 1926 and 1929. This building was extended in the tenth century when Dunstan remodeled the conventual buildings on a Benedictine plan, and parts of Dunstan's works were uncovered in the 1950s.

Most of the excavations within the abbey have been of poor quality and did little more than uncover and trace building foundations of the Medieval period. The problems are summarized in M. Aston and R. Leach (1977), which also provides a list of excavation references. A large ditch running north-south below the transepts of the medieval abbey church was investigated in 1956–1957 and claimed as a Dark Age feature, a *vallum monesterium* (monastery wall) (Radford 1981), but the complete absence of any dating evidence raises many doubts about this interpretation. A massive ditch was sectioned in Magdalene Street, west of the precinct, in 1984–1985, and a radiocarbon (C-14) date from wood near its base suggests that it was constructed in the tenth century, possibly as the western boundary of the monastery (Hollinrake and Hollinrake 1992a); its size was similar to the one found in 1956.

The northern line of the pre-twelfth-century monastic precinct is known for part of its length. Excavations in 1988 and 1992 revealed an 18-m-wide ditch whose top silts contained twelfth–thirteenth-century pottery (Hollinrake and Hollinrake 1992b). This feature must, therefore, date to the eleventh century or earlier, and it is probably

G

best interpreted either as a part of Dunstan's tenth-century works or as an early Norman construction. The later medieval precinct has been fossilized by the layout of the road system. The size of the Norman and Saxon (or earlier) precincts, however, is only poorly understood, although various authorities have attempted to reconstruct the boundaries (see Rahtz 1993:94).

The greater part of the medieval precinct has not been subject to archaeological investigation, and a survey by C. Hollinrake and N. Hollinrake of parch marks that appeared within the grounds during a prolonged drought in 1986 detected many previously unknown buildings, structures, and earthworks (Rahtz 1993:95–97).

In the later Medieval period, the abbey was constantly enlarged up to the eve of the Dissolution (Henry VIII's dissolution of monasteries and nunneries and confiscation of their property). It was a great landowning house whose monks concentrated their energies on the improvement and management of their estates (see Carley 1988).

The Parish Outside the Town

A rescue excavation in 1986–1987 revealed a canal that linked the River Brue and the abbey, c. 1 mile long and dated by C-14 dates and pottery to the mid-tenth century (Hollinrake and Hollinrake 1992a). This canal, which could have had a dual practical (transport of building materials) and ceremonial (entry of royal entourages) role, taken together with a massive ditch found in 1984, reflects the scope of mid-tenth-century construction works and the importance of Glastonbury during this period. Three English kings were buried in the abbey in the tenth century, and the national treasure was deposited there for a short period (see Stenton 1943, 1971:447).

Excavations on Beckery island, c. 2 km southwest of the abbey and overlooking the old course of the River Brue, revealed a small Saxon monastic satellite of the abbey dating from the seventh–eighth centuries. The foundations of a wooden Saxon chapel and later Saxon and medieval rebuilding of the same in stone, together with a medieval priest's house, were recorded, and a Saxon cemetery of male inhumations (plus one female and two children) was excavated. Beckery was one of a number of small "satellite" foundations, intimately connected to the main monastery, scattered through the surrounding moors and on the Tor (Rahtz and Hirst 1974).

The Town

In comparison with the abbey and the important historical sites of the Tor and Beckery, excavations within the town have been small and, without exception, rescue led, reacting to development threats.

The town of Glastonbury was dependent upon inhabitants of the abbey providing the services that catered to pilgrims, travelers, and traders as well as the daily needs of the monastery. Small-scale excavation at the Tribunal, a medieval townhouse and once erroneously thought to be the abbey's courthouse, suggest that the High Street properties were laid out in the twelfth century (Hollinrake and Hollinrake 1992c). Further small-scale excavation to the rear of Northload Street and on Dod Lane confirmed that this was the period when the town was planned, and surviving abbey documents contained within the Great Chartulary (Watkin 1948) bear witness to the twelfth century as a period of expansion and planned settlement.

The medieval town was small, with burgage plots (city lots) recorded on High Street, Benedict Street, Northload Street, parts of Chilkwell Street, and Dod Lane. Bove Town was apparently an area of small farms in the thirteenth century. The main street was High Street, or Great Street, which ran west from St. John's Church to the junction of Northload Street and Benedict Street. This was where the fifteenth-century pilgrims' inn, the George, stood, and, immediately adjacent, the modern Crown Inn is on the site of an inn belonging to Bruton Priory. The south side of High Street was probably the medieval marketplace, and the abbot's courthouse was situated there. During the Medieval period, the main gate into the abbey was off the marketplace opposite St. John's Church, in contrast to the later main entrance off Magdalene Street. It is possible that St. John's Church was deliberately sited opposite the main entrance to the abbey and that this took place in the tenth century as part of Dunstan's reforms, enclosing the monastery and providing a new lay church at the same time.

There are two medieval churches in Glastonbury: St. John the Baptist (the original parish church) and St. Benignus. The latter, although totally rebuilt in the early sixteenth century, is aligned on the axis of the monastic church and the Lady Chapel, an arrangement normally only found in pre-Norman religious sites, such as nearby Wells and Canterbury (see Rodwell 1981). Excavations in the chancel of St. John's, which was extensively rebuilt in the fifteenth century after the collapse of the central tower, revealed the plan of an early, and smaller, chancel. The foundations of this structure contained human bone, suggesting that they had been cut through an earlier graveyard (see Rahtz 1993:102). St. John's was the "mother" church to St. Benignus, which was consecrated as a chapel of St. John's in A.D. 1100. Although positive dating evidence for the foundation of St. John's was not forthcoming, as the senior church it must have predated the consecration of the Chapel of St. Benignus, and the abbey always claimed St. John's as a Saxon foundation.

St. John's had a *hospitium* (hospital) attached to it. This was demolished in the thirteenth century and refounded as the Hospital of St. Mary Magdalene in 1247 just outside the town limits, probably, as its dedication and site suggest, as a leper hospital, although it later became an almshouse. There was a second hospital, or almshouse, built in the fifteenth–sixteenth centuries in the northwest corner of the monastic precinct. On the periphery of the town were two slipper chapels used by pilgrims before they entered Glastonbury. The first, situated in Bove Town, was dedicated to St. James; the second, southwest of the town, on the road to Ponters Ball, was dedicated to St. Dunstan.

The Abbey Barn, northeast of the precinct on Bere Lane, is a fine fourteenth-century building whose orientation is markedly different from the roads around it. It may mark the position of an earlier road aligned on the Saxon marketplace, traces of which may have been recorded during the parch mark survey of 1986.

The abbots of Glastonbury created two parks outside the town: Wirral Park immediately west of the monastery and Norwood Park on the eastern edge of the island. Both entailed the closure of existing roads into Glastonbury, creating new roads in their place outside the park boundaries.

Glastonbury was one of the last monasteries to surrender (c. 1540) to King Henry VIII (1491–1547). The ending was violent and sudden, with the last abbot being hanged, drawn, and quartered on the Tor. The town survived the destruction of the abbey as a small regional market center, with industries specializing in the tanning and processing of sheepskins, and tourism also an important factor in its economy.

FURTHER READINGS

Aston, M., and I. Burrow. *The Archaeology of Somerset: A Review to 1500 A.D.* Taunton: Somerset County Council, 1982.

Aston, M., and R. Leach. *Historic Towns in Somerset.* Bristol: Committee for Rescue Archaeology in Avon, Glostershire, and Somerset, 1977.

Bowen, E.G. Britain and the British Seas. In *The Irish Sea Province in Archaeology and History.* Ed. D. Moore. Cardiff: Cambrian Archaeological Association, 1970. pp. 13–28.

Carley, J.P. 1985 *The Chronicle of Glastonbury Abbey.* Bury St. Edmunds: St. Edmundsbury Press, 1985.

———. *Glastonbury Abbey.* London: Guild, 1988.

Carr, J. Excavations on the Mound, Glastonbury, Somerset, 1971. *Proceedings of the Somerset Archaeology and Natural History Society* (1985) 129.

Dumville, D.N. *Wessex and England from Alfred to Edgar: Six Essays on Political, Cultural, and Ecclesiastical Revival.* Bury St. Edmunds: Boydell, 1992. See especially the essay titled Ecclesiastical Lands and the Defence of Wessex, 1992.

Ellis, P. Excavations at Silver Street, Glastonbury, 1978. *Proceedings of the Somerset Archaeology and Natural History Society* (1982) 126:17–31.

Finberg, H.P.R. *The Early Charters of Wessex.* Leicester: Leicester University Press, 1964.

———. Ynyswitrin, and Sherborne, Glastonbury, and the Expansion of Wessex. In *Lucerna: Studies of Some Problems in the Early History of England.* London: Macmillan, 1964, pp. 83–115.

———. *West-Country Historical Studies.* Newton Abbot: David and Charles, 1969. See especially the essay titled St. Patrick at Glastonbury, pp. 70–88.

Garmonsway, W.H. *The Anglo-Saxon Chronicle.* London: J.M. Dent, 1972 (1982).

Hill, D. *An Atlas of Anglo-Saxon England.* Oxford: Basil Blackwell, 1981.

Hollinrake, C., and N. Hollinrake. The Abbey Enclosure Ditch and a Late-Saxon Canal: Rescue Excavations at Glastonbury, 1984–1988. *Proceedings of the Somerset Archaeology and Natural History Society* (1992a) 136:73–94.

———. An Archaeological Watching Brief on the Rear of No. 44 High Street, Glastonbury. Unpublished Report to Somerset County Council, 1992b.

———. Excavations at the Tribunal, Glastonbury. Unpublished Report to Somerset County Council, 1992c.

Pearce, S.M. *The Kingdom of Dumnonia.* Studies in History and Tradition in South Western Britain, A.D. 350–1150. Padstow, Cornwall: Lodenek, 1978.

Radford, C.A.R. Glastonbury Abbey before 1184: Interim Report of the Excavations, 1908–64. In Medieval Art and Architecture at Wells Cathedral. *British Archaeological Association Conference Transactions* (1981) 4:110–134.

Rahtz, P. Excavations on Glastonbury Tor, Somerset, 1964–6. *Archaeological Journal* (1970) 127:1–81.

———. *Glastonbury.* London: Batsford/English Heritage, 1993.

G

Rahtz, P., and S. Hirst. *Beckery Chapel, Glastonbury, 1967–8.* Glastonbury: Glastonbury Antiquarian Society, 1974.

Robinson, J. Armitage. *The Times of St. Dunstan.* Oxford: Clarendon, 1923.

Rodwell, W. The Lady Chapel by the Cloister at Wells and the Site of the Anglo-Saxon Cathedral. In Medieval Art and Architecture at Wells Cathedral. *British Archaeological Association Conference Transactions* (1981) 4:1–9.

Scott, J. *The Early History of Glastonbury.* An Edition, Translation, and Study of William of Malmesbury's *De antiquitate Glastonie ecclesie.* Bury St. Edmunds: St. Edmundsbury Press, 1981.

Stenton, F.M. *Anglo-Saxon England.* Oxford: Clarendon, 1943 (1971).

Stevenson, W.H., ed. *Asser's Life of King Alfred.* Oxford: Clarendon, 1904.

Warner, R. *History of the Abbey of Glastonbury and the Town of Glastonbury.* Bath: Richard Critwell, 1826.

Watkin, Dom A. *The Great Chartulary of Glastonbury.* Vols. 59, 63, 64. Taunton: Somerset Records Society, 1947, 1948, 1956.

Charles Hollinrake and Nancy Hollinrake

Goudelancourt

The Necropolis

The necropolis of Goudelancourt-les-Pierrepont in northern France was excavated from 1981 to 1987. Discovered in the middle of farm fields during plowing, the site consisted of two contemporary, but distinct, cemeteries: 458 tombs were excavated; 324 were part of the first cemetery, and 134 of the second.

The general layout of a necropolis in two cemeteries is rare. The most likely hypothesis is that a group, perhaps a family, more religious than the others, desired to be set apart from the rest of the population and did so by abandoning the original cemetery and creating the second one. From one cemetery to the other the orientation of the tombs is different. The tombs were found in a south-southwest/north-northwest direction in the first and in a distinctly west/east direction in the second.

Dug into a bank of chalk, the graves were of a more or less rectangular shape, rounded off at both ends. The size of each tomb depended on the size of the individual. Several big communal graves were uncovered in which the individuals were placed side by side.

At Goudelancourt, the rituals practiced at burial were not original. No cremations were discovered. The practice of burying an individual dressed was the rule. For this reason, assorted clothing accessories, such as buckles and belt buckles, were found *in situ,* as well as different items indicating the social rank of the deceased: weapons for the men, jewelry for the women.

In many cases, the deceased was found with some pottery placed at the feet. The wealth of these graves was well known and led to plundering: barely 10 percent of the graves were found intact. The only outside traces of the sepulchers were a few stelae, or stones, that outlined the individual in certain graves.

In general, the deceased were buried lying on their backs with their heads to the west. Their arms were either placed alongside their bodies, folded over the pelvis, or a combination of the two.

Burial in open ground was used in 60 percent of the cemetery. It is the predominant rite in the second cemetery, where 75 percent of the burials took place in open ground. Wooden caskets or coffins were found in 37 percent of the graves. All of the existing sarcophagi were destroyed by plowing the fields. A decorated stone and numerous fragments testify to their existence.

In spite of the destruction caused by farmwork and pillaging, the number of objects found is quite large: ceramics, weapons, clothing accessories, and jewelry. All are characteristic of the sixth and seventh centuries.

A chronological study of each object indicates that there were four phases of occupation of the necropolis. Phase 1, from c. A.D. 530–540 to 560–570, corresponds to the creation of the first cemetery. Phase 2, from c. A.D. 560–570 to 580–590, saw the creation of the second cemetery. Phase 3 lasted from A.D. 580–590 to 620–640, and Phase 4 extended from A.D. 620–640 to 680–690. Phases 2 and 3 are best represented in the Goudelancourt necropolis. Both cemeteries experienced concentric development.

An anthropological study was conducted on 40 percent of the individuals. As in other sites, there was a small proportion of children—only 12 percent. The mortality rate of young adults (age eighteen–thirty years) was high. The study showed that the living conditions for the population of Goudelancourt were very difficult and deteriorated in the sixth–seventh centuries due to epidemics of the Black Plague.

Infant and child mortality was high: slightly more than 25 percent of infants died before the age of one year, and 33–50 percent of children died before the age of five. Life expectancy at birth was thirty-five years.

Researchers were able to reconstruct the living population based on a series of indicators. There were 126 individuals in a community of 21 families. The existence of the large second cemetery seems to support the hypothesis of two distinct population groups.

Housing

The settlement was discovered 150 m south of the necropolis and excavated from 1988 to 1992. Spread over an area of 1.5 ha, it had all the characteristics of a farming and domestic community of the Merovingian Era.

Numerous ditches, various remnants from the houses, several ovens, drainage ditches, and a well were excavated. The main structures that were unearthed were huts with dug-out foundations 30–70 cm deep. The huts had either two, four, or six support posts, with two-post huts the most numerous.

The uses of these huts seem to have been purely domestic: animal shelters, toolsheds, garrets, and various workshops. However, it is quite possible that some of the huts, probably the largest, were used as workshops as well as living quarters such as dormitories.

The outlines of five buildings were discovered, all by alignments of postholes. Each building had a rectangular or trapezoidal shape and an area larger than that of the huts. These buildings were probably at the center of the settlement's economic activity and used as barns, stables, or large workshops. Many metal deposits were found near one of the buildings, suggesting that one of the inhabitants worked with iron, perhaps as a blacksmith.

One building was noticed immediately because it was quite different from the others. This building measured 8.5 m long × 6 m wide and had a framework of sixteen support posts. Three of these posts were ridgepoles in the center of the building and supported the roofing. The other thirteen were part of distinctly parallel walls. An entrance with a canopy was built in the northeast. In the southwest corner, the remains of a hearth were perfectly visible. The discovery of this hearth is exceptional and is proof that this building was nothing other than a home.

The discovery of a pair of huts 160 m to the west points to the probability of other farm buildings located to the west of the site in the valley. Follow-up excavations will allow researchers to determine whether Goudelancourt-les-Pierrepont was a site composed of several isolated farming communities spread out in the valley, or a succession of hamlets, or perhaps a one-street town.

A. Nice

Grove Priory

Grove Priory in Bedfordshire is one of the most extensive and complete monastic and manorial sites to have been excavated in Great Britain; the demesne buildings and their surroundings were under almost continuous investigation from 1973 to 1986, when all but the fishponds were destroyed by a sand quarry. Its special status as a royal manor and alien priory generated copious and useful documentation, including an *1155 Extent* and fourteenth-century bailiff's accounts, which is complementary to the equally rich excavation evidence. The site produced a wide variety of well-preserved structural material, sequences of industrial features, large quantities of ceramics and other artifacts, and environmental evidence. Pioneer independent (archaeomagnetic) dating was carried out during the last years of excavation.

A total of 20,000 m² of buildings and courtyards were excavated in detail, with a further 7 ha examined under more difficult rescue conditions, enabling the history of the site to be followed from the mid-eleventh century through to the eighteenth.

The completeness and scale of the excavation have allowed a detailed analysis of the whole settlement through time. Although a rural excavation, its palimpsest of buildings has given it an urban character, including stratified sequences of buildings. One of the special aspects identified, and one that could only be discovered when studying a site in the circumstances of complete and detailed excavation, is that the overall layout of the site was mathematically planned, conforming in considerable detail to a grid based on a rod, pole, or perch. This planned layout was first extended, and then replanned on a different alignment. Both buildings and boundary lines relate closely to the grid, which was used as a guide for a lengthy campaign of building.

Although there is both prehistoric and Saxon (sixth–seventh-century) activity on the site, the story begins in earnest in the mid-eleventh century. The royal manor of Leighton has an entry in the *Domesday Book,* and it may be that some of the complex of structures excavated by the Bedfordshire County Archaeology Service are eleventh-century buildings belonging to the royal manor. These are likely to be some of the higher-status timber buildings.

The *1155 Extent,* compiled by the constable of England, appears to order a number of new, and quite specific, agricultural buildings needed after the depredations of the Anarchy (the chaos associated with the reign of King Stephen and the civil war that broke out between

G

Stephen and Matilda in 1138). Total lack of reference to other types of structure implies that the contemporary administrative, service, and domestic structures survived pillaging and neglect, and some of these have been tentatively identified. Only nine years later, the royal manor was gifted by Henry II (1133–1189) to the house of Fontevrault in Anjou in place of a generous annuity by Henry I (1069–1135). The manor cum priory seems to have been exploited as a major agricultural enterprise, or grange, with a view to sending as much cash as possible to the motherhouse. Nothing like a conventional claustral complex (church and cloister) was uncovered. One of the major masonry buildings, a chamber block, was converted to a chapel as part of the systematic and prolonged campaign of building. A small cemetery was excavated, probably dating to c. 1220, when the rights of sepulture (the rights to bury people) were granted to the priory.

The demesne settlement evolved into three distinct courts of buildings. One was agricultural, and one contained both agricultural and service buildings. The third, carefully defined and defended by wooden fences and then stone walls, contained the ecclesiastical complex, the royal quarters (for the royals continued to use the manor as if it were still their own), and substantial service buildings, including kitchens, a workshop, and a smokehouse.

At the beginning of the fourteenth century, when the king brought all the alien houses into his own hand, Grove appeared to revert to a royal manor with resident chaplin. There were frequent royal visits both during the priory period and later, and royal quarters have been identified. The manor was held by a number of royal ladies, including Princess Mary, daughter of Edward I (1239–1307), herself a nun of the Fontevrautine nunnery at Amesbury. A number of agricultural buildings survived with a surprising amount of detail recorded.

Later, toward the end of the fifteenth century when the demesne block was separated from the rest of the manor, the lower court was virtually abandoned. Most of the medieval buildings were demolished, and a grand timber-framed manor house with plaster floors constructed over the remains of the medieval hall; this new hall may have been built for Princess Cecily, mother of Edward IV (1442–1483). The bay windows overlooked the entrance to the great outer court, and the land at the back was turned into gardens, reusing some of the remnant medieval structures. The sixteenth century saw a gradual decline, and the property went into private hands. A new manor was built a few yards away on the other side of the boundary stream, and the old manorial buildings were dismantled. Last to go was the chapel, robbed so thoroughly that it could be seen as a rectangular depression in the meadow called Chapel Field.

Ten phases have been identified within the Medieval and post-Medieval periods. It has been possible to trace new building, demolition, reduction and expansion in size, and repairs and renovation, as well as changes in function and status. The postexcavation analysis is in its final stages. The archive will be deposited with Luton Museum, where some of the artifacts are already on display.

FURTHER READINGS

Baker, Evelyn. The Medieval Travelling Candlestick from Grove Priory, Bedfordshire. *Antiquaries Journal* (1981) 61 (Part 2):336–365.

———. Grove Priory and the Royal Manor of Leighton, Bedfordshire. *Bedfordshire Magazine* (1983a) 18:321–327.

———. Grove Priory and the Royal Manor of Leighton: Interim Report on the Excavation from 1973–1981. *Council for British Archaeology Group 9* (1983b) 4:5–9.

Blair, J. Hall and Chamber: English Domestic Planning, 1000–1250. In *Manorial Domestic Buildings in England and Northern France.* Ed. G. Meirion-Jones and M. Jones. Occasional Papers, no. 15, London: Society of Antiquaries, 1993, pp. 1–21.

Webster, Karen. The Excavation and Conservation of a Knife and Shears Set from Grove Priory in Bedfordshire. *Bedfordshire Archaeology* (1988) 18:57–63.

Evelyn Baker

H

Haithabu

Haithabu (Danish Hedeby) is the site of the Viking Age and early medieval town situated south from the River Schlei near the city of Schleiswig, Schleswig-Holstein, Federal Republic of Germany. An enormous semicircular ringwork consisting of an impressive rampart and an outside ditch has been preserved from the Viking Age. Both the ditch and the rampart form the fortification of the early town of Haithabu to the north, west, and south (Fig. 1). The rampart is still very well preserved. Today it is 4–5 m high and 5–10 m wide. A fortification of such dimensions was unlikely to have been created at once; it was probably the result of several periods of construction that gradually created the monument that is preserved today.

The semicircular rampart is 1300 m long and encloses an area of 24 ha. It is presumed that nearly the entire interior of

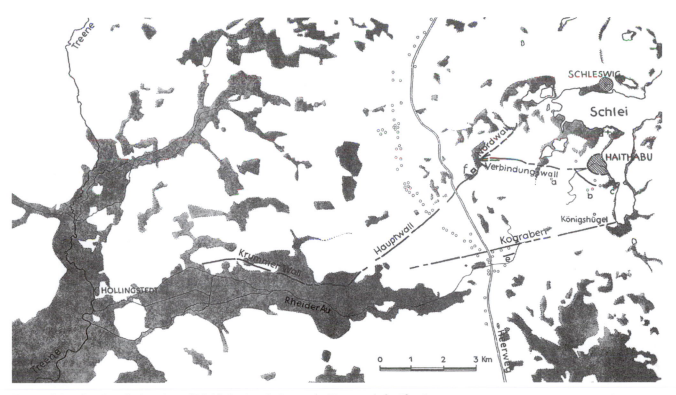

FIG. 1. Map showing the location of Haithabu in relation to the Danewerk fortifications.

the rampart was covered with Viking Age occupation. However, since only 5 percent of the area at Haithabu has been excavated, additional excavations may provide surprising results.

Haithabu cannot be treated in isolation by archaeologists. It must be seen instead in the context of many other sites that are, directly or indirectly, related to the Viking town of Haithabu. The first of these is the Tyraburg, a fortification at the northern end of the town wall. There are well-preserved grave mounds in the area that are attached by a very narrow strip of land to the Tyraburg. The Tyraburg, which is also called Hochburg, seems to have been a center of political power and rule.

Another important feature of Haithabu's topography is that the semicircular rampart, or Halbkreiswall, is divided into two parts: a northern one and a southern one (Fig. 2). The two parts are separated by a little stream (German Bach), which is of great importance because it forms a guideline for the topographical development of the center of Haithabu. Lines of buildings were excavated on both banks of the Bachbett. Many of them were dwellings, but others were used for trade and handicraft activities. The Bach not only served as a line separating the two parts of the settlement, it was also a major source of archaeological information as a result of the archaeological remains enclosed in its various layers. These archaeological layers provide a complete stratigraphic sequence (the Bachbett-Stratigraphy) for Haithabu. The Bachbett-Stratigraphy provides detailed archaeological information about the beginning, the flourishing, and the end of Haithabu. Its layers provide crucial information concerning the absolute and relative chronology of the site. It can, for example, be shown that the Halbkreiswall was constructed above older settlement structures termed the Südsiedlung (southern settlement) and a cemetery with human burials. A large part of the Südsiedlung has been excavated. Recent excavations have traced settlements in the open fields around Haithabu. Some of these may have already been in existence when the Halbkreiswall was constructed; others must have been constructed at the same time as the wall.

Haithabu is located close to the isthmus between the Baltic and the North Sea, the end of the River Schlei. It is c. 7 km wide at this point. Hollingstedt, the western end of the Danewerk (Danevirke), is located at its western end. The Danewerk is an enormous rampart that crosses the Jutish isthmus in a west-to-east direction and ends at the western part of the Haithabu Halbkreiswall (see Fig. 1). There are additional fortifications connected to the main rampart of the Danewerk—the Nordwall, the Bogenwall, the Verbindungswall, the Doppelwall, and, most important, the Kograben. The Kograben and the Hauptwall enclose a nearly triangular area south and west of the Viking town of Haithabu.

The whole system of ramparts, ditches, and fortifications subsumed under the name the Danewerk forms an enormous barrier or barricade that was erected by the Danish kings against Saxon invasions from the south. This barrier functioned on several occasions between the eighth and the nineteenth centuries. H.H. Andersen, a Danish archaeologist, has carried out several excavations on the Danewerk. He distinguishes three main phases of its construction. Dendrochronological (tree-ring) investigations from the most ancient wooden structures of the Danewerk date the most ancient building activities to A.D. 737.

Archaeological prospection has demonstrated that archaeological finds are spread all over the interior of the Halbkreiswall. It is presumed that the density of occupation is highest along both banks of the stream (Bach) crossing the middle of the town area. The overwhelming majority of the house constructions come from this central part of the settlement. An enormous number of finds were recovered during excavations that took place from 1900 to 1980.

Excavations have shown that stone buildings did not exist in Haithabu; buildings were constructed exclusively of timber. Waterlogged layers had preserved an enormous number of wooden pieces belonging to houses of differing construction and function. Wooden substructures made of oak and other trees underlay the foundations of the houses. Details of the wooden wall constructions were discovered in an excellent state of preservation. The walls of the houses were formed of wooden planks fitted into one another. Stave construction was widely used in the central part of Haithabu, but wattle was also used for parts of the house walls. The roof construction consisted of pairs of rafters with various functions. Houses were built of different dimensions, depending on their use. In addition to dwellings and buildings with economic uses, other wooden structures, including bridges, fences, wooden ways, and geometric structures of the town plan, have also been excavated. There is no doubt that a geometric town plan consisting of vertical and horizontal lines existed in Haithabu. The buildings fit into a checkerboard pattern. The excavations showed that houses of different construction and function existed in Haithabu. These houses were between 3.5 × 17 m and 7 × 17.5 m in

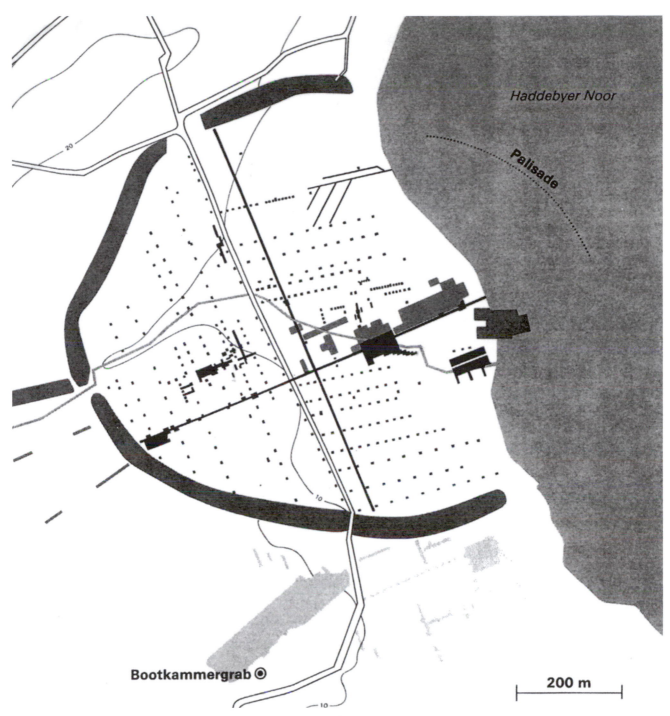

FIG. 2. Map of Haithabu showing the main areas of excavation and the fortifications surrounding the site.

size. They were all constructed of three naves that lay parallel to one another. The roofs were covered with grass or reeds. The walls were constructed of planks that fit into one another (stave construction). Oak was used exclusively in the construction of these houses. Overall, oak was used in 62 percent of Haithabu construction. A great variety of

wooden construction pieces were recovered, including wells, floors, doors, walls and planks, and small bridges over the Bachbett.

Daily life in tenth–twelfth-century Haithabu is reflected mainly in the small finds. Various types of weapons were recovered, including swords, shields, fragments of long

H

bows, axes, arrowheads, and lances. Warfare and trade were common occupations of the inhabitants of Haithabu. They traveled overseas for trade and/or warfare. Three shipwrecks can be seen in the Viking museum at Haithabu. Another group of finds consists of textile fragments. These finds are so rich that it will be possible to reconstruct the styles and functions of clothing for men and women during the Viking period. Fragments of leather come from different types of shoes. An anorak- or parkalike article of clothing was also known. Spinning and weaving activities can be traced by spindle whorls and loom weights, as well as by the various types of textiles.

Jewelry of various shapes and quality has been excavated at Haithabu. Brooches and fibulae made of gold or silver and decorated in filigree or animal style were popular and attractive to women of the upper classes. They may have been produced by foreign craftsmen or have been products of native craftsmen. Those who used these precious objects may have belonged to the upper classes of Haithabu society. There was a decided need for decorated objects in various kinds of wood, metal, leather, and other materials. Six styles of decoration can be distinguished. Their motifs show intertwined animal bodies; other pieces are decorated with plant elements like acanthus leaves or with geometrical ornamentation. The molds that were found at Haithabu are evidence for the local and foreign production of these artifacts.

As soon as the excavators discovered that organic finds were excellently preserved in great numbers, they took special care of this important group of remains. These organic remains provided evidence of how the inhabitants of Haithabu cultivated and used different sorts of grain and other plants. Wild plants such as nuts were collected; apples and plums were cultivated. Fishing along the banks of various rivers and lakes played an important role in feeding the large population. Herring predominated, making up 38.8 percent of all fish; perch was in second place. Animal bones were found in great numbers during the Haithabu excavations. They provide valuable evidence both for the breeds of cattle used and for the problem of where the inhabitants obtained their livestock.

Animal bones and all other domestic refuse from the settled areas were carried out of the inhabited zones and thrown into the sea. The animal bones demonstrate that pigs were the most numerous animals used at Haithabu, followed by cattle, sheep, and goats. Porridge was the most common meal besides meat.

There is no doubt that social differences existed in Haithabu's population. They can be seen not only in the quality of the diet, but also in the clothes and household inventories. Tools and implements differ, depending on the needs of the different classes and social groups at Haithabu.

The single graves and cemeteries are another source of information about the social life at Haithabu. About twelve thousand graves are known from Haithabu and the surrounding areas, but only about fifteen hundred of them have been excavated. The majority of the graves are situated in cemeteries. A cemetery containing barrows with Slavonic inventories is located near the "Hochburg." The older phase of Haithabu's occupation is represented by burials in wooden coffins.

A cemetery that was in use during the ninth and tenth centuries is located inside the Halbkreiswall close to the dwellings. Most of the graves contain bodies with grave goods. The chamber graves form a particularly outstanding group of graves. They are constructed of timber and are c. 3.4 × 2.6 m in size. A rich woman is buried in one of these chambers; her grave contains precious grave goods such as glass beads, a bronze vessel, a chessboard, and a trunk with a handle ending in an animal's head. Many objects in this burial were of outstanding quality in gold and silver.

Another noble grave is the so-called boat-chamber grave from Haithabu. It may have belonged to a king or to one of his nearest relatives. The boat-chamber grave contained the burials of three noblemen with their extremely rich inventories, reflecting a royal personage with his nearest followers, who may have followed him not only in life but also in death. It should be noted that, as opposed to the small group of royal or noble burials, the great majority of the burials are of "normal" or poor quality. The variety of the graves in Haithabu reflects a society marked by wide differences, ranging from those of royal or noble status down to the "average men" who may have worked as craftsmen, peasants, workmen in the harbor, or even slaves.

As an important trading place, Haithabu brought together goods and products from the whole of Europe, especially from the north. Trading connections with the Carolingian Empire, Russia, the Baltic, and Arabia can be identified by imported goods of various kinds. Silver coins were minted in Haithabu. A group of twenty-five bronze bars was recovered from the harbor at Haithabu. Bulk articles came in as imports, including millstones and pottery from the Rhine and building stone from the volcanic areas near Koblenz and the Moselle Valley. All these activities made Haithabu a place that had clearly surpassed the limited framework of agrarian existence; it was on its way to becoming a community of real urban character. This picture is consistent with the existence of a monetary system for local and foreign use, trade relations with various areas and countries, craft production, social differentiation, population agglomeration, and another important feature of urban existence: writing, as seen in the runic inscriptions on stone and wood.

Spiritual and religious life in Haithabu shows two different elements. On the one hand, pagan objects have been found, such as amulets, small figures of gods, and a Thorshammer (a pagan symbol associated with the Norse god Thor). On the other hand, there are objects that clearly indicate that Christianity had already entered Haithabu's society, such as a circular fibula showing Christ in a mandorla (an oval-shaped frame). Apparently, both religions, pagan and Christian, existed in Haithabu at the same time. Widespread trading and commercial interests may have prevented conflicts between the different religions of those who lived in Haithabu or those who came in from abroad. There is no doubt that Haithabu and a few comparable sites are phenomena in a historical process that leads from very simple trading places, to more extended and better organized ones, to early towns like Haithabu and comparable sites such as Birka in Swe-

den, Kaupang in Norway, Dublin in Ireland, and Dorestad in the Netherlands (Fig. 3). Seen in this perspective, Haithabu is not simply a single item of archaeological knowledge; rather, it is a model for the transition from the rural existence of the migration and early Medieval periods to early urban and, ultimately, true urban existence. This model could not have been created without archaeologists and historians asking new questions that led them into new fields of inquiry. The Haithabu excavations are, therefore, to a great degree, part of the creation of a new kind of archaeology—the archaeology of settlements (Seidlungsarchaeologie)—that opens up new fields for research activities. These new questions require a new type of archaeology, the kind that has been practiced only since the 1960s.

FURTHER READINGS

Andersen, H.H., H.J. Madsen, and O. Voss. *Danevirke.* 2 vols. Copenhagen: Jysk Arkeologisk Selskabs Skrifter, 1976.

Behre, K.E. Die Ernährung im Mittelalter. In *Mensch und Umwelt im Mittelalter.* Ed. B. Herrmann. Stuttgart: Deutsche Verlags Anstatt, 1986, pp. 74–87.

Bronsted, J. *The Vikings.* Trans. Kalle Skov. New York: Penguin, 1980.

FIG. 3. Map of Europe showing the location of Haithabu in relation to other important early medieval sites.

H

Capelle, T. *Der Metallschmuck von Haithabu: Studien zur wikingischen Metallkunst.* Neumünster: K. Wachholtz, 1968.

Ellmers, D. *Frühmittelalterliche Handelsschiffahrt in Mittel- und Nordeuropa.* Neumünster: K. Wachholtz, 1972.

Jankuhn, H. *Haithabu: Ein Handelsplatz der Wikingzeit. 8, neubrarbeitete und stark erweiterte Auflage.* Neumünster: K. Wachholtz, 1986.

Janssen, W. *Die Importkeramik von Haithabu.* Die Ausgrabunden in Haithabu 9. Neumünster: K. Wachholtz, 1987.

Klindt-Jensen, O. *The World of the Vikings.* London: Allen and Unwin, 1970.

Liestol, A. *Runenstäbe aus Haithabu-Hedeby.* Berichte über die Ausgrabungen in Haithabu 6. Neumünster: K. Wachholtz, 1973, pp. 96–119.

Müller-Wille, M. *Das Bootkammergrab von Haithabu.* Berichte über die Ausgrabungen in Haithabu 8. Neumünster: K. Wachholtz, 1976.

Schietzel, K. Handwerk und Handel in Haithabu: Probleme der Interpretation. *Zeitschrift für Archäologie* (1979) 13:91–99.

———. *Stand der siedlungsarchäologischen Forschung in Haithabu: Ergebnisse und Probleme.* Berichte über die Aurgrabungen in Haithabu 16. Neumünster: K. Wachholtz, 1981.

Walter Janssen

SEE ALSO
Birka; Danevirke; Emporia; Vikings

Hamburg

Settlements have been erected on the tongue of land located between the junction of the Alster and Bille Rivers in northern Germany since prehistoric times. Continuous settlement of Hamburg began in the late Saxon period. Later, a fortification of two circular ditches, 48 m in diameter, protected this small village in the eighth century. At this time, Slavic pottery indicates, there were some influences from the east, but it is not clear if the Slavs themselves settled in this area.

Shortly after 817, a Carolingian earthwork was erected with its entrance at the west side. West of it, we find a *suburbium* (suburb) and, to the south, at the river side, a harbor. Between 831 and 834, Ansgar, the archbishop of Hamburg and Bremen, raised the dome of his cathedral at Hamburg, but the whole location was destroyed in 845 by a Danish invasion.

The dome was reerected in 858, and it seems that the settlement was repopulated as well. During the eleventh century, the location developed rapidly. C. 1035, Archbishop Bezelin built a tower for his own security, and another archbishop's castle existed at the east end of the settlement from 1012 to 1066. Two other castles at the west end (Alsterburg and Neue Burg) were erected by the dukes of Billung, but we have archaeological evidence from only one of these monuments. The Slavic invasions and destructions of 983, 1066, and 1072 were unable to interrupt the development of the site. In 1188, the Neustadt was founded and obtained a city charter, which was extended to the old city in 1225. Later, Hamburg played an important role in the Hanseatic League.

Archaeological research at Hamburg goes back to the late fifteenth century but became very important right after 1945, when the center of the town was rebuilt after the destructions of World War II. Hamburg was one of the earliest locations of medieval archaeology in Germany. Excavations took place at many sites in the old town. In addition, the site of the Carolingian fortification and the dome, which was pulled down in 1804–1807, was excavated from 1947 to 1957 and from 1979 to 1987. Inside the dome, the remains of the cenotaph of Pope Benedict V, who died at Hamburg in 965, were discovered. Many other excavations, especially in the former *suburbium,* have clarified the chronology of medieval pottery at Hamburg and the influence of Slavic ceramics.

In 1989, a new campaign began to research the first settlement in the marsh land south of the earliest center on the River Bille. This settlement developed on an island now called Reichenstraße. The first evidence of human activity in this region dates to the ninth century. Later, flooding of the River Elbe forced the settlers to use fill to raise the ground level by more than 2.5 m. Every lot in the settlement had its own wooden construction. The lots were all nearly the same size, 8 m wide and c. 70 m deep. This construction dates to the thirteenth century. The objects found in the excavations indicate that mostly craftsmen settled in this area.

FURTHER READINGS

Busch, R., ed. *Bodendenkmalpflege in Hamburg.* Hamburg: Hamburger Museum of Archaeology, 1989.

———. *Medieval Urban Archaeology in the City of Hamburg.* In press.

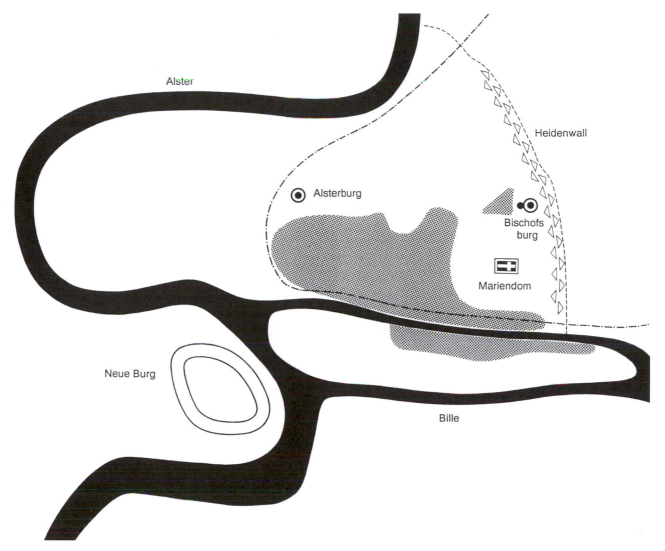

Hamburg, eleventh century.

Lobbedey, U. Northern Germany. In *European Towns.* Ed. M.W. Barley, London: Academic, 1977, pp. 127–157.

Schindler, R. *Ausgrabungen in Alt-Hamburg.* Hamburg: Verlag Gesellschaft der Freunde des vaterländischen Schul- und Ereichungswesens, 1957.

R. Busch

SEE ALSO
Germany

Hamwic
See Emporia.

Hartlepool

Hartlepool is a headland on the northeast coast of England (NZ 528 338). It comprises a ridge of limestone protruding into the North Sea with cliffs in all directions except the west, where a steep slope leads down to a natural harbor. The evidence suggests that the Anglo-Saxon monastery was sited on the ridgetop and the medieval town was based on the slope and around the harbor.

Anglo-Saxon Monastery
In the late A.D. 640s, Hilda was appointed abbess at Heruteu, and, in 655, K. Oswiu of Northumbria gave his daughter, Aelffled, into her care there. In 657, Hilda and

Aelfled moved to Whitby to establish a double monastery similar to that at Heruteu, on land given by Oswiu. Hilda and succeeding abbesses of Whitby retained control of the monastery at Heruteu (Colgrave and Mynors 1969).

Heruteu has been traditionally associated with Hartlepool, and this was confirmed by the find of a cemetery with namestones at Cross Close in the late nineteenth century (Cramp 1984). Further work has confirmed this

identification and revealed a number of components of the monastery. Two cemeteries and one group of buildings are now known, and the position of the religious focus has been adduced from this information (Fig. 1).

The cemetery with the namestones is known only through newspaper reports and brief notes, but the evidence suggests north-south burial in association with the namestones, and this is assumed to be the cemetery of the

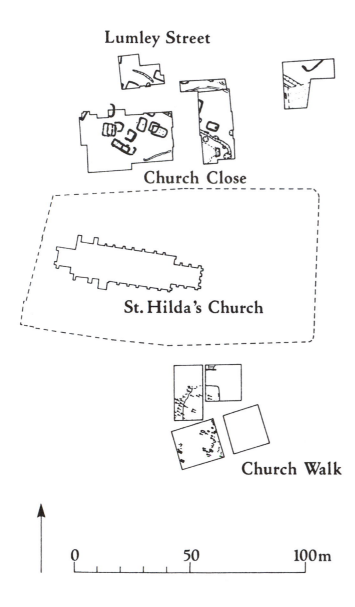

Lumley Street

Church Close

St. Hilda's Church

Church Walk

0   50   100m

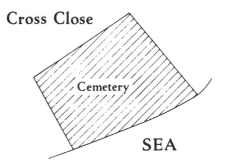

Cross Close

Cemetery

SEA

FIG. 1. Hartlepool Anglo-Saxon monastery.

professed of the community (Cramp 1984; Cramp and Daniels 1987).

The second cemetery, at Church Walk, contained both male and female burials and infants. There was horizontal stratification within the cemetery, with the infants sited in a distinct group to the southeast of the others. A second distinct group of graves with stone kerbing lay to the southwest of the main group. Radiocarbon dating confirmed that the cemetery was of the monastic period.

Excavations at Lumley Street and Church Close (Cramp 1976; Daniels 1988) revealed a group of small earthfast timber buildings that demonstrated Anglo-Saxon construction techniques but were much smaller than the typical Anglo-Saxon hall. In the mid-eighth century, a number of these buildings were cut off at ground level and stone footings inserted, making them comparable to the excavated buildings at Whitby (Rahtz 1976). The buildings have been interpreted as cells used by the professed for study and prayer.

The excavations at Church Close also revealed a substantial internal boundary of the monastery, in the backfill of which were the remains of small metalworking crucibles and molds. The most important is a design of a calf, the symbol of Saint Luke, which is depicted with a trumpet and can be paralleled by trumpeting Lion and Angel figures from the *Lindisfarne Gospels* (Cramp and Daniels 1987) (Fig. 2).

The positioning of these elements of the monastery, when compared to the sites at Whitby, Jarrow, and Monkwearmouth (Cramp 1976), suggests that the religious focus lies in the area to the east of the present medieval church rather than under it.

The archaeological evidence from Church Close suggests that the monastery was abandoned toward the end

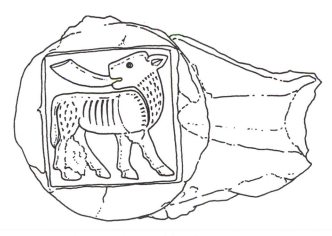

FIG. 2. Calf metalworking mold; scale 3:2.

of the eighth century. There was no evidence of deliberate destruction of the site.

Medieval Town

There was a hiatus between the Anglo-Saxon monastery and the medieval town when there was no substantial settlement on the headland. The medieval town was a deliberate plantation, probably by the Brus family, following the Norman Conquest (1066). The first documentary reference to it dates from 1171, when a military force landed there. Its economy was based on coastal trade and fishing. It played a major role in supplying the bishop and the monastery at Durham, and it served as a provisioning center during the Scottish Wars of the late thirteenth and the fourteenth centuries.

Excavations have revealed an initial semirural phase of the planned town (Daniels 1990) prior to the development of an urban economy, but the town developed rapidly from the mid-thirteenth century. This development was prompted by substantial investment by the Brus family through the construction of a large church and Franciscan friary (Fig. 3).

The waterfront comprised a mix of timber and stone docks and open foreshore, with reclamation taking place throughout the Medieval period (Daniels 1991). The initial earthfast timber buildings built parallel to the frontage gave way to structures placed gable end to the street and with ground floors, at least, of stone (Daniels 1990). St. Hilda's Church dates from the late twelfth to the early thirteenth centuries and is of substantial proportions, reflecting its role as a status symbol for the town. Its construction was immediately followed by that of the Franciscan friary, which could offer sanctuary by 1243 and which had reached its final form of double nave and choir by the third quarter of the thirteenth century (Daniels 1986a).

While the Scottish Wars brought prosperity, they also brought the risk of Scottish attack. In 1315, the town was raided, and subsequently the inhabitants petitioned the king to construct defensive walls, the townspeople having already dug a ditch across the peninsula. Murage grants (grants to construct walls) were made throughout the fourteenth century, and a substantial wall, comprising round and square towers, was constructed. The harbor was defended by two massive towers with a boom chain between preventing access to enemy shipping. One stretch of town wall survives on the southern beach, although the Sandwell Gate feature is an insertion of the fifteenth century. The construction of the Sandwell Gate

H

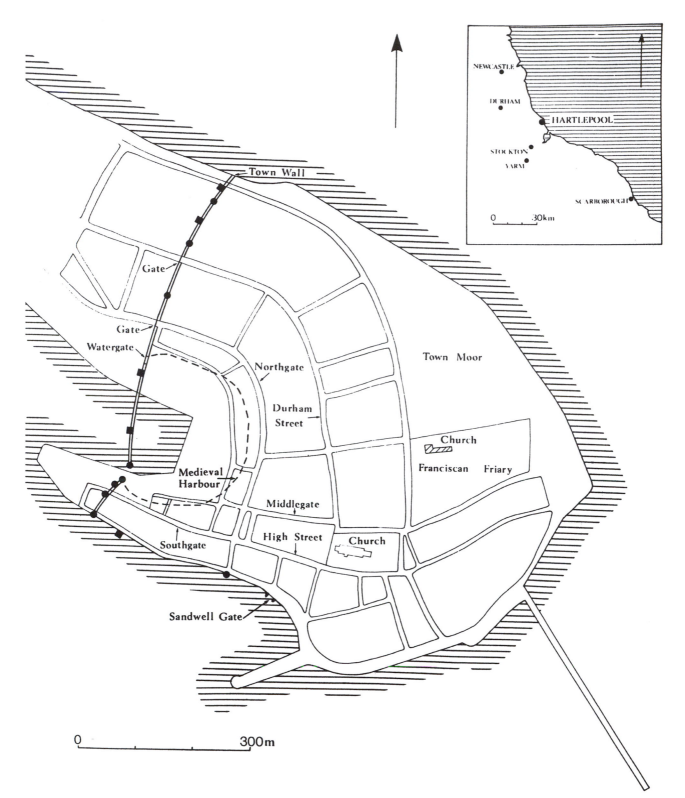

Town Wall

Gate

Gate

Watergate

Northgate

Durham
Street

Town Moor

Church

Franciscan   Friary

Medieval
Harbour

Middlegate

High Street

Church

Southgate

Sandwell Gate

0   300m

NEWCASTLE

DURHAM

HARTLEPOOL

STOCKTON

YARM

SCARBOROUGH

0   30km

FIG. 3. Medieval Hartlepool.

is contemporary with the construction of a pier that allowed boats to beach at the gate (Daniels 1986b).

The archaeological evidence suggests a lengthy period of decay of the town from the end of the fifteenth century, which was reversed only by the nineteenth-century construction of docks linked by rail to the Durham coalfield.

FURTHER READINGS

Colgrave, B., and R.A.B. Mynors. *Bede's Ecclesiastical History of the English People.* Oxford: Clarendon, 1969.

Cramp, R.J. Monastic Sites. In *The Archaeology of Anglo-Saxon England.* Ed. D. Wilson. Cambridge: Cambridge University Press, 1976, pp. 210–252.

———. *Corpus of Anglo-Saxon Stone Sculpture: Durham and Northumberland.* London: British Academy, 1984.

Cramp, R.J., and R. Daniels. New Finds from the Anglo-Saxon Monastery at Hartlepool, Cleveland. *Antiquity* (1987) 61:424–432.

Daniels, R. The Excavation of the Church of the Franciscans, Hartlepool, Cleveland. *Archaeological Journal* (1986a) 143:260–304.

———. The Medieval Defences of Hartlepool, Cleveland: The Results of Excavation and Survey. *Durham Archaeological Journal* (1986b) 2:63–72.

———. The Anglo-Saxon Monastery at Church Close Hartlepool. *Archaeological Journal* (1988) 145:158–210.

———. The Development of Medieval Hartlepool: Excavations at Church Close, 1984–85. *Archaeological Journal* (1990) 147:337–410.

———. Medieval Hartlepool: Evidence of and from the Waterfront. In *Waterfront Archaeology.* Ed. G.L. Good, R.H. Jones, and M.W. Ponsford. CBA Research Report 74. London: Council for British Archaeology, 1991, pp. 43–50.

Rahtz, P. The Building Plan of the Anglo-Saxon Monastery of Whitby Abbey. In *The Archaeology of Anglo-Saxon England.* Ed. D.M. Wilson, Cambridge: Cambridge University Press, 1976, pp. 459–462.

Robin Daniels

Hedges

The medieval landscape was divided by hedges, streams, ditches, dry-stone walls, wooden fences, and temporary "dead hedges" made of cut thornbushes. Many boundaries, especially in open-field systems, were marked only by balks (strips of uncultivated land) or not marked at all. Hedges were a common demarcation, especially around private fields, meadows, woodlands, and commons and along roads and parish boundaries. The classic hedged regions were in west, south, and east England and northwest France, but hedges probably occurred locally in most of Europe except Spain.

A medieval hedgerow was a strip of trees and bushes like an American fencerow. It served as a barrier to prevent livestock from straying, as a means of defining an ownership boundary, as a shelter for cattle, and as a source of timber and wood. Hedges could originate by people planting them or by people not getting rid of the trees and bushes that sprang up naturally along balks, fences, and walls. They could be managed by coppicing (felling trees in a cycle of years and allowing them to grow again from the stump, thus producing a perpetual succession of poles and twigs) or pollarding (cropping branches for fuel, or leaves for feeding animals) or plashing (half-cutting and intertwining the stems to form a barrier).

Hedges are difficult to detect in excavations. Field boundaries in general go back to the Neolithic. There is some evidence for hedges in Iron Age and Roman Britain (first–fourth centuries A.D.). Hedges were known to the Romans in Italy and Belgium, and hedges and hedgerow trees are abundantly recorded in English documents and place names from the eighth century onward. Their numbers probably increased over time.

Many medieval hedges are still extant. They are best known in England, where they can be identified by their sinuous shapes and massive banks, by their composition of many species of tree and shrub, and by the ancient pollard trees and coppice stools that they contain.

FURTHER READINGS

Pollard, M.D., M. Hooper, and N.W. Moore. *Hedges.* London: Collins, 1974.

Rackham, O. *The History of the [British and Irish] Countryside.* London: Dent, 1986.

Oliver Rackham

SEE ALSO
Woodland

Helgö

Helgö was a trade and manufacturing center on the island of Helgö in Lake Mälaren, c. 20 km west of Stockholm, Sweden. The island of Helgö consists mostly of rock and moraine hillocks around a clay-filled valley. It lies like a plug at the west end of one of the remaining fairways

H

through Mälaren, near the passage through Södertälje and c. 15 km southeast of Birka.

The valley in the east of the island is surrounded by a number of groups of buildings on terraces, some cemeteries containing approximately two hundred mounds and stone settings, and a prehistoric fortress. The site was uncovered in 1950 through the accidental unearthing of gold coils and a bronze ladle. This initiated almost thirty years of archaeological excavations, mainly under the leadership of Wilhelm Holmqvist. As a result, more terraces and cemeteries were discovered, many of them now excavated. The site dates from c. A.D. 400–1000.

The occupied area of the site consisted of groups of terraces, mainly supporting buildings of indigenous longhouse type, but there were also some sunken-featured buildings. Each group contained buildings devoted to specific functions, not necessarily all in use at the same time.

Building Groups 1, 2, and 3 were the largest. Each contained material from many periods, but internal continuity is uncertain. It appears that only one or two terraces were occupied simultaneously, and it is possible that activities moved from one place to another from time to time.

The remains of intensive manufacture, particularly ironsmithing and bronze casting, were discovered everywhere on the site. Trading contacts were represented by a great quantity of foreign objects: sherds of glass, bronzes, and pottery. The largest hoard of late Roman *solidi* (coins) to be found in mainland Sweden was discovered, on two separate occasions, immediately west of the settlement.

The most remarkable assemblage of finds was discovered on the central terrace—in Foundation 1 in Building Group 2. One building, c. 30 m long and with its roof carried on posts, contained hundreds of sherds of glass beakers from the Merovingian period, some pieces of gold foil decorated with human figures, and locks and keys, plus prestige objects such as a Coptic bronze ladle, fragments of a large decorated silver dish, an "Irish" (probably west European) crozier, and a Buddha statuette from north India. This assemblage dates predominantly from the eighth century, but some Arabic coins from the beginning of the ninth century were also discovered in association with it.

To the east and below Building Group 3, comprising a number of narrow terraces, there was a huge rubbish heap composed of ninety thousand fragments of molds and c. 300 kg of crucible fragments; they were all from a workshop that was in use A.D. 400–650. This was the first migration period and Merovingian period bronze-casting workshop to have been discovered. The most important objects made here were square-headed (relief) brooches and clasp buttons of migration period types. Research into this material continues.

The finds of most recent date came from the most westerly building group, Building Group 1. They were mainly of Viking Age type and most from ironsmithing.

Numerous cemeteries were found on the land above the settlement. Two remain unexcavated. The excavated examples produced grave goods covering the entire occupation period, but only exceptionally were the finds of a higher status than those normally found in cemeteries in the surrounding countryside.

A simple prehistoric fortress with no signs of settlement lay above Building Group 2. Another "prehistoric fortress" stood farther to the west, but this was probably an enclosure around a Bronze Age burial cairn.

The remarkable finds from Helgö initiated a wide-ranging debate about the character of the site. The building groups on the terraces were originally thought to be roughly contemporary and to represent a protourban society dependent on trade and manufacture. More detailed research has shown that the building groups were occupied over many centuries but not always simultaneously, and that the cemeteries were of virtually the same character as those in the rest of the Mälaren hinterland. The number of graves in the cemeteries showed that there could never have been more than, on average, a population of twenty.

On the other hand, the finds from the settlement itself are quite different from those found on "normal" settlements, and the emphasis on manufacture such as bronze casting and ironsmithing is quite exceptional. Modern opinion is that Helgö was probably a specialized economic zone within an extensive estate around the prehistoric and medieval royal manorial site of Hundhamra, which faces it across the strait. Hundhamra contains many high-status great mounds dating from the eighth century, the final *floruit* of Helgö.

The particularly rich finds from the migration and Merovingian periods (i.e., before the Viking Age) suggest that Helgö's manufacture and trade were preeminent before the trading center of Birka on Björkö grew up at the beginning of the Viking Age, c. A.D. 800. But Helgö lived on, perhaps as a purely agricultural settlement. In the High Middle Ages, there was still an important estate with the name Helgö; by the late Middle Ages, it was called Bona.

FURTHER READINGS

Early Medieval Studies. Vols. 1–8. Antikvariskst Arkiv 38–40, 46, 50, 53–54, 57. Stockholm: KVHAA, 1970–1975.

Holmqvist, W., A. Lundström, H. Clarke, et al., eds. *Excavations at Helgö.* Vols. 1–12. Stockholm: KVHAA, 1961–.

Lundström, A., ed. *Thirteen Studies on Helgö.* SHM Studies 7. Stockholm: Statenshistoriska Musuem, 1988.

Björn Ambrosiani, translated by Helen Clarke

SEE ALSO

Birka

Herpes

The Merovingian cemetery of Herpes, in the Charente département in southwestern France, was discovered in 1886 and excavated by a local antiquary, Philippe Delamain. The graves were situated on either side of a Roman road linked to the main route from Saintes to Limoges, which lay 3 km to the south. They were densely grouped and cut into the chalky marl at a depth of up to 2 m. There were no sarcophagi or coffins, but many of the graves contained stone blocks. The skeletons were in good condition, oriented with their heads to the west, and often accompanied by a glass or a pottery vessel.

The male graves contained iron knives, iron, silver and copper-alloy buckles, iron spearheads, seaxes, and axes, but no swords or shields. The female graves were richer, yielding both jewelry and everyday items, including earrings, amber and glass beads, buckles, and a variety of radiate-headed, rosette, bird, and square-headed brooches, as well as finger rings, chatelaines, iron shears, and copper-alloy tweezers.

In an area of France characterized by burials in sarcophagi with relatively few grave goods, Herpes is remarkable for both its mode of burial and the abundance of finds. It has generated controversy since its discovery. First identified as Visigothic, it is now seen as belonging to a small group of cemeteries, situated between Saintes and Angoulême, that suggest the introduction of a strong Frankish element into the local population at the beginning of the sixth century.

The cemetery is also notable for the Anglo-Saxon pieces found there, directly comparable to material from Kent in England and the Isle of Wight, although whether this represents actual emigration, intermarriage, or trading links has been fiercely debated. Recent discoveries of similar material from northern France help place these objects in context, although Herpes remains the only site in the southwest with such a concentration of imported finds.

Unfortunately, interpreting the significance of the Herpes cemetery remains problematic, due to the difficulties posed by the surviving documentation. No plan exists of the site, and the brief monograph that the excavator, Delamain, produced in 1892 is not a detailed cemetery report but a collection of articles, which had previously appeared elsewhere, together with drawings of a mere 144 objects. It covers only material from the first nine hundred graves and illustrates only one grave group, a woman buried with a gold-and-garnet finger ring, an inscribed silver finger ring, a pair of gilt-silver animal brooches, a pair of cloisonné garnet disc brooches, a pair of gilt-silver radiate-headed brooches, and a pottery vessel. The contents of eighteen other graves are listed in M. Deloche's work on finger rings, *Les anneaux sigillaires* (Signet rings) (1900), but these are not fully illustrated, and attempts to identify these objects among the surviving material have met with limited success. Excavations continued until at least 1893, by which time a total of sixteen hundred burials had been unearthed, a figure given in Delamain's report on the Biron cemetery published in 1898. A second volume dealing with the finds from these later graves was planned but never published.

The listing of grave groups by Deloche and the recent discovery of an excavation diary for the period February–May 1893, together with other original documentation, indicate that other records did once exist but are now lost. Some scholars have cast doubt on the integrity of the existing material, believing it to be an admixture of sites from Delamain's collection, rather than the surviving material from Herpes, and it has to be admitted that only a relatively small number of pieces can be securely identified from contemporary illustrations. The possibility remains that some of the objects may be from other cemeteries or collections.

The Delamain collection was dispersed in 1901. Most of it was sold to the collector Edouard Guilhou, who retained the finger rings (present whereabouts unknown) and put the rest up for sale in 1905, when it was purchased by the British Museum. Other pieces were purchased by a rich German industrialist, Johannes von Diergardt, who gave some objects, since lost, to the Museum für Vor- und Frühgeschichte in Berlin. The remainder of his collection is now in the Römisch-Germanisches Museum in Cologne. A number of objects

H

from the site, previously thought to be from northern France, have been identified in the J. Pierpont Morgan Collection in New York.

FURTHER READINGS

Delamain, P. *Le cimetière d'Herpes.* Angoulême: Société Archéologique et Historique de la Charente, 1892.

Deloche, M. *Etude historique et archéologique sur les anneaux sigillaires et autres des premiers siècles du moyen âge.* Paris: E. Leroux, 1900.

de Ricci, S. *Catalogue of a Collection of Gallo-Roman Antiquities Belonging to J. Pierpont Morgan.* Paris: Imp. de l'Art, C. Berger, 1911.

Guilhou Collection. *Catalogue des objets antiques et du moyen âge . . . provenant de la collection de M. Guilhou dont la vente aura lieu à Paris du jeudi au samedi 18 mars 1905.* Paris: n.p., 1905.

Haith, C. Un nouveau regard sur le cimetière d'Herpes (Charente): Actes des VIIIe journeés internationales d'archéologie mérovingienne de Soissons 9–12 juin 1986. *Revue archéologique de Picardie* (1986) 3–4: 71–80.

James, E. *The Merovingian Archaeology of South-West Gaul.* BAR Supplementary Series 25. Oxford: British Archaeological Reports, 1977.

Marin, J.Y. *Les Barbares et la Mer.* Caen: Musée de Normandie and Toulouse: Musée des Augustins, 1992.

Werner, J. *Katalog der Sammlung Diergardt: Die Fibeln.* Berlin: Gebr. Mann, 1961.

Catherine Haith

History and Archaeology: A Theoretical Perspective

The mutual relationships between archaeology and history can be considered on the basis of the links between each of them and anthropology. This seems to be a realistic criterion for measuring the distance or closeness of the cognitive perspectives of archaeology and history. Historical knowledge is situated between that which is material (tangible objects) and that which is nonmaterial (traditions, texts). The relationship between the disciplines of archaeology, history, and both social and cultural anthropology is therefore crucial. The relationship between these three disciplines is constantly undergoing change, as a function of their historical development and changing research aims. These formally distinct scientific disciplines, each possessing autonomous academic status, are however characterized by a high degree of overlap and a mutual dependence which is not often sufficiently appreciated. In reality, as Marc Bloch wrote, there is only one "science of man," "of men in time." It would be more correct to discuss here the different methods of historical research within the various cooperating disciplines, all of which study the human past.

We are currently witnessing a new stage in the development of historical thought. For nearly a century history has been seeking inspiration and useful methods from other sciences of man. After geography, sociology, economics, and demography, attention has now turned to anthropology—here considered in broad terms, both a science of physical variability in man and a science of society and culture. As a result, we see it as the investigation of a wide spectrum of phenomena, examples of which include the relationship between biology and cultural behavior, incorporating extra-economic values in the sphere of economic behavior, medieval consanguinity; or political and cultural anthropology. The influence of the anthropological approach is particularly visible in all these cases; the object of study becomes symbols, senses, and meanings detectable in various attributes of material culture. This anthropological approach is not a distinct and individual field of investigation; it can be found in many disciplines, not only archaeology, but also history, history of art, etc.

A very significant analysis of the relationship between history and ethnology has been made by C. Lévi-Strauss. Both history and ethnology have social life as the object of research and better knowledge of man as their goal. They share the same method with differing emphasis on its various research procedures. Both these disciplines are distinguished by the choice of complementary perspectives: history organizes its data in relation to conscious manifestations, ethnology in relation to the unconscious conditions of social life.

Even though in a broadly conceived archaeology there are components of both approaches, it is prehistoric archaeology, well described as "le summum de l'ethnologie," which is especially close to social and cultural anthropology. Classical archaeology, on the other hand, because of its close links with ancient history, philology, and history of art, is closer to history. Medieval archaeology appears to constitute an area of the mutual influence and overlap between both these approaches. While, on one hand, archaeological data are complemented by written evidence, on the other, we see strong links with ethnographic investigation. There also occur together here (to a greater extent than in other branches of archaeology) the investigation of both idiographic components (usually considered as proper for the historical approach) and nomothetic ones, to which contemporary cultural anthropology aspires. Social and cultural anthropology can constitute a practical system of reference at various levels of the investigative process—from analysis through interpretation to explanation and synthesis. A second such system is constituted by historiography and, in particular, by information derived from written sources. Medieval archaeology seems therefore (together with ethnoarchaeology) to constitute a natural field in which to search for links between "monuments" and "documents" and a way of integrating the various types of sources of knowledge of the social past.

Archaeological sources, as a rule, provide information about certain relations, states, and situations formed during the historical process; written sources, first and foremost, provide information about events. In this sense, documents such as acts and chronicles reflect aspects of reality essentially different from those which we re-create on the basis of excavated evidence. The first, to use the terminology of Lévi-Strauss, inform us about unconscious conditions; the second about conscious manifestations of social life.

The formation of the archaeological record (continuous, although not at a constant rate in time and space) is a process of cumulative deposition of things that man creates, transforms, accumulates, and leaves behind. The preserved part of these material correlates of human presence and activity becomes, upon its progressive discovery, a source of information about the social past.

The creation of the written record, on the other hand (discontinuous and evidently intermittent in time and space), is a process of making information permanent with the intention of its transmission to contemporaries and/or descendants. Thus, in this manner the written record, where it is present, partially overlaps with the potentially enormous and continuously generated mass of archaeological materials.

Archaeological sources not only serve as a basis for "prolonging history backwards," but also yield new qualitative data which enrich the vision of subsequent stages of historical development. These sources allow us to go beyond the frontier of "the world with history." They allow us to "recognise the structure and course of the creators of history, and of those to whom history was not given."

Increasingly the Middle Ages are becoming conceived of as a period of coexistence between the "world with his-

tory" and the broad social area with "insufficient" or even "lack of history." The only available witness of their existence and role are the material remains, without which the imposing monuments and urban complexes of the medieval European landscape would not have been possible. Access to the significant information contained in this buried and excavated material is in many cases especially difficult.

More archaeologists are now prepared to substitute the previously dominant substantive approach with a structural one, using a semiotic description of cultural reality. This has provided the impetus for new ways of conceptualizing archaeological evidence. In historiography, the change of perspective is expressed most suggestively by M. Foucault dealing with the notions of "document" and "monument," and the relationship between them. The traditional understanding of the document, as Le Goff (commenting on Foucault) underlines it, contains the concept *"docere,"* the deliberate making permanent of information with the purpose of transmitting it to someone else. The document is conceived as something which informs us of that which concerns he who made it. In reality a document is de facto always a monument. It is something that shapes rather than informs, with a purpose *"impressionare."* The interpretation of Le Goff allows us to understand more clearly the meaning of Foucault when he writes that history today is that which transforms "documents" into "monuments" and that which uncovers (where traces left by people are being read) an ensemble of elements which should be distinguished, divided into groups, evaluated, linked together, and joined into entities. He also states that while archaeology gains sense only through the reproduction of historical discourse, so now history is tending towards archaeology—towards the intrinsic description of the monument.

In conclusion, just as the historian transforms "documents" into "monuments," the archaeologist does the opposite; "monuments" appear to him as "documents." So the scholars meet halfway, crossing the line of demarcation which sharply divided archaeological and written sources until recently in the consciousness of many researchers. This fact makes possible (as recently emphasized especially by Hodder, Patrik, and Carver) a more objective confrontation, not of the types of sources themselves, but of the information contained in them. This would open further perspectives for the process of explanation based both on written sources and excavated data.

Two particularly promising fields of advance in this direction are ethnoarchaeology and historical archaeology,

H

medieval archaeology having an especially important role. This is, however, dependent on the dialogue between historians and archaeologists ceasing to be, as experience too often has shown can be the case, a "dialogue of the deaf."

FURTHER READINGS

Bloch, M. *The Historian's Craft.* Manchester: Manchester University Press, 1954.

Burgiere, A. L'anthropologie historique. In *La nouvelle histoire,* ed. J. Le Goff and J. Revel. Paris: Retz-C.E.P.L., 1978, pp. 37–61.

Carver, M.O.H. Digging for Data: Archaeological Approaches to Data Definition, Acquisition and Analysis. In *Lo scavo archeologico: dalla diagnosi all'edizione,* ed. R. Francovich and D. Manacorda. Firenze: Edizioni All'Insegna del Giglio, 1990, pp. 45–120.

Fehring, G. *The Archaeology of Medieval Germany: An Introduction.* London and New York: Routledge, 1991.

Foucault, M. *L'archéologie du savoir.* Paris: Éditions Gallimard, 1977.

Hodder, I. *Symbols in Action: Ethnoarchaeological Studies of Material Culture.* Cambridge: Cambridge University Press, 1982.

Le Goff, J. *Intervista sulla storia di Francesco Maiello.* Roma: Latenza, 1982.

Lévi-Strauss, C. *Anthropologie structurale.* Paris: Librairie Plan, 1958.

Patrik, L.E. Is there an archaeological record? In *Advances in Archaeological Method and Theory,* vol. 8, ed. M.B. Schiffer. New York: Academic Press, 1985, pp. 27–62.

Tabaczyński, S. The Relationship between History and Archaeology: Elements of the Present Debate. *Medieval Archaeology* (1993) 37:1–14 (for further arguments and references).

Wolf, E.R. *Europe and the People without History.* Berkeley: University of California Press, 1982.

Stanisław Tabaczyński

Hofstaðir

Hofstaðir is located on the River Laxa near Lake Myvatn in northern Iceland. First excavated in 1908 by D. Brunn and F. Jonsson, Hofstaðir was long identified as a pagan temple site based on place-name evidence and local tradition. Brunn's excavation revealed an exceptionally large long hall, a circular depression filled with animal bones and charcoal, and some traces of earlier structures. Brunn and Jonsson concluded that the great hall had been a temple and feasting hall, and it has since figured in controversies about the nature of pre-Christian Nordic religion. Since 1992, new investigations have been carried out under the leadership of the Archaeological Institute of Iceland (directed by Adolf Friðriksson and Orri Vesteinsson) in cooperation with the North Atlantic Biocultural Organization (NABO). Major well-stratified collections of animal bones, archaeobotanical remains, and artifacts dating to c. A.D. 875–1050 are combined with soil micromorphology and the study of tephra (volcanic ash layers) in a multidisciplinary attempt to better understand the complex interactions of humans and landscape at the time of the initial colonization of Iceland. The circular depression is a pithouse (with a terminal radiocarbon date calibrated to A.D. 880±40), filled by later midden material, and several phases of early turf buildings documented below the great hall excavated by Brunn. While the site clearly functioned as a full-scale farm, a row of cattle skulls buried along the side of the hall hints at some ritual elements as well. Excavations continue, and updates are available through the NABO Web site, www.geo.ed.ac.uk/nabo/home, and the new series Archaeologica Islandica.

Thomas H. McGovern

Hungary
Roman Pannonia

The area of modern Hungary extends west and east of the two great rivers of the Danube and Tisza. In the east lies the Great Hungarian Plain, fertile grassland once renowned for horse breeding; to the west, lowland slowly gives way to the rougher highland of the Austrian and Italian Alps. In antiquity, the western half of Hungary comprised the Roman province of Pannonia, facing Sarmatian tribes across the Tisza.

Under Rome, the Danube had formed a fortified frontier *(limes)* protecting a healthy scattering of colonies, townships, and rural settlements. These sites tended to lie close to the Danube and to Lakes Fertö and Balaton. Forest cover and marshland perhaps filled much of the interior of the province, although drainage works from the later third century denote a boom in rural activity. From the A.D. 170s, barbarian assaults and military insurrections led to increasing insecurity, prompting continuous reinforcement of the frontier, although the strong military presence also allowed for urban development, particularly at the governors' seats of Savaria, Sopianae, Siscia, and Sirmium. Christianity was established from an early date, with each of the larger towns housing a bishop;

however, a significant factor was the Pannonian adherence to the Arian creed, and survival of this may be visible after the mid-fifth century. Churches and Christian cemeteries are attested at most towns, notably Sopianae and Gorsium, and at villas, too. The fourth century also marks the rise of a group of large, planned fortified complexes of c. 350 × 300 m set rearward of the Danube (Héténypuszta, Ságvár, Környe, Kisárpás, and Keszthely-Fenékpuszta), which may have acted as supply bases for the *annona* (army rations) or were a rearward guard to the *limes,* controlling communications toward Italy.

From 374, Roman Pannonia suffered repeated Sarmatian and Quadic incursions, leading to the progressive breakup of Roman control along the Middle Danube. A.D. 378 saw the disastrous Roman defeat at Adrianople at the hands of the Visigoths, and subsequently hordes of Goths, Huns, and Alans rampaged through Pannonia, countered only by being granted lands on which to settle. The year 395 is often quoted as one of major destruction by invading Marcomanni, Huns, and Goths; then, in 401, Vandals pushed through, followed in 402 by Alaric's Visigoths, who were pushed back out of Italy and fobbed off with the military command of Pannonia. In 405, Radagaisus's army marched through, prompting the flight of many Pannonians to Italy; the Visigoths pushed into Italy again in 408, leaving Pannonia clear, but, by 420–425, the Huns had established themselves in the Hungarian Plain and controlled much of Pannonia. The old province was finally ceded to the new conquerors between 427 and 433.

Excavations of *limes* forts and of late Roman and Hun period cemeteries reveal through ceramic evidence a strong settlement from c. 375 of "barbarian" federates, groups, or even tribes of allied Germans used to aid in the Roman defense. Their presence is attested in various forts into the fifth century, coinciding in many cases with revisions in the frontier defensive system in terms of fort shrinkages, blocking of gates, and desertion of certain watchtowers. The frontier troops seem to have been unable to oppose the various waves of attack, although, as in Roman Noricum, there are indications of "Roman" survival well into the fifth century. For example, the last phase of activity at Pone Navata (Visegrád-Sibrik), postdating the desertion of the late Roman watchtower, comprised traces of three semisunken huts *(Grubenhäuser)* set over and within ruinous Roman structures and associated with various "barbarian" finds. Elsewhere, early fifth-century building work is predominantly in drystone or features poor stonework bonded with earth or clay, as evi-

dent at Vindobona and Carnuntum, where such walls overlay collapsed buildings or ran across roads. In the same period, burials begin to occur within the walls. Coins extend into the reign of Honorius (395–423) and, in a few rare cases (e.g., Carnuntum, Quadrata), into those of Theodosius II (408–450) or Valentinian III (425–455), but overall they suggest a cutoff coinciding with the Hunnic occupation of Pannonia.

Huns, Goths, and Suebi

Information for the hundred years between the end of Roman Pannonia and the Lombard occupation that began in 547 is scattered and imprecise. There is little to prove a persistence of settlement, save stray finds of Hunnic, Germanic, or even Christian character of fifth–sixth-century date occurring near or within forts like Brigetio, Aquincum, and Intercisa. How far these finds, as with finds in much later contexts, denote a physical presence of barbarian groups *within* the old Roman settlements, *outside* their walls, or in distinct sites *away* from them, and how far they imply the survival of a romanized population, remains to be established. A maintenance of churches is certainly witnessed at sites like Fenékpuszta, Gorsium, and Sopianae, while grave finds at Fenékpuszta help demonstrate Christian groups persisting at least into the sixth century.

Hunnic period finds include the distinctive cauldrons, examples of which come from or near the Roman sites of Intercisa, Törtel, and Várpalota. Wealthy tombs are known near Sopianae, Szekszárd, Pannonhalma, Aquincum, and Lebeny, all equipped with swords, horse fittings, and fine dress items. Potentially, this evidence signifies a Hunnic reuse of many fortified centers, but such occupation is not directly attested by archaeology or by the written sources. Indeed, Attila (d. 453) chose the Central Hungarian Plain, an open nonurbanized expanse, as the Hunnic heartland. Fringe territories such as Pannonia were probably given over to allied tribes such as the Alans, Goths, Heruls, and Sciri. These tribes adopted Hunnic dress and traits and likewise displayed wealth in death. Artificial skull deformation is often viewed as a distinguishing mark of the Hunnic confederacy, although the tradition was certainly maintained after the Hunnic demise. Indeed, fifth-century Pannonia features many examples, very few of which relate to Mongolid stock. For example, at Mözs, eleven of twenty-eight inhumations had deformed skulls, the bulk of which stem from the third generation of burial here, beginning c. 430 and marked by finds such as crescent earrings, plate, and chip-carved brooches.

H

Similar finds at Szabadbattyán near Gorsium included eastern, nomadic mirrors. Elsewhere, Szabadbattyán-type finds seemingly mark a continuity of late Roman cemeteries, which may suggest the incorporation of former federate groups into the Hunnic fold. If their role had long been to occupy Roman defenses, then it can be argued that this role was maintained under Hunnic overlordship.

The dissolution of the Hunnic Empire in 454–455 saw the emergence of a number of barbarian kingdoms along the Middle Danube, whose territorial confines cannot be firmly fixed, given that the various tribes long preserved Hunnic-style attributes. However, the overall zones of influence are broadly understood, and finds are accorded ethnic appurtenance largely on the basis of location. In the period to 472, Ostrogothic power was dominant in former Pannonia but was centered primarily in the area south of Lake Balaton. Beyond this, Heruls may have controlled the northwest region, while the northeast appears a virtual no man's land, with the Suebic Kingdom largely set over the Danube. In the east, the Great Hungarian Plain was already under the sway of the Gepids.

After 473, when the Ostrogoths moved eastward, and, subsequently in 489, when they moved westward to Italy, Suebi and Heruls may have extended their control into Transdanubia, but the bulk of Pannonia lacked any guiding power. The Gepids did, however, establish a foothold by occupying the city and territory of Sirmium. However, the archaeology of this time period is restricted and confused. In the case of the Ostrogoths, it is argued—without material support—that palaces existed in the fortified centers of Fenékpuszta, Sopianae, and Sirmium. Certainly, sources like the historian Jordanes still refer to towns like Sirmium and Bassiana but give no details as to their physical well-being.

From the late fifth century, Suebic weapon graves and rich female burials occur in northern and eastern Pannonia (e.g., Brigetio, Környe, Intercisa, and Gorsium) extending south to Szekszárd and as far west as Savaria. Distinctive elements are the bronze- or gilded-silver-knobbed bow brooches with chip-carved spiral decoration and polyhedral earrings. Again, finds imply a relationship with former Roman settlements. At Aquincum, there was a hoard datable to 526 buried in the amphitheater; at Gorsium, graves lay close to the larger basilica. Yet, actual "Germanic" settlement traces in this period are limited to sunken-featured buildings at Mohács, Szak, and Fenékpuszta; the buildings, at least, verify German settlers within the walls of a Roman site.

Lombards and Gepids

In 526, the Suebic Kingdom, covering northern Pannonia and zones north of the Danube, was conquered by the Lombards, expanding eastward from Lower Austria and Moravia. Subsequently, in 547–548, the Byzantine Emperor Justinian (c. 482–565) gave the Lombards the towns of Noricum and the Pannonian fortresses—effectively, southern Pannonia. In so doing, the Lombards came to oppose the Gepid Kingdom that lay over the Danube, focused on the Tisza and Maros Rivers but extending as far as Transylvania.

Gepid settlement was predominantly village based but with occasional possession of the Danubian cities of Sirmium and Singidunum. In contrast, the Lombards occupied an area in which Roman towns and forts appear as ongoing concerns. However, proof of Lombard reuse is lacking, being dependent on the presence of burials in the immediate proximity or stray finds from within these sites. Urban survival is nonetheless attested by reference to bishops at Scarbantia (Sopron) and Sopianae (Pécs). Lombard cemeteries reveal a more highly militarized society than is evident from Gepid burials, although Lombard tombs have suffered less from ancient looting. Dress items indicate high technical and artistic skills within each tribe. Distinctive among the Gepid repertoire are eagle-headed buckles, perhaps derived from Ostrogothic models, while Lombard metalwork reveals a ready assimilation of Roman/Mediterranean, local Germanic, and Ostrogothic designs.

After the death of Justinian in 565, Byzantine diplomacy turned in favor of the Gepids. In response, the Lombards allied themselves with the powerful Avars, likewise discarded by Byzantium, and in 567 invaded Gepidia and crushed the Gepid army. The Avars besieged Sirmium and mopped up remaining Gepid resistance in central Hungary. As part of the treaty, the Lombards departed for Italy and ceded Pannonia to the Avars.

From Avars to Magyars (A.D. 568–997)

Avar success in Hungary spilled over into raids south into the Balkans and Greece, westward against the Franks, and northwestward against the Slavs. In 626, however, a heavy defeat outside Constantinople countered Avar eastward expansion. Instead they extended control into southern Slovakia and eastern Lower Austria, although here they faced a new Slavic state.

The huge donatives received from Byzantium and kept either as gold coin or melted down to make ornaments attest Avar settlement throughout the Carpathian Basin, but with a focus on the Danube-Tisza region. Their early nomadic character is reflected in the restricted size of their later sixth–early seventh-century cemeteries and in accompanying burials of warhorses. Only from the mid-seventh century do larger cemeteries emerge to imply fixed settlements. However, while more than thirty thousand Avar period burials are known, the number of excavated and identified Avar village sites is small. Some of the earliest Avar period cemeteries occur in Danubian Pannonia, notably those at Környe, Várpalota, Szekszárd, and Kölked. Best documented are Környe and Kölked, where the earliest grave finds, datable to the last quarter of the sixth century, exhibit a high Germanic content, even if burial was in Avar guise (with weapon and horse burial, with stirrups, bows, and nomadic belts for males; with beaded necklaces and globular earrings for females). Környe yielded 152 graves covering the period 568–650 and included 20 horse graves. Germanic features included shields, lances, axes, short and long swords, and belt fittings. Anthropological study revealed no Mongolid component; instead, a composite settlement including Gepids, Sarmatians, and possible Lombards and natives is suggested. At Kölked-Feketekapu, two cemetery zones were excavated: one contained 681 graves of sixth–eighth-century date; the other, a cluster of small graveyards, contained 366 graves and was set within and around a planned village containing 140 semisunken houses. In the outer cemetery, early finds showed weapons, dress, and pottery of Germanic character that became "Avarized" over time. In the village area, Germanic and Avar components are roughly equal, with Avar material dominant from c. 680.

The persistence of Gepid-style artifacts (e.g., stamped pottery, iron buckles, cleavers) within Hungary may denote a sizable survival of Gepids in the Carpathian Basin under Avar rule, giving support to the documentary reference to them as an ethnic group still in the later ninth century. Although Gepid finds continue in Siebenburgen (the eastern part of former Gepidia), no material exists between here and the Danube, their former heartland. Rather, "Gepidized" cemeteries occur in Transdanubia, suggesting an enforced transplantation of Gepid-German groups across the Danube after 568 to provide a buffer zone to the Avar center. How extensive the actual Avar presence was here remains to be determined.

From 791, Charlemagne's Frankish armies began campaigns against the Avars, attacking along the Danube and from Italy. Victory came in 803 with the surrender of the Avar Zodan, *princeps Pannoniae*. Subsequently, despite insurrections, Carolingian rule extended over two zones: Pannonia Inferior controlled by the duke of Friuli, and Pannonia Superior (from the Danube to the Drau) under the duke of the East and the archbishop of Salzburg. Carolingian power did not extend to all of eastern Pannonia, however, since here Charlemagne maintained Avar vassal princes. Farther east, Avar rule persisted, with Carolingian logistics too stretched to contemplate annexation.

The subsequent rise of Bulgar power modified the power structures in Hungary. The Bulgars gained military control of much of the Carpathian Basin and, through an invasion of southeast Pannonia in 826–829, displaced remaining Avars and forced the Carolingians to divide their lands into smaller units. Archaeologically, virtually nothing is known of this Carolingian interlude except signs of renewed activity at Fenékpuszta and the distribution of Carolingian-type lances. It is doubtful that the Carolingians sought to repopulate or redevelop Pannonia. Too little time was available in any case. In 883, Duke Svatopluk of Moravia devastated eastern Pannonia for twelve days; then, in 894, the Magyars crashed across the Danube and overwhelmed Pannonia, thereby completing their rapid conquest of Hungary.

These disparate Maygar forces resembled the nomadic Avars in their heyday, with more thought on booty than on establishing a fixed territorial base. Crushing defeats in 955 and 970, however, halted their expansionist aims in Europe and forced a more static lifestyle upon them. Ranked cemeteries are attested within the Carpathian Basin from the Conquest period (894 onward), sited close to village communities and to large fortified tribal/clan centers. Trade with Byzantium, Italy, and Germany is attested from the first half of the tenth century, and the need for markets and ports of call prompted the reemergence of protourban settlements, leading in the later tenth century to a centralization of Magyar society. The Danube emerged once again as a vital traffic route and secured the rise of Esztergom and later Buda as royal capitals, while the adoption of Christianity from 973 led to the establishment of bishoprics. Along the Danube, many Roman centers were revived, with churches appearing within their ruinous walls but with secular zones located outside. For example, the fourth-century bridgehead of Contra Aquincum was donated in the mid-tenth century by the Magyar Prince Taksony to the Bulgarian nobles Billa and Boscu. A church and associated cemetery developed here, but the extant fortress walls were largely demolished as Pest developed into a thriving merchant town. Elsewhere, Roman remains provided quarries for church construction. Best known is the building program

H

of Stephen I from 997 for his capital of Székesfehérvár, which saw the massive robbing of nearby Roman Gorsium. Within a few generations, therefore, Hungary had been established as a major new political power. This gave impetus, finally, to urbanization in the Great Hungarian Plain, boosting the new state's economic strength.

FURTHER READINGS

Böna, I. *The Dawn of the Dark Ages: The Gepids and the Lombards in the Carpathian Basin.* Budapest: Corvina, 1976.

————. Die Verwaltung und die Bevölkerung des karolingischen Pannoniens. *Mitteilungen des Archäologischen Instituts Ungarns* (1985) 14:149–160.

Christie, N. The Survival of Roman Settlement along the Middle Danube: Pannonia from the Fourth to the Tenth Century A.D. *Oxford Journal of Archaeology* (1992) 11:317–339.

Dienes, I. *The Hungarians Cross the Carpathians.* Budapest: Corvina, 1972.

Gerevich, L., ed. *Towns in Medieval Hungary.* Budapest: Akademiai Kiado, 1990.

Holl, I. The Development and Topography of Sopron in the Middle Ages. In *Towns in Medieval Hungary.* Ed. L. Gerevich. Budapest: Akademiai Kiado, 1990, pp. 96–102.

Kiss, A. Das Gräberfeld und die Siedlung der awarenzeitlichen germanischen Bevolkerung von Kolked. *Folia Archaeologica* (1979) 30:185–192.

————. Die Goldfunde des Karpatenbeckens von 5.–10. Jahrhundert. *Acta Archaeologica Academiae Scientiarum Hungaricae* (1986) 38:105–145.

————. Das Weiterleben der Gepiden in der Awarenzeit. In *Die Völker Südosteuropas im 6. bis 8. Jahrhundert.* Ed. B. Hänsel. Südosteuropa Jahrbuch 17. Berlin: 1987, pp. 203–218.

Kovács, L. Bemerkungen zur Bewertung der frankischen Flugellanzen im Karpatenbeckens. *Mitteilungen des Archäologischen Instituts Ungarns* (1978–1979) 8–9: 97–119.

Menghin, W., T. Springer, and E. Wamers, eds. *Germanen, Hunnen, und Awaren: Schätze der Völkerwanderungszeit: Die Archäologie des 5. und 6. Jahrhunderts an der mittleren Donau und der ostlich-merowingische Reihengräberkreis.* Nurnberg: Verlag Germanisches Nationalmuseum, 1987. (Exhibition Catalog).

Salamon, A., and J. Erdelyi. *Das völkerwanderungszeitliche Gräberfeld von Környe.* Studia Archaeologica 5. Budapest: Akademiai Kiado, 1971.

Soproni, S. *Die letzten Jahrzehnte des Pannonischen Limes.* Munich: Beck. Münchner Beiträge zur Vor- und Frühgeschichte, vol. 38. 1985.

Neil Christie

SEE ALSO
Buda

Hunting

During the Middle Ages, traditional hunting of wild mammals and birds was transformed by new environmental, legal, and economic developments. Birds; furbearers; hares; dormice; seals; porpoise; great whales; wild (and feral) pigs; wild sheep; wolves; foxes; bears; aurochs; red, roe, and fallow deer; elk (known as moose in North America); and reindeer were all exploited in different parts of Europe. Animal products were frequently collected as tribute, tax, and tithe in lieu of money. Hunting techniques varied with target game and local custom. Bow and arrow were traditional weapons for hunting large game and birds throughout Europe. Parts of simple, light crossbows have been recovered from early medieval sites in Scandinavia and northern Britain, and these may have been hunting weapons. A variety of forms of crossbows and bolts were developed by the mid-Middle Ages for hunting large game, birds, furbearers, and whales. Portable firearms existed by the fourteenth century, but they were not effectively adapted to hunting purposes until much later.

A variety of other weapons were also adapted to hunting, especially for use by nobles. Specialized spear forms were developed to allow footmen to hold dangerous prey (like wild boar and bears) at bay, while some horsemen employed spear-pointed swords. Stationary facilities and weapons were also employed. Deadfall and mechanical traps were used for bears, wolves, foxes, and wolverines. Birds were often flushed into nets, and nets and seines were used to take fish.

The use of dogs was an important part of hunting techniques as well. Both nobles and commoners kept dogs for hunting; in some areas near hunting preserves, commoners were obliged to keep dogs to aid large noble-run hunts. Likewise, commoners were obliged to keep dog packs to control local dangerous predators. The use of dogs for such specific tasks resulted in the formulation of specialized breeds. Predatory birds were tamed for the hunting of birds and small game. Class differences were reinforced by legal restrictions on possession of certain species.

While hunting techniques were varied, the motives for hunting in the Middle Ages can be identified as falling into at least four major patterns: (1) subsistence supplements for peasant communities; (2) provisioning elite households; (3) destruction of predators and competitors; and (4) market, or "cash," hunting.

Subsistence Supplements for Peasant Communities

In most parts of Europe, hunting provided only a minor part of daily subsistence to peasant agriculturalists, but hunting and snaring of birds and small mammals may have provided a valuable supplement to a diet increasingly dominated by cereal grains. An exception may be provided by the varied communities of the Atlantic fringe, where seabird colonies, small whales, seals, and stranded great whales played a more important role in peasant subsistence. In Iceland, stranded whales were regularly fought over, and, in the climatically vulnerable northeast, harbor seals played an important supplementary role. In Greenland, beyond the limits of cereal agriculture even during the medieval warm period (prior to A.D. 1310), seals and caribou played a still more important role in daily subsistence. Animal-bone collections from settlement areas in Greenland are often more than half seal bone, and isotopic analyses of human remains and studies of dental morphology indicate a diet very different from that of other medieval Europeans.

Provisioning Elite Households

Medieval elites continued the ancient tradition of strongly carnivorous elite feasting both to attract and hold retainers and to mark the interactions of different levels of feudal society. Large game animals were required in substantial numbers to support elite household meat consumption without unduly depleting domestic herds and flocks. Elite hunting was progressively elaborated with ritual and specialized dress and weaponry but retained a very real dietary component throughout the Middle Ages (as bone collections from secular and ecclesiastical contexts indicate). Increasingly formalized and restrictive sport hunting and legal game conservation measures thus formed part of a complex marking differential access by elites to resources needed for their own maintenance and display.

Destruction of Predators and Competitors

As peasant settlement and urbanization expanded and population grew throughout the thirteenth century, field and flocks invaded many formerly forested areas, and domestic mammals increasingly competed for forest resources and suffered from predators. The destruction of predators was an explicit goal of much elite hunting in eastern and central Europe down to the early modern period, and there is little question that increased hunting pressure was a major element in widespread land clearance during the High Middle Ages.

Market, or "Cash," Hunting

A variety of animal products became significant trade items in medieval Europe, and demand in the urbanizing core occasionally seems to have been strong enough to generate a specialized market-oriented hunt. In Russia and Arctic Scandinavia, skins of martins, ermine, squirrel, and other small furbearers became major trade items (and were integrated into the sumptuary laws as markers of merchants and noble classes). Rare game products and live animals, including polar bears and birds of prey, also figured in prestige-goods exchange among elites during the Viking period (c. 800–1050) and afterward. A specialized trade in reindeer hides and antlers may have extended back to the Viking period in northwest Europe, providing raw material for clothing and a wide range of household objects. The distant Greenland colony apparently maintained a remarkable long-range hunt into the High Arctic to secure walrus hides and ivory, polar bear skins, and the occasional live polar bear (as a royal gift). Perhaps the most influential market hunt was to be the developing Basque hunt for baleen whales. Beginning in the Bay of Biscay prior to 1200, by the end of the Middle Ages this uniquely profitable marine hunt had brought Europeans back to the northeasternmost shores of North America.

A repeated theme in the development of medieval hunting is the increasingly successful attempt by elites to restrict access to large game animals. While there is abundant evidence extending back into prehistory for the use of wild species as a supplement to agriculturalists' diets, and strong indication of a special elite role in hunting large mammals back to the early Iron Age, we know very little about the mosaic of traditional management strategies prior to c. A.D. 800. By the onset of the High Middle Ages (c. 1100), secular and ecclesiastical elites throughout Latin Christendom were increasingly successful in restricting regular hunting of deer, boar, and large wildfowl (swans, herons) by commoners. The increasingly draconian "forest laws" designed to establish exclusive hunting preserves from what had probably been a communally managed resource may reflect continued resistance by commoners, articulated in Britain by the many varieties of the Robin Hood legend.

H

Another theme in the development of hunting during the Middle Ages is increasing conflict between steadily expanding population (especially during the later thirteenth century) and arable cultivation and the habitats of woodland species. While the Anglo-Norman forest laws predate the major increases in later medieval population, there can be little doubt that later protectionist measures (including the fortification of woodlands in some areas) were prompted by increasing pressure on steadily shrinking woodlands by peasant agriculturalists. As in the modern developing world, fuel collection and charcoal burning probably accelerated habitat destruction as population density increased. The survival of many of Europe's wild species up to the present is probably the result of the self-interested efforts of medieval aristocrats, as well as the retreat of settlement following the Black Death and the onset of the Little Ice Age in the fourteenth century.

FURTHER READINGS

Brusewitz, Gunnar. *Hunting: Hunters, Games, Weapons, and Hunting Methods from the Remote Past to the Present Day.* New York: Stein and Day, 1969.

Christophersen, Axel. *Håndverket i Forandring: Studier i Horn og Beinhåndverkets Utvikling i Lund, ca. 1000–1350.* Acta Archaeologica Lundensia Series in 4. No. 13. Lund: CWK Gleerup, 1980.

Cummins, John. *The Hound and the Hawk: The Art of Medieval Hunting.* London: Weidenfeld and Nicolson, 1988.

Davis, Simon. *The Archaeology of Animals.* New Haven: Yale University Press, 1987.

Gilbert, John M. *Hunting and Hunting Reserves in Medieval Scotland.* Edinburgh: John Donald, 1979.

Grant, A. The Significance of Deer Remains at Occupation Sites of the Iron Age to the Anglo-Saxon Period. In *The Environment of Man: The Iron Age to the Anglo-Saxon Period.* Ed. M. Jones and G. Dimbleby. BAR British Series 87. Oxford: British Archaeological Reports, 1981, pp. 205–212.

Maltby, Mark. *The Animal Bones from Exeter, 1971–75: Faunal Studies on Urban Sites.* Exeter Archaeological Reports 2. Sheffield: Department of Archaeology and Prehistory, Univ. of Sheffield, 1979.

McGovern, T.H. Cows, Harp Seals, and Churchbells: Adaptation and Extinction in Norse Greenland. *Human Ecology* (1980) 8:245–277.

Proulx, Jean-Pierre. *Whaling in the North Atlantic from Earliest Times to the Mid-19th Century.* Ottawa: Parks Canada, 1986.

Steensberg, Axel, and J.L. Ostergaard Christensen. Store Valby. *Historisk-Filosofiske Skrifter* (1974) vol. 8, no. 1, part I: 405–454.

Vebæk, C.L. Hunting, by Land and by Sea, and Fishing in Medieval Norse Greenland. *Acta Borealia* (1991) 1:5–14.

Sophia Perdikaris and Jim Woollett

SEE ALSO
Forests

Hyde Abbey

Hyde Abbey was one of the great monastic houses of medieval England. Founded in Winchester by King Alfred the Great and completed by his son King Edward the Elder in A.D. 903, it was originally located beside the seventh-century Old Minster, the cathedral church of Wessex. During the tenth century, this New Minster was closely associated with the royal family; interred there were the bodies of King Alfred (849–899); his wife, Ealhswith; King Edward the Elder (899–924) and two of his sons; and later King Eadwig (ruled 955–959).

After the Norman Conquest (1066), changes in the center of Winchester caused the monastery to move to the northern suburb of Hyde in 1110, accompanied by royal remains and holy relics (St. Judoc, St. Grimbald, St. Valentine, and the splendid gold cross donated by King Canute). The renamed Hyde Abbey was seriously damaged during fighting between the supporters of King Stephen (1097–1154) and the Empress Matilda (1102–1167) in August 1141; the rebuilt church is said to have had a great tower with eight bells, and, later, miracles associated with the remains of St. Barnabus enhanced the reputation of the monastic house as a pilgrimage site. Over the years, the site of Hyde Abbey has yielded finely carved capitals decorated with classical motifs that have been cited as physical evidence for the twelfth-century Renaissance.

In 1538, Hyde Abbey was surrendered to King Henry VIII's commissioners. The monastic buildings were demolished, and the ensuing years saw on the site a Tudor urban mansion, a Georgian prison, and, finally, the present terraces of Victorian brick houses. Hyde Abbey's gatehouse and its parochial church, St. Bartholomew's, are the only surviving medieval structures. John Leland, Henry VIII's historian, recorded that lead tablets bearing the names Alfred and Edward were found in tombs in front of the great altar at Hyde (Minns 1914). During construction of the Bridewell in 1788, a large, lead-lined stone coffin was found at a location again said to be in front of the high altar. The bones were tipped out, the coffin broken up and reburied, and the lead sold (Bogan 1986). A contemporary sketch plan indicates that the visible remains of the abbey church were no more than low mounds of rubble (Howard 1798). In 1866, an amateur antiquary, John Mellor, excavated part of the site and found human bones, claiming them to be the remains of Alfred the Great. They were eventually reburied outside the east end of St. Bartholomew's Church (Bogan 1986).

Since 1972, limited archaeological work has taken place in the monastic enclosure, but not at the Victorian terrace that covered the site of the abbey church. A noticeable slope east of the terrace, just within a city park, suggested to the authors the site of the chancel, relatively undisturbed since its demolition. In 1992, a telecommunications-cable trench encountered solid masonry there; subsequent testing extended the area of masonry, and large-scale excavation was planned for three seasons. The 1998 work discovered thick Tudor demolition rubble covering the site but removed and replaced in parallel trenches dug by the antiquarian Mellor. No floor levels remained; walls had been robbed to the foundations or totally removed. Late medieval walls had been built over earlier monastic burials, and fire-damaged reused stones testified to a previous structure. All the burials but one were in coffins made of chalk blocks. The south wall of the church was found to be 2 m wide and made of flint rubble, faced with ashlar masonry. Attached to it, a small, apsidal side-chapel sug-gests that the chancel had a triple-apse east end, not uncommon among Benedictine churches. The width of the church may have been as much as 26 m, and an ambulatory would have surrounded a 14-m-wide presbytery and choir. Almost all the finds are building related; noteworthy are a range of decorated glazed floor tiles and carved stonework from a screen, probably from a side altar.

FURTHER READINGS

Biddle, M. Felix urbis Winthonia: Winchester in the Age of Monastic Reform. In *Tenth Century Studies*. Ed. D. Parsons. London and Chichester: Phillimore, 1995, pp. 123–140.

Biddle, M, ed. *Winchester in the Early Middle Ages*. Winchester Studies 1. Oxford: Clarendon, 1976.

Bogan, A. Where Is King Alfred Buried? *Winchester Cathedral Record* (1986) 55:27–34.

Grierson, P. Grimbald of St. Bertin's. *English Historical Review* (1940) 55:329–361.

Howard, H. Enquiries Concerning the Tomb of King Alfred, at Hyde Abbey, near Winchester. *Archaeologia* (1798) 3:309–312.

Minns, G., ed. The Itinerary of John Leland in Hampshire. *Proceedings of the Hampshire Field Club* (1914) 6.

Yorke, B. The Bishops of Winchester, the Kings of Wessex, and the Development of Winchester in the Ninth and Early Tenth Centuries. *Proceedings of the Hampshire Field Club* (1984) 40:61–70.

Eric Klingelhofer and Kenneth Qualmann

I

Ipswich

Archaeological excavations in Ipswich since 1974 have shown that the town was founded in the seventh century, probably by the East Anglian Royal house whose burial ground lies at Sutton Hoo, 15 km northeast of the town. The settlement appears to have been urban in its functions from birth, acting as the sole international port and craft-production center for the entire Kingdom of East Anglia until the ninth century. Thereafter, with the foundation of major towns at Norwich and Thetford, its market hinterland was reduced in size and its growth restricted. The seventh–eighth-century town appears to have covered c. 20 ha, mainly on the north side of the River Orwell centered on the crossing that was bridged by the tenth century. Burial took place outside the occupation area on the rising heathland immediately to the north. The largest group of burials excavated so far was found during excavations in 1988–1989 south of the Buttermarket. A variety of burial practices were present among the hundred or so inhumations, including chamber graves and small barrows. Grave goods were present with many burials. One burial produced a sword, spears, belt fittings, and two glass palm cups, paralleled by Alamannic burials of the seventh century.

Shortly after c. A.D. 800, the town grew suddenly to c. 50 ha in what appears to be a deliberate expansion based on a gridiron street system laid out on the unoccupied heathland to the north of the earlier town.

The economy of the middle Saxon (c. A.D. 600–c. 850) town was based on craft production and international trade. Craft industries included weaving, metalworking, bone working, and leather working, but these were overshadowed by a major pottery industry. The product, Ipswich ware, is unusual in that it was wheel made and kiln fired, whereas most areas of England continued to produce handmade pottery during this period. Its comparative quality ensured a widespread distribution throughout the whole of East Anglia and beyond, as far as Yorkshire and Kent, indicating a massive hinterland for the town at this point.

The town was also an important international port trading with the Frankish Empire. If the imported pottery present is a reliable guide, most trade was with the Rhineland and what is now northern France and Belgium. Other than pottery and German lava millstones, few imported objects have been found. Wine is likely to have been imported, probably in wooden barrels that have been excavated on a number of sites and appear to be of German origin.

Little is known about the detailed layout of the town, but most of the present-day streets appear to be of Anglo-Saxon origin. Buildings were of timber construction and similar in form to their rural counterparts. The central area of the town has produced evidence of intensive craft activity, with buildings close together and against street frontages, whereas, toward the edge, they appear sparser, with associated evidence for agricultural activity.

Shortly after A.D. 900, the town was first surrounded with defenses, probably during the Danish occupation (c. 879–918). The town grew very little during the late Saxon period (c. 850–1066). Its economy continued to be based on craft production and trade. The latter was marked by the development of local and regional trade and a reduction in international trade, especially after the tenth century.

A castle was established after 1086, but it was demolished by 1176. The earthen town defenses were enlarged in 1203, eventually including three stone gates. The

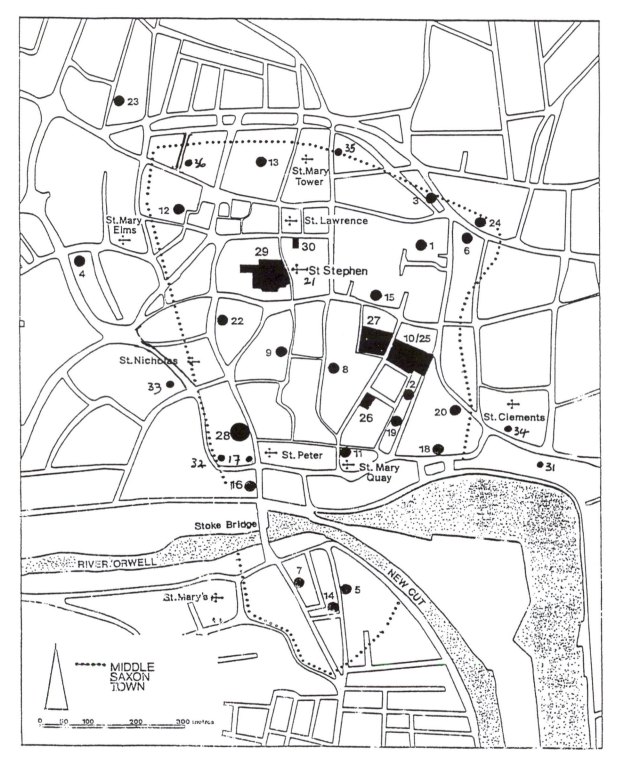

182 Excavation in Ipswich. Key to sites: *1*, Cox Lane; *2*, Shire Hall Yard, 1959; *3*, Old Foundry Road; *4*, Elm Street; *5*, Great Whip Street; *6*, St. Helen's Street, 1975; *7*, Vernon Street; *8*, Lower Brook Street; *9*, Turrett Lane; *10*, School Street; *11*, Foundation Street/Star Lane; *12*, Arcade Street; *13*, Tower Ramparts; *14*, Little Whip Street; *15*, Tacket Street; *16*, Bridge Street; *17*, St. Peter's Street/Greyfriars Road; *18*, Key Street; *19*, Shire Hall Yard, 1982; *20*, Fore Street; *21*, St. Stephen's Church; *22*, St. Nicholas Street; *23*, St. George's Street; *24*, St. Helen's Street, 1983; *25*, School Street/Foundation Street; *26*, Smart Street/Foundation Street; *27*, Wingfield Street/Foundation Street; *28*, Greyfriars Road, 1986; *29*, St. Stephen's Lane; *30*, Buttermarket; *31*, Neptune Quay; *32*, Greyfriars Road, 1989; *33*, Franciscan Road; *34*, 85–87 Fore Street; *35*, Northgate Road Library; *36*, Crown and Anchor, Westgate Street.

medieval town expanded outside the defended areas with suburbs around the extramural churches of St. Matthew, St. George, St. Margaret, St. Helen, and St. Clement. Five religious houses were established in the town: the Austin Canons, c. 1130, with a second foundation by 1162; the Blackfriars, 1263; the Whitefriars, c. 1278; and the Greyfriars before 1298. Both the Blackfriars and the Whitefriars have been extensively excavated. The town remained a craft-production center, a market town for East Suffolk, and an international port, overshadowed in East Anglia by the regional center of Norwich.

FURTHER READINGS

Hodges, Richard. *Dark Age Economics.* London: Duckworth, 1982.

Redstone, L.J. *Ipswich Through the Ages.* Ipswich: East Anglian Magazine, 1948.

Wade, Keith. Ipswich. In *The Rebirth of Towns in the West, A.D. 700–1050.* Ed. R. Hodges and B. Hobley. CBA Research Report 68. London: Council for British Archaeology, 1988, pp. 93–100.

———. The Urbanization of East Anglia: The Ipswich Perspective. In *Flatlands and Wetlands: Current Themes in East Anglian Archaeology.* Ed. J. Gardiner. East Anglian Archaeology Report 50. Ipswich: Suffolk County Planning Department, 1993, pp. 144–151.

Keith Wade

SEE ALSO

Emporia; Ipswich Ware; Norwich; Sutton Hoo; Thetford

Ipswich Ware

Coil-built and made on a slow wheel or tournet, Ipswich ware was well fired in permanent kilns in a reduced atmosphere to a gray color. Production of this pottery, which is dated to c. 650–c. 850, was the first to be carried out at an industrial level in England since the end of the Roman period (c. A.D. 400). The industry flourished in the great trading and manufacturing port of Ipswich (Suffolk), and there is at present no evidence that Ipswich ware was made anywhere else. There is abundant dating evidence for its use in the eighth century, but its starting and end dates are not certain. Negative evidence shows that it was not circulating before the mid-seventh century, and a takeover by Thetford-type wares in the later ninth century is well attested.

Chance finds of kilns and dumps of wasters were made in the northeast part of middle Saxon (c. 600–850)

Ipswich during the early twentieth century, but to date only one kiln, which was operating in the ninth century, has been accurately recorded under modern conditions. This was found in 1988 during formal excavations on the Buttermarket site some distance from the main production area.

The most common form is the jar, squat and globular with a sagging base and a simple upright or everted rim in a narrow range of shapes. Pitchers with a D-spout and strap handle, and sometimes lugs, also occur, as do more specialized forms, such as lamps, bowls, and bottles. Fabrics range from smooth and fine sandy to coarse sandy with a distinctly pimply feel and appearance caused by profuse quartz grains. Burnishing is sometimes found on pitchers. Decoration, in the form of simple incised geometric designs and stamped motifs, is confined to large jars and pitchers. Definite chronological developments in either forms or fabrics have not yet been identified.

The ware is commonly found in Norfolk and Suffolk, the heartland of the Kingdom of East Anglia, on occupation sites of varying size, status, and function, but it does not occur in cemetery contexts. It was also traded in small quantities throughout the eastern counties, from the south coast of Kent to York, and as far west as western Northamptonshire in the Midlands. Pitchers form a larger portion of assemblages at the outer limits of the distribution than in East Anglia, and a greater proportion of larger jars, perhaps traded as containers, are found on sites outside Norfolk and Suffolk.

A major research project begun in 1995 aims to answer outstanding problems and uncertainties concerning provenance and fabric definition, while the analysis and publication of a number of key excavated sites in East Anglia and elsewhere, in particular Brandon, Flixborough, and Ipswich itself, will answer aspects of chronology.

FURTHER READINGS

Hurst, J.G. Saxo-Norman Pottery in East Anglia. Part II: Thetford Ware. *Proceedings of the Cambridge Antiquarian Society* (1957) 51:37–65.

———. The pottery. In *The Archaeology of Anglo-Saxon England.* Ed. D.M. Wilson. London: Methuen, 1976, pp. 283–348.

West, S.E. Excavations at Cox Lane (1958) and at the Town Defences, Shire Hall Yard, Ipswich (1959). *Proceedings of the Suffolk Institute of Archaeology* (1963) 29:233–303.

Andrew Rogerson

I

SEE ALSO

Ipswich; Thetford-Type Ware

Ireland

The chronological definition of medieval Ireland for the archaeologist is somewhat different from that of the historian. Both archaeologists and historians agree that the Middle Ages began in the fifth century with the coming of Christianity to Ireland and the beginning of written records. Historians normally date its end to just before the middle of the sixteenth century, but, archaeologically, the settlement patterns remained largely medieval in nature until the Cromwellian Conquest in the seventeenth century.

The great divide in the medieval period is the Anglo-Norman Invasion of 1169–1170, which utterly changed the material culture of much of Ireland. In the pre-Norman period, the dominant settlement was the dispersed ringfort, usually an annular earthwork with a shallow fosse (ditch) and an internal bank. In the west and the north, these were often constructed of stone and are known as *cashels;* in the east, they are often called *raths.* The archaeological evidence for these settlements is often very limited; nevertheless, the majority of excavated examples date to the first millennium A.D., with a concentration at the latter end of the period. They primarily functioned as single-family farming units of the free element in early Irish society, with pastoralism often the predominant form of agriculture associated with them. Excavations at Lisleagh in County Cork and at Deerpark Farm in County Antrim have produced evidence of circular wooden houses dating to this period, as well as evidence for metalworking. A variant of the ringfort was the *crannóg,* an island habitation site in a lake, of which more than a thousand are known to have existed. Like the ringfort, its economy was dominated by mixed farming. Prehistoric hillforts and promontory forts were also reused in this period, and there is contemporary historical evidence for the existence for some form of nucleated settlements, although confirmation from archaeology has yet to appear.

The other major settlement features of the pre-Norman landscape were the monasteries and the Viking towns, the latter mainly located along the east coast. Some of the larger monasteries, such as Armagh, Clonmacnoise in County Offaly, and Glendalough in County Wicklow, were functioning as urban centers from the tenth century onward as the ecclesiastical fame of these settlements attracted merchants, students, and craftsmen from the surrounding areas. The Vikings, who raided Ireland from the end of the eighth century, soon started settling down in the island and set up major ports at Dublin, Waterford, Wexford, Cork, and Limerick, to name the most important. Excavations in Dublin and Waterford have located the extent, layout, and wealth of these Hiberno-Norse towns, which played a significant part in the Viking trading empire.

With the coming of the Anglo-Normans in 1169–1170, the settlement pattern of Ireland profoundly changed. This small force of men, operating in an unfriendly environment, constructed campaign castles all over eastern Ireland. These motte-and-bailey and ringwork castles were constructed out of materials that were readily available everywhere: earth and wood. The main difference between them was that the motte, or earthen mound, whose profile resembled that of a Christmas pudding, relied for its defensive strength on its height, whereas the ringwork castle was usually sited on a naturally defensive location with its fosse and palisaded perimeter bank composing its main defensive elements. All together, c. 350 examples of mottes and at least fifty ringwork castles are known in Ireland. It is often difficult to identify accurately the ringwork castles in the modern landscape because their morphology closely resembles that of the much more prolific pre-Norman ringforts. The motte castles in Ireland, which are some of the latest known examples in Europe, are usually small and often lack surviving baileys. These baileys were associated rectilinear earthworks where the Anglo-Norman family would actually have lived.

These earthworks were soon replaced by stone castles at important locations in the Anglo-Norman Lordship, where the Crown or a powerful Anglo-Norman lord had the financial and constructional resources necessary to build one of these mighty edifices. The earliest examples of these were built at Carrickfergus in County Antrim and at Trim in County Meath at the end of the twelfth century and the start of the thirteenth. There have been excavations at both castles, although the work at Trim has probably been more extensive. D. Sweetman's excavations there in the 1970s produced artifacts dating to the late thirteenth to early fourteenth centuries, which he linked to the occupation of the castle by the Justiciar, Geoffrey de Geneville, from 1254. The dendrochronological (tree-ring) analysis of some of the timbers in the keep have revealed that its construction commenced at the end of the twelfth century.

These early castles had rectangular keeps within strong curtain walls, but, as the thirteenth century progressed, newer types of castles were constructed. A further development was the polygonal keep, of which there are also several examples, including Athlone, which guarded the important bridge across the River Shannon, and Shanid in County Limerick. There was also the continued use of rectangular keeps, such as Seafin in County Down, excavated by D.M. Waterman in the 1950s.

At some time in the thirteenth century, the concept of having a separate keep was abandoned, and the main defensive element became the curtain walls with a strongly fortified gate tower. One such castle was Castle Roche in County Louth, which was located on a naturally defensive ridge. Constructed c. 1236 by Lady Rohesia de Verdun, it is the only recorded example of a seigneurial castle in Ireland being built by a woman. There was also a small group of castles, found mainly in the Province of Leinster, that did not conform to this pattern. These castles featured a square keep with round towers at each angle and were often surrounded by a rock-cut fosse. One of the best-preserved examples is located at Ferns in County Wexford, which was excavated by Sweetman of the Office of Public Works from 1972 to 1975, before a major program of conservation work, which is now completed. Although no medieval occupation evidence was found in the keep's interior, Sweetman was able to date the window loops to the first quarter of the thirteenth century, as they were architecturally similar to those at Chepstow Castle in Monmouthshire, England.

Three major thirteenth-century keepless castles were located at important urban centers: Dublin, Limerick, and Kilkenny. Excavations in the mid-1980s at Dublin Castle, the center of royal administration in medieval Ireland, have revealed its massive moat, more than 20 m wide and 9 m deep, in which were found artifacts dating from the thirteenth to the eighteenth centuries. The original medieval causeway and the junction between the castle and the town wall were also revealed during the excavations.

The last major group of large seigneurial castles were mostly built in Connacht in the later thirteenth century. The most sophisticated example is located at Roscommon and represents the apogee of Irish castle construction in the 1280s. It comprises an almost rectangular court, 50 × 41 m, with powerful D-shaped towers at each corner, a strongly fortified gatehouse in the middle of the eastern curtain wall, and a smaller postern on the western wall.

Along with the military encastellation of the country, Anglo-Norman settlers, especially from western England, came over to settle the Irish Lordship. Many of them were attracted by the favorable land tenure on offer in a large number of the villages that were set up in the eastern half of the island. These were given the status of boroughs, although they were no larger than corresponding English villages, and R.E. Glasscock has coined the name *rural boroughs* for them. The great Anglo-Norman lords of the area granted their inhabitants a charter of liberties whereby they became burgesses with their own court and the right to tax themselves outside the harsh feudal system that operated throughout the rest of the Lordship, all for a low fixed rent each year. Because we do not possess any accurate population figures for medieval Ireland, we do not know how many of these villages were set up and have since been abandoned. However, aerial photography has been very useful in identifying possible sites where there is a general absence of documentary evidence. Although there is one brief reference to a settlement at Kiltinan in County Tipperary in 1432, it is only aerial photography that reveals the extensive rectilinear earthworks and hollow way of this significant medieval village, which unhappily has now been disturbed by plowing. Even where there is extensive historical evidence, such as for Newtown Jerpoint in County Kilkenny, cartography and aerial photography combine to reveal the extent and layout of this important rural borough, which guarded a major bridging point across the River Nore from the thirteenth to the seventeenth century.

More than 750 examples of medieval moated sites were mapped by the middle of the nineteenth century. Many of these rectangular earthworks, averaging 2,000–3,000 m² in area and delimited by a fosse and internal bank, were the defended manor houses of middle-range Anglo-Norman lords. They were mainly occupied from the thirteenth to the early fourteenth century. Unlike in England, where many examples are located within or close to medieval villages, most Irish examples are in dispersed locations along the periphery of the Lordship, where they would have been most exposed to raiding by the indigenous Irish. Only six sites have been archaeologically excavated, with Rigsdale in County Cork producing the most chronologically exact dating evidence for its occupation. In the excavation in 1977, Sweetman found two pennies of King Edward I (1239–1307) dating to c. 1300 in the site's occupation layers. One of these coins was found in association with sherds of Saintonge polychrome pottery. He also located the plinth of a gatehouse, the foundations of an unfinished hall, and a stone latrine to its immediate east. The available evidence would indicate

I

that this manor house was probably overrun during the Desmond Rebellion in the 1320s.

The mapped moated sites are mainly concentrated in the eastern half of the country, and there is a surprising lack of them in Ulster. As Anglo-Norman settlement penetration here was less dense than it was farther south, small mottes were still being used as defensive centers rather than the more lightly defensive moated sites. It is salutary to realize that we know about the locations of these moated sites only because their fosses and internal banks survived into the nineteenth century, when they were mapped by the Ordnance Survey, a comprehensive geographical and mapping survey of Britain and Ireland sponsored by the British government. Thus, the unmoated manor houses of the period would be much more difficult to identify archaeologically, although only the most secure parts of the Anglo-Norman colony would have possessed a significant number of them.

The Anglo-Normans were also largely responsible for the foundation of the network of towns and cities that still survive in Ireland, except for the western periphery, which always remained under indigenous Irish control. B.J. Graham has mapped more than three hundred examples of boroughs and market towns and has shown that the most urbanized counties were Louth, Kildare, and Dublin. There have been major excavations in Armagh, Carrickfergus, County Antrim, Dublin, Cork, Limerick, and Waterford. Smaller excavations have also taken place in urban centers such as Drogheda in County Louth, Downpatrick in County Down, and Wexford, among others.

These urban excavations have revealed that all of these major towns were thriving throughout the expansionary thirteenth and early fourteenth centuries. However, there were also difficulties—such as those experienced by Wexford and, less significantly, by Dublin—when their port areas started to silt up. Dublin got over this by using Dalkey and Howth as outports and then transporting goods overland from them, but Wexford went into steep decline from the end of the thirteenth century, probably exacerbated by its too close proximity to New Ross in County Wexford and Waterford, two of the most important east-coast ports.

Excavations in Dublin from the 1960s onward have elucidated more than 10 percent of the medieval walled town. The earliest excavations concentrated upon the Hiberno-Norse period (tenth–twelfth centuries), especially as many of the later medieval layers had been destroyed by the large cellars constructed in the Georgian period (1714–1830). More than 150 post-and-wattle houses of this era were located in the Wood Quay/ Fishamble Street area, and the wide range and sophistication of the artifacts recovered in the National Museum of Ireland excavations all testify to the political and socioeconomic wealth of the Hiberno-Norse town. More recent excavations have revealed more about the Anglo-Norman phase of occupation, such as the discovery of two of the thirteenth-century mural towers of the city. In the Cornmarket area in the west of the city, traces of the first Anglo-Norman defensive ditch have been excavated. This was replaced in the thirteenth century by another ditch, which was in use until the fifteenth century. Much waste from a thirteenth-century bronze workshop was also recovered from this fill. Most of the recent excavations have produced pottery, metal, and wooden artifacts of the thirteenth and early fourteenth centuries, as well as enormous collections of leather goods and animal, fish, and bird bones. These all illustrate the wide-ranging nature of Dublin's trade throughout the Middle Ages.

Excavations in the center of Waterford, around Arundle Square, have produced more than 200,000 artifacts and many structures dating from the tenth century to the postmedieval period. Indeed, more than 20 percent of the walled city has been archaeologically excavated beginning in 1986. The parish church of St. Peter and its associated graveyard were fully excavated. Skeletal evidence from this cemetery will give medieval archaeologists unparalleled information about the diet and living conditions of the medieval urban population of the city. As well, more than eighty post-and-wattle houses dating from the eleventh century were also uncovered. On top of them lay some larger timber structures from the twelfth and early thirteenth centuries, including a complex stone-and-wood structure, whose purpose is still unknown. Six cellared structures from the eleventh century were also exposed, the greatest number located in any Irish town to date.

In Cork, urban excavations have revealed the foundations of Skiddy's Castle, built in 1445, and the stone foundations of the College of Holy Trinity-Christchurch, built in 1482. Some medieval street frontages and portions of the town wall have also been excavated. More recently, the church and claustral area of the Dominican house of St. Mary de Insula, founded in the early thirteenth century, were excavated prior to their being covered over by a development.

After all the socioeconomic traumas of the first half of the fourteenth century, many settlements went into decline. However, this period also saw the construction of up to seven thousand tower houses in Ireland. These were the single stone towers, sometimes surrounded by a defensive court or bawn, that were designed to provide a protected home for a lord and his family from the later fourteenth century until the widespread use of gunpowder made them obsolete in the seventeenth century. In the west, more than ninety friaries were established in the fifteenth century, all indicators of the wealth that still survived in Ireland even in the most difficult circumstances. But it was in the seventeenth century, with the Cromwellian Conquest of the country, that the medieval pattern of settlement was altered irrevocably to usher in the early modern period.

FURTHER READINGS

Barry, T.B. *Medieval Moated Sites of South-East Ireland.* BAR British Series 35. Oxford: British Archaeological Reports, 1977.

———. *The Archaeology of Medieval Ireland.* London and New York: Routledge, 1988.

Edwards, N. *The Archaeology of Early Medieval Ireland.* London: Batsford, 1990.

Hurley, M.F. Late Viking Age Settlement in Waterford City. In *Waterford History and Society.* Ed. W. Nolan and T.P. Power. Dublin: Geography Publications, 1992, pp. 49–72.

Ryan, M.F., ed. *The Illustrated Archaeology of Ireland.* Dublin: Country House, 1991.

Wallace, P.F. *The Viking Age Buildings of Dublin.* 2 Vols. Dublin: Royal Irish Academy, 1992.

Terry Barry

SEE ALSO
Cashels; Crannógs; Dendrochronology; Raths

Irish Sea Province
See Glastonbury.

Iron Age

While approaches to the formation of the early medieval world that are based upon the written sources of the time emphasize the role of late Roman and Germanic traditions, an archaeological approach shows that the pre-Roman peoples of temperate Europe also played a significant part in the development. When Roman armies conquered Gaul (the lands between the Pyrenees and the River Rhine, most of which is France today) between 58 and 51 B.C. and the regions south of the River Danube in 15 B.C., those territories were inhabited by peoples, most of them known as Celts, who possessed highly developed cultures and traditions. Writings by Roman observers such as Julius Caesar (100–44 B.C.) provide us with some information about these Iron Age populations, and, through the techniques of archaeology, we can learn much more. Following the conquest, many of these peoples were incorporated into the Roman Empire, but many preserved their traditions during the centuries of Roman rule.

The Iron Age in Europe

The final period of prehistory in Europe is known as the Iron Age, following the Stone Age and the Bronze Age. Scholars have been studying the European Iron Age intensively for well over 150 years, and we now have a good understanding of changing patterns of settlement, economic activity, social structure, and ritual behavior. According to scholarly consensus, the Iron Age began c. 800 B.C. and ended with the start of the Roman period, c. 50 B.C. in Gaul and 15 B.C. east of the Rhine. The time between 800 and 450 B.C. is known as the early Iron Age, or Hallstatt period, and that between 450 B.C. and the Roman Conquest as the late Iron Age, or La Tène period. Many of the characteristic features of the early Middle Ages, including settlement patterns, house types, crafts, commerce, burial practices, and artistic traditions, are foreshadowed by developments in the prehistoric Iron Age.

The first large communities with concentrated craft and trade activity formed during the early Iron Age, and they can be called Europe's first towns. They appeared c. 600 B.C. and were situated on hilltops and surrounded by substantial defensive walls. The best-studied example is the Heuneburg in southwestern Germany, and similar sites have been investigated in France, Switzerland, and the Czech Republic. Craft workers at these centers manufactured objects of many different materials, including iron, bronze, textiles, pottery, bone and antler, lignite and jet, and gold. Goods imported from abroad included coral from the Mediterranean, amber from the Baltic shores, and silk from the East. In many respects, these early Iron Age craft and trade centers resemble those of the early Middle Ages, especially the commercial sites of the fifth–ninth centuries on the North Sea and Baltic coasts, such as Helgö, Birka, Ribe, and Dorstad.

Richly outfitted burials containing gold ornaments, bronze vessels, exotic imports, and four-wheeled wagons occur at the centers, and they contrast sharply with the

I

modest graves of the majority of the people. The evidence suggests a strongly differentiated society, with a small elite acquiring sizable quantities of wealth, probably through the manufacturing and trade at the centers.

Among many changes that took place during the fifth century B.C., at the beginning of the late Iron Age, the style of ornamentation known as La Tène, or Celtic, art began. It incorporated elements adapted from Mediterranean traditions, including spirals, tendrils, blossoms, and mythological creatures. The evolution of this style of decoration can be traced directly from these fifth-century-B.C. origins to the early medieval Celtic art of Britain and Ireland.

During the early part of the late Iron Age, centers such as those of the early Iron Age were lacking in temperate Europe. The landscape was occupied by small agricultural settlements—farmsteads and villages. But important developments were taking place in technology. Ironworking was especially important, because tools made of iron and its alloy, steel, were employed for many tasks, including agricultural production and building. The increasing availability and quality of such implements made possible advances in the efficiency of many kinds of work. Iron ore is abundant throughout temperate Europe, and, from the fourth century B.C. onward, most communities smelted their own iron and forged the tools they needed. By the end of the prehistoric Iron Age, more than two hundred kinds of iron tools were in use. Other major crafts included bronze casting, still important for making ornaments; the manufacture of glass jewelry; and leather working.

The earlier part of the late Iron Age was characterized by a standard burial practice across much of temperate Europe. Bodies were laid out flat on their backs, sometimes in coffins or on boards. Women were outfitted with ornaments, especially bronze rings (worn on the neck, arms, fingers, and legs), ornate bronze pins known as *fibulae,* and beads of glass, amber, and stone. Men were often buried with sets of iron weapons, including long swords, spears, and shields. Very rich graves were rare during this period, but variations in burial equipment suggest that significant status differences existed among individuals.

The second half of the second century B.C. was a period of major change. Large fortified settlements known as *oppida* were established throughout the central regions of temperate Europe, with massive walls of earth, stone, and timber enclosing as much as several hundred acres of land. They were sited at naturally defensible loca-tions, especially on steep-sided hilltops and on peninsulas formed by river bends. These were the largest communities of prehistoric Europe, and some, such as Manching in Bavaria and Stradonice in Bohemia, can be considered urban in character, with populations in the thousands and with evidence of preplanned settlement layouts, dense occupation, intensive industrial activity, and extensive commerce. Manufacturing, especially in iron, was on a much larger scale than at the early Iron Age centers, and a whole range of new tools were being made. These included iron plowshares, colters, and scythes, all of which contributed to an increase in agricultural efficiency. Locks and keys are numerous on the *oppidum* settlements. A differentiated coinage in gold, silver, and bronze indicates the emergence of a money economy.

The causes of the sudden establishment of these great walled settlements are not fully clear. Evidence suggests a period of exceptional military activity, including migrations of peoples from the north and conflict among communities within central Europe, but whether external or internal factors were predominant in the development of the large fortified settlements is still uncertain. Written accounts by Roman and Greek authors and archaeological evidence indicate significant interactions at this time between the Celtic peoples of central regions of the continent and Germanic peoples to the north.

At the same time that the *oppidum* settlements were established, significant changes occurred in ritual activity. Burial practice changed to cremation, and in most regions few goods were placed in graves. A new type of ritual site became common, consisting of a rectangular plot of land enclosed by a raised bank. In one corner of the interior was typically a large building, indicated by sizable postholes, and also within the enclosure were often one or more deep shafts dug into the ground, into which objects were thrown, apparently as votive offerings. The practice of making offerings, including sacrificed animals as well as manufactured goods such as swords and personal ornaments of metal, was common in prehistoric Europe, but new was the construction of the enclosures as artificial places for such activity; in earlier periods, offerings were made in springs, rivers, lakes, and caves. In addition, many hoards of precious metal were buried, some consisting of gold or silver coins, others composed of coins and rings. These hoards can be interpreted in two different, but not mutually exclusive, ways: as treasure buried for safekeeping during times of conflict and as offerings to deities accompanying requests for aid and protection.

The Roman Conquest

The great walled settlements and the intensive industrial and commercial activities at them ended around the middle of the first century B.C. In Gaul, Julius Caesar led Roman armies to conquer the Celtic peoples. East of the Rhine, most of the *oppida* were given up around the same time, under conditions that are not well understood. With the Roman Conquest of the lands south of the Danube in 15 B.C., a new phase began under the enforced peace of the Roman Empire. The peoples who inhabited the unconquered regions across the Rhine and Danube frontiers maintained their traditional ways of life, but they were much influenced through their interactions with the Roman world.

In the past few decades, archaeologists working in the Roman period have turned their attention increasingly to the native peoples within the Roman territories. They are finding that much of the pre-Roman Iron Age traditions survived during the Roman period, including settlement patterns, burial practices, ritual behaviors, and styles of metalwork and pottery. The extent of survival of such prehistoric cultural patterns varied in different regions. The so-called Celtic Renaissance of the third century A.D. was a vivid expression of some of these traditions.

Conclusion

When the archaeological evidence from the Iron Age and from the early Medieval period are compared, we see many striking similarities. In both contexts, the cultural landscape was dominated by farms and small villages, but manufacturing and trading centers also played a role. Buildings were constructed with post frames and wattle-and-daub walls, remains of both of which survive archaeologically. In many cases, burial practices were similar, especially when we compare the well-outfitted graves of the earlier part of the late Iron Age and those of the Germanic kingdoms of the early Middle Ages. In both contexts, men often were outfitted with sets of iron weapons, women with bronze and glass jewelry. Many of the late Iron Age rectangular enclosures remained in use during the Roman period, and in some instances Gallo-Roman temples were erected directly on top of them, as at Ribemont in northern France. Some investigators have argued that such temples were the direct forerunners of the first Christian churches in the same regions.

We need to ask to what extent such similarities that are apparent archaeologically represent real continuity and to what extent they reflect responses to similar social, political, and economic conditions in the two periods. Much recent work on Roman period archaeology shows that Iron Age traditions were maintained in some places, but we do not yet have a good overview of the situation for any part of Europe. To learn more about this question, we need intensive regional investigations. Circumstances of cultural survival and change were different in different places, depending upon local political and economic conditions, and they changed with time. During the migration period at the beginning of the Middle Ages, there was considerable movement of peoples throughout Europe, yet the evidence does not show complete replacement of populations. Most likely, the majority of people remained in their home landscapes. Recent discoveries suggest that much exciting work remains to be done on this subject to help us understand the role of the pre-Roman Iron Age cultures in the formation of medieval Europe.

FURTHER READINGS

Barrett, J.C., A.P. Fitzpatrick, and L. Macinnes, eds. *Barbarians and Romans in North-West Europe.* BAR International Series 471. Oxford: British Archaeological Reports, 1989.

Collis, John. *The European Iron Age.* New York: Schocken, 1984.

King, Anthony. *Roman Gaul and Germany.* Berkeley and Los Angeles: University of California Press, 1990.

Megaw, Ruth, and Vincent Megaw. *Celtic Art.* London: Thames and Hudson, 1989.

Wells, Peter S. *Farms, Villages, and Cities: Commerce and Urban Origins in Late Prehistoric Europe.* Ithaca: Cornell University Press, 1984.

———. Iron Age Temperate Europe: Some Current Research Issues. *Journal of World Prehistory* (1990) 4:437–476.

Peter S. Wells

SEE ALSO

Birka; Bohemia: Early Medieval Villages; Emporia; Helgö

Ironworking

Iron was an indispensable component of life in medieval Europe. Iron was utilized in subsistence activities (as plowshares and sickle blades), in craft production (as carpenters' saws and axes), and in warfare (as swords and armor). Despite the importance of iron to the people of

I

medieval Europe, relatively little is known about medieval iron. Questions such as the amount and frequency of iron usage in daily life are essentially unstudied. Much of what is known is based on metallographic analyses of arms and armor. Although these studies are of great use, they present a distorted picture of the overall technical level and product quality of medieval iron since many of the artifacts that have survived and have been studied are elite items made with particular care for the wealthy.

Medieval iron was usually wrought iron. Wrought iron, a very tough and strong metal, is essentially a pure form of iron with a low carbon content. It is poorly suited for use in edged tools, such as axes and knives, because it is so soft. Steel, a harder alloy of iron and carbon, was available to medieval smiths and was used to make cutting tools, although it remained scarce and expensive. An indication of the relative values of wrought iron and steel comes from fourteenth-century England, where steel cost £3 a ton, five times the price of wrought iron (Steane 1984). Cast iron, a high carbon variety of iron, was not used in Europe until the very end of the medieval period.

Iron is a common element in the Earth's crust, and good sources of iron were widespread in Europe. Consequently, at least limited iron production occurred in most areas. A few areas, such as southern Germany and northern Spain, became known for especially high quality iron goods, such as armor and swords, and these items were traded widely. Most iron, however, was made and used regionally, leaving widely scattered archaeological remains of small-scale production, often no more than one or two furnace bottoms and a few tons of iron slag.

Production of Iron

The archaeological study of iron production is largely dependent upon the examination of waste products: slags, cinder, and furnace remains. In medieval Europe, iron itself was relatively valuable and so was generally carefully handled and sold or traded away from the production centers. Waste products were of little value and tended to remain at or near iron-production centers. The techniques of medieval iron production have been studied through excavation, scientific analysis, and experiments with replica furnaces. The technical processes used to produce iron in Europe remained essentially the same from the early Iron Age, c. 600 B.C., through the end of the Medieval period. As a result, a wide range of examples may be used to study medieval wrought-iron production.

Virtually all iron in medieval Europe was made by direct process smelting. Direct process smelting is so

called because the iron product may be removed from the furnace and directly worked—wrought—by a blacksmith. Direct process smelting is a simple, although inefficient, method that is well suited to small-scale or part-time operations. Most known medieval iron-production sites have only a few tons of slag present, representing a total useful production of perhaps no more than a ton or two of iron. The ratio of slag to iron is extremely variable, depending upon ore quality and the methods used to process it, but a 4:1-to-8:1 ratio of slag to finished iron is a reasonable estimate. In the smelting process, iron oxide, an ore, is reduced to metallic iron. The basic process may be summarized by the following chemical equation:

$$FeO + CO + heat \text{ (energy)} \rightarrow Fe + CO_2$$

The equation, in words, is the following: iron oxide + carbon monoxide + heat = iron + carbon dioxide. In practice, the process is more complex. No ore is pure iron oxide. Other materials are present and need to be separated into a slag before workable iron is obtained. The most common mineral present in medieval slag was fayalite, Fe_2SiO_4. Slag production was a wasteful process since two iron atoms were consumed for every silicon atom that was removed. Because of the wasteful nature of the process, only very rich ores could profitably be smelted in medieval furnaces.

Smelting furnaces remained similar thoughout Europe during the Medieval period. Although variations did exist, a typical furnace may be defined. The furnaces were small and roughly circular, often with an internal diameter of no more than 30–40 cm. A total height of 1.2 m is estimated for a medieval furnace, and walls, 20–30 cm thick, were constructed of clay or a mixture of clay and stone. Only rarely do more than the lowermost portions of these furnaces survive. Operating temperatures were so low that the clay walls of the furnace were not completely baked into a ceramic that could remain intact after the furnace was abandoned. Consequently, the archaeological remains of furnaces are often limited to the thin skin of a well-fired furnace base, while the remainder of the wall will have decayed, leaving only a shadow in the ground, similar to a post mold.

Three ingredients are necessary to operate a direct process furnace successfully: fuel, ore, and air. In more elaborate furnaces built in the late Middle Ages, a limestone flux was added. The flux helped form a more free-flowing slag that was less wasteful of iron. Most medieval furnaces were top charging. In these furnaces, the fuel and the ore, which together are known as the *charge,* were

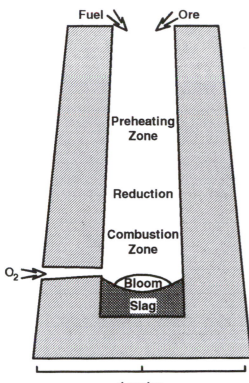

Typical medieval smelting furnace used in iron production.

added through the top opening through which the exhaust gases also escaped. Temperatures in direct process furnaces were not hot enough to melt iron, although the slags were at least partially fluid. The fluid slags drained away, leaving behind iron particles that welded together with some residual slag into a spongy mass known as *iron bloom.*

The slag and bloom accumulate at the base of the furnace. In some furnaces, the fluid slags were removed through a small tap hole in the base; in others, the slag was allowed to build up in a pit below the furnace. Solid iron bloom was removed after each smelting cycle. In small, low furnaces, bloom would be pulled out through the top. In larger furnaces, bloom was removed through a hole knocked in the side of the furnace or through a previously built opening that was blocked up during the smelting cycle. Quantities of iron bloom were small. In a typical small shaft furnace of the type described above, 2 kg of bloom per cycle was a reasonable level of production (Crew 1991).

Bloom Consolidation and Smithing

The spongy iron bloom produced in direct process furnaces needed to be consolidated into useful billet or bar iron before a smith could fashion an implement. Bloom consolidation is a time-consuming and wasteful process. A full day's work by a smith was needed to consolidate 2 kg of bloom into a billet (Crew 1991). Up to half the weight of the bloom was lost in the consolidation process. Some of the lost material was entrapped slag, but the rest was potentially useful iron. Archaeological evidence for smithing includes hearths that are shaped like shallow bowls. During excavation, these hearths are frequently confused with the bases of smelting furnaces. This confusion is understandable since these hearths were sometimes made from the bases of abandoned smelting furnaces. Additional evidence for the smelting process is provided by distinctively shaped cakes of slag, iron slag, fuel ash, and the like. These cakes are known as PCBs (plano-convex bottoms) because their curved shape reflects the bowl-shaped bottoms of smithing hearths. The PCBs often have a depression at the top where the blast of the bellows pushed the slags and other materials to the side. Detailed studies of PCBs are just beginning and may eventually allow archaeologists to determine the particular smithing activities that were occurring at the time a given PCB was formed.

Once bar iron was produced, medieval smiths were capable of making iron objects of virtually any shape. Although they were often quite conservative stylistically, medieval smiths were not lacking in technical ability. Even in areas such as Ireland, northern England, and Scandinavia, which were remote from centers of metallurgical innovation, analyses of artifacts have shown that medieval smiths used a wide range of steeling methods and welding techniques (see Scott 1990). There is great variation in the quality of medieval iron objects, and this variation can be interpreted in a number of different ways. One plausible explanation is that the range in quality reflects not only variations in technical skill, but also economic considerations. In other words, high-quality iron items were purchased by those who could most easily afford them.

One of the most technically challenging smithing activities was the construction of an iron-and-steel blade. As steel was expensive and scarce, only a thin layer of steel was welded onto the edge of an iron core or sandwiched between two iron layers. In more elaborate pieces, a pattern-welded blade could be made. In pattern welding, layers of iron and steel are alternated, resulting in a blade that combines the strength and toughness of wrought iron with the sharp cutting edge of steel.

I

Variations in Medieval Iron

Although iron in medieval Europe may be considered a largely stable, uniform commodity, there were important developments that affect the archaeological record of iron production. One of the most interesting is the presence and use of Damascus, or Wootz, steel. Wootz steel, which was probably manufactured in India, was imported to Europe through the Middle East (Damascus); hence, its contemporary name. Wootz steel was a very high quality cementation steel that could be made into excellent blades. It was produced from wrought iron that had been brought into contact with a carbon source, such as charcoal, at a sufficiently high temperature in the absence of oxygen so that some of the carbon was absorbed by the iron, chemically transforming it into steel. The surface of Wootz steel was marked with characteristic light and dark lines. It was so highly valued that similar lines were often etched into non-Wootz European blades to imitate the appearance of Wootz steel.

The introduction of water power in iron production was of even greater technological significance. The earliest evidence for bellows driven by water wheels was in 1408 at a bloomery owned by the bishop of Durham (Tylecote 1976). The use of these bellows spread quickly and was followed shortly thereafter by the use of water-driven trip hammers for working the bloom. These innovations allowed larger quantities of air to be forced into a furnace and larger quantities of bloom to be worked at one time. Not surprisingly, larger furnaces soon followed. The trend toward larger furnaces was particularly marked in Germany, where, by the middle of the fifteenth century, the so-called *Hochofen* was in use (Gilles 1952). Essentially a small blast furnace, the *Hochofen* enabled smiths to produce cast iron in a continuous fashion, laying much of the groundwork for modern metallurgy.

A final aspect of the archaeology of medieval iron concerns the use of early-modern historical sources. Just as continuity in technologies allows Iron Age evidence to be used, so, too, is it possible to make use of postmedieval written documents. The most important historical works are two sixteenth-century volumes that provide the first contemporary technical descriptions of metal production. The books are *The Pirotechnica* by Vannoccio Biringuccio (1540) and *De re metallica* by Georgius Agricola (1556). Although much of the actual science in these books has been proved incorrect, these sources provide otherwise unavailable insights into early ironworking methods and organization. These data aid in the reconstruction of medieval ironworking technology from archaeological evidence.

FURTHER READINGS

Agricola, Georgius. *De re metallica,* 1556. Trans. Herbert Hover and Lou Hover. New York: Dover, 1950.

Biringuccio, Vannoccio. *The Pirotechnica.* 1540. Trans. Cyril Stanley Smith and Martha Teach Gnudi. New York: Dover, 1990.

Crew, Peter. The Experimental Production of Prehistoric Bar Iron. *Journal of the Historical Metallurgy Society* (1991) 25(1):21–36.

Gilles, Josef. Der Stammbau des Hochofens. *Archiv für des Eisenhuttenwesen* (1952) 23:407–415.

Scott, B.G. *Early Irish Ironworking.* Belfast: Ulster Museum, 1990.

Steane, John. *The Archaeology of Medieval England and Wales.* Athens: University of Georgia Press, 1984.

Tylecote, Ronald. *A History of Metallurgy.* London: Metals Society, 1976.

Carl Blair

SEE ALSO
Iron Age

Italy

A Difficult Start

As in every European country, the beginning of medieval archaeology in Italy is related to the interest in national antiquities that began in the nineteenth century and was deeply associated with the definition of a particular national identity. As in France, Germany, and England, early medieval furnished burials were considered the first and most obvious material evidence marking the beginning of the Middle Ages and national history. There was, however, one very important difference; while the Merovingians and the Anglo-Saxons were considered the legitimate ancestors of the nineteenth-century French and English nations, the Lombards, who settled in Italy in 568, were considered by nineteenth-century Italian historical tradition as the invaders of Italy and the polluters of the original and native Roman state structure. While looking for Lombard graves, Italian archaeologists were, therefore, looking for evidence of the fate of their Roman ancestors (La Rocca 1993).

Nevertheless, a substantial number of burials were recorded and collected, especially between 1880 and 1900; these finds are still the principal material evidence for the Lombard period in Italy. It is worth mentioning the burial sites of Testona (Turin province), excavated in 1877, where about four hundred furnished Lombard graves were found, and Nocera Umbra (Perugia) and Castel Trosino (Ascoli Piceno), excavated at the beginning of the twentieth century (republished in Jorgensen 1992). While only a short notice was published for Testona that did not indicate which objects were related to each grave (Calandra and Calandra 1883), the other two sites were published in a scientific and an exhaustive way (Pasqui Paribeni 1919; Mengarelli 1902). Unfortunately, this was not the general standard for archaeological publications of the period. The majority of the Lombard sites were often badly excavated and recorded by amateurs—directors of local museums, collectors of weapons, and art historians—who did not have any experience in archaeological method. Their main interest was in finding and publishing specific objects from early medieval graves and not in recording contexts. This attitude was encouraged by art historians who included Lombard gold brooches and crosses in their repertories of "barbarian art"; these objects were presented as evidence for decadence from Roman times.

The political separation between the Lombard conquerors and the Latin victims strongly limited archaeology's role in the study of early medieval life. The presence of the Lombard invaders could be detected only in furnished graves; settlement archaeology could not be used because there was not yet an interest in using building techniques to distinguish between different cultural groups. Lombard graves did not stimulate an interest in, and approaches to, early medieval material culture on the whole. In France and Britain (Higham 1992; *Actes du Colloque International* 1978), Anglo-Saxon and Merovingian furnished graves, settlement patterns, and building techniques were studied as the basis of the material culture of national "prehistory," while, in Italy, Lombard material culture was seen as the illegitimate interference of uneducated invaders.

The interest in Lombard grave goods was further weakened during the Fascist regime, whose ideology was entirely devoted to the celebration of the Roman imperial splendor. The few scholars who persisted in publishing "German antiquities" were officially accused of studying unimportant matters and of denying "the supremely Italian character of ancient Rome" (Manacorda 1982). After 1925, it is very difficult to find even one publication about early medieval remains, and one could say that, at this stage, Italian medieval archaeology was already dead. Instead, Lombard artifacts were the objects of several typological studies by German and Swedish scholars who were looking for the dispersed traces of German antiquities in Europe.

After World War II, it was a legal historian, Gian Piero Bognetti, who again attracted attention to the Lombard past and redefined its role in Italian history with the help of material evidence. Bognetti stressed the substantial break in the institutional and political history of Italy created by Lombard settlement. For Bognetti, the Italian Middle Ages began in 568. His studies were, therefore, structured by the strong contrasts between Lombard and late antique society; while the former was primitive and dominated by German-warrior ideology, the latter was highly complex and dominated by bureaucracy. This opposition was also seen in the material aspects of society, including building techniques, urban settlement, and the development of fortified centers. The site of Castelseprio (Varese province), where Bognetti found a Lombard church decorated with frescoes of Byzantine influence, became the paradigm for a further development in historical interpretation in the mid-1950s (Bognetti 1948). Bognetti argued that the Italian Middle Ages were created by Lombard culture, strongly modified in its structure and content by its relationship with Byzantium. Material culture was considered important evidence for cultural interaction. Bognetti, therefore, invited a Polish team of archaeologists from the School of Material Culture at Warsaw to excavate at Castelseprio. The Polish team published its first report in 1964, and only then did Italian medieval archaeology have a new beginning. For a summary of the research, see Hensel and Tabaczyńsky (1981).

A New Discipline

Bognetti's influence in renewing the interest in medieval material culture in Italy varied depending on the local archaeological tradition. In the area of Rome and in Liguria, interest in early medieval and late antique remains had a long and independent tradition that was related to studies of Christian archaeology (i.e., the study of early Christian cemeteries and basilicas). In Liguria, the work of Nino Lamboglia, although devoted principally to the history of early Christian architecture, was conducted by excavating urban sites of great importance, including Albenga and Ventimiglia. These were Roman towns that lost their political and institutional position during the early Middle Ages. The Istituto di Studi Liguri, a fruitful

I

collaboration of prehistorians and classical archaeologists, was soon devoted to the study of pottery and its distribution during late antiquity and the early Middle Ages. It is in this context that we can understand the seminal work of Tiziano Mannoni, who, combining his profound knowledge of mineralogy with extensive fieldwork, proposed a typology of medieval fine wares and coarse wares from the fourth century to the fifteenth for the western part of Liguria (Mannoni 1975). The main interests of the Genoese group called Centro Ligure per la Storia della Cultura Materiale were building techniques, pottery, and the excavation of settlements. Together with the local archaeological authorities, this group managed to excavate several small sites in Genoa during rebuilding work, providing a sample of the stratigraphy of the city center (Blake et al. 1978).

Since the 1960s, historians and geographers have focused their attention on the peculiarity of the medieval landscape with the aid of aerial photographs of the Campagna Romana made by the British School at Rome. In Florence and Tuscany, in particular (Francovich 1973), but also in Piedmont, written sources were used for the first time to study changing settlement patterns, including the relationship between castles, churches, and villages during the eleventh–thirteenth centuries (Settia 1973). Written sources were collected to explain the complex movements of dispersed villages to hilltop settlements. The monumental buildings (castles and churches) were then studied not merely as objects, but in connection with the process of the transformation of medieval power. Meetings of the Genoa, Florence, and Turin groups were based from the beginning on the mutual relationship between historians and archaeologists. In 1974, the national magazine *Archeologia medievale* was founded, and medieval archaeology was, indeed, presented as a new academic discipline, characterized by specific aims, techniques, and methodology. The first editorial of this magazine was devoted to the explanation of the connection between medieval archaeology and prehistoric methods of investigation. The aims of medieval archaeology were defined as the "history of material culture studying the material aspects of activities devoted to production, distribution and consumption of goods and the conditions of these activities in their changes and relationship to the historical process" (*Archeologia medievale* 1974:8).

From 1974 to 1980, Italian medieval archaeology was made up of a multidisciplinary set of scholars. Its interest initially focused on the late Middle Ages, for which the abundance of written sources and archaeological evidence could provide an ideal common ground to compare the methods and results of research. The conferences held by *Archeologia medievale* focused on historiographical themes in which geographers, settlement historians, archaeozoologists, and archaeologists could debate and compare their specific results. Their subjects, including the history of rural settlements (*Archeologia medievale* 1980) and the history of diet (*Archeologia medievale* 1981), reflected the interest in a multidisciplinary approach. At this stage, the study of the late Middle Ages was profoundly revitalized by its relationship with archaeology, especially studies of pottery typology and production, while the early Middle Ages were set aside, left to the interests of early Christian archaeologists and the specialists in Lombard grave goods.

Towns and Countryside

In 1984, an English-Italian team promoted an exhibition about the stratigraphy and archaeological evidence for the history of north Italian towns from the prehistoric period to the late Middle Ages. The exhibition was held in Milan (Lombardy), where the substantial amount of building work since World War II was responsible for significant destruction of archaeological deposits in the city. The construction of a new underground railroad in the city center was an important opportunity to use archaeology to record the stratigraphic development of the city from prehistoric to modern times. Following the experience of English archaeologists, especially in London, Italian archaeologists tried to determine the amount of archaeological deposits that were still intact in all the cities of the region, proposing a strategy for future excavations (*Archeologia urbana in Lombardia* 1985). It was a real experiment, because, before the 1980s, stratigraphic excavations in northern Italy were rare and had been primarily conducted by university researchers. The activity of Lancaster University in Pavia was particularly noteworthy (Ward-Perkins et al. 1978), and it also produced a synthetic evaluation of archaeological deposits in the old Lombard capital (Hudson 1981).

In the 1984 exhibition, special attention was paid to the early medieval phases of the cities; here archaeology would play a particularly important role due to the lack of written sources from the sixth to the tenth centuries. The early medieval towns showed a pattern of substantial decay from the monumental Roman past. Archaeological evidence, recovered by extensive excavations, apparently confirmed the historical interpretation of the Belgian Medieval historian Henri Pirenne (1862–1935). For Pirenne, substantial modifications to the late antique urban structure were caused by a decline in long-distance commerce, which was provoked by the Arab invasion of the Mediterranean during the seventh century. The main center of Roman trade was then blocked, dividing Europe into two distinct areas (the northern one administered by the Franks, and the southern one dominated by the Arabs). The lack of long-distance trade would have profoundly altered the urban economy and the material characteristics of the towns themselves. From the seventh century onward, the old network of Roman towns would have been destroyed; towns would, therefore, have lost their special identity and functions (Barker and Hodges 1981). Research undertaken on the early medieval stratigraphy of cities that maintained their institutional position as episcopal sees, like Brescia and Milan, supported this interpretation of a sharp decline of the urban system itself, with evidence for abandonment of settlement in the Roman *insulae* (city blocks), a decline in the quality of building techniques, and a striking difference between the accumulation of archaeological deposits in the Roman town (thin layers) and the early medieval ones (thick layers of dark earth). This would support an interpretation of a ruralization of towns, which is also documented by contemporary written evidence. Wooden houses, identifiable only by small post-holes, took the place of the urban *villae* built in stone and bricks; the paving of Roman streets was abandoned; and public monuments were ruined and spoiled (Brogiolo 1989).

This pattern of economic and demographic decline proposed by R. Hodges and D.B. Whitehouse (1983), based on the abandoned Roman city of Luni, stimulated archaeological research on early medieval Italian cities. From 1984 onward, the number of stratigraphic excavations in towns increased sharply, and the National Superintendency (the national antiquities authority) was entrusted with the recovery of these data. Archaeologists and historians contributed to the ongoing debate on the form of early medieval towns. Archaeologists stressed other differences between early medieval and late antique towns, in an attempt to reshape the terms of one traditional Italian historiographical theme (i.e., the continuity between the Roman and early medieval city). They called attention to the substantial difference between late antique and early medieval urban society in the donation of monumental buildings to their city as a means for advancing a political career (Ward-Perkins 1984). The lack of fiscal control made early medieval kings a lot poorer than their imperial predecessors; the decline in the

quality of private and public buildings was thus related to the fact that less money was available for building rather than to a general demographic crisis. Urban graves, which had previously been used to emphasize the abandonment of the city centers, were located in old public areas, like theaters and amphitheaters; therefore, they cannot be used to show the abandonment of private houses. The example of Verona, one of the most important northern Italian cities during the early Middle Ages, proved that the changing physical appearance of the city was not connected to the loss of the city's role as a seat of public and episcopal power, nor was it related to an assimilation between city and countryside. Instead, the use of the land inside the town was reshaped to conform to the needs of a new society (Hodges and Hobley 1988).

Castles and Seigneurial Power

Another important point of discussion between historians and medieval archaeologists was the origins of fortified hilltop settlement, a process normally called *incastellamento* after the research of Pierre Toubert in the Sabina region (Toubert 1973). Toubert's work showed a complex phenomenon of territorial reshaping of dispersed settlement organized by the local aristocracy: during the ninth and tenth centuries, the dispersed population was invited to live inside fortified settlements for protection against danger. In this way, the owner of the castle could better exercise his rights of power and control over the rural population. The castral revolution would radically change the pattern of settlement, concentrating it only in hilltop villages, which were created by aristocratic initiative, and later stimulating a new territorial organization based on castles. Toubert's model was adopted by historians and archaeologists, but it was also criticized on the basis of local examples (Noyé 1988; Settia 1984; Wickham 1978, 1985). From an archaeological perspective, the first experiments in the classification of these settlements were designed to verify documentary evidence (Francovich 1973). During the 1980s, archaeological excavations showed the differences between castles as seats of institutional power and the material history of the castles themselves. Since then, archaeological research has tried to develop models based on material evidence and not on written sources. As a result, the problem of the origins of castles has been profoundly modified. Archaeological excavations undertaken in Molise, Puglia, Tuscany, and at the important site of Montarrenti showed that settlements were slowly moving up to hilltop sites during the sixth and seventh centuries on their own. Only two

I

centuries later were these settlements fortified by a seigneurial power; the revolutionary character of the *incastellamento* did not consist of seigneurial initiatives but in giving juridical significance to a spontaneous movement of peasants (*Archeologia medievale* 1990).

The contribution of medieval archaeology in reshaping historical problems, especially for the early Middle Ages when written sources are limited, was also evident in the reappraisal of the most traditional theme of Italian archaeology—Lombard graves and church archaeology. Although few new sites have been found since the beginning of the twentieth century (regional lists of sites have been published in *Studi medievali* since 1973), the principal Lombard cemetery, found in Trezzo d'Adda (Bergamo province), has been studied in connection with landscape and settlement history (Roffia 1986). The important excavation of the Carolingian monastery of San Vincenzo al Volturno in the Molise region, by the British School at Rome (Hodges 1993), has not only examined the traditional architectural aspects of the surviving buildings, it has also studied the material culture of the site (tile and pottery production, the architectural and decorative apparatus, and the large number of frescoes and stone inscriptions throughout the monastic complex) as a means of communicating the power of the Benedictine monks to the local peasants and landholders. A series of surveys made of hilltop villages owned by the monastery has shown an integration between the monastery's economy and its possessions and the material influence of the monastery on the surrounding territory.

FURTHER READINGS

Actes du Colloque international sur l'Abbé Cochet et l'archéologie au XIXe siècle. Rouen: Académie de Rouen, 1978.

Archeologia medievale (1974) 1:8.

Archeologia medievale (1990) 1:introduction.

Barker, G., and R. Hodges. Archaeology in Italy, 1980: New Directions and Mis-Directions. In *Archaeology and Italian Society: Prehistoric, Roman, and Medieval Studies.* Ed. G. Barker and R. Hodges. Oxford: British Archaeological Reports, 1981, pp. 1–16.

Blake, H. McK., T.W. Potter, and D.B.Whitehouse, eds. *Papers in Italian Archaeology I.* BAR Supplementary Series 41. Oxford: British Archaeological Reports, 1978.

Bognetti, G.P. Santa Maria Foris Portas di Castelseprio e la storia religiosa dei Longobardi. In *Santa Maria di Castelseprio.* By G.P. Bognetti and A. Capitani D'Arzago. Milan: Instituto Treccani degli Alfieri, 1948, pp. 15–511.

Brogiolo, G.P. Brescia: Building Transformations in a Lombard City. In *The Birth of Europe: Archaeology and Social Development in the First Millennium A.D.* ed. Klaus Rondsberg. Annalecta Romana Instituti Danici Supplementum 16. Rome, 1989. pp. 156–165.

Bussi, Rolando, and Alberto Molinari, eds. *Archaeologia urbana in Lombardia.* Modena: Panini, 1985.

Calandra, C., and E. Calandra. *Di una necropoli barbarica scoperta a Testona, in Atti della Società di Archeologia e Belle Arti per la provincia di Torino* (1883) 4:17–52.

Francovich, R. *Geografia storica delle sedi umane: I castelli del contado fiorentino nei secoli XII e XIII.* Florence: Olscaki, 1973.

Hensel, W., and S. Tabaczyński. *Archaeologia Medioevale Polacca in Italia.* Wrocław: Zakład Narodowy Imienia Ossolińskich Wydawnicłwo Polskiej Akademii Nauk, 1981.

Higham, N. *Rome, Britain, and the Anglo-Saxons.* London: Seaby, 1992.

Hodges, R., ed. *San Vincenzo al Volturno 1: The 1980–1986 Excavations. Part I.* London: British School at Rome, 1993.

Hodges, R., and B. Hobley, eds. *The Rebirth of Towns in the West, A.D. 700–1050.* CBA Research Report 68. London: Council for British Archaeology, 1988.

Hodges, R., and D.B. Whitehouse. *Mohammed, Charlemagne, and the Origins of Europe: Archaeology and the Pirenne Thesis.* London: Duckworth, 1983.

Hudson, P. *Archeologia urbana e programmazione della ricerca: L'esempio di Pavia.* Florence: Edizioni All'Insegna del Giglio, 1981.

Jorgensen, L. Castel Trosino and Nocera Umbra: A Chronological and Social Analysis of Family Burial Practices in Lombard Italy (6th–8th Cent. A.D.). *Acta Archaeologica* (1992) 62:1–58.

La Rocca, C. Uno specialismo mancato: Esordi e fallimento dell'archeologia medievale italiana alla fine dell'Ottocento. *Archeologia medievale* (1993) 20:13–43.

Manacorda, D. Per un'indagine sull'archeologia italiana durante il ventennio fascista. *Archeologia medievale* (1982) 9:443–470.

Mannoni, T. *La ceramica medievale nella Liguria Occidentale.* Genoa: Instituto di Studi Liguri, 1975.

Mengarelli, R. La necropoli barbarica di Castel Trosino. In *Monumenti Antichi dell'Accademia dei Lincei,* 12. Rome: n.p., 1902.

Noyé, G., ed. *Structures de l'habitat et occupation du sol dans les pays méditérranéens: Les méthodes et l'apport de l'archéologie extensive.* Rome: Ecole Française de Rome, 1988.

Pasqui Paribeni, A. La necropoli barbarica di Nocera Umbra. In *Monumenti Antichi dell'Accademia dei Lincei,* 25. Rome: n.p., 1919.

Roffia, E., ed. *La necropoli longobarda di Trezzo sull'Adda.* Florence: Edizione All'Insegna del Giglio, 1986.

Settia, A.A. "Villam circa castrum restringere": Migrazioni e accentramento di abitati sulla collina torinese nel basso Medioevo. *Quaderni Storici* (1973) 24:905–944.

———. Castelli e villaggi nell'Italia padana. Naples: Liguori, 1984.

Toubert, P. *Les structures du Latium Médiéval: Le Latium méridional et la Sabine du IXe siècle à la fin du XIIe siècle.* Rome: École français de Rome. Bibliothéques des Ecoles Françaises d'Athènes et de Rome, 1973, p. 221.

Ward-Perkins, B. *From Classical Antiquity to the Middle Ages: Urban Public Building in Northen and Central Italy, A.D. 300–850.* Oxford: Oxford University Press, 1984.

Ward-Perkins, B., H. Blake, S. Nepoti, L. Castelletti, and G. Barker. Scavi nella Torre Civica di Pavia. *Archeologia medievale* (1978) 5:77–272.

Wickham, C. Settlement Problems in Early Medieval Italy: Lucca Territory. *Archeologia medievale* (1978) 5:495–503.

———. *Il problema dell'incastellamento in Italia Centrale: L'esempio di San Vincenzo al Volturno.* Florence: Edizioni All'Insegna del Giglio, 1985.

Cristina La Rocca

SEE ALSO

Lombards

J

Jarlshof

The multiperiod site (Bronze Age to Medieval period) at Jarlshof on the southern tip of Shetland produced the first examples of Viking/Norse architecture in the Northern Isles. The long period of occupation at Jarlshof resulted in extensive midden deposits, but the house floors themselves were kept fairly clean so relatively few artifacts were found in them. The vast majority of finds came from the various midden deposits that have been dated on the basis of these finds. The houses were dated based on their stratigraphic relationship with these dated midden deposits.

The parent farmstead was dated by J.R.C. Hamilton (1956) to A.D. 800–850. This consisted of a dwelling house that may have had bowed walls and three associated outhouses enclosed by a wall. Over the next several centuries, a number of other structures were built and modified. These changes have been divided into seven phases. Subsequent houses were built perpendicular to the parent farmstead and often included a byre at one end. Phase 5 marks the beginning of the late Norse period with major changes occurring throughout the settlement. For example, House 1 was enlarged and a byre added; House 2 was demolished; House 3 was converted from a dwelling house to a byre; and Houses 6 and 7 were built. Houses 6 and 7 were shorter than the earlier ones, although byres were soon added. The final Norse phase of occupation has been dated to the thirteenth century when decline was evident on the site.

Viking and Norse artifacts found at Jarlshof include large quantities of soapstone-vessel fragments, but S. Buttler (1989) has found that the Shetland material is not well suited for detailed typological studies because, in general, it is not well made. The Shetland sherds are often coarse, so attributes such as rim form and wall angle are not useful in building stylistic groups. Instead, Hamilton grouped the Jarlshof sherds into groups such as "small round" (earlier vessels), "large round" (all phases), "rectangular" (late eleventh century or later), and "handled." Provenance studies of the Shetland soapstone material have not yet been successful.

Soapstone was also used for loom weights, spindle whorls, and line sinkers or fishing weights. The latter are common in the later phases at Jarlshof, indicating that fishing now played a dominant role in the economy. This trend has also been noted at other sites in the Northern Isles (e.g., Sandwick). Finally, baking plates are present in the later phases of Jarlshof; they appear in the Norwegian town material c. A.D. 1100.

The combs found at Jarlshof were useful for dating various parts of the site. A late ninth–early tenth-century Viking-type comb with animal head terminals is similar to examples from Birka and Århus, as well as Orkney. Jarlshof also produced combs from later periods when copper-alloy rivets took the place of the earlier iron rivets. These included short double-sided combs with finer teeth on one side than the other and single-sided combs also common in medieval Scandinavia.

FURTHER READINGS

Bigelow, Gerald F. Sandwick, Unst, and Late Norse Shetland Economy. In *Shetland Archaeology.* Ed. Brian Smith. Lerwick: Shetland Times, 1985, pp. 95–127.

———. Domestic Architecture in Medieval Shetland. *Review of Scottish Culture* (1987) 3:23–28. Edinburgh: John Donald and the National Museums of Scotland.

J

Buttler, Simon. Steatite in Norse Shetland. *Hikuin* (1989) 15:193–206. Moesgård: Forlaget Hikuin.

Curle, Alexander O. Dwellings of the Viking Period. In *Viking Antiquities in Great Britain and Ireland*. Part 6. Ed. Haakon Shetelig. Oslo: H. Aschehoug, 1954, pp. 7–64.

Hamilton, J.R.C. *Excavations at Jarlshof, Shetland*. Edinburgh: HMSO, 1956.

Barbara G. Scott

SEE ALSO
Birka; Northern Isles

Jelling

Jelling (in Jutland, Denmark) has a series of dynastic Viking monuments built in the middle decades of the tenth century by King Harald Bluetooth (r. 935–985) and his father, King Gorm (d. 935). The royal character is emphasized by the dimensions and the quality of the individual monuments. They also demonstrate the transformation of a complex of pagan monuments into one of Christian significance. The two earliest phases of the monuments date from late pagan times, while the latest phase is Christian. The main linear axis was retained throughout. The conversion itself, which took place c. 965, is celebrated by the great rune stone. One of its pictures shows Christ, and its inscription reads: "King Harald commanded these monuments/memorials to be made in memory of Gorm his father and in memory of Thyre his mother—that Harald who won for himself the whole of Denmark, and Norway, and made the Danes Christian."

Until recently, there have been many questions relating to the relative chronology of the individual monuments, but most of these were elucidated during the 1980s and 1990s. The first major monument was probably a 170-m-long ship-setting related to a Bronze Age mound that forms the base of the later North Mound (Fig. 1*A–C*, 1*L*). This is by far the longest ship-setting known in Scandinavia, although only minor parts of it are preserved, mainly under the later South Mound. The smaller of the two Jelling rune stones, the original position of which is unknown, may once have formed the prow of this ship-setting. If this is indeed so, it would have been Gorm's memorial to his queen. The stone's inscription reads: "King Gorm made these monuments in memory of Thorvi (Thyre), Denmark's adornment." It is not known where Thyre is buried.

The second building phase encompassed the erection of the North Mound, which covered the northern tip of the ship-setting and the Bronze Age mound itself (Fig. 1*D–E*). This is Denmark's largest burial mound, c. 65 m in diameter. It contained a wooden burial chamber that was investigated in the nineteenth century. In it were found the remains of a few prestigious grave goods, including the silver cup whose ornament gave its name to the Jellinge style of Viking art, and some others with masculine attributes. No skeletal remains were found. Dendrochronology indicates that the burial chamber was closed in the year 958 or 959; it was probably the pagan burial place of King Gorm, constructed on the orders of his son and successor, Harald.

The changes in Jelling due to the conversion in c. 965 must have taken place according to a major overall plan. One of the new elements of this third building phase was Harald's great rune stone (Fig. 1*H*). Through its inscription and by reason of its position, it provides a clue to the whole monument; the stone was, and still is, the very center of the site. Another grand mound, the South Mound (Fig. 1*F–G*), was also erected but without a burial chamber. Dendrochronology indicates that the construction of this mound probably did not start before c. 970. It covered much of the old ship-setting, which thus lost its meaning. Perhaps the South Mound was a new memorial to King Harald's mother, Thyre (instead of the ship-setting), and a memorial to Harald himself. It is the largest mound from ancient times in Denmark.

Further, a large timber church (Fig. 1*K*) was built between the two mounds. The church was c. 30 m long and is known from postholes found by excavation under the present stone church (which is the fourth church on the site and dates from c. 1100). Toward the east end of the nave of the first church was a wooden burial chamber that was constructed at the same time as the church itself. This held the disarticulated bones of a man who had initially been buried elsewhere. This was probably the second grave, the Christian grave, of King Gorm, who had first been buried in the pagan North Mound and then translated to the new church after Harald's acceptance of Christianity.

In its Christian form, King Harald's Jelling comprised (Fig. 1*E–K*): the North Mound, now without a grave; the recently built South Mound which never had a grave; a royal burial church probably containing the reburied bones of King Gorm; King Gorm's rune stone for his queen, now situated at an unknown place; and King Harald's rune stone.

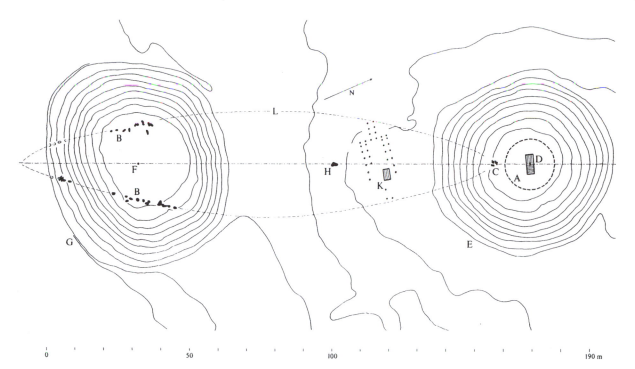

FIG. 1. Plan of the Jelling monuments (contours at 1-m interval): *A*, Bronze Age mound; *B–C*, large stone or stone sockets in the ground beneath the mounds; *D*, burial chamber of the North Mound; *E*, North Mound; *F*, central post in the South Mound; *G*, South Mound; *H*, King Harald's rune stone; *K*, postholes and burial chamber from the first church in Jelling; *L*, reconstruction of suggested ship-setting. (Drawing by Knud J. Krogh, after Krogh and Olsen 1993.)

This stone is a huge, largely semipyramidal granite boulder, c. 270 cm high, whose entire surface is covered with script, pictures, and ornament (Fig. 2). The three faces are bound together by their framing ornament, large knots, and continuous inscription. The first face carries the beginning and main part of the inscription. The second face displays a large prancing animal entwined with a snake. This is a splendid example of the Mammen style of Viking art and the first occurrence in Scandinavia of this combination of animal and snake. The exact meaning of the composition is lost, but from now on the motif became popular and was used in many media for more than a century. The third face depicts Christ fully dressed with outstretched arms and a crossed halo and entwined

FIG. 2. The three faces of King Harald's rune stone. Because of damage to the stone, no ornamental links can be seen between the stone's first and second faces. (Drawing by Thora Fisker, after Moltke 1985, but the sequence of pictures is rearranged.)

J

with foliated interlace. This picture is the earliest-known representation of Christ in Denmark and the earliest sculptural example in Scandinavia. Exact prototypes are not known. Underneath, the text ends with the words "and made the Danes Christian." The stone was probably once painted in vivid colors to enhance the script, ornament, and pictures, but no color survives here. The artist responsible for this well-planned and innovative rune and picture stone seems to have developed the idea of a traditional Danish rune stone, drawing his inspiration partly from the illuminated books so closely related to the new religion.

King Harald may have planned his own grave in Jelling—there is space for another body next to the grave found in the church. He was, however, killed c. 987 in a rebellion led by his son Sven Forkbeard and was probably buried in Roskilde in Sjælland. After Harald, Jelling lost its importance, which is why so much is preserved there today.

FURTHER READINGS

Fuglesang, S.H. Crucifixion Iconography in Viking Scandinavia. In *Proceedings of the Eighth Viking Congress.* Ed. H. Bekker-Nielson, Peter Foote, and Olaf Olsen. Odense: Odense University Press, 1981, pp. 73–94.

———. The Axehead from Mammen and the Mammen Style. In *Mammen: Grav, kunst og samfund i vikingetid.* Ed. M. Iversen. Højbjerg: Jysk Arkæologisk Selskab, 1991, pp. 83–107.

Jacobsen, L., and E. Moltke. *Danmarks Runeindskrifter.* Vols. 1–2. København: Munksgaard, 1941–1942. pp. 66 ff.

Kornerup, J. *Kongehøiene i Jellinge.* Kjøbenhavn: Det Kongelige Nordiske Oldskrift Selskab, 1875.

Krogh, K.J. The Royal Viking-Age Monuments at Jelling in the Light of Recent Archaeological Excavations. *Acta Archaeologica* (1982) 53:183–216.

———. *Gaden om Kong Gorms grav: Historien om Nordhojen i Jelling* (The Riddle of Gorm's Grave: The Story of the North Mound in Jelling). Royal Viking Monuments in Jelling 1. Herning: Poul Kristensen, 1993.

Krogh, K.J., and O. Olsen. From Paganism to Christianity. In *Digging into the Past: Twenty-Five Years of Archaeology in Denmark.* Ed. S. Hvass and B. Storgaard. København: Det Kongelige Nordiske Oldskrift Selskab and Jysk Arkæologisk Selskab, 1993, pp. 233–236.

Moltke, E. *Runes and Their Origin: Denmark and Elsewhere.* Trans. P. Foote. Copenhagen: National Museum of Denmark, 1985, pp. 202–223.

Nielsen, K.M., et al. Jelling Problems: A Discussion. *Mediaeval Scandinavia* (1974) 7:156–234.

Roesdahl, E. *Viking Age Denmark.* London: British Museum, 1982, pp. 171–179.

———. *The Vikings.* Second Edition. London: Penguin, 1998, pp. 161ff. and passim.

———. King Harald's Rune Stone in Jelling: Text, Script, and Images. In *Image, Text, and Script: Studies on the Transformation of Visual Literacy, c. 400 A.D.–c. 800 A.D.* Ed. X. Barral i Altet and M. Mostert. Leiden: Brill, in press.

Wilson, D.M., and O. Klindt-Jensen. *Viking Art.* 2nd ed. London: Allen and Unwin, 1980, pp. 95–123.

Else Roesdahl

SEE ALSO
Dendrochronology

Jewelry

Medieval European jewelry encompasses a full range of objects from humble clothes fastenings of the days before zippers and Velcro, to emblems of royalty and lavish ornaments distinguishing the elite. While jewelry has been relegated to the so-called minor or decorative arts, the archaeological significance of jewelry is certainly not minor—it communicates to us a wealth of information about the age, gender, marital status, ethnicity, rank, status, and beliefs of its bearers. Analysis of materials and techniques can also inform us about trade, economy, and workshop practices. Only a few jewelry-manufacturing techniques develop substantially during the Medieval period, but the sources of information about jewelry—archaeological, written, and pictorial—change significantly from the early to the later part of the era. The most distinct differences are between the pagan protohistorical cultures of northern Europe until c. A.D. 1000 and the Christian cultures focused on the Mediterranean regions with strong antique influences. As Christianity spreads northward, this distinction becomes blurred.

Types of Jewelry

Jewelry was worn by men, women, and children, although women usually wore more varieties of artifact types. Men's adornments included practical brooches and buckles, as well as signets and garters. Clerics, too, wore jewelry, especially rings and insignia of their office. Children's jewelry was often downsized to suitable proportions for them to wear and reflected beliefs in the prophylactic virtues of certain materials, such as coral placed around the neck to defend infants from harm.

Different styles of dress and conventions for expressing status required various jewelry types, but there are some prevalent forms across medieval Europe. In the earlier Middle Ages, men as well as women sometimes wore earrings. Women used hairpins of metal or bone to fasten cloth headpieces, and their clothing was secured at the shoulders by pairs of decorative brooches. Necklaces were worn around the neck, sewn to the dress, or fastened to shoulder brooches. Among amulet types were bracteates, thin gold disks impressed with zoomorphic designs, hanging from suspension loops. Pins or brooches were the most ubiquitous clothing fasteners for both men and women of all ranks and classes. The stylistic development and geographic variations of brooch types have led to their exhaustive analysis and typological classification by archaeologists and art historians. For example, Anglo-Saxon brooch types have been classified into at least the following types: saucer, annular (ring), penannular (broken ring), quoit, disc, bow, long or cruciform, square-headed, equal-armed, trefoil, bird, and animal. Several of the types are variations of the *fibula* (clasp), known from the Roman type, with its name reflecting its resemblance to the human leg bone. The square-headed brooch is an elaborated fibula consisting of an arched bow between a head plate covering the attachment of a coiled spring on the reverse and a foot concealing the catch plate for the spring. Both head and foot provided fields for profuse decoration. Armlets and bracelets might be glass bangles, and wrist clasps were a specifically Anglo-Saxon variety of cuff fastening. Finger rings were made of various materials. Costumes also required miscellaneous buckles, clasps, and strap mounts. Girdles were worn by men and women to hold everyday objects, including toilet articles and keys.

Christianity did not bring any particular modification in jewelry-making techniques, although some changes in forms were prompted by new costume styles. Earrings were hardly worn in the later Middle Ages, but other types of head adornment became prominent, including the chaplet, garland, circlet, frontlet, and coronet. The ring brooch, a simple type that depends on the pull of cloth against the ring to hold its pin in place, remained popular, but pendants and necklaces began to overtake its prominence with a change in fashion to low-cut bodices. New types include phylacteries, wearable reliquaries containing the remains of saints. Chains became a Venetian specialty in the twelfth century. Girdles remained in use, but paternoster and rosary beads for counting prayers were hung from them in the later Middle Ages. Goldsmiths also answered the demand for jewel-adorned vestments and other sumptuous articles for use in the service of the church. As gems became more obtainable with the expansion of trade with India beginning in the thirteenth century, the emphasis shifted from the glitter of gold filigree and granulation toward glowing precious stones. The display of wealth through jewels increased until laws were instituted in the fourteenth century to regulate the types of jewelry that were allowed to be worn by persons of different status.

Sources of Metals and Other Raw Materials

Although gold, silver, and some semiprecious stones occur in Europe, many materials used in jewelry production imply long-distance trade. Gold occurs naturally in usable metallic form as veins in quartz or in its weathered sediments as alluvial (or placer) gold, recovered from river sands by panning. Although gold is fairly abundant in eastern Europe, Austria, Spain, and Ireland, very little was removed from these regions during the early Middle Ages. Most gold used at this time originated from ancient Roman stocks recycled from coins, ingots, and outdated or damaged jewelry.

Gold was not always the most precious of metals. Silver was the prestige material of choice in western Europe from c. A.D. 700 until c. 1200, when new sources of gold were exploited in the Rhine Valley. During this period, gold supplies accumulated in the Byzantine east, retaining its high status there, and the silver trade was controlled by Arab merchants. Silver, which must be smelted from mineral ores, had been produced since ancient times in many regions of Europe but also was melted and reused. The base metals of copper, bronze, and iron were used for lower-status utilitarian jewelry, such as pins and belt buckles. Tin for bronze working was obtained primarily from Cornwall and Spain, but copper was more abundant. Iron from bog ore and other sources was found throughout Europe.

Other materials besides metal employed in jewelry include ivory, bone, glass, and stones and stonelike objects. Readily obtained walrus ivory and bone could be worked into simple pins and rings. Glass, made from silica, lime, and soda, was formed into beads and pendants but also was inserted into metal jewelry by methods of inlay and enamel. Much early medieval glass was Roman in origin, but later it was produced elsewhere, including the Rhineland. Stones could be drilled with a bow drill to

J

make independent beads or inlaid into more complex jewelry. European semiprecious stones and similar materials include amber, fossilized pine resin, from Baltic shores; quartz from the Alps; rock crystal from Germany, Switzerland, and France; and jet, fossilized remains of trees from Spain and Whitby in England. India was the ultimate source of garnets used in early medieval western Europe as a result of earlier Roman luxury trade. Amethysts from the eastern Mediterranean were also recycled from Roman stocks. Classical cameos (stones with differently colored layers cut away to form designs) and intaglios (stones into which designs were engraved) were reset in medieval rings and inlays. Coral from the Mediterranean, agates from India, pearls from the Persian Gulf, and lapis lazuli from Afghanistan also were prized. Rubies and sapphires from India, Ceylon, Arabia, and Persia were exploited only during the later Middle Ages, and cut diamonds were introduced from India in the fourteenth century.

Sources of Information about the Jewelry-Making Craft

Information about techniques for producing medieval jewelry comes from historical and archaeological sources and from examination of the artifacts. The most important historical source is *De diversis artibus* (Of Diverse Arts), a manual written by Theophilus, a monk in Westphalia, Germany, c. 1120–1130. An Englishman in Paris, Alexander of Neckham (1157–1217), also wrote a description of a contemporary goldsmith's workshop. For the later Medieval period, there are occasional written contracts specifying manufacturing methods for specific commissioned objects.

Archaeologically, certain debris and tools imply the presence of jewelers' workshops: touchstones for testing gold purity, waste from separating precious metals from ores, glass rods for enameling, crucibles with residue from melting metals, broken mold fragments, and tools, including hammers and tongs. Though a source of heat for melting metal and glass is necessary, charcoal fires for jewelry making are difficult to distinguish from ordinary domestic hearths. The Anglo-Saxon royal treasury site at Winchester and Viking sites such as Birka, Hedeby (Haithabu), and Ribe are notable for workshop remains of the eighth–tenth centuries. In a few cases, analysis of styles, techniques, and tool marks has permitted tentative identification of the output of a single craft worker or workshop.

Common historical sources of the later Middle Ages concerning jewelry—wills, inventories, and payment accounts—inform us about the owners of objects rather than about their makers. Late Roman, as well as later medieval, sources disclose that customers were responsible for supplying the metal, as coins or disused jewelry, and expensive materials such as gemstones for commissioned pieces. Goldsmiths also produced a stock of common items, including rings and brooches that could later be engraved with wearers' names.

Since jewelry making did not require an extensive workshop, many goldsmiths worked alone or with a single assistant. Workshops in later urban centers such as London and Paris employed several goldsmiths and apprentices. Royal palaces and monasteries often had their own workshops. Nearly all documented goldsmiths were men, but widows occasionally took over their husbands' businesses. Burnishing, a small part of the jewelry-making process, was performed by women.

Pictorial sources informative of jewelers' workshops include numerous late medieval illustrations of goldsmiths and their patron saints. St. Eligius, bishop of Noyon and Tournai (641–660), was known for his engraving and silversmithing, and St. Dunstan, a Benedictine monk who became archbishop of Canterbury (960–988), was also reputed to be a metalworker. Paintings, woodcuts, engravings, manuscript illuminations, and sculptures depict these popular patrons of jewelers' guilds working with hammer and anvil.

Fabrication

Most gold jewelry was produced from an ingot hammered into a malleable flat sheet, which was further hammered or shaped into the basic forms of the object. The components were then joined and decorated with granulation, filigree, inset stones, or enamel. Decorative patterns were made directly onto sheet metal by means of several methods. *Repoussé* is the general term for designs hammered and punched from the back; work from the front side is called *chasing*. Simple designs were impressed onto sheet gold by pushing it down onto a die with wooden tools. The sheet, placed over a resilient bed of resin, lead, wood, wax, or leather, was further embellished by driving punches or stamps into it from the back, as on Scandinavian migration period (A.D. 450–600) gold bracteates. Inscriptions or decorative patterns could be chased using a chisel-like tool to displace the metal or engraved with a sharp implement to gouge out metal strips.

Casting, which was more common for silver and bronze than for gold, requires the use of a mold into which molten metal is poured. The ancient casting process was called *cire perdue,* or "lost-wax," a technique in which a wax model is melted (and thus "lost") when metal melted in a crucible is poured in to replace the wax. In this process, the mold must be broken to release the final casting, so each cast is unique. During the Medieval period, the two-piece mold largely replaced the lost-wax process; however, even with two-piece casting, molds were seldom reused, as we know from fragments of broken molds for Viking period (ca. 800–1050) oval brooches at Birka in Sweden. Instead, a fresh mold impression was made from a template. After casting, pieces were filed and rubbed with burnishing stones, and examples from the same pattern are no longer identical.

Most metal jewelry was assembled from numerous components by mechanical methods of folding, riveting, and attaching pieces with wires or solder. Chains were assembled by a loop-in-loop method, with each oval loop soldered and threaded through the previous one. Soldering bonds two pieces of metal together by placing between them an alloy of slightly lower melting temperature than the metals to be joined. When heat is applied, the joining solder in the form of small clippings or powder melts, flows, and, when cool and solidified, joins the parts.

Applied Decoration

Filigree consists of ornamental small wires soldered to a gold background. Single or twisted, plain or beaded wires were formed into circles, spirals, and rosettes. Wire was made by twisting, hammering, and rolling metal strips or rods until approximately circular in section. Decorative "beaded" wire resembling a line of small beads was manufactured by rolling a circular-section wire across a multiple-edged die. Drawn wire, generated by pulling metal through draw plates with round-sectioned holes, was introduced in the seventh century but came into general use in the ninth century.

Granulation refers to the application of tiny spherical granules of gold, or less commonly silver, that were soldered to the surface of jewelry. The grains were not difficult to manufacture—small pieces of gold heated on charcoal roll up into spheres less than a millimeter in diameter due to surface tension—but they were difficult to place accurately and solder successfully to a background. They were usually massed into patterns to cover a section of an object. Filigree and granulation often were used together, as on the magnificent migration period golden collars from Västergötland and Öland, Sweden. The tedious soldering of these small components continued in Scandinavia and eastern Europe after nearly dying out in much of Europe c. A.D. 1000.

To make jewelry appear more valuable, its surface could be plated or gilt, such as the silver brooches from the Szilágy-Sómlyó hoard from northern Romania. Gold plating results from gold foil pressed or hammered over a core of another material, such as silver or bronze or even wood or ivory. Gilding is gold leaf attached to a metal surface with an adhesive. Surfaces could also be tinned for a shiny appearance by dipping in molten tin.

Much medieval jewelry is characterized by its colorful appearance, thus earning the name *polychrome.* Colors were created with enamel, essentially colored glass fused to a metallic base, usually gold. Two basic varieties of enamel are *cloisonné,* bounded by individual cells *(cloisons)* created by soldering vertical strips of metal onto the surface, and *champlevé,* placed in recesses carved from the background. The c. 700 Irish Celtic Tara brooch is an example of cloisonné, and twelfth-century ecclesiastical pieces from Limoges represent the acme of *champlevé.* In both types, broken or powdered glass is inserted and then the work is heated. When the glass reaches its melting-point, it fuses and penetrates the metal surface.

Inlay was also used to achieve polychrome effects. Jewelry was inlaid with colored stones, glass, amber, and other substances that were cut to shape and cemented with resin and filler into cells formed by metal strips soldered to a background. Glowing red garnets inlaid over a brilliant gold-foil background were typical of early Anglo-Saxon jewelry, such as the artifacts from Sutton Hoo decorated with more than four thousand garnets. Also from Sutton Hoo is inlaid *millefiori* glass, composed of glass rods of various colors and diameters fused together to form intricate patterns and then sliced across into small sections. Semiprecious gems used in the early medieval period could be polished with sand or ground between two flat stones. *Faceting* of hard gemstones, including emeralds and sapphires, developed in the fourteenth century with the use of abrasives such as emery (aluminum oxide).

Archaeological and Other Sources of Information about Jewelry

The jewelry available for study must be only a small and nonrepresentative sample of that which was worn in the

J

past. Whether worn as personal adornment, emblem of rank, symbol of wealth, or for practical necessity, many objects must have been accidentally lost or purposely melted down. The survival of medieval jewelry depended upon several factors: burial customs, accidents of survival and discovery, the degree of sentimental attachment, and the amount of jewelry in use in any given period.

Gold is not affected by corrosion, so gold jewelry survives when buried in the ground even though it may be dented or smashed. In the early Middle Ages and in the pre-Christian cultures of northern Europe, the custom of burying the dead with possessions accounts for much extant jewelry, although pieces without documented provenance fill the collections of most museums. Jewelry is also found in hoards consisting of objects deliberately buried and hidden, presumably with the intention to recover the deposit later. Many metal objects have been found as stray finds, perhaps scattered from looted burials or hoards or, more likely, due to accidental loss. In the past, these finds were often noticed by farmers working close to the ground without mechanized equipment; in recent decades, such finds have been surpassed by those made with metal detectors.

Many examples of early medieval jewelry are stray finds recovered from contexts that cannot be firmly dated by archaeological means. Such objects are identified based primarily upon comparison of provenanced and unprovenanced finds and dated through association with more closely dated find combinations, especially coins. There is no scientific method to date metals comparable to radiocarbon dating for organic materials or thermoluminescence for ceramics, so dating by art-historical stylistic methodologies is still the norm, with emphasis upon typological classification of ornamental styles.

For the later Medieval period, we have more numerous historical and pictorial sources about jewelry, jewelers, and their patrons, but we have less archaeological information. In the largely Christian society, the deceased were not buried with as much personal equipment as in the pagan period. Jewelry of the later period rarely comes from excavated cemeteries but survived due to historical significance, family sentiment, or pure chance. Through historical sources such as inventories, wills, chronicles, and literature, we know that jewelry was given as tribute to bolster political alliances and as gifts for births, birthdays, and weddings and was passed down as heirlooms. While we assume for the earlier Middle Ages that jewelry was worn to indicate status or wealth, to display religious

affiliation, or to bring amuletic protection, we have documentary evidence of these explanations for the later period. From as early as the thirteenth century, sumptuary laws regulating the types of jewelry worn inform us about the extravagance of the rich. These laws were enacted in Italy to control the conversion of too much money into lavish adornments and to maintain elite status by limiting access to gold; during the fourteenth century, such edicts spread through Europe. Portraits of the later Middle Ages illustrate subjects wearing luxuries regulated by these statutes. Far from an art of minor importance, fine metalworking placed jewelers at the forefront of medieval artisans, and jewelry of the entire Middle Ages is significant archaeologically, revealing much about socioeconomic patterns, social organization, and the status of its wearers.

FURTHER READINGS

Arrhenius, Birgit. *Merovingian Garnet Jewellery: Emergence and Social Implications.* Stockholm: Almqvist and Wiksell, 1985.

Axboe, Morten. On the Manufacture of the Gold Bracteates. *Frühmittelalterliche Studien* (1982) 16:302–307.

Backes, Magnus, and Regine Dölling. *Art of the Dark Ages.* New York: Abrams, 1969.

Bayley, Justine. Anglo-Saxon Non-Ferrous Metalworking: A Survey. *World Archaeology* (1991) 23(1):115–130.

———. Goldworking in Britain: From Iron Age to Medieval Times. *Interdisciplinary Science Reviews* (1992) 17(4):314–321.

Benda, Klement. *Ornament and Jewellery: Archaeological Finds from Eastern Europe.* Prague: Artia, 1967.

Boehm, Barbara, and Elisabeth Taburet-Delahaye. *Enamels of Limoges, 1100–1350.* New York: Metropolitan Museum of Art, 1996.

Campbell, Marion. Gold, Silver, and Precious Stones. In *English Medieval Industries: Craftsmen, Techniques, Products.* Ed. John Blair and Nigel Ramsay. London: Hambledon, 1991, pp. 107–166.

———. *An Introduction to Medieval Enamels.* London: Victoria and Albert Museum, 1983.

Cherry, John. *Goldsmiths.* Medieval Craftsmen Series. Toronto and Buffalo: University of Toronto Press, 1992.

Egan, Geoff, and Frances Pritchard. *Dress Accessories, c. 1150–1450.* Medieval Finds from Excavations in London 3. London: Museum of London, 1991.

Evans, Joan. *A History of Jewellery, 1100–1870.* 2nd ed. Boston: Boston Book and Art, 1970.

Hines, John. *Clasps, Hektespenner, Agraffen: Anglo-Scandinavian Clasps of Classes A-C of the Third to Sixth Centuries A.D.: Typology, Diffusion, and Function.* Vitterhets Historie och Antikvitets Akademien. Stockholm: Kungl, 1993.

Hougen, Bjørn. *The Migration Style of Ornament in Norway.* 2nd ed. Oslo: Universitetets Oldsaksamlingen, 1967.

Janes, Dominic. The Golden Clasp of the Late Roman State. *Early Medieval Europe* (1996) 5(2):127–153.

Jessup, Ronald. *Anglo-Saxon Jewellery.* Aylesbury, Buckinghamshire, UK: Shire Publications, 1974.

Kornbluth, Genevra. *Engraved Gems of the Carolingian Empire.* University Park: Penn State University Press, 1995.

László, Gyula. *The Art of the Migration Period.* Coral Gables: University of Miami Press, 1974.

Lightbown, Ronald W. *Mediaeval European Jewellery, with a Catalogue of the Collection in the Victoria and Albert Museum.* London: Victoria and Albert Museum, 1992.

Mackeprang, Mogens. *De Nordiske Guldbrakteater* (with English summary). Jysk Arkæologisk Selskab Skrifter 2. Århus: Universitetsforlaget, 1952.

Newman, Harold. *An Illustrated Dictionary of Jewelry.* London: Thames and Hudson, 1981.

Ogden, Jack. The Technology of Medieval Jewelry. In *Ancient and Historic Metals: Conservation and Scientific Research.* Ed. David A. David, Jerry Poday, and Brian B. Considine. Marina del Rey: Getty Conservation Institute, 1994, pp. 153–182.

Oldeberg, Andreas. *Metallteknik under Vikingatid och Medeltid* (with English summary). Stockholm: Seelig, 1966.

Ross, Marvin C. *Catalogue of the Byzantine and Early Mediaeval Antiquities in the Dumbarton Oaks Collection.* Vol. 2: *Jewelry, Enamels, and Art of the Migration Period.* Washington, D.C.: Dumbarton Oaks Center for Byzantine Studies, Trustees for Harvard University, 1965.

Schadt, Hermann. *Goldsmiths' Art: Five Thousand Years of Jewelry and Hollowware.* Stuttgart and New York: Arnoldsche, 1996.

Speake, George. *Anglo-Saxon Animal Art and Its Germanic Background.* Oxford: Clarendon, 1980.

Steingräber, Erich. *Antique Jewellery: Its History in Europe from 800 to 1900.* New York: Praeger, 1957.

Tait, Hugh, ed. *Jewelry, Seven Thousand Years: An International History and Illustrated Survey from the Collections of the British Museum.* 2nd ed. New York: Abrams, 1987.

Theophilus. *Theophilus: On Diverse Arts: The Foremost Medieval Treatise on Painting, Glassmaking, and Metalwork.* Ed. and trans. John G. Hawthorne and Cyril Stanley Smith. New York: Dover, 1979.

Walters Art Gallery. *Jewelry, Ancient to Modern.* New York: Viking, 1980.

Webster, Leslie. *Aspects of Production and Style in Dark Age Metalwork.* Occasional Paper 34. London: British Museum, 1982.

Whitfield, Niamh. Round Wire in the Early Middle Ages. *Jewellery Studies* (1990) 4:13–28.

———. Some New Research on Gold and Gold Filigree from Early Medieval Ireland and Scotland. In *Outils et ateliers d'orfèvres des temps ancients.* Ed. Christiane Eluère. Saint-Germain-en-Laye: Société des Antiquitiés Nationales et au Château de Saint-Germain-en-Laye, 1993, pp. 125–135.

Youngs, Susan, ed. *"The Work of Angels": Masterpieces of Celtic Metalwork, Sixth–Ninth Centuries A.D.* Austin: University of Texas Press, 1990.

Nancy L. Wicker

SEE ALSO

K

Kootwijk

Kootwijk is a village in the heart of the Veluwe region (part of the Dutch province of Gelderlands), north of the Lower Rhine River in the Netherlands. In the drift-sand area south of the village (which happens to be the largest "desert" of the Netherlands), large-scale excavations, which provided a clear picture of the settlement history of the area from before the desert formation, were carried out in the 1970s by the University of Amsterdam. Evidence of occupation from the Mesolithic onward was found, but the investigation was especially focused on the settlements from the Roman period (second–third centuries) and the early Middle Ages (sixth–eleventh centuries). The latter are dealt with here.

The Veluwe is one of the few regions of the Netherlands where settlement continuity from early prehistoric times is evident, despite some demographic dips and cultural and ethnic changes (for instance, between the third and the sixth centuries A.D.) (Fig. 1). The area consists of high, sandy ground—mainly glacial formations and windblown deposits—surrounded by damp lowland, which, for the most part, was not cultivated until the late Middle Ages. Conditions on this high ground were apparently good enough for a self-sufficient economy, despite the low fertility of the soil and its susceptibility to erosion. The economic significance of the Veluwe in the early Middle Ages, as was shown archaeologically, was not, however, due to agriculture but to large-scale iron production that took place in the woodland hills east of Kootwijk. Although probably involved in this industry and trade (and benefiting from it, as the amount of imported pottery shows), Kootwijk at that time (seventh–tenth centuries) was primarily an agrarian settlement, as most settlements of the Veluwe were.

As was shown in detail in Kootwijk, the location of prehistoric and protohistoric settlements was strongly influenced by the presence of a certain combination of soil types, the infrastructure (main roads), territorial behavior (an ideal distance to neighboring settlements), and—although less obvious in the archaeological record—by the history and mental aspects of the cultural landscape.

FIG. 1. The location of Kootwijk and the Veluwe.

K

Within a confined area, the settlements moved around in their territories, dispersed, or contracted, depending on the social and economic conditions of the time. In the tenth and following centuries, major changes took place; population growth, expansion to other soil types due to improved manuring methods, deforestation, and severe loss of usable land by wind erosion altered the cultural landscape on the high ground considerably. In this period, the wet border zone of the Veluwe was colonized, which produced a new generation of settlements (for example, Kootwijkerbroek as a subsidiary of Kootwijk). Apart from demographic and economic factors, climatic conditions also played a role in these changes as far as the tenth century is concerned. Analyses of a former pool and a number of wells at the Kootwijk settlement showed that the average precipitation in part of the tenth and early eleventh centuries was lower than has ever been recorded since. This was the very period of the birth of the desert of Kootwijk.

The archaeological evidence of medieval Kootwijk is derived from four geographically separate nuclei in the area (Fig. 2): a small hamlet (*A*) and a single farm (*B*) from the Merovingian period; a large nucleated settlement from the eighth–tenth centuries (*C*); a small, completely eroded settlement from the eleventh–twelfth centuries; and some stray finds from the twelfth century onward in the present village. No cemeteries were found. It is likely that these elements, as well as smaller settlements, still await discovery or were destroyed by wind erosion, as were parts of the settlements mentioned. Representative parts of settlements *A*, *B*, and *C* were excavated. The most complete picture of both the archaeological and ecological evidence was derived from the large Carolingian village *C*.

Settlement History

The early medieval settlements (and the predecessors from the Iron Age and Roman period as well) were located at the southern edge of an area of relatively fertile soils that were used as arable land. It is not yet clear if a new foundation was made in the late sixth or early seventh century (data from the fourth–fifth centuries are missing). Nevertheless, hamlet *A* came into existence then. It was composed of a small number of fenced-in farmsteads (two of them were excavated) consisting of a main building (average length 15 m), a few sunken huts, and some other outbuildings. During the seventh century, the single farmstead *B* was founded. The finely built, large, slightly boat-shaped house (length 25.5 m) suggests that we are dealing here with local elite.

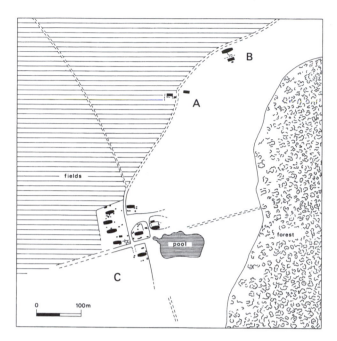

FIG. 2. Early medieval Kootwijk (not all settlements are contemporary): *A* and *B* coexisted in the second half of the seventh century; *C* came into being in the first half of the eighth century.

In the early eighth century, both settlements disappeared; at the same time, or not much later, the nucleated settlement *C* was founded near a small pool. During the eighth century, the settlement grew from eight farms to about twenty. The structure of the enclosed farmsteads, as well as the building traditions, prove cultural continuity. As in the previous period, all the main buildings (boat-shaped houses with an average length of c. 20 m) were oriented in a more or less east-west direction. The axis of the village was formed by a road that remained in use after the desertion of the adjacent farms. In general, the structure of the village suggests that it was planned. Although historical evidence about this village is lacking, it might be suggested that the reallocation of the Kootwijk area was caused by the reorganization of landed property after the integration of this realm into the Frankish Empire. The presumed new large landowner of Kootwijk should be sought outside this peripheral region, for any clear evidence of social differentiation, as in the previous period, is missing from this settlement.

During its existence, the village gradually moved in a southerly and easterly direction. Obviously, farmyards adjacent to fields were often turned into arable land after desertion, while new farmsteads were created only at the other side of the village (the wasteland side). In this silent way, the structure of the village altered considerably. The picture of the later phases is rather incomplete because the eastern part was severely affected by wind erosion. This process of internal reallocation indicates a certain degree of community organization. In this sense, we can speak of a "village."

C. A.D. 1000, the settlement was deserted. However, the fields, which were already affected by sand drifts, continued to be used for a while by people from neighboring dispersed farms (only a distant settlement was detected). In the end, the blowing sand drove all settlement to the area of the present village.

The Carolingian Village

The excavated inventory of settlement *C* consists of fifty-four boat-shaped farmhouses (combining a dwelling area with a byre) (Fig. 3), c. 30 barns, c. 10 granaries, 190 sunken huts, 55 wells, and other less identifiable constructions. The sunken huts—shallow pits covered by a roof supported by two posts—were small and probably functioned as storage cellars. Apart from the wells, which were built in the pool area, there were no specific concentrations of certain elements. Smithing activities, however, could be identified at only two farmsteads (Fig. 4).

To the north and west of the settlement stretched the fields, which were partly excavated. The data from the tenth century provided the clearest picture of the allotment system and the method of plowing. Very small plots (0.02–0.1 ha) were found next to the village. These probably served as intensively exploited gardens (for growing, e.g., horsebeans), which were manured periodically by fenced-in cattle. The allotment system of the adjacent field area was less clear (some plots of 0.2 ha were found

next to the garden area). This appears to be some sort of infield-outfield system (the infields were part of a three-field system, and the outfields lay fallow for long periods and were then used as pasture). Mainly rye, oats, barley, and flax were grown.

The domestic livestock consisted of cattle, pigs, sheep (and goats), and horses. The possibilities for grazing in the vicinity were limited, especially for cattle and horses. It is therefore suggested that the wetlands at the western border of the Veluwe were used for grazing on a transhumant basis. The evidence for the agricultural system in the earlier centuries is less clear. In the Merovingian period, the emphasis probably lay on pig and cattle breeding in the forest for meat production.

The Kootwijk settlements were not rich in precious-metal objects, coins, and glass. However, a great deal of the pottery was imported from areas like the German Rhineland and the Eifel region, which is quite unusual in the sandy districts north of the Rhine. There must have been very close connections with trading centers in the river area, enhanced by the export of iron from the Veluwe.

Culturally, the Kootwijk settlements belonged to a large group that stretched from the Netherlands north of the Rhine to Denmark. There are, however, differences that should be explained in social terms. The magnate farms of Warendorf in Germany and Vorbasse in Denmark show evidence for social differentiation that is not seen in settlements of the Kootwijk type. The single-aisled longhouse with outer posts is a regional variant of a type that was found, for example, in the central Netherlands (Dorestad), Drenthe (Odoorn, Gasselte), Westphalia (Warendorf), and Niedersachen (Dalem). In Kootwijk, the boat shape (in some cases constructed with the aid of

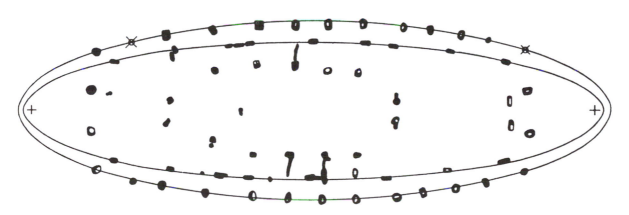

Fig. 3. A Kootwijk house, second half of the eighth century: the ellipse as the basis for the layout of the ground plan.

K

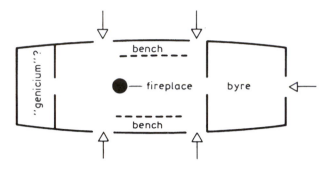

FIG. 4. The internal organization of an early medieval Kootwijk house.

pure ellipses, see Fig. 3 and Fig. 4) had already developed by the late seventh century. This fashion, which certainly had some symbolic meaning, soon conquered large parts of northwestern Europe.

FURTHER READINGS

Heidinga, H.A. *Medieval Settlement and Economy North of the Lower Rhine: Archeology and History of Kootwijk and the Veluwe (The Netherlands).* Assen/Maastricht/ Wolfboro: Van Gorcum, 1987.

————. From Kootwijk to Rhenen: In Search of the Elite in the Central Netherlands in the Early Middle Ages. In *Medieval Archaeology in the Netherlands: Studies Presented to H.H. van Regteren Altena.* Ed. J.C. Besteman, J.M. Bos, and H.A. Heidinga. Assen/Maastricht: Van Gorcum, 1990, pp. 9–40.

Groenman-vanWaateringe, W., and L.H. van Wijngaarden-Bakker, eds. *Farm Life in a Carolingian Village: A Model Based on Botanical and Zoological Data from an Excavated Site.* Studies in Pre- en Protohistorie 1. Assen/ Maastricht/Wolfboro: Van Gorcum, 1987.

H.A. Heidinga

SEE ALSO
Netherlands

L

Langobards

See Lombards.

Leighton, Royal Manor of

See Grove Priory.

Llangorse Crannóg

Llangorse Lake, the largest natural lake in south Wales, covers an area of c. 150 ha but is generally only a few meters deep. In the middle of the nineteenth century, the lake level was lowered as the result of drainage operations on the River Llynfi, the main lake outlet. Shortly afterward two local antiquarians, Edgar and Henry Dumbleton, visited the lake and noted traces of timbers projecting out of the water around a small stony island. The Dumbleton brothers were aware of the investigations of artificial islands, or crannógs, in Ireland and Scotland as well as the publication of the "Swiss Lake Villages" (waterlogged Neolithic and Early Bronze Age villages that were revealed after a drought in the 1850s) and recognized the site as being a crannóg. Trenching and recording of timbers were undertaken, and the Dumbletons showed the site to be an artificial mound on top of brushwood, reeds, lenses of sand, and peat. The crannóg was edged by more than one arc of vertical oak piles, while additional round wood piles stood beyond the island edge. Substantial quantities of animal bone and a few undated fragments of pottery, bronze, leather, and stone were found (Dumbleton 1870).

After the late nineteenth century, crannóg exploration in Britain and Ireland declined, and Llangorse, as the only known example in Wales, faded from archaeological sig-

nificance. In 1925, a logboat (dugout canoe) was found 400 m east of the site, and the Romano-British typological date given to the boat was tentatively applied to the site. In the 1970s, a radiocarbon date of A.D. 814 ± 60 was taken for the boat, and, although the 1920s' conservation technique was regarded as a possible source of contamination, this date was locally attributed to the crannóg (McGrail 1978:233–236).

In 1987, a new survey was begun on the site by staff and students of the University of Wales, Cardiff, stimulated by increasing crannóg exploration in Ireland and Scotland. Although the site was undated and doubt had been cast on the identification of the site as a crannóg, it was clear from surface traces of split-oak planks, brushwood, and the nature of the stony mound that Llangorse was, indeed, a genuine crannóg.

The initial survey confirmed the basic accuracy of the Dumbletons' plans, and two dendrochronological dates indicated construction after the mid-ninth century A.D. These quite late dates suggested that the site could be identified with a documented place destroyed by a Mercian (English) army in A.D. 916, and it seemed likely that the crannóg was a royal residence of the local Welsh Kingdom of Brycheiniog (Campbell and Lane 1989).

Five seasons of survey and limited excavation have now been undertaken on the site by a joint team from the University of Wales, Cardiff, and the National Museum of Wales (Redknap and Lane 1994). This has shown that the site is an artificial island, c. 40 × 30 m, built on an underlying peat shallow or small island. The crannóg may have been extended over a period of a few years from an initial D-shaped platform, as the oak palisade revetment to the site has a number of arcing extensions. A wattle fence,

L

supported externally by vertical round wood stakes, may represent a preliminary construction phase shortly before the oak planks were driven into the lake silts. Within the wattle fence, layers of regularly laid brushwood provide a "raft," or platform, that had been stabilized on the top with horizontal oak beams pinned down by pegs. A carefully laid layer of sandstone rubble overlaid this and presumably provided a stable platform for buildings. Outside the oak palisade, a number of roughly concentric lines of round wood were traced, indicating either external walkways or other structures external to the main crannóg. Underwater searching to the north produced evidence of a pile-supported causeway or bridge running toward the nearby northern shore of the lake (Redknap 1991:17–25).

No structures or stratified deposits remain on top of the crannóg mound, probably as a result of fluctuating lake levels and erosion. However, complex stratified silt and charcoal deposits lie to the north in the lee of the crannóg, and systematic underwater searches to the south and west of its eroding edge recovered quantities of artifacts. These include bone combs, shale and glass rings, copper-alloy mounts and pins, crucible fragments, textiles, leather, and a few wooden objects. The most important items are a fragmentary eighth–ninth-century pseudopenannular brooch of Irish type, a fragment of an insular enamel-decorated reliquary house shrine of similar date, and a spectacular carbonized fragment of an elaborate embroidered textile decorated with stylized animals and birds.

Dendrochronological samples have given sapwood dates in the summers of A.D. 889, 890, and 893, but the precise chronology of the site and whether its construction was extended over several seasons is still to be confirmed. Although no structures were excavated on the surface of the mound, the recovery of artifacts, carbonized grain, and animal bones makes it clear that this was a settlement site and probably a residence of high status.

The historical sources support this hypothesis. In A.D. 916, according to the *Anglo-Saxon Chronicle,* Aethelflaed, daughter of King Alfred of Wessex (849–899) and effectively queen of Mercia, sent an army into Wales and destroyed Brecenanmere and captured the king's wife and thirty-three other persons. Brecenanmere was the English name for the lake. It seems likely that this attack was on the crannóg, which appears to have been occupied for a fairly short time and has signs of destruction by fire. Medieval charters from Llandaff Cathedral near Cardiff confirm a royal presence in the area. Llangorse was said to have been given to the church with a substantial estate in

the eighth century by the kings of Brycheiniog, and it may have been a royal burial ground. The monastery of Llangorse was also the site of a meeting between the king and the bishop in A.D. 925 (Campbell and Lane 1989).

Consequently, it seems likely that the crannóg was a royal residence of the local kings, built c. A.D. 889–893 and destroyed by the Mercians in A.D. 916. However, Llangorse is the only known crannóg in Wales, and there are no others in the British Isles known outside Scotland and Ireland. The best parallels for Llangorse are from Ireland, where crannógs are common in the later first millennium A.D. It seems likely that Llangorse represents Irish influence and perhaps the activities of Irish craftsmen. The origin legend of the local Welsh kingdom, Brycheiniog, claims descent from Brychan, son of an Irish father and a Welsh mother. This is normally assumed to refer to events in the fifth–sixth centuries A.D., when Irish ogham inscriptions indicate an Irish presence in this part of Wales, but it may represent much later contacts between Ireland and Wales in the Viking period (c. 800–1050). If the crannóg was destroyed in A.D. 916, this type of residence may have been perceived as unsuccessful, with the result that no other crannógs were built in Wales, although modern survey may yet produce other examples.

There are no further references to the Llangorse site until the late twelfth century, when the Cambro-Norman writer Gerald of Wales referred to local stories that the lake contained sunken buildings and landscapes. A sixteenth-century manuscript refers to pieces of timber and frames of houses visible in the lake. By the nineteenth century, these local observations and folktales had become an account of a royal palace drowned due to the wickedness of the inhabitants. Although this is an international folk *topos,* it seems likely that observation of the crannóg and perhaps knowledge of its royal status underlie the developing story.

Only small-scale excavation has taken place at Llangorse. It has suffered from erosion and tourist damage, and current plans focus on methods of preserving the site. However, even the limited work undertaken so far has shed dramatic light on a very poorly understood period of Dark Age Wales, and we have a very unusual phenomenon—a unique archaeological site that is also identified in the historical record.

FURTHER READINGS

Campbell, E., and A. Lane. Llangorse: A Tenth-Century Royal Crannóg in Wales. *Antiquity* (1989) 63:675–681.

Dumbleton, E.N. On a Cranoge, or Stockaded Island, in Llangorse Lake, near Brecon. *Archaeologia Cambrensis,* 4th ser., (1870) 1:192–198.

McGrail, S. *Logboats of England and Wales.* BAR 51. Oxford: British Archaeological Reports, 1978.

Redknap, M. *The Christian Celts: Treasures of Late Celtic Wales.* Cardiff: National Museum of Wales, 1991.

Redknap, M., and A. Lane. The Early Medieval Crannóg at Llangorse, Powys: An Interim Statement on the 1989–93 Seasons. *International Journal of Nautical Archaeology,* (1994) 23(3):189–205.

Alan Lane and Mark Redknap

SEE ALSO
Crannógs

Lombards

Although late entrants to the barbarian migrations, the Lombards (Langobards, or "Long Beards") were one of the more successful Germanic tribes, establishing a kingdom in Italy that endured for more than two centuries. They are remarkable for the fact that, unlike most other major Germanic groupings of the fifth and sixth centuries A.D., such as the Franks, who are recorded only from the third century, the Lombards are, in fact, listed in the first century A.D. in the Roman historian Tacitus's *Germania* (Ch. 40): "famous because they are so few."

Tacitus locates the Lombards in the area of the Lower Elbe in Lower Saxony, a zone featuring numerous large urnfields (e.g., Putensen). Although reference is made to Lombards invading Roman Pannonia in c. 170 along with some Obii, it seems likely that these were mercenary war bands and that the bulk of the Lombard people remained in the region of Hamburg into the third or even fourth century A.D. Archaeologically, however, the early Lombards are indistinct from neighboring tribal groupings, and few artifact types known from the Elbe urnfields can yet be traced along the presumed route of the subsequent Lombard migration. The late eighth-century *Historia Langobardorum* (History of the Langobards) of Paul the Deacon provides the essential historical and semi-legendary guide to the Lombards' Scandinavian origins and subsequent migration from their base on the River Elbe through Bohemia and Moravia to Lower Austria, the northern fringes of the former Roman province of Noricum, by c. A.D. 500. Here the Lombards become archaeologically visible through their row-grave cemeteries containing finds such as pottery and brooches that reveal links with the old presumed homeland and with the Saxons in particular. In two stages, in 526 and 546, the Lombards subsequently expanded into former northern and southern Pannonia (western Hungary). It seems clear that a residual Latin population persisted here, as reflected in Lombard settlement in and around late Roman Danubian forts and towns such as Aquincum (Budapest), Ulcisia Castra (Szentendre), and Scarbantia (Sopron). So far, cemeterial data alone are available, but these provide good indicators, through weapon and jewelry types, of a highly militarized and stratified society. A key zone of interest was the Danube on the eastern border of Pannonia, where further Lombard expansion was strongly opposed by the Gepids.

In Pannonia, the Lombards were recognized as allies of Byzantium (as were the Lombards' enemies, the Gepids), and troops were loaned for campaigns with the Byzantine army against Ostrogothic Italy. The devastating effects of the Gothic War (535–554) gave the opportunity for renewed Lombard migration and conquest, and they duly entered Italy in A.D. 568–569, abandoning Pannonia to the Avars. Rapid military campaigns against an ill-prepared Byzantine administration in Italy allowed the Lombard king and dukes to carve out major territorial gains between 570 and 605, subduing most of the northern regions of the peninsula and controlling large areas of central and southern Italy. The Byzantines were forced back onto the coasts, with their defense focused on Ravenna and Rome. Lombard rule was centered in the north on the capital of Pavia and articulated between various urban-based dukedoms, notably Cividale, Verona, Brescia, Trento, Spoleto, and Benevento. Paul the Deacon's *History* also records various military fortifications in the Alpine regions, and this image is extended through the evidence of place names such as *fara, warda,* and *sculca.* As yet, little is known archaeologically of Lombard settlement types. Excavation in the urban centers of Verona, Milan, and Brescia generally depict fairly crude housing among ruined Roman structures, continuing a trend of decay apparent since the fifth century. Excavations at the forts of Invillino and Castelseprio, meanwhile, indicate that the Lombards were maintaining defensive sites active since late Roman times.

The Lombards are far better documented through their extensive cemeteries, which are best represented in northern and central Italy. Key excavated sites include Nocera Umbra, Castel Trosino, Testona, and Cividale. Grave finds from these testify to the survival and evolution of manufactures from Pannonia and to the progressive

L

adoption of Mediterranean styles or motifs. The speed of this adoption or acculturation remains disputed, however, given that coins are largely absent. Simultaneously, the grave goods also demonstrate the maintenance of a strongly militarized society, with parade equipment as emblems of the elite, as illustrated in the stunning finds recently made at Trezzo sull'Adda near Milan. Burial with grave goods terminates in the later seventh century, coinciding with a general adoption of Catholic Christianity from 680. Although previous kings, queens, and nobles had professed Catholicism, most of the nobility were Arian Christians, while the bulk of the Lombard folk probably remained pagans. From the late seventh century, Catholic Lombard kings expressed piety through church and monastic foundations, and, in northern towns like Brescia, Pavia, and Cividale, sculpture and art signify the start of a notable artistic flourish.

Law codes were issued in Latin under Kings Rothari (636–652), Grimoald (662–671), Liutprand (712–744), Ratchis (744–749), and Aistulf (749–756). Whereas the seventh-century laws embody rather antiquated Lombard customs, and thereby provide a useful context to the mute cemetery evidence, the eighth-century issues testify to an increasing complexity in Lombard society and to the declining power of the central royal authority in the face of a strong nobility. These late laws stand in contrast with the contemporary evidence of high-cultural activity in the Lombard zones.

Lombard rule in the north was curtailed in A.D. 774 through conquest by the Frankish king Charlemagne (742–814). Although Charlemagne maintained Lombard functionaries in office, many nobles chose to flee south to the Principality (formerly Duchy) of Benevento. Benevento enjoyed a brief period of architectural and artistic vigor before political fragmentation saw the breakaway of centers such as Salerno and Capua. Though fragmented, independent Lombard rule nonetheless persisted, albeit with difficulties, into the eleventh century.

FURTHER READINGS

Bóna, I. *The Dawn of the Dark Ages: The Gepids and the Lombards in the Carpathian Basin.* Budapest: Corvina, 1976.

Christie, N. Langobard Weaponry and Warfare, A.D. 1–800. *Journal of Roman Military Equipment Studies* (1991) 2:1–26.

———. *The Lombards.* Oxford: Basil Blackwell, 1994.

Fischer Drew, K. *The Lombard Laws.* Philadelphia: University of Pennsylvania Press, 1973.

Kiszely, I. *The Anthropology of the Lombards.* BAR S61. Oxford: British Archaeological Reports, 1979.

Melucco Vaccaro, A. *I Longobardi in Italia.* Milan: Longanesi, 1981.

Menghin, W. *Die Langobarden: Archäologie und Geschichte.* Stuttgart: Konrad Theiss Verlag, 1984.

Menis, G.C., ed. *I Longobardi.* Exhibition Catalog. Milan: Electa, 1990.

Roffia, E., ed. *La necropoli longobarda di Trezzo sull'Adda.* Ricerche di Archeologia Altomedievale e Medievale 12–13. Florence: All'Insegna del Giglio, 1986.

Wickham, C. *Early Medieval Italy: Central Power and Local Society, 400–1000.* London: Macmillan, 1981.

Neil Christie

SEE ALSO
Italy

London

The archaeological discovery of Saxon London is an object lesson for anyone believing that archaeological theory and fieldwork need not be connected. The city of London is one of the best-documented settlements in Anglo-Saxon England, both in terms of contemporary documentary sources and in terms of what can be gleaned from later sources about conditions pertaining in the sixth–eleventh centuries. Despite this, the location and the nature of settlement in London during this period, especially in the earlier centuries up to the end of the ninth century, have been a source of speculation and contention from the days of Sir Mortimer Wheeler, whose work begins the scientific study of Saxon London (Wheeler 1927, 1935). It continued through the early 1980s, when a spate of articles appeared, all stimulated by two papers published simultaneously by M. Biddle and A.G. Vince in 1984, which suggested that, in common with several other seventh–ninth-century trading centers, the port and main settlement of London lay outside the Roman walled city on a "green field" site. This period of speculation was brought to a neat conclusion with the discovery of extensive archaeological evidence for settlement to the west of the Roman city, along and behind the Strand, an area of London along the Thames. Despite criticism from place-name scholars, this settlement has been termed Lundenwic in recent archaeological literature. The name Lundenwic was current in documentary sources from the early eighth century to the late ninth century and undoubtedly did refer, in most cases, to the

Strand settlement. Indeed, it appears to have been commemorated in the name of an area of the Strand occupied in the Medieval period by a triangular market Aldwych. However, it is claimed that the name may well have been one of several used for London, depending on the context. When referring to the defensive aspects of the site, the name Lundenburh (or variants) was preferred; when the name was used as a mint mark, it was either shortened to Lundonia or appeared as Lundonia Civit.

The End of Late Roman London

The chronology of the decline of late Roman London is another area of contention. On the one hand, the archaeological evidence for settlement in the late fourth to early fifth centuries is limited to a small strip along the Thames, from the site of the Roman London Bridge to the southeast corner of the city, where a part of the city defenses underlying the Tower of London has been shown to have been built from fresh materials at the very end of the fourth century. On the other hand, there is evidence to suggest that the extensive cemeteries that formed a halo around the walled city continued to be used at least until the end of the fourth century. These imply the continued existence of a substantial population.

Romano-British Survival?

There is no positive archaeological evidence for the continued occupation of London after the breaking of ties with the Roman Empire in the early fifth century, but the visit of St. Germanus to Britain in the early fifth century, a mention of the continued worship at the shrine of St. Alban in Gildas, and the reference in the *Anglo-Saxon Chronicle* to the conquest of the Britons by Anglo-Saxons along the northern scarp of the Chilterns all suggest that parts of what was to become the territory of the East Saxons had remained in British hands for several generations. Whether London itself was part of this British enclave is unknown.

Early Anglo-Saxon Settlement

Evidence for the settlement of Germanic peoples within the Thames Valley is present both to the east and to the west of London from the middle of the fifth century. By the sixth century at the latest, occupation can be demonstrated on rural settlements within a few miles of the city, although there is very little evidence from this period either from within the walled city or from the Strand. These finds do, however, include burials with stone sarcophagi accompanied by glass bowls dated to the later sixth or the seventh century from the site of the later Church of St. Martin-in-the-Fields discovered in the early eighteenth century.

Metropolis of the East Saxons

In 604, London was chosen as the seat of the bishop of the East Saxons, following their conversion to Christianity. The Benedictine scholar Bede (c. 672–735), writing in the early eighth century, describes London as the metropolis of the East Saxons and a trading center. What the term "metropolis" meant to Bede and whether he was describing the settlement of his own day or that of the early seventh century is a matter of debate. Later traditions, however, suggest that the newly founded cathedral was endowed with considerable estates, mainly in what was to become Middlesex, on the north bank of the Thames. There is no reason to doubt that this cathedral stood close to the site of the later St. Paul's Cathedral within the walls of the Roman town. How much of the interior of the walled city was under the direct control of the bishop is unknown. By the end of the Anglo-Saxon period (but after the movement of settlement back within the walls), the cathedral lay within a clearly defined, perhaps even notionally defendable, precinct.

Political Control in the Sixth–Eighth Centuries

Two patterns can be seen in the political overlordship of London during the seventh and eighth centuries. First, the Kingdom of the East Saxons had more powerful neighbors to both the north and the south. Early on, probably from some time in the late sixth century, Essex had been under the overlordship of the Kingdom of Kent. Then followed a period in which East Anglia exerted an influence upon the kingdom, followed by the reassertion of Kent, at least in London itself. During the eighth century, however, the kings of the midland Kingdom of Mercia became overlords of the East Saxons. Early in the eighth century, Mercian kings were granting land in the western parts of the kingdom without reference to the East Saxon king, and, soon after, this area is referred to as the land of the Middle Saxons, later Middlesex. Mercia retained direct control of London until the collapse of the kingdom in the 880s, with the exception of a short period in the 820s when Egbert of Wessex (802–839) overran Mercia and issued a coin with the name London upon it as a commemoration of the event.

The Seventh–Eighth Centuries

The nature of London during this period is illustrated by three sources: numismatics, archaeology, and a series of

L

documents issued by the kings of Mercia that granted remission of toll at the port of London.

Two series of coins are known with mint marks indicating a London source. The first was a gold coinage of the early to mid-seventh century, and the second was a debased silver *sceatta* coinage, Rigold's Series L. Other coins were probably issued in London, but opinions vary as to which ones.

Archaeological evidence exists for a waterfront, dated to the later seventh century by dendrochronology, and for a large, probably undefended area of settlement beyond the waterfront. Analysis of animal bone from excavations within this area suggests that the settlement may be divided into a meat-consuming area at the core and surrounding sites where animal husbandry may have been practiced. Too little has been excavated yet to tell whether the settlement had a grid of streets, nor can anything be said about the existence or the nature of properties within the settlement. A flat-bottomed ditch found at Maiden Lane is interpreted as a late attempt to defend a part of the settlement, but there is otherwise no evidence for any physical boundary. The extent of land pertaining to the settlement is probably indicated by a mid-tenth-century charter granting the area to the Abbey of Westminster. No direct evidence for the location of churches within the settlement exists. Westminster was probably founded only in the late eighth century on the island of Thorney on the western boundary of the settlement, while three of the parish churches have more or less good claims to belong to this period: St. Martin-in-the-Fields, St. Andrew's Holborn, and St. Bride's Fleet Street.

Late Eighth–Ninth-Century Developments

To judge by the distribution of stray finds and evidence from controlled excavations, the later eighth and early ninth centuries were a period of prosperity in London. Soon after this, however, the fortunes of the town declined. The exact chronology of the decline is uncertain. It might start with the taking of the town by Egbert or with the succession of Viking raids that London suffered from 841 onward and that were undoubtedly responsible for a hoard found at the Middle Temple, in the Fleet Street area. A date of c. 850 for the abandonment of the Strand settlement and its relocation within the Roman walls has been put forward by T. Tatton-Brown (1986), and similar early dates have been proposed by those working on materials recovered from the Strand-area excavations. Nevertheless, there is still much in favor of the view that the record under the year 886 in the

Anglo-Saxon Chronicle refers to the relocation of the settlement under the direction of Alfred the Great (849–899), although numismatic opinion would place the actual event a few years earlier.

The Alfredian Town

Archaeological evidence for the London of Alfred is difficult to find, probably because the initial foundation was not an immediate success. Documents known as the *Queenhithe Charters* are the clearest evidence for conditions in the town and, indeed, the clearest evidence for royal policy toward town development in this period. They indicate that the rudiments of the street grid in the western part of the walled city had been laid out before the end of the ninth century and that trading was allowed both on the streets (as at Cheapside, which continued to be the site of street markets well into the Medieval period) and on the foreshore in front of the Roman riverside wall. Whether royal policy extended to the provision of churches or whether these were entirely the responsibility of those to whom blocks of land within the street grid were granted is not known. The only intramural church known to have existed is St. Paul's Cathedral itself.

London in the Reign of Edward the Elder

In all probability, the upturn in London's fortunes can be dated to the tenth century, in the reign of Edward the Elder (899–924). Archaeological evidence points to the street grid in the eastern part of the walled city being in existence by this time, effectively doubling the size of the settlement, and this period saw the removal of the Viking threat with the recapture of Essex and the southeast Midlands from Viking armies that had settled there from the 870s onward. To judge by the chronology of the reconquest, it would seem that London must have been in a crucial position both for campaigns to the north—at Hertford and Bedford, for example—and to the east—at Maldon.

The Late Tenth–Early Eleventh Centuries

Evidence for the increased pressure on space within the walled city is provided by a series of excavations that show that, while initially buildings were placed away from the street frontages, later they were erected along the street frontages. Subsequently, new streets were provided to allow access to the backs of these properties and to the Thames waterfront, and finally these streets, too, were lined with buildings.

Dendrochronological (tree-ring) dating of timbers from the southern piers of London Bridge show that there was a bridge from at least the tenth century. The bridge features in saga accounts of attacks upon the city in the early eleventh century, and a cache of iron tools and weapons discovered near the bridge decorated in Ringerike style has been linked to these events, either as a loss in battle or as a deliberate ritual deposit made afterward.

Some indication of the character of London in the early eleventh century comes from excavations along the waterfront from which pottery imports from the Rhineland, the Low Countries, and northern France have been retrieved. Documentary sources amplify this evidence and show that, from at least this period, a royal palace existed within the walled city, probably on the site of the Cripplegate fort on the northwest side of the walled circuit. This palace was abandoned in the reign of Edward the Confessor (1002–1005) with the construction of a palace at Westminster and the transformation of the abbey into a royal mausoleum.

Although excavations inside the walls have demonstrated that empty space still existed within the city, it is to the eleventh century that the beginnings of London's suburbs can be dated. Excavations in Aldergate, Bishopsgate, Aldgate, High Holborn, Fleet Street, the Strand, and across the Thames in Southwark show that these streets were built up by the end of the century, probably in the years immediately before the Norman Conquest.

London and the Norman Conquest

The importance of London within the late English state can be seen clearly in the actions of William the Conqueror (c. 1028–1087) after the Battle of Hastings (1066). Clearly, London was seen as the capital of the kingdom and the place where a new king should be crowned. In addition to this symbolic significance, it is also clear that the future king was wary of the military capabilities of the town's inhabitants. Rather than make a frontal assault on the town, William circled around it, approaching finally from the north. The town surrendered to William without a fight, but it is probably significant that one of the new king's first actions was to order the construction of the White Tower, dominating the southeastern corner of the town. Recent excavations have made the shadowy documentary references to a western castle, Baynard's Castle, much clearer, showing that a timber castle had been constructed overlooking the southwestern quarter, the western approach to the city, and the Cathedral of St. Paul. Whether for reasons of military strategy or as a result of pressure for space, the riverside wall was demolished within years of the Conquest and its site occupied by a riverside road, Thames Street, soon to be lined with houses, churches, and wharves. By this period, therefore, the walled city of London, although only c. 180 years old, had taken on many of the features that were to dominate its topography for the remainder of the Medieval period.

FURTHER READINGS

Biddle, M. London on the Strand. *Popular Archaeology* (July 1984): 23–27.

———. A City in Transition, 400–800. In *The City of London*. Ed. Mary D. Lobel. The British Atlas of Historic Towns 3. Oxford: Oxford University Press, 1989.

Cowie, B., and R. Whytehead. Lundenwic: The Archaeological Evidence for Middle Saxon London. *Antiquity* (1989) 63:706–718.

Demsem, R., and S. Seeley. Excavations at Rectory Grove, Clapham, 1980–81. *London Archaeologist* (1982) 4 (7):177–184.

Dyson, T. Two Saxon Land Grants at Queenhithe. In *Collectanea Londiniensia: Studies . . . Presented to R. Merrifield*. Ed. J. Bird, H. Chapman, and J. Clark. Special Paper 2. London: London and Middlesex Archaeological Society, 1978, pp. 200–215.

———. London and Southwark in the Seventh Century and Later. *Transactions of the London and Middlesex Archaeological Society* (1980) 31:83–95.

———. Early Harbour Regulations in London. In *Bergen 1983: Conference on Waterfront Archaeology in Northern European Towns*. Ed. A. Herteig. Bergen: Historisk Museum Bergen, 1985, pp. 19–24.

Gem, R.D.H. The Origins of the Abbey. In *Westminster Abbey*. Ed. C. Wilson. London: Bell and Hyman, 1986, pp. 6–21.

Haslam, J. Excavations on the Site of Arundel House in the Strand WC2, in 1972. *Transactions of the London and Middlesex Archaeological Society* (1975) 26:221–242.

———. Parishes, Churches, Wards, and Gates in Eastern London. In *Minsters and Parish Churches: The Local Church in Transition, 950–1200*. Ed. John Blair. Oxford: Oxford University Committee for Archaeology, 1988, pp. 35–43.

Hill, C., M. Millett, and T. Blagg. *The Roman Riverside Wall and Monumental Arch in London: Excavations at Baynard's Castle, Upper Thames Street, London, 1974–76*. Special Paper 3. London: London and Middlesex Archaeological Society, 1980.

Horsman, V., C. Milne, and G. Milne. *Aspects of Saxo-Norman London I*. Special Paper 11. London: London and Middlesex Archaeological Society, 1988.

Pritchard, F.A. Late Saxon Textiles from the City of London. *Medieval Archaeology* (1984) 28:46–76.

Redknap, M. The Saxon Pottery from Barking Abbey. Part 2: The Continental Imports. *London Archaeologist* (1992) 6 (14):378–381.

Rigold, S.E. The Sutton Hoo Coins in Light of the Contemporary Background of Coinage in England. In *The Sutton Hoo Ship Burial I.* Ed. R. Bruce-Mitford. London: British Museum, 1975, pp. 653–677.

Steedman, K., T. Dyson, and J. Schofield, eds. *Aspects of Saxo-Norman London III: The Bridgehead and Billingsgate to 1200.* Special Paper 14. London: London and Middlesex Archaeological Society, 1992.

Stewart, I. Anglo-Saxon Gold Coins. In *Scripta Numeria Romana.* Ed. R.A.G. Carson and C.M. Kraay. London: Spink and Son, 1978, pp. 143–172.

Sutherland, H. *Anglo-Saxon Gold Coinage in Light of the Crondall Hoard.* Oxford: Oxford University Press, 1948.

Tatton-Brown, T. The Topography of Anglo-Saxon London. *Antiquity* (1986) 60:21–30.

Vince, A.G. The Aldwych: Saxon London Discovered. *Current Archaeology* (1984) 93:310–312.

———. New Light on Saxon Pottery from the London Area. *London Archaeologist* (1984) 4 (16):431–439.

———. The Economic Basis of Anglo-Saxon London. In *The Rebirth of Towns in the West, A.D. 700–1050.* Ed. R. Hodges and B. Hobley. CBA Research Report 68. London: Council for British Archaeology, 1989, pp. 83–92.

———. *Saxon London: An Archaeological Investigation.* London: Seaby, 1990.

———, ed. *Aspects of Saxo-Norman London II: Finds and Environmental Evidence.* Special Paper 12. London: London and Middlesex Archaeological Society, 1991.

Watson, B. The Excavation of a Norman Fortress on Ludgate Hill. *London Archaeologist* (1992) 6 (14):371–376.

Wheeler, R.E.M. *London and the Vikings.* Museum Catalog 1. London: London Museum, 1927.

———. *London and the Saxons.* Museum Catalog 6. London: London Museum, 1935.

White, W. *The Cemetery of St. Nicholas Shambles.* Special Paper 9. London: London and Middlesex Archaeological Society, 1988.

Whytehead, R., and L. Blackmore. Excavations at Tottenham Court, 250 Euston Road, NW1. *Transactions of the London and Middlesex Archaeological Society* (1983) 34:73–92.

Whytehead, R., and R. Cowie, with L. Blackmore. Excavations at the Peabody site, Chandos Place, and the National Gallery. *Transactions of the London and Middlesex Archaeological Society* (1989) 40:35–176.

Alan Vince

SEE ALSO
Dendrochronology; England

Lübeck

The city of Lübeck is located on the River Trave in northern Germany. In the Middle Ages, it became the first western city on the Baltic coast, the turntable of north European trade, and the head of the Hansa. It is an important center of Slavic and urban archaeology.

After the migration period (fifth to eighth centuries) and in the course of Slavic colonization of central Europe, two geoeconomically and geopolitically related places developed. The Slavic fortified capital of Liubice-Old Lübeck represents the stage of early urban development, while German Lübeck evolved into a fully developed city.

Liubice-Old Lübeck

The intensively settled early Slavic Citadel I, erected in 819, with its western settlement, already played an important role in long-distance trade in the ninth century. After a temporary loss of importance, a new building phase, the late Slavic Citadel II, took place in 1055–1056 under Prince Gottschalk of the Obodrit dynasty, who had a monastery or convent built, probably the cruciform wooden church that has been excavated. After a further building phase in which Citadel III was built under King Heinrich (1087–1089), Old Lübeck became the central capital of the great west Slavic Obodrit Empire and attained its greatest political and economic importance. A three-part layout governed all features of the early city: (1) the citadel was the center of military rule, administration, and ritual with its stone *Königsgrabkirche* (king's burial church), mint, and highly specialized crafts; (2) the suburb (southern settlement) was characterized by timber blockhouses and various handicrafts; and (3) the harbor and foreign-merchant settlement *(Kesselbrink)* had its own church on the opposite riverbank. In 1138, destruction followed in the wake of internal Slavic clashes. Old Lübeck was surrounded by a ring of agrarian, unfortified settlements (Fig. 1).

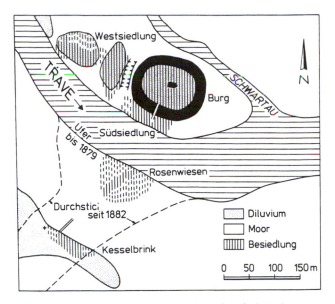

FIG. 1. Liubice–Alt (Old) Lübeck: Slavic fortified residence dating from the end of the eleventh century to the beginning of the twelfth century (after Kempke 1988).

Lübeck

The movement of the fortified settlement of Old Lübeck and its place name 6 km upriver formed the foundation of German Lübeck in 1143. However, this foundation, which was repeated in 1159, did not prove to be the prototype of the modern western chartered city of the twelfth century, as planned. German Lübeck did, however, join together several areas and several centuries of Slavic settlement on the hill between the Wakenitz and the Trave Rivers. These consisted of a fortified settlement that dominated water and land routes in the north with a large suburb, long-distance trade route, harbor, and growing areas of settlement. By 1095, German Lübeck had already experienced extensive settlement growth, so that, with gradual emigration from the capital of Old Lübeck, it was well established by the destruction of Old Lübeck in 1138. Thus, the founding of the German Lübeck in 1143 represents nothing more than the development and restructuring of the three-part, harbor-oriented market settlement under the protection of the count's castle (Fig. 2).

German Lübeck consisted of the castle in the north, a harbor with a shore market and foreign-merchant settlement in the middle, and a cathedral with a bishop's seat in the south. The second founding in 1159 made Lübeck a city in a legal sense. After 1181, political, economic, and legal expansion led to a fully developed city. Internal and external expansion gradually brought about a uniform, fortified settlement construction. After a period of local autonomy, the city was made subject only to the Holy Roman Emperor in 1226, and a governmental and topographic center was constructed around the market and town hall.

The city plan and layout of the plots were clearly not simply a result of the foundation plan. The road system consisted of an obviously older, long-distance trade route at the center and of a bundle of routes radiating vertically and perpendicularly from the harbor. The system was conceptualized by 1159 at the latest and was carried out gradually. It was completed by 1217–1220 in the west along the River Trave, after the abandonment of the foreign merchants' shore markets, which were built in an early medieval tradition. The restructuring of northern European trade, with a shift in the market's function, led to a new and significantly different type of harbor settlement. Initially, the ground plots laid out by law were large square blocks, loosely covered with buildings. Later, the plots were more typically long and narrow parcels. The subdivision of the plots and the dense development mirrored the growth in the population and the economy, occurring in large part from the end of the twelfth through the fourteenth centuries.

In terms of house construction, the traditional single-story post buildings in Lübeck were replaced by multiple-story upright framework constructions on sillbeams with a large hall (*Dielenhaus*) as early as the last quarter of the twelfth century. Towering structures appeared as a new architectural type: first, wooden *Kemenaten* (heated apartments); then early thirteenth-century stone structures, as well as great halls of brick (*Saalgeschosshaus*) with upper stories. These houses were owned by the social upper class. In the second half of the thirteenth century, monumental floored houses built of brick (*Dielenhaus*) appeared for the first time in response to the marketing of bulk goods.

Economic developments and technological innovations mirrored the rapid rise of Lübeck as a leading Hanseatic town. To improve land traffic, the inner-city streets were surfaced with wood-board construction beginning shortly after 1159. A system of waterworks with wooden pipes was established in Lübeck in the thirteenth century, as early as anywhere else in Europe. Wells and cisterns of a different construction superceded this system. By the late twelfth century, Lübeck was the only city on the Continent where a multifaceted production of

L

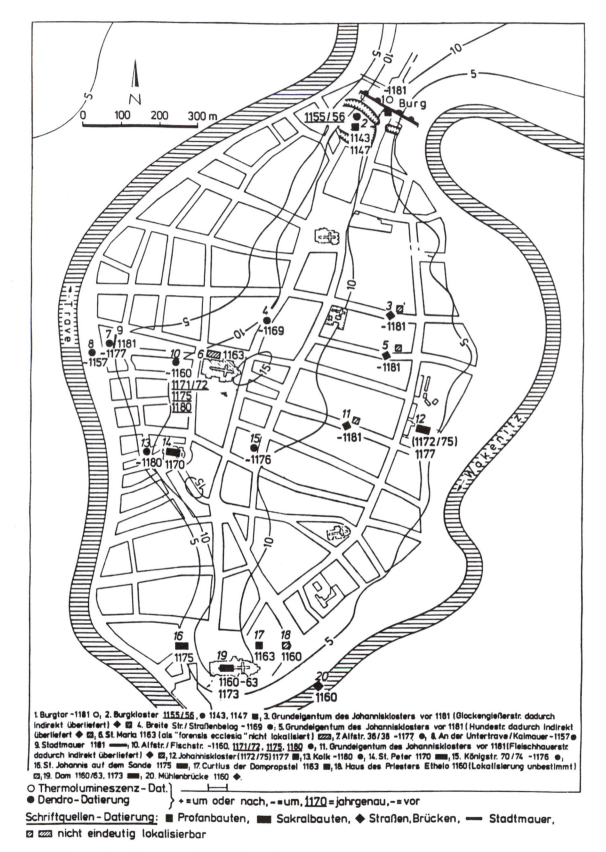

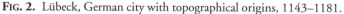

1. Burgtor ~1181 ○, 2. Burgkloster <u>1155/56</u>, ● 1143, 1147 ■, 3. Grundeigentum des Johannisklosters vor 1181 (Glockengießerstr. dadurch indirekt überliefert) ◆ ☑ 4. Breite Str./Straßenbelag ~1169 ●; 5. Grundeigentum des Johannisklosters vor 1181 (Hundestr. dadurch indirekt überliefert ◆ ☑, 6. St. Maria 1163 (als "forensis ecclesia" nicht lokalisiert) ▨, 7. Alfstr. 36/38 ~1177 ●, 8. An der Untertrave/Kaimauer ~1157 ● 9. Stadtmauer 1181 ━━━, 10. Alfstr./Fischstr. ~1160, <u>1171/72</u>, <u>1175</u>, <u>1180</u> ●, 11. Grundeigentum des Johannisklosters vor 1181(Fleischhauerstr. dadurch indirekt überliefert) ☑, 12. Johanniskloster (1172/75) 1177 ■, 13. Kolk ~1180 ●, 14. St. Peter 1170 ■■■, 15. Königstr. 70/74 ~1176 ●, 16. St. Johannis auf dem Sande 1175 ■■■, 17. Curtius der Dompropstei 1163 ■■■, 18. Haus des Priesters Ethelo 1160 (Lokalisierung unbestimmt) ☑, 19. Dom 1160/63, 1173 ■■■, 20. Mühlenbrücke 1160 ◆.

○ Thermolumineszenz – Dat.
● Dendro – Datierung ⎱ +=um oder nach, ~=um, <u>1170</u>=jahrgenau, ~= vor

<u>Schriftquellen – Datierung:</u> ■ Profanbauten, ■■■ Sakralbauten, ◆ Straßen, Brücken, ━━━ Stadtmauer,
☑ ▨ nicht eindeutig lokalisierbar

FIG. 2. Lübeck, German city with topographical origins, 1143–1181.

high-quality glazed ceramics took place. At an equally early date, it also possessed workshops for the production of other types of ceramic vessels and bronze casting. From the end of the thirteenth century onward, uniquely large bakery ovens appeared in Lübeck. These bakeries were used to supply oceangoing vessels.

In terms of the far-reaching questions of social and economic structure, additional knowledge was gained when it was possible to associate selected archaeological data with the many written historical sources that are available from the end of the thirteenth century onward. This is true not only for economic history, but also for social history: domestic material culture is known both qualitatively and quantitatively from study of the complex of finds obtained through systematic excavations. Clear differences in domestic material culture are obviously useful in defining the broad spectrum of social classes.

The long and complicated development from its early urban Slavic roots to a German harbor and market resulted in Lübeck's gradual transformation to a fully developed city that can be considered urban by all criteria. This development was characterized by unforeseen changes in topography, ground plot, and urban structure, by technological innovations, and by economic transformations. The founding of Lübeck was not a static act; rather, it was a process that is paralleled in the development of other leading cities in medieval Europe.

FURTHER READINGS

Fehring, G.P. Archaeological Evidence from Lübeck for Changing Material Culture and Socio-Economic Conditions from the Thirteenth to the Sixteenth Century. *Medieval Archaeology* (1989) 33:60–81.

———. Die Entstehung von Lübeck. *Zeitschrift für Archäologie* (1991a) 25:223–236.

———. Die frühstädtische Burgwall-Siedlung Alt Lübeck in jungslawischer Zeit. In *Siedlungen und Landesausbau zur Salierzeit, Teil 1.* Ed. Horst Wolfgang Böhme. Sigmaringen: Jan Thorbecke Verlag, 1991b, pp. 233–261.

———. Origins and Development of Slavic and German Lübeck. In *From the Baltic to the Black Sea: Studies in Medieval Archaeology.* Ed. D. Austin and L. Alcock. London: Unwin Hyman, 1991c, pp. 251–266.

———. Stadtarchäologie in Lübeck, 1973–1993. *Zeitschrift für Archäologie des Mittelalters* (1995) 22: in press.

Gläser, Manfred, ed. *Archäologie des Mittelalters und Bauforschung im Hanseraum, Festschrift G.P. Fehring.* Schriften des Kulturhistorischen Museums Rostock 1. Rostock: Konrad Reich Verlag, 1993.

In addition to the articles listed above, the primary sources for this topic are found in *Lübecker Schriften zur Archäologie und Kulturgeschichte (LSAK)* 1–23 (1978–1993). For further comparisons, see *Häuser und Höfe in Lübeck* 1, 1988–4, 1993.

Güner P. Fehring

SEE ALSO
Brunswick; Germany; Water Supply

M

Markets

Theoretical Frameworks for Medieval Markets

The picture of medieval economies based largely on the historical record between the fall of Rome in the fifth century and the end of the Middle Ages around 1500 was unquestioned until recent times. Historian Henri Pirenne's thesis became the primary interpretive framework for the economic transition between late antiquity and the Middle Ages. In this model, the Roman organization of Europe persisted far into the Medieval period, and, as European trade with the Mediterranean was cut off by Moslem expansion, rulers of the Dark Ages slowly developed their region's agricultural economies.

However, archaeological investigations since the late 1970s have revised or even reversed the theories of the development of post-Roman economies. Archaeological evidence has recently demonstrated that, in much of Europe, the sociopolitical structure and market economy of Rome disintegrated between A.D. 400 and 500 and was replaced by many complex regional systems.

Marketplaces in medieval Europe stemmed from a number of different cultural traditions and socioeconomic and political environments. Their locations and interactions passed through many stages of development in which their function, organization, and administration were transformed.

Trade and exchange can be studied in terms of local and long-distance socioeconomic transactions, and archaeological evidence of markets can be studied on different scales. By studying the synchronic geographic locations and interaction of market sites throughout Europe, and then following their diachronic transformations, long-term change and interregional interaction may be examined. On an intermediate scale, research may focus on individual market sites and their hinterlands, and on a smaller scale by examining the functioning of individual workshops, crafts quarters, and artifact distributions. All of these perspectives are vital to the interpretation of marketplace archaeology.

The Early Middle Ages Inside and Outside the Former Empire

The market traditions of early medieval Europe and their trajectories differ among the core of the former Roman Empire, in which the populace was substantially romanized; the less-romanized provinces like England; and the non-Roman buffer areas such as Free Germany, Scandinavia, Ireland, and the Slavic lands, which were wholly outside the empire but interacted with Rome on a secondary basis.

The market economy of the Roman provinces was based on manufacturing and the import and export of goods among the cooperating members of a single political and economic entity. According to recent interpretation of archaeological evidence, with the decline of Rome after A.D. 450, and perhaps somewhat earlier, these provinces were transformed into regional and subregional systems, and markets largely lost their character as interregional and long-distance trade centers. Investigations in Italy illustrate the collapse of such trade between the fifth and the seventh centuries through a strong decline in trade amphorae from Africa and the eastern Mediterranean, as well as the abandonment of commercial harbors. While some former Roman towns in southern Europe maintained their urban character, though at a reduced level, western European towns and the markets

M

they fostered were either greatly reduced or largely abandoned between A.D. 450 and 700. Long-distance commercial exchange and, with it, the interregional market system collapsed.

Scandinavia and Free Germany, though not part of the imperial political structure, had significant economic contact with the empire, trading utilitarian goods such as leather, foodstuffs, and slaves for Roman prestige goods for elite consumption. Elite-controlled ports, such as the archaeological sites of Gudme and Dankirke in Denmark, each with a complement of craftspeople, were well established in the north by A.D. 500. Located at sacred centers and assembly places where people gathered for socioreligious purposes, local elites could control the distribution of the prestige imports. Even after the collapse of the empire, trading places that had been established flourished until the ninth century.

The Age of Emporia (A.D. 700–1000)

While interregional trade in subsistence and commercial goods eroded with the fall of Rome, local rulers and magnates of the early Medieval period maintained long-distance trade in luxuries to solidify and maintain political and social relationships with their peers, as well as to obtain the symbols of their rank in local society. The sites that served as points of entry for elite goods such as precious metals and gems, tableware and glass, wine, textiles, and weapons are commonly called *emporia*.

Many emporia have been extensively excavated, including Ipswich and Hamwic in England; Birka, Ribe, Kaupang, and Hedeby (Haithabu) in Scandinavia; Quentovic and Dorestad on the Rhine; Staraya Ladoga in Russia; and Wollin in Poland.

Obtaining imports and taxing the commerce were both primary concerns of local leaders. In return for their tax and toll payments, merchants could expect protection from raiders and thieves, and the presence of officials to witness agreements and transactions and enforce the laws of fair trade.

Artifacts of such elite control are seen in the physical remains of administration and fortification, whose labor and organization only rulers could supply. In Scandinavia, nondefensive boundary earthworks surround some eighth- and ninth-century markets such as Ribe and Löddeköpinge. These are interpreted as defining the extent of the elite-administered market, where the laws that regulated trade were in effect. In Dorestad, property and boundary markings between traders indicate careful regulation of space. Other markets, such as Hedeby in Denmark and Ipswich and Hamwic in England, had protective fortifications between the seventh and the tenth centuries.

Urban Markets of the Later Middle Ages

The emporia were vulnerable to collapse in that they were linked to changing local political conditions. By the turn of the millennium, they were largely replaced by other types of markets. These often developed around various types of fortified elite settlements. By the tenth and eleventh centuries, many of these had developed into towns with regional, competitive markets. An example is Mikulcice in Czechoslovakia, an eighth-century fortress with evidence of attached craft specialists and long-distance trade. During the ninth and tenth centuries, dependent nonelite settlements clustered around the fortified site and an urban center appeared, with marketplace and resident craftspeople. Hamburg, Lübeck, and Brandenburg in Germany have a similar record. Such sites, along with the surviving old Roman cities, formed the core of the marketplace hierarchy of the later Middle Ages.

The Archaeology of the Marketplace

Structures erected for marketplace transactions are often temporary or seasonal and, therefore, can be difficult to identify in the archaeological record. In much of northern and western Europe, small sunken-floored houses that served as workshops and market stalls were a feature of the marketplace. Unlike their ephemeral surface architecture, their deep floor layers often escape destruction and provide information on site layout and contain many artifacts. In Löddeköpinge in Sweden, the floors of the sunken-floored houses consisted of alternating occupational layers and sterile sand, indicating a market of a seasonal or occasional nature.

Artifact assemblages at market and production sites are complex and rich: sawn bone and horn fragments from comb and tool manufacturing, fragments of crucibles and molds used in metal casting, molten glass wasters from bead manufacture, ceramic wasters and kilns, weaving and spinning implements, butchered animal bones, as well as the tools of such trades, are often found in connection with markets. In some conditions, wood and leather items may be preserved. Scales, weights, and balances may be recovered, as well as the keys that opened the merchant's locked coffers, coins, and, in some areas, artifacts such as rune-covered split tally sticks that merchants used to keep track of debts, or the accounts and trade transactions scribbled on birchbark and preserved at Novgorod in Russia.

As mentioned above, workshop boundaries and property divisions, which reflect the long-term regulation of manufacture and trade and the planned layout of streets and blocks by central authority, are important artifacts in themselves.

Although a more detailed historical record exists in the later Middle Ages, the archaeological study of marketplace workshops, wharves, and warehouses provides a record of the unwritten concerns and strategies of the manufacturer, the merchant, and the middleman whose activities transformed Europe's economy and society during this vital period.

FURTHER READINGS

Barley, M.W. *European Towns: Their Archaeology and Early History.* London: Academic, 1977.

Callmer, J. Production Site and Market Area. *Meddelanden från Lunds Universitets Historiska Museum 1981–82* (1983) 7:135–165.

———. Recent Work at Åhus: Problems and Observations. *Offa* (1984) 41:63–75.

Clarke, H., and B. Ambrosiani. *Towns in the Viking Age.* London: Leicester University Press, 1991.

Fehring, G. *The Archaeology of Medieval Germany: An Introduction.* London: Routledge, 1991.

Frandsen, L., and S. Jensen. Pre-Viking and Early Viking Age Ribe. *Journal of Danish Archaeology* (1987) 6: DL121.J68rm.

Grandell, A. Kredithandel med tillhjälp av karvstock (Credit Transactions with the Aid of the Tally Stick). *Fornvännen* (1986) 81:121–128.

Hedeager, L. Empire, Frontier, and the Barbarian Hinterland: Rome and Northern Europe from A.D. 1–400. In *Centre and Periphery in the Ancient World.* Ed. M. Rowlands and K. Kristiansen. Cambridge: Cambridge University Press, 1987, pp. 125–140.

———. Money Economy and Prestige Economy in the Roman Iron Age. In *Trade and Exchange in Prehistory.* Ed. B. Hårdh. Lund: Acta Archaeologica Lundensia, 1988, pp. 147–153.

Hodges, R. *Dark Age Economics: The Origins of Towns and Trade, A.D. 600–1000.* London: Duckworth, 1982.

———. Emporia, Monasteries, and the Economic Foundation of Medieval Europe. In *Medieval Archaeology.* Ed. C. Redman. Binghamton: Medieval and Renaissance Texts and Studies, 1989, pp. 57–72.

Hodges, R., and D. Whitehouse. *Mohammed, Charlemagne, and the Origins of Europe: Archaeology and the Pirenne Thesis.* London: Duckworth, 1983.

Ohlsson, T. The Löddeköpinge Investigation I: The Settlement at Vikshogsvägen. *Meddelanden från Lunds Universitets Historiska Museum 1975–76* (1976) (1):59–161.

———. The Löddeköpinge Investigation II: The Northern Part of the Village Area. *Meddelanden från Lunds Universitets Historiska Museum 1979–80* (1980) 5:68–111.

Randsborg, K. The Town, the Power, and the Land: Denmark and Europe during the First Millennium A.D. In *Centre and Periphery: The World Archaeological Conference at Southampton.* Ed. T. Champion. London: Unwin Hyman, 1989, pp. 207–223.

———. *The First Millennium A.D. in Europe and the Mediterranean.* Cambridge: Cambridge University Press, 1991.

Sawyer, P. Early Fairs and Markets in England and Scandinavia. In *The Market in History.* Ed. B.L. Anderson and A.J.H. Latham. Dover: Croom-Helm, 1986, pp. 59–77.

Schietzel, K. Haithabu: A Study on the Development of Early Urban Settlement in Northern Europe. In *Comparative History of Urban Development in Non-Roman Europe.* Ed. H.B. Clarke and A. Simms. BAR International Series 255. Oxford: British Archaeological Reports, 1985, pp. 147–181.

Thompson, M.W. *Novgorod the Great.* London: Evelyn, Adams, and Mackay, 1967.

Tina Thurston

SEE ALSO
Birka; Emporia; Haithabu; Ipswich; Lübeck; Novgorod; Quentovic

Material Culture as an Archaeological Concept

The systematic division of culture into its components has matured progressively. Anthropologists, preoccupied mostly with dealing with cultures substantively, initially dealt with it in an *ad hoc* manner. A. Weber in 1912 appears to have been the first to have made the dichotomy ("material"—"spiritual") and to have expanded it to a trichotomy in 1920 (civilizational process—social process—cultural movement) in the present specific sense. This three-fold segmentation of culture, despite considerable differences in the terms used, has been shared by several authors, both anthropologists and archaeologists. This classification has had a wide usage in research practice. The distinctive qualities of the main

M

categories of this segmentation of culture ("Reality culture"—"Social culture"—"Value culture") are most adequately presented by A.L. Kroeber.

In historiography, K. Lamprecht in 1885 appears to have been among the first to apply the notion and method of "material culture" in his studies on economic life in medieval Germany. In France a similar material concept—but in the larger context of the civilizational process—was, from its origin, one of the postulates of the so-called school of synthesis of H. Berr. The continuation and development of this approach is due to the program of structural history, originated by L. Febvre and M. Bloch and their *Annales* school.

A belief that the material conditions of social existence should be studied was connected in European archaeology and historiography with a concept of science, oriented first of all towards explanation and not only towards describing historical reality. This was a vision of a global history, although investigated primarily from the perspective of economic history, which was in harmony with the theoretical conviction of the basic importance of economic factors in history. A concrete manifestation of this trend was the creation of multidisciplinary Institutes of Material Culture (in 1919 in the USSR and 1953–1954 in Poland) within their respective Academies of Sciences.

In the 1960s the significant scientific trends in archaeology lean towards a concept of material culture and show tendencies to develop scientific methods connected with the analysis of this culture. In the 1960s and 1970s research on material culture, considered as an integral element of *la nouvelle histoire*, has been considerably enlivened, undoubtedly under the influence of joint Polish-French research on medieval archaeology, and draws directly on Polish and Soviet experience. In Italy, the impact of these experiences is still evident. In Austria in Krems there is an "Institut für Realienkunde des Mittelalters und der Frühen Neuzeit." A telling example of this trend is the unprecedented development of the so-called new archaeology in the United States and particularly of the "analytical archaeology" in Great Britain which focuses interest on the construction of a general model for archaeological entities—components of a sociocultural system as a unitary whole.

Material culture is ordered here as a structured hierarchy of systems from the lowest level (attribute and artifact) to more complex ones such as artifact and type, assemblage and culture, culture and culture group, culture group and technocomplex. These entities which are defined on the basis of numerical taxonomy show regularities in syntactic interrelations between various levels of this hierarchy. Clarke's (1968) model, however, indicates the theoretical possibilities in the realm of analysis of the "fossil" record rather than the current practice of the archaeologist's craft.

Thus the notion of material culture and its interpretation, in a developed and critical form, constitute the basic concepts in the building of archaeological theories about the social past. There are different views of material culture that have been set out in current theory. There are first of all Childe's two axioms. First, that artifacts (implements, tools, facilities) reflect the economic and social conditions that produce them and that we can, therefore, learn about these conditions from the artifacts. Second, he pointed out that we should treat artifacts as concrete expressions and embodiments of human thoughts and ideas, albeit, our cognitive abilities, beyond the realm of technical knowledge, are still greatly limited.

The basic premise of the New Archaeology is that the patterning of material culture reflects human behavior albeit modified by postdepositional processes. Conceived correctly, this "fossil" record could constitute, as Binford (1962) stresses, a base for a critical reading of that pattern as a "systematic and understandable picture of the total extinct cultural system."

The discovery of the material dimensions of culture is undoubtedly related to archaeological finds. Modern archaeology is able to recover and, eventually, more precisely to date these objective correlates of human behavior. This allows a broadening of observations of contemporary (primitive and complex) societies on a previously unimaginable diachronic scale. In particular it allows the creation of an empirical basis for the examination of history as a process joining within itself a multiplicity of times: from the rapidly changing superficial level of events, through conjunctional cycles, to underlying long-term trends. History, as well demonstrated in the work of F. Braudel, becomes a science selecting the long time as a natural framework for understanding the past. Access to the really significant information potentially contained in the archaeological materials is, however, often particularly difficult.

As argued by the post-processualists, material culture has a meaningful context, so that its creation, use, and deposition must be analyzed as having symbolic significance. Hodder (1986) wrote "Material culture does not just exist. It is made by someone. It is produced to do something. Therefore it does not passively reflect society—rather, it creates society through the actions of individuals." For this reason it must be seen as an active agent affecting actions, behavior, and culture. "Individuals and societies construct their own social reality, and material culture has an integral place within that construction" (Renfrew and Bahn 1991).

The perception of the meaningful content of "material culture" makes possible a better recognition of the mutual relations always unifying human behavior and material culture in one system, a system in which the role of internal social conflicts is a matter to be more fully considered and in analysis of which a purely positivist approach can no longer dominate. This has led to the current emphasis on the cognitive anthropology and archaeology, seeking a reconstruction of the grammar of culture, i.e., the patterns of thinking of members of a particular group. This permits us to enter more deeply into the meaning of things constituting the material equipment of a culture. It seems that research on contemporary living societies (ethnoarchaeology) and literate ones (classical and post-classical archaeology) constitutes a particularly promising field of analysis. These are the domains of study in which the excavated material can be confronted with sources of another type and in which a critical moment of passage from our conceptual categories, i.e. the "etic" approach, to their conceptual categories, i.e. the "emic" approach, seems to be possible.

It follows that archaeological material cannot be treated exclusively as a specific type of fossil. The alternative to the "palaeontological" treatment becomes the "textual" model. This model treats the excavated evidence as "meaningfully constituted," and thus in its structure comparable in many ways to texts. This allows the use in all investigations of "material culture," methods of analysis similar to those employed in linguistics.

To what extent can these various approaches used to define and to conceive material culture explain problems such as the dilemma posed, for example, by dichotomies: social norms-individual behavior; mental reality-material reality; subject-object? It seems that none of these approaches, although perfectly appropriate in specific cases, entirely captures the complexity implied in the notion of "material culture." It now seems that the formulation of "laws of culture processes" as universal laws like those of physics may not necessarily be the only fruitful path toward explanation in archaeology. The *consensus ommium* does not exist. The various approaches can therefore operate simultaneously as fruitful research strategies.

FURTHER READINGS

Binford, L.R. Archaeology as Anthropology. *American Antiquity* (1962): 28:217–225.

Bloch, M. *The Historian's Craft.* Manchester: Manchester University Press, 1954.

Carandini, A. *Archeologia e cultura materiale. De "lavori senza gloria" nell'antichita a una politica dei beni culturali.* Bari: De Donato editore, 1975.

Childe, V.G. *Progress and Archaeology.* London: Watts, 1944.

———. *Society and Knowledge: The Growth of Human Tradition.* New York: Harper, 1956.

Clarke, D.L. *Analytical Archaeology.* London: Methuen, 1968.

Hensel, W., and S. Tabaczyński. The Institute of the History of Material Culture of the Polish Academy of Sciences. Achievements of the last thirty years. *Acta Academiae Scientiarum Polonae* (1983) 3–4:129–159.

Hodder, I. *Symbols in action: Ethnoarchaeological studies of material culture.* Cambridge: Cambridge University Press, 1982.

———. *Reading the Past.* Cambridge: Cambridge University Press, 1986.

Hodder, I., ed. *The Meaning of Things. Material Culture and Symbolic Expression.* London: Unwin Hyman, 1989.

Hodder, I., Shanks, M., Alexandri, A., Buchli, V., Carman, J., Last, J. and G. Lucas. *Interpreting Archaeology. Finding Meaning in the Past.* London and New York: Routledge, 1995.

Kluckhohn, C., and A.L. Kroeber. Culture. A Critical Review of Concepts and Definitions. *Papers of Peabody Museum of American Archaeology and Ethnology* (1952) 47 (1).

Kroeber, A.L. *The Nature of Culture.* Chicago: University of Chicago Press, 1952.

Patrik, L.E. Is there an archaeological record? In *Advances in Archaeological Method and Theory,* vol. 8. Ed. M.B. Schiffer. New York: Academic Press, 1985, pp. 27–62.

Pesez, J.-M. Histoire de la culture matérielle. In *La nouvelle histoire.* Ed. J. Le Goff, R. Chartier, and J. Revel. Paris: Retz-C.E.P.L., 1978, pp. 98–130.

McGuire, R.H. *A Marxist Archaeology.* San Diego and New York: Academic, 1992.

Renfrew, C., and P. Bahn. *Archaeology. Theories. Methods and Practice.* London: Thames and Hudson, 1991.

Shanks, M., and C. Tilley. *Reconstructing Archaeology.* Cambridge, Mass.: Harvard University Press, 1987.

M

Tilley, C., ed. *Reading Material Culture: Structuralism, Hermeneutics and Post-Structuralism.* Oxford: Basil Blackwell, 1990.

Trigger, B.G. *A History of Archaeological Thought.* Cambridge: Cambridge University Press, 1989.

Stanisław Tabaczyński

Medieval Place Names
See Place Names.

Merovingian Archaeology
See France.

Messuage

The term *messuage* reached the English language from Norman French in the post-Conquest period. It derives from the Latin term *mansa* and often occurs in Latin texts (e.g., as *mesura* or *mesuagium*). Its basic meaning is "a dwelling house," but it was regularly used for both the residence itself and the entire dwelling plot, and it is in the latter sense that it is normally used in a modern archaeological context. When applied to a peasant farmstead, the term *messuage* is, therefore, directly equivalent to *toft*.

These terms do on occasion, however, convey slightly different connotations. The term *toft* is generally used exclusively in modern parlance to refer to the space directly associated with a peasant farmstead, whether in a village or as part of a dispersed settlement pattern. While it is often used in this same context, *messuage* is also used for settlement enclosures of higher status and particularly for manorial complexes and moated sites. This corresponds to the commonplace occurrence of the term in late medieval documents such as *Inquests Post Mortem* and wills, wherein it often refers to the "capital messuage" (in Latin, *mensuagium capitale* or similar). In brief, *messuage* has a wider range of applications than *toft*, although the two do overlap to a marked extent and are often synonymous. The use of medieval French and Middle English by different sectors of medieval society in Britain has influenced the context in which these very similar terms have been deployed in the postmedieval period.

N.J. Higham

SEE ALSO

Toft

Mills and Milling Technology

In its essentials, the milling process entailed the reduction of cereal grains to either flour or meal by the rubbing and shearing action of stones. By the Medieval period, this process was increasingly, but by no means exclusively, being effected by water-powered mills. During the early Medieval period, simple rotary querns (from O.E. *cweorn*, O.H.G. *quirn*), which consisted of two small-diameter disc-shaped stones with a central pivot and a wooden crank handle, were a common household item. They have frequently turned up on early medieval English and Irish settlement sites. In England, querns of imported lava from the Mayern-Niedermendig area of Germany are relatively common on middle to late Saxon sites. During the Medieval period, the simple rotary quern underwent an important technical change that enabled the distance between the rotating upper and stationary lower stone to be more easily regulated. By extending the axle through the base of the lower stone and allowing it to pivot on an adjustable beam, it became possible to exert greater control over the distance between the stones (a process called *tentering*), a factor that directly affected the coarseness of the flour or meal. More recent finds from a Russian settlement site of the late twelfth–early thirteenth century and Hungarian rotary querns of the eleventh–thirteenth centuries indicate that tentering beams were used and that querns of this type were often driven from the rim, by means of a rope girding the rim of the upper millstone.

Two basic types of water-powered mill were used in medieval Europe and in the contemporary Islamic world. The first of these mills employed a horizontal waterwheel set on a vertical axle, in which one revolution of the waterwheel produced a corresponding revolution of the upper millstone (Fig. 1). In the second type of watermill, the motion of a waterwheel set on a horizontal axle was communicated to a pair of millstones via wooden gearwheels set at right angles to each other (Fig. 2). The latter variety of watermill, the *vertical mill*, had effectively replaced the horizontal-wheeled (sometimes called the *Norse mill*) variety in most of central and northern Europe by the end of the Medieval period. A large number of early medieval horizontal-wheeled mill sites have come to light in Ireland, many of which have been dated by dendrochronology to the seventh–eleventh centuries A.D. The huge corpus of Irish mill components includes almost complete mill buildings, the earliest-known examples of horizontal waterwheels; the wooden water-feeder chutes, or penstocks, associated with them; and tentering beams for adjusting the millstones. In England, a well-preserved Saxon site, dated by dendrochronology to the ninth century, has been excavated at Tamworth, Staffordshire, while at Earl's Bu in the Orkney Islands the remains of a Viking Age example have come to light. A Saxo-Norman example has been excavated at Raunds in Northhamptonshire, and a slightly later example at Old Windor in Berkshire. In Denmark, remains of wooden structures at Omgard (c. A.D. 800), Ljorring (c. A.D. 960), and Borup Ris (eleventh century) have been interpreted as those of horizontal-wheeled mills.

Vertical-wheeled mills dating to the seventh century have been investigated at Little Island, County Cork, in Ireland and at Old Windsor in Berkshire, England. At Little Island, a double horizontal-wheeled mill (see Fig. 1)

and a vertical-wheeled mill (see Fig. 2) operated side by side, the earliest-known close association of both types of mill in medieval Europe. As in the case of the majority of the excavated horizontal-wheeled mills, most of the medieval vertical-wheeled mills that have come to light in Europe had substantial wooden foundations. The foundations of the mill at Castle Donnington in Leicestershire, England, and of a two-phase (thirteenth- and fourteenth-century) mill at Patrick Street, Dublin, Ireland, for example, were constructed with large wooden beams. However, while early medieval horizontal waterwheels have been excavated in Ireland, only a small number of vertical waterwheels associated with grain mills have thus far been excavated. The remains of a waterwheel

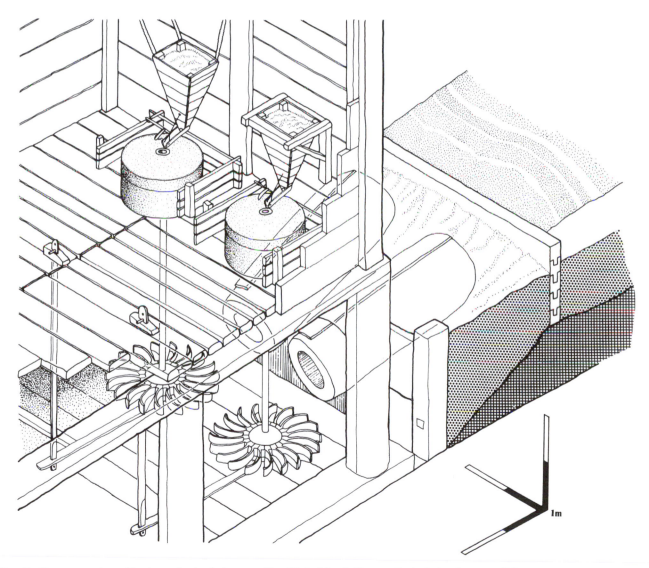

FIG. 1. Reconstruction of horizontal-wheeled watermill at Little Island, County Cork, Ireland, c. A.D. 630.

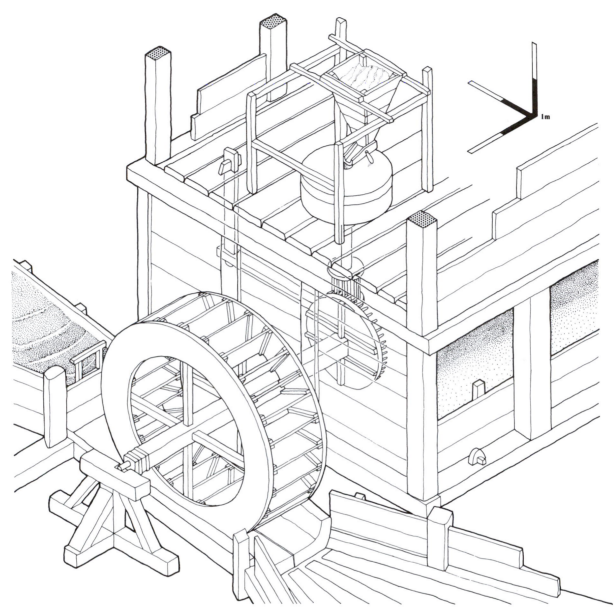

FIG. 2. Reconstruction of vertical-wheeled watermill at Little Island, County Cork, Ireland, c. A.D. 630.

4 m in diameter were found at the site of a medieval mill at Ahrensfeld near Hamburg, Germany. Contemporary examples of waterwheels, used to power other industrial processes such as ironworking, have proved to be smaller. The waterwheel at Chingley forge, Kent (c. A.D. 1300–1350), for example, was 2.47 m in diameter, while that at Batsford, Kent, was 2.6 m in diameter.

It is generally believed that the first geared windmills were developed in southeastern England, the earliest recorded examples of which were at work by the 1180s.

By the 1190s, windmills were in existence in France. For the most part, however, windmills were essentially a supplement to water-powered mills. The early English examples were *post mills,* which consisted of a wooden framework supporting the wind sails and the mill machinery. The mill framework pivoted upon a large main post, which enabled the entire framework to be turned, when necessary, to suit changes in the direction of the wind. A pair of cross beams set into a specially prepared *mill mound* provided support for the main post, and it is often the mound that remains on high ground when all other traces of the windmill have gone. In some cases, the cross beams appear as crop marks on aerial photographs (e.g., Shelford, Nottinghamshire), although a number of mounds have been excavated (e.g., Bridlington, Yorkshire, c. A.D. 1500), and the cross beams of one example at Linford in Buckinghamshire have yielded a radiocarbon (C-14) date of A.D. 1220±80.

FURTHER READINGS

Crossley, David. *Post-Medieval Archaeology in Britain.* London: Leicester University Press, 1990.

Holt, Richard. *The Mills of Medieval England.* Oxford: Basil Blackwell, 1988.

Rahtz, Philip, and Robert Meeson. *An Anglo-Saxon Watermill at Tamworth.* London: Council for British Archaeology, 1992.

Reynolds, Terry S. *Stronger Than a Hundred Men: A History of the Vertical Waterwheel.* Baltimore: Johns Hopkins University Press, 1983.

Rynne, Colin. The Introduction of the Vertical Watermill into Ireland: Some Recent Archaeological Evidence. *Medieval Archaeology* (1989) 33:21–31.

Selmeczi Kovaks, Attila. Querns Historical Layers: Technical Regression. *Ethnologia Europaea* (1990) 20:35–46.

Colin Rynne

SEE ALSO
Raunds

Mont Dardon

Mont Dardon (Commune of Uxeau, Department of Saône-et-Loire, France) was a locus for Neolithic and Bronze Age activity and the site of an Iron Age hillfort; in the later Iron Age (La Tène), its summit was sacred to the Celtic goddess of horses, Epona. During the Gallo-Roman period (first to the fourth centuries), sacred observance on Dardon's summit also included the Roman god of commerce, Mercury.

From the late Gallo-Roman period until the seventh century, sparse archaeological remains on Mont Dardon suggest a period of temporary abandonment. After this period of disuse, significant activity took place once again on the mountain in the following medieval phases.

During the phase of Christian expansion begun in the seventh century, venues perceived as being apart from the evils of the world were sought; rural, remote, and abandoned areas were optimal locations for religious shrines, chapels, and monastic establishments. Mont Dardon meets all three of these criteria for sites of medieval Christian buildings.

The site of Mont Dardon also lies at the point where the boundaries from three communes come together (Issy l'Evêque, Ste. Radegonde, and Uxeau). Medieval chapels were often situated at such politically neutral boundaries, which connoted the older Celtic idea of otherworldliness at border and in-between places. It was additionally a common practice to locate Christian edifices on the sites of earlier "pagan" shrines. The association of Dardon with the Celtic goddess Epona and a Gallo-Roman fanum qualify Mont Dardon in this regard.

Sometime in the seventh century, a cemetery was begun in the area of the citadel, as evidenced by fragments of monolithic sandstone sarcophagi, ceramics, a bronze clasp, and a ring. This activity continued until the ninth century (c. A.D. 850), when a small rectangular building—dated by ceramics found in a construction trench—was erected in the citadel area. The building could not be fully excavated and is thus not securely identified, but it may be a Carolingian Era chapel or some other type of religious edifice (a shrine or anchorite's abode) connected with the cemetery.

This building shares its south wall with a single-naved stone chapel that includes an altar, circular apse, and tower; it is radiocarbon (C-14) dated to A.D. 950–1050. It could not be determined whether the earlier building continued in use as an annex to the chapel or was destroyed at the time of the chapel's construction. Both buildings are constructed of unworked granite fieldstones, set in clay for the earlier building and in yellowish mortar for the chapel. The chapel was plastered inside and out. From the lack of roof tiles, both buildings apparently had timber-and-thatch roofs. Layers of carbon suggest burning episodes for both buildings.

At the end of the tenth century or the beginning of the eleventh century, a third structure was built at the northeast edge of the summit and was connected to the chapel by a curtain wall. Also at this time, a cemetery was created on the southeastern apse-end of the church, consisting of two rows of fetus and infant burials. A twelve-to-fifteen-year-old female was buried under the floor of the two-story tower located at the opposite end of the chapel from the apse. Remains of three other children ranging in age from three to seven years were found around the chapel, as well as fragmentary remains of other infant burials. In the eleventh century, the chapel fell into disuse and its

M

tower began service as a dwelling, as evidenced by the domestic refuse found on its floor. In the twelfth century, the citadel of Mont Dardon was fortified by earthworks and a bank-and-ditch system.

There has been no established chronological sequence of medieval pottery for the Arroux Valley, and comparisons have had to be made with surrounding regions. The ceramics point to attenuated trade and a reliance on local production. The sparse remains of green-glazed wares and gray common wares indicate limited use of the citadel area from the twelfth to the fifteenth centuries, after which habitation of the site was abandoned.

Specific historical references to the chapel have not been found. The exact ownership of the chapel and its relationship to the contemporaneous priory in the nearby village of Uxeau, as well as the ownership of the area when the later domestic habitation took place, are not known. Preliminary investigations point to one or another of the monastic establishments in the important medieval city of Autun, 40 km to the north-northeast, as having authority over the site.

FURTHER READINGS

Berry, Walter E., and Carole L. Crumley. Rapport annuel: Les fouilles du Mont Dardon (Saône-et-Loire), 1979. *Echos du passé* (1980) 43:1–26.

Berry, Walter E., Paul R. Green, and V. Ann Tippitt. Archaeological Investigations at Mont Dardon. In *Regional Dynamics: Burgundian Landscapes in Historical Perspective*. Ed. Carole L. Crumley and William H. Marquardt. San Diego: Academic, 1987, pp. 41–119.

Crumley, Carole L. Les fouilles du Mont Dardon, 1976. *La physiophile* (1977) 86:93–102.

———. Archaeological Reconnaissance at Mont Dardon, France. *Archaeology* (1983) 36(3):14–17, 20.

———. A Diachronic Model for Settlement and Land Use in Southern Burgundy. In *Archaeological Approaches to Medieval Europe*. Ed. K. Biddick. Kalamazoo: Medieval Institute, 1984, pp. 239–243.

———. *Le Mont Dardon: Lieu de culte, de l'age du fer au moyen âge*. Bourgogne Archéologique 13. Dijon: Les Amis du Dardon, le Ministère de la Culture (DRAC-Bourgogne), et le Conseil Général de Saône-et-Loire, 1993.

Crumley, Carole L., and Walter E. Berry. Les fouilles du Mont Dardon, 1977: Rapport annuel. *Echos du passé* (1978) 39:13–32.

———. Les fouilles du Mont Dardon, 1978: Rapport annuel. *Echos du passé* (1979) 41:17–40.

Crumley, Carole L., and William H. Marquardt, eds. *Regional Dynamics: Burgundian Landscapes in Historical Perspective*. San Diego: Academic, 1987.

Elizabeth A. Jones and Carole L. Crumley

SEE ALSO
France

Mucking

The English site of Mucking in southeast Essex provided the first opportunity to excavate an Anglo-Saxon settlement and its burials together. The site includes the most extensive and one of the earliest settlements and cemeteries found in England so far. It is most well known, however, as the site of a possible settlement of Germanic mercenaries, stationed in the early fifth century to guard the Thames against invasion, although this interpretation has come under attack in recent years.

Rescue excavations on the gravel terrace of the Thames at Mucking were carried out from 1965 until 1978. Although there was agricultural use of the land until the 1960s, the 18 ha that were investigated revealed a multiperiod landscape that may have lasted from the Paleolithic until the Anglo-Saxon period.

The settlement consisted of at least 53 posthole buildings and 203 *Grubenhäuser* (sunken-featured buildings) (Hamerow 1993). Metalwork, glass, imported pottery, certain types of Anglo-Saxon pottery, and coins indicate that the settlement was occupied from the first half of the fifth century until at least c. 685, and probably into the eighth century.

It appears that the proportion of grass-tempered pottery increased in the sixth and seventh centuries, while by the seventh century, less pottery, and decorated pottery in particular, was produced.

Nearly all the *Grubenhäuser* are of the two-post type, with the majority laid out according to the two-square module: the areas to either side of the central doors consist of two approximately equal quadrangles. No sequence of types could be found apart from the late date for the largest huts. There was little evidence of plank construction, wattle and daub, or true occupation levels. The sunken hollows appear to have been the floor level. A few hearths and pits, plus workshop debris, were found.

The settlement, which appears to have been a hamlet, shifted through time, as did several similar settlements on the Continent. Such settlement mobility may have been widespread in early and middle Saxon England. The initial phase of settlement was quite dense. In the sixth century, the main focus shifted northward; this second phase consisted of fewer buildings, and occupation may have been briefer and more dispersed. During the third phase, the settlement shifted to the northeast and was relatively dense, with some deliberate alignment of buildings. In the seventh century, the settlement shifted away from the edge of the terrace and consisted of widely dispersed farmsteads.

There was an absence of well-defined properties or boundaries or much planned layout. There are no large or central buildings. The population appears to have been about a hundred, with a minimum of ten posthole buildings and fourteen *Grubenhäuser* standing at any one time.

There are two cemeteries that lie c. 150 m apart (Hirst and Clark, forthcoming). A relative chronology will be established using computer seriation based on the association of artifact types within each grave and the similarity of the graves to each other on these grounds.

There are some similarities between the cemeteries. Both contain objects that date from the first half of the fifth century to the seventh century. In both cemeteries, the earliest graves, at least the most obvious ones, were weapon burials (Evison 1981).

Unfortunately, there is little bone evidence, although body position can be deduced by stains. Poor bone preservation precludes detailed demographic inferences, and independent associations of specific artifact types with particular age classes or sexes cannot often be made. Nevertheless, both cemeteries appear to have consisted of family groups. Both indicate a degree of wealth and social hierarchy. Part of the value of the cemeteries lies in the well-preserved organic stains, particularly structural features, consisting of such items as coffins, pillows, and biers.

There are, however, a number of dissimilarities between the two cemeteries. Cemetery I is incomplete due to gravel quarrying and consists of at least sixty-three graves. Its original extent is hard to define, but it must have been smaller than Cemetery II. Cemetery II is complete and consists of at least 275 graves. In Cemetery I, nearly all the graves are oriented with the head to the southwest, with very little intercutting. In Cemetery II, the orientations are varied, with somewhat more intercutting.

Work remains to be done on the spatial development of the cemeteries. Within Cemetery II, however, the earliest graves, from the first half of the fifth century, appear to have been concentrated at the eastern end of the cemetery. In contrast, the latest graves appear to have been located on the eastern edge of Cemetery I. These graves

are laid out in possible rows, both north-south and east-west. Cemetery I does not appear to have been enclosed, whereas the distribution of the graves in Cemetery II appears to have been influenced by a Roman ditch system. Cemetery II overlaps the settlement slightly, while Cemetery I does not.

Unlike Cemetery I, where only two cremations that cannot be securely dated were found, there are c. 480 cremations in Cemetery II. Indeed, in Cemetery II there were nearly twice as many cremations as inhumations. The cremations had sustained some damage from the clearance of the topsoil. They both cut and were cut by the graves. It is difficult to date them precisely as few datable artifacts are found, but these suggest fifth- and sixth-century cremations. To date the cremations more closely, the distribution and correlation of artifact types, the bone evidence, and ceramic data (including the types of fabric, stamps, and other decoration, as well as general vessel groups based on overall similarity) will be examined.

Some comparisons between the settlement and the cemeteries can be made. The stamp-decorated ceramics from the cemetery are, on the whole, similar to those found on the settlement. In a few cases, identical dies were used. The pottery stamps from the settlement appear to have their closest parallels to the west, north, and south, linked by the Thames.

Analysis of the pottery has also shown that the fabric groups, which appear to be locally made, in both the settlement and the cemeteries are also similar, but the proportion of forms is not. In the cemetery, there is a far higher proportion of highly decorated vessels. Faceted carinated bowls are almost entirely restricted to the settlement, while a narrower range of shapes consisting almost exclusively of jars, and bossed jars in particular, is found in the cemeteries.

There is an overlap of artifact types between the settlement and the cemeteries. Tools, however, are rarely found in the cemeteries, and the graves have produced many decorative or costume artifacts and weapons that have not been found in the settlement.

The question of continuity from the Roman to the Anglo-Saxon period is problematic. Although there is clear evidence for continuity of land use, there was no phase of overlap or integration between the Romano-British and Anglo-Saxon communities. In the early post-Roman period at least, some of the surviving earthworks continued to serve as boundaries, although Roman ditches, such as the one that partly delimited the extent of Cemetery II, were now silted up. By the sixth century, it is clear

M

that there were links to Saxon, Anglian, and Kentish areas, reflected primarily in the costume.

The field patterns have been examined by Chris Going (1993:22). A field system was established, probably in the middle Anglo-Saxon period, and the settlement density diminished greatly. The site reverted principally to agricultural use. A new Saxon-Norman or later field system evolved and seems to have lasted into the nineteenth century. The main medieval feature appears to have been a windmill erected in the twelfth–thirteenth centuries that was dismantled in the fifteenth–sixteenth centuries.

FURTHER READINGS

Evison, V.I. Distribution Maps and England in the First Two Phases. In *Angles, Saxons, and Jutes: Essays Presented to J.N.L. Myres.* Ed. V.I. Evison. Oxford: Clarendon, 1981, pp. 126–167.

Going, C. Middle Saxon, Medieval, and Later. In *Excavations at Mucking.* Vol. 1: *The Site Atlas.* By Anne Clark. London: English Heritage/20 British Museum Press, 1993, p. 23.

Hamerow, H. *Excavations at Mucking.* Vol. 2: *The Anglo-Saxon Settlement.* London: English Heritage/British Museum Press, 1993.

Hirst, S., and D. Clark. *Excavations at Mucking.* Vol. 3: *The Anglo-Saxon Cemeteries.* London: English Heritage/British Museum Press, forthcoming.

Dido Clark

SEE ALSO
West Stow

N

Nautical Archaeology in the Mediterranean

The Medieval period saw important developments in the construction and design of ships, maritime commerce, and naval warfare in the Mediterranean. A traditional *shell-first* method of hull construction, in which frames (ribs) were added to an already erected shell of hull planking edge-joined together by mortise-and-tenon joints that were the principal source of hull strength, evolved into a *frame-first* method, less wasteful in labor and wood, in which hull planking was fastened to already erected frames, now the principal source of strength. The new method, requiring the application of precise measurements and geometry to achieve desired hull shape, brought into being the science of naval architecture. The lateen sail, affording a marginal increase in mobility, was preferred over the square sail in a now less tranquil sea. Attempts to combine the speed of the rowed warship with the capacity of the sailed merchantship led to the great merchant galleys that, toward the end of the period, linked the Mediterranean, Black Sea, Atlantic, and North Sea with fast, reliable service. In the fourteenth century, the introduction of the northern European stern rudder and the innovation of using square and lateen sails together on the same ship made possible larger sailing ships that better accommodated an increasing volume of trade. In naval warfare, the Greco-Roman objective of sinking enemy ships with a waterline ram gave way to that of effectively concentrating missile and incendiary firepower preparatory to boarding and capture by heavily armed marines; naval tactics changed little with the subsequent introduction of cannon.

Unfortunately, we have few details about these and other developments dating earlier than c. A.D. 1200: just a few instructive ship representations, none of warships, some Byzantine naval manuals and sea laws, and some surviving papers of Jewish merchants living in Egypt in the eleventh–thirteenth centuries. After 1200, ship representations (including warships) become quite numerous, naval warfare accounts more detailed, and texts on economic matters far more abundant. Mid-thirteenth-century contracts for the building and leasing of ships at Genoa and Venice for Saint Louis's Crusades and the *Fabrica di galere,* a 1410 Venetian shipbuilding treatise, have yielded, and continue to yield, much information on the design and construction, rigging, and equipment of major ship types but leave many fundamental questions unanswered.

To date, the contribution of shipwreck archaeology has been modest, since adequately published excavations have been few and far between. The first medieval-shipwreck excavation in the Mediterranean was conducted in the years 1961–1964 at Yassī Ada, Turkey. The ship, which sank in or shortly after 626, was Byzantine, quite possibly a church-owned vessel that had a priest-captain and was carrying c. 800 amphoras of wine that may have been collected as taxes in kind. It had a galley with a tile roof and a tile firebox with iron grill (the first well-documented examples of such structures) equipped to prepare food for a large number of people. The hull was built in the shell-first manner up to the waterline, but the mortise-and-tenon joints were extremely small and widely spaced; hull strength resided primarily in the framing. The hull was built frame first above the waterline. These and other economical construction features made the ship more affordable than a comparable Roman vessel had been.

Hull remnants excavated in a marsh at Pantano Longarini in southeastern Sicily in 1965 were thought to have

N

belonged to a large Byzantine merchantship of over 300 tons capacity. A new, unpublished reconstruction demonstrates, however, that the vessel had been an otherwise unknown type of lighter for off-loading heavy cargo.

Off the nearby port of Marzamemi, also in the 1960s, prefabricated marble architectural elements for a church were recovered from a Byzantine wreck of the mid-sixth century. These marbles were a product of the Emperor Justinian's effort to promote religious unity in the Empire through a standardization of church architecture.

Between the late 1960s and the mid-1970s, three tenth-century wrecks were partly excavated on the southern coast of France at Agay, Bataiguier, and Rocher de l'Estéou. All three ships had cargoes of millstones and Islamic pottery from western North Africa or Spain that included oil lamps, pitchers, jugs, and large storage jars with capacities of up to 1,000 l. The Agay and Bataiguier ships also carried copper vessels, and the Agay ship, at least 250 bronze ingots. The Agay ship's hull remnants were examined underwater. The hull's bottom was flat, and no mortise-and-tenon joints were detected in the planking. It is assumed, but not certain, that the ships were Islamic. Probably sailing westward toward Italy, they represent a commerce otherwise unknown.

From 1977 to 1979, the wreck of a Byzantine ship of c. 30-ton capacity was excavated at Serçe Limanī on the southern Turkish coast. The ship had sunk c. 1025 while carrying from Moslem Syria toward Constantinople diverse, often small cargoes (cargo diversity protected profits in a period of increasing free trade), including glass cullet and glassware; small lots of Islamic glazed, fine, and coarse ware; wine in reused Byzantine amphoras; raisins; and sumac. Several hundred glass vessels restored from two-thirds of a ton of broken glassware cullet constitute an unusually comprehensive collection of medieval Islamic glassware that reveals for the first time the Syrian regional glassware style. Both the glassware and the pottery from this well-dated wreck have caused chronological revisions for medieval Islamic glassware and glazed wares. Almost ninety piriform Byzantine amphoras with more than two dozen distinct, precise-capacity sizes shed considerable light on Byzantine wine capacity systems and marketing. There were no mortise-and-tenon joints in the hull's planking; substantial framing had been erected before planking was begun. The builder employed precise measurements and elementary mathematical progressions to obtain simple hull lines, a flat bottom, straight sides, and a boxlike hold that maximized capacity.

Since the 1980s, excavations have been carried out on the wreck of a merchant galley that sank at Cala Culip on the Spanish Costa Brava in the second half of the fourteenth century. The vessel was carrying cargoes of pottery from Granada, meat, nuts, and fruit. Ship's pottery from Languedoc suggests that the galley was heading for the southern coast of France. The flat-bottomed hull was built frame first, and an identifying Roman numeral and several score lines on each frame give valuable insights into how the desired hull shape was achieved.

Interest in medieval wrecks has much increased during the 1990s with new excavations in Israel, Syria, Turkey, Italy, and Spain. What we know about medieval seafaring in the Mediterranean may soon be much more comprehensive and detailed.

FURTHER READINGS

Bass, George F., ed. *A History of Seafaring Based on Underwater Archaeology.* London and New York: Thames and Hudson/Walker, 1972.

———. The Shipwreck at Serçe Liman, Turkey. *Archaeology* (1979) 32:6–43.

Bass, George F., and Frederick H. van Doorninck Jr. *Yassī Ada I: A Seventh-Century Byzantine Shipwreck.* College Station: Texas A&M University Press, 1982.

Lewis, Archibald R., and Timothy J. Runyan. *European Naval and Maritime History, 300–1500.* Bloomington: Indiana University Press, 1985.

Parker, A.J. *Ancient Shipwrecks of the Mediterranean and the Roman Provinces.* BAR International Series 580. Oxford: British Archaeological Reports, 1992.

Steffy, J. Richard. *Wooden Ship Building and the Interpretation of Shipwrecks.* College Station: Texas A&M University Press, 1994.

Frederick H. van Doornick Jr.

SEE ALSO
Shipbuilding

Netherlands

Though some medieval sites were investigated by archaeologists at various times since the early nineteenth century, medieval archaeology came into its own in the Netherlands only during the second half of the twentieth century. Some of the possibilities of medieval archaeology first became apparent with the draining of the former Zuiderzee (South Sea, now the Ijselmeer, or Ijsel Lake, northeast of Amsterdam). The new lands thus exposed revealed traces of settlements and hydraulic works largely unknown from written documents. During the 1930s and 1940s, W.C. Braat and P.J.R. Modderman were able to date these traces to the late Middle Ages, based largely on the rapidly expanding knowledge of medieval ceramics in northwestern Europe.

Medieval archaeology received implicit institutional recognition in 1950 with the establishment of the Rijksdienst voor het Oudheidkundig Bodemonderzoek (State Service for Archaeological Investigations, or ROB). From then onward, any restorative work on historical monuments was to be accompanied by excavations designed to uncover and document all historical evidence. Because most historical monuments in the Netherlands date from the late Middle Ages or later, late medieval archaeology became a regular subject of research as churches, castles, and town centers damaged or destroyed during World War II were restored or rebuilt. Additionally, the postwar building boom as well as extensive landscape leveling and reconstruction brought to light much evidence of not only prehistoric but also medieval settlements. In particular, there was a revival of interest in Merovingian cemeteries, which eventually led to the investigation of the settlements to which they belonged.

An institutional focus for medieval archaeology was provided in 1960 with the appointment of H.H. van Regteren Altena to head a new department of town-center archaeology at the Instituut voor Prae- en Protohistorie (IPP) at the University of Amsterdam. With growing numbers of students attracted to this new emphasis, the position held by van Regteren Altena was first converted into a lectureship (1974) and eventually a full professorship (1980) in medieval archaeology. While medieval archaeology was thus developing a distinct institutional identity at the University of Amsterdam, similar developments also took place elsewhere. For example, the Biologisch-Archaeologisch Instituut (BAI) at the University of Groningen and the Archaeological Institute of the Free University of Amsterdam (AIVU), both founded to pursue prehistoric archaeology, began to extend their research focus into the Middle Ages as well. Finally, the Archeologische Werkgemeenschap voor Nederland (Archaeological Working Group for the Netherlands, or AWN) brought together large numbers of amateur archaeologists, who, collectively and as individuals, have made valuable contributions to medieval archaeology in the Netherlands.

Much medieval archaeological research in the Netherlands since World War II has proceeded in two major directions. The first is settlement archaeology, which has been aimed primarily at establishing the continuity of settlement from late Roman or prehistoric times into the early Middle Ages, as well as investigating the settlement systems of the Merovingian and Carolingian periods to which individual settlements belonged. Almost always multidisciplinary in approach and often large in scale, these efforts have gone a long way toward producing a picture of early medieval settlement in the Netherlands that is more concrete and dynamic than could ever be created from documents alone.

The best-known and most important excavation of a medieval settlement site in the Netherlands is the early medieval commercial center of Dorestad. Long known from historical records as a Carolingian emporium, a port of entry into the Frankish Empire with toll and mint privileges, it was only recently that archaeologists could identify Dorestad with a specific site in the central Netherlands, at the place where the Lower Rhine split into the Lek and Kromme Rijn Rivers. Though the earliest excavations at Dorestad were carried out during the mid-nineteenth and early twentieth centuries, the first modern fieldwork began in 1953 and continued especially in the years 1967 to 1977, when large sections of Dorestad were investigated by the ROB. In all, c. 30 ha were laid bare, including much of the old harborfront found under the present Hoogstraat, or High Street. Among the finds were extensive complexes of wooden streets and causeways or wharfs. An adjacent agrarian zone and a cemetery (containing more than two thousand inhumations) have also seen extensive investigation. The variety and richness of finds, much of which remain to be analyzed and published, have verified Dorestad's importance as a Carolingian emporium. The excavation at Dorestad, meanwhile, has become the model for the investigation of other early medieval riverbank settlements at Maastricht, Nijmegen, Medemblik, and Deventer.

Dorestad had close trading connections with the districts inhabited by Frisians during the early Middle Ages, the entire coastal lowland from southwestern Netherlands into and through northwestern Germany. In 1991, the BAI and the IPP began a joint excavation of an early medieval dwelling mound, or *terp* (German *Wierde*) at Wijnaldum, in the province of Friesland, along the north coast of the Netherlands and within the heartland of Frisian settlement. This particular *terp* is believed to have

N

been the residential site of a member of the ruling elite of the early medieval Frisians. The evidence accumulated so far, including large numbers of coins and fine jewelry, supports that belief, though all attempts to associate the finds with a historically attested individual have so far failed.

Other Carolingian sites have been excavated on higher and drier terrain. One of the most important of these was near Kootwijk, c. 35 km northeast of Dorestad in the sandy hills of the Veluwe district. Four campaigns that teamed archaeologists with members of other disciplines were carried out there by the IPP beginning in 1971, and these efforts eventually came to be the core of a larger socioeconomic research project designed to reconstruct what is now referred to as a "nucleated region" during the early Middle Ages. Kootwijk, it became clear, lay on the periphery of a larger hierarchical network of settlements, and much research in the higher-lying south and central portions of the Netherlands since then has been aimed at revealing this network more fully.

A series of continuing excavations begun in 1981 by the IPP and the AIVU makes up a major component of the Kempen Project, a multidisciplinary effort to reconstruct the villa system that existed during the early Middle Ages in the Kempen region, south of Dorestad and Kootwijk, in south-central Netherlands, along the Belgian border. In particular, researchers are seeking to understand how early medieval settlement in the region changed through extended contacts with Frankish core regions to the south. Additional projects aimed at the same period are underway in the southeastern part of the Netherlands, including the eventual total excavation of a presumed villa along the Maas/Meuse River.

One of the most interesting settlements to be investigated so far falls outside the primarily early medieval focus of projects mentioned above. The excavations carried out by the IPP between 1978 and 1982 in Assendelft, c. 15 km northwest of Amsterdam, revealed a village that was fairly typical of new settlements founded during the eleventh and twelfth centuries on formerly uninhabited peat bogs that had to be drained before settlement could take place. Not only were the remnants of individual houses uncovered, but a gradual movement of the village westward over time was detected. The work carried out at Assendelft represents the first large-scale investigation of a reclamation village so typical of the Holland portion of the Netherlands (i.e., the western coastal district) during the High and late Middle Ages.

The second major tack of medieval archaeology within the Netherlands today is a continuing focus on urban archaeology, uncovering the physical remains of former townscapes and documenting the material culture of urbanites. Since the 1960s, fifteen cities and towns in the Netherlands have developed their own departments of archaeology with at least some responsibility for covering the Medieval period. Though most urban excavations have been relatively small in scale and opportunistic in nature, they have greatly increased our knowledge of urban life, especially during the late Middle Ages, by supplementing what can be learned from documents.

Medieval archaeology, despite its relatively recent emergence as a distinct area of research, has compiled an impressive record in the Netherlands. Not only has it been able to provide much information to flesh out and fill in gaps of knowledge, it has, in fact, provided information for times and places for which no documentary record exists.

FURTHER READINGS

Besteman, J.C., J.M. Bos, and H.A. Heidinga, eds. *Medieval Archaeology in the Netherlands: Studies Presented to H.H. van Regteren Altena*. Ed. J.C. Besteman, J.M. Bos, and H.A. Heidinga. University of Amsterdam Instituut voor Prae- en Protohistorie Studies in Prae- en Protohistorie 4. Assen: Van Gorcum, 1990.

———. *Graven naar Friese koningen: De opgravingen in Wijnaldum*. Franeker: Van Wijnen, 1992.

Besteman, J.C., and H. Sarfatij. Bibliographie zur Archäologie des Mittelalters in den Niederlanden 1945 bis 1975. *Zeitschrift für Archäologie des Mittelalters* (1977) 5:163–231.

Brandt, R.W., W. Groenman-van Waateringe, and S.E. van der Leeuw, eds. *Assendelver Polder Papers 1*. University of Amsterdam Instituut voor Prae- en Protohistorie Cingula 10. Amsterdam: IPP, 1987.

Es, W.A. van, and W.J.H. Verwers. *Excavations at Dorestad 1: The Harbour, Hoogstraat I*. Nederlandse Oudheden 9. Amersfoort: ROB, 1980.

Groenman-van Waateringe, W. The Assendelver Polders Project: Integrated Ecological Research. In *Integrating the Subsistence Economy*. Ed. Martin Jones. BAR International Series 181. Oxford: British Archaeological Reports, 1983, pp. 135–161.

Heidinga, H.A. *Medieval Settlement and Economy North of the Lower Rhine: Archaeology and History of Kootwijk and the Veluwe (the Netherlands)*. University of Amsterdam Instituut voor Prae- en Protohistorie Cingula 9. Assen: Van Gorcum, 1987.

Heidinga, H.A., and G.A.M. Offenberg. *Op zoek naar de vijfde eeuw: De Franken tussen Rijn en Maas.* Amsterdam: De Bataafsche Leeuw, 1992.

Smink, E.H. Bibliography of Dutch Medieval and Post-Medieval Archaeology, 1976–1987. In *Medieval Archaeology in the Netherlands: Studies Presented to H.H. van Regteren Altena.* Ed. J.C. Besteman, J.M. Bos, and H.A. Heidinga. University of Amsterdam, Instituut voor Prae- en Protohistorie, Studies in Prae- en Protohistorie 4. Assen: Van Gorcum, 1990, pp. 325–361.

Theuws, F., A. Verhoeven, and H.H. van Regteren Altena. Medieval Settlement at Dommelen: Parts I and II. *Berichten van de Rijksdienst voor het Oudheidkundig Bodemonderzoek* (1988) 38:229–430.

The collections of papers published in the series Rotterdam Papers: A Contribution to Medieval Archaeology are especially important for medieval urban archaeology in the Netherlands.

William H. TeBrake

SEE ALSO
Emporia; Kootwijk

Nidaros
See Trondheim.

Nonnebakken
See Trelleborg Fortresses.

Normandy: Castles and Fortified Residences

In Normandy, castles of the fifth–ninth centuries remain largely unknown. The sparse network of castles was centered primarily on towns fortified during the late Roman Empire (Bayeux, Rouen, etc.) and, to a lesser extent, on the late antique rural *castra* (e.g., Cherbourg) and was completed by several fortifications erected against the Vikings in the ninth century (Pont de l'Arche, Eure). The establishment of the ducal dynasty in 911, followed by its rise, and then its fall in 1204, changed the situation and led to the development of castles associated with individual families. The first dukes depended on the network of earlier fortresses, which they reoccupied (e.g., Cherbourg)

and sometimes strengthened by the addition of strong points (e.g., a keep at Rouen in the last [?] third of the tenth century). The large castles that they created in the tenth and eleventh centuries were of the same kind; they were spacious, irregular enclosures of several hectares, as at Caen (5 ha at c. 1050), or more regularly shaped, as at Fécamp (10 ha in the tenth century, then an ellipse of 2 ha at c. 1000–1025). Keeps are rare, and the quadrangular tower gate continues to form the major part of the fortification. The elements that form the basis of princely architecture are found on the interior: the hall (16×8 m at Caen; 16.5×5.8 m and later 20×5 m at Fécamp), the private apartments, and the chapel. Despite the precocious use of stone for the fortifications and principal buildings (end of the tenth century and beginning of the eleventh century at Fécamp), the layouts remain rather conservative, with the exception of the remarkable keeps. The spread of private castles remained limited until 1030–1035. They were essentially the work of the ducal family who erected them in vulnerable frontier areas (e.g., Ivry keep, Eure, end of the tenth century).

The construction of fortifications increased as a result of the crises of succession that struck the dynasty and provoked waves of seigneurial emancipation. The first crisis (1035–1047) primarily concerned Lower Normandy, and the second (1087–1106) affected Upper Normandy more profoundly. These crises continued into the twelfth century (1035–1151). They led to a flurry of castle building in both stone and wood. Motte-and-bailey castles predominated; they were constructed not only by dukes (e.g., Gaillefontaine, Seine-Maritime), but also by lesser aristocrats. At present, the oldest example known through excavation is Grimbosq (Calvados, c. 1040), the work of the Taisson family. Several ringworks complete the network (Plessis-Grimoult, Calvados, first half of the tenth century; Audrieu, Calvados, twelfth century).

The progressive strengthening of the dukes' authority in the twelfth century had several consequences. The spread of masonry fortifications accelerated; true castles were gradually reserved for the rich. The dukes strengthened the military potential of their fortresses by developing strong points and strengthening the curtain walls within them. Henri I (1106–1035) constructed a series of large square or oblong keeps (such as Arques, Seine-Maritime, 20×20 m; Caen, 27×24 m; Domfront, Orne, 26×22 m; Falaise, Calvados, 26×23 m; and Vire, Calvados, 14×13 m). He improved the defenses of the castles by adding towers to them and by breaking up the surfaces (as

N

seen in the well-defended quadrangular enclosure around the keep at Rouen). Henri II (1133–1189) increased the number of flanking towers constructed along the ramparts (Gisors, Eure; Fécamp) and established the type of geometric castle (Fécamp, 46 × 24 m) with a reduced surface area and numerous towers and projections. This represented a significant development in France from the end of the twelfth and the beginning of the thirteenth centuries onward. The high aristocracy did not fall behind, as seen by the large oblong keep of Chambois (21 × 15 m), the work of a familiar of Henri II. The lower and middle ranks of the aristocracy turned toward semifortified manor houses beginning in the second half of the twelfth century. These small, moated sites served as both seigneurial residences and centers for working the land and possessed only rudimentary defenses. A prototype, dated to 1150–1204, has been excavated at Rubercy (Calvados).

The increasing French military pressure on the frontier from the last third of the twelfth century led to the strengthening and construction of a certain number of princely castles that, like the famous example of Château-Gaillard (Eure), integrated a maximum number of innovations (reduction of the surface area, well-defended curtain walls, breaking up of the defenses, buttressed keep, etc.). The western frontier of the duchy was carefully protected.

The surrender of Normandy to France in 1204 led King Philippe Auguste (1165–1223) to build a number of military constructions to solidify and symbolize his power. At Rouen, he abandoned the ancient ducal fortress to construct a new polygonal castle endowed with a large round tower and placed at an elevation that dominated the city. At Caen, he surrounded the old keep with a curtain wall heavily flanked with towers. At Falaise, Gisors, Lillebonne (Seine-Maritime), and Vernon (Eure), he added a large circular keep in the midst of the older ducal fortresses.

The upheavals at the end of the Middle Ages, especially the Hundred Years' War (1337–1453), led to much defacement and destruction. The times were favorable for castle renovation and construction, as much for the French as for the English. The curtain walls were strengthened by heightening them, by adding additional flanking towers (Arques, Tancarville, Seine-Maritime, etc.), by concentrating the defense on their summits, and by more effectively protecting their access (at Caen, the English constructed a barbican facing toward the city that they distrusted). The new castles are classics of their era.

At Rouen, beginning in 1419, the English King Henry V (1387–1422) erected a *palatium,* which was in fact a beautiful quadrangular fortress (1.7 ha) flanked by circular bastions that he built to affirm his authority. The reconstruction of the second half of the fifteenth century was mostly devoted to manors where residential concerns and civil preoccupations led to many monumental constructions. The external defensive outline lost much of its aggressiveness while not rejecting it entirely. Martainville (Seine-Maritime), constructed at the very end of the fifteenth century by a merchant of Rouen, is a good example of this transitional architecture.

FURTHER READINGS

de Bouard, M. *Le château de Caen.* Caen: Centre de Recherches Archéologiques Médiévales, 1979.

Renoux, A. *Fécamp: Du palais de Dieu au palais ducal.* Paris: CNRS, 1991. Includes numerous bibliographic references.

A. Renoux

SEE ALSO
Castles

Northern Isles

The Northern Isles of Scotland comprise the island groups of Orkney and Shetland. The Shetland archipelago lies 160 km off the north coast of Scotland and 350 km west of Bergen, Norway. The Orkney islands lie just off the northern tip of Caithness and are almost completely made up of old red sandstone, which is ideal for drystone building and has been used in construction from the Neolithic onward. Trees exist in the Northern Isles only where protected from the wind, although Orkney is fertile while Shetland is covered with peat and some heather and grass. The climate is damp and windy with cool summers and mild winters.

The Viking Age is usually dated from c. A.D. 800 until c. A.D. 1050, although the start may be pushed back into the eighth century, and the close is also debated. In the Northern Isles, the Viking period is followed by the Norse period, variously defined as A.D. 1050–1500 and A.D. 1050–1300 (the period A.D. 1300–1500 is then the Medieval period).

Our sources for the Northern Isles include place names, documents, medieval Icelandic sagas, especially *Orkneyinga saga (OS),* and the archaeological evidence. Icelandic sagas written in the late twelfth–early thirteenth

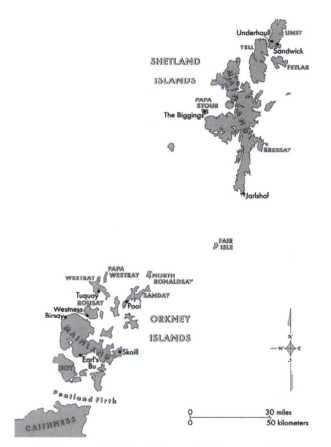

Map of Orkney and Shetland showing the location of the major archaeological sites.

resembling either a cloverleaf or a figure-of-eight. In contrast, Viking/Norse structures were rectilinear. Viking/Norse settlements were often built directly on top of previous native occupation, some of which go back to the Neolithic.

The Northern Isles were brought under more direct Norwegian political influence with the imposition of earls from Norway in the late ninth century. After 1195, Shetland was governed directly from Norway, but Orkney retained its earldom status until the Northern Isles were pawned by Christian I (1426–1481) of Denmark-Norway to the king of Scotland in 1469. Even then, some estates were retained by Norwegian landholders and some contacts continued.

Pagan Norse burials are almost nonexistent in Shetland but have been found in Orkney, including boat burials at Westness, Rousay, and Scar, Sanday. Archaeologically the Viking/Norse presence is usually recognized by the rectilinear architecture, typically Viking/Norse artifacts such as combs, and, especially, the use of soapstone instead of ceramics. Baking plates, or bakestones (round grooved pieces of soapstone possibly used for baking flatbread), are found in Norwegian towns after c. A.D. 1100 and also in Shetland, though rarely in Orkney. Soapstone is native to Shetland, although some was probably brought from Norway, but it had to be imported to Orkney. Remains of stone-and-turf Viking/Norse structures can be seen easily at several sites (e.g., on the Brough of Birsay, at the Earl's Bu at Orphir, and eroding out of the cliff face at the Norse/medieval site of Tuquoy, Westray).

Most of the excavated sites on Orkney were high-status sites, especially those in the Birsay Bay area. Only four Viking/Norse habitation sites have been excavated in Shetland. Underhoull and Sandwick are not high-status sites, while the Biggings, Papa Stour, was in the hands of elite families closely tied to Norway for several hundred years. Artifacts and the internal arrangement of the houses at the Norse/medieval sites of Sandwick and the Biggings show continued close contacts with Norway.

The most important Norse settlement site in the Northern Isles is Jarlshof on the southern tip of Shetland. Here there are remains of stone-and-turf Norse houses from the ninth to thirteenth centuries, which underwent modification through time, as well as native occupation dating back to the Bronze Age.

Farm mounds, known in northern Norway, are also found on Sanday and North Ronaldsay, Orkney. These poorly understood mounds of accumulated settlement debris are often the site of current farm buildings.

centuries mention the Northern Isles—*OS* is actually set there—but these sagas were written by Icelanders long after the original Norse settlement. The *Historia Norvegiae,* possibly written in Orkney c. A.D. 1200 but surviving in a late fifteenth-century manuscript, is the source for the longstanding belief that the Vikings ravaged and plundered the islands and that the initial Viking settlement was extremely violent, something for which there is no archaeological evidence but which the overwhelmingly Norse place names seem to support. However, there seems to have been a peaceful Pictish-Norse interface on a few sites where Pictish material culture appears in early Norse layers.

A few radiocarbon (C-14) dates indicate some Viking settlement may have occurred as early as c. A.D. 800, although large-scale settlement probably began no earlier than the mid-ninth century. The first Vikings in the Northern Isles met the native farming population, the poorly understood Picts. Pictish houses were cellular,

N

Work conducted in the 1970s and 1980s indicates that the Pictish Church was well established before the Viking settlement, and the "papay" place names indicate that monastic communities survived the initial Viking incursions. The Brough of Birsay, a tidal island, was probably the focus of pre-Viking Church activity, as well as Norse political power, and, in the eleventh century, Earl Thorfinn built his minster in Birsay.

The twelfth century saw the construction of a number of churches (e.g., the Orphir round church, possibly inspired by the church of the Holy Sepulchre in Jerusalem; and St. Magnus Cathedral, Kirkwall, showing the influence of both Durham Cathedral and Nidaros Cathedral in Trondheim, Norway). These illustrate Orkney's wealth and far-flung connections in this period.

Recently archaeologists have stressed paleoenvironmental studies in an attempt to reconstruct the Norse economy. Animal bone, fish bone, seeds, pollen, and insects have been carefully analyzed. In the Viking period, bere/barley, oats, and flax were all cultivated, and animal husbandry played an important role. There was a significant increase in deepwater fishing at the end of the eleventh century, at least in Shetland and Caithness. In Shetland, these fish were channeled through the Hanseatic *kontor* (privileged trading settlement) in Bergen until the fifteenth century, when traders from northern Germany began to trade directly with Shetland. Regular contacts failed to develop with Orkney, perhaps because its grain surpluses were seen as a disruptive influence.

FURTHER READINGS

Batey, Colleen, Judith Jesch, and Christopher D. Morris, eds. *The Viking Age in Caithness, Orkney, and the North Atlantic.* Edinburgh: Edinburgh University Press, 1993.

Crawford, Barbara E., ed. *Scandinavian Scotland.* Leicester: Leicester University Press, 1985.

———. *St. Magnus Cathedral and Orkney's Twelfth-Century Renaissance.* Aberdeen: Aberdeen University Press, 1988.

Crawford, Barbara E., and Beverly Bolin Smith. *The Biggings, Papa Stour, Shetland: The History and Archaeology of a Royal Norwegian Farm.* Edinburgh: Society of Antiquaries of Scotland, Monograph Series no. 15 (1999).

Curle, C.L. *Pictish and Norse Finds from the Brough of Birsay, 1934–74.* Edinburgh: Society of Antiquaries of Scotland, 1982.

Fenton, Alexander, and Hermann Pálsson, eds. *The Northern and Western Islands in the Viking World: Survival, Continuity, and Change.* Edinburgh: John Donald, 1984.

Hamilton, J.R.C. *Excavations at Jarlshof, Shetland.* Edinburgh: HMSO, 1956.

Hedges, John. Trial Excavations on Pictish and Viking Settlements at Saevar Howe, Birsay, Orkney. *Glasgow Archaeological Journal* (1983) 10:73–124.

Hunter, John. *Rescue Excavations on the Brough of Birsay, 1974–82.* Edinburgh: Society of Antiquaries of Scotland, 1986.

Morris, Christopher D., and D. James Rackham, eds. *Norse and Later Settlement and Subsistence in the North Atlantic.* Glasgow: University of Glasgow Department of Archaeology, 1992.

Renfrew, Colin, ed. *The Prehistory of Orkney, B.C. 4000–1000 A.D.* Edinburgh: Edinburgh University Press, 1990.

Ritchie, Anna. Excavation of Pictish and Viking-Age Farmsteads at Buckquoy, Orkney. *Proceedings of the Society of Antiquaries of Scotland* (1977) 108:174–227.

Small, Alan. Excavations at Underhoull, Unst, Shetland. *Proceedings of the Society of Antiquaries of Scotland* (1966) 98:225–248.

Smith, Brian, ed. *Shetland Archaeology.* Lerwick: Shetland Times, 1985.

Thomson, William P.L. *History of Orkney.* Edinburgh: Mercat, 1987.

Barbara G. Scott

SEE ALSO
Animal Husbandry; Birsay; Jarlshof; Picts

Norton Priory

Excavations were carried out at the site of Norton Priory (Runcorn, Cheshire) in northwest England from 1971 until 1983, making it one of the most fully explored monastic sites in Europe (Greene 1989) and contributing to the revolution in knowledge of medieval monasticism that archaeology produced in the last quarter of the twentieth century. Research and publication is continuing. The Augustinian Priory was founded in 1134 by the barons of Halton, whose castle overlooks the site, and was endowed by them with extensive lands and other properties not only in Cheshire and Lancashire but as far afield as Nottinghamshire and Oxfordshire. Subsequent benefactions were made principally by the powerful Dutton family, the knightly retainers of the barons.

The excavation revealed considerable information about the construction history of the priory and the lifestyle of its inhabitants. It also proved possible to examine the surrounding landscape of the manor of Norton, which was owned by the canons. This estate must have been the source of oak timbers that were used in the construction of temporary accommodation for the brethren in the years following the foundation. Large post-pits containing the preserved stumps of oak posts, the traces of two phases of timber buildings, were found to the west of the masonry buildings; the canons would have occupied the timber-aisled halls until first the church and then the domestic buildings were completed in stone. The layout of the masonry buildings followed the most common pattern, with the church placed on the north side of a square cloister that was flanked by an arcaded cloister walk with the dormitory range to the east, the refectory on the south, and the cellarer's range on the west. Kitchens were found in the southwest part of the site, and to the west was the outer courtyard.

The church began life as a simple Romanesque structure built with sandstone ashlar walls to a cruciform ground plan. However, in the late twelfth century, it was extended to the west and east. Soon afterward, the cloister, the refectory, and the cellarer's range were demolished and enlarged. The chapter house and the latrine block were doubled in size. This dramatic expansion is consistent with the growth in Norton's endowment and indicates a doubling of the number of canons from the original thirteen. The excavation revealed other modifications to the priory, including the rebuilding of the cloister to a particularly fine design following a fire in 1236 and further expansions of the church with the construction of a north aisle and an east chapel to house a shrine. The north transept chapel also expanded to house burials of the Dutton family, whose coat of arms appeared on mosaic tiles made in the early fourteenth century. Extensive areas of tile flooring were found in the church, and the kiln in which they were fired was located and excavated. Experiments on the techniques used by the tile makers, including the construction and firing of a replica kiln, were carried out, revealing much important information (Greene 1981).

Research on the excavated skeletons produced evidence of stature, diet, and disease, while animal, bird, and fish bones illuminated aspects of the canons' diet. The management of water was also investigated, and an impressive system of moats, fishponds, water mill, drains, and supply pipes was revealed. Norton, which had been raised to the rank of mitred abbey in 1391 (Greene 1979), was closed as part of Henry VIII's dissolution of the monasteries in 1536. The excavation examined the subsequent history of the site, including the conversion of the monastic buildings to a Tudor mansion and its replacement by a Georgian country house in the eighteenth century. The latter was demolished in the 1920s, leaving the site to become abandoned and overgrown. Today, however, the excavated site forms part of an award-winning museum that attracts many thousands of visitors every year.

FURTHER READINGS

Greene, J. Patrick. The Elevation of Norton Priory, Cheshire, to the Status of Mitred Abbey. *Transactions of the Historic Society of Lancashire and Cheshire* (1979) 128:97–112.

———. Experimental Archaeology in England. *Archaeology* (1981) 34(6):24–31.

———. *Norton Priory.* Cambridge: Cambridge University Press, 1989.

———. *Medieval Monasteries.* Leicester: Leicester University Press, 1992.

J. Patrick Greene

Norwich

Norwich, the county town of Norfolk, lies in the heart of East Anglia, an area of relatively low landscape relief and rich agricultural soils in eastern England. It stands astride the River Wensum, which, east of the city, joins the River Yare and flows to the North Sea at Great Yarmouth. Gravel terraces constricted the riverside marshes, providing good, relatively flat, areas for early settlement.

Norwich is not a Roman foundation. The Roman town of Venta Icenorum lies c. 5 km to the south and now survives as an open field defended by a bank and wall. While there is evidence of considerable prehistoric and Roman activity in the greater Norwich area, the earliest occupation that can be associated with the later medieval city dates from the eighth century A.D. This takes the form of middle Saxon place names and artifacts, both of which suggest settlement on either bank of the River Wensum. Models of urban development in the 1970s and 1980s have suggested a number of small, discrete nucleated villages, although the most recent discoveries may imply more linear development along each riverbank.

The largest corpus of eighth- and ninth-century pottery and other finds recovered to date has been from the north bank of the river. This area seems also to have been the center of an Anglo-Scandinavian borough, established by the Danes following the conquest of East Anglia in the late ninth century. While there is not any documentary evidence to suggest such a borough, Danish place names, artifacts and church dedications imply a small but growing community, one that excavation indicates was defended by a bank and ditch from the beginning of the tenth century.

East Anglia fell to the West Saxon King Edward the Elder (r. 899–924) in 917. Edward's successor, Athelstan, had coins minted in Norwich, the mint signature being the earliest epigraphic reference to the settlement. Norwich, therefore, appears to have been of significance as an administrative center, although documentary evidence is absent until the 980s, and little archaeological evidence has been recovered, possibly reflecting the lack of excavation in the most sensitive area, immediately north of the river.

C. A.D. 1000, occupation of the south bank became more intense. Archaeological excavations here frequently recover large quantities of late Saxon material, and it is very probable that a planned town was established at this time. Elements of this survive in the modern topography, but much was lost in the late eleventh century by the establishment of the castle and cathedral precincts and in the thirteenth century with the creation of the Franciscan Friary. Archaeological research is seeking to explore the late Saxon town and has revealed evidence of houses, churches, cemeteries, commercial waterfronts, and industrial areas.

The Norman Conquest of England in 1066 led to the establishment of major institutions in Norwich. The castle was probably under construction by 1068 and was besieged as early as 1075 (much of the area has now been excavated, including the massive earthwork defenses). The seat of the bishopric was moved to Norwich in 1094, and construction of the cathedral and its attendant close was started in 1096. A borough for the Franci de Norvic, the Frenchmen of Norwich, was created west of the castle around a large new marketplace. Expansion southward along the river seems to have occurred from c. 1100. A house of a twelfth-century Jewish financier survives here, while, north of the cathedral, a further stone building has been excavated and preserved. The town also expanded northward in the first half of the twelfth century. A planted suburb was created by the bishop, and marginal development occurred along axial streets. Again, excavation has recovered evidence of early streets, buildings, cemeteries, trade, and industrial activity.

The concentration of secular and ecclesiastical authority in Norwich as a result of the Norman Conquest, probably building on pre-Conquest trends, meant that Norwich had become an extremely important market, industrial town, and administrative center by the thirteenth century. It is likely that its population was greatly in excess of twenty thousand; it was served by more than sixty parish churches and contained some thirty monastic institutions and dependencies. Examples of churches and other ecclesiastical institutions have been excavated archaeologically. From 1260 onward, the city began to be fortified, ultimately having a defensive wall nearly 5 km long with forty towers and twelve gates. The enclosed area was larger than that of London, and the river was crossed by five bridges, the greatest number of any medieval English city.

Much of the wealth of the city was founded upon the cloth trade. Worsted cloth, often produced in the surrounding countryside, was finished in Norwich and marketed by city merchants. Remains of a dyeworks has been recovered by excavation, while a large cloth-merchant's hall from the fifteenth century survives. Archaeological deposits frequently contain evidence of trade beyond the region, especially across the North Sea to the Baltic, Germany, the Low Countries, and northern France.

The city suffered economic decline in the sixteenth century, exacerbated by disastrous fires in 1507 (remarkable evidence for which has been seen in excavations) and by the Reformation (a substantial area of the medieval Franciscan Friary, dissolved at this time, has been excavated). The traditional cloth industry was revived after 1568, however, by the establishment of New Draperies, largely founded by "Strangers," immigrants from the Low Countries. The Strangers laid the basis for extraordinary wealth in the seventeenth and early eighteenth centuries, so much so that Norwich was known as the Second City between about 1660 and 1730.

Despite twentieth-century slum clearance and bombing in World War II, Norwich remains rich in historic buildings. More than thirty medieval churches survive, as well as the cathedral, the castle, and two medieval bridges. Much of the city wall still stands. More than fifteen hundred buildings predate 1830, with structures of the sixteenth and seventeenth centuries being particularly important. The city is also exceptionally well endowed with late medieval documentation, but much of the earlier history of the settlement relies upon archaeological excavation and survey.

FURTHER READINGS

Ayers, B.S. *English Heritage Book of Norwich.* London: Batsford, 1994.

Blomefield, F. *An Essay towards a Topographical History of the County of Norfolk, Continued by Parkin.* Vols. 3–4. London: William Miller, 1806.

Brown, P. *Domesday Book: Norfolk.* Chichester: Phillimore, 1984.

Campbell, J. Norwich. In *Historic Towns.* Vol. 2. Ed. M.D. Lobel. Baltimore: Johns Hopkins, 1975, pp. 1–25.

Carter, A. The Anglo-Saxon Origins of Norwich: The Problems and Approaches. *Anglo-Saxon England* (1978) 7:175–204.

Fernie, E. *An Architectural History of Norwich Cathedral.* Oxford: Clarendon, 1993.

Green, E.B., and R.N.R. Young. *Norwich: The Growth of a City.* Norwich: Norfolk Museums Service, 1981.

Hudson, W.H., ed. *The Streets and Lanes of Norwich: A Memoir by J. Kirkpatrick.* Norwich: Norfolk and Norwich Archaeological Society, 1889.

Hudson, W.H., and J.C. Tingey, eds. *The Records of the City of Norwich.* Norwich: Jarrold, 1906, 1910.

Sandred, K.I., and B. Lindstrom. The Place-Names of Norfolk. *English Place-Name Society* (1989) 61: pt. 1.

Archaeological excavations are nearly all published in the journal *Norfolk Archaeology* and the monograph series East Anglian Archaeology. Work from the 1980s onward appears in the latter; Norwich volumes include nos. 13 (1981), 15 (1982), 17 (1983), 26 (1985), 28 (1985), 37 (1987), and 58 (1993).

Brian S. Ayers

Novgorod

Novgorod (literally, "new town") is one of the oldest Russian towns. The town is mentioned in connection with an invitation to settle by the Scandinavian prince in 859 A.D. This invitation was undertaken by multiethnic tribes (Slavonic and Finnish), who settled on fertile soils along Lake Ilmen in the eighth–ninth centuries. However, it was only in the tenth century that they settled the territory on which modern Novgorod is located.

In twelfth–fifteenth centuries, Novgorod was a capital of the northwestern Russia. It had a republican form of government, a developed economy, and a high culture. Novgorod's state structure differed from south Russia's, where the prince was in charge of the state. In fact, Novgorod was a parliamentary republic; governors *(Posad-*

niks) and representatives to the *veche* (popular assembly) were elected from the *boyars* (members of old nobility in Russia). The basis of the administrative-territorial structure of Novgorod were independent, self-ruled quarters (Nerevskiy, Slavenskiy, Ludin, Plotnitzkiy, Zagorodskiy). Each of them had its own administration and its own *veche.*

The territory of Novgorod (Novgorod's land) spread as far as the White Sea in the north, and the Ural Mountains in the east. Novgorod shared a border with lands of other Russian principalities in the south and Pskov's land in the west. Because of its convenient geographic position (Novgorod was located at a crossroads of the most important east European waterways, which had a connection with the Baltic Sea), Novgorod was the largest center of medieval international and domestic Russian trade. The town connected Russia, western Europe, Byzantium, and the Muslim East.

In 1478, as a result of a critical political struggle between the Novgorod Republic and the Grand Principality of Moscow, as well as internal conflicts between Novgorod's *boyars,* Novgorod and all its possessions became a part of Moscow's lands, which became a basis for the formation of the centralized Russian state.

The Archaeology of Novgorod

The remains of life in medieval Novgorod were deposited in a deeply stratified (2–6 m) cultural layer. Artifacts of nonorganic (metal, stone, glass, clay) as well as organic (wood, bone, leather, birchbark) materials are well preserved in the soil. The splendid state of preservation of Novgorod's cultural layer and all the artifacts found there make Novgorod a classic source for the history of life in medieval Russia.

Systematic archaeological research began in Novgorod in 1932. The volume of archaeological work in Novgorod, the quantity of artifacts found there, and the scientific research based on them make Novgorod the most important site for Russia and for European medieval archaeology in general. During sixty years of excavations in Novgorod, whole blocks of the medieval town with various buildings, pavements, and amenities were found. The wooden roadways of the town streets provided a key to the town's chronology. These roads first appeared in the tenth century and existed until the eighteenth century in the same location. The excellent preservation of wood permitted the use of dendrochronology (a method of dating based on annual tree rings).

N

The collection of artifacts consists of more than 150,000 individual finds, made of all known medieval materials. The artifacts and other materials discovered included tools, pottery and tableware, warrior's weapons and horsemen's equipment, details of house architecture and the remains of furniture, industrial raw and waste materials from craftsmen's work, clothes and shoes, ornaments and musical instruments, articles of applied art as well as imported articles, toys for children and games for adults, grain, and fruits of domestic as well as imported southern plants.

The discovery of birchbark documents (letters scratched on birchbark with a metal stick) became the biggest event of Russian twentieth-century archaeology. These letters can most definitely be called new kinds of written historical sources. The first such letter was found in 1951. By the end of the summer of 1993, their number had reached 753. Taking into account the conditions and the state of preservation of the cultural layer in various parts of Novgorod, it is possible to estimate that there were, perhaps, more than twenty thousand birchbark documents within Novgorod. These documents were discovered in the layers dating from the eleventh to the fifteenth centuries and describe medieval town life so completely that other writings cannot possibly be compared to them. An infinite variety of texts were found: complaints of peasants and orders of feudal lords, notes of usurers and testaments, military messages and letters of merchants, school exercises and notes on literature, family correspondence and marital contracts. The discovery of the unique letter 752, found in the layer dating from the late eleventh–early twelfth centuries, became a great sensation. This is a letter from a young woman, settling the relationship with her lover.

The discovery through linguistic analysis that these letters represent an old town dialect is of great importance for the history of Novgorod. It was found that this dialect is different from common Russian and is closely related to the languages of western Slavs. This, in turn, completely changed the scientific view of the origins of Novgorod and the formation of the ancient Russian state. According to the newest research in linguistics, archaeology, and anthropology, the first migrations to Novgorod's land were mainly from the south coast of the Baltic Sea (the territory of western Slavs) and not from the south (Dnieper area) as was previously believed.

The other important discovery in the archaeology of Novgorod were town properties, which can provide infor-mation about the formation of the town's territory as well as the social structure and the role of different social groups in the town's social life.

The majority of town properties discovered during Novgorod's excavation belonged to *boyars,* the richest and the most influential people in Novgorod's society. *Posadniks* were chosen from their class. Properties of some of the *posadniks* were investigated in different parts of the town. In addition, the properties of merchants and free citizens from nonprivileged families were also discovered. The discovery of the properties of the artist Olisey Grechin, who lived at the end of the twelfth century, became a sensation. The archaeological investigation of this property was a priceless investment in the history of ancient Russian art, which was previously largely anonymous. The value of archaeological material for the study of the decorative as well as the applied art of Novgorod has now been recognized.

During the excavations, it was revealed that not only jewelry and the products of applied art, but also items of everyday use (spoons, knife handles, combs, chair backs, children's cradles, details of houses, and sledges) were decorated with carvings, fanciful ornament, or the depictions of fantastic as well as real animals. The skillful use of different forms of ornament demonstrates the aesthetic values of residents of Novgorod and their highly developed sense of harmony.

The discovery in Novgorod of different musical instruments, such as wooden stringed instruments (*gusli, gudok),* pipes, *vargani,* and rattles, was of particular significance for studies of medieval music. The collection of medieval instruments from Novgorod appears to be unique in the range of instrument types, in their chronological span (eleventh–fifteenth centuries), and in the quantity of articles discovered (about seventy).

Studies of handcraft industries, trade, and their relation to the economic development of the town were also revealed through archaeological research. The discoveries of craftsmen's tools and devices used for various professions, debris and half-finished articles, raw and waste materials, and the large number of finished goods illustrate the developed handcraft industries in Novgorod. Trade was necessary to supply raw materials (precious and nonferrous metals, amber, carved stones, rare woods). Finished handcraft products of foreign origin appeared in the large collection in small numbers.

The excavations in Novgorod produced many data on life in medieval Novgorod. They provided previously unknown information to virtually every branch of medieval scholarship. Every new season of excavation brings new discoveries, solves certain problems, and raises new questions.

FURTHER READINGS

Yanin, V.L., E.N. Nosov, A.S. Khoroshev, A.N. Sorokin, E.A. Rybina, V.I. Povetkin, and P.G. Gaidukov. *The Archaeology of Novgorod, Russia.* Monograph Series 13. Lincoln: Society for Medieval Archaeology, 1992.

Elena Rybina

SEE ALSO
Dendrochronology

O

Offa's Dyke

A vast system of bank-and-ditch earthworks runs along the Marcher lands between England and Wales, originally between Mercia and the independent Welsh principalities. The largest is securely dated to the reign of Offa, king of Mercia (757–796). There is considerable research in progress on which earthworks belong to this system known as Offa's Dyke (Fig. 1).

The southern stretch on the River Wye is being actively investigated, while the northern stretch south of Prestatyn is now demonstrated to be a twelfth-century boundary structure. The proven dyke consists of the length from Treuddyn (near Mold) in the north to just south of the River Wye in the south—in other words, the traditional frontier between Mercia and Powys.

The central section may be a defense built against raids from the Welsh Kingdom of Powys by Offa in the early years of his reign. The evidence for this consists of the siting of the monument and the inscription of a cross known as the Pillar of Eliseg. Together they point to a series of bloody raids by the Welsh into Mercia (England) and the response, early in the reign of Offa, of the building of a fortified patrol line. The defense consists of a simple bank and ditch (always on the Welsh side) that is so sited as to command the views to the west. No associated structures (forts, fortlets, or gateways) have yet been discovered, although marking-out banks have been excavated under the bank. The dyke should be a major resource for evidence of the habitat and agriculture of the region in the eighth century.

The dyke forms the core of a popular long-distance footpath through wonderful scenery and fascinating small market towns. The path runs "from sea to sea" and has led to an increase in the interest in the dyke.

FURTHER READINGS
Hill, D., and M. Worthington. *Offa's Dyke,* forthcoming.
David Hill

SEE ALSO
Wat's Dyke

Open Fields

Preenclosure agriculture operated by means of field systems that are referred to as *open fields, common fields,* or *subdivided fields.* The term *open fields* is used here.

F. Seebohm, writing in 1883, was the first to describe the main elements of English open fields. Further studies were made by P. Vinogradoff in 1892, by F.W. Maitland in 1897, and, in 1915, H.L. Gray published the first national account of English field systems. A.R.H. Baker and R.A. Butlin edited a series of essays in 1973 that further showed the variety and complexity of British field systems.

The field systems of England fall into two main classes, those of the highland zone and those of the lowland zone. The highlands have a low amount of arable land as a percentage of the township area, contrasting with the extensive arable land of much of the lowland zone. The lowlands can be further subdivided into three main regions: the Midlands, the Southeast, and Yorkshire. The Midland zone is the most complicated and familiar and is described first.

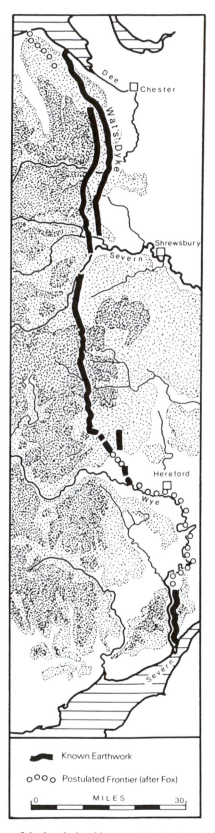

FIG. 1. Map of the borderland between England and Wales showing the location of Offa's Dyke and Wat's Dyke.

Legend:
— Known Earthwork
○○○○ Postulated Frontier (after Fox)

MILES
0   30

The Midland Region

In the Midlands, the wide open expanse of arable land was subdivided into many small, arable strips called *lands* that lay in blocks called *furlongs.* The furlongs were grouped into a few large areas called *fields,* which were open and hedgeless. The fields occupied most of the available area in a township (the smallest unit of an agricultural system that formed a complete, self-contained farming regime) and were frequently cultivated using a two- or three-year rotation, one year being fallow. There were common grazing rights over the fallow at certain times. A farm, called a *yardland,* consisted of c. 25 acres (10 hectares) of land (the amount varied greatly from village to village), lying not in a block but scattered in strips throughout the township, with no two strips lying together.

Individual lands vary from about a quarter to half an acre. They became ridged as a result of plowing in a clockwise motion beginning at the middle and finishing at the outside, leaving a furrow. A counterclockwise motion was adopted in the fallow season to take some of the soil back and maintain a low ridge. The purpose of ridging was for soil drainage; the furrow acted as an open drain that formed a clear demarcation between lands. The ends of most lands were curved, so that the whole land took the shape of a very elongated, mirror-image of an "S."

Meadow, like arable land, was owned in narrow strips. Animals were kept out of hay meadows until mowing time, when grass was marked into strips with stakes and cut by the proprietors. The meadows were then used for common grazing during the remainder of the season. Woods were a limited resource in many parts of England but formed part of the overall economy of "forest" townships, being subject to common grazing rights as well as supplying woodland products. Some townships shared woodland, and some had their own wood lying detached at a distance.

Physical remains of ridge and furrow and linear earthworks at furlong boundaries survive in the modern landscape. Methods of archaeological survey can be used to make reconstructions of medieval fields, and documentary evidence enables fields and furlongs to be identified (Hall 1982, 1984).

Written sources relating to open fields can be found in schedules of charters and deeds, called *terriers.* The most complete and important records are *field books,* which list every strip in a township, giving details of all fields, furlongs, and lands. Usually, the quantity of land and the name of the owner are stated; sometimes there is more information, such as the type of tenure, the name of the tenant, and the precise measurement of the lands. Some field books relate to contemporary maps. It is probable that all parishes had field books. A few medieval examples are known; Cambridge has one from the fourteenth century, and two for Northamptonshire date from c. 1410 and 1433 (Hall 1995). Later field books are common.

Open fields were controlled by a complex series of agreements and orders made by manorial or village courts. Commonly, Midland field systems were run on a two- or three-fold cultivation. Northamptonshire evidence shows that townships were mainly two-field in the thirteenth century, changing continuously until most villages operated a three-course system by the eighteenth century. The number of fields was greater than three in some places after A.D. 1500, although they were usually grouped into three blocks for cropping. Multiple fields occurred in many of the forest townships, probably caused by assarting (removal of trees and bushes to form arable land).

As well as the widespread change from two to three fields within one township, there are examples of amalgamation of separate systems during the fifteenth and sixteenth centuries. Partial enclosure caused rapid field changes; several townships enclosed one of their three fields between 1590 and 1650 and rearranged the remaining two into three new smaller ones.

Manorial demesnes, or *home farms,* occur as two types, lying either in compact blocks of land or dispersed throughout the fields. There were probably always these two forms; no evidence has been found for the conversion of one into the other, with the implication that one type was an original layout.

Yardland sizes varied according to topographical location. Small yardlands were characteristic of regions of good soil, and large yardlands were found in areas where there was once woodland or heath. Large yardlands are attributed to intakes of marginal land made after an initial fixed-size yardland allocation.

Regular ordering of lands occurred in many field systems. Analysis of terriers and field books shows that probably all townships had their lands laid out in a regular manner. An ordered structure seems to have been created before the thirteenth century, since the older the record the more likely it is to show tenurial regularity. The number of yardlands in many cases directly relates to the *Domesday* assessment of 1086.

Changes in Agricultural Practice

After 1400, there were changes in land use in open fields, mostly involving contraction of the amount of arable land and an increase in the grass area. These changes were made possible because of population decline during the fourteenth and fifteenth centuries, when less grain was needed.

The most common type of increase of grass was to lay down arable land, by agreement, to form a "cow pasture" for village herds. Examples from the fifteenth–eighteenth centuries are known. Parts of furlongs, and sometimes whole furlongs, were left to grass over permanently, in which case they were called *leys.* Leys appear primarily in the fifteenth and sixteenth centuries.

Narrow strips of grass called *balks* were formed by plowing a few furrows away from the ridge of a particular land, leaving them to grass over. Balks were used to mark out significant groups of lands, such as blocks of demesne. By the seventeenth and eighteenth centuries, balks were often left between every land as greensward.

Small pieces of grass were introduced after c. 1550 by leaving 8–18 m unplowed at lands' ends. When all furlongs were treated in this manner, the net result was that each was surrounded by a band of grass. Other small grass areas, called *rick places,* were formed at the end of a group of lands and used as platforms for stacks or ricks.

There are different types of ridge and furrow; all described above were of the early open-field type. Ridges were plowed after enclosure in the nineteenth century and are distinguished from the older ones in that they are straight and parallel to at least one modern field hedge. Some are wide, c. 12 m across, but narrow ridges only a few feet wide are also known (Murray 1813).

Dating and Origin

There has been controversy in the past about the dating of ridge and furrow and whether it corresponded to that recorded on preenclosure plans. M.W. Beresford and J.K.S. St. Joseph (1979:25–37) have used comparisons of aerial photographs with contemporary plans to show that, in many cases, ridge and furrow was in existence in the sixteenth century. Earlier dating (to the thirteenth century) can be demonstrated where there is coincidence of physical survival and particular events recorded in documents.

Archaeological data show that strip fields are no older than the Saxon period, since they overlie many settlement sites of the period c. 450–750. The historical evidence shows directly that named furlongs existed in the twelfth century, and analysis of relationships between yardlands and the *Domesday* fiscal returns of 1086 shows that medieval farms were in existence at that time. It seems,

O

therefore, that field systems were created before 1066, according to the yardland data, and after c. A.D. 750 from the archaeological findings. Strips were laid out on a large scale initially, with long lands stretching more than 1.5 km across major pieces of topography—from brook to brook or from a settlement to its township boundary. In the Midlands, an undulating terrain, often of a clayey nature, necessitated the subdivision of long strips and realignment of the new blocks (generally by turning them through 90°) to satisfy natural drainage. This process led to formation of furlongs before the twelfth century.

The Midland system operated in a central region of England running from south Durham to Somerset, being well developed in the Midlands. It was characterized by a high percentage of arable land on which village animals supplemented shortage of fodder by grazing fallow land. This necessitated uniform distribution of arable land to make available large fallow blocks; the whole system was controlled by complex regulations.

Other Regions

Lowland. In East Anglia and southeastern England, strips of similar dimensions to those of the Midlands were farmed, but no ridges were plowed because soil was light and required little drainage. Manorial regulations were similar.

On the Yorkshire Wolds and in Holderness, there was no checkerboard pattern of furlongs; fields were divided into very long simple strips up to a mile long, as first set out. There was some ridging, and the percentage of arable land was high, leading to a system of common fallowing similar to that found in the Midlands. In the East Anglian Fens, long ditched strips called *darlands* were used. These were not ridged, and the fen had an abundant supply of hay and pasture grounds. Long strips have many parallels in continental Europe, particularly in the east, where they are associated with the expansion of the Carolingian Empire in the eighth century (Nitz 1988).

Upland. In regions of England with high ground supporting heath and moor, mainly in the west and north, conditions were less suitable for arable land, and it formed a small percentage of the total township area. Ridging frequently developed where there was plowing and ample pasture for animals. A highly developed communal grazing system with uniform dispersal of arable land did not occur, and the complex (late) introduction of grass into arable lands was not necessary.

FURTHER READINGS

Baker, A.R.H., and R.A. Butlin. *Field Systems of the British Isles.* Cambridge: Cambridge University Press, 1973.

Beresford, M.W., and J.K.S. St. Joseph. *Medieval England.* 2nd ed. Cambridge: Cambridge University Press, 1979.

Gray, H.L. *English Field Systems.* London: Merlin, 1915.

Hall, D.N. *Medieval Fields.* Aylesbury: Shire, 1982.

———. Fieldwork and Documentary Evidence for the Layout and Organization of Early Medieval Estates in the English Midlands. In *Archaeological Approaches to Medieval Europe.* Ed. K. Biddick. Studies in Medieval Culture 18. Kalamazoo: Medieval Institute, 1984, pp. 43–68.

———. *The Open Fields of Northamptonshire.* Northampton: Northamptonshire Record Society, 1995.

Maitland, F.W. 1897. *Domesday Book and Beyond.* London: Fontana edition (1960).

Murray, A. *A General View of the Agriculture of the County of Warwick.* London: McMillan, 1813, p. 130.

Nitz, H-J. Settlement Structures and Settlement Systems of the Frankish Central State in Carolingian and Ottonian Times. In *Anglo-Saxon Settlements.* Ed. D. Hooke. Oxford: Basil Blackwell, 1988, pp. 249–273.

Seebohm, F. 1883. *The English Village Community.* London: Kennicat, 1971 reprint.

Vinogradoff, P. *Villeinage in England.* Oxford: Oxford University Press, 1892.

David Hall

SEE ALSO
Forests; Woodland

Orkney
See Northern Isles.

Ostrów Lednicki
Ostrów Lednicki is a small island in the middle of Lake Lednica in Wielkapolska, western Poland, where Duke Mieszko I (c. 930–992) built a defended capital with a stone castle and church in the mid-tenth century, and where, theoretically, his baptism took place in 966, signaling the beginning of the Christian Polish nation. The site has been excavated annually since the 1960s, sponsored by the Polish government, and today the island is the cen-

ter of a museum complex dedicated to researching and interpreting the history of the Polish state.

Beginning in the tenth century, the lake area was populated with regularly spaced villages around its perimeter, all of which participated in a local redistributive system that provisioned the island. The island itself consisted of an extramural settlement and defended royal enclosure. A circular earth-and-timber rampart defined and protected the enclosure, which contained a mortared stone castle and attached chapel. An adjacent church with royal cemetery was built later, in the second half of the tenth century, and served either the clergy or the elite inhabitants of the enclosure. Excavations have revealed two bridges connecting the island to the east and west banks of the lake, constructed in 954 and 963, respectively. The western bridge was destroyed in 1038–1039 by Bretislaw of Bohemia, but the eastern bridge functioned well into the twelfth century. Precious-metal workshops have also been uncovered on the lakeshore at the foot of the western bridge, associated with Mieszko's Court. Underwater excavations around the island have helped determine the early medieval water level and appearance of the island and have recovered archaeological evidence for both subsistence and military activity in the tenth and eleventh centuries.

Thalia Gray

SEE ALSO
Polish State, Early

P

Paleoethnobotany

Paleoethnobotany may be defined as the study of the cultivation or exploitation of plant resources by early human communities. Many of the data come from archaeological excavations. The initial focus of paleoethnobotanical research was the investigation of the origins and spread during prehistory of agriculture, so that the Middle Ages tended to be neglected. The recognition that plant remains from medieval sites could be informative, particularly for periods predating documentary sources and for low-status undocumented sites, is a comparatively recent development. Even now, far more information is available from northern and western Europe, where medieval archaeology has had a high profile, than in the south and east.

Plant material may be preserved by one of several processes. Charring (carbonization) during crop processing or in granary fires has resulted in the preservation of abundant crop remains at many sites. In anoxic waterlogged deposits, such as latrine pits, microbial activity is inhibited, so that uncharred seeds, fruit stones, and other dietary residues have been preserved. Material has also been preserved by mineralization, as impressions on daub or pottery, and by desiccation, particularly in standing medieval buildings in which straw was used for thatch or insulation. Plant remains preserved by these means provide a basis for addressing some significant economic questions. On the most basic level, it is possible to establish which crops were cultivated, how production changed through time, and how crops were utilized and consumed.

The diverse climatic and edaphic conditions of Europe permitted cultivation of a wide range of cereals and pulses,

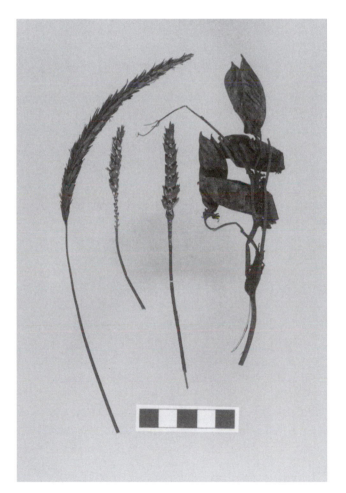

Desiccated crop remains from fifteenth-century buildings in southern England (Steeple Claydon, Bucks; and Tisbury, Wiltshire): *left to right,* rye *(Secale cereale),* bread wheat *(Triticum aestivum),* rivet wheat *(Triticum turgidum),* and pea *(Pisum sativum).* The material is blackened by soot from open hearths. Scale graduated in cm. (Material kindly supplied by John Letts, University of Oxford.)

P

including wheats (einkorn, emmer, rivet and macaroni wheats, bread wheat, and spelt), barley (two and six row, hulled and naked), oats, rye, broomcorn and Italian millets, beans, vetches, bitter vetch, lentils, peas, and chickpeas. In the south, the olive and grape were staples. Flax and hemp, grown principally for fiber, were widely cultivated. Fruits, nuts, oil seeds, herbs, and dye plants were cultivated as climate and soils permitted.

Where sufficient work has been done, it is possible to reconstruct the history of particular crops. Rye, for example, was introduced to Europe in prehistory as a weed of other cereals. By the Iron Age, it was being grown as a crop in several areas, and it later spread as a result of population movements in the post-Roman period. It was in the Middle Ages, however, that cultivation expanded massively in northwest Europe. Rye permitted cultivation in areas marginal for arable farming—impoverished sandy soils or upland areas—where yields of other cereals were poor. It is possible that the spread and intensification of rye growing was related to population pressure.

Agricultural production, however, is influenced not just by ecological considerations but by cultural preferences: food and drink are characteristic features of any culture. Evidence for the ways in which crops were consumed is sometimes obtained. For example, thirteenth–fourteenth-century fire deposits at Bergen, Norway, included abundant charred sprouted barley intended for use as malt for brewing, associated with remains of sweet gale, formerly a flavoring for ale. The requirements of medieval Bergen for malt must have influenced production elsewhere, for the barley from this site is thought, on the evidence of associated weed seeds, to have been imported.

Cultural and economic changes inevitably had effects on crop production. In southern Britain during the Roman period, agriculture, based on the production of spelt wheat, was associated with an infrastructure of specialized plant-processing equipment, such as corn driers and large granaries, and linked via an efficient transport system to an international market. The collapse of the Roman Empire in the fifth century and the arrival of Germanic peoples removed the economic basis of this system, and there was a reversion to largely subsistence farming. Over this period, spelt was replaced as the staple crop by free-threshing wheat and, as elsewhere in northwest Europe, rye. Results from West Stow, England, however, show that spelt cultivation continued until at least the mid-fifth century. This points to a degree of agricultural continuity rather than immediate replacement of spelt by

the free-threshing cereals. Other changes in production in this area during the Medieval period are less confidently explicable in terms of population movements and cultural change. Free-threshing tetraploid wheat, probably rivet, appears to have been introduced in the eleventh century. It is tempting to link this to the Norman Conquest of Britain in 1066, but at present paleoethnobotanical evidence from the likely source area of northern France is lacking.

Other forms of cultural contact, such as trade, are reflected by the appearance of exotic foodstuffs in the paleoethnobotanical record. Figs, for example, grown in southern Europe, are almost unknown in the north until the tenth century, but huge numbers of seeds in later medieval latrine pits point to large-scale importation of dried fruits. Other exotic southern foods identified from seeds at sites in northern and central Europe include walnut, grape, almond, date, pomegranate, and rice, some of which, on climatic grounds, must represent imports rather than introductions. Indirect evidence for wine imports comes from barrels recovered from archaeological sites. At Ipswich, England, an oak barrel gave a tree-ring sequence (A.D. 539–744) matching sequences from mid-south Germany, and ninth–tenth-century barrels of silver fir from Haithabu, northern Germany, are thought to have come from the Upper Rhine. Long-distance trade in spices is attested by finds of pepper and cardamom from sites in Germany and Switzerland.

In recent years, much paleoethnobotanical research has focused on the interpretation of plant remains in terms of activities at a given site: were the occupants, for example, engaged in crop production and processing, or did they obtain ready-processed crops from other sites? Clearly, this would be a reflection of site status and function. Ethnographic studies of crop products and by-products at modern Greek and Turkish peasant villages have provided an analogue for interpreting material from archaeological sites. It has proved possible to define the composition, in terms of grain, chaff, straw, and weed seeds, of products from the successive stages of threshing, winnowing, and sieving necessary in cereal processing. Statistical comparison of paleoethnobotanical samples with modern ones gives a basis for interpreting them. An example of the application of this approach comes from the work at a sixth–ninth-century hilltop site in the valley of the Biferno in Molise, Italy, excavated during a study of *incastellamento* (settlement nucleation) in this part of Italy. Most charred cereal samples were found to consist of more than 70 percent grain, with few chaff or weed-seed impurities. The absence of harvest waste, at least in the area excavated, suggests that the site was more than a simple peasant village and may have obtained its cereal requirements from other subsidiary sites. It is probable that similar work along these lines in other areas will help define economic relationships between sites.

Where *groups* of contemporary sites have been studied, it is possible to develop regional models of land use and agriculture. Plant remains from sites in the coastal areas of Germany and the Netherlands have been extensively investigated. Along the low-lying North Sea coast, there were extensive areas of salt marsh, subject to tidal inundation, on which settlements on artificial mounds, termed *terpen* in Dutch and *wurten* in German, were occupied during the early Middle Ages. The eighth–tenth-century wurt Elisenhof at the mouth of the Eider is an example. Remains of marsh and grassland plants indicate importation of animal fodder to the site, and it seems that cattle grazing was the predominant component of the site's economy. However, there was also some arable farming on creek levees. The horsebean was the main crop, with barley, oats, and flax/linseed. From the associated weed seeds, it is suggested that agriculture was confined to the summer months, thereby avoiding the potentially disastrous effects of saltwater flooding of fields in winter storms. This remarkable exploitation of an extreme and hazardous environment persisted along this coastline until the eleventh century, when seawalls were constructed to protect settlements and their fields.

The emphasis in this brief review on agricultural production should not obscure the importance of "wild" plant communities, many of which were managed so as to maximize production of desired resources. A wide variety of plant communities provided animal fodder. Salt marshes have already been mentioned, and many sites have produced plant remains indicating haymaking in grasslands from alluvial to montane. In the north and the west, heaths and moors, managed by controlled burning and grazing, also supplied fodder, besides a variety of other raw materials, such as mosses for rope, insulation, and sanitary purposes, and wild fruits, such as cloudberry, dwarf cornel, and bilberry. In the Netherlands, the use of *plaggen*—sods cut in heathland areas and enriched with dung from stalled animals—as manure actually resulted in an expansion of heathlands. Wild-plant foods, such as rose, hawthorn, sloe, and blackberry, were collected in deciduous woodland areas, but the principal use of woodland was to supply fuel and constructional wood. Excavations in waterlogged deposits at medieval towns and cities commonly produce abundant wood, attesting to the management of woodlands by coppicing or pollarding. Coppiced trees are cut near the base to produce new shoots, while pollarded trees are cut 8–12 feet (c. 2.5–4 m) above ground level, usually to preserve the new shoots from domestic animals. The purpose of coppicing and pollarding was to produce roundwood stems, while standard trees provided larger timber.

Recent paleoethnobotanical research has begun to reveal the diversity of agricultural production and exploitation of "wild" plant resources across medieval Europe. It was these economic activities that largely shaped the face of modern European landscapes.

FURTHER READINGS

Behre, K.-E. *Die Pflanzenreste aus der Fruehgeschichtlichen Wurt Elisenhof.* Bern and Frankfurt: Lang, 1976.

———. The History of Rye Cultivation in Europe. *Vegetation History and Archaeobotany* (1992) 1:141–156.

Krzywinski, K., S. Fjelldal, and E.-C. Solvedt. Recent Palaeoethnobotanical Work at the Medieval Excavations at Bryggen, Bergen, Norway. In *Site, Economy, and Environment.* Ed. B. Proudfoot. BAR International Series 173. Oxford: British Archaeological Reports, 1983, pp. 145–169.

Moffett, L. The Archaeobotanical Evidence for Free-Threshing Tetraploid Wheat in Britain. In *Palaeoethnobotany and Archaeology.* Ed. E. Hajnolova and B. Chropovsky. International Workgroup for Palaeoethnobotany, Eighth Symposium, Nitra-Nove Vozokany, 1989. Nitra: Archaeological Institute of the Slovac Academy of Sciences, 1991, pp. 233–243.

Murphy, P. The Cereals and Crop Weeds. In *West Stow: The Anglo-Saxon Village.* Vol. 1. By S. West. East Anglian Archaeology Report 24. Ipswich: Suffolk County Planning Department, 1985, pp. 100–108.

Van der Veen, M. An Early Medieval Hilltop Settlement in Molise: The Plant Remains from D85. *Papers of the British School at Rome* (1985) 53:211–224.

Van Zeist, W., K. Wasylikowa, and K.-E. Behre. *Progress in Old World Palaeoethnobotany.* A Retrospective on the Occasion of Twenty Years of the International Work Group for Palaeoethnobotany. Rotterdam and Brookfield: A.A. Balkema, 1991.

Peter Murphy

SEE ALSO
Dye Plants; West Stow; Woodland

P

Parks

A park in the medieval sense is an area of private land in which the owner keeps deer (or wild cattle or wild boar). They were confined by a wall or a strong fence called a *park pale*.

The Romans had kept deer and other animals in parks. The idea spread to other countries, especially to England, where parks became abundant in the twelfth century and in the thirteenth century were a major feature of the landscape. The chief animal of parks was the fallow deer. Unlike forests, English parks usually had at least some woodland.

The original function of parks was as formal deer farms and status symbols; the ability to eat deer was a privilege of at least minor aristocracy. Parks also functioned as places in which to hold ceremonial hunts and as formal landscapes surrounding great houses. Both these functions, however, were mainly postmedieval developments.

A medieval park can be recognized in the field by its outline, a compact shape often defined by a bank or a wall; sometimes a parish boundary has been deflected to conform to the park shape. There may be remains of the building called the *park lodge* and of internal compartments for excluding deer from parts of the park in which the trees were growing again after a recent felling. Occasionally, medieval trees themselves may survive; these do not necessarily prove that the park is medieval, for it was the custom in later periods to preserve ancient trees when creating a new park.

FURTHER READINGS

Rackham, O. *The History of the [British and Irish] Countryside.* London: Dent, 1986.

Oliver Rackham

SEE ALSO

Forests; Woodland

Picts

It was the Romans who gave the native peoples of northern Britain the name we know them by today—the Picts, Picti, or Painted Ones—first recorded in A.D. 297. The name refers to the people who lived beyond Hadrian's Wall, the northern Roman boundary of the time. We do not know what these peoples called themselves, so the nickname remains. As with the name, so the people have remained a mystery for many centuries. Even in the 1950s, the Picts were referred to in archaeological terms as a problem.

An anonymous twelfth-century Norwegian historian wrote:

The Picts were little more than pygmies in stature. They worked marvels in the morning and evening building towns, but at midday they entirely lost their strength and lurked through fear in little underground houses.

Combined with comments concerning the tradition of body painting or tattoos, the Picts were thus remembered in school history books.

The reality seems to have been somewhat different. It is true that one of the most distinctive hallmarks of Pictish culture, the symbol stone that is found throughout areas of Pictish presence in both northern and southern Scotland, still evokes mystery and controversy over the meaning of the images carved on the stones. However, evidence of distinctive settlement types is now available, as well as forms of burial and jewelry, and the picture is somewhat clearer than in preceding decades.

The Picts were a group of indigenous peoples in Scotland, named first in the third century A.D. and recognized into the early ninth century when the Kingdom of the Picts came to a gradual end under political pressure from both Scots and Vikings. During the intervening years, however, Pictland and the tribal confederacies centered in northern Pictland (Sutherland to Orkney) and southern Pictland (centered in Fife and Angus) developed a quite distinctive material culture and history. Throughout both main centers, the place-name record can help identify a Pictish presence; the presence of such elements as *pit-* in the place name, as in Pittenweem or Pitlochry, is distinctively Pictish. Historical records of the Pictish kings themselves do not begin until the sixth century, and by the end of that century Pictland was being converted to Christianity. This had a profound effect on Pictish art in its many forms, and art is one of the main sources of evidence for the Picts.

The earliest carved symbol stones (Class I) probably date to the period up to the mid-sixth century and include incised symbols—animals, mirrors, combs, and others—on stone that has barely been shaped. Following these and the advent of Christianity, the stones are roughly shaped and have a wide range of symbols as well as a cross on one face (Class II). These are followed by Class III symbol stones, which are carefully shaped and prepared with elaborate cross designs as a dominant fea-

P

ture. Class III stones date to the late eighth–ninth centuries, and some show figural embossed scenes. Scattered widely throughout north and south Pictland, these symbol stones appear in isolation (especially Class I) and may represent boundary markers or even burial stones. Those that appear in large collections may possibly have been brought from a nearby churchyard. There are some examples of symbol stones that include inscriptions in ogam, a linear script that is often unintelligible, but, where this can be read, a personal name is often included. It is not clear what the symbols represent, and only in the case of the later pieces with elaborate cross designs can a precise function for the stones be suggested. These stones remain something of a mystery.

The incised symbols, which include fish, crescents and V-rods, dumbbells, serpents, mirrors, and combs, are distinctively Pictish. Some of these motifs also appear in metalwork; for example, silver chains with incised dumbbells are known from southern Pictland. However, the penannular brooches of a form found in the St. Ninian's Isle treasure in Shetland (a massive Pictish hoard deposited in the late Pictish period) were being manufactured in Orkney. The identification of these as Pictish rests on their forms and associated information rather than the presence of incised symbols.

Recent archaeological advances in our understanding of the Picts have been great. The view of Picts retiring to live in holes in the ground is hard to dispel. Underground structures, *souterrains,* are common features in Pictland. It would be too easy to see them as impractical refuges for endangered Picts. The evidence suggests, however, that these were underground stores for small surface buildings. Other buildings have been identified as Pictish houses; these are of a very distinctive cellular, almost amoebic, form, built of stone with flagstone floors. Although they are still not common, examples have been excavated in Birsay at Buckquoy. The Pictish houses at Birsay are quite different in plan from the succeeding Viking buildings.

One final area of progress in identifying and studying the material culture of the Picts is that of burial monuments. The use of round or square stone cairns with stone kerbs around them has been identified at several sites in Pictland. In some cases, such as Watenan, Caithness, the cairn may have been surmounted by a symbol stone. The cairn itself was set on clean sand. A stone coffin or cist containing an extended body was laid out beneath the sand. Usually, there are no grave goods with these burials, but the distinctive method of burial serves to mark it as Pictish.

It has taken several decades to demythologize the Picts to this extent, but the results of recent archaeological research have altered traditional views about them.

FURTHER READINGS

Friell, J.P.G., and W.G. Watson. *Pictish Studies: Settlement, Burial, and Art in Dark Age Northern Britain.* Oxford: British Archaeological Reports, 1984.

Ralston, I., and J. Inglis. *Foul Hordes: The Picts in the North-East and Their Background.* Aberdeen: University of Aberdeen Anthropological Museum, 1984.

Ritchie, A. *Picts.* Edinburgh: HMSO, 1989.

Colleen Batey

SEE ALSO
Birsay; Scotland, Dark Age

Pilgrim Souvenirs

Pilgrimage was the main reason that the majority of people during the Medieval period undertook lengthy journeys in peacetime. Most religious shrines catered for the great numbers of travelers on pilgrimages, and for their own revenues, by providing mementos to suit every purse, commonly in the form of a brooch or badge of lead-tin alloy. Recent finds, especially in London, where hundreds of these badges have been excavated from closely dated deposits, give some idea of the great range of cheap souvenirs brought home by returning pilgrims from across much of western Europe and beyond. These mass-produced trinkets, from journeys to shrines of both officially recognized and unofficial saints, are among the most immediately attractive and intriguing of widespread medieval finds. They often feature a representation of the saint together with some readily recognized attribute relating to miracles performed or to the manner of martyrdom.

The murder of Archbishop Thomas Becket (c. 1118–1170) in Canterbury Cathedral in 1170 quickly gave rise to a cult of considerable importance, for which *ampullae* (small vessels, mainly of tin to hold holy water) were produced in substantial numbers. The remarkable variety of designs and the range of quality of Canterbury souvenirs, ampullae, and badges over the next three centuries are difficult to parallel among survivals from any other center. Large numbers of Canterbury mementos have been found in London, but there is also a significant scatter across Britain and much of northern Europe. The majority of Becket ampullae have the martyrdom scene on one

P

face with three knights in full armor attacking the archbishop, and on the other the archbishop giving a blessing. Several have an openwork frame with the legend "Thomas is the best healer for the pious sick" in Latin. They almost all have two handles by which they could be worn suspended from a string or a ribbon around the neck, as wear on one face frequently attests. Canterbury's exceptionally prolific brooch souvenirs frequently refer to specific sights in the cathedral. The murder weapon kept there is commemorated by miniature swords, some of which are accurate replicas that can be drawn from a metal scabbard that is furnished with a pin for attachment. The head reliquary, in which the part of Becket's skull that was cut off at the murder was held, is represented by several hundred surviving badges of his mitred bust (the more elaborate versions having an openwork canopy), relatively few of which are from the same mold. The martyr's tomb set with jewels and other offerings is reproduced on other brooches, as are scenes from his last journey back from exile in France by sea (Becket in a ship) and then overland to Canterbury (Becket on horseback). A few parts of the stone molds in which some of the these souvenirs were cast have been unearthed in Canterbury. A particularly skilled mold maker, working for Canterbury in the late fourteenth century, is responsible for the finest surviving martyrdom souvenirs and for brooches the size of latter-day postcards commemorating visits to the shrine of Our Lady Undercroft (also at Canterbury Cathedral but not related directly to the cult of Becket). Pendants in the form of "Canterbury bells," of hard pewter alloy so that they could be rung, were yet another successful line in Becket souvenirs, popular in the fourteenth century particularly. Like many other English and Continental cult centers, Canterbury turned during the late fifteenth and early sixteenth centuries, at a time when pilgrimage was in general decline, to souvenirs stamped in copper-alloy foil. A few silver-foil mementos with Becket's head also appear among finds from this immediately pre-Reformation period, but the pedestrian workmanship does not match the precious material. The establishment of the Protestant Church after 1536 in England by Henry VIII (1491–1547) put an effective end to the centuries-old tradition of pilgrimage and its souvenirs, not only at Canterbury but across the country.

Other shrines that were, from the numbers of finds now known, particularly popular include those of Our Lady of Walsingham in Norfolk and the Holy Rood of Boxley in Kent (the Rood, an elaborate crucifix, was even-tually burned publicly in London at the Reformation). Slightly less lasting in popularity were ampullae from Bromholm Priory, as well as badges from the shrines of the English protomartyr St. Alban at St. Albans and those for the unofficial saint, John Schorn, based at Windsor and North Marston in Buckinghamshire in the later Medieval period. Schorn was a local rector whose feats as an exorcist are commemorated in badges showing him standing in the pulpit, with the devil to one side looking out of a large boot into which he had just been conjured as the result of an encounter between the two.

The badges found at Salisbury include souvenirs from most of the important shrines in England and several abroad, with an emphasis that does not occur elsewhere on the local cults of St. (Bishop) Osmund, the founder of Salisbury Cathedral, and of Our Lady of Salisbury. Similarly, East Anglian cults are prominent among a wide range of souvenirs found in Norfolk.

Foreign cults are well known from pilgrims' souvenirs found widely in Britain. The Continental fashion was for badges to have small rings at the corners, by which they could be sewn in place on a garment, rather than a pin at the back. They also tend to place less emphasis on openwork, a prominent feature among those of English origin. The Holy Land itself is unrepresented by finds of this kind, but souvenirs of journeys to Rome (usually with the images of St. Peter and St. Paul, respectively, holding their symbols of a key and a sword) are known in some numbers from excavations. The important Spanish shrine of St. James at Compostela is represented by badges in the form of a scallop shell, originally the distinguishing motif of this particular cult, which became widely used as a symbol for all pilgrims.

Several routes to these and other major cult centers, such as Cologne (the Three Kings) and Paris (St. Denis), can be reconstructed from finds in Britain from shrines along the way, some of which remain well known while others are more obscure today. Souvenirs from Mont St. Michel depict the archangel bestriding the stricken Satan, while those from the less famous shrine of St. Josse (also on the north coast of France) depict the saint as a bearded and hooded figure holding a staff and a rosary, and those from the shrine of John the Baptist at Amiens copy the round face of the reliquary of the supposed fragment of the saint's skull that drew pilgrims there. A late thirteenth-century souvenir of a visit by a Londoner to Toulouse in the southern part of France provides the sole surviving, detailed indication of the form of the image of the local Madonna, the focus for pilgrims there.

Toward the end of the Medieval period, a number of secular badges, including political ones relating to factions prominent in the Wars of the Roses in England (1455–1485), began to appear, and even some of the religious souvenirs include political motifs. This trend is particularly evident in the many badges found in London and elsewhere from the Windsor-based cult of the "martyred" Lancastrian king Henry VI. Henry's death at Yorkist hands was seized upon for propaganda by the new Tudor dynasty, and the cult was fostered as a means of damaging the reputations of potential rivals for the throne in the early years of Henry VII's reign (1485–1509). The number and variety of Henry VI badges found in London indicates considerable popular support at street level in the capital for this cult. On the Continent, other causes are evident among secular badges, and there is also a range with explicit sexual motifs.

A number of badges remain unidentified, but new finds continue to provide fresh information. The discoveries over the past twenty-five years have transformed the picture available of these popular trinkets and have provided an array of images of varied quality to add to knowledge of this facet of medieval religious art.

FURTHER READINGS

Jones, M. The Secular Badges. In *Heilig en Profaan*. Ed. H.J.E. van Beuningen and A.M. Kolderweij. Rotterdam Papers 8. Cothen: Stichting Middeleeuwse Religieuze en Profane Insignes, 1993, pp. 99–109.

Spencer, B. Medieval Pilgrim Badges. In *Rotterdam Papers: A Contribution to Medieval Archaeology*. Ed. J.G.N. Renaud. Rotterdam: Coordinate Commissie van Advies Inzake Archaeologisch Onderzoek Binnen het Ressort Rotterdam, 1968, pp. 137–153.

———. King Henry of Windsor and the London Pilgrim. In *Collectanea Londiniensia*. Studies in London Archaeology and History presented to Rolph Merrifield. Ed. Joanna Bird, Hugh Chapman, and John Clark. Special Paper 2. London: London and Middlesex Archaeological Society, 1978, pp. 235–264.

———. *Medieval Pilgrim Badges from Norfolk.*. Norfolk: Norfolk Museums Service, 1980.

———. Pilgrimage. In *The Age of Chivalry*. Ed. J. Alexander and P. Binski. Exhibition catalog. London: Royal Academy of Arts, 1987, especially pp. 218–224.

———. *Pilgrim Badges and Secular Souvenirs*. Medieval Catalog 2. Salisbury: Salisbury and South Wiltshire Museum, 1990.

Geoff Egan

Place Names

The most direct contribution made by place-name studies to archaeological knowledge consists of references in place names to archaeological remains. In England, most of these references date from the period known as the Dark Ages, which followed the collapse of the Roman Empire in the fifth century A.D. The majority of place names in England are in the Old English language, which was brought into the country by the Anglo-Saxons, who became the dominant ethnic group. These immigrant Anglo-Saxons came into a country that was liberally sprinkled with monuments of prehistoric and Roman date. They saw these remains not as the work of their own ancestors but as elements in a landscape that they appraised with the fresh, sharp eyes of peasant farmers, and their comments, though based on visual impressions rather than folk memory or archaeological knowledge, are sufficiently precise to be of practical interest to modern archaeologists. It has become commonplace for teams of rescue archaeologists prospecting the route of a new motorway or the site of a building complex to be guided to the most interesting areas by "archaeological" terms incorporated in field names.

The Anglo-Saxon perception of prehistoric sites in England involved a classification according to assumed functions of burial or defense. Prehistoric burial mounds, which are numerous today, would have been much more numerous in the fifth century, and many that are now diffuse plow spreads would have been higher and sharper when the Anglo-Saxons saw them. The words most frequently used by the Anglo-Saxons for tumuli were *beorg* (modern *barrow*) and *hlāw* (which becomes -*low* in place names). The Scandinavians who settled in eastern and northern England in the late ninth and early tenth centuries used the Norse word *haugr* for burial places, and this becomes -*how* in such names are Spellhow ("speech mound," referring to a tumulus that was the marker for an assembly place).

The words *beorg, hlāw,* and *haugr* are not foolproof guides to the presence of tumuli. They can be used for natural hills as well as artificial ones, and the frequent siting of tumuli on commanding eminences adds to the uncertainty. But there are many instances in which these words certainly refer to burial mounds, and, if a place name containing one of them occurs in an area where there is no natural hill, the archaeologist should accord them serious attention.

Modern archaeologists adopted the word *barrow* as a technical term for a tumulus because it survived in that

P

sense in southwest England, an area that attracted much early archaeological attention. The communal burial places of the Neolithic period were covered by long earthen banks, and these were called "long barrows" by the Anglo-Saxons, as they are by archaeologists today. Old English *langan beorge* has become Lambrough in Bibury, Gloucestershire, and Longborough near Moreton-in-the-Marsh in the same county, and near both villages the long barrows are still to be seen. The round barrows of later periods, which were raised over single burials, sometimes have names that show that they had been robbed when the Anglo-Saxons saw them. Idel Barrow, in Upton St. Leonards, Gloucestershire, contains the Old English *īdel* (modern *idle*), "empty, useless"; and Brokenborough, "broken barrow," in Wiltshire probably refers to a tumulus with the familiar robber's hollow in the top. Tumuli were often chosen as meeting places. Modbury in Dorset is Old English *gemōthbeorg*, or "moot barrow."

In the seventh century, the Anglo-Saxons adopted a custom of building burial mounds for the most elevated members of their society. In naming these, they preferred the word *hlāw* to *beorg*. An Anglo-Saxon princely burial in Buckinghamshire gave rise to the village name Taplow. The mound is in the churchyard there, and the rich grave goods are in the British Museum. Roman tumuli are referred to by *beorg* in Thornborough, Buckinghamshire, and by *hlāw* in Bartlow, Cambridgeshire. Groups of tumuli are referred to in such names as Twemlow in Cheshire, and Tomlow, "two lows," in Warwickshire and Rumbelow in Staffordshire (Old English *thrimhlāwum*, "three lows").

For prehistoric monuments that they judged to have been built for defensive purposes, the Anglo-Saxons most frequently used the word *burh* (dative *byrig*), or "fort." The nominative *burh* usually becomes *borough*, and the dative *byrig* is most frequently represented by *-bury*. This "fort" word and the "tumulus" word *beorg* are sometimes confused in early spellings of place names, but, if there are good records, the philologist can usually say which word is more likely to be involved.

Among the most striking remains of earlier cultures encountered by the Anglo-Saxons were the great hillforts of the Iron Age, and many of these have names ending in *-bury*, like Cadbury, Danebury, and Oldbury. The word was also used for the houses of upper-class Anglo-Saxons, which were "forts" because they were surrounded by a ditch and a palisade; toward the end of the Anglo-Saxon period, it came to mean "town," which is the sense of the modern "borough." This late sense is found in the names of some towns that grew up at the gates of tenth-century monasteries, like Peterborough and Bury St. Edmund. Investigation of field names ending in *-bury* has, on a number of occasions, led to the discovery of defensive earthworks, invisible now on the ground but sometimes discernible in air photographs.

Some prehistoric earthworks have names beginning with *Grims-* or *Grimes-*. These contain oblique references to the god Woden, who was known as *Grim*, "the masked one," because of his habit of going about in various disguises. There are a number of linear earthworks called Grimsditch or Grimsdyke. In Suffolk, a group of hollows left by Neolithic flint mining is called Grimes Graves, and a large Bronze Age enclosure on Dartmoor in Devon is called Grimspound. Woden also has earthworks and tumuli ascribed to him under his proper name, as in the great earthwork called Wansdyke in southwest England; a village in Kent called Woodnesborough, "Woden's tumulus"; and Wednesbury, "Woden's fort," near Birmingham.

Roman remains are impressive today, and they must have been much more so when the Anglo-Saxons first saw them. The usual Old English term for a Roman site with an enclosing wall (whether town or fort) was *ceaster*, borrowed from the Latin *castra*. This occurs by itself, as in Chester, Caister, and Caistor, but it is more frequently combined with *tūn*, the most common Old English term for a settlement, as in Chesterton and Casterton, or with topographical words, as in Chesterford and Chesterfield. Most frequently, it occurs as the final element in a compound, as in Silchester, Dorchester, Worcester, Exeter, and Wroxeter. Sometimes, as in Dorchester, Exeter, and Wroxeter, *ceaster* has been added to the Romano-British name of the town, which the Anglo-Saxons must have learned from the descendants of Romano-British people. Roman roads (which remained important throughout the Middle Ages) were called *strǣt* (a borrowing from the second part of Latin *via strata*), and villages or towns called Street, Streatham, Stretton, Stratton, Stratford, Stretford, Streetley, and Streatly lie on, or very close to, the major roads of Roman Britain. Bath derives its name from the ruins of the structures that enabled the Romans to use the hot springs there as a major recreational source. Places called Wickham and Wykeham are on sites of small Roman towns. This name derives from the Old English *hām*, or "settlement," and *wīc*, which is a borrowing from the Latin *vicus*.

The above account details some ways in which place names refer directly to prehistoric and Roman remains. In a less direct way, place names are important to the archaeologist as general guides to the state of the landscape and the density and type of settlement patterns in early times. Every student of landscape and settlement history should be aware of the evidence contained in place names, which is summarized in the books by K. Cameron (1988) and M. Gelling (1988, 1993) listed below.

FURTHER READINGS

Cameron, K. *English Place-Names.* 4th ed. London: Batsford, 1988.

Ekwall, E. *The Concise Oxford Dictionary of English Place-Names.* 4th ed. Oxford: Clarendon, 1960.

Gelling, M. *Signposts to the Past: Place-Names and the History of England.* 2nd ed. Chichester: Phillimore, 1988.

———. *Place-Names in the Landscape: The Geographical Roots of Britain's Place-Names.* London: Dent, 1993.

Nicolaisen, W.H.F., M. Gelling, and M. Richards. *The Names of Towns and Cities in Britain.* 2nd ed. London: Batsford, 1986.

Spittal, J., and J. Field. *A Reader's Guide to the Place-Names of the United Kingdom.* Stamford: P. Watkins, 1990.

M. Gelling

SEE ALSO
Rescue Archaeology

Poland
See Polish State, Early.

Polish State, Early

The early Polish state lay in the valleys of the Oder and Vistula Rivers in the center of the north European Plain between the Carpathian Mountains and the Baltic coast; to the east lay the Kievan ("Russian") state, to the south were the Moravian and Bohemian states. Since 1945, the frontiers of the modern state have been broadly similar in extent to the boundaries of the early medieval state, stimulating new interest in research into its origins. The written sources give little information about this area before the eleventh century, and archaeology is a major source of data. After World War II, a large-scale program of intensive multidisciplinary studies was undertaken to investigate the beginnings of the Polish state in connection with the millennium of the first historical mentions of the state in the 960s. In an innovative project (1946–1966) that has generated a vast literature, many aspects of the process of the formation and the functioning of the state were investigated. Most of the major centers and many minor sites were excavated; between 1946 and 1966, more than 240 sites (enclosed and open settlements, towns, cemeteries, architectural remains) were investigated. The silver hoards from Polish territory were also inventoried and fully studied, and almost all the relevant information in the written sources was reexamined. The project also led to methodological innovations that were later utilized elsewhere; for the first time, Marxist paradigms were used in Polish archaeology, to interpret the investigated phenomena in socioeconomic terms. The cooperation between archaeology and other historical and natural-science disciplines was a notable feature of this project. The process of state formation turned out to be more complex than had previously been thought, and it demonstrates great territorial and organizational variability between the period of formation of the state and its transformation in the thirteenth century into something approaching the western European model.

Slav settlement had begun to stabilize in this area toward the end of the sixth century; by the ninth century (as in other Slav territories), a number of strong tribal groupings had developed here. Among them were the Polane of Great Poland, the Vislane of Little Poland, and several groups in Silesia and along the Pomeranian coast. The Polane and the Vislane show signs of growing influence and economic growth in the ninth century, while the Pomeranians formed part of a system of long-distance exchange (evidenced by Arab silver hoards and single-coin finds along the Baltic coast). None of these groupings can be considered states; the southern areas (Silesia and Little Poland) were under Bohemian influence in the earlier part of the tenth century, though neither eastern nor western neighbors were strong enough to establish political control of the Oder-Vistula watershed. Social organization in all these areas seems to have been fragmented and personal, based around the strongholds (*grody*), most of which are best interpreted as elite centers. These are often the focus of settlement clusters; many *grody* have settlements immediately outside the defenses, as well as scattered in the hinterland. These settlement clusters are surrounded by areas devoid of settlement. Several of these clusters form groups separated by wider blanks in the settlement pattern. These probably equate with the tribal groupings known from the written sources (and some that are unknown from written records). The archaeological evidence demonstrates a notable increase in the number of settlements and in the quality of cultural material throughout the eighth and ninth centuries.

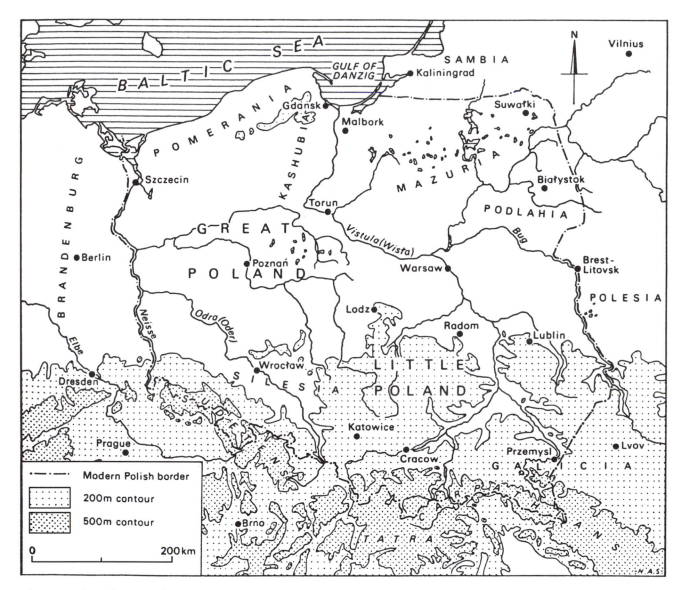

The geography and regions of modern Poland (after Bursche and Taylor 1991:589).

In the A.D. 960s, circumstances allowed the prince of the Polane tribe, Mieszko I (c. 930–992) of the Piast dynasty, to subdue several of the neighboring groups, beginning the process of territorial aggrandizement and institutionalization of power leading to the formation of a state. This was centered at first on the old tribal centers of Gniezno and Poznan in Great Poland. In many areas of Poland, former tribal centers seem to have been destroyed and replaced by new ones. Mieszko's son Bolesław (r. 992–1025) united Little Poland and Krakow (later to be the medieval capital) with the kingdom and attempted to ex-

pand east and west. The extent to which the subject tribes felt themselves to be ethnically related to the Polane, however, may be judged by the frequency with which the early state split up. (Pomerania was held only briefly for a number of times before the fifteenth century; even the central part of the state dissolved into feudal statelets ruled by minor princes of the Piast dynasty between 1138 and 1333.) The new state was officially recognized by the German emperor Otto III (980–1002) at the Congress of Gniezno in A.D. 1000, and in 1025 the coronation of Bolesław took place. This did not, however, prevent increasing conflict with the Ottonian German Empire in later years and frequent invasions from the west, ultimately leading to the loss of parts of the western territories, especially Silesia and western Pomerania (which became part of Poland again only in 1945).

Under Mieszko and Bolesław, the state underwent a number of important socioeconomic transitions. The most striking features were the dynamic growth of the new social system and similar progress in the diversification of culture. The archaeological evidence indicates that this period saw marked social stratification, an increase in craft specialization, a rise in living standards, and a further demographic increase (it is estimated that 1.25 million people inhabited late tenth-century Poland in an area of 250,000 km²). It is difficult at this stage to decide whether these phenomena are causes or effects of the state-formation process.

One of the most important ideological changes was the conversion to Christianity in 966. At first, the new religion most strongly affected only the upper echelons of society and major centers, penetrating only slowly into the rural communities. In A.D. 1000, Poland was able to establish its own ecclesiastical organization (independent of the German Empire) with the archbishopric at Gniezno. These changes are visible in the archaeological record; inhumation now becomes common, at first in rural cemeteries, as well as beside churches, but the burial beside churches becomes the rule by the middle of the twelfth century. The first inhumations (tenth–twelfth [?] centuries) have grave goods in a pagan fashion. The most spectacular traces of the new ideology, however, are a number of monuments of "pre-Romanesque" churches, both of basilican and central plan, from a number of sites (Gniezno, Poznan, Ostrów Lednicki, Kracow).

The social structure of the early Polish state broadly resembled that of Carolingian feudalism. The ruler moved among several royal centers *(sedes regni principales)* with his Court and personal troops *(druzina),* while a count palatine handled administrative matters. Local administration was based on the *grody,* with power in the hands of an elite hierarchy answerable to the holders of the most important regional centers (which were later known as *castellanies).* These were entrusted with wide military, administrative, judicial, and fiscal powers over the people residing in the neighborhood. In densely settled areas, the radius of influence of the center did not exceed 14 km, though territories were larger on the fringes of the state. It seems that, through the armed men attached to the five hundred or so *grody* in early Piast Poland, the state exercised a monopoly of armed force. The *grody* were also the centers where tribute was exacted. The *grody* of the centralized state were inhabited by large groups of lords and strong military garrisons, which led to a growing demand for consumer goods. These demands were satisfied by the extensive luxury trade and also stimulated local production. The *grody* were additionally supplied by a system of "services," in which, in order to make use of and to spur rural production, the Piast monarchy controlled the output of craftsmen specializing in certain branches of production, according to a carefully conceived plan. The names of some villages responsible for providing certain services or personnel evidenced in the written sources have survived in Poland to the present day (e.g., *Sokolniki* [falconers], *Piekary* [bakers], *Skotniki* [cattle herders], and *Winiary* [vintners]). The elaborate system operated within its fundamental framework from the middle of the tenth century to the end of the eleventh. Craftsmen also inhabited the settlements immediately adjacent to the stronghold. By the end of the eleventh century, the system of services was being replaced by local exchange of products from a variety of workshops. The state also tried to control trade routes; Gdansk was founded in the last decades of the tenth century to try to capture some of the Baltic trade from other centers on the Baltic coast. It is in this context that we should view the first attempts at minting a coinage by the first kings (at first mainly for prestige). At about this time, the flow of Arab silver into the Baltic dries up. Material from c. 350 hoards and more than 150 single finds of coins from settlements and graves serves as evidence of the two pecuniary functions of silver money: thesaurization (the formation of a treasury) and as currency, providing reliable evidence for the changing structure of monetary circulation. Silver hoards of the period after 950 contain many western European coins (English, Danish, and German, including some especially minted for trade with the Slavs), as well as fragmented silver jewelry, which was clearly used as a medium of payment (by weight). By the second half of the eleventh century, however, we find coinage (including, from the reign [1058–1079] of Bolesław the Bold, coins from Polish mints) being used on an increasing scale as an element in the formation of local markets. Silver hoards, characteristic of the period of the rise of the new society, become much rarer from the second half of the eleventh century, and from this period we have more numerous mentions in the written sources of markets, both rural and attached to *grody.*

The process of urbanization had its beginnings in the settlements of craftsmen in and near the *grody,* presumably

P

even before state formation. As elite centers, these sites also functioned as political and administrative centers, as well as nodal points in exchange networks. The settlements *(podgřodzia)* adjacent to the *gřody* became the focus for the economic development of the late eleventh century. Some of them had been surrounded by earthen and timber ramparts like the *gřody* themselves, though they each performed a different function. The *podgřodzia* were relatively small built-up areas (which may sometimes have had a regular plan and wooden streets) and housed a motley population: members of the elite, members of the military garrison, merchants, innkeepers, artisans, and servants, as well as fishermen or peasants. Although little is known about the social conditions of life and work of these people, it seems that they were settled by the will of the lords of the *gřody* or settled there of their own accord. Part of their output was presumably due to the lords of the *gřody.* Written sources mention markets adjacent to many *podgřodzia.* Archaeological evidence shows the increase in craft specialization and consequent technical improvement from the mid-tenth century onward in a number of crafts (pottery, shoemaking and leather work, bone and antler work, and fine metalworking). It was not, however, until the formation of local exchange networks that these centers took on most of the characteristics of medieval towns.

FURTHER READINGS

Barford, P. Paradigms Lost: Polish Archaeology and Post-war Politics. *Archaeologia Polona* (1993) 31:257–270.

Bosl, K., A. Gieysztor, F. Graus, M.M. Postan, and F. Seibt, eds. *Eastern and Western Europe in the Middle Ages.* London: Harcourt Brace Jovanovich, 1970.

Bursche, A., and T. Taylor, eds. A Panorama of Polish Archaeology. *Antiquity* (1991) 65:583–721.

Gieysztor, A., S. Kieniewicz, E. Rostworowski, J. Tazbir, and H. Wereszycki, eds. *History of Poland.* Warsaw: Panstwowe Wydawnictwo Naukowe, 1968.

Hensel, W. *The Beginnings of the Polish State.* Warsaw: Polonia, 1960.

———. The Origin of Western and Eastern European Slav Towns. In *European Towns: Their Archaeology and Early History.* Ed. M. Barley. London: Academic, 1977, pp. 373–390.

Hensel, W., L. Leciejewicz, and S.Tabaczyński. En Pologne médiévale: L'archéologie au service de l'histoire. *Annales Economies Civilisations* (1962) 17:209–238.

Leciejwicz, L. Medieval Archaeology in Poland: Current Problems and Research Methods. *Medieval Archaeology* (1976) 20:1–15. London.

———. Medieval Archaeology and Its Problems. In *Unconventional Archaeology: New Approaches and Goals in Polish Archaeology.* Ed. R. Schild. Wroclaw: Ossolineum, 1980, pp. 191–211.

———. Medieval Archaeology in Eastern Europe. In *The Study of Medieval Archaeology.* Ed. H. Andersson and J. Wienberg. Stockholm: Almqvist a. Wiksell Int, 1993, pp. 75–83.

Topolski, J. *An Outline History of Poland.* Warsaw: Interpress, 1986.

P.M. Barford and S. Tabaczyński

SEE ALSO
Ostrów Lednicki

Poultry

The keeping of poultry, or domestic birds, was common throughout all of medieval Europe. The most popular species kept were the chicken *(Gallus gallus)* and the goose *(Anser anser).* Less frequently, domestic duck *(Anas platyrhynchos)* and pigeon *(Columba livia)* were reared. A number of other bird species are known to have been kept at this time (pheasant, peafowl, and partridge), but these were not true domesticates and are not dealt with here.

Domestic chicken had been well established in Europe during the Iron Age and the Roman period. However, its dietary and economic importance increased substantially in the Medieval period, as indicated by archaeozoological finds that show a significant increase in the proportion of identifiable chicken remains relative to mammalian species throughout central Europe.

The value of poultry is well documented in the historical records, with domestic chickens (and geese) and/or their eggs commonly used to pay rents and fines. Egg production is strongly implied by the recovery of predominantly adult bones from archaeological deposits throughout Europe and by the reconstructed sex ratio of populations that strongly favors female birds. Furthermore, the recovery of broken long bones and the use of X-rays can reveal deposits of medullary bone in the shaft, indicative of laying females within the population. Fragments of eggshell have been recovered by careful sieving of some sites, but little work has been done on the identification of such material.

Fowls would also have been an important source of meat, and medieval flock structure from a number of central European sites has been compared to that of modern-day multipurpose fowls. Documentary evidence indicates that caponization (male sterilization) may have been practiced to increase meat yields, but this is difficult to verify archaeologically.

Backyard chicken rearing in towns was common, and fowls probably had to forage for their food among domestic waste. Some evidence for malnutrition can be found in the faunal remains; at medieval Nantwich in Britain, for example, a chicken sternum exhibited marked bending, which has been linked to a deficiency condition. Similar evidence has been found at the site of Wood Quay in Dublin. Another indicator of less sophisticated poultry-rearing techniques at this time is the general decline in chicken height and robusticity after the Roman period in Europe. Birds bred in rural areas, however, may have fared better.

In medieval Europe, there seems to be little evidence for more than one or two different breeds, and selective breeding was probably not attempted until the late Medieval and post-Medieval periods. In parts of the Netherlands and Poland, there is evidence for both a small and a large breed of fowl in the early Medieval period, which may have been kept separately.

Osteologically, domestic chicken is very similar to the domestic guinea fowl (Numida meleagris), which was first introduced into Europe from Africa during the Roman period. Documentary references to guinea fowl exist for both medieval Britain and France, but the bones of guinea fowl have not yet been identified archaeologically. This is not surprising, given that an osteological guide for their differentiation appeared only recently in the literature (MacDonald 1992), and thus the situation is perhaps in need of reappraisal.

The rearing of domestic geese was largely confined to low-lying, marshy environments. In these areas, the goose would have been at least as economically important as chicken, with a greater potential meat yield. Geese were more commonly consumed in towns than in the rural areas in which they would have been raised, and they were well suited to being driven to market on foot. The geese may have been sold alive, or already butchered, as at Wood Quay in Ireland, where there is good evidence for systematic longitudinal butchering of the birds, to be sold in two halves, with the low-meat-bearing feet and wingtips already removed. In some areas, drainage of the wetlands to increase agricultural productivity may have led to a decline in the goose population over time.

In most archaeological contexts, the bones of adult geese predominate, which may indicate the importance of egg production. However, at some high-status sites, such as Barnards Castle (London), there is evidence for the consumption of goslings.

A further economic function of the goose was the production of feathers, with goose feathers favored as quills for writing and as flights for arrows.

Duck bones are only rarely encountered in archaeological deposits of this period and never in large numbers. Furthermore, it is difficult to distinguish osteologically between wild and domestic species. That domestic ducks were kept is known from documentary sources; at Winchester (England), for example, a city ordanance dating to 1380 bans both ducks and geese from the main streets. Like geese, ducks could be driven to market on foot and were probably of some economic significance in terms of both egg and meat production.

The remains of domestic pigeons are also rare. This may be due to the fact that they were kept in dovecotes by wealthy landowners and were of little significance to the economy as a whole. Charlemagne (742–814) is known to have kept ornamental pigeons. The practice is thought to have spread from France to England in the mid-thirteenth century.

FURTHER READINGS

Astill, G., and A. Grant, eds. *The Countryside of Medieval England*. Oxford: Basil Blackwell, 1988.

Benecke, N. On the Utilization of the Domestic Fowl in Central Europe from the Iron Age Up to the Middle Ages. *Archaeofauna* (1993) 2:21–31.

Coy, J. The Provision of Fowls and Fish for Towns. In *Diet and Crafts in Towns: The Evidence of Animal Remains from the Roman to the Post Medieval Periods*. Ed. D. Serjeantson and T. Waldron. BAR British Series 199. Oxford: British Archaeological Reports, 1989, pp. 25–40.

Ervynck, A. The Role of Birds in the Economy of Medieval and Post-Medieval Flanders: A Diversity of Interpretation Problems. *Archaeofauna* (1993) 2:107–119.

Hutton MacDonald, R., K.C. MacDonald, and K. Ryan. Domestic Geese from Medieval Dublin. *Archaeofauna* (1993) 2:205–218.

MacDonald, K.C. The Domestic Chicken (*Gallus gallus*) in Sub-Saharan Africa: A Background to Its Introduction

P

and Its Osteological Differentiation from Indigenous Fowls (Numidinae and *Francolinus* sp.). *Journal of Archaeological Science* (1992) 19:303–318.

Mason, I.L., ed. *Evolution of Domesticated Animals.* New York: Longman, 1984.

Prummel, W. *Excavations at Dorestad 2: Early Medieval Dorestad, an Archaeozoological Study.* Amerstoort: ROB, 1983.

Sidell, E.J. A Methodology for the Identification of Avian Eggshell from Archaeological Sites. *Archaeofauna* (1993) 2:45–51.

R. Hutton MacDonald and K.C. MacDonald

Prague

The beginnings of Prague are closely linked to the foundation of Prague Castle, located on the Hradčany spur near a ford over the Vltava (Moldau) River, where, as early as the late ninth century, a tripartite hillfort enclosed by a ditch and a rampart was established. The seat of the Czech Přemyslid princes was transferred there from Levý Hradec at a time when the Slavic hillforts around the Prague Basin (Šárka, Butovice, and Zámka) were losing their function.

The conversion of the Czech Prince Bořivoj to Christianity had led, prior to 885, to the construction of the Church of the Virgin Mary on the western bailey of Prague Castle. Cultural links between the Czech princes and the Great Moravian state were reflected in grave goods from the late ninth and early tenth centuries recovered from a cemetery in the northern forefield of the castle, as well as in the architecture of this church.

The topography of the Prague Basin, with terraces and deep valleys eroded by the Vltava, was of fundamental importance in the development of the Prague settlement agglomeration. The shallow riverbed near the Štvanice Islands and close to the Hradčany spur enabled caravans of traders and merchants to cross the river. The castle was of great strategic value as a new Přemyslid residence, overlooking the junction of the roads coming from the west and leading farther north, east, and south after crossing to the right bank. By the mid-tenth century, church buildings had been erected in the central part of the hillfort (the tripartite Basilica of St. George and the Rotunda of St. Vitus both reflecting Byzantine influences), as had the royal palace, close to which stood the stone throne where Czech sovereigns were elected until the twelfth century. In addition to stone buildings, the hillfort area also contained wooden huts.

The establishment of a mint, which produced silver denarii after the mid-tenth century, was a sign of the prosperity of the Přemyslid domain. A real building boom began in the years 1060–1069, with the construction of both the Basilica of St. Vitus and the bishop's house underway; the latter was not completed until the early twelfth century. In the twelfth century, the fortifications of the castle continued to be extended and underwent extensive alterations. In 1135, Prince Soběslav I began new stone ramparts and had a new palace set up within the enclosure; the Chapel of All Saints was attached to it.

Craftsmen settled on the southern slopes of Prague Castle, taking advantage of the terraces (Nebovidská, 182–185 m above sea level [a.s.l.], Újezdská, 188.5 m a.s.l.), which offered shelter from the excessive flooding of the Vltava on the eastern side. Their settlements have been archaeologically documented from both halves of the ninth century (by evidence obtained from Sněmovni ulice [Street] Nos. 37/III, 176/III). At the turn of the tenth century, the area extended northward in the direction of Pětikostelni náměstí (No. 28/III) and east of the present-day Malostranské náměstí (nam., or Square), the occupied area extending continuously from St. Thomas Monastery to Maltézské náměstí.

In the first half of the tenth century, the hillfort at Vyšehrad on the right bank of the Vltava began to play an active role, protecting the southern approach to the Prague Basin. The hillfort, which was already occupied in the early part of the century, contains the remains of a cruciform sacred building found beneath the foundations of the Basilica of St. Lawrence. The existence of a princely seat is very likely. After the mid-tenth century, a local mint was at work, coining the denarii of the ruling princes. The significance of Vyšehrad increased under the reign of Prince (later King) Vratislav I, who transferred his seat there from the castle and had a palace built, joined by a bridge to the chapter house, which was established in the eleventh century independently of the Prague bishopric. The Church of St. Peter was built in the area of the chapter house, a three-aisled Romanesque basilica with a double choir. The Basilica of St. Lawrence already stood outside the royal compound (Fig. 1).

In connection with the transfer of the princes' seat to Vyšehrad, a certain decline in the settlement below the castle is apparent, reflected archaeologically in the abandonment of the wooden semisunken houses on the western edge of the area. The cessation of iron production, which was not resumed until the mid-twelfth century as is indicated by two smelting pits containing fill from the

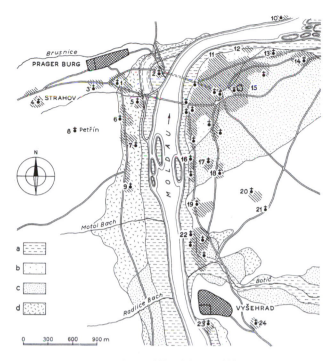

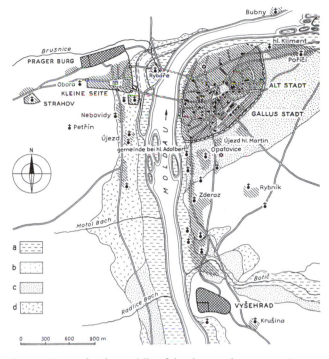

FIG. 1. Prague up to the middle of the twelfth century: *1,* Malostranské nám (Square); *2,* Klárov area, village of Rybáře, with settlement (eighth–thirteenth century) and St. Peter's Church; *3,* area of the village of Obora with settlement and St. John's Rotunda; *4,* Strahov with cemetery before monastery; *5,* Maltézské Nám., Monastery of the Knights of St. John; *6,* Hellichova ulice (Street), village of Nebovidy with the Church of St. Lawrence; *7,* village of Újezd with St. John's Church; *8,* Petřín hill with St. Lawrence; *9,* Sts. Philipe and James Church; *10,* St. Clement Church in the village of Bubny; *11,* Monastery of Cyriacs; *12,* Na Františku, Convent of St. Clara (St. Agnes Monastery); *13,* St. Clement Church; *14,* St. Peter in Petrská ulice, *Vicus theutonicorum; 15,* Nám. Republiky, St. Benedictus with command post; *16,* St. Adalbert Church; *17,* village of Opatovice; *18,* St. Lazar Church; *19,* Zderaz; *20,* village of Rybník with St. Longin Church (today St. Stephan); *21,* Na bojišti St. John; *22, Vicus Wissegradensis* (today Vyšehradská ulice); *23,* village of Podolí; *24,* village of Krušina. Key to geomorphology (after Záruba): *a,* Holocene alluvia in the Vltava Valley; *b,* alluvial terrace IV; *c,* alluvial terrace IV, the Maniny Terrace; *d,* slope screes and clay.

FIG. 2. Prague by the middle of the thirteenth century: Prague Castle, Lesser Town, Strahov Monastery, Knights of St. John, s.c. Queen Judith's Bridge (1158–1172), Old Town (Staroměstské náměstí), St. Gallus Town, and Vyšehrad Castle.

1169, along with the Basilica of St. Mary beneath the Chain. To the north, a bishop's manor was built in the twelfth century to ensure the safety of travel from the right riverbank; it became the seat of the Prague bishops in the early thirteenth century (Fig. 2).

Farther to the north, a settlement called Rybáře was located, lying on an island formed between an older river channel and the course of the Vltava. Nine occupational phases, in which the earliest agricultural community dates to the ninth century, show the development of a settlement that soon acquired a manufacturing character. The twelfth century saw the extension of the settled area southward (features in Karmelitská ulice No. 450/III show evidence of manufacturing).

The earliest cemeteries were situated outside the occupied area: in the southwest with the Church of St. John from the twelfth century to the early thirteenth where the settlement of Obora later appeared, and also in the north around the Churches of St. Michael (at No 171/III) and St. Martin (Nos. 177/III and 16/III) situated closer to the slopes of Hradčany. The extension of settlement southward

late twelfth and early thirteenth centuries, also hints at decline.

The occupied area was extended, reaching as far as a false channel of the Vltava; the settlement near present-day Maltézské náměstí is referred to as Trávnik. On its site, a command post of the Order of the Knights of St. John (the Knights Hospitalliers) was established prior to

is shown on the site of the later community of Nebovid, where a nonfarming settlement, which is referred to in written sources as the *vicus,* was located near the Church of St. Lawrence in the twelfth century. This settlement overlaid the cemetery.

Another settlement district was at Újezd, where a site dating to between the early twelfth and mid-thirteenth centuries was uncovered near a ninth–tenth-century cemetery (No. 609/III). The site of the community is delimited by Říční (No. 425) and Besední Streets (the area of the greenery in the present-day road) and by the space east of the Church of St. John in Všehrdova Street. Outside the whole settlement district are isolated settlement features from the courtyard of Tyršův dům.

During the late twelfth and early thirteenth centuries, the settlements developed independently, a situation that came to an end in 1257, when King Přemysl Ottakar II (1230–1278) had the population expelled and founded the Lesser Town of Prague by colonization. In the second half of the thirteenth century, an urbanization process had started in which the early medieval settlements (towns) were transformed into a High Medieval city. The settlements were gradually incorporated into surrounding building developments, and the borders of the city were delimited by a belt of fortifications built by Charles IV in the mid-fourteenth century (Fig. 3).

During the late eleventh century, the center of the city's life began to move from below the castle to the opposite bank of the river, where the floodplain of the Vltava and its tributaries offered favorable conditions for the development of iron manufacturing.

The distribution and density of workshops suggest that the settlement proceeded from the river to the unoccupied space on the right riverbank. In the area below Vyšehrad, such workshops were located along the Botič Stream (Na Slupi and Vyšehradská Streets and around the Church of St. Mary on the Lawns), and eleventh-century cemeteries were situated on the edge of the occupied area in Podolská třída and Na hrádku. Settlements also tended to center along the route leading from Vyšehrad to the north and along the edge of the river terrace (190.2 m a.s.l.). These included the sites at Na Zderaze and—on the floodplain—Na Struze, as well as Opatovice, a site around the Rotunda of the Holy Cross and its graveyard, V Konviktu, Náprstkova ulice (outside No. 292), Betlémské náměstí (No. 8/100), one on the edge of the floodplain and the terrace in Husova ulice, and another around the Church of St. Valentine at the junction with Karprova ulice; there the occupied area extended farther onto the terrace, where a settlement with a cemetery was located between the ends of Bartolomějská and Martinská Streets.

Settlement features were also uncovered in Jilská ulice and in Malé náměstí, where, after the abandonment of the previous settlement site, a linear cemetery was established that contained 118 burials datable to the mid-twelfth century. The route of a late twelfth-century road was found in the subsoil, joining that linking the ford to Štvanice Island to the western end of Kaprova ulice.

To the north, in the floodplain, was a settlement centering on the Pinkas Synagogue, another in the area of the Cyriac Monastery, and a third under the Church of Sts. Simon and Judas. Settlement features can also be found on the eastern edge of the riverbank (e.g., the horizon beneath the St. Agnes Cloister layer, which includes the surrounding area as far as the Church of St. Castulus, the settlement around the Church of St. Clement, and a site in Petrské náměstí).

The southern edge of the Old Town area was also gradually filled with settled communities forming a belt called Újezd; this included the church of St. Martin, mentioned in written records prior to 1140, and twelfth- and thirteenth-century settlement features. Similar features were found at Uhelný trh (Square) by the Church of St. Gallus.

Inhumation burials of the ninth–tenth centuries were found at Celetná ulice (No. 558), northeast of the later core of the Old Town, as was an eleventh-century cemetery at Dlouhá třída (Fig. 4).

Foreign merchants soon began to mix with the population of the area below the castle, settling down in unoccupied spaces near the trade routes and close to the fords. In addition to a first report given by Ibrahim ibn Jakob (965–966), who mentions the presence of merchants from neighboring countries—particularly other Slavs and Jews—there is also evidence of German tradesmen from the site at Na Poříčí. A privilege accorded by Soběslav II (1173–1178) entitled these merchants to use their own legislation, and their community, the *vicus teutonicorum,* had its own church.

Jews as an ethnic community are mentioned as located both on the left bank below the castle and on the right below Vyšehrad, as well as in the Old Town after 1091; the special character of burials found at the cemetery in Bartolomějská ulice suggests the presence of another ethnic group, the Romany.

Trade was enhanced, and the population below the castle and on the opposite bank increased, as a result of the building of the stone Queen Judith Bridge between

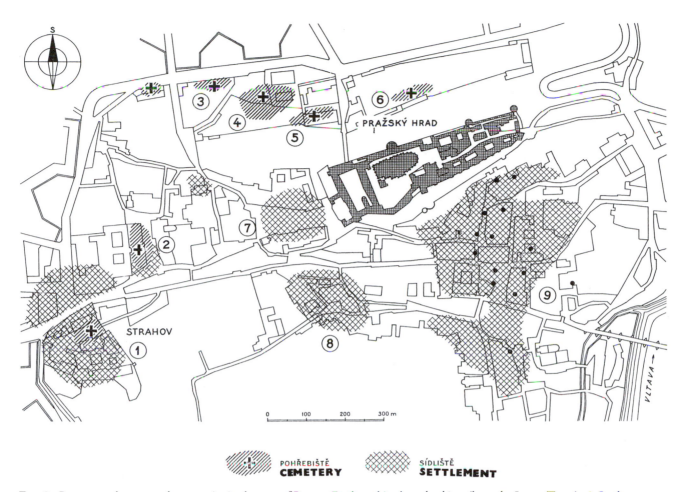

FIG. 3. Prague: settlement and cemeteries in the area of Prague Castle and in the *suburbium* (later the Lesser Town): *1,* Strahov, settlement (seventh–twelfth centuries) and cemetery (ninth–tenth centuries); *2,* Loreta Square with early Slavic cemetery (sixth–seventh centuries); *3,* Jelení ulice, cemetery (ninth–tenth centuries); *4,* Lumbe Garden (zahrada), cemetery (ninth–tenth centuries); *5,* Jízdárna (Royal Riding School), cemetery (ninth–tenth centuries); *6,* Míčovna (ball field), cemetery (ninth–tenth centuries); *7,* Hradčanské nám., settlement (eleventh–twelfth centuries); *8,* village of Obora with St. John's Rotunda (cemetery from the eleventh century); *9,* Malostranské nám., *suburbium* below Prague Castle, settlement east of Malostranské nám. from the eighth to the middle of the twelfth century, in No. 626 Josefská ulice, settlement from the end of ninth century.

1158 and 1172, replacing the mid-tenth-century wooden bridge. On the right bank were communities called Ve struze, Opatovice, Újezd sv. Martina, Rybník, Chudobice, Poříčí, and Újezd sv. Klimenta. In the beginning of the twelfth century, the Prague agglomeration already had a regular market where fairs were held every Saturday. In the late twelfth century, when the concentration of buildings became denser, a fortified manor belonging to the Czech princes appeared on its eastern edge, later serving as a customs house and a haven for foreign merchants (when it was called the Ungelt).

The twelfth century saw more expansion and an increase in the number of sites, with smelting and casting workshops (forges) on the right bank. The earlier sunken houses were replaced by ashlar-built manorial buildings with more rooms and stories. In addition to privately owned churches—elongated rotundas—there were also sacred institutional buildings of Christian orders such as the Knights Templar and the Teutonic Knights (e.g., the Basilica of St. Castulus and the Church of St. Benedictus with its command post), as well as those of the Dominicans near the Judith Bridge.

FIG. 4. Prague Old Town with s.c. Gallus Town (Havelské Město): + cemeteries, = churches, – Roman houses, ... alluvial terrace IV, the Maniny terrace. *1,* Jewish Ghetto; *2,* St. Castulus Church; *3,* St. Benedictus; *4,* town wall; *5,* Týn area; *6,* St. Virgin Church before Týn area; *7,* Staroměstské nám.; *8,* St. Gallus Church; *9,* St. Michael; *10,* St. Martin in the Wall; *11,* St. Stephen; *12,* St. Cross; *13,* St. Andreas; *14,* St. Philipe and James; *15,* Aegidius Church; *16,* St. Lawrence; *17,* St. John "Na zábradlí" in the Ballustrade; *18,* s.c. Judith Bridge; *19,* St. Clement; *20,* St. Mary "Na louži"; *21,* St. Martin-Minor; *22,* St. Valentin; *23,* St. Linhart; 23. Monastery of Cyriacs, settlement from the twelfth century to the thirteenth; *24,* Sts. Simon and Juda, settlement from the twelfth century; *25,* Na Františku, Convent of St. Clara (St. Agnes Monastery) (settlement began in the thirteenth century); *26,* Ovocný trh (Square), settlement from the twelfth century to the early thirteenth, later the Gallus Town. *A,* cemetery in Bartolomějská ulice; *B,* Malé nám., settlement and cemetery from the twelfth century; *C,* cemetery around of St. Michael (begun in the twelfth century); *D,* cemetery (tenth century) in Celetná ulice; *E,* Dlouhá ulice, cemetery (begun in the twelfth century). (All figures drawn by St. Novák.)

During the twelfth and the early thirteenth centuries, the density of the population of what later became the Old Town reached its highest level (with c. 3,500 people), accompanied by a building boom. The seeds of the autonomy of the later-independent town were provided by the king's appointment of an administration and a judicial official, mentioned c. A.D. 1212, who was also put in charge of supervising the town market.

The right-bank settlements were protected on the northern side by a stone rampart and ditch. The town's new class also incorporated some of the German settlers, who, in the early thirteenth century, had moved from the Poříčí site closer to the Old Town market. The town's area, delimited by the city walls, also incorporated the Nova Civitas Circa s. Gallum (Havelské Město). Thus, a major phase in Prague's evolution into a medieval city had been accomplished; by the late thirteenth century, the city comprised as many as three parts: the Greater Town of Prague (later the Old Town), the planned Havelské Město, and the Lesser Town of Prague (Malá Strana). The whole development culminated later, under Charles IV in the mid-fourteenth century, when Prague was further extended to include a belt of the newly designed New Town of Prague (Nové Město), with fortifications linking it to the Vyšehrad.

FURTHER READINGS

Boháčová, I., J. Frolík, P. Chotěbor, and J. Žegklitz. Bývalý biskupův dům na Pražském hradě. *Archaeologia historica* (1986) 11:117–126.

Borkovský, I. Pohřebiště obchodníků z doby knížecí v Praze (A merchant cemetery dating to the epoch of the princes of Prague). *Slavia antiqua* (1948) 1:460–484.

———. *Pražský hrad v době přemyslovských knížat* (Prague Castle at the time of the Přemyslid Princes). Prague: Československá Akademie Věd (Academia), 1969.

———. *Svatojiřský klášter a bazilika na Pražském hradě.* Prague: Ceskoslovenská Akademie Ved (Academia), 1975.

Carek, J. *Románská Praha* (Der romanische Prag). Praha: Universum Praha, 1947.

———. K rekonstrukci vývoje a rozlohy raně feudální Prahy (On the reconstruction of the development and of the beginning of early feudal Prague). *Pražský sborník historický* (1966) 3:10–43.

Ciháková, J., and J. Draganová. K vyvoji osídlení jádra Malé Strany v dobe Premyslovcu. (On settlement history of the core of Malá Strana [Lesser Quarter of Prague] under the Premysl dynasty). *Staletá Praha* (1992) 22:89–109.

Dragoun, Zd. Archeologický výzkum rotundy Sv. Jana Křtitele pod Pražským hradem v r. 1986 a 1987 (Archaeological Research on the Rotunda of St. John the Baptist below Prague Castle in 1986–87). *Archaeologia historica* (1988a) 13:103–146.

———. K Vývoji jednoho staroměstského bloku (The development of an old city house block). *Archaeologia Pragensia* (1988b) 9:103.

Frolík, J. Osídlení západního předpolí Pražského hradu před vznikem města Hradčan (Settlement of the Area of the Prague Castle Prior to the Foundation of the Town of Hradčany in the Czech Republic). *Archeologické rozhledy* (1986) 38:73–85.

Frolík, J., and J. Boháčová. Archologický výzkum Pražského hradu v 80. letech (Archaeological Research on the Prague Castle in the 1980s). *Staletá Praha* (1992) 22:71–88.

Hásková, J. *Vyšehradská mincovna na přelomu 10. a 11. století* (The mint at Vyšehrad at the turn of the 10th and 11th centuries). Prague: Sborník Národního muzea, sv. 29 (1975) No. 3.

Hlavsa, V., and J. Vančura. *Malá Strana: Menší město pražské* (A small aspect of the smaller city of Prague). Prague: SNTL-Nakladatelsví Technické Literatury, 1983.

Hrdlička, L. Předběžné výsledky výzkumu v Praze 1, na Klárově. *Archeologické rozhledy* (1972) 24:644–663.

———. Outline of Development of the Landscape of the Prague Historical Core in the Middle Ages. *Archeologické rozhledy* (1984) 36:638–652.

Hrdlička, L., Z. Dragoun, and J. Richterová. Praha 1, Staré Město (Prague 1; the old town). *Pražský sborník historický* (1981) 13:165–174.

Huml, V. K osídlení vltavského brehu Starého a Nového Mesta prazského ve 12. a 13. století (On the settlement of the banks of the Moldau in the old and new cities of Prague in the 12th–13th centuries). *Pražský sborník historický* (1981) 14:50–64.

———. Research in Prague: An Historical and Archaeological View of the Development of Prague from the Ninth Century to the Middle of the Fourteenth Century. In *From the Baltic to the Black Sea: Studies in Medieval Archeology.* Ed. D. Austin and L. Alcock. London: Unwin Hyman, 1990, pp. 267–284.

———. On the Settlement of the St. Gallus Town before Its Annexation to the Old Town Prague. *Archeologia Polski* (1992) 37(1–2):201–207.

P

Huml, V., Z. Dragoun, and R. Nový. Der archäologishe Beitrag zur Problematik der Entwicklung Prags in der von 9. bis zur Mitte des 13. Jahrhunderts und die Erfassung der Ergebnisse der historisch-archäologischen Erforschung Prags. *Zeitschrift für Archäologie des Mittelalters* (1990–1991) 18–19:33–69.

Janáček, J. Úvod (Introduction). In *Přaha středověká* (Prague in the Middle Ages). Ed. E. Poche, J. Janáček, J. Homolka, J. Kropáček, D. Líbal, and K. Stejskal. Prague: Panorama, 1983, pp. 7–47.

Ječný, H., J. Čiháková, S. Kršáková, H. Olmerová, D. Stehlíkova, L. Špaček, and M. Tryml. Praha v raném středověku (Prague in early medieval times). *Archaeologia Pragensia* (1984) 5(2):211–288.

Ječný, H., and H. Olmerová. Historie a proměny jednoho bloku při hradbách Starého Města pražského (The history and transformation of a block near the walls of the old city of Prague). *Staletá Praha* (1992) 22:21–70.

Kalina, T. Příspěvek k založení Starého Města a k vývoji jeho areálu ve 13. stol. *Historická geografie* (1972) 8:73–104.

Kašička, F., and B. Nechvátal. *Vyšehrad pohledem věků* (Wyssegrad in light of the centuries). Prague: Správa Národní Kulturní Památky Vyšehrad, 1985.

Kejř, J. Zwei Studien über die Anfänge der Städtverfassung in der böhmischen Ländern. *Historica* (1968) 26:81–142.

Merhautová, A. *Raně středověká architektura v Čechách, Praha* (Early Medieval Architecture in Bohemia, Prague). Prague: Československá Akademie Věd (Academia), 1971, pp. 204–296.

Nechvátal, B. K stavebně historickému vývoji baziliky sv. Petra a Pavla (A contribution on the building history of St. Peter and Paul on the Wyssegrad). *Uměni* (1974) 22:113–138.

———. K nejstaršímu vývoji kapitulního okrsku na Vyšehradě. *Archaeologia Pragensia* (1984) 5:81–86.

———. Závěrečná etapa archeologického výzkumu v bazilice sv. Petra a Pavla na Vyšehradě (The final phase of archaeological research on St. Peter and Paul's Basilica on the Vyšehrad). *Archaeologia historica* (1988) 13:417–422.

Nový, R. K počátkům středověké Prahy (On the beginning of medieval Prague). *Documenta Pragensia* (1984) 4:27–42.

Píša, V. Románské domy v Praze (Roman houses in Prague). *Ochrana pamiatok-Monumentorum tutela* (1971) 7:85–174.

Pokorný, O. Historicko-geografické pojetí vzniku Prahy a původu jejího jména (Historical-Geographic Concept of the Origin of Prague and the Origin of Its Name). *Sborník feské geologické společnosti* (1985) 3:200–209.

Reichertová, K. Bývalý klášter bl. Anežky Přemyslovny v Praze 1, Na Františku (Das ehemalige Kloster sel. Agnes von Böhmen in Prag 1, Na Františku, Ergebnisse der Archäologischen Untersuchungen). *Archaeologia Pragensia* (1986) 10:133–204.

Richterová, J. Výzkum v Ungeltu čp. 636/637 Praha 1, Staré Město (Die Untersuchungen im sog. Ungelt-Hof [Nr. 636/637] Praha 1, Altstadt). *Archaeologia historica* (1979) 4:21–31.

Smetánka, Z., L. Hrdlička, and M. Blajerová. Výzkum slovanského pohřebiště za Jízdárnou Pražského hradu v r. 1973 (The 1973 excavation of Slavic churchyard outside the Stables of Prague Castle). *Archeologické rozhledy* (1974) 26:386–405.

Smetánka, Z., L. Hrdlička, and T. Durdík. Archeologické výzkumy na Pražském hradě od roku 1971. *Staletá Praha* (1980) 10:94–107.

Špaček, L. Nové nálezy při stavbě metra na Můstk (Neue Funde beim Bau des Metro) *Archaeologia historica* (1978) 3:381–386.

———. Výzkum v Petrské ulici. Příspěvek k datování středověké hmotné kultury. *Archaeologia Pragensia* (1984) 5:71–80.

Tomas, J. Problematika studia dějin Prahy v období raného feudalismu: Vývoj pražské raně feudální městské aglomerace (The problem of the study of the history of Prague in the period of early feudalism). *Archaeologia Pragensia* (1984) 5(1):35–56.

Třeštík, D. K počátkům Prahy. *Folia historica Bohemica* (1980) 2:325–334.

Tryml, M., and J. Zavřel. K počátkům středověkého osídlení jižní části Maslé Strany (On the Origins of Early Medieval Settlement of the S Part of the Lesser Quarter). *Staletá Praha* (1992) 22:109–126.

Turek, R. Die Anfänge der Prager Siedlungskonzentration. In *Probleme des frühen Mittelalters in archäologischer und historischer Licht*. Berlin: Institute of the History of the German Academy of Sciences/Herausgebener von H.A. Knorr, 1966, pp. 130–140.

———. Praha jako rezidenční sídlo českého středověku (Prague as a prince's residence in the early Middle Ages). *Archaeologia Pragensia* (1984) 5(1):27–33.

Varhaník, J., and J. Zavřel. K počátkům kostelů sv. Jana Křtitele a sv. Vavřince na Malé Straně. *Zprávy Klubu za starou Prahu* (1987): 45–55.

Záruba, Q., and J. Pašek. Vývoj reliéfu území vnitřní Prahy. *Ochrana památek* (Sborník Klubu za starou Prahu na rok) (1960):47–51.

Václav Huml, translated by R. Pulchartová assisted by A. W.D. Millar

Pre-Viking Scandinavia

The Iron Age in Scandinavia was a mosaic of contrasting settlement patterns, political events, and spiritual symbolism and a period of vigorous social change. Although the term *Iron Age* is used as a blanket label for almost fifteen hundred years of Scandinavian history, many distinct regional traditions developed. These differences are related to each area's proximity to the coast and to continental Europe, as well as the different cultural origins of the inhabitants.

The Scandinavian Iron Age is divided into the Older Iron Age and the Younger Iron Age. In Denmark, the Younger Iron Age is recognized as beginning at A.D. 400, while in Norway it begins at A.D. 570. The Older Iron Age includes the pre-Roman Iron Age (450 B.C.–A.D. 0), the Older Roman period (A.D. 0–200), the Younger Roman period (A.D. 200–400), and the migration period (A.D. 400–570). The Younger Iron Age has two parts: the Merovingian period (A.D. 570–750) and the Viking Age (A.D. 750–1030).

Although there have been extensive debates about dating in the Iron Age, the purpose here is not to define the detailed chronology of the period but rather to concentrate on the archaeological record of settlement patterns and political movements that brought the Scandinavian Iron Age to its conclusion and ushered in the Viking Age—the final period in the Iron Age—which resulted in colonization and contact with peoples beyond known boundaries.

There are some important questions that underline the issues surrounding this period. Why and how were settlements established and how did they shift and change? What were the political forces that initiated and accompanied those changes?

The indigenous Bronze Age traditions were characterized by a uniformity of styles of metalwork. Circular ornaments are found in almost all of south and central Scandinavia and in the Schleswig/Holstein region of Germany, while the rectangular style is present in east Finland. Despite years of contact with iron-producing Celts in northern Europe, iron production was not adopted in the Nordic regions until 450 B.C., with the beginning of the pre-Roman Iron Age.

Until the very early first century A.D., the archaeological record of the Iron Age shows a continuation of late Bronze Age burial practices with cremation graves having little or no surface marking. Most graves included sparse grave goods, but there are a few exceptionally rich finds from graves in Denmark. The silver Gundestrup Cauldron was found dismantled in a bog and was probably left on the bog's surface as a symbol of destruction. Such acts of ceremonial destruction, presumably of war loot, were common practice at the time. However, the cauldron's origin and function are subject to dispute. One other find is a war find, a five-piece boat, the *Hjortspring*. Other objects from this period are decorative needles and belt buckles, some rectangular shields, and occasional swords, most of which were associated with bodies from sacrificial contexts.

The style of ornamentation in jewelry as well as weapons indicates contacts with the La Tène complex of central Europe, one of the "Celtic"-style complexes of Europe. The changes in this period are mainly in armor, with the introduction of the *spatha*, a long sword with no point and a particularly long handle. However, the houses and some rock carvings are typologically the same as those recovered from the preceding Bronze Age.

A number of changes occurred during the transition from the Older Roman period to the Younger Roman period in Denmark, Norway, and Sweden. A Nordic style of craft work with some Roman attributes emerged at this time in armor, in weapons, and in pottery that imitated Roman bronze vessels. Some Roman imports, such as Frankish and Germanic glass produced in the Rhine region, have been recovered from archaeological contexts. Occasionally, Roman-made weapons such as the *gladius*, a short, heavy-bladed sword, are also found. The difference between burial practices in the "Older" and the "Younger" periods is in the quantity of grave furnishings rather than the quality. Grave goods are more plentiful in all graves during the Younger Iron Age, but some graves are associated with exceptionally rich and variable collections of goods. The Nydam ship burial from a bog in Schleswig is such a burial. Many researchers have suggested that this concentration of wealth indicates the presence of chiefly burials and have inferred the development of a hierarchical society during the Younger Iron Age, especially in Denmark. Many bodies recovered from bogs belong to the Younger Roman period and indicate that ritual sacrifice continued.

Social and economic ranking may also be illustrated in village layouts. Although, in southern Scandinavia, village

P

structure is much the same as it was in the Neolithic, in the Younger Iron Age one of the houses is distinctively larger, a trend that becomes marked in the next period.

The migration period (A.D. 400–570) is also called the Older Germanic period in Denmark. The former term is misleading in reference to Scandinavia, since, with the collapse of the Roman Empire in the fifth century A.D., there is migration in all of Europe except Scandinavia. The migration period is thought to have been a period of crisis. In many areas, the number of graves is reduced, and there is a contraction of settlements noted that is associated with the plague of Justinian, which spread across Europe in 549 and may have been yellow fever.

During the migration period, differentiation in houses, graves, and personal decoration increases. The low mounds and cremation burials of the Roman period are replaced by fewer, but larger, mounds, 20–25 m in diameter, that contained inhumations within stone cysts. The location of ritual practices changes from bogs to solid ground, but the secret sacrifices of goods and people continues.

The ornaments found in this period are spectacular and mark the florescence of the true Nordic style. This is perhaps a stylistic development linked to the taste of the new dynasties in Denmark. At this time as well, the Nordic animal figurines emerge. Their origin has been disputed for a long time, though some have tried to link them to Scythian art. The small silver fibulae of the Roman period expand in size and are now mostly gold. Weaponry also changes from the Roman *gladius* sword to the Viking one-handed sword.

Also in the migration period, there is also a sudden and very late appearance of hillforts. A number of them seem to defend transportation and trade routes while protecting the local population. They are often found on the fringes of farm clusters and villages, such as the hillforts along the present Swedish border, near Lake Mjosa in Norway, and nearby Larvik.

Another explanation for the crisis noted in this period is the reorganization of the land. New boundary markers were erected around old farms, and a number of farms were abandoned at this time. Clearance cairn fields stop c. A.D. 500, marking a decline in forest swidden agriculture and the transition to agricultural intensification and extensive deforestation. Agricultural production is reorganized on a larger scale. Land is used on a permanent basis, which may indicate better soil management and manuring but is more labor intensive. Forest clearance also suggests expanded livestock production. At this time, there emerges a political organization with a land-owning aristocracy that is supported by taxation and/or land rents, added factors in discouraging swidden agricultural settlement (a kind of slash-and-burn agriculture).

The earlier chronologies were reconstructed on the basis of graves. In the transition to the Younger Iron Age, there is an increase in silver, and a reduction in gold, ornamentation. Gold, which had once been imported from the Romans, is replaced by silver, coming to the Nordic countries from the Arab world via the Volga route. This is the time when central Europe was becoming Christian under the influence of the Carolingian Empire, while Scandinavia and the Baltic remained pagan.

There is a mixture of burial customs in this period, including inhumation and cremation burials. We also find a combination of both large and small mounds. In the area of Stavanger in Norway, there is great variety in the shape of surface markings—from triangular, to boat burials, to wooden and chamber burials. The content of the graves shows a marked increase in iron objects and, in Norway, many more weapons.

There is also a change in dress styles at this time. The fibulae resemble the Celtic ring-shaped ones. Women's dress changes; buttons are replaced by shoulder straps, and oval-shaped brooches are worn in pairs. On the coast and along the inland fjords, the graves and the farms are found closer to the water, indicating that transportation, trade, and communication are more important. The sail was introduced c. A.D. 600–650, and the fixed steering oar to starboard replaced hand-held oars. In the Merovingian period (A.D. 570–750), there are single- and double-edged one-handed swords. The shields are round, and the lances that first appeared in the migration period become smaller.

Isolated burial mounds replaced the mound fields, a development that may be connected to an increase in the number of single-family farms. More cash crops were being produced, and the exploitation of mountain regions beginning c. A.D. 700–750 signals increased production of iron, furs, and other sub-Arctic products for sale. The reindeer-trapping system intensified, along with the production of soapstone and the extraction of bog ore. The production of pottery in Norway and in most of Sweden ceased. Pottery production continued in Scania and in Denmark, but, throughout the Nordic regions, there was an increase in foreign ceramic imports. The decreased number and isolation of the mounds, combined with increased population densities, suggests that labor-intensive burials were becoming more prestigious.

The beginning of the Viking period finds Scandinavia with an internationally recognized aristocracy who inhabited farms such as Åker, Borre, and Avaldsnes. New ports of trade, which were previously called towns, such as Birka, Kaupang, and Ribe, make their appearance. Most flourished c. A.D. 800, but the majority died out shortly thereafter. These ports are in isolated locations, enclose a small, permanent population, and are involved primarily in a long-distance luxury trade maintained by the aristocracy in glass, glass beads, slaves, and jewelry. The ports were either abandoned or transformed into medieval towns such as Bergen, Oslo, Vågan, and Nidaros in Norway. What separates these towns from the earlier ports is the presence of ecclesiastical and secular institutions of power. They were tax-collecting, administrative centers with a small army in residence. Only later in the Middle Ages did artisans' production become an important component of town life.

By the ninth century, "national" kingdoms began to emerge. The king was still elected, but there were now rules for dynastic inheritance. The king usurped judicial, legal, and policing authority from the kin-based lineages, so that both the tasks and the power are more centralized. This was reinforced by expanding the small permanent army present in each town to form a tax-collection system. However, most of these kingdoms fell apart before the Middle Ages. State formation requires relative stability, and Scandinavia was in political and social turmoil at the time. Previously uninhabited lands were colonized. Migration into the Baltic region and Russia continued to bring ethnically Norse people into contact with diverse distant populations. Within Scandinavia, there was an internal expansion, and more farms were established in the interior. There is also outward expansion, sometimes called raiding and sometimes trading, but quite often both aspects were combined. In England, the Danelaw was established as a colony so that the Danes could collect taxes from the English. The voyages of the time took the Norse as far east as Constantinople (modern Istanbul) and as far west as the New World.

The only "typical" aspect that marks the whole Iron Age is chronological change and variation in the economy—from mixed farming, husbandry, and subsistence fishing and hunting to cash cropping, commercial hunting and fishing, and trade. The Iron Age ends in Scandinavia with the introduction of Christianity and the beginning of the northern Middle Ages c. A.D. 1030.

FURTHER READINGS

Baudou, Evert, et al. *Archaeological and Palaeoecological Studies in Medelpad, North Sweden.* Kungl. Vitterhets-, Historie och Antikvitets Akademien. Stockholm: Almquist and Wiksell, 1978.

Bronsted, Johannes. *Danmarks Oldtid.* Vol. 1–3. Copenhagen: Gyldendal, 1957–1960.

Calissendorff, Karin, et al. *Iron and Man in Prehistoric Sweden.* Trans. and Ed. Helen Clarke. Stockholm: Jernkontoret, LT, 1979.

Collis, John. *The European Iron Age.* London: Batsford, 1984.

Glob, P.V. *The Bog People: Iron Age Man Preserved.* Ithaca: Cornell University Press, 1969.

Hald, Margrethe. *Ancient Danish Textiles from Bogs and Burials: A Comparative Study of Costume and Iron Age Textiles.* Trans. Jean Olsen. Copenhagen: National Museum of Denmark, 1980.

Hedeager, Lotte. *Iron Age Societies: From Tribe to State in Northern Europe, 500 B.C.–A.D. 700.* Trans. John Hines. Oxford: Blackwell, 1992a.

———. Kingdoms, Ethnicity, and Material Culture: Denmark in a European Perspective. Trans. John Hines. In *The Age of Sutton Hoo: The Seventh Century in North-Western Europe.* Ed. M.O.H. Carver. Woodbridge: Boydell, 1992b, pp. 279–300.

Klindt-Jensen, Ole. *Foreign Influences in Denmark's Early Iron Age.* Kobenhavn: Munksgaard, 1950.

Linturi, Elvi, ed. *Iron Age Studies in Salo.* Helsinki: Finnish Antiquarian Society, 1986.

Megaw, J.V.S. *Art of the European Iron Age: A Study of the Elusive Image.* Bath: Adams and Dart, 1970.

Megaw, J.V.S., and T.C. Champion, eds. *Settlement and Society: Aspects of West European Prehistory in the First Millennium B.C.* Leicester: Leicester University Press, 1985.

Myhre, Bjorn. The Royal Cemetery at Borre, Vestfold: A Norwegian Centre in a European Periphery. In *The Age of Sutton Hoo: The Seventh Century in North-Western Europe.* Ed. M.O.H. Carver. Woodbridge: Boydell, 1992, pp. 301–313.

———. *The Beginning of the Viking Age: Some Current Archaeological Problems.* In press.

Näsman, Ulf. The Germanic Iron Age and Viking Age in Danish Archaeology. *Journal of Danish Archaeology* (1989) 8:159–187.

Ramquist, Per H. *Gene: On the Origin, Function, and Development of Sedentary Iron Age Settlement in Northern*

P

Sweden. Umeå: University of Umeå Department of Archaeology, 1983.

Randsborg, Klavs. *The Viking Age in Denmark: The Formation of a State.* London: Duckworth, 1980.

Samson, Ross, ed. *Social Approaches to Viking Studies.* Glasgow: Cruithne, 1992.

Sawyer, P.H. *Kings and Vikings: Scandinavia and Europe, A.D. 700–1100.* London: Methuen, 1982.

Sellevold, Berit Jansen. *Iron Age Man in Denmark.* Vol. 3 of *Prehistoric Man in Denmark.* Kobenhavn: Kongelige Nordisk Oldskriftselskab, 1984.

Stjernquist, Berta. *Gardlosa: An Iron Age Community in Its Natural and Social Setting.* Lund: CWK Gleerup, 1981.

Widgren, Mats. *Settlement and Farming Systems in the Early Iron Age: A Study of Fossil Agrarian Landscapes in Ostergotland, Sweden.* Stockholm: Almquist and Wiksell, 1983.

Sophia Perdikaris

SEE ALSO

Birka; Emporia; Iron Age; Trondheim

Q

Quentovic

In 1984, the location of Quentovic had not been satisfactorily established, although many possibilities had been put forward over the previous 140 years. The place name is variously rendered but means "the market on the Canche." The Canche is a river with a large estuary c. 29 km south of Boulogne in northern France. Quentovic, known from documents and coins minted there, was the principal early medieval port of the Frankish homelands and the recognized port of entry for the hosts of Anglo-Saxon pilgrims traveling to Rome. The evidence suggested that the port flourished from the sixth century A.D. but is no longer heard of after the middle of the ninth century except for a tenth-century coinage that claims to be struck at Quentovic but is of types struck by, and bearing the name of, the ninth-century Charles the Bald (823–877).

Various sites along a 14-km stretch of the River Canche, from its mouth at Etaples to the head of the tide at Montreuil, had been suggested, but Roman pottery kilns and pottery and bone disturbed in drainage improvement suggested a new site in the hamlet of Visemarest situated on the south bank of the Canche and c. 7 km from its mouth. The modern Canche has been canalized and is now 0.5 km to the north of the hamlet (Fig. 1). After initial fieldwork, which showed that Carolingian pottery was to be found there, although there was no evidence of any structures from a surface examination, a program of survey and excavation was instigated by the University of Manchester with the cooperation of the French authorities.

In ten seasons, sixty-four *sondages* (test trenches) were excavated on a grid pattern designed to place one sondage in each 100-m square, although local conditions pre-

vented this from being rigorously applied. Each sondage was 4 × 1 m in area and excavated to the top of the occupation layer, which showed as a layer of gray-black sand or as features filled with this material and cut into the clean, light-colored sand that was the natural estuarine deposit here. The early medieval layers were not excavated, thus preserving the integrity of the site; their position, section, and plan were recorded together with any finds from the upper layers. It was possible in this way to establish the limits of the early medieval site. On the plan (Fig. 2), filled circles indicate occupation, and open circles indicate sondages without settlement levels. The port of Quentovic seems to have been set to the west of a possible Roman routeway that carries the road between the river crossing at Beutin and the village of La Calotterie today. To the south, the evidence suggests that there was a branch of the River Canche flowing at the foot of the valley side. To the north, an ancient trackway, now disused, overlies a bank of earth revetted with wattle fencing. Wattle from this fencing has given a radiocarbon date centered on A.D. 760. To the west of the settlement, the slightly lower ground was probably tidal marsh or a shallow lagoon. The area occupied is more than 45 ha and is directly comparable in area to other western European emporia of similar date, such as Hamwic (Saxon Southampton), Dorestad, London, and Ipswich.

The area excavations looked at a part of the northern limit of the port (*N1–2* on the plan), at a central location where geophysical survey had suggested occupation (*1985–1986* on the plan), and at two low mounds to the south that had revealed human bones during drainage operations and were threatened by plowing (*M1* and *M2* on the plan).

Q

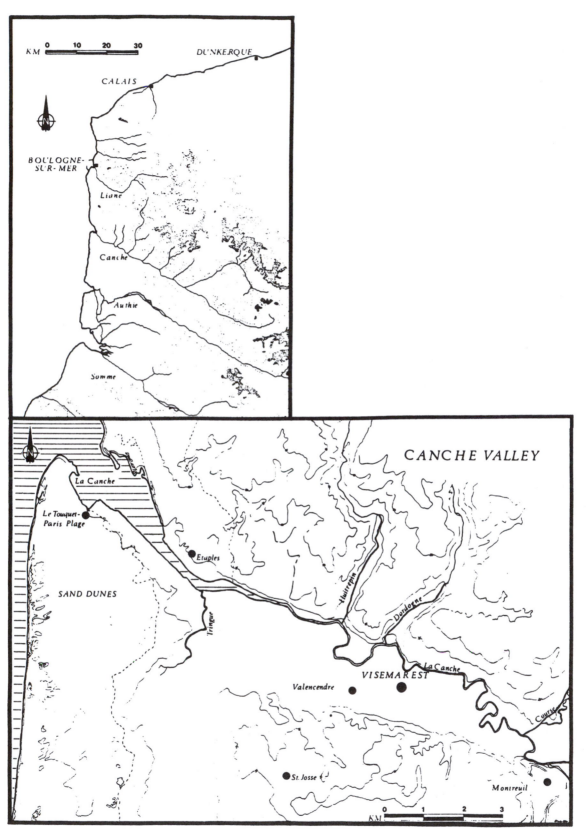

FIG. 1. Location map of northern France and the Canche Valley showing Visemarest.

could be clearly defined within this layer until the lowest levels were reached, when the bases of a series of intercutting pits were revealed.

The two burial mounds examined in the southern part of the town presented some interesting questions. Mound 1 was examined first, and disarticulated bone, some but not all plow damaged, was found together with fully articulated skeletons in shallow graves unaccompanied by grave goods. Some of the bodies had been covered with chalk blocks. There was no dating evidence except that, in the cleaned section of a drainage ditch, which cut the northern side of the mound, a rich black occupation layer could be seen below the level of the burials. An area to the north of the drainage ditch was opened and confirmed that the burials ceased after a short distance and that there was considerable early medieval occupation debris below and beyond them. A similar pattern was found in the initial investigation of the southern mound. A single radiocarbon date from one of the skeletons from Mound 1 centered on a date of A.D. 715. A silver coin, a series G *sceatta,* dating to c. A.D. 720, confirmed this dating, which was very much earlier than the stratigraphy had suggested.

A further season of excavation at the southern mound revealed that there had been considerable workshop activity before the mound was constructed. The mound was constructed of chalk blocks and a gravelly sand that is found on the adjacent plateau but not in this area of the valley bottom. The workshops themselves were not identifiable, but areas of waste from the manufacture of bone and antler combs were found. Nearby was an area rich in worked and unworked pieces of amber, some unworked jet, an amethyst bead, fired clay beads, and the silver surround and base plate of an unfinished composite brooch; a jewelry workshop seems a likely interpretation. It was noted that the pottery found in these workshop levels did not contain a class of pottery known as Beauvais red-painted ware that was prolific elsewhere in the port's occupation levels. As red-painted ware is thought to have reached this area of northern France in the mid-ninth century, it seemed that the workshops must predate this. Three further radiocarbon dates were obtained, two from skeletons within Mound 2 and one from the remains of a large vertical timber found within the mound, its foundation pit cutting into the subsoil. The skeletons gave dates centering on A.D. 715 and 640, and the date of the timber centered on A.D. 805. Again, a very early date for the settlement below the burials is suggested, although the pottery evidence is clearly Merovingian and Carolingian and

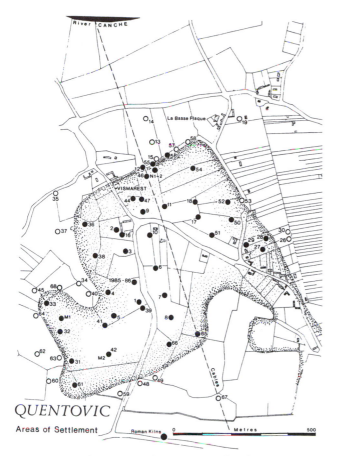

FIG. 2. Map of Quentovic showing areas of settlement.

The northern excavation was the first to reveal the early medieval waterfront, although sondages 12, 13, 14, and 15 had indicated the limit of occupation. The line of the waterfront was checked in sondages 55 and 56, where it was present but moving southeast and off the alignment of the trackway. It was absent in sondages 57 and 58. An area 15 × 15 m behind the waterfront was excavated, and early medieval occupation was evident in the earliest features cut into the natural sand. These features had been considerably disturbed by a later farmhouse dated on the pottery evidence to the eleventh–fifteenth centuries.

The areas excavated in 1985 and 1986 were the first to be opened. The reason for the good geophysical results was quickly revealed in the remains of the foundation walls of a rectilinear building. The pottery associated with these remains was medieval, perhaps as late as the fifteenth century. The walls and surfaces of this period sealed the early medieval phase, which in this area consisted of a very richly humic, black layer containing large quantities of animal bones and shell, consistent with food waste, and early medieval pottery sherds. No features

Q

not Gallo-Roman. Pottery kilns of the Gallo-Roman period were found on the river terrace to the south of the port and were excavated in 1973 prior to road widening. The Gallo-Roman pottery is quite different in form and decoration (Couppe and Vincent 1973) from early medieval pottery.

The aim of these investigations was to identify and define the limits of the early medieval settlement at Vismarest. This has been achieved, and the location of the site, the size of the area occupied, and the range of artifacts and raw materials found leave little doubt that this is, indeed, the lost emporium of Charlemagne, known as Quentovic.

Clearly, there are still many questions remaining to be answered, and only large-scale open-area excavations with appropriate funding can hope to answer them adequately. The preliminary work of confirming the location and defining the area of the site was undertaken mainly by adult students of the Department of Extra-Mural Studies at Manchester University, people who are not available to undertake full-time commitments to archaeological exca-

vation of the type required. Almost all the site is pasture, so it is not under threat and can await a future initiative.

FURTHER READINGS

Couppe, J., and F. Vincent. L'officine de potiers de La Calotterie. *Bulletin de la Commission Départmentale des Monuments Historiques du Pas-de-Calais* (1973) 9:209–220.

Hill, David, David Barrett, Keith Maude, Julia Warburton, and Margaret Worthington. Quentovic Defined. *Antiquity* (1990) 64:51–58.

Hill, David, Margaret Worthington, Julia Warburton, and David Barrett. The Definition of the Early Medieval Site of Quentovic. *Antiquity* (1992) 66:965–969.

Leman, P. Contribution à la localisation de Quentovic ou la relance d'un vieux débat. *Revue du Nord* (1981) 63(251):935–945.

Margaret Worthington

SEE ALSO

Emporia; Ipswich; London

R

Radiocarbon Age Determination

Radiocarbon age determination, popularly known as carbon-14 (C-14) dating, was developed by Willard Libby (1908–1980) in 1949. While the method is most often used to date prehistoric sites, radiocarbon age determination has increasingly been used to date organic materials recovered from medieval sites. The method is based on carbon, an element that is present in all living things. The most common isotope of carbon is a light, stable isotope, carbon-12; however, all living plants and animals also contain trace quantities of a heavier, radioactive isotope of carbon, carbon-14. Small quantities of radioactive ^{14}C are constantly being formed in the Earth's upper atmosphere. Both ^{14}C and ^{12}C combine with oxygen to form carbon dioxide (CO_2) one of the most common gases in the Earth's atmosphere. Carbon dioxide is absorbed by plants during photosynthesis, a process by which plants convert CO_2 and sunlight into food and oxygen. When plants absorb CO_2 from the atmosphere, they absorb large quantities of ^{12}C and trace amounts of ^{14}C. As these plants are eaten by animals who are, in turn, eaten by other animals, radiocarbon is spread throughout the food chain. Therefore, living plants and animals will contain the same small proportion of ^{14}C that exists in the Earth's atmosphere. (The ratio of ^{12}C to ^{14}C in the Earth's atmosphere is about eight hundred billion to one.)

When an organism dies, it ceases to take up any new radiocarbon. The radioactive carbon that is present in the organism's tissues decays at a known rate. This rate is known as the *half-life,* or the amount of time needed for the half the radioactive atoms to decay. The half-life of radiocarbon is 5730 ± 30 years. Thus, by measuring the amount of radioactive carbon that remains in a sample of organic material, archaeologists can estimate the amount of time that has elapsed since that organism died. This is the principle that underlies radiocarbon age determination. (See Renfrew 1973 for a detailed summary of the assumptions that lie behind the radiocarbon dating method.)

The advantage of radiocarbon dating over other methods is that it can be used on a wide range of organic materials, including charcoal, wood, bone, and shell. Traditional radiocarbon dating requires c. 25 g of the organic material for laboratory analysis. The material is cleaned and converted to a gas by burning, and its radioactivity is measured over a period of two weeks. This count is used to estimate the amount of radiocarbon remaining in the sample. A newer procedure known as the AMS (accelerator mass spectrometry) method uses an accelerator and a mass spectrometer to measure directly the amount of ^{14}C remaining in the sample (Hedges and Gowlett 1986). The AMS technique allows much smaller samples—even single grains of wheat or barley—to be dated.

Radiocarbon age determinations are expressed in years B.P. (before present). The present has been defined arbitrarily as A.D. 1950. Radiocarbon dates always include a plus-or-minus factor (e.g., 1250 ± 50 years B.P.) because radiocarbon dates are not absolute ages; they are statements of probability. The date of 1250 ± 50 B.P. means that there is approximately a 66 percent (two out of three) chance that the true age of the archaeological sample will fall between 1200 and 1300 B.P. (i.e., between A.D. 650 and 750). The ± 50 years is a statistical measure known as a *standard deviation.*

R

FURTHER READINGS

Hedges, R.E.M., and J.A.J. Gowlett. Radiocarbon Dating by Acceleraor Mass Spectrometry. *Scientific American* (1986) 254:100–107.

Renfrew, Colin. *Before Civilization: The Radiocarbon Revolution and Prehistoric Europe.* Cambridge: Cambridge University Press, 1973.

Pam J. Crabtree

Raths

In the early Christian period (c. A.D. 500–1200) in Ireland, most people lived in single-family farmsteads scattered around the countryside. One of these types of settlements was the rath, or ringfort. Raths are by far the most numerous type of settlement site from the early Christian period in Ireland, and estimates of the number of surviving raths range from thirty thousand to sixty thousand. A rath consisted of a circular enclosure, formed by digging a ditch and piling up the earth from the ditch, which created the characteristic structure of a bank with an external ditch. The average diameter of a univallate (i.e., having only one bank and ditch) rath was c. 30 m.

Raths are, for the most part, located in low-lying areas of Ireland, such as the middle part of the country. They were most likely associated with some surrounding land, on which the inhabitants of the rath grazed their animals and planted their crops. There were usually several buildings inside the rath that appear to be houses and storage areas. These buildings were often made of wood or wicker, such as those at the rath at Deer Park Farms, County Antrim (Lynn 1989). It seems unlikely that the ditch and bank that surrounded the raths of early Christian Ireland were built purely for defensive purposes, as they were usually not very high or substantial. A more plausible explanation for the enclosure of houses in this manner is to provide a small measure of security for the livestock owned by the rath dwellers. The rath structure was probably just enough to keep the livestock from escaping and to keep the wild animals from making a meal of the livestock during the night.

There were also some multivallate raths in early Christian Ireland (i.e., raths that had two or three sets of the bank-and-ditch structures). These additional banks and ditches were probably symbols of the greater wealth of the inhabitants of the settlement, rather than additional defenses. Building more than one ditch and bank probably indicates that the inhabitants of the rath could count on the labor of people outside the immediate family. The ability to muster a larger labor force indicates that the multivallate-rath dwellers most likely had higher status and more wealth than did the average, univallate-rath dweller.

FURTHER READINGS

Edwards, Nancy. *The Archaeology of Early Medieval Ireland.* Philadelphia: University of Pennsylvania Press, 1990.

Flanagan, Laurence. *A Dictionary of Irish Archaeology.* Dublin: Gill and Macmillan, 1992.

Hamlin, Ann, and C.J. Lynn, eds. *Pieces of the Past: Archaeological Excavations by the Department of the Environment for Northern Ireland.* Belfast: HMSO, 1988.

Lynn, C.J. Deer Park Farms. *Current Archaeology* (1989) 113:193–198.

O'Kelly, Michael J. *Early Ireland.* Cambridge: Cambridge University Press, 1989.

O'Ríordáin, Seán P. *Antiquities of the Irish Countryside.* 5th ed. London and New York: Routledge, 1991.

Maura Smale

SEE ALSO
Ireland

Raunds Area Project

The Raunds Area Project is a major landscape project providing important information about the processes of village formation and development in midland England. Through the joint venture of the Northamptonshire County Council and English Heritage, a series of large-scale archaeological excavations and related work was carried out in and around Raunds between 1977 and 1992. The careful field survey of c. 40 km² of surrounding countryside enables the results to be set in their contemporary landscape and is supplemented by detailed documentary studies, artifact analyses, and archaeoenvironmental investigations.

The Raunds area encompasses the four medieval parishes of Raunds, Stanwick, Hargrave, and Ringstead, which together extend from river valley to clay upland. They reach from the floodplain meadows and terrace gravels of the River Nene across the mainly permeable geologies of the valley slopes to the Boulder Clay Plateau of the former "forest" of Bromswold.

The project was partly conceived as an investigation of the lowest levels of rural society with the aim of documenting the social and economic changes of the last fifteen hundred years. Within this time span, the major components of the project comprise North Raunds, where three separate excavations, at Furnells Manor, Langham Road, and Burystead, have together investigated the development of a manor and its immediate hinterland; and West Cotton, where the archaeological evidence includes a late Saxon manor and subsequent medieval tenements.

The interaction between the inhabitants of the densely populated landscape of the late Roman period and the newly arrived Saxons is still poorly understood. The early part of the Saxon period, however, appears to have heralded a decline in the number of individual settlements. People settled on lighter soil usually at either side of a stream, possibly in loose clusters of timber halls and sunken huts.

The colonization of the landscape remained dispersed until the tenth century, when it rapidly coalesced into the familiar pattern of the four main communities and related hamlets. Although the initial laying out of the open-field strip system has yet to be dated, the formalization of village settlement took place at around the time of the Danelaw (the time when the eastern part of England was under Danish law and custom). Land parcels were created, indicating a scheme of large-scale planning within a relatively short period.

The focal point of each settlement appears to have been an enclosed group of large buildings, each constructed with wall trenches; they can be identified as embryonic manors. The arrangement of these sites seems to have followed a common pattern, comprising a long, narrow hall (the Long-Range) surrounded by ancillary buildings set around a courtyard.

Not all of the attendant attributes were shared. The manor of Furnells in North Raunds possessed an adjacent church, but at West Cotton there was only an associated mill. Such variation may reflect status as much as differences in ownership and economy. Furnells Manor was probably the seat of a thegn, with West Cotton possibly held by a sokeman (freeman).

Later in the Medieval period, the manorial holding at West Cotton was replaced by a series of peasant tenements in a toft-and-croft arrangement. The first frontages also appeared in North Raunds, and the Furnells Manor house was rebuilt in stone in the thirteenth century. These changes coincided with the production of cash crops, as indicated by contemporary documents and demonstrated in the archaeological record by the widespread occurrence

of malting ovens. They probably denote the shift toward a more market-based economy.

Any nascent prosperity was halted by the onset of the Black Death in 1347 and the change toward pastoralism in the late Medieval period. At West Cotton, these factors combined with the specific problems of soil erosion and consequent flooding to cause the abandonment of the settlement in the first half of the fifteenth century. Despite partial desertion and contraction, Raunds has survived until today, and even with subsequent economic and social changes, including rapid expansion in the nineteenth century due to the footwear industry, its layout retains a core of recognizable medieval streets and associated tenements.

FURTHER READINGS

Audouy, M. *North Raunds, Northamptonshire: Excavations, 1977–87.* English Heritage Archaeological Reports. London: English Heritage, in press.

Boddington, A. *Raunds Furnells: The Anglo-Saxon Church and Churchyard.* London: English Heritage, 1996.

Chapman, A. *West Cotton: A Study of Medieval Settlement Dynamics: Excavations at West Cotton, Raunds, Northamptonshire 1985–89.* English Heritage Archaeological Reports. London: English Heritage, in press.

Parry, S. *Raunds Area Survey: An Archaeological Study of the Landscape of Raunds, Northamptonshire, 1985–92.* English Heritage Archaeological Reports. London: English Heritage, in press.

Brian Dix

Rescue Archaeology

Rescue archaeology, or the carrying out of investigations in advance of the destruction of archaeological deposits, has been one of the main ways in which medieval archaeology has obtained much of its information. While carefully controlled research excavations have been important, the wide range of data have largely been collected by salvage, either by interested antiquarians, amateurs, and the public or within effective rescue operations.

Although medieval archaeology as a distinct discipline did not begin to emerge until the 1950s and is still hardly a coherent discipline in some parts of Europe, there has long been an interest in rescuing fragments of antiquity from destruction. Many fine objects, particularly from burials of the migration period (fifth and sixth centuries) or objects such as tile, sculpture, and armor were recovered and added to antiquarians' collections from activities

R

such as agriculture, building work, and gravel extraction. For example, the grave of Childeric, the king of the Merovingian Franks who died in 481, was recovered in 1653, and a great many Anglo-Saxon cemeteries in England were discovered in the early and mid-nineteenth century in this way. Although these important finds were recorded or preserved, there was usually no active searching for such material in advance of development.

In the later nineteenth century, some efforts began to be made to record disappearing evidence in a more structured way. Within towns, various developments led to finds or structures being uncovered, whether medieval churches in London (England) from the 1870s or during laying of sewers in Lund (Sweden) from 1889. Canals and then particularly railways led to many discoveries, such as urban deposits in Olso (Norway) and numerous Anglo-Saxon burials and associated finds in England.

Amateur efforts in a number of cities led to small-scale excavations or larger efforts inadequate to the task. Prague Castle (Czech Republic) was one of the few places where, from 1925, consistent interest was taken in rescue archaeology in advance of conservation and building. Even so, during the first half of the twentieth century, the plotting of finds locations and the excavation of assemblages from rubbish pits and other closed deposits gradually led to the accumulation of much information in towns such as Coventry, London, and Oxford (England), Trondheim (Norway), and Visby (Sweden). Some rural rescue excavations took place, such as on the early medieval settlement of Gladbach (Germany) in 1937, but these were rare.

The beginnings of formal rescue began during World War II, and excavations in advance of airfields and other installations were undertaken in England. However, it was with the need for massive rebuilding in urban centers across all of Europe after the war, and the appearance of more government-controlled planning and spending in both the Western democracies and in the new Socialist republics to the east, that rescue archaeology began to develop.

The repair of bomb-damaged medieval structures and rebuilding on vacant plots during the 1940s and 1950s led to opportunities for large-scale excavations never previously seen in towns. Efforts can be seen across Europe, but with different emphases. This related to survival of deposits, research interests, and also the amount of information already obtained from earlier data collection. Thus, London provided few secular buildings at this stage because nineteenth-century cellars had already removed all traces, but pits, wells, and religious buildings were the focus of attention. In Germany, there was a particular interest in churches, as at Köln and Trier, though more specifically urban issues were addressed at centers such as Hamburg and Magdeburg. In Warsaw (Poland), excavations took place before the Old Town and its walls were reconstructed, and this pattern of archaeological excavation followed by sympathetic rebuilding has been subsequently developed over decades at the Baltic port of Elblag. Once this momentum began, other causes of redevelopment also led to rescue excavation. The fire at the Bryggen wharf in Bergen (Norway) proved the catalyst for a massive and very influential excavation during the 1950s; another important site of this period was Ribe (Denmark). In the 1960s, the program of work at Winchester (England) began, and this had a profound influence over much of Europe. A coordinated program of rescue excavation linked to clear research questions was undertaken, and this led to important methodological developments with regard to site recording and stratigraphic sequencing of deposits using a matrix.

In the 1970s, development continued, and the quantity and quality of data that could be recovered were by now obvious to some archaeologists. This led in Britain to the establishment of the pressure group Rescue and the demand for greater resources to be put into excavation in advance of destruction. In Britain, state intervention in both the level of funding and statutory protection was traditionally low, so it took considerable lobbying of politicians and galvanizing of the media to produce the considerable upsurge in funds during the 1970s. The nature of the problem was made explicit in a series of publications, notably *The Erosion of History: Archaeology and Planning in Towns* by C. Heighway (1972) and *The Future of London's Past* by M. Biddle, D. Hudson, and C. Heighway (1973). The basic argument propounded was that the archaeological heritage should be recovered before destruction. Rather than prevent development and its concurrent damage to the archaeological resource, this should be rescued by excavation and recording. The assumption made was that "preservation by record" would allow future generations of archaeologists to use the collected data to answer all sorts of as yet unformulated questions about the past. Towns featured prominently in the publicity, but rural threats were also highlighted, notably gravel extraction along river valleys where aerial photography was revealing extensive settlement, and motorway construction that provided transects across the landscape and the resultant discovery of numerous hitherto unknown sites (Rahtz 1974).

In other parts of Europe, the recognition of the need for rescue archaeology took various forms. In Ireland, the threats to urban deposits, including well-preserved remains of the Viking town at Wood Quay (Dublin), led to mass public demonstrations and some admission of the need for a strategy for rescue archaeology. In much of western Europe, there was some recognition of the need for rescue work without the vocal lobbying necessary in Britain and Ireland, though some countries preferred to devote most resources to research projects directed through professional institutes. Examples of major urban projects that developed from the 1970s include those at Tours (France), Trondheim and Oslo (Norway), Antwerp, Ghent, and Bruges (Belgium), and Dorestadt (Netherlands). In Sweden, urban archaeological methods were developed by a national archaeological unit. Rural projects in western Europe and Scandinavia tended to develop after urban archaeology, in the later 1970s and 1980s, but in the Netherlands and Germany they were then conducted on a large scale. This trend has now spread to France.

In the Socialist countries, state investment in archaeology could be heavy and led to some major programs of work in advance of destruction. Though constrained by ideological concerns in the type of information to be collected and the way it could be interpreted, work took place on a grand scale in both urban and rural contexts. An example of an integrated approach is that in and around Most (Czech Republic), where both the town and the villages in the hinterland have been studied prior to open-cast mining. Extensive research on all types of settlement and burial sites was undertaken prior to massive hydroelectric schemes in the former Soviet Union on both the Don and the Volga Rivers. Urban archaeology was highlighted first in Novgorod and, from 1967, spread to the 115 designated historic towns in Russia.

The assessment of threats not only in major centers but also in smaller towns was undertaken in many European countries, and campaigns of work were carried out in some. Units were usually set up on a city or a county basis to undertake rescue work, largely funded with central-government money, though often with local-government funding also. However, the research direction was often vague or nonexistent. Individual spectacular discoveries such as waterfronts at Trig Lane and Billingsgate, London, or tenements at Coppergate, York, were, by the scale of investigation and the quality of waterlogged deposits, bound to produce significant results. In other cases, information collected was either poorly structured or redundant. It gradually became clear that there was an accumulating backlog of excavated material yet to be processed and published and that much of this material could not be used to answer anything but the most basic of questions. In a few notable cases, a clear research strategy was linked to the rescue work, allowing selection between threatened sites and certain types of deposits within them, for example at Hamwic (early medieval Southampton, England). A similar problem of information overload has been experienced elsewhere in Europe, often leading to conflicts in the allocation of resources between further rescue excavation and the study of material already recovered.

The publication of results has lagged badly behind in all urban excavations, but different strategies have been applied in each city, even within England. In London, great emphasis has been placed on unpublished but detailed stratigraphic archives and finds databases, combined with particular thematic volumes on both settlement evidence and finds. In York, a series of fascicules have been published intermittently under various thematic headings, sometimes on a site-by-site basis, in other cases reviewing material from the city as a whole.

In the 1980s and 1990s, there was an increased reluctance of governments in the West to fund rescue archaeology. In the East, the end of Socialist power structures meant that state support also diminished dramatically. There has been an increased interest in developer funding, a particularly important concept with regard to major construction and extraction activities. In England, Ireland, Sweden, and some other European countries, developer funding has become the norm. The result has been an increased interest by developers in minimizing the need for rescue archaeology. This change was also promoted by the government in England, with the issue of Planning Policy Guidance Note 16, *Archaeology and Planning* (1990), widely referred to as PPG16. Henceforth, preservation *in situ* is presumed to be the reaction to threat rather than rescue archaeology. A significant step in formulation such a policy was taken at York, where a survey of the city by Ove Arup and Partners and York University, *York Development and Archaeology Study* (1991), proposed that archaeological deposits should be evaluated through a deposit model and suggested ways in which development could take place while mitigating the damage, primarily through the use of piling. This solution to funding rescue archaeology, attractive to both state and private sponsors of enforced excavation, is likely to be widely emulated throughout Europe. This will result in

R

far less excavation being undertaken, at least in historic urban centers. In many countries, limited evaluation of the archaeological resource is undertaken with the intention of minimizing damage to the resource rather than carrying out large-scale excavation in advance of destruction. Likewise, rural management schemes, often linked to wider environmental protection, have allowed sites to be preserved, and blanket forestry has been replaced with selected areas being left unplanted. Motorways and pipelines now may be moved slightly to avoid the most sensitive and significant sites. Rescue archaeology will continue to exist and will be important for the recovery of information about the Middle Ages, but not on the scale seen in the 1970s and 1980s.

FURTHER READINGS

Archaeology and Planning. Planning Policy Guidance Note 16. London: HMSO, 1990.

Biddle, M., D. Hudson, and C. Heighway. *The Future of London's Past.* London: Rescue, 1973.

Heighway, C. *The Erosion of History: Archaeology and Planning in Towns.* London: Council for British Archaeology, 1972.

Mytum, H., and K. Waugh, eds. *Rescue Archaeology: What's Next?* York: University of York Department of Archaeology/Rescue, 1987.

Ove Arup and Partners and York University. *York Development and Archaeology Study.* York: University of York, 1991.

Rahtz, P., ed. *Rescue Archaeology.* Harmondsworth: Penguin, 1974.

Harold Mytum

SEE ALSO

Emporia; England; Hamburg; London; Novgorod; Polish State, Early; Prague; Sweden; Trondheim; Urban Archaeology

Ribe

See Emporia.

Roads

There has been little study of roads in the Medieval period, despite their undoubted importance to the growth of the whole medieval trading system. Much has been written about the growth of towns and trade, but any study of the routes along which most of that trade was conducted has been meager, principally because of the lack of good archaeological, documentary, and cartographic evidence. Trying to establish the growth of the medieval road network is a problem in historical geography, to which archaeology provides only limited clues.

Of course, some trade (particularly of heavy and bulky goods) went by river, but for most trade this was not an option, as many places were distant from navigable water, or the rivers flowed in the wrong direction. However, the rivers themselves exerted a strong influence on where towns grew, providing a classic chicken-and-egg situation.

The lack of study has led to a number of myths about medieval roads and travel, notably that roads were poor and travel difficult (especially in winter or wet weather), that few people traveled, and that water travel was used for preference. It has become clear that the roads were, in most cases, adequate for the traffic, even in inclement weather, that many people traveled, and that water transport was used as part of the overall transport system if it was available.

Archaeological Evidence

There was little deliberate road building between the collapse of the Roman Empire in the fifth century A.D. and the early modern period. There are a few instances of roads being engineered or surfaced, usually where they had to cross boggy ground; trees, branches, bundles of twigs, and stones were used in different locations. However, in Britain, for example, there was little building of new roads until c. 1800, when new techniques were pioneered by John McAdam (1756–1830) and Thomas Telford (1751–1834).

Throughout most of medieval Europe, the Roman roads continued to be used; their construction was sufficiently robust to make them usable for many centuries. The evidence for their use lies in the documentary record and in the simple fact that many Roman roads are still in use today, buried under modern tarmac. The archaeological evidence for them is usually much clearer than for medieval roads.

However, in the Medieval period, although very few new roads were built, many came into existence, roads that "made and maintained themselves" (Flower 1923) by the habitual passage of traffic. The medieval concept of a road was that it was a right-of-way or an easement rather than a strip of land of fixed width. In England, travelers had the right to diverge from an impassable section of road, even to the extent of trampling crops. This meant that roads sometimes spread out laterally as a set of multiple tracks as travelers sought to find the easiest line of travel; some routes across open ground may have been more than a mile wide. Medieval roads like these are best seen on aerial photographs, especially if they survive only as crop marks, though the extent of modern plowing has destroyed much evidence.

Where roads had to climb hills, they also tended to fan out into multiple tracks. Here, however, the roads were eroded not only by the passage of horses and carts, but also by rain, the roads acting as stream channels. Where the channels were overdeepened, they became known as *holloways,* or sunken roads (*hohlweg* in German), and can be up to 9 m deep.

There are several fundamental archaeological problems related to medieval roads. The first is that roads that were not engineered or surfaced tend to disappear from the landscape or be destroyed or buried under modern roads. The second is the difficulty of ascribing a date to any surviving tracks; they may date from any time before, during, or after the Medieval period. An excellent example of the problem is presented by the mile-wide multiple tracks of the prehistoric Icknield Way, at the foot of the Chiltern Hills in England. One of the tracks was "romanized"; several were no doubt in use during the Medieval period; and many remain as tracks today.

Better dating evidence can be gained from bridges, since the date of their construction is often known, and this allows crucial river-crossing points to be fixed. But the problem of which came first, road or bridge, remains.

Other Evidence

To study medieval roads, one has to begin in the library by looking at the documentary sources including contemporary and modern maps.

Good evidence sometimes comes from maps, though large-scale cartography did not really begin in Europe until the sixteenth century and the accurate and detailed depiction of roads not until the nineteenth century in most areas. However, there are a few notable exceptions, such as the Gough map of Britain (c. 1300–1360), which depicts c. 4,700 km of roads, and Erhard Etzlaub's Romweg map (1500) showing routes to Rome from central Europe.

Postmedieval maps, of whatever scale and date, may also show roads that had been in use in medieval times. Estate plans (dating from the mid-sixteenth century in England) usually depict local roads and tracks, and there are often many others types of maps, including specific road books. However, such sources must be used with care, and never as the sole evidence, as they date from several hundred years after the Medieval period. Systematic, national, large-scale mapping (from the nineteenth century) provides an excellent base on which to plot information and also depicts old roads, or features associated with them, still visible at that date.

Documentary references to roads are potentially a most useful form of evidence and are extremely varied in nature. But records of the movements of traders rarely survive in any comprehensive form. The best record for England is that of Roger of Nottingham, who was buying wheat in the area around the River Trent in 1324. When the government was buying grain to supply its armies, records have sometimes survived, and these *Purveyance Accounts* give details of the cost of moving food, as well as the routes and modes of transport used. But, again, such movements are unlikely to be typical of the movement of foodstuffs in general.

The movements of medieval monarchs are well recorded; most of the daily movements of the English monarchs are known from the time of King John (1189 onward). They provide an extremely valuable source, even if their movements are unlikely to reflect the patterns of travel as a whole. The monarchs did, however, travel around the country throughout the year, complete with numerous carts and wagons, strongly suggesting that travel was not unduly difficult. There are records of a few individual travelers such as pilgrims and bishops, but most travel was a routine business and went unrecorded.

Place names (including field and road names) can provide useful evidence. Roads are frequently mentioned in legal documents as boundaries to estates, and place names are generally well documented, have a good geographical spread, and tend to persist even after the feature they describe has disappeared. The status or condition of the road may sometimes be inferred from how it is described; a few English examples include *paeth, straet, high road, magna strata, via regia, herepath* (army road), and *stayngate* (stony road). Similar examples can be found throughout Europe; in Germany, the most common names are *Weg* and *Strasse.* Names are not always reliable, and their authenticity must be checked; the so-called Pilgrims' Way leading to Canterbury along the North Downs is, in fact, an eighteenth-century romantic invention, and the route probably saw few medieval pilgrims. Equally, the naming of a road after a specific use, such as Saltway, Abbots' Way, or even the common term *packhorse track* (even if historically correct) should not be taken to imply that the road was used for a single purpose. A *via regia,* for

R

example, was unlikely to have been used solely by medieval monarchs.

Some documents are less reliable. There are several references to impassable roads in early court cases; for example, in 1386 the abbot of Chertsey allowed two 8-ft (2.4-m) -deep "wells" to exist in a high road and was prosecuted for claiming the goods of a man who had drowned in one of them. The problem with such cases is that the selection is biased since the instances of good roads are never reported.

Conclusion

The study of medieval roads requires the synthesis of a wide range of data from archaeology, air photographs, documents, place names, and maps, nor is it possible to study medieval roads in isolation. The roads served a purpose, and thus the whole geography of the medieval economy must be investigated to see how the interlocking systems of production, towns, and trade were linked by the ever-changing transportation system. It must be remembered, too, that the transport system included coastal and river routes as well as roads.

FURTHER READINGS

Edwards, J.F., and B.P. Hindle. The Transportation System of Medieval England and Wales. *Journal of Historical Geography* (1991) 17(2):123–134.

Flower, C.T. Public Works in Medieval Law. *Selden Society* (1915) 32 and (1923) 40.

Hindle, B.P. The Road Network of Medieval England and Wales. *Journal of Historical Geography* (1976) 2(3): 207–221.

———. *Medieval Roads.* Princes Risborough: Shire Archaeology, 1989.

———. *Roads, Tracks, and Their Interpretation.* London: Batsford, 1993.

Brian Paul Hindle

Roman Empire, Collapse of

One of the most renowned subjects of historical inquiry is the collapse of the Roman Empire. The disintegration of so powerful and so resilient a state has inspired research and speculation for many centuries. Despite so much attention, it remains unresolved why the Roman Empire disintegrated. In fact, the more the topic has been examined, the more complex and multifaceted it has become. Until recently, though, however much the questions multiplied, the evidence of written history stayed pretty much the same.

In recent decades, the amount of relevant evidence has been increased rapidly by modern archaeological research. This new information is beginning to change the condition of the discourse greatly, but it has so far been gathered mostly within the context of the questions and disputes based on the written evidence. This context can best be described through a brief summary of the traditional narrative history of the empire's disintegration (Fig. 1 depicts the empire's extent at various times).

The Roman Empire originated as territories subjected by the city of Rome, but by the second century A.D. it had evolved into one of the largest and most complex preindustrial states ever, held together by powerful economic and cultural ties as well as the political forces still notionally centered at Rome but including persons from throughout the empire. During the third century, however, there developed a pattern of political crisis and fragmentation of authority. Emperors were set up and overthrown in rapid succession by the armies, and civil wars between the candidates of rival armies resulted in the separation of some regions from the central administration for years or even decades. Meanwhile, the political disorder and disruption of the military allowed and encouraged increasingly strong incursions by Persian armies, Germanic warbands, and North African nomads.

During the decades c. A.D. 300, the political situation stabilized and central authority was reestablished, but the institutions of government and society had changed considerably during the crisis. During the fourth century, there were usually two or more coregent emperors, each taking responsibility for administering and defending a portion of the empire. The most common division was into two halves, roughly corresponding to long-standing cultural zones: the West, where Latin was the written language, and the East, where Greek was the foremost written language. Symbolic of this process was the creation of a second imperial capital, parallel to Rome, at Byzantium, renamed Constantinople.

In the later fourth and early fifth centuries, a new set of military crises afflicted the empire, during which substantial groups of Germanic-speaking people from central and eastern Europe moved into the empire while retaining their own military organization and often refusing to acknowledge Roman control. By the 450s, most of the Latin West was under the dominion of various Germanic warlords, and the collapse of the western imperial admin-

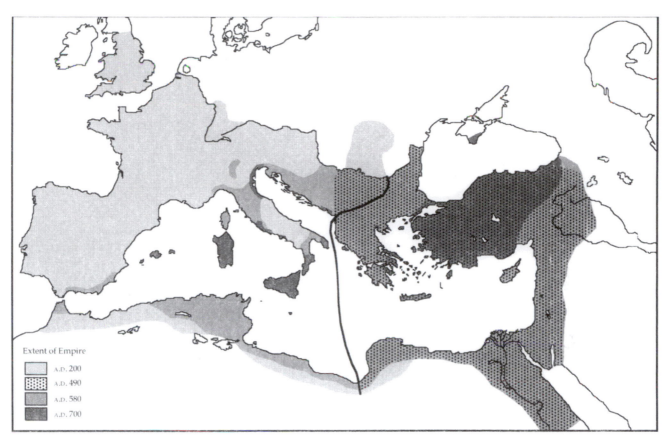

FIG. 1. Extent of the Roman Empire: the heavy line divides the western, predominantly Latin-using, section of the empire from the eastern section, which wrote mostly in Greek. Parts of Sicily and southern Italy were also at times predominantly Greek using. The various shadings indicate the areas more or less controlled by the empire around four points in time: the years 200, 490, 580, and 700. For the latter two especially, there is some uncertainty about which areas to include, due partly to poor documentation but mostly to uncertainties (inherent in collapse) about districts whose status was ambiguous or transitional.

istration was formalized in 476 when one of these warlords deposed the last western emperor.

Toward the end of the fifth century, then, the former extent of the Roman Empire had come to include several effectively independent kingdoms: the Vandals in North Africa, the Suevians in northwestern Spain and Portugal, the Visigoths in Spain and southern France, the Burgundians in eastern France, the Ostrogoths (later followed by the Lombards) in Italy, and the Franks in northern France. The eastern half of the empire, however, remained under the Roman emperor based at Constantinople. In this portion, the Roman administration and military remained much as before.

Between 533 and 561, a series of military expeditions from the eastern empire returned parts of the West to Roman rule: North Africa, Sicily and Sardinia, Italy, and the southeastern coast of Spain. Much of this recovery proved ephemeral, though; most of Italy was lost again by 574, and the foothold in Spain was lost by 624. At the same time, Roman control over the eastern provinces of the empire was shaken by Slavic and Persian invasions. Even as the empire struggled to repair itself, a new force emerged to the south.

In 632, the leaders of the new religion of Islam in Arabia began a project of military expansion. Within twelve years, their armies had conquered almost half of the remaining Roman Empire (and other areas as well) and, in so doing, deprived it of much of its army and most of its tax base. By 700, the empire had been reduced to a fragment of its former self, consisting of Constantinople

R

plus its navy and army and the scattered districts that the military could still control. The Roman Empire as formerly conceived no longer existed, and the Byzantine Empire that reemerged in the eighth and ninth centuries was something quite different.

This sequence of events is well enough known in itself; the difficulties arise when one seeks to explain why events turned out in this way rather than in some other. The long history of research has produced hundreds of attempted explanations for the fall of Rome, ranging from the trivial (e.g., the empire fell because its army was defeated) to the bizarre (e.g., lead poisoning or race mixture destroyed the Roman people). Most of these efforts seek to place the political events in some more general context. However, despite what might seem at first glance to be an overabundance of written sources, there are many crucial issues for which the historical sources provide no conclusive evidence. In particular, the economic and social conditions are widely thought to be of crucial importance for understanding the political events, but the written sources yield only biased, rhetorical, or anecdotal comments on these matters.

Archaeology has become important, therefore, as a method for more objective measurement of the changes taking place in late antiquity. This includes not only evaluation of some of the suggested causes of disintegration, but also different ways of describing the process itself.

The concept of *collapse* or *disintegration* can be interpreted in a number of ways. The most obvious sense is the replacement of Roman government by other regimes in various parts of the empire. The historical sources allow one to estimate the decline in the amount of territory governed by the Roman emperors (indicated by the heavy line in Fig. 2; see also Fig. 1). Collapse can also be interpreted as change in the structure of the empire. The empire in 700 was not simply a smaller version of the empire in 200; it had become less centralized and less integrated in the course of its diminution. The course of this change is not clear from historical sources, however; one can sometimes argue for both increasing centralization and decreasing governmental control for the same periods.

The production of coinage is one example of an archaeological measure of centralization or disintegration within the Roman administration. Ancient states minted coins as a standardized means for paying governmental expenditures; precious metals (gold and silver) were used for the more important payments. As it happens, Roman coinage frequently has mint marks or other indications of

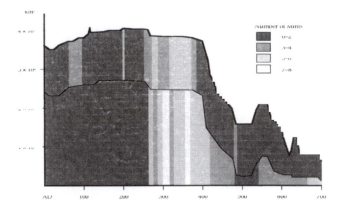

FIG. 2. Coin production and size of the Roman Empire, A.D. 1–700: the upper curve represents the total area of the empire, divided by the lower curve into two portions, the lower representing the Latin West and the upper the Greek East (as defined in Fig. 1). Within each portion, the intensity of shading indicates the number of mints in that part of the empire producing precious-metal coins under Roman administration (local coinages have been excluded except Asian *cistophori* and Alexandrian *tetradrachms*). Sources: R.A.G. Carson, *Coins of the Roman Empire* (London: Routledge, 1990); Michael F. Hendy, *Studies in the Byzantine Monetary Economy, c. 300–1450* (Cambridge: Cambridge University Press, 1985); David R. Sear, *Greek Imperial Coins and Their Values* (London: Seaby, 1982).

the place of minting. Since all money from the same mint has passed through a single administrative office, the existence of relatively few separate regional mints should indicate greater concentration of the flow of major sums of money within the government. Likewise, many separate mints would indicate dispersed management of governmental resources. The number of mints is not a direct or an exact measure of administrative decentralization, since some offices minted very large amounts of coin for large areas, while others produced very limited issues; it may, however, be seen as a rough ordinal index. The shading in Fig. 2 shows the number of mints in the eastern and western parts of the empire in relation to the territorial shrinkage of the empire.

The pattern of precious-metal minting indicates that the empire became much less centralized after 250; the East became more centralized by the fifth century, but centralized administration was not established in the areas later reconquered in the West. Being based on the higher-value coins, this pattern applies primarily to the major, higher-level functions of government, such as maintenance of the army. A similar study of base-metal (low-value) coinage would be misleading, because before 250 much of the base-metal coin (unlike precious-metal coin) was produced by local communities, but this in itself suggests that the lower-level functions of government became much more centralized after 250. Thus, the operation of government shows a general trend toward regional separation, even if it became to some degree more centralized within these regions, but this trend was later erased in the East though not in the West. Once areas passed out of Roman control, the same trend usually continued, with many local mints operating increasingly independently.

The concept of *collapse* can also be understood as extending beyond the political and administrative realm to encompass society in general. Obviously, society cannot be said to have collapsed totally, since life continued and many aspects of Roman culture endured, but archaeology shows that, in most parts of the erstwhile empire, life in the eighth century was very different from life in the second century. Roman culture had typically featured well-appointed towns, a densely populated rural landscape, and an active and diverse economy. By the eighth century, most of these towns were either reduced to vestiges with few inhabitants or abandoned altogether. The population had declined greatly in most areas, leaving occasional small villages where there had once been scores of farms and villas. Finally, the economy in many areas had been reduced to local self-sufficiency at a low level of production.

To trace these changes as they developed not only describes this aspect of the process of collapse, it also brings in the question of causes. Much of the argument over why the empire collapsed involves argument over change within the empire after c. 160. In particular, were there internal changes that could have produced collapse and, if so, of what nature? The written documentation is neither specific enough nor quantitative enough to be conclusive on such important matters as whether the economy was declining or the population was shrinking. In fact, many historians in the past have dismissed these possibilities on the ground that such general internal changes could not account for the differences in collapse between West and East.

It is in this regard that archaeological evidence has had the most impact so far. It is now clear that significant economic changes occurred throughout the sequence and that the regional variation in economic trends corresponds surprisingly well to the regional variation in political collapse.

The most important, although not the easiest to prove, of these concerns the population. Decline in population would mean fewer taxpayers, fewer recruits for the army, and so on; in other words, it could contribute strongly to political collapse. Whether it occurred or not, though, has been fiercely disputed by historians. In recent decades, archaeologists have begun systematic examination of particular areas for the presence of Roman and post-Roman sites, making it possible to compare the number and the extent of settlements of various periods. This has revealed a much more dynamic situation than previously envisioned; population appears to have been growing or declining all the time, with considerable differences between different regions of the empire (Fig. 3). Most important for the issue of collapse, population appears to have begun to decline in the West by the second century and had reached low levels by the fifth century (when imperial administration collapsed there), whereas population reached a maximum in the East during the fifth and sixth centuries (when imperial power became centered in

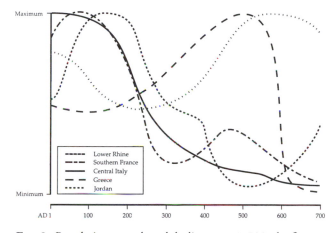

FIG. 3. Population growth and decline, A.D. 1–700: the five curves represent estimates of the changing population densities of five regions of the empire: the Lower Rhine Valley, southern France, central Italy, central Greece, and Jordan. There is no absolute vertical scale; each curve is standardized relative to the local maximum settlement density during this period. Sources: This graph has no secure factual basis; it is merely a subjective impression based on numerous regional studies of rural and urban settlement, such as those cited by Klavs Randsborg, *The First Millennium A.D. in Europe and the Mediterranean* (Cambridge: Cambridge University Press, 1991), and those in R.F.J. Jones et al., eds., *First Millennium Papers,* BAR International Series 401 (Oxford: British Archaeological Reports, 1988), and G. Barker and J. Lloyd, eds., *Roman Landscapes: Archaeological Survey in the Mediterranean Region,* Archaeological Monographs of the British School of Rome 2 (London: British School of Rome, 1991).

R

the East). The timing of political collapse in a region thus tended to follow depopulation.

The pattern is not as unequivocal as Fig. 3 makes it seem, however. The patterns of changing numbers of known sites are clear, but questions have been raised about how well this represents changing population. Estimates of when sites were occupied are normally based on the types of pottery found there, but in many areas the local pottery sequence is poorly known, so that the sites are dated mostly on the basis of small quantities of imported pottery. Thus, it has been suggested that the changes in number of sites known reflect changing patterns of trade rather than changing population. At present, the matter is unresolved, but in the few areas where the local pottery is reasonably well known, such as southern France, the patterns of site abundance resemble Fig. 3 anyway, supporting the inference of population change, though the degree of change is less drastic than it might appear without this knowledge.

Considering the magnitude of population decline apparent in the West by 300, it is noteworthy that much of the system of production survived, though in reduced form, until after the replacement of imperial rule. Agricultural production in most areas continued to yield marketable surpluses that landowning elites could convert into luxury goods and empirewide influence; craft specialists continued to produce a wide range of consumer goods. Before 650 (earlier in the northwestern provinces), however, this system finally became so attenuated as almost to have disappeared in most regions, the main exception being the Levant, where economic and demographic collapse did not occur until well after the end of Roman rule.

Political strength depends not only on the infrastructure of population and production, but also on the connections holding the parts together. In addition to the administrative centralization described above, there is also an economic aspect exemplified by the amount of long-distance trade within the empire. This can be measured to some extent by the frequency of shipwrecks in the Mediterranean Sea. Over the long run, periods with much shipping should yield many shipwrecks, and periods with little shipping should yield few, as long as one makes allowance for the varied amounts of underwater research in different areas (quite a lot in southern France and very little in Lebanon, for example).

Figure 4 shows the changing relative frequency of shipwrecks for the Mediterranean as divided into three parts (western, central, and eastern). For all three zones, the peak is in the first century; it is notable, however, that shipping in the West declined sharply, reaching a low level before 400, but in the East it remained intermittently strong until after 700. While this difference may be, in part, simply a consequence of the earlier decline of population in the West, it implies in any case that the regular economic traffic necessary for maintaining a unified regional system broke down largely in advance of the collapse of Roman control.

Although it is clear that economic processes involving both local population and long-distance trade were important among the causes of collapse, this observation cannot be considered to solve the whole problem. Noting that depopulation, for example, seems to have been a factor in political change raises the question of what caused the depopulation. Although many possible causes have been suggested, including epidemic disease, soil deterioration, and excessive taxation, the detailed research needed to construct and test such models has barely begun.

It may in any case be missing half the point merely to ask why the Roman Empire collapsed: as historian Edward Gibbon commented, "instead of inquiring why the Roman Empire was destroyed, we should rather be

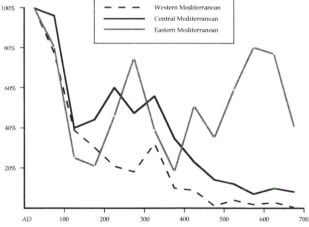

FIG. 4. Frequency of shipwrecks in the Mediterranean, A.D. 1–700: the three lines represent relative numbers of shipwrecks per fifty-year interval for the western Mediterranean (France, Algeria, and westward), the central Mediterranean (Italy, Croatia, Tunisia, Libya, and Malta), and the eastern Mediterranean (Greece, Egypt, and eastward). There is no absolute vertical scale; each line has been standardized by setting its maximum at 100 percent. Frequencies have been estimated by dividing each instance evenly over its estimated date range. Source: A.J. Parker, *Ancient Shipwrecks of the Mediterranean and the Roman Provinces,* BAR International Series 580 (Oxford: Tempvs Reparatvm, 1992).

surprised that it had subsisted so long" (Gibbon 1995: vol. 2, p. 509). Few states have maintained themselves over such a large area for so long, and no other has unified the entire Mediterranean Basin. One manifestation of this, probably both cause and consequence, was a degree of cultural assimilation that has influenced all subsequent cultures there.

Complete cultural unity did not occur, as mentioned already in the case of language, nor was it sought. However, the educated upper classes throughout the empire came to share many values, beliefs, and practices; some elements of this culture were spread more generally throughout society, such as the Latin language (in the western provinces) and the Christian religion (which, despite its Near Eastern roots, in its developed form is mostly a product of provincial Roman culture and owes its success to its adoption by the Roman state). By the eighth century, there was no longer a shared elite culture for the whole Mediterranean Basin; it was divided among barbarian western Europe, the Greek-speaking Byzantine Empire, and the new Arabic culture of the Islamic caliphate. All of these, however, derived many parts of their cultural traditions from their shared Roman heritage. In this sense, then, the Roman civilization did not collapse; it continued to evolve throughout the vicissitudes of political change.

The changes that constitute the end of antiquity and the beginning of the Middle Ages are not easy to summarize. The predominant theme of recent scholarship on this era is variation. Imperial control was collapsing in some regions while it flourished in others; population and trade declined in some areas while they expanded in others; some aspects of culture and society broke down while others did not. The most important conclusion is that collapse was not a simple event or a uniform process. Some changes are clearly correlated, but different regions and different elements of the Roman system took different trajectories. Dissecting the various changes and understanding how they are related, in terms of the archaeological evidence unhindered by the literary sources, are the foremost challenges at present in the study of the Roman Empire's collapse.

FURTHER READINGS

Burnett, A. *Coinage in the Roman World*. London: Seaby, 1987.

Gibbon, Edward. *The History of the Decline and Fall of the Roman Empire*. Ed. David Womersley. New York: Viking Penguin, 1995.

Jones, A.H.M. *The Later Roman Empire, 284–602*. Oxford: Basil Blackwell, 1964.

Randsborg, Klavs. *The First Millennium A.D. in Europe and the Mediterranean*. Cambridge: Cambridge University Press, 1991.

Rollins, A.M. *The Fall of Rome: A Reference Guide*. Jefferson: McFarland, 1983.

David Yoon

SEE ALSO
Coinage; Lombards; Visigoths

Rostock

The city of Rostock lies 13 km from the open Baltic Sea (Fig. 1) in northern Germany. Nevertheless, in the Middle Ages this location had the advantages of a coastal town because the River Warnow could be traveled by seagoing ships up to this point. The 400-m-wide Warnow Valley at Rostock reflects the course of an Ice Age crack feature of melting ice. Above the reaches of the Lower Warnow, which is more than 100 m wide, the river originally was divided into two branches so that the areas around the Petrikirche and the Nikolaikirche appeared as an island. The city itself extended from a 12-to-14-m-high debris-marl-plateau, which was cut through by an Ice Age melt-water channel. Its favorable position in a sheltered hinterland and its location on a west-east trade route were major reasons for the rise of Rostock as an important city of the Hanseatic League in the southern Baltic Sea area.

Both eastern Germany and the Warnow Valley were originally settled by the Slavs (Fig. 2). The name Rostock was mentioned for the first time by the Danish historian Saxo Grammaticus in the year 1160. At that time, a castle of the same name was taken by Danish troops and was burned, along with the idol located there. The Slavic word *roztoc* was closely connected to the locality of the castle. It marked the position where the river widened; this waterfall was the place where the Warnow, previously only 50 m wide, suddenly expanded and entirely filled the Ice Age bed, which was more than 100 m wide. The bridge at this location was the last spot at which the Warnow could be crossed in the early historic period. The castle, which is no longer visible on the surface, was located in the so-called Petribleiche; small portions of it were examined. Its location satisfied important ground conditions for a castle in the late Slavic period: a well-sheltered location in the swampy Warnow marsh, a position favorable to trade on an old coastal trade route, a

R

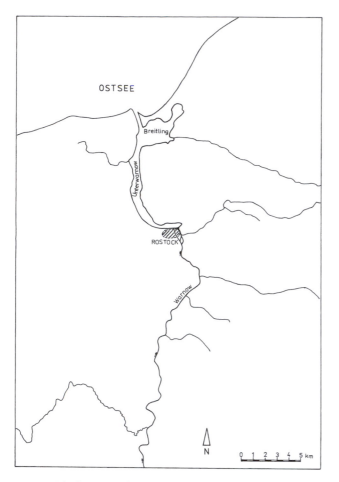

FIG. 1. The location of Rostock on the River Warnow.

location on a navigable river, and control over a large hinterland.

According to dendrochronological (tree-ring) investigations, by the beginning of the twelfth century (at the latest) the established castle possessed a wall built of tree trunks as well as a forecastle. Corresponding with the castle in the marsh, a Slavic settlement of the same age can be detected lying to the west on the island of Altstadthügel (old city hill) near the Petrikirche. Archaeological investigations, as well as virtually every building development on this hilltop, have exposed late Slavic graves and settlement layers, which hitherto could be dated only generally to the twelfth century on the basis of ceramics. A large number of finds imported from Scandinavia and from the old German settlement region west of the River Elbe verify the far-reaching trade relations of this settlement,

which may also have functioned as a market under the protection of the castle. Burned layers observed in many graves indicate the eventual simultaneous destruction of the castle and the settlement in 1160.

Restoration of the castle in 1170 is demonstrable archaeologically and through inferences from written sources. A document from the year 1189 gives accurate information concerning the appearance of the castle and settlement at that time. It mentions that the power of Rostock was displayed in Rostock's castle by the enfeoffed Slavic Prince Nikolaus, with a market now located by the castle as well as a Christian church with a chaplain resident there. There is still no written reference to the true medieval city of Rostock at the end of the twelfth century; however, historians accept that the first German settlers and merchants arrived between 1180 and 1190. That would correspond with the oldest archaeologically recognizable German settlement horizon on the Altstadthügel, which can be dated through ceramics and certain brick remains to the twelfth century or the beginning of the thirteenth. A paved road leading from the west in the direction of the Petrikirche, as well as remains of a wood house and cellar of log-type construction, belong to this period. At present, we know as little about the exact time of the founding as we do of the appearance of the first urban settlement. One can only suspect that the houses of the craftsmen and the merchants were grouped with a church and a marketplace. The expansion of this settlement (c. 200 × 150 m), which is understood accurately as a result of excavation, geological peculiarities, and historical knowledge, coincides well with the 10-m contour line around the Petrikirche.

The medieval city of Rostock appears in documents for the first time in 1218, when the Slavic Prince Heinrich Borwin I of the settlement confirmed the town charter of Lübeck. Thus, a functioning urban entity must already have existed at this time. When the influx of settlers very quickly exceeded the capacity of this first Altstadt (old city), it resulted c. 1230 (1232, first reference) in a second city founding, the Mittelstadt (middle city) around the Marienkirche, and c. 1250 (1252, first reference) in a third city founding, the Neustadt (new city) around the Jakobikirche. All were originally free-standing urban constructions with a city hall, a market, and a parish church. They were first joined formally in 1265.

Natural borders continued to exist between these three cities. The Grube (ditch), a branch of the Warnow, divided Altstadt and Mittelstadt; the Faule Grube (foul

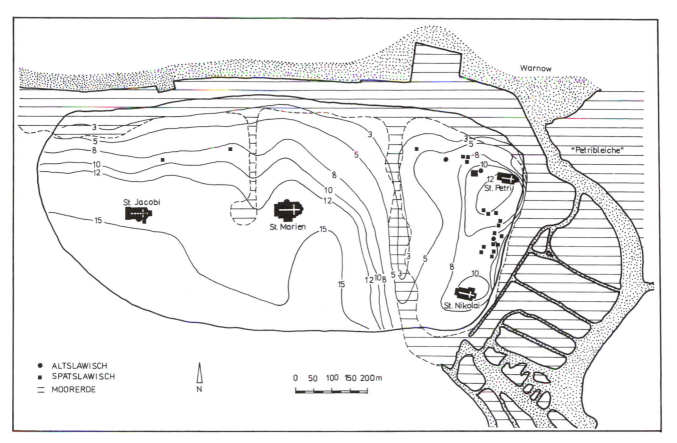

FIG. 2. The location of Slavic finds in the Rostock area. The maps are based on a 1908 topographic study.

ditch), a mud-filled Ice Age gutter, separated Mittelstadt from Neustadt. These ditches, which gradually became mud-filled depressions, as well as the bank of the wide Lower Warnow that dropped off gently to the north, were used for settlement for the first time in the thirteenth century as a result of costly measures of land reclamation/development. Geological and archaeological investigations have revealed that minimally all areas lying below the 5-m contour line originally lay considerably deeper in flood areas of the Warnow or else were mud filled. The open country up to at least the 5-m contour was initially made more elevated and cultivatable through extensive deposits of settlement waste of all kinds (household trash, manure, wood waste, and clay from building excavations). These processes could be explored in an exemplary fashion on the west side of the Altstadthügel in the area of the Katharinenkloster, where the land-reclamation and development layers, dendrochronologically dated to c. 1234, originate.

The erection of a uniform (standardized) city wall in the second half of the thirteenth century then marked the final medieval city borders, which were supposed to contain Rostock into the nineteenth century.

FURTHER READINGS

Hofmeister, Adolf. Zur historischen Topographie Rostocks. *Beiträge zur Geschichte der Stadt Rostock* (1907) 4 (Heft 4):1–13.

Krause, Ludwig. Zur Rostocker Topographie. *Beiträge zur Geschichte der Stadt Rostock* (1925) 13:12–82.

Lisch, Georg Christian Friedrich, and Vincent Heinrich Mann. Beiträge zur älteren Geschichte der Stadt Rostock. *Jahrbücher für mecklenburgische Geschichte und Altertumskunde* (1856) 21:3–50.

Mulsow, Ralf. Stadtkernforschung am Alten Markt in Rostock. *Archäologisches Korrespondenzblatt* (1992) 22:441–448.

R

———. Stadtarchäologie in Rostock: Ein Überblick. In *Archäologie des Mittelalters und Bauforschung im Hanseraum.* Ed. Manfred Gläser. Schriften des Kulturhistorischen Museums in Rostock 1. Rostock: Konrad Reich Verlag, 1993, pp. 47–52.

Olechnowitz, Karl Friedrich. *Rostock von der Stadtrechtsbestätigung im Jahre 1218 bis zur bürgerlich-demokratischen Revolution von 1848–49.* Rostock: Hinstorff, 1968.

Schäfer, Heiko. Das archäologische und bauhistorische Forschungssproject Katharinenkloster zu Rostock. In *Archäologie des Mittelalters und Bauforschung im Hanseraum.* Ed. Manfred Gläser. Schriften des Kulturhistorischen Museums in Rostock 1. Rostock: Konrad Reich Verlag, 1993, pp. 347–352.

Warnke, Dieter. Rostock-Petribleiche: Eine slawische Fürstenburg des 12. Jahrhunderts. In *Archäologie des Mittelalters und Bauforschung im Hanseraum.* Ed. Manfred Gläser. Schriften des Kulturhistorischen Museums in Rostock 1. Rostock: Konrad Reich Verlag, 1993, pp. 155–160.

Ralf Muslow

SEE ALSO
Lübeck

S

St. Abb's Head

See Scotland: Early Royal Sites.

Saint-Nicolas D'Acy

The priory of Saint-Nicolas d'Acy, situated 3 km west of the royal city of Senlis (Oise, France), is a Cluniac priory that was a daughter house of the Cluniac monastery of Saint-Martin-des-Champs in Paris. Founded as a church in 1098 by Robert, a lay advocate, it was occupied from the beginning of the twelfth century by a group of Parisian monks following an increased endowment given by Guy de la Tour, a knight close to the king. This monastic establishment maintained its community of ten monks up to the time of the French Revolution (1789).

The site of the priory was excavated over four seasons from 1983 to 1986. The archaeological research program was designed to reconstruct the plan of this simple Cluniac monastery and its evolution during the Middle Ages and the modern period. The monastic buildings were arranged around a square cloister attached to the south of the church, which served as both a parish church (nave) and a priory (transcept and sanctuary). These orderly buildings appear perfectly adapted to the size of the monastic community and its *familia* (i.e., the roughly fifty persons who lived on the manor within the priory grounds). The priory was remarkably well organized for a lasting monastic way of life. The medieval layout dates to the second half of the twelfth century, with minor additions in the following century. This monastery did not suffer from the disturbances at the end of the Middle Ages. In the sixteenth century, even though most of the buildings were in good repair, successive priors decided to change the arrangement of the buildings in response to practical necessities and new spiritual needs.

In addition to reconstructing the layout of the priory, a multidisciplinary study of the site and its surroundings was made possible by the use of data from archaeology, history, studies of the human and natural environment, ceramic analyses, numismatics, and physical anthropology. Three subjects were particularly emphasized. The first concerns the mechanisms by which the monastic community was established around the church built in the second half of the eleventh century. The monks waited approximately half a century before constructing regular buildings in stone. The second aspect relates to the impact of the priory on its environment along the Nonette Valley between the great forests of Chantilly to the south and Halatte to the north, including the monastic hamlet, its real-estate holdings, water supply, and relations with the laity. The final aspect is devoted to mortuary archaeology (rites and practices) and the anthropological study of certain monks and lay individuals who were buried in three principal zones: the parish cemetery, the church *(ad Sanctos),* and the priory (cloister galleries and chapter house). This study allowed for the development of important hypotheses concerning the relationship of the monks with the external world, the politics of burial, and the state of health of the populations having relations with the priory. The discovery of intentionally damaged or bent coins of the twelfth century in the fill of certain tombs, as well as the types of tombs (constructed, semiconstructed, characterized by the presence or absence of a coffin or by the presence or absence of a stone basin supporting the head), their placement, their partial disturbance, and the study of the positions of

S

the skeletons have provided valuable information on all aspects of the role and religious character on a Cluniac monastery.

FURTHER READINGS

Ligny, F. Le prieuré de Saint-Nicolas d'Acy: Archéologie extensive. *Revue Archéologique SITES* (1991) 44: 25–28.

Porée, B. Us cas de dynamisme technique médiéval et moderne: Témoingage de la poterie du prieuré de Saint-Nicolas d'Acy (Beauvaisis). *Revue Archéologique SITES* (1992) 51:31–36.

Racinet, P. Deux fouilles sur des prieurés clunisiens en Picardie: Saint-Nicolas d'Acy et Notre-Dame de Nanteuil-le-Haudouin. Les aspects monumentaux. *Histoire Médiévale et Archéologie* (Publications du CAHMER, Université de Paris 13) (1991a) 4:73–80.

———. Un prieuré moyen de l'ordre de Cluny en Picardie: Saint-Nicolas d'Acy (XIe-XVIIIe siècles). *Revue Archéologique de Picardie* (1991b) 1–2:21–163.

Racinet, P., F. Laphung, M. Pereira da Salva, and O. Cussenot. Vie et mort dans le prieuré clunisien: Archéologie funéraire et anthropologie à Saint-Nicolas d'Acy (Oise). *Heresis* (1990) 2:195–228.

Philippe Racinet

Sandy Flanders: Early Medieval Settlement

The inquiry into the early medieval occupation history of sandy Flanders—a flat region dominated by unfertile sandy soils, located in northwestern Belgium between the coastal plain and the River Scheldt—was for long limited to the one-sided analysis of the scarce written sources. These included several *vitae sanctorum* (saints' lives), early Carolingian deeds of sale, and some place names and were thus suited only for defining the broad picture. They led to the interpretation of a chaotic and dark fifth century, with the slowly incoming Salian Franks taking the place of the sparse Gallo-Roman population that had fled to the south. Then came a phase of reconstruction, due to a strong impulse from the southern town of Tournai on the River Scheldt, where the Merovingian elite was grouped. This impulse generated a massive colonization move toward the northern sand area during the sixth and seventh centuries, which itself led to more stable settlement structures (hamlets, villages) and to social control by the new land-based rulers.

Since the 1980s, intense but often small-scale archaeological research has brought more clarity and depth to this picture. The first surprise came with the discovery and partial excavation of several Germanic settlements, which were already established within the Roman Empire from the late fourth century onward. Sites such as those at Asper, Kruishoutem, Sint-Martens-Latem, and Sint-Gillis-Waas often produced relevant indicators like sunken huts or uncommercial, handmade pottery brought along from Saxon or Frankish territories in the Netherlands and northern Germany. These sites seem to demonstrate that small groups of Germanic farmers had been able to settle south of the border before the downfall of Rome in northern Gaul c. A.D. 410. The same picture emerges in the Campine and Lower Meuse area, as can be seen at Donk, Neerharen-Rekem, and Voerendaal. The early Germanic sites of sandy Flanders were, it seems, often occupied throughout a major part of the fifth century, and they sometimes even show some kind of continuity of occupation during the Merovingian colonization phase.

Settlements and cemeteries from the late fifth and sixth century are still infrequent in the archaeological record. It seems that the completely rural occupation of the area at that time consisted of very small communities, a maximum of two or three households, that settled here as part of larger social groups. Some of their cemeteries, especially those with one or two rich weapon graves with long swords, indicate the presence of a clan leader.

In the course of the seventh century, the settlement structure becomes more stable, under the influence of the Merovingian nobility. Larger rural entities, probably focused around major *villae*, and more extensive pagan cemeteries made up of rows of graves with a dominant southwest-northeast orientation occur at this time, as can be seen in the Scheldt Basin at Beerlegem and Sloten (Gent/Port-Arthur). From this period onward, some commerce and nonrural settlement may start to develop again, especially near the Scheldt and Lys Rivers and in the neighborhood of the old late Roman military structures. It is clear that by now the waterways have taken the place of the collapsed Roman road network as the main arteries for communication and transport.

From the middle of the seventh century onward, the crucial settlement of Gent, on the confluence of the Lys and the Scheldt, took the lead in the final Christianization of sandy Flanders. Especially its two abbeys, Saint Peter and Saint Bavo, became crucial factors in the conversion of the inhabitants of this preurban settlement. The Christianization of the countryside was much slower and occurred only in the eighth century. Abbeys, such as those in Gent, Dikkelvenne, and Elnone, played an important role. Another distribution channel for Christianity were royal Merovingian possessions, parts of which were formerly Roman imperial property. A research project in Kruishoutem is investigating the reasons for an obvious continuity between a Roman *vicus* (small town) centered on an important pagan sanctuary and a medieval settlement with a Christian chapel or church named for Saint Peter.

FURTHER READINGS

Van Doorselaer, A., ed. *De Merovingische beschaving in de Scheldevallei, Kortrijk.* Westvlaamse Archaeologica Monografieën 2. Kortrijk: 1981.

Vermeulen, F. *Tussen Leie en Schelde: Archeologische inventaris en studie van de Romeinse bewoning in het zuiden van de Vlaamse Zandstreek.* Buitengewone Reeks 1. Gent: AIV, 1992.

Vermeulen, F., M. Rogge, and L. Van Durme, eds. *Terug naar de bron: Kruishoutem archeologisch doorgelicht.* Buitengewone Reeks 2. Gent: AIV, 1993.

Frank Vermeulen

Scandinavia

See Pre-Viking Scandinavia.

Scotland, Dark Age

By A.D. 1100, much of north Britain could be legitimately described as Scotland; before then, north Britain consisted of a number of regionally based kingdoms whose fortunes, influences, and boundaries were in a constant state of flux. Nevertheless, Scotland's particular history in the Middle Ages and later makes it valuable to discuss Scottish medieval archaeology from the fifth century onward. During this period, four peoples with distinctive cultural traditions coalesced into a coherent medieval state in a region not overendowed with natural resources. Scotland provided the medium that not only linked Ireland with Northumbria, but also contributed significantly to the creation of great works of art and literature. The evidence for Dark Age (A.D. 400–1100) Scotland is biased heavily in favor of the Church and the aristocracy, who not only dominated secular dealings but also controlled powerful ecclesiastical networks.

Northern Britain contains dramatic geographical variations that made the effective governance of the mainland with its Highland interior very difficult until the eighteenth century. The islands on its western and northern seaboard only compounded the problem of exercising centralized control. On the mainland, a major north-south division is created by the broad valleys of the Forth and the Clyde Rivers. This central belt is moderately fertile and has always attracted settlement, but the great agricultural wealth of the country is concentrated in the eastern coastal regions, where fertile soils and moderate rainfall are especially suited to cereal cultivation. To the west, the ground becomes more mountainous, wetter, and less fertile. These west Highlands are cut by sea inlets into innumerable peninsulas and islands. As a consequence, the sea provides the most efficient means of travel in the western and northern coastal region, and here seafaring encouraged intellectual as well as commercial exchange.

In the fifth century, following the final lapse of Roman authority in Britain, four peoples were recognized as inhabiting northern Britain. They possessed separate languages and were internally divided into a several petty kingdoms. The least well known of the native Celtic inhabitants were the Picts, who dwelled in the east, north of the River Forth. The other native Celts, the Britons, who occupied the country to the south and west of the River Clyde, are more familiar in language and literature because they were, in effect, the northern Welsh. The Scots were incoming Celts, who crossed the Irish Sea to settle on the west coast in the area known as Argyll. They maintained close political and cultural ties with their Irish homeland. The Angles were a Germanic people who had migrated from the Continent to northern England; as their kingdom in Northumbria grew in stature, they began to encroach upon the southeast, for a time exercising power as far north as the Forth.

The notion of four peoples, as spoken of by the English Benedictine scholar Bede (c. 672–735), finds material expression, most conspicuously in sculptured stone monuments. Most of these are explicitly Christian, but a group of more than 150 standing stones bearing inscribed symbols that are found in Pictland have an ambiguous religious orientation (Fig. 1; Fig. 2). These Pictish symbols include animal representations and abstract motifs, but there is no universally accepted interpretation of the stones themselves. It seems most likely that they are a local manifestation of memorial stones, which were widespread in Britain and Ireland in the fourth–sixth centuries. Although many of the symbol stones are found in the vicinity of later churches, there is nothing explicitly Christian about the symbols. However, the symbols do reappear on a later series of stone crosses that are clear expressions of Christianity.

FIG. 1. The Pictish symbol stone at Aberlemno with the cross executed in deep relief. (Photograph: Historic Scotland.)

FIG. 2. The reverse of the Aberlemno stone with symbols at the top and a battle scene below. (Photograph: Historic Scotland.)

S

The symbol stones foreshadow the elaborate stone sculptures, which begin to appear all over Scotland a century or so after the conversion and which are the most significant relics of this period. The regionalization reflected in the sculpture is partly the result of the different paths the conversion to Christianity followed.

Over time, saints' relics became the objects of pilgrimage, and cults came to play an important political role. The most important cults tended to focus on the saint identified with the conversions. Direct archaeological evidence for the earliest stages of Christianity is rare, if only because it is not clear what form the earliest religious establishments would have taken. An exception is provided by the small group of Latin inscriptions that are found in southern Scotland, particularly in the southwest. These provide the earliest datable evidence for Christianity in the north and support the tradition that the first missionary, Ninian (c. 360–432), established a church in Whithorn perhaps in the early fifth century. This site was later developed into an Anglo-Saxon monastery and became one of the principal pilgrimage destinations in Scotland.

The establishment of a monastic community on Iona in 563 by the Irish nobleman Columba (c. 521–597) is the principal religious event of early Scottish history. Iona became the center of an extremely influential network of monasteries that extended into Ireland and northern England. For much of this period, it was the preeminent ecclesiastical center in northern Britain and had a profound influence on liturgical, spiritual, and artistic matters. The archaeology of Iona consists largely of sculptured stone monuments, including some of the most impressive High Crosses anywhere. The early Christian monastery has been obscured by a late medieval refoundation, and the only visible structural remains are those of the monastic enclosure wall, or *vallum*. This is typical of most of the other known early monastic sites, in which the carved stone monuments are the most prominent features and the circular vallum is often the only upstanding element. What is atypical is Iona's significance in historical terms. This can be measured crudely by the importance we attach to the books produced in its scriptorium: the *Vita Columba*, a set of annals now encapsulated within the *Annals of Ulster*, and, arguably, the *Book of Kells*.

There is no great Pictish missionary of the stature of Columba or Ninian, but filling the hagiographical void stands the most important body of early Christian sculpture in Britain. These sculptures attest to widespread Christianity in Pictland by the seventh century. The most distinctive of these monuments are massive slabs standing 2–6 m high. Typically, they feature an elaborately ornamented cross carved in relief on one side, while the reverse usually presents a figurative scene, which is rarely religious. A substantial proportion also have Pictish symbols on the figurative side. The finest of these share the same decorative repertoire seen in the contemporary illuminated manuscripts and fine metalwork. Despite the clear Christian iconography, the most arresting aspect of these monuments is the prominence of the secular elements.

In the later Middle Ages, the conversion of the Strathclyde Britons was attributed to the efforts of St. Kentigern, to whom Glasgow Cathedral is dedicated. However, there is no archaeological evidence for an early Christian establishment at Glasgow, while the greatest concentration of early medieval sculpture in the region is to be found at Govan, a few miles down the Clyde. Although there is no historical documentation to accompany this large collection of burial memorials and ecclesiastical sculpture, it was probably a cult center established by the kings of the Britons in Strathclyde, which served both as a pilgrimage site and as a royal cemetery.

To date, there have been no pagan Anglian burials, so typical of the English settlement farther south, found in Scotland. This is because, by the time the presence of the Anglo-Saxons was felt in Scotland, they had become Christian. At the apogee of Northumbrian influence in the mid-seventh century, their influence stretched west to Whithorn, and there was even a bishopric established at Abercorn on the Forth. Fragments of stone crosses in the Anglo-Saxon style are the principal physical evidence of this presence, but, remarkably enough, the best of all Anglo-Saxon crosses is preserved nearly complete at Ruthwell. Not only does it contain a finely executed set of iconographic images, but it also features the "Dream of the Rood" (a lyrical meditation written by the ninth-century poet Cynewulf) inscribed in runes.

The most graphic images of secular life to survive anywhere in Dark Age Britain are those on the Pictish stones. They include vivid representation of members of the aristocracy engaged in the hunt, at war, or simply attired as warriors. Not only do they animate the material record, they also underscore the significance of the warrior ideology for the nobility. The link they establish through this combination of secular and religious imagery underpinned the social order dominated by the nobility.

From a landscape perspective, the most conspicuous aspects of the archaeology of the nobility are their residences, which were often located on prominent craggy eminences. The most important of these combine residential, ceremonial, and manufacturing aspects within their unmortared stone walls. Typically, these fortified hills have a central residential structure surrounded by one or more enclosures where retainers and craftsmen could live and work. The exceptional examples, with royal associations, also have features of a ceremonial nature. The most well known and extensively excavated example is Dunadd in Argyll, which was a center for one of the dynasties of the Scots (Fig. 3). A series of similar sites have been identified and excavated recently, including the Strathclyde British center at Dumbarton and the Pictish ones at Dundurn and Burghead.

Besides providing secure and impressive residences for the elite, these sites were centers where artisans plied their trade. In all excavated cases, these residential sites have provided evidence for fine metalworking in the form of fragments of molds, metal and enamel scraps, and trial pieces. At the Mote of Mark, a large range of manufacturing debris suggests that the artisans were working in both Celtic and Anglo-Saxon styles (Fig. 4). These sites also produce the greatest evidence for foreign commerce represented by imported Continental pottery. It is possible to see these places as centers from which exotic and rare goods were distributed to the loyal followers of the elite. The traces of ceremonial activity, as at Dunadd and Burghead, suggest that they may also have been the settings of royal ceremonies.

The impact of the Vikings was as strongly felt in Scotland as anywhere in Britain. The Northern and Western Isles were a natural stopping-off place en route between Norway and the Irish Sea. The Scandinavian settlement

FIG. 3. The craggy knoll occupied by the hillfort of Dunadd in Argyll. (Photograph: Historic Scotland.)

FIG. 4. The Hunterston brooch, which could have been made in either Ireland or western Scotland. A Scandinavian runic inscription on its reverse may testify to a Viking raid. (Photograph: National Museum of Scotland.)

of the north was so substantial that the Celtic language was completely replaced. New forms of building were introduced, as can be seen in the excavations at Jarlshof in Shetland, and a new power elite was established whose links were with the Norse in Scandinavia. The Orkney Islands became the center of an independent earldom with its main center at Birsay. Here, excavations help chart the transition from a Pictish center to a Norse one. Elsewhere, the impact of the Vikings may be recognized in the elaborate burials, often in boats, that have been excavated over the years. These frequently contain goods acquired from Scotland, England, or Ireland.

Raiding was a major aspect of the Scandinavian contact with Scotland and most conspicuously caused the Abbey of Iona to be abandoned c. A.D. 800. On the east coast, raiding is often cited as a contributing factor in the downfall of the Pictish kingdoms, and the instability in the east may have paved the way for the Scot Kenneth Mac Alpine to add the kingdom of the Picts to his dominion c. A.D. 843. This established the dynastic basis for the medieval state and firmly oriented it toward the east coast. This movement toward a feudal kingdom was manifest negatively by the evidence of the abandonment of the hillforts as the principal centers of authority and positively by the strengthening of the nonmonastic Church in the east of the country.

FURTHER READINGS

Alcock, Leslie. Early Historic Fortifications in Scotland. In *Hill-Fort Studies.* Ed. G. Guilbert. Leicester: Leicester University Press, 1981, pp. 150–181. This initial survey has been followed up by a program of excavation, the reports of which are to be found in the *Proceedings of the Society of Antiquaries of Scotland.*

———. *Economy, Society, and Warfare among the Britons and Saxons.* Cardiff: University of Wales Press, 1987.

Allen, J.R., and J. Anderson. *The Early Christian Monuments of Scotland.* Edinburgh: Society of Antiquaries of Scotland, 1903. Reprinted, Forfar: Pinkfoot, 1993.

Crawford, Barbara. *Scandinavian Scotland.* Leicester: Leicester University Press, 1987.

Driscoll, S.T., and M.R. Nieke, eds. *Power and Politics in Early Medieval Britain and Ireland.* Edinburgh: Edinburgh University Press, 1988.

Ritchie, Graham, and Anna Ritchie. *Scotland: Archaeology and Early History.* London: Thames and Hudson, 1981.

Royal Commission on the Ancient and Historic Monuments of Scotland. *Argyll.* Vols. 1–8. Edinburgh: HMSO, 1971–1992. An inventory with detailed descriptions of the sites and monuments in the Scottish heartland.

Thomas, Charles. *The Early Christian Archaeology of North Britain.* Oxford: Oxford University Press, 1968.

Wainwright, F.T., ed. *The Problem of the Picts.* rev. ed. Perth: Methven, 1980.

Stephen T. Driscoll

SEE ALSO
Birsay; Jarlshof; Northern Isles; Picts; Scotland: Early Royal Sites; Scotland, Medieval

Scotland: Early Royal Sites

In early historic Scotland, broadly the sixth–ninth centuries A.D., numerous historical notices refer to activities and events—sieges, burnings, destructions, rebuildings—at identifiable places with royal connections. Such invaluable guides to major sites of the period have been exploited in a series of excavations and other research from 1973 to 1993. This account gives references to the general program and basic methodologies, historical, archaeological, and radiometric; cites a broad generalizing summary; and gives brief site accounts to emphasize major results.

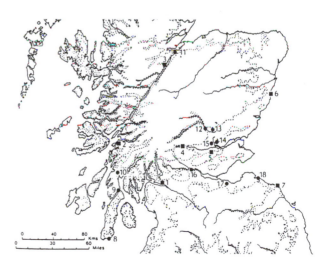

Map of Scotland showing the location of early royal sites. *Sites excavated 1974–1984: 1,* Dumbarton; *2,* Dunollie; *3,* Urquhart; *4,* Dundurn; *5,* Forteriot; *6,* Dunnottar; *7,* St. Abb's Head. *Other sites with historical references: 8,* Dunaverty; *9,* Tarbert; *10,* Dunadd; *11,* Inverness; *12,* Dunkeld; *13,* Clunie; *14,* Scone; *15,* Inveralmond; *16,* Stirling; *17,* Edinburgh; *18,* Dunbar.

S

St. Abb's Head

At St. Abb's Head (NGR NT 9168), a clifftop fort, enclosing c. 3 ha with a timber palisade, was identified. The fort type is British, but here the name Coludesburh and the radiocarbon (C-14) dates indicate that it was an Anglian construction. Subsequently, it formed the *vallum,* or enclosure wall, for the Northumbrian monastery founded by St. Æbbe c. A.D. 634.

Dunollie Castle

At Dunollie Castle (NGR NM 8531), a site frequently mentioned in the *Annals of Iona,* several phases of earthwork defense spanning the seventh–tenth centuries A.D. were uncovered beneath the masonry castle. The earliest work may have been a simple oval drystone fort, to which the outer enclosure was added. There is evidence for metal- and bone working and Continental imported pottery. The published account discusses the disputed dating, social status, and supposed Irish connections of such forts.

Dundurn

At Dundurn (NGR NN 7023), it was possible to explore a fort of the sixth–ninth centuries A.D., with no late medieval overlay. The plan was of a distinctive Scottish type, the nuclear fort—one with a central enclosed nucleus on a prominent hill, with dependent enclosures on the lower slopes. Excavation demonstrated that this complex plan had developed by additions to the original nucleus. In a discussion of such plans ranging from Scotland to central Europe, it was recommended that the term *hierarchically organized* was preferable to *nuclear* because it places an appropriate emphasis on the social structure implied by the plan. The outer enclosure may have been intended to protect cattle and, more important, horses against raiders. Finds were scarce but included ornaments of bronze and glass and evidence for metalworking.

Alt Clut

Alt Clut, Dumbarton (NGR 4074), produced evidence for the timber-laced defense of the *civitas Brettonum munitissima* referred to by Bede (c. 672–735) in his *Ecclesiastical History of the English People.* This had been destroyed by Norse raiders from Dublin in A.D. 870, the rubble of the rampart becoming vitrified (i.e., fused) by burning. Finds included the most northern examples of amphorae imported from the east Mediterranean, as well as imports of glass and pottery from western Europe. The site controls a good natural harbor at the junction of tidal waters with two rivers giving access to a large hinterland. Discussion centers on the importance of such harbor sites in northern and western Britain c. A.D. 450–850, and the site report includes a gazetteer, complete to 1990, of both coastal and inland sites of the period.

Forteviot

Fieldwork at Forteviot (NGR NO 0517) explored evidence for the eighth-century political center of successive Pictish and Scottish kings. The palace itself lies under the modern village, but a carved stone arch is witness to a royal chapel. Aerial photography suggests that the area was one of great ceremonial and ritual importance back into the third millennium B.C. and also reveals a Christian burial ground and enclosure east of the village. A study was also made of the Dupplin cross, which overlooks Forteviot as a permanent statement of royal power legitimated by divine right and military might.

Urquhart

A reference in the *Life of St. Columba,* together with earlier recovery of vitrified rubble, had led to the expectation of finding a vitrified fort beneath the later medieval castle of Urquhart (NGR NH 5328). It was found, however, that the early fort had been destroyed by later building works, but C-14 dates suggested occupation going back to the fifth–seventh centuries. The early fort may have taken the form of a citadel and lower enclosure (i.e., a hierarchically organized plan). Wider fieldwork made it possible to speculate on the landed estate of the sixth-century potentate resident in the citadel.

Dunnottar Castle and Bowduns

No trace was found of Dun Fother (*Annals of Ulster* A.D. 681; 694) beneath Dunnottar Castle (NGR NO 8883), but, at the north side of the sheltered Castle Haven (of which the castle formed the south side), the large promontory of Bowduns (NGR NO 8884) was shown to have been defended by a large ditch and bank not inappropriate for a sixth-century fort. Overlooked by Bowduns is Dunnicaer, a near-inaccessible sea stack, which earlier had yielded five slabs carved with early Pictish symbols. These are now published. The stack itself may be regarded as a Pictish cult focus.

FURTHER READINGS

Alcock, L. A Multi-Disciplinary Chronology for Alt Clut, Castle Rock, Dumbarton. *Proceeding of the Society of Antiquaries of Scotland* (1976) 107:103–113.

———. Early Historic Fortifications in Scotland. In *Hill-Fort Studies*. Ed. G. Guilbert. Leicester: Leicester University Press, (1981) pp. 150–180.

———. The Activities of Potentates in Celtic Britain, A.D. 500–800. In *Power and Politics in Early Medieval Britain and Ireland*. Ed. S.T. Driscoll and M.R. Nieke. Edinburgh: Edinburgh University Press, 1988, pp. 22–46.

Alcock, L., and E.A. Alcock. Reconnaissance Excavations on Early Historic Fortifications and Other Royal Sites in Scotland, 1974–84: Dunollie Castle, Oban, Argyll, 1978. *Proceedings of the Society of Antiquaries of Scotland* (1987) 117:119–147.

———. Reconnaissance Excavations on Early Historic Fortifications and Other Royal Sites in Scotland, 1974–84: Alt Clut, Clyde Rock, Strathclyde, 1974–75. *Proceedings of the Society of Antiquaries of Scotland* (1990) 120:95–149.

———. Reconnaissance Excavations on Early Historic Fortifications and Other Royal Sites in Scotland, 1974–84: A. Forteviot, Perthshire, 1981; B. Urquhart Castle, Inverness-shire, 1983; C. Dunnottar, Kincardineshire, 1984. *Proceedings of the Society of Antiquaries of Scotland* (1992) 122:215–287.

Alcock, L., E.A. Alcock, and S.T. Driscoll. Reconnaissance Excavations on Early Historic Fortifications and Other Royal Sites in Scotland, 1974–84: Dundurn, Strathearn, Perthshire, 1976–77. *Proceedings of the Society of Antiquaries of Scotland* (1989) 119:189–226.

Alcock, L., E.A. Alcock, and S.M. Foster. Reconnaissance Excavations on Early Historic Fortifications and Other Royal Sites in Scotland, 1974–84: Excavations near St. Abb's Head, Berwickshire, 1980. *Proceedings of the Society of Antiquaries of Scotland* (1986) 116:255–279.

Bede, The Venerable, Saint. *Bede's Ecclesiastical History of the English People*. Ed. Bertram Colgrave and R.A.B. Mynors. Oxford: Clarendon, 1992.

Leslie Alcock

SEE ALSO
Scotland, Dark Age; Scotland, Medieval

Scotland, Medieval

The period between the mid-eleventh century and the beginnings of the Calvinist Reformation (1540) saw the small, regionally restricted kingdoms of the early Middle Ages replaced by a state founded upon the national kingship of the Scots. The kingdom expanded from its core in eastern coastal districts so that by the end of this period royal authority included an area that approximates modern Scotland. The Northern and Western Isles were by this time nominally, if not effectively, part of the realm. This expansion was secured in spite of the serious attempts by the English to add Scotland to their dominion during the later thirteenth and early fourteenth centuries. The dramatic expansion and ultimately successful defense of the realm have tended to obscure the rather more prosaic questions of how the institutions of the state were physically constituted and in some cases imposed upon the countryside.

Archaeology is well placed to contribute to this latter study, particularly by providing a material context for the social changes engendered by the development of the state. What might be thought of as Celtic social practices relating to land tenure and lordship were gradually eroded and reshaped into a familiar feudal appearance (Barrow 1981). Gaelic was also transformed from the tongue of the ruling elite to the speech of those who lived at the extreme limit of royal authority in the Highlands and Isles. In its place, the new language of Scots evolved from Anglo-Saxon and Cumbric.

The social changes, such as the development of an increasingly differentiated and powerful aristocracy, can be seen by looking at the castles and churches, which are the principal monuments of the age. Town life formally constituted in the burghs also begins in this period, although the country remained overwhelming rural and agrarian until the modern period. This rural majority remains the most obscure historically, and there has been little archaeological work directed at correcting this deficiency.

Castles, by contrast, have been well studied and have emerged as one of the modern icons of Scottishness (MacGibbon and Ross 1887–1892; Cruden 1960; Tabraham 1990). Medieval castle and church building seems to spring afresh during the middle eleventh century, after an extended period of close to two centuries (A.D. 850–1050) that has left few physical traces. These buildings represent new attempts to expand the scale of lordship, often under direct royal authority. Inevitably, a number of significant castles were sited on places of previous political importance, in part because of intrinsic geographical advantages, but also to capitalize on the traditional associations. Although the provision of fortified dwellings for the elite is well documented in the early Medieval period, continuity of the political status of such sites can be difficult to substantiate, even in the case of Edinburgh Castle

S

where one can argue for continuous settlement since Roman times (MacIvor 1993).

Contact with Norman military architecture and feudal knighthood came via the English Court, particularly during the later eleventh and the twelfth centuries. Traditional royal strongholds at Edinburgh, Stirling, and Dunbarton were reestablished, although their form remains unknown (Fig. 1). For instance, all that survives of the earliest royal castle at Edinburgh is St. Margaret's Chapel, which is a fragment of a larger masonry structure built in the late eleventh or early twelfth century (Fernie 1986). By virtue of their remoteness, the Highlands and Isles have preserved the bulk of the early stone castles, where the various maritime lordships established fortified strongholds. These were plain rectangular enclosures with simple battlements and modest towers that relied to a fair degree on the natural strength of rocky headlands, as at Castle Sween, Skipness, and Dunstaffnage. These structures illustrate that, by c. 1200, serious castles were being built even in remote areas and that Celtic lords were executing works that demonstrated a good awareness of prevailing feudal practices.

Classic Norman inspiration is reflected in the more than three hundred motte-and-bailey castles that are found on the Scottish mainland (see Higham and Barker 1992:311–318 for synopses of excavated sites in Scotland). The greatest concentrations are to be found in the southwest (especially Galloway) and the northeast. The motte is a conspicuous relic of the policy to settle loyal followers in those areas in which royal authority was weak (Simpson and Webster 1985). Although these mottes did offer a degree of protection, they should be recognized principally as the centers of estates, which were established as the basis for feudal rule. In many cases, the timber castle that originally crowned the earthen mound was replaced by masonry work, as at Crawford in Lanarkshire and Duffus in Moray. Perhaps more often the restrictions of the motte form led to its abandonment and the construction of later estate centers nearby, as at the Bass of Inverurie, Aberdeenshire, built c. 1180. Here, the motte survives in a pristine state, because it was replaced by a moated castle and later a mansion on an adjacent site.

During the thirteenth century, the most impressive, nonroyal castles were built in the more fertile river valleys of the mainland, where not only was it possible to follow Continental architectural developments, there was also money to execute them. The most spectacular of these castles, at Caerlaverock (built c. A.D. 1277), Bothwell,

and Kildrummy, were built by major magnates and featured round donjons (stone towers), massive gate towers, and projecting corner towers from the curtain walled enclosures (Fig. 2).

The Wars of Independence (1296–1314), in which Scotland successfully resisted various attempts by the English to annex the country, created a prolonged period of unrest during which little major building was undertaken. This lull extended until the middle of the fourteenth century; when it ended, a new castle form, the towerhouse, emerged to become the template for elite architecture for the rest of the Middle Ages. In their pure form, towerhouses consist of a series of rooms stacked one upon another connected by an internal spiral staircase. Usually, the main public hall was built over a vaulted storage and kitchen area. Private accommodations were on the upper floors. These efficient structures were usually the dominant elements of a large complex of buildings, as was the case with David's Tower in Edinburgh Castle (begun A.D. 1367–1368) and at Threave, Dumfriesshire (begun c. A.D. 1370) (Good and Tabraham 1981). The practice of building towerhouses gradually was extended to most levels of the aristocracy, and they were still being built after A.D. 1600 (Fig. 3).

The towerhouse was so popular with all levels of the nobility that few late castles were built in any other style. The main exceptions are the royal palaces, in which the provision of public and domestic space became increasingly elaborate. Although Edinburgh Castle was largely bypassed by Renaissance building developments and became the primary fortress of the realm (MacIvor 1993), the other palaces—at Stirling, Linlithgow, Falkland, and Holyrood—adopted nondefensive plans and Renaissance decorative treatments.

The earliest stone churches are closely contemporary with the earliest castles and are found in rich agricultural lands of east-central Scotland in the former Pictland (Donaldson 1985; Cruden 1986). These include freestanding round towers (in the Irish fashion) at Abernethy and Brechin, but more typically the towers were square and incorporated into small churches, the most spectacular of which is St. Rule's at St. Andrews (Fig. 4). These buildings are generally thought to date to the late eleventh or early twelfth centuries (Fernie 1986) and were followed in the mid-twelfth century by accomplished Romanesque churches, such as the one that survives at Leuchars, Fife. Apart from those works at previously established monasteries, they represent the material consequences of the formalization of the parochial system.

FIG. 1. Edinburgh Castle, a royal castle, which by the end of the Middle Ages had become the principal stronghold of the realm. Over the years, it has been much rebuilt to repair the damage occasioned by frequent disputes with England. (Photograph: Historic Scotland.)

FIG. 2. Kildrummy Castle, built by one of the major landowners, the Earl of Mar, during the course of the thirteenth century. It had an unusually active military history, which ended only in the eighteenth century. (Photograph: Historic Scotland.)

The early twelfth century saw the introduction of new religious orders, both at older monastic establishments and as new foundations. The foundation in A.D. 1070 of a Benedictine house at Dunfermline under the patronage of Queen (ultimately Saint) Margaret (c. 1045–1093) marked a significant development in introducing Continental monastic orders. The principal surviving remains of the abbey is the fine early twelfth-century Romanesque church, which is reminiscent of Durham Cathedral. In the following generation, the endowment of new abbeys increased, partly in response to the royal endowment of Jedburgh (begun c. 1138) and Melrose (Fawcett 1985). All the great abbeys are now ruinous; nevertheless, the ruins exhibit fine examples of late Romanesque and Gothic work that illustrate their wealth and, indirectly, their political significance (Fig. 5).

The formalization of the parochial system naturally called for the development of the cathedrals. In the east-central region, this involved the elevation and refurbishment of traditional ecclesiastical centers (Donaldson 1985; Cruden 1986), most of which were already blessed with important relics. In national terms, the most important relics were at the archbishopric of St. Andrews, where the remains of the cathedral, various associated chapels, and the bishop's castle all survive as ruins and give some impression of the magnificence of the see. In the north and west, new cathedrals were established in the twelfth century. The greatest of these was at Glasgow, whose holdings extended throughout southwest Scotland and whose fiscal sophistication was reflected in the frequent appointment of its bishops as royal chancellor. Glasgow is the only Scottish cathedral to have survived the Reforma-

FIG. 3. Craigievar Castle, Aberdeenshire, stripped of its surrounding wall and outbuildings. This towerhouse, built between 1610 and 1626, displays the local Renaissance style known as Scots Baronial with its characteristic flamboyant towers and crenellations. (Photograph: Royal Commission on the Ancient and Historical Monuments of Scotland.)

FIG. 4. The tower of St. Rule's within the ecclesiastical precinct at St. Andrews is the most splendid of the early towered churches; it was probably built before A.D. 1200. (Photograph: Historic Scotland.)

tion intact, and, although dedicated in A.D. 1136, it was completely reconstructed during the thirteenth century in a mature Gothic style, which is most notable for its elaborate crypt (Cruden 1986; Fawcett 1985).

While fortifications and churches had a long history, the development of town life in Scotland came late. It is hard to say just how late, despite considerable attention to the archaeology of towns (Lynch et al. 1988). The royal charters for burghs go back to the early twelfth century, when the Crown started to take serious measures to increase its revenue base. However, it is unlikely that these charters represent entirely new foundations in every case; unfortunately, with the exception of Perth, little pre-twelfth-century material has been discovered by excava-

tion. There are hints of early Scandinavian influences in some of the burghs (Crawford 1987), with hints at development along the lines of the Irish emporia, but archaeological confirmation for this does not yet exist.

Despite their late start, the burghs came to provide a major source of income and financial independence for Scotland. Perth and St. Andrews possess medieval gridded street plans, but elsewhere, even at Edinburgh, the burgh consists of no more than one or two main streets. The High Street usually features a wide space, which provided a marketplace and along which long narrow plots were fronted. The dominance of a single street gave rise to a strung-out, linear plan. Distinctively, the Scottish burghs belonged to a single parish, which in all the principal

FIG. 5. The late fourteenth-century work in the east end of Melrose Abbey. Little survives of the monastery apart from the church itself. (Photograph: Historic Scotland.)

towns led to the construction of substantial churches that in architectural form and scale rivaled the abbeys and the cathedrals.

Both large and small burghs handled the local agricultural commerce, and the relative wealth was determined by the wealth of the hinterland (Lynch et al. 1988). Agricultural goods also provided important export goods, which were supplemented with more exotic materials, such as pelts and freshwater pearls. International commerce went in two directions, east and south, with England being the largest trading partner. Consequently, the most developed towns emerged on the east coast—Berwick, Edinburgh (with its port at Leith), Dundee, Perth, and Aberdeen. For much of its history, Berwick was Scotland's second-largest burgh. However, because it occupies the border, it frequently changed hands, and, despite possessing the finest walls of any Scottish town, it is now technically within England. Substantial commercial links were established with the Baltic countries as well as the Low Countries. In archaeological terms, Aberdeen stands out as the best understood of the major burghs (Murray 1982). The maturity of burghs as major components of Scotland's social, financial, and cultural composition was confirmed in the foundation of universities at St. Andrews, Aberdeen, and Glasgow, all of which were in existence by the mid-fifteenth century.

S

FURTHER READINGS

Barrow, G.W.S. *Kinship and Unity.* Edinburgh: Edinburgh University Press, 1981.

Crawford, Barbara. *Scandinavian Scotland.* Leicester: Leicester University Press, 1987.

Cruden, Stewart. *The Scottish Castle.* Edinburgh: Spurbooks, 1960.

———. *Scottish Medieval Churches.* Edinburgh: John Donald, 1986.

Donaldson, Gordon. *Scottish Church History.* Edinburgh: Scottish Academic Press, 1985.

Fawcett, Richard. *Scottish Medieval Churches.* Guidebook. Edinburgh: HMSO, 1985.

Fernie, Eric. Early Church Architecture in Scotland. *Proceedings of the Society of Antiquaries of Scotland* (1986) 116:393–412.

Good, George L., and Christopher J. Tabraham. Excavations at Threave Castle, Galloway, 1974–78. *Medieval Archaeology* (1981) 25:90–140.

Higham, Robert, and Philip Barker. *Timber Castles.* London: Batsford, 1992.

Lynch, Michael, Michael Spearman, and Geoffrey Stell, eds. *The Scottish Medieval Town.* Edinburgh: John Donald, 1988.

MacGibbon, David, and Thomas Ross. *The Castellated and Domestic Architecture of Scotland.* Vols. 1–5. Edinburgh: David Douglas, 1887–1892.

MacIvor, Iain. *Edinburgh Castle.* London: Batsford, 1993.

Murray, Charles, ed. *Excavations in the Medieval Burgh of Aberdeen, 1973–81.* Monograph 2. Edinburgh: Society of Antiquaries, 1982.

Simpson, Grant G., and Bruce Webster. Charter Evidence and the Distribution of Mottes in Scotland. In *Essays on the Nobility of Medieval Scotland.* Ed. K.J. Stringer. Edinburgh: John Donald, 1985, pp. 1–24.

Tabraham, Christopher. *Scottish Castles.* Guidebook. Edinburgh: HMSO, 1990.

Stephen T. Driscoll

SEE ALSO
Castles; Emporia; Scotland, Dark Age; Scotland: Early Royal Sites

Shetland
See Northern Isles.

Shipbuilding

Many people think of the Middle Ages as a retrogressive period. While that might be true for the early Middle Ages, when compared to the high standard of civilization in Roman times, it is not at all true for the late Middle Ages. In particular, the development of techniques for constructing and handling ships was progressive, so by the end of the Middle Ages the result was a type of western European ship that was superior to all other ships in the world. This superiority was based mainly on the following advances in shipbuilding: the introduction of the carvel construction of the hull; the introduction of the stern rudder; the establishment of sheltered living quarters underneath the fore- and aft-castles; the partition of one large sail into several smaller ones to be hoisted on three masts; and the placement of the ship's guns in the hull behind gun ports.

This type of ship could be navigated across all oceans by means of a compass, instruments for astronavigation, and sea charts. The home ports of these ships not only had shipyards that were willing and able to include all these new arrangements while making sure that the ships remained secure and watertight even under the worst conditions of bad weather, they also had ship owners who wanted these improvements made to their ships in order to use them for more and more profitable trade. Though each of these new elements of shipbuilding and ship handling had a different origin, they all came together to form the specific pattern of shipping that started the European domination of the world that was to continue for centuries. Not one of these elements had been developed with the specific aim of facilitating the European domination of the world. By developing this or that element or by combining some of them for the first time, people just tried to make their own shipping more effective. Thus, toward the end of the Middle Ages, a superior type of ship and the means to handle it were at hand at a time when the Portuguese and the Spaniards were willing to expand European influence to other continents.

In short, medieval shipbuilding is more than just the specific methods of joining wooden strakes to get watertight vessels. Medieval shipbuilding resulted in a product that changed the face of the world.

At the beginning of the Middle Ages, ships were built based on the experience of three major and several minor shipbuilding traditions that all had roots deep in prehistory but that differed very much one from another. Within each tradition, boats and ships had specific shapes and methods of construction. Archaeological finds reveal

FIG. 1. Constructions of the sides of ships: *a,* hulk-shaped boats; *b,* boats of Nachen type (Rhine); *c–f,* different clinker constructions: *c,* with short iron nails; *d,* with rebent iron nails (cogs); *e,* with iron rivets (Viking ships); *f,* hidden clinker construction; *g–i,* carvel constructions: *g,* with rebent iron nails; *h,* with treenails; *i,* mortise-and-tenon construction.

that one of the best indicators for the different traditions is the different techniques by which the strakes were joined (Fig. 1). Using this indicator, even small fragments of a wreck can be classified according to their shipbuilding tradition. The first shipbuilding tradition recognized by archaeologists in the nineteenth century was that of the Viking ships and their predecessors. The gently curved hulls of these ships were made from very thin strakes, split radially from oak trunks. Each upper strake partly overlapped the strake below it at the outside and was kept together by iron rivets driven through the overlap (Fig. 1*e*). When the shell was finished, light ribs were inserted. The result was a light and flexible boat or ship that was very seaworthy and quick. In Scandinavia, the roots of this tradition can be traced back to bark canoes of the early Bronze Age. This tradition found its way to England with the Anglo-Saxon immigration in the fifth century A.D., and the Slavonic invaders of the southern Baltic coast learned how to build these boats from those few Germans who did not emigrate. In all these areas, boats of this tradition were built continuously until the twentieth century. Although the Vikings sailed the most seaworthy of these ships via Iceland and Greenland as far as North America (Newfoundland) c. 1000 A.D., this shipbuilding tradition had limited influence on the development of the oceangoing ships of the explorers. During the wars of the thirteenth century, English ships of this tradition were fitted out with *castles* (i.e., towerlike platforms that enabled the crossbowmen to shoot their arrows from a high standpoint) (Fig. 2). People found shelter underneath these platforms in bad weather and started to make closed living quarters for the first time on board ships in the North Sea and the Baltic.

The second of the three major shipbuilding traditions is not one homogeneous tradition but consists of a group of more or less related traditions that differ in many details across central and western Europe. All these traditions had developed from mere dugouts of rather solid and inflexible build. Although these dugouts served as the

FIG. 2. English ship (in the tradition of the Viking ships) with side rudder and towerlike castle for crossbowmen. Seal of Dunwich, thirteenth century.

bases for big and sophisticated ship constructions throughout the Middle Ages, small dugouts were built continuously for many purposes; these vessels included fishing boats, ferries, supports for floating water mills, and even cargo vessels, especially in rivers.

The simplest way to make boats (on a dugout base) bigger than the original tree trunks was to collect several dugouts alongside one another, fasten them together with the aid of crossbeams, and cover them with a platform of boards. Many medieval ferries were constructed in this way to take horse carts and cattle from one side of the river to the other. A second method of getting bigger boats was to fasten additional strakes on top of the dugout. In the Middle Ages, people in different areas used different techniques to attach additional strakes to the upper part of the dugout (Fig. 1*a–d*). The most sophisticated way to enlarge a dugout was to split it lengthwise into two halves, place bottom strakes between both halves, and nail all these elements to the bottom timbers using treenails. The result is a boat with a flat, flush-laid bottom, in which the half-dugouts make the transition from the bottom to the sides and serve as chine girders (i.e., form a kind of backbone for the boat) so that no keel is needed for longitudinal strength. For bigger boats, one or two additional strakes are put on top of the half-dugouts.

Flat-bottom boats of this type were used in rivers, lakes, and shallow tidal waters along the shore from at least the early Bronze Age to the end of the Middle Ages. In seagoing vessels of this construction, sailors did not like an angled chine. They preferred to sail in boats with smooth cross-sections to prevent hard rocking in the waves. In Celtic Europe during the late La Tène and Roman periods (c. 200 B.C.–A.D. 400), large, long, iron nails were used to join the solid frames and strakes (Fig. 1*g*). By this time, shipwrights were able to construct strong vessels of a special carvel (i.e., ships built with planks meeting flush at the seams); these ships were built along the Atlantic coast of France and along both sides of the English Channel. After the collapse of the western Roman Empire, there was a lack of iron, and shipwrights reduced the use of iron nails to the utmost minimum. The transition from iron to wooden nails in the early Middle Ages resulted in ordinary carvel construction (Fig. 1*h*) and was the first of the five steps toward the development of the ships used by the Spanish and Portuguese explorers. For a while, the carvel construction was a regional method of shipbuilding. The way in which this technique began to influence the Mediterranean art of shipbuilding has not been adequately studied. From Brittany, it was introduced to the North and Baltic Seas in the fifteenth century.

From pre-Roman Iron Age times, the cog was the native type of vessel used along the southern shores of the North Sea and in its rivers. The cog had a flat carvel bottom like the Romano-Celtic boats, but its steep sides rose from the bottom at almost a right angle. The sides were not carvel built but were made of a specific clinker construction; the overlap of the strakes was fastened with iron nails, and the points of the nails were rebent into the timber (Fig. 1*d*). The same technique for securing the nailing was used in the Romano-Celtic boats to fasten the frames to the strakes (Fig. 1*g*). This is an indication of the interrelationships among the many different shipbuilding techniques of Continental Europe.

In the early Middle Ages, Frisian merchants sailed the cog in the shallows of the Wattenmeer. Toward the end of the eighth century, cogs were introduced to the Baltic from the port of Haithabu in Schleswig-Holstein. When the Hanseatic League was founded in 1159, along with the foundation of the first Hanseatic town of Lübeck in the southwest corner of the Baltic, the Hanseatic merchants took over the Frisian cog, which still had its characteristic side rudder. As Hanseatic trade expanded rapidly, there was a strong demand for bigger cogs, which could no longer be maneuvered by the typical side rudder. Toward

the end of the twelfth century, the stern rudder was adapted to the Hanseatic cog and remained its characteristic feature. It proved to work very well and was subsequently used on other big European ships.

In the late thirteenth century, wooden towers with high platforms for crossbowmen were installed on Hanseatic cogs, following the English pattern described above. Underneath these platforms, people were sheltered against the rain. Boards were used to close the sides against the wind and weather. The town seal of Stralsund, Germany, carved in 1329, provides the first evidence for this innovation (Fig. 3). This first room underneath the aft-castle was reserved for the men aft of the mast, including the captain, merchants, and others. At the end of the fourteenth century, a small room underneath the forecastle was constructed for the crew only, and from this time forward the room for the crew was called the *foc'sel.* Without these rooms on board ships, it would not have been possible to make long, transoceanic journeys. With the addition of these rooms, the cog had come to the end of its development.

To identify the fourth step toward the ships of the explorers, the partition of the sails, one must look to the third major shipbuilding tradition, Mediterranean shipbuilding. In the Mediterranean, ships continued to be built following the older Roman patterns throughout the

FIG. 3. Hanseatic cog with closed living quarters underneath the aft-castle. Seal of Stralsund, 1329.

Middle Ages. A characteristic feature is mortise-and-tenon construction (Fig. 1*i*), which kept the light, flush-laid strakes together so that the shell could be finished before the ribs were inserted. During the Middle Ages, mortise-and-tenon construction was gradually converted to ordinary carvel construction (Fig. 1*h*); thick, strong strakes were no longer fastened to one another but were instead just fastened to strong ribs by treenails. Thus, in late medieval times, the Mediterranean shipwrights adopted the techniques of strong, heavy carvel construction that shipwrights along the Bay of Biscay had practiced since pre-Roman times and that influenced the development of ship construction in the Mediterranean.

The most striking Mediterranean contribution to the oceangoing ships of the European explorers is the division of the one big sail into several smaller ones on several masts. Since these small sails could be hoisted one after another by the same small crew, ships with several small sails could be handled by a relatively small crew, even when the total area of all the sails was larger than that of a ship with one big sail. Roman cargo vessels already had two sails, both square rigged. The main mast held a large main sail, and a second mast in the foreship held a small sail called an *artemon*. Other Roman ships already had lateen sails, triangular sails extended by a long yard slung to the mast. Late medieval ships in the Mediterranean tended to have three masts, the first two with square sails and the last with a lateen sail. This arrangement of sails resulted in such good maneuverability that, by 1470, it was even adopted in the Baltic. It was first introduced, along with carvel construction, on the ship called *Peter of Danzig*.

This ship was already equipped with firearms, which were positioned relatively high in the fore- and aft-castles like the crossbows in older ships. Heavy weights placed high in the ship have very bad effects on stability; heavy weights should be placed as deep in the hull as possible. The solution to this problem was found in Flanders, as is shown on the seal of Maximilian, the prefect of Burgundia, from 1493 (Fig. 4). The heavy guns were placed on a special gun deck underneath the main deck, and a special gun port was cut through the side for each gun. The gun port could be closed with a lid and made watertight for sailing in strong winds when the guns could not be used.

Thus, at the end of the Middle Ages, the Occident was able to produce a ship that was strong enough to withstand all the storms and waves of long-term ocean sailing, sheltered enough to make life possible for the sailors for months even under the worst weather conditions, maneu-

FIG. 4. Three-masted ship of carvel construction with living quarters in the fore- and aft-castles and with gun ports. Seal of Maximilian, prefect of Burgundia, 1493.

verable enough to sail to all the shores of all the oceans and back again, and armed like a fortress and more aggressive than any other ship of any nation of the world. Those who sailed these ships were able to sail wherever they wanted and could easily carry their superiority to any point on the other side of the ocean. These ships suddenly appeared, and no one was able to resist them.

After the migration period, medieval shipbuilding began in the ruins of former Roman towns and in rural districts outside the former Roman Empire under relatively poor economic conditions and with limited resources (e.g., wooden nails instead of iron ones). Shipbuilders in each region used a range of different techniques, with very little exchange of ideas or methods. In the course of the Middle Ages, when former Roman towns began to flourish again and new towns were founded outside the Roman Empire and when merchants began to play a predominant role in economic life, a strong demand developed for effective vessels as a means of transportation. Shipwrights became citizens of towns, even though the shipyards required so much space that they were located just outside the town walls. These urban shipyards were the basis for the accelerating development of new ideas in shipbuilding, with a new readiness to learn from the shipbuilding traditions of other countries

S

with which they came in contact through shipping and trade.

In late medieval towns, shipwrights no longer depended on local resources for their raw materials, as they did in the early Middle Ages. C. 1380, for example, the shipwright of the Hanseatic cog at Bremen obtained the bent timbers for her frames from the forests near the town and the moss for caulking from the neighboring moors. However, he obtained the long, straight oaks for the keel, stem and stern posts, strakes, and crossbeams from the mountains along the Upper Weser River through trade. The tar was imported from the Baltic, the hemp for the ropes from the east, and the iron for the nails, bolts, anchor, and caulking clamps from an unknown area. As early as 1200, the cog makers started to use a saw to cut the oak trunks into strakes instead of splitting them. In the second half of the thirteenth century, cranes with tread wheels were erected along the banks of harbor towns to remove and replace the masts of ships if necessary. Toward the end of the Middle Ages, urban gun making became an important feeder service for shipbuilding. In medieval towns, shipbuilding was a key industry, producing the predominant means of transportation for the town's own merchants; in the late Middle Ages, some towns even built new ships for foreign merchants. The shipyards kept the economy going through the imports of raw materials and by employing subcontractors. They included smiths for the various iron objects needed in great quantities (e.g., eight thousand caulking clamps for one cog) or large sizes (e.g., anchors) and for tools; weavers and sail makers for sails; rope makers and tar heaters; and, toward the end of the Middle Ages, even compass makers and gun founders. Last but not least, ships were the largest movable objects in any medieval society, so raising the money to build a ship was always a problem. Unfortunately, little research has been done on how medieval ships were financed.

Each new ship required a lot of secondary activities before it was ready to sail for the first time. The skipper had to hire his crew and to provide victuals, water, and other supplies. The merchants had to collect the cargo, and many hands were needed to pack it and process it through customs. In summary, nearly the whole harbor town made its living from the products of the shipyards.

FURTHER READINGS

Ellmers, Detlev. Loose Objects Found in Shipwrecked Cogs (in German with English summary). *Deutsches Schiffahrtsarchiv* (1965) 18:207–232.

Gardiner, Robert, ed. *Cogs, Caravels, and Galleons: The Sailing Ship, 1000–1650.* Annapolis: Naval Institute Press, 1994.

Keidel, Klaus-Peter, and Uwe Schnall, eds. *The Hanse Cog of 1380.* Bremerhaven, 1985.

Lahn, Werner. *The Hanse Cog of Bremen.* Vol. 1: *Structural Members and Construction Processes* (in German with English summaries). Schriften des Deutschen Schiffahrtsmuseums 30. Hamburg: E. Kabel, 1992.

Unger, Richard W. *The Ship in the Medieval Economy, 600–1600.* London: Croomhelm, 1980.

Villain-Gandossi, Christiane, Busuttil, Sulvino, and Paul Adam, eds. *Medieval Ships and the Birth of Technological Societies.* Vol. 1: *Northern Europe.* Malta: European Coordination Center for Research and Documentation in Social Sciences, 1989.

D. Ellmers

SEE ALSO
Boatbuilding; Haithabu; Lübeck.

Shrewsbury

Shrewsbury, the county town of Shropshire, lies in the English Midlands on the upper reaches of the River Severn, in an area containing a succession of settlements with regional central-place functions. The historic urban core occupies a high and naturally defensible site within a loop of the river. The earliest nonagricultural occupation that can be deduced from later documentary evidence is monastic—two minsters of middle Saxon date (650–850), one (St. Mary's) a probable royal foundation, the other (St. Chad's) episcopal. Two further churches (St. Alkmund's and St. Juliana's) are likely to represent monastic foundations of the ninth or tenth century, and two smaller churches of the eleventh century also had some of the characteristics of minster status. The exceptional concentration of minster churches on the site cannot yet be fully explained but points to a regional importance not apparent from surviving documentary or archaeological sources (Bassett 1991). Shrewsbury appears to have shared in the urban revival of the late ninth and early tenth centuries. The town is first mentioned in 901 as *civitate Scrobbensis;* it appears next as *Scrobbesbyrig*—the fortified place in the district of The Scrub—in 1006. That it had been a defended settlement for some time can also be inferred from the minting of coins there from the reign of Aethelstan (925–939). The *Domesday Book* records a total of 252 households in the town on the eve of the Norman Conquest (1066).

Archaeological evidence for the Anglo-Saxon ecclesiastical presence adds little to the written evidence: the foundations of a pre-Norman apsidal church were found at St. Mary's in 1864, and eleventh-century grave covers and small headstones remain there; charcoal burials and a cruciform eighth–ninth-century stylus were excavated at St. Chad's in 1890; fragments of a stone frieze of possible ninth-century date have been discovered in a cellar. Late Saxon domestic occupation is known archaeologically only from excavated latrine pits bearing mainly Stafford-type (Chester-type) ware of probable tenth- or earlier eleventh-century date and from a single fragment of a stake-and-post-built structure associated with the same pottery.

Some elements of the early medieval geography can be inferred from features recorded much later. The King's Market lay between St. Alkmund's and St. Juliana's in their shared churchyard, in an oval open space at the center of the town site. The market was moved to a newly cleared, more spacious site in 1261. The dispersal of market functions may have begun earlier. Pride Hill, a main street bordering the high ground, appears to have been widened to create a livestock market. On one side, large house plots with regulated frontage widths were laid out with extensive backlands parceling out the alluvial zone below and giving access to watercourses, arguably for grazing. The other alluvial fringes of the town site were similarly treated.

There are some documentary indications that the pre-Norman defenses ran across the neck of the river loop on the line of a later wall and ditch. The Norman motte-and-bailey castle was similarly sited to control landward access to the town. The *Domesday Book* records the loss of 52 houses during its construction, probably to create an open area that was later consolidated as an outer bailey. The town's perimeter was defended by stone walls, built mainly in the first half of the thirteenth century as a response to Welsh incursions. The new walls bisected the domestic plots stretching down from the high ground to the river, and some replanning of streets took place to maintain access to the backlands. As Shrewsbury's military role as a strategic border town declined, parts of the town wall were colonized by high-status domestic buildings; so, too, was the outer bailey, and the castle itself was relegated to use as a prison.

Norman impact on the substantial presence of the Church began with the foundation of a Benedictine abbey in the 1080s on a high-status suburban site across the river. All the town churches were rebuilt before the end of the twelfth century. Three friaries established on riverside extramural sites in the thirteenth century undoubtedly attracted popular devotion at the expense of older institutions, but they have had only limited archaeological attention. Investigations at the Benedictine abbey have shown that its precinct was walled in stone for the first time probably in the later twelfth century. The abbey underwent several minor episodes of expansion up to c. 1400 involving (as at the friaries) wetland reclamation. From the mid- to late thirteenth century, the riverside edge of the monastic outer court was occupied by an unusual range of stone buildings that combined waterfront functions with other accommodation. A new kitchen was built on reclaimed ground by the outer court c. 1400. Excavation here found deeply stratified waterlogged deposits, one of which (inexplicably) contained one of the earliest-known pieces of English hallmarked silver.

The earliest-known surviving generation of medieval houses is a group of large high-status sandstone buildings with their principal room at first-floor level. In most cases, these were probably halls, but some may have been private chambers associated with hall ranges that have not survived. Only a minority of the wealthiest can now be identified with particular individuals or families from documentary records. Timber-framed buildings begin to survive in some numbers from the fourteenth and fifteenth centuries; many were speculatively built shops. On Pride Hill, one of the principal medieval streets, large early medieval plots appear to have remained intact after c. 1300, with stone halls over undercrofts set back behind wide, shop-lined street frontages.

FURTHER READINGS

Baker, N.J., J.B. Lawson, R. Maxwell, and J.T. Smith. Further Work on Pride Hill, Shrewsbury. *Transactions of the Shropshire Archaeological and Historical Society* (1993) 68:3–64.

Bassett, S. Anglo-Saxon Shrewsbury and Its Churches. *Midland History* (1991) 16:1–23.

Carver, M.O.H. Early Shrewsbury: An Archaeological Definition in 1975. *Transactions of the Shropshire Archaeological Society* (1975) 59, III (for 1973–1974).

N.J. Baker

Skeletal Populations

The Medieval period consists of two major archaeologically identified horizons: early Medieval (post-Roman)

S

and late Medieval. The early Medieval period (fifth–tenth centuries) is equivalent to the migration period or Dark Ages, and the late Medieval period (eleventh–fifteenth centuries) is equivalent to the High and late Middle Ages. This distinction has influenced the study of medieval skeletal populations such that the two have become quite separated in intent and purpose.

Studies of the early Medieval period have concentrated on documenting the arrival of presumed immigrant Germanic peoples in lands once controlled politically by Rome. These studies often employ a direct historical approach that attempts to fit archaeological remains into a documented historical sequence (see James 1989 for a review of the approaches). The direct historical approach has led to many studies of cemeteries and their diagnostic grave goods to the detriment of settlement sites and other types of archaeological contexts. Comparatively little effort has been expended on the analysis of the human remains and on questions of social structure from either archaeological or physical anthropological study of burial contexts. There is, therefore, considerable debate over the interpretation of the burials. For example, does the reconstructed mortuary rite reflect status, lineage, family, or personal inspiration? Physical anthropological evidence has often been credulously applied in an attempt to identify ethnic or family groups from skeletal remains, to document various presumably non-Christian, and therefore pagan, cultural practices, such as ritual suttee, beheading, or live burial, and to trace the emergence of high-status individuals.

Research on skeletal populations from the late Medieval period has largely resulted from the building boom that Europe experienced in the 1970s and 1980s. Many once-urban cemeteries have been unearthed and cleared to make way for modern buildings with their deep foundations. Although the archaeological output from these excavations has been impressive, the reporting of human remains has suffered from a lack of adequately informed researchers. This has resulted in inadequate treatment and poor integration with the archaeological reports. Specialist reports on human remains are often appended to, or contained within, a larger archaeological report on the site with little or no cross-referencing (Wells and Cayton 1980; Marlow 1992; Cross and Bruce 1989), or the specialist reports appear as separate volumes before or after the publication of the archaeological context. The unfortunate result is that the evidence becomes difficult to use for comparative purposes and the various specialist studies tend to become separated in subsequent syntheses. This situation is reflected in general reviews of later medieval archaeology in which the burial remains have received scant attention, although related subjects, such as parish churches, churchyards, grave inclusions, and burial orientation, have been covered.

The largest published assemblages from this time period include 1,041 individuals from St. Helen-on-the-Walls parish church, York (Dawes and Magilton 1980); 234 individuals from the parish church of St. Nicholas Shambles, London (White 1988); and 402 individuals from the parish and monastic cemeteries of St. Andrews, Fishergate, York (Stroud and Kemp 1993).

There has been a long-standing interest in morphological change in European populations (biological distance studies). Alterations in cranial, femoral, and tibial shape as measured by the cranial, platymeric, and platycnemic indices have been noted through time. Although relatively easy to measure and identify, the cause of such changes remains poorly understood, and the genetic significance they may have, if any, has not been completely demonstrated. Growth and developmental processes and the contribution of plastic change in response to differential activity or habitual posture could equally account for the trends observed. The most often cited of these changes is the apparent increase in the breadth of the cranial vault through time in western European populations (Brothwell 1981; Rösing and Schwidetsky 1984; White 1988; Stroud and Kemp 1993). Nonmetric analyses of discrete traits have also been used in an attempt to identify family groupings within late medieval cemetery populations. Most of these attempts have been inconclusive (White 1988; Dawes and Magilton 1980), perhaps hampered by an overemphasis on cranial traits, many of which become unidentifiable in fragmentary remains, and by the use of deficient trait lists that often include some traits that are of dubious value. G. Stroud and B.L. Kemp (1993), however, employ an approach that combines archaeological context and phasing with metric and nonmetric analyses. They have made a firmer assessment of relatedness among individuals by noting the occurrence of dolichocrany (long-headedness), hypodontia, and crowding and rotation of teeth in relation to burial within the nave of a church serving a Gilbertine monastic community at Fishergate in the city of York.

Most of the paleodemographic analyses of late medieval cemetery populations have revealed sex-dependent biases in the analyzed samples. J. Dawes and J. Magilton

(1980) demonstrated a greater proportion of females in the St. Helen-on-the-Walls parish cemetery in York, while W. White (1988) reported a greater number of male skeletons in the parish church of St. Nicholas Shambles, London. These differences are likely due to sample bias and are not statistically significant. Stroud and Kemp (1993), however, have demonstrated a marked difference between the mid-eleventh–twelfth-century parish population and that of the later thirteenth–sixteenth-century monastic cemetery at St. Andrews, Fishergate, York. The sex ratio of males to females was 1.4:1 in the earlier period and 3.2:1 in the later period when the cemetery served the monastic community. This discrepancy likely relates to prescribed burial restrictions. The later group also contained a skewed age profile, containing only 15.6 percent of individuals who died before their twentieth year, while the earlier group contained 36.4 percent who died before that age. In addition, individuals thought to represent the remains of medieval canons, buried to the east of the presbytery, demonstrated a greater longevity, with 66 percent of individuals living beyond age forty as compared to only 44 percent of both males and females at St. Helen-on-the-Walls and only 31 percent of males and females of the earlier of the two cemeteries at St. Andrews, Fishergate. At the cemetery of St. Helen-on-the-Walls (Dawes and Magilton 1980), 27 percent of the population had died in childhood, as had 17.5 percent of the population at the cemetery of St. Nicholas Shambles (White 1988). These mortality profiles are in keeping with data from the earlier lay cemetery at Fishergate, attesting to high infant and child mortality. The lower infant and child mortality at the later Fishergate cemetery is commensurate with a high-status monastic site.

Females appear to have had somewhat shorter lifespans throughout the early and late Medieval periods (Brothwell 1972; Dawes and Magilton 1980; Marlow 1992), while today females tend to have longer lifespans than do males (Waldron 1989). This difference has been attributed to the greater physical demands of childbearing, birth, and weaning of infants in the Middle Ages. There may be, however, a systematic underageing of female skeletons that has not been detected. Stature estimates have been recorded as a measure of nutrition and also to gauge physical trends in human populations. Medieval stature estimates indicate reduced stature for both males and females when compared to modern European samples (Waldron 1989). M. Marlow (1992) reports a range of stature from 1.53 to 1.92 m for males and from 1.42 to 1.54 m for females from a series of British skeletal collections spanning the early and late Medieval periods.

In many cases, paleopathological studies are the only published treatments of skeletal assemblages. These studies of ancient disease have developed from a case-study format to a more holistic approach that attempts to monitor the health status of human populations in response to socioeconomic, cultural, and environmental conditions. Chief among the potentially environmentally linked diseases is rheumatoid arthritis, a seriously debilitating disorder, which has increased steadily in frequency. Today this disease affects 2.5 percent of the U.S. population and 3 percent of the English population (Manchester 1983). Considerable research effort has been concentrated on determining the antiquity and prevalence of rheumatoid arthritis in past populations and, through complementary environmental data, on determining the conditions under which the disorder existed in the past. Medieval populations have been crucial to such research, as it is in the Medieval period that evidence of an erosive condition resembling rheumatoid arthritis is seen in a European population, possibly for the first time (Rogers et al. 1981). One case resembling rheumatoid arthritis has been found in the skeleton of a woman from an urban context in London (Rogers et al. 1991). Other arthropathies (joint diseases) have also been the subject of study. The degenerative disorder osteoarthritis is the most common paleopathological condition identified. It may be related to repeated activity or posture and it is age related—that is, it is more prevalent in the older age categories (Rogers et al. 1987). That osteoarthritis is more than an age-related phenomenon seems clear. At St. Andrews, Fishergate, for example, the most frequent site of osteophytosis associated with a diagnosis of osteoarthritis is the spine. The spinal affectation demonstrated sufficient variation in the degree of involvement to argue for causative factors other than simply the ageing process.

Another arthropathy, diffuse idiopathic skeletal hyperostosis (DISH), has been well documented in medieval skeletons. This disease is characterized by the ossification of the anterior longitudinal ligament of the spine and of other ligaments and tendons throughout the body. It is a disease that is increasingly prevalent in older individuals, especially in older males tending toward obesity and suffering from diabetes, and affects about 10 percent of males and 7 percent of females over seventy years of age in modern populations (Rogers et al. 1985; Waldron 1985). In the Medieval period, this disorder has a higher prevalence

S

in cemeteries associated with ecclesiastical houses, perhaps due to environmental or dietary factors that remain incompletely specified. Other arthropathies documented from medieval sites include ankylosing spondylitis (distinguished from DISH by its sacroiliac involvement), gout, and Reiter's disease or psoriasis (Rogers et al. 1981).

Another prominent modern malady, neoplastic disease, has also been documented in medieval skeletons, although there remains doubt as to its prevalence and diagnosis and to the carcinogenic factors likely responsible for the disease in the past (Gladykowska-Rzeczycka 1991; Anderson et al. 1992). Analysis of medieval populations and their archaeological context (e.g., the prevalence of this disease in urban versus rural communities) may eventually reveal trends that may be used to better understand modern affectation. Less fatal, though often socially quite informative in documenting violence in the past, are traumatic lesions. Traumatic lesions have been studied to document wounds received in large-scale violence such as warfare (Knowles 1983) and as a measure of medical acumen (Roberts 1991).

Infectious diseases are still of great medical concern in many parts of the modern world and in certain populations. Infectious disease is divided into two types: specific infection (in which the causative agent, bacterial or viral, and etiology, often expired droplet infection, is known) and nonspecific (in which the causative agent is unknown). Only the former will be reviewed here. Medieval populations suffered from many infectious diseases that today have a much more restricted distribution.

Leprosy, tuberculosis, and syphilis (treponemal disease) are all identifiable by their skeletal manifestations, although these changes are usually derived from a chronic infection, so the proportion of people that had the disease is likely actually greater. There are few examples of leprosy in the seventh–tenth centuries (Wells 1962; Manchester 1981), and it is not until the twelfth century that the evidence increases. The disease seems to have a rural distribution in the earlier period and a more urban one in the latter Middle Ages. The rise in leprosy hospital foundations in the thirteenth and fourteenth centuries may indicate a greater prevalence of the disease, although, due to confusion over the etiology of the disease and social factors, many nonleprous individuals resided in these institutions (Roberts 1986), and some leprous individuals are found in other cemeteries (Brothwell 1958). Few leprosy hospitals have been excavated, although nearly two hundred were founded in Britain alone during the Medieval period. Those that have been excavated throughout

Europe have produced skeletal manifestations of the disease (Møller-Christensen and Borge 1952; Wells 1962; Farley and Manchester 1989; Lee and Magilton 1989).

Tuberculosis is a disease transmitted to humans by infected humans or other animals, usually domesticated cattle. It is associated with animal husbandry, increased population density, and the development of urbanism. The disease is diagnosed from lytic destruction of the vertebral column and of the major weight-bearing joints (hip and knee). In contrast to plentiful medieval documentary evidence for tuberculosis, the skeletal evidence is scarce. Although Roman cases are known (Stirland and Waldron 1990; Wells 1982), there are no published reports of cases from the Medieval period. There are, however, unpublished references to the disease.

Debate about the development and transmission of treponemal disease (syphilis) is well known. The date of Columbus's first voyage (A.D. 1492–1493) plays a prominent role in the arguments. Three theories have been proposed to explain the course of the disease in the past: a New World origin, an Old World origin, and a unitarian model, which includes both an Old and a New World origin for the disease (Baker and Armelagos 1988). The disease manifests itself in four forms: pinta (a disease of the soft tissue only), yaws, treponarid (endemic syphilis), and venereal syphilis. Skin-to-skin contact and venereal transmission are the most common forms of spread. Urbanism, with its increased population density, plays a prime role in this dissemination. The skeletal evidence in the Old World is rare, and various theories have been tendered to explain this apparent paucity. Some of the external signs of syphilis resemble leprosy, and many afflicted individuals may have been interred in leprosy hospital cemeteries. There are some cases of treponemal disease dated to the Medieval period and from pre-1493 archaeological contexts (Dawes and Magilton 1980; Stirland 1991b). Radiocarbon dating of these individuals is in progress and may provide fuel for further debate.

Dental health has long been a concern of biological anthropologists working with medieval remains. The dentition reveals much information about diet, likely documenting the advent of refined sucrose in the late Medieval period (Moore and Corbett 1971, 1973) and perhaps reflecting socioeconomic differences within cemetery populations (Watson 1993). The dentition has also been studied in relation to markers of physical stress, which appear most frequently on the incisors and canine teeth as linear bands or pits in the enamel. These manifestations, along with porotic hyperostosis (a pitting of the external surface of the cranial vault), cribra orbitalia (a porosity and thinning of the bone in the roof of the orbits), and general periosteal porosity (indicative of localized infection of the soft tissue enveloping bones), have been used in assessments of general health during growth and development. A.L. Grauer (1993) found that, although these conditions were prevalent in some frequency in the poor medieval parish of St. Helen-on-the-Walls and increased in their frequency with age, most adults had survived these episodes despite their likely socioeconomic disadvantages.

Several researchers have begun work on the biomechanical alterations to bone that indicate repetitive behavior, in an attempt to identify occupations from medieval skeletal remains (Knüsel et al. 1992; Knüsel and Göggel 1993; Stirland 1985, 1990, 1991a, 1993). These alterations are produced through the normal process of bone remodeling in response to the strain created by muscular exertion. They are identifiable as alterations in surface morphology, cross-sectional area, density, and overall shape, asymmetry, and proportion of bones. These plastic alterations to bone, when coupled with osteoarthritic analyses, may eventually contribute to an understanding of the developmental process of the latter and provide insights into human adaptation to various environments. It may eventually be possible to monitor the changing social status of certain occupational specialists through time by an analysis of their funerary contexts. An integrated archaeological and bioanthropological approach is, therefore, desirable here as in other studies.

FURTHER READINGS

Anderson, T., J. Wakely, and A. Carter. Medieval Example of Metastic Carcinoma: A Dry Bone, Radiological, and SEM Study. *American Journal of Physical Anthropology* (1992) 89:309–323.

Baker, B., and G. Armelagos. The Origin and Antiquity of Syphilis: Palaeopathological Diagnosis and Interpretation. *Current Anthropology* (1988) 29:703–737.

Brothwell, D.R. Evidence of Leprosy in British Archaeological Material. *Medical History* (1958) 2:287–291.

———. Palaeodemography and Earlier British Populations. *World Archaeology* (1972) 4:75–87.

———. *Digging Up Bones.* London: British Museum (Natural History), 1981.

Cross, J.F., and M.F. Bruce. The Skeletal Remains. In *Three Scottish Carmelite Friaries: Excavations at Aberdeen, Linlithgow, and Perth, 1980–1986.* Ed. J.P.

Stones. Monograph Series 6. Edinburgh: Society of Antiquaries of Scotland, 1989, pp. 119–142.

Dawes, J., and J. Magilton. The Cemetery of St. Helen-on-the-Walls, Aldwark. The Archaeology of York, Vol. 12: The Medieval Cemeteries. London: Council for British Archaeology, 1980.

Farley, M., and K. Manchester. The Cemetery of the Leper Hospital of St. Margaret, High Wycombe, Buckinghamshire. *Medieval Archaeology* (1989) 33: 82–89.

Gladykowska-Rzeczycka, J. Tumors in Antiquity in East and Middle Europe. In *Human Paleopathology: Current Syntheses and Future Options.* Ed. D. Ortner and A. Aufderheide. Washington: Smithsonian Institution Press, 1991, pp. 251–256.

Grauer, A.L. Patterns of Anemia and Infection from Medieval York, England. *American Journal of Physical Anthropology* (1993) 91:203–213.

James, E. Burial and Status in the Early Medieval West. *Transactions of the Royal Historical Society,* 5th ser. (1989), 39:23–40.

Knowles, A.K. Acute Traumatic Lesions. In *Disease in Ancient Man.* Ed. G.D. Hart. Toronto: Clark Irwin, 1983, pp. 61–83.

Knüsel, C.J., and S. Göggel. A Cripple from the Medieval Hospital of Sts. James and Mary Magdalene, Chichester, England. *International Journal of Osteoarchaeology* (1993) 3:155–166.

Knüsel, C.J., Z.C. Chundun, and P. Cardwell. Slipped Proximal Femoral Epiphysis in a Mediaeval Priest. *International Journal of Osteoarchaeology* (1992) 2:109–119.

Lee, F., and J. Magilton. The Cemetery of the Hospital of St. James and Mary Magdalene, Chichester: A Case Study. *World Archaeology* (1989) 21:273–282.

Manchester, K. A Leprous Skeleton of the Seventh Century from Eccles, Kent, and the Present Evidence for Leprosy in Britain. *Journal of Archaeological Science* (1981) 8:205–209.

———. *The Archaeology of Disease.* Bradford: University of Bradford Press, 1983.

Marlow, M. The Human Remains. In *An Anglo-Saxon Cemetery at Norton, Cleveland.* Ed. Stephen J. Sherlock and Martin G. Welch. CBA Research Report 82. London: Council for British Archaeology, 1992, pp. 107–120.

Møller-Christensen, V., and F. Borge. Leprous Changes in a Material of Medieval Skeletons from the St. George's Court, Næstved. *Acta Radiologica* (1952) 37:308–317.

Moore, W.J., and M.E. Corbett. The Distribution of Dental Caries in Ancient British Populations II. Anglo-Saxon Period. *Caries Research* (1971) 5:151–168.

———. The Distribution of Dental Caries in Ancient British Populations II. Iron Age, Romano-British, and Medieval Periods. *Caries Research* (1973) 7:139–153.

Roberts, C. Leprosy and Leprosaria in Medieval Britain. *M.A.S.C.A. Journal* (1986) 4(1):15–21.

———. Trauma and Treatment in the British Isles in the Historic Period: A Design for Multidisciplinary Research. In *Human Paleopathology: Current Syntheses and Future Options.* Ed. D. Ortner and A. Aufderheide. Washington: Smithsonian Institution Press, 1991, pp. 225–240.

Rogers, J., T. Waldron, and I. Watt. Erosive Osteoarthritis in a Medieval Skeleton. *International Journal of Osteoarchaeology* (1991) 1:151–153.

Rogers, J., I. Watt, and P. Dieppe. Arthritis in Saxon and Medieval Skeletons. *British Medical Journal* (1981) 283:1668–1670.

———. Palaeopathology of Spinal Osteophytosis, Vertebral Ankylosis, Ankylosing Spondylitis. *Annals of Rheumatic Diseases* (1985) 44:113–120.

Rogers, J., T. Waldron, P. Dieppe, and I. Watt. Arthropathies in Palaeopathology: The Basis of Classification according to Most Probable Cause. *Journal of Archaeological Science* (1987) 14:179–193.

Rösing, F.W., and I. Schwidetsky. Comparative Statistical Studies on the Physical Anthropology of the Late Medieval Period (A.D. 1000–1500). *Journal of Human Evolution* (1984) 13:325–329.

Stirland, A. A Possible Correlation between Os Acromiale and Occupation in the Burials from the Mary Rose. In *Fifth Annual Proceedings of the European Palaeopathology Association.* Siena: EPA, 1985, pp. 327–334.

———. The Late Sir Thomas Reynes: A Medieval Identification. *Journal of Forensic Sciences* (1990) 30:39–43.

———. Diagnosis of Occupationally Related Paleopathology: Can It Be Done? In *Human Paleopathology: Current Syntheses and Future Options.* Ed. D. Ortner and A. Aufderheide. Washington: Smithsonian Institution Press, 1991a, pp. 40–47.

———. Pre-Columbian Treponematosis in Medieval Britain. *International Journal of Osteoarchaeology* (1991b) 1:39–47.

———. Asymmetry and Activity-Related Change in the Male Humerus. *International Journal of Osteoarchaeology* (1993) 3:105–113.

Stirland, A., and T. Waldron. The Earliest Cases of Tuberculosis in Britain. *Journal of Archaeological Sciences* (1990) 17:221–230.

Stroud, G., and R.L. Kemp. Cemeteries of the Church and Priory of St. Andrew, Fishergate. *The Archaeology of York: The Medieval Cemeteries 12/2.* London: Council for British Archaeology, 1993.

Waldron, T. DISH at Merton Priory: Evidence for a 'New' Occupational Disease? *British Medical Journal* (1985) 291:1762–1763.

———. The Effects of Humanisation on Health: The Evidence from Skeletal Remains. In *Diet and Crafts in Towns: The Evidence of Animal Remains from the Roman to the Post-Medieval Periods.* Ed. D. Serjeantson and T. Waldron. BAR British Series 199. Oxford: British Archaeological Reports, 1989, pp. 55–73.

Watson, P. Dental Findings. In Cemeteries of the Church and Priory of St. Andrew, Fishergate, by G. Stroud and R.L. Kemp. *The Archaeology of York: The Medieval Cemeteries 12/2.* London: Council for British Archaeology, 1993, pp. 242–250.

Wells, C. A Possible Case of Leprosy from a Saxon Cemetery in Beckford. *Medical History* (1962) 6:383–386.

———. A Leper Cemetery at South Acre, Norfolk. *Medieval Archaeology* (1967) 11:242–248.

———. The Human Burials. In *Romano-British Cemeteries at Cirencester.* Ed. A. McWhirr, L. Viner, and C. Wells. Cirencester: Cirencester Excavations Committee, 1982, pp. 135–202.

Wells, C., and H. Cayton. The Human Bones. In *Excavations at North Elmham Park, 1967–1972.* Ed. P. Wade-Martins. East Anglian Archaeology Report 9. Gressenhall: Norfolk Archaeological Unit, 1980, pp. 247–372.

White, W. *The Cemetery of St. Nicholas Shambles.* London: Museum of London/London and Middlesex Archaeological Society, 1988.

Christopher J. Knüsel and Charlotte Roberts

SEE ALSO
Cemeteries and Burials

Slavs
See Early Slav Culture.

Snape

The Snape Anglo-Saxon cemetery lies in the extreme northeast corner of the present parish of Snape, Suffolk, England. The River Alde, a major estuary, flows 2.5 km to the south, and the North Sea is 7 km to the east. Sutton Hoo lies 17 km to the southwest.

The site has been known since 1862, when it was visible as a group of nine or ten large burial mounds, up to 25.5 m in diameter and 2 m tall. Three of the mounds were excavated by the local landowner, and one was found to contain the plundered remains of a ship burial. Like the more famous example from Sutton Hoo, the ship was of clinker-built and riveted construction. It was at least 14 m in length. The grave contained within it had already been robbed but produced some interesting finds. A pair of spearheads indicates a male burial, while the remains of a glass "claw beaker" and, principally, a magnificent gold ring (now in the British Museum) show that the man was of the highest status. The ring is unique in Anglo-Saxon England but can be paralleled among high-status continental European graves. The paucity of finds makes dating difficult, but the ring and the claw beaker suggest a date of burial c. A.D. 550.

The 1862 excavators also found a number of cremation burials, indicating that the burial mounds were part of a larger cemetery. Excavations on the site from 1986 to 1991 concentrated on the surrounding cemetery, studying a total of sixty inhumation and cremation burials threatened by destruction from plowing. An estimated 20 percent sample of the site was excavated, providing a reliable basis for deductions about the nature of the whole cemetery. It had dimensions of c. 200 × 70 m and probably contained one thousand burials, with cremations and inhumations in equal proportions. The cemetery started as a cremation cemetery, perhaps in the later fifth century. Cremation continues to the end of the site's use in c. 625, with inhumation burials taking place from c. 550 onward. It may be that the ship burial initiated the inhumation phase. The original focus for the cemetery was perhaps a Bronze Age burial mound, the intact urn from which was found within the ship burial mound.

The excavations provide unique detail about the nature and variety of pagan Anglo-Saxon burial rites. The layout of the corpses was significant, with three possible body positions (flexed, extended, extended with feet crossed). In several graves, planks and branches of charred oak were placed in the grave during backfilling, as part of the ritual. Especially interesting were the containers in which the bodies were placed. Their traces, preserved as soil stains by the acidic sand, could be reconstructed in three dimensions. Some bodies had been placed in coffins (apparently without lids); others were on biers, which could be full- or half-length; in three cases, the body had been placed in a grave, the sides and base of which were lined with a coarse textile, possibly a rug; in two cases, the body had been placed in a small (3-m) wooden dugout canoe. This latter burial rite offers a unique and interesting contrast to the better known and more splendid ship burials. One of the boat graves had a horse's head, complete with bridle and bit, in a pit adjacent to it. In another grave, part of a boat was buried above the body.

There was an equal variety in the cremation burials, and the remains of a cremation pyre were found.

This variety of burial rite indicates that pagan Anglo-Saxon religion (at least insofar as burial was concerned) required commitment, was highly organized, and demanded a number of clearly defined choices (cremation or inhumation, position of body, inclusion of charred wood, type of container, and so forth). This interpretation fits well with the little available written evidence, which suggests a wide variety of deities worshiped in numerous different ways. The Snape evidence also points to ethnic origin as the main determinant of religious belief, with Scandinavian, Saxon, Anglian, and Frisian influences being apparent. The population was clearly diverse.

The recent excavations at both Snape and Sutton Hoo have clarified the relationship between the two sites. They are clearly linked by the occurrence of boat burial (which remains unique to the two sites), by their proximity, and by their survival as visible barrow cemeteries in similar locations, on heathland near a major East Suffolk estuary. They are linked more generally by a parallel variety of burial rite. All the variations noted at Snape were also found at Sutton Hoo (albeit on a grander scale), pointing to common ethnic origins.

Differences between the two sites are equally significant. In the first place, Snape is clearly the earlier of the two sites. As Snape comes to an end in c. 625, Sutton Hoo starts. The second difference is that, while Snape is a folk cemetery, containing the full range of pagan Anglo-Saxon graves, Sutton Hoo contains only the graves of the elite or of those bound to them.

If Sutton Hoo is the first burial ground of the Wuffinga kings of East Anglia, then Snape represents an earlier phase in the kingdom's emergence. It is arguable that the Snape ship burial, with its superb gold ring, is that of a king, perhaps an early member of the Sutton

S

Hoo dynasty whose power was confined to that immediate area of southeast Suffolk and who was buried among his "folk," a community of people whose religious beliefs reflected their recent history as immigrants from a wide area of northwest Europe.

FURTHER READINGS

Carnegie, S., and Filmer-Sankey, W. A Saxon Cremation Pyre from the Snape Anglo-Saxon Cemetery, Suffolk. *Anglo-Saxon Studies in Archaeology and History* (1993) 6:107–112.

Filmer-Sankey, W. A New Boat Burial from the Snape Anglo-Saxon Cemetery, Suffolk. In *Maritime Celts, Frisians, and Saxons.* Ed. S. McGrail. London: Council for British Archaeology, 1990, pp. 126–134.

———. Snape Anglo-Saxon Cemetery: The Current State of Knowledge. In *The Age of Sutton Hoo.* Ed. M.O.H. Carver. Woodbridge: Boydell and Brewer, 1992, pp. 39–52.

Filmer-Sankey, W., and T. Pestell. *The Snape Anglo-Saxon Cemetery.* East Anglian Archaeology, forthcoming.

William Filmer-Sankey

SEE ALSO
England; Sutton Hoo

Spain, Early Medieval

Early medieval Spain is not yet well understood archaeologically; it is both a cause and a consequence of this that sites of the period have received little attention until recently. The archaeological evidence is, therefore, very uneven in quantity and quality, and much of the important recent work has not yet been synthesized. However, using what information is available, and using also the absence of evidence where this seems meaningful, it is already possible to add much to what is known from the scanty and difficult historical sources.

Historically, the years between 400 and 900 are marked by a number of major events: the collapse of Roman rule between 409 and 475, the establishment of authority in Spain by the Visigoths between 456 and 475, the conquest of the Visigothic Kingdom in 711 by Arabs and Berbers who established an Islamic regime that dominated most of the Iberian Peninsula for centuries, and the creation between 718 and 813 of a number of small principalities in northern Spain that became the forebears of modern Spain and Portugal. These events normally provide the framework for defining time periods to describe the history. The

archaeological evidence does not fit very neatly into this framework, however. The major periods discernable in the material remains (with very general, approximate dates) are an attenuated persistence of Hispano-Roman culture from 400 to 600, a "Dark Age" from 600 to 800, and new growth of diverse regional cultures after 800.

Much of Spain was under Roman rule for six centuries, and the Roman Era did not end abruptly with the collapse of Roman administration there. That the Spanish (Castilian), Catalan, and Portuguese/Galician languages are direct descendants of the Latin brought by the Romans attests to the lasting importance of Roman culture. Roman imperial administration in Spain was finally disrupted by Germanic invaders during the decades after 409, but the population had become Roman in culture and institutions. In fact, although government fell entirely into the hands of Visigoths and Suevians between 409 and 475, archaeologically there is virtually nothing Germanic to be seen in the culture of their kingdoms.

In most aspects of culture—architecture, domestic artifacts, settlement, trade—there is more continuity than change from the fourth century to the fifth. The most immediate changes reflect the changed political environment specifically. The government of the Roman Empire had been powerful and active; the new kingdoms, ruled by peoples without traditions of administrative government, were less ambitious. Thus, for example, the Roman government had constructed many public works, produced much propaganda, and minted huge quantities of coin in a wide range of denominations for its expenditures. After c. 400, there is much less evidence for such governmental activity, except the minting of small quantities of coin in one or two denominations.

There is perhaps surprisingly little change to be seen in the basic economic patterns. The most salient features of the human landscape remained the Roman towns and the villas that served as residences for wealthy aristocrats and centers for their extensive landholdings. The towns were smaller and the villas more self-contained than during the height of the Roman Era, but in this there was little difference from the last century or two of Roman rule. In some areas, the number of recognized sites is noticeably less than for the fourth century, possibly indicating a decline in population. Also, settlement in some places shifted to more remote and defensive hilltop locations, perhaps because of increased violence and instability in the absence of Roman government.

Both towns and villas represent an economy in which surplus production could be concentrated and converted into wealth. The artifacts in the towns and villas, moreover, demonstrate the persistence of a market economy in which this wealth could be transformed into the products of specialist craftsmen or imports from overseas. Most items of trade have perished, of course, but pottery and other nonperishables give some indication of the patterns of trade. Although Spain and North Africa were no longer part of the same empire—in fact, their governments were often at odds—considerable quantities of North African fine table pottery were imported into Spain as late as the sixth century. Pottery from the eastern Mediterranean arrived also, though in much smaller quantities. Some continued exchange with the rest of western Europe may be discerned from finds of coins.

The real transition from classical antiquity to the Middle Ages in Spain occurred during the century between 550 and 650. The most clearly discernible change is the gradual disappearance of foreign imports. By c. 600, imported pottery was quite rare and largely restricted to the eastern coast of Spain; by c. 650, imports had ended altogether. This is important not just for what it indicates about changed economic conditions but because the imported pottery is at present the most useful material for dating late ancient sites. In Spain, where the local pottery in most areas has been little studied until recently, early medieval sites without imported pottery generally have been difficult to recognize unless they have metal adornments (especially belt buckles) or architectural stone carving, which occur mostly in graves and churches, respectively. Thus, for some centuries after 600, it is difficult to identify evidence for what people did except when they went to church or died.

The problem of finding archaeological evidence is most severe for the period between 600 and 800. However, the reasons why it has been so difficult to clarify this period, together with the small amount of evidence that has been recognized, suggest major changes in the culture and the conditions of life. The pottery of this period has been relatively little studied not just because it is locally produced, but also because it is too unattractive to be of interest within the art-historical values of traditional medieval archaeology. The pottery types that have recently been identified as products of the seventh or eighth century were produced on a small scale without much investment of skill or technology and were made in a limited range of utilitarian shapes, mostly plain cooking pots. In the fourth and fifth centuries, most pottery was made using the potter's wheel; this is typical where full-time craft specialists are producing large amounts of pottery

for sale. By the seventh century, the potter's wheel had largely ceased to be used. In all, it seems that the economic system in which wealth was exchanged for the products of skilled urban craft specialists had broken down.

Excavations within the towns support this picture of collapse. Historical sources indicate some sort of continuity of use of many towns throughout the early Middle Ages, but this use must have been very limited between 600 and 900. Excavations in towns used in both Roman and medieval times generally find the earliest medieval level (of the tenth century or later) directly on top of a late ancient level (of the sixth century or earlier), with no intervening use of the location. With the collapse of both external and internal trade, most towns must have become almost empty shells, with a few religious and political locations (and little else) remaining in use.

What little can be discerned of the settlement pattern suggests crisis for the rural population as well. The Roman pattern of dispersed villas and farms located primarily in the most productive lowland locations cannot be traced beyond the beginning of the seventh century. Instead, the trend toward settlement in remote, defensible hamlets was greatly augmented. In southeastern Spain, where the early medieval pottery is best known, sites attributed to the seventh–tenth centuries are small, few in number, and almost all located in defended hilltop locations. The sites of this period contain very little that could not have been produced by a purely local economy with minimal specialization.

This apparently impoverished, depopulated landscape continues to dominate the evidence for the ninth century, although it is modified by the first signs of the florescence of medieval Spain. In some areas, the later medieval sequence of known sites and pottery types begins in the ninth century; in most other areas, it begins in the tenth century. Where evidence is available, sites of the ninth and tenth centuries are noticeably more common than sites of the seventh and eighth centuries, suggesting new population growth after 800.

External trade also began to reemerge by the tenth century, helping to create increased regional diversity in the cultural traditions. Southern and eastern Spain, under Islamic rule, began to show influences from other Arab regions in North Africa and the Near East, while the Christian enclaves in northern Spain began to show ties to the rest of western Europe. One of the earliest but also most spectacular examples of this trend is the Great Mosque in Córdoba. The mosque was begun in the 780s,

S

using Roman architectural techniques and even masonry salvaged from Roman buildings. It was built in a blend of eastern Roman and Visigothic-period Hispano-Roman styles to create an Islamic structure for an Arab ruler. The later medieval cultures of Spain evolved in this manner from the ninth-century remnants of Roman heritage in the context of new economic, political, social, and cultural circumstances.

FURTHER READINGS

Caballero Zoreda, Luis. Observations on Historiography and Change from the Sixth to the Tenth Centuries in the North and West of the Iberian Peninsula. In *The Archaeology of Iberia: The Dynamics of Change.* Ed. Margarita Díaz-Andreu and Simon Keay. London: Routledge, 1996. pp. 235–264.

Collins, Roger. *Early Medieval Spain: Unity in Diversity, 400–1000.* London: Macmillan Education, 1983.

Dodds, Jerrilyn. *Architecture and Ideology in Early Medieval Spain.* University Park: Pennsylvania State University Press, 1990.

Glick, Thomas F. *From Muslim Fortress to Christian Castle: Social and Cultural Change in Medieval Spain.* Manchester: Manchester University Press, 1995.

Gutiérrez Lloret, Sonia. Production and Trade of Local and Regional Pottery in Early Medieval Spain (Seventh–Ninth Centuries): The Experience of the Southeast of the Iberian Peninsula. *Boletín de Arqueología Medieval* (1992) 6:9–22.

Keay, Simon. The End of Roman Spain. In *Roman Spain.* Berkeley: University of California Press, 1988, Chapter 9.

Palol, Pedro de, and Max Hirmer. *Early Medieval Art in Spain.* New York: Abrams, 1967.

Reynolds, Paul. *Settlement and Pottery in the Vinalopó Valley (Alicante, Spain), A.D. 400–700.* BAR International Series 588. Oxford: Tempus Reparatum, 1993.

Salvatierra Cuenca, Vicente. The Origins of Al-Andalus (Eighth and Ninth Centuries): Continuity and Change. In *The Archaeology of Iberia: The Dynamics of Change.* Ed. Margarita Díaz-Andreu and Simon Keay. London: Routledge, 1996, pp. 265–278.

David Yoon

SEE ALSO
Visigoths

Spong Hill

Spong Hill is on the southern edge of the parish of North Elmham in central Norfolk, East Anglia, England. North Elmham was the site of a bishop's see in the later Saxon period, later replaced by Norwich. The Anglo-Saxon cemetery at Spong Hill was first recorded in 1711, but systematic excavation began only in 1969. Between 1972 and 1981, the whole cemetery was excavated. The site is published in the East Anglian Archaeology series, and the finds are the property of the Norfolk Museums Service.

Evidence of prehistoric, Roman, and medieval activity was recovered as well as the cemetery, which dates to the fifth and sixth centuries A.D. and is the largest of its type to have been fully excavated in England. Part of a contemporary settlement was excavated along with the cemetery in 1984, but field and aerial surveys suggest that several small settlements existed in the area during the early Saxon period, all of which initially buried their dead at Spong Hill.

The full extent of the cemetery was established, but many cremations had been destroyed or damaged by earlier pot hunters and by agricultural activity. About twenty-four hundred cremations were found, in conditions varying from intact to fragmentary. The original total is estimated to have been more than three thousand. Fifty-seven inhumations were also excavated.

The cremations were contained in handmade, badly fired pots, most decorated with incised, plastic, or stamped patterns. About 70 percent contained grave goods. Melted glass beads, brooches, spindle whorls, and ivory rings were buried with women, who had been laid out for cremation in their clothing and jewelry in the same way as for ordinary burial. Other cremations contained sets of miniature iron razors, tweezers, and shears, often with bone combs and playing pieces. These occurred in graves of all ages and both sexes, but with a tendency toward adult males. There was no equivalent among the cremations for the male inhumations with weapons.

Relative wealth and trade contacts are represented by glass vessels, sword fittings, ivory, bronze vessels, and bronze-bound buckets.

Individuals of both sexes and all ages were buried at Spong Hill, although there was underrepresentation of children and infants. Animal bones were also identified in nearly half of all the cremations, including substantial parts of some carcasses, not just deposits of joints of meat. Horse bones were found most frequently, in 227 burials. Other domestic species (sheep/goat, cattle, pig, and dogs), occasional wild species (deer, bear, beaver, hare), birds, and fish were also identified.

Some cremations contained the remains of more than one individual, often an adult with a child. In others, bones and grave goods from one burial had been shared between two pots. At least 650 cremations (around 25 percent) had been buried in the same pit together with one or more others.

Products of the same potter or workshop could be identified through impressions of the same stamp die on several pots or other idiosyncratic features. The largest such groups include seventy or more pots.

The detailed chronology of the site is still unclear. Burial groups and stamp-linked pots provide an independent basis for identification of contemporary burials within the site. Spatial patterning of some types of pottery and grave goods suggests a radial development of the cremation cemetery. Relatively early burials, with the closest affinities to Continental material, are found in the middle, whereas the stamp-linked pots, produced later, when local potters had emerged, were buried in clusters around the edge of the cemetery. In absolute terms, the cemetery seems to have begun by the middle of the fifth century A.D. and to have gone out of use c. A.D. 600.

The inhumations lay along the northern edge of the cemetery. Few bones survived in the acid sandy soil, but there were traces of wooden coffins. The earliest, No. 40, was a large rectangular grave containing a sword, a shield, a spear, and a bucket. Around it was a ring ditch, 10 m in diameter, the last trace of a mound. Cut into the ditch were four small graves; two at least were female. Another large ring ditch cut the first, and at least two other inhumations in this area were surrounded by smaller ditches. The few cremations here may have been deliberately buried in the middle of inhumation grave pits or nearby. A similar mixture of burial rites has been observed elsewhere, for example at Snape and Sutton Hoo. Other inhumations were overlain by a number of cremations. The cremation cemetery seems to have existed before and after the period of the inhumation burials. The pottery and metalwork buried in graves of both rites is the same, so the inhuming group were probably not of different origin from those cremating their dead. Although the ring-ditch graves appear to be burials of people of some rank, not all inhumations were rich, nor all cremations poor.

The finds from Spong Hill in general support Bede's claim that the Angles, who settled East Anglia, came from Angeln in Schleswig-Holstein, since that is where the closest Continental parallels are to be found. Only the idea of stamped decoration on pottery seems more likely to have come instead from Lower Saxony. The motifs used for the stamps may include some with pagan religious significance. It is unlikely that the incoming Anglo-Saxons completely replaced the indigenous Romano-British population, but so many aspects of burial practice and material culture changed so profoundly in eastern Britain during the fifth century that some significant immigration must have taken place. However, some of those buried at Spong Hill could have been of British origin, using new Germanic burial practices. The range of age, sex, and elaboration of burial deposit suggests that the cemetery was used by all, or most, of the local population and not set aside for an elite, whether native or foreign.

The cemetery at Spong Hill went out of use as part of the long-term trend that led to the abandonment of the early, large pagan cemeteries and to the beginning of the medieval Christian pattern of local village graveyards.

FURTHER READINGS

Hills, C.M. The Anglo-Saxon Cemetery at Spong Hill, North Elmham, Norfolk, Part I: Cremation Catalog. East Anglian Archaeology Report 6, 1977a.

———. A Chamber Grave from Spong Hill. *Medieval Archaeology* (1977b) 21:167–176.

———. Anglo-Saxon Cremation Cemeteries, with Particular Reference to Spong Hill. In *Anglo-Saxon Cemeteries 1979*. Ed. P.A. Rahtz, T. Dickinson, and L. Watts. BAR British Series 82. Oxford: British Archaeological Reports, 1980, pp. 197–207.

———. Anglo-Saxon Chairperson. *Antiquity* (1980) 54: 52–54.

———. Animal Stamps on Anglo-Saxon Pottery in East Anglia. *Studien zur Sachsenforschung* (1983) 4:93–110.

Hills, C.M., and K.J. Penn. The Anglo-Saxon Cemetery at Spong Hill, North Elmham, Norfolk, Part II: Cremation Catalog. East Anglian Archaeology Report 11, 1981.

Hills, C.M., K.J. Penn, and R.J. Rickett. The Anglo-Saxon Cemetery at Spong Hill, North Elmham, Norfolk, Part III: Inhumations. East Anglian Archaeology Report 21, 1984.

———. The Anglo-Saxon Cemetery at Spong Hill, North Elmham, Norfolk, Part IV: Cremations. East Anglian Archaeology Report 34, 1987.

McKinley, J. Spong Hill: The Cremations. In *Burial Archaeology: Current Research, Methods, and Developments*. Ed. Charlotte Roberts, Frances Lee, and John

S

Bintliff. BAR British Series 211. Oxford: British Archaeological Reports, 1989, pp. 247–248.

Richards, J.D. *The Significance of Form and Decoration of Anglo-Saxon Cremation Urns.* BAR British Series 166. Oxford: British Archaeological Reports, 1987.

Catherine Hills

SEE ALSO
Snape; Sutton Hoo

Stoneware

Stoneware seems to be the most important and specific contribution that Germany made to the medieval European ceramic arts. In the strict sense, stoneware is fused. Its porosity should be less than 2 percent, so it is ideal for drinking, serving, and storing liquids. In reality, there are many products that do not fit this modern scientific definition but seem to have been intended as stoneware by medieval potters. This can be seen in the specific formal and technological execution of these products; only the full vitrification of the sherd is lacking. This incomplete vitrification must be caused by the use of inappropriate clays and, particularly in the thirteenth century, by problems of reaching the necessarily high temperatures of c. 1200–1300°C.

In addition to the fused, mostly gray, sherd, an outside glaze is typical of most stonewares. These glazes are mostly brown to red and later grayish in color. Few of these glazes have been analyzed, but they usually seem to be mixtures of slip with iron or manganese oxides, ash glaze, or, from the fourteenth century onward, salt glaze. Wares with fully fused sherds are real stoneware. Wares with mostly fused sherds and, with the exception of some Rhenish wares, invisible or barely visible tempering can be regarded as proto-stoneware. (Proto-stoneware has a hard but only partly fused sherd, often with a slip, and shows the same forms as the other groups.) In reality, the differentiation is not easy without scientific analyses, but these cannot be discussed here in detail. There is an urgent need both for a scientific databank to test the archaeological classifications and for thorough research on the production sites, which is largely lacking.

Nearly vitrified pottery was produced in Carolingian potteries at Mayen (Eifel), but it was not before c. A.D. 1200 that the development of stoneware began in what was then the most prominent ceramic region of Germany near Cologne. There were several places in the Rhineland during the late twelfth and the thirteenth centuries where the production of specific hard wares showing tendencies toward fusion took place. These production centers cannot be differentiated in detail because of a lack of thorough research. They include the Vorgebirge, which was the dominant older center with places like Pingsdorf and later the town of Brühl, and Langerwehe and Raeren-Eynatten in Belgium, as well as Brunssum-Schinveld in South Limburg. Other regions that participated in the general development were the North Eifel (Binsfeld, Speicher), Mayen and the Middle Rhine near Koblenz and Mainz (Urbar, Düppenhausen, Aulhausen), and the Westerwald (Grenzau, Grenzhausen, Niederzeuzheim). Siegburg played an important role and was the innovative center. There, c. A.D. 1250, a typical ash-glazed light gray ware with visible artificial quartz tempering was invented. Art historians and archaeologists call this *near-stoneware,* but from a scientific perspective it is real stoneware. In this period, there is also a shift to new forms. C. 1300, the manufacture of classical Siegburg stoneware without visible mineral components began, although it seems that mass production did not start before the second quarter of the fourteenth century. This was the last step toward a domination of this type of ware in most parts of central Europe.

It must be stressed, on the other hand, that the other Rhenish potteries did not change their wares so radically, and on the whole there seems to be a much longer transitional period. Outside the Rhineland, except for Waldenburg, near- and proto-stonewares seem to dominate throughout the later Middle Ages.

The imitation of both the fabric and the forms of Rhenish stoneware is typical of many potteries of international, regional, and local importance even in the sphere of earthenware. Yet, research must be done on a much larger scale to obtain more insights in this most complex matter. The most restricting factor seems to have been the rarity of highly plastic clays. So, after a period of establishment of a series of production centers for proto- and near-stoneware in the thirteenth century in the Rhein and Main region, Hesse, and Lower Saxony, a crisis due to massive imports of high-quality Rhenish stoneware forced some other potteries to close or to neglect their manufacture of stoneware type between c. 1350 and 1450.

During the later fourteenth and the fifteenth centuries, a smaller number of centers specialized in stoneware; the most important seem to have been Siegburg and some places in the Vorgebirge; Langerwehe and Raeren; Speicher and Mayen (Eifel); Höhr-Grenzhausen (Westerwald); Dieburg, Großalmerode, Michelsberg, and Dreihausen (Hessen); Coppengrane and Duingen (Lower Saxony); Waldenburg (Saxony); and Lusatia and Lostice (Moravia). For most potteries, there is still an urgent need for systematic research, but generally it is evident that the center of the development in many respects remained in the Rhineland, whereas other ceramic regions were receptors of these innovations. Also, there is a chronological gradient from west to east that reflects the diffusion of technological knowledge.

It is probably no coincidence that stoneware was invented in a crucial period of technical and economic change. It can be regarded as the most prominent type of later medieval ceramic tableware. This is reflected in its considerable formal variety, its influence on earthenware, and its unusually wide distribution. During the thirteenth century, for the first time, many different and sometimes plastically decorated forms of jugs, beakers, pitchers, and flasks were made for more differentiated functions than before. The basic forms are handy jugs, both bellied and slim, but there are numerous variations in detail, including vessels with special functions like aquamaniles, miniature vessels, and figures of knights and animals. In some regions, horizontal roulette decoration was quite common c. 1230–1320; it is often combined with horizontal strips and a collared rim. In other places, stoneware was decorated only with horizontal cordons on the belly, shoulder, neck, and rim as well as a frilled base. Anthropomorphic applications are rare before c. 1500 and seem to be restricted to an early phase and to the period c. 1400. Generally, only a rather small selection of the many vessel forms produced were exported in long-distance trade.

In contrast to northwest Europe, where pewter-glazed wares dominated, in central Europe stonewares were preferred from c. 1250. During the fourteenth century, the mass production of stonewares swamped the market, particularly in the zones of activity of the Hanseatic merchants, including north Germany and the countries around the Baltic and North Sea. In south Germany and the other central European countries, there are few Rhenish imports, but there are some imports from centers like Dieburg, Waldenburg, and Lostice. There are no doubt differences between the trading areas of potteries. The only place with an overall distribution seems to have been Siegburg, perhaps because of its high quality, but also on the basis of the Cologne trade. In England, Langerwehe and later Raeren products were much more common. Lower Saxon near-stoneware was common in north Germany and in areas around the Baltic Sea but not in north-

west Europe. Other potteries like Dieburg and Mayen seem to have had a more regional distribution. Still, this was much more than that of an average earthenware pottery, whose distribution area was only c. 30–50 km.

During the fourteenth and fifteenth centuries, the formal variety was much reduced. Vessels became more standardized and mostly undecorated. At the end of the Middle Ages, particularly in the transition phase to the Renaissance during the first half of the sixteenth century, new types of decoration and new forms appear. The most typical are jugs with face masks (particularly in Raeren) and generally molded applications (from c. 1400, foremost in Siegburg). The frilled base so typical of medieval stoneware also occurs until this time. Most of the older centers survived to early modern times, but some (e.g., Siegburg) lost their former importance, and others (e.g., Westerwald) developed a leading position.

FURTHER READINGS

Beckmann, Bernhard. *Der Scherbenhügel in der Siegburger Aulgasse.* Rheinische Ausgrabungen 16. Bonn, 1975.

Davey, Peter, and Richard Hodges, eds. *Ceramics and Trade: The Production and Distribution of Later Medieval Pottery in North-West Europe.* Sheffield: University of Sheffield Publications, 1983. See especially articles by Hurst (Langerwehe), Janssen (Netherlands), and Stephan (German Stoneware).

Gaimster, David R.M., Mark Redknap, and Hans-Helmut Wegner, eds. Zur Keramik des Mittelalters und der beginnenden Neuzeit im Rheinland. BAR International Series 440. Oxford: British Archaeological Reports, 1988. See especially articles by Redknap (Mayen) and Stephan (Stoneware, Definition).

Hähnel, Elsa. 1987, 1992 *Siegburger Steizeug.* Bestandskatalog 1, 2. Köln: Führer und Schriften des Rheinischen Freilichtmuseums und Landesmuseums für Volkskunde in Kommern 31, 38.

Klinge, Eckhard. *Siegburger Steinzeug.* Düsseldorf: Kataloge des Hetjens-Museums, 1972.

Reineking-von Bock, Gisela. *Steinzeug.* 3rd ed. Köln: Katalog des Kunstgewerbemuseums Köln, 1986.

Hans-Georg Stephan

Survey

In archaeology, *survey* is a somewhat ambiguous term. To American archaeologists, it principally connotes the physical search for previously unrecorded sites and features in a landscape. To British archaeologists, the term can also refer

S

to the compilation of an inventory of sites of a certain class from documentary sources or to the mapping of a site. No narrowing of the definition of *survey* will be attempted here, since historical sources constitute a prime resource for medieval archaeology in Europe. Site inventories culled from documents are termed *paper surveys,* while surveys that are undertaken in the field to discover previously unrecorded sites are termed *reconnaissance surveys.*

One cannot speak of *survey* solely in relation to settlement sites. Nonsite features such as field boundary walls, cattle ways, lynchets, and springs are equally legitimate objects of *survey.* The indeterminate nature of unexcavated surface indications usually compels the archaeologist to record everything that is encountered.

In the present day, reconnaissance surveys are undertaken with nearly the same frequency in Europe as excavations. However, there is far less written on survey strategy than there is on excavation methodology. This is more true for the British Isles than for the United States, where a lively debate over survey strategy transpired in the 1960s and 1970s in connection with the overall debate over sampling, instigated by the practitioners of the "new archaeology" (see Flannery 1976a,b; Hill 1967; Plog 1976; Nance 1983; Redman 1974). In the British Isles, archaeological survey, called *fieldwork* or *field walking,* has a venerable pedigree going back to the nineteenth century. However, the techniques and strategy of fieldwork are seldom explicitly discussed in the British literature.

In Europe, systematic, problem-oriented reconnaissance surveys specifically targeting medieval settlement do occur (e.g., Barrett 1980; Cunliffe 1972; Foard 1978), but these are not common. As examples of the more numerous kinds of surveys, one might first cite nationally mandated surveys of extant medieval remains in cities and towns (e.g., Bradley 1985). There have also been efforts to develop national registers of all settlements of a certain class, such as British and Irish moated settlements (Åberg 1978; Åberg and Brown 1981; Barry 1977). Then there are the surveys of the archaeological remains of regions, including counties, baronies, and parishes, which have included medieval sites in addition to sites and features dating to other periods (e.g., Cuppage 1986; Fleming and Ralph 1982; Hayfield 1980, 1987; Lacy 1983; O'Sullivan 1986; Stout 1984). Lastly, there are rescue surveys prompted by the construction of roadways or pipelines.

A wide range of techniques can be utilized in field surveys. In medieval archaeology, survey is usually initiated with a paper survey of documentary sources and old maps. It has also become standard practice to study and make maps from existing aerial photographs or to undertake an aerial reconnaissance prior to walking the land. This step cuts down the costs of foot survey and enhances the accuracy of maps made on the ground. Besides aerial photography, other remote-sensing techniques such as magnetometers and phosphate sampling are used increasingly in extensive surveys.

The methodology that is employed to discover sites is contingent upon the visibility of the sites in a specific region. In rural northern Europe, most structures of the Middle Ages were constructed of perishable or nondurable materials. Vegetation covers the ground surface, and agricultural activities carried out over centuries have leveled and churned sites. Under these conditions, a field is walked only after it has been freshly plowed, and sites are identified through the observation of artifact densities (Cunliffe 1972; Foard 1978; Hayfield 1987). It is best if teams of surveyors make systematic sweeps through these fields to ensure uniform coverage, but many surveyors opt instead for a haphazard walk through a field, termed *random walking* (Foard 1978:358; Hayfield 1987:7), possibly due to labor constraints.

In stony regions with thin soil, cover sites are often visible on the surface. A reconnaissance survey of sites and features of the early Middle Ages in the eastern half of the rugged karstic limestone uplands known as the Burren in northern County Clare, Ireland, exemplifies this situation. The Cahercommaun Project set out to reconstruct the social structure and boundaries of a chiefdom of the eighth–ninth centuries A.D. through a survey of settlements and contemporary field boundary wall systems (Gibson 1990). The settlements dating to this period generally have thick enclosing walls of limestone, ensuring uniform preservation.

Land in most of the rural British Isles is enclosed by innumerable field boundaries, and in the Burren these are made of stacked limestone slabs. This fact, together with the ruggedness of the terrain and the large number of small landowners whose permission must be gained before survey can be undertaken, places serious limitations on any sampling procedure employing linear or quadrangular transects of uniform, arbitrary dimensions and orientation. In deference to these factors, the "grid and system" procedure was utilized (Coles 1972:16–18). All the existing fields within a townland were numbered, and each of these was walked by crews of three in systematic sweeps.

Rather than survey a random sample of fields, an attempt was made to walk all the fields within a townland. The justification for this procedure lay in the nature of the region's archaeological record. From the Neolithic period on, settlements in the Burren uplands were observed to be positioned within networks of field boundary walls that extended for kilometers beyond the sites. The project sought to study settlements not in isolation but as they existed within an associated system of fields and cemetery areas. A randomized sampling system would be incapable of revealing these interrelated systems.

Establishing the ultimate boundaries of a survey is another problem that confronts the archaeologist. In a contract or parish survey, the area to be surveyed is predetermined. In a research survey, however, the boundaries must be established through considerations of the goals of research, the duration of the project, and the available labor. Carole Crumley has advocated an open-ended survey design to define the archaeological and ecological structure of a region (1979), which she implemented in her study of the Burgundy region in the late prehistoric period and early Middle Ages (Crumley et al. 1987). This approach is quite sensible given the fact that these aspects are usually unknown at the onset of research.

Crumley's design was adopted by the Cahercommaun Project. Survey expanded outward by townlands from the chiefdom's probable center at the eighth–ninth-century cashel site of Cahercommaun. However, the density of sites and features, dense vegetation, and the ruggedness of the topography made it impossible to survey two of the initial townlands completely within the initial three-season run of the project. In retrospect, a more systematic approach that prioritized the areas to be surveyed within the region might have been preferable.

FURTHER READINGS

Åberg, F.A., ed. *Medieval Moated Sites.* CBA Research Report 17. London: Council for British Archaeology, 1978.

Åberg, F.A., and A.E. Brown. *Medieval Moated Sites in North-West Europe.* BAR International Series 121. Oxford: British Archaeological Reports, 1981.

Barrett, G.F. A Field Survey and Morphological Study of Ring-Forts in Southern Co. Donegal. *Ulster Journal of Archaeology* (1980) 43:39–51.

Barry, T.B. *The Medieval Moated Sites of South-Eastern Ireland: Counties Carlow, Kilkenny, Tipperary, and Wexford.* BAR 35. Oxford: British Archaeological Reports, 1977.

Bradley, J. The Medieval Towns of Tipperary. In *Tipperary History and Society.* Ed. W. Nolan. Dublin: Geography Publications, 1985, pp. 34–59.

Coles, J. *Field Archaeology in Britain.* London: Methuen, 1972.

Crumley, C.L. Three Locational Models: An Epistemological Assessment for Anthropology and Archaeology. In *Advances in Archaeological Method and Theory.* Vol. 2. Ed. M.B. Schiffer. New York: Academic, 1979, pp. 141–173.

Crumley, C.L., W.H. Marquardt, and T.L. Leatherman. Certain Factors Influencing Settlement during the Later Iron Age and Gallo-Roman Periods: The Analysis of Intensive Survey Data. In *Regional Analysis: Burgundian Landscapes in Historical Perspective.* Ed. C.L. Crumley and W.H. Marquardt. New York: Academic, 1987, pp. 121–172.

Cunliffe, B. Saxon and Medieval Settlement-Pattern in the Region of Chalton, Hampshire. *Medieval Archaeology* (1972) 16:1–12.

Cuppage, J., ed. *Corca Dhuibhne: Dingle Peninsula Archaeological Survey.* Ballyferriter: Oidhreacht Chorca Dhuibhne, 1986.

Flannery, K.V. Sampling on the Regional Level. In *The Early Mesoamerican Village.* Ed. K.V. Flannery. New York: Academic, 1976a, pp. 131–136.

———. The trouble with regional sampling. In *The Early Mesoamerican Village.* Ed. K.V. Flannery. New York: Academic, 1976b, pp. 159–160.

Fleming, A., and N. Ralph. Medieval Settlement and Land Use on Holne Moor, Dartmoor: The Landscape Evidence. *Medieval Archaeology* (1982) 26:101–137.

Foard, G.R. Systematic Fieldwalking and the Investigation of Saxon Settlement in Northamptonshire. *World Archaeology* (1978) 9(3):357–374.

Gibson, D.B. *Tulach Commáin: A View of an Irish Chiefdom.* Ann Arbor: University Microfilms International, 1990.

Hayfield, C. Wharram Percy Parish Survey. In *Fieldwalking as a Method of Archaeological Research.* Ed. C. Hayfield. Occasional Papers 2. London: Directorate of Ancient Monuments and Historic Buildings, 1980, pp. 26–33.

———. *An Archaeological Survey of the Parish of Wharram Percy, East Yorkshire.* BAR British Series 172. Oxford: British Archaeological Reports, 1987.

S

Lacy, B. *Archaeological Survey of Co. Donegal.* Lifford: Donegal Co. Council, 1983.

Nance, J.D. Regional Sampling in Archaeological Survey: The Statistical Perspective. In *Advances in Archaeological Method and Theory.* Vol. 6. Ed. M.B. Schiffer. New York: Academic, 1983, pp. 289–356.

O'Sullivan, P., ed. *Newcastle Lyons: A Parish of the Pale.* Dublin: Geography Publications, 1986.

Plog, S. Relative Efficiencies of Sampling Techniques for Archaeological Surveys. In *The Early Mesoamerican Village.* Ed. K.V. Flannery. New York: Academic, 1976, pp. 136–158.

Redman, C.L. *Archaeological Sampling Strategies.* Module in Anthropology 55. Reading: Addison-Wesley, 1974.

Stout, G. *Archaeological Survey of the Barony of Ikerrin.* Roscrea: Roscrea Heritage Society, 1984.

D. Blair Gibson

SEE ALSO
Cashels

Sutton Hoo

Sutton Hoo is the site of an early medieval burial ground located beside the River Deben, c. 12 km upriver from the North Sea in Suffolk, southeast England [NGR TM 288 487]. Nineteen mounds have been recognized so far, of which twelve were examined by archaeological excavation in the twentieth century. Six of these proved to have been cremations, one was a chamber grave, one a horse burial, one a child, and two were ship burials, one of them producing the richest assemblage from any British burial. There were forty other burials, not beneath mounds, the majority unfurnished, a number showing evidence for decapitation or hanging. All the burials that have been dated belong to the late sixth to late seventh centuries A.D., the time of the conversion of the Anglo-Saxons to Christianity.

Investigations

There have been at least five different investigations of the site. First, it has been discovered that the site was extensively explored in the mid-nineteenth century; at least six mounds (Mounds 2, 3, 4, 5, 6, 7) had been cut by large trenches running east-west, but no finds have survived. Then, in 1938, Mounds 2, 3, and 4 were reopened by Basil Brown on behalf of the landowner, Mrs. E. Pretty. The fragmentary finds showed them to have been Anglo-

Saxon, and one (Mound 2) included iron rivets typical of early medieval ship construction. In 1939, Brown opened Mound 1 for Mrs. Pretty and discovered the intact ship burial that made the site famous. The burial chamber that lay amidships was excavated by Charles Phillips, and the outline of the ship was investigated by Commander Hutchinson. The magnificent treasure recovered from the burial chamber was found under English law to belong to the landowner, Mrs. Pretty, who donated it to the British Museum where it may be seen. In the period 1966–1971, a team from the British Museum, led by R.L.S. Bruce-Mitford, reexcavated the site of the Mound 1 ship burial and explored the prehistoric settlement first contacted by Brown. After the final publication of the Mound 1 ship burial in 1975–1983, a new campaign of research was launched by the Society of Antiquaries of London and the British Museum, under the direction of M.O.H. Carver, University of York. One hectare of the cemetery was opened, including the excavation or reexcavation of eight mounds and thirty-nine other burials; 12 ha of adjacent land were mapped by remote sensing, and the Anglo-Saxon settlement of the Deben Valley was explored in collaboration with the Suffolk Archaeological Unit. The fieldwork of this campaign was concluded in 1993.

Prehistory

The Anglo-Saxon cemetery was coincident with a prehistoric settlement. In the late Neolithic/early Bronze Age, pits were dug containing Beaker pottery, a roundhouse was constructed, and the land was divided into units c. 0.5 ha in area. In the later Bronze Age, the land was divided into new units with stake fences; in the Iron Age, it was redivided again into small fields marked by earth banks. These fields were exploited in the Roman period to grow unidentified crops (which may have included vines), and the banks were still visible when the Anglo-Saxons initiated their cemetery. The prehistoric sequence has produced some fifty thousand finds of pottery and flint.

Early Medieval Burial Rites

The Sutton Hoo cemetery is notable for the variety of its burial rites. In Mounds 4, 5, 6, 7, and probably 18, the body had been cremated and the burnt bone wrapped in a cloth and placed in a bronze bowl in a shallow pit under the mound. In Mound 3, the cremation had been heaped on a wooden piece. In Mound 17, the body of a young man had been placed in a coffin with a sword and a purse; under the coffin lay a shield and outside it lay two spears, a cauldron, a bucket, a haversack, a wooden tub, and the bridle of a horse. The horse itself lay in a pit parallel and adjacent to the human burial and under the same mound. The very small Mound 20 covered the burial of a child in a coffin, accompanied by a miniature spear and a buckle. Under Mound 14, the burial, probably a female, had been placed in a wooden chamber. Under Mound 2, there was also a chamber, which had originally contained the richly furnished grave of a man. A ship, c. 20 m long, had been placed over the chamber and the mound piled on top of this. In Mound 1, the chamber had been built inside the ship, which itself was placed in a deep trench. The mound had been heaped over the chamber and the ship together. In the chamber, the dead man had lain in a coffin, with a heap of clothing, shoes, and toiletries at his feet. His accoutrements included a baldric with shoulder clasps and gold buckle, a helmet, a sword, and a purse containing thirty-seven coins; nearby were a set of gaming pieces, two drinking horns, and six maplewood bottles. At the head (east) end of the coffin were stacked or suspended three spears, three angons, a large ornate hanging bowl, a Coptic bowl, a lyre in a beaver-skin bag, a set of ten silver bowls, two silver spoons, an iron "standard," and a whetstone "scepter." At the foot (west) end was a great silver dish, a lamp, an axehammer, a mailcoat, three cauldrons, a tub, and a bucket. The assemblage also had a rich array of textiles deriving from clothing and hangings.

The sizes of the mounds have varied greatly. Mound 20, the smallest, was only c. 2 m in diameter, as indicated by its ditch. Mound 1, the largest, was originally c. 30 m in diameter. Mound 2 was c. 20 m in diameter and had stood c. 4 m high. The remainder were between 5 m and 15 m in diameter.

Three other groups of burials have been found in the cemetery that were not under mounds. Group 1 consisted of twenty-three graves clustered together on the eastern periphery. Three of the bodies were prone, three kneeling, two beheaded, one hanged, and one arranged in a large grave in a splayed posture accompanied by a wooden artifact resembling an ard (a scratch plow). Group 2 consisted of twenty-one graves arranged radially or tangentially around Mound 5. Six of the bodies in these graves were beheaded, one hanged, four prone, and one dismembered. The first of the Group 2 burials was put in place immediately after the construction of Mound 5, and burials continued to be added in the neighborhood of Mound 5 until after the construction of Mound 6. Group 3 graves were furnished: one to the west of Mound 5 had con-tained a bronze fitting and a glass bead; two to the east of Mound 5 contained adolescents, one, probably male, equipped with buckles and knife, and the other, probably female, furnished with leather bag and chatelaine.

Early Medieval Art

The richest assemblage found in this or any Anglo-Saxon cemetery was that found in the ship burial under Mound 1: 263 objects were recovered, of gold, silver, bronze, iron, wood, textiles, leather, and other materials, deriving from fifty-eight artifacts originally placed in the grave. Of these, twenty-six were imported from abroad. The acid sand had, however, severely reduced the organic materials, often past recognition. The sword, baldric, and purse were worked in gold with cloisonné garnets and mille-fiori glass. This polychrome jewelry, among the finest known from the early Middle Ages, features ribbon animals in Salin's style II. The sword may be Frankish, but the remainder of the jewelry, featuring characteristic mushroom-shaped garnets, is thought to be local. The silverware, a great dish carrying stamps of Anastasius (A.D. 491–518), silver bowls incised with a cruciform design, and two spoons carrying the inscriptions "Saulos" and "Paulos," respectively, are thought to have originated in Byzantium. The bronze hanging bowls carry escutcheons of red enamel and millefiori glass set in raised trumpet scrolls and are attributed to northwest Britain or Ireland. The helmet and the shield are closely related to examples found in ship burials at Vendel and Valsgårde in Sweden. The thirty-seven gold coins are tremisses, minted in Merovingian France. Some of the textiles, particularly the finer cloak fabrics, have been traced to the eastern Mediterranean.

In the more modest horse burial beneath Mound 17, there was a bridle with an iron snaffle bit, and buckles and connectors in silvered iron and gilt bronze, carrying zoomorphic ornament. There are numerous fragments of ornamental metalwork in silver and gilt bronze from the other mounds. Together, Sutton Hoo has produced the best evidence in northwest Europe for the work of the early seventh-century artist and artisan. The zoomorphic ornament looks back to sixth-century Anglo-Saxon, Scandinavian, and Frankish polychrome and *kerbschnitt* jewelry and forward to the early insular Gospel books such as the *Book of Durrow* (Northumbria or Iona, 660–675) and *Durham A II 10* (Northumbria, 650–700).

Of the two ships, only that under Mound 1 survived well enough to be measured. It was a clinker-built timber

S

vessel and, at 27.3 m, is the longest known from the early Middle Ages. It had nine strakes on each side, fastened with more than fifteen hundred iron clench nails. The keel was a plank, and the gunwales carried "thorn-shaped" tholes against which the oars were pulled. No evidence survived for a mast, but experiments have shown that the ship could easily have sailed. There were repairs in the hull, indicating that the ship had seen service and had not been built especially for the funeral.

Date

1. *Historical.* The Mound 1 ship burial is attributed to Raedwald, who is recorded by Bede as being a king of East Anglia who converted to Christianity and reverted to paganism, on the grounds of its wealth, its location in East Anglia, and its mixture of Christian symbolism and pagan burial rites. The death of Raedwald is recorded as A.D. 624 or 625. 2. *Stylistic.* The polychrome jewelry and zoomorphic ornament can be placed after 550 and before A.D. 650. 3. *Numismatic.* The coins in the purse were originally dated to c. 650, then redated by J. Lafaurie to c. 620, a date favored by Bruce-Mitford and the analysis of John Kent. A date of c. 600 has been suggested for their collection (Stahl in Kendall and Wells 1992). 4. *Radiocarbon dates* have been obtained from the beeswax in the Mound 1 lamp (A.D. 480–570), from a piece of wood in Mound 1 (A.D. 560–650), from Group 1 burials (A.D. 540–700, 680–820), from Group 2 burials (A.D. 650–955, 650–780), and from a Group 3 burial (A.D. 670–830).

Interpretation

Most scholars have considered Sutton Hoo to be a burial ground of the early kings of East Anglia and datable to the early seventh century. For H.M. Chadwick, Mound 1 was the resting place of Raedwald, who was important enough to attract the epithet *bretwalda* (overlord or great king). The researches of Bruce-Mitford (1975–1983) developed this thesis, emphasizing the Swedish connections of Raedwald's family, the Wuffas, which he saw as being signaled in the burial. Carver (1986, 1992, 1993, 1998) interprets the Sutton Hoo cemetery as a political and ideological statement. The people of East Anglia acquired kings only in the late sixth century and inaugurated for them special regalia (the "standard" and the "scepter") and a separate burial. The new aristocracy felt their autonomy, pagan ideology, and traditional allegiance with the Scandinavian peoples threatened by the political ambitions of Christianity and the Franks and reacted by carrying out extrav-

agant and theatrical burials, featuring ritual killing and Scandinavian practices such as cremation under mounds and the burial of ships.

FURTHER READINGS

Bruce-Mitford, R.L.S. *The Sutton Hoo Ship-Burial.* 3 Vols. London: British Museum Press, 1975–1983.

Carver, M.O.H. Sutton Hoo in Context. *Settimane di Studio* (1986) 32 (Centro Italiano di Studi sull'Alto Medioevo, Spoleto):77–117.

———, ed. *The Age of Sutton Hoo.* Woodbridge and Rochester: Boydell, 1992.

———. *Sutton Hoo Research Committee Bulletins, 1983–93.* Woodbridge and Rochester: Boydell, 1993.

———. *Sutton Hoo: Burial Ground of Kings?* Philadelphia: University of Pennsylvania Press, 1998.

Farrell, R., and C. Neuman de Vegvar, eds. *Sutton Hoo: Fifty Years After.* American Early Medieval Studies 2. Oxford, OH: Miami University Department of Art, 1992.

Kendall, C.B., and P.S. Wells, eds. *Voyage to the Other World.* Minneapolis: University of Minnesota Press, 1992.

Martin Carver

SEE ALSO
Barrows; Cemeteries and Burials; Sutton Hoo Regional Survey

Sutton Hoo Regional Survey

The Anglo-Saxon cemetery at Sutton Hoo in England was the center of a major research program between 1983 and 1993, and, as part of this project, an area survey was carried out to put this important site into its local context. The survey will form the basis for a regional research program that aims to understand the settlement patterns and social hierarchy of the Kingdom of East Anglia.

The survey area chosen was centered on Sutton Hoo and the Deben Valley in southeast Suffolk. Between 1983 and 1989, c. 5,000 ha of arable land were systematically searched for surface finds. The survey covered an area of 134 km^2 that is bisected by the River Deben, with two-thirds of the area on light soils derived from sand and gravel and the remainder on heavier boulder clay deposits. The area that was examined represents nearly all of the cultivated land in what is a predominantly arable region. In all cases, each plot of land was walked at 20-m intervals in order to locate concentrations of material that might represent past activity areas. When Anglo-Saxon pottery scatters were located, a more detailed examination ensued using a systematic 25-m square method to build up a reliable database that can be used to rank sites by size and density of ceramic finds. In addition, metalwork scatters of Anglo-Saxon date located by local metal-detector users were also examined in detail for surface finds. The survey took advantage of the exceptional post-Roman ceramic tradition in East Anglia, which allows the early Anglo-Saxon period (early/mid-fifth century to c. A.D. 650), with its tradition of handmade wares, to be distinguished from the middle Saxon period, with its distinctive Ipswich ware (produced c. A.D. 650 to c. A.D. 850), and the late Saxon period, with its Thetford-type wares (produced c. A.D. 850 to c. A.D. 1150).

In the Roman period, southeast Suffolk had a relatively high rural population with clear evidence for extensive land exploitation. The site density for the period up to c. A.D. 400 was one site per km^2 on the heavier clay soils and half that on the lighter soils. The survey results point to a large number of farms in a dispersed settlement pattern over a well-organized landscape. Coin evidence from these sites indicates that an economic decline had set in at least by the late fourth century. While settlement and cemetery sites for the following early Anglo-Saxon period are rarer in the landscape and harder to locate due to the fragile nature of pottery types in this era, clear evidence has been recovered from the lighter soils in the Deben and Fynn Valleys that indicates that these areas began to fill up again in the late fifth and the sixth centuries. Metalwork finds also point to a more widespread phase of settlement in the early and mid-fifth century than had previously been thought. This is shown by recent discoveries of equal-arm and supporting-arm brooches in the area. During this period, the adjoining areas of heavier soils appear to have seen only intermittent use, with little clear evidence for settlement.

It was during the seventh century that the basis for later medieval settlement was laid. This was the period of Sutton Hoo and the foundation of the trading port of Ipswich when the Wuffinga dynasty reached the peak of its influence in an independent kingdom of East Anglia. Through comparison of ceramic collections from early and middle Saxon sites it is apparent that a major settlement shift took place in the seventh century. The Sutton Hoo area survey located twelve scatters of middle Saxon Ipswich-ware pottery sherds. All these pottery scatters represent probable settlements sites of the seventh–ninth centuries, and all of them lie close to present parish churches. It is notable that the only middle Saxon pottery scatter with clear evidence for continuity from the preceding early Anglo-Saxon period is at Rendlesham and is probably the royal vill mentioned by Bede in his *Ecclesiastical History of the English People.* Finally, it should be noted that a period of middle-to-late Saxon (ninth–tenth-century) settlement expansion was identified from the surface survey results. This phase of expansion led to the foundation of the minor settlements recorded in the *Domesday Book.* The majority of these settlements never achieved parish status. The survey results indicate that the basic structure of the settlement pattern and the later parochial system was present by the mid-ninth century.

FURTHER READINGS

Newman, J. East Anglian Kingdom Survey: Final Interim Report on the South-East Suffolk Pilot Survey. *Bulletin of the Sutton Hoo Research Committee* (1989) 6:17–20.

———. The Late Roman and Anglo-Saxon Settlement Pattern in the Sandlings of Suffolk. In *The Age of Sutton Hoo.* Ed. M.O.H. Carver. Woodbridge and Rochester: Boydell, 1992, pp. 25–38.

Wade, K. Regional Survey. *Bulletin of the Sutton Hoo Research Committee* (1986) 4:29–31.

John Newman

SEE ALSO
Ipswich; Ipswich Ware; Survey; Sutton Hoo; Thetford-Type Ware

Sweden

In Swedish archaeology, the Medieval period covers the time span from c. 1100 to 1500, or more specifically 1520, Martin Luther's breach with the Catholic Church. The starting point has been placed as early as 1000 or as late as 1200 for various parts of the country. Earlier portions of the Continental Medieval period are encompassed in Sweden by the migration period (375–550), the Vendel period (550–800), and the Viking Age (800–1050), subdivisions of the pagan Iron Age, whereas medieval archaeology comprises the period of the ascendancy of the Catholic Church in Sweden. Medieval archaeology in Sweden is discussed here as archaeology of the Middle Ages within the geographical confines of the modern Swedish state rather than the boundaries of medieval Sweden. This excludes Finland but includes the former Danish provinces of Scania, Blekinge, and

S

Halland and the Norwegian provinces in the west, especially Bohulän.

Development of the Discipline

The subject of medieval archaeology has been taught in Sweden at Lund University since 1962, with the first doctoral degree granted in 1976. The first professor of the field, Erik Cinthio, was succeeded by Hans Andersson in 1987. Medieval archaeology has been considered almost synonymous with historical archaeology in Sweden. Before inaugurating the academic study of medieval archaeology at Lund, work in this field was carried out by specialists from other disciplines, especially history and art history. Medieval archaeology struggled to attain its own niche, and some have described it as a field with an identity crisis. The journal *META,* published since 1979 by the Society for Medieval Archaeology in Lund, has served as a Swedish-language forum for vigorous discussion of the theory, methods, and goals of medieval archaeology as its study matures.

In the 1960s and 1970s, Swedish medieval archaeology was dominated by urban archaeology in the southern province of Scania. This largely resulted from the ancient monuments law, which stipulates that archaeological investigations must be carried out when any modern development will affect previous occupation layers. The most extensive excavations were concentrated in historical urban centers of southern Sweden during the building boom of this period, and it is here that Swedish medieval archaeology was born. During the 1990s, the focus began to shift from purely urban archaeology to studying relationships between urban centers and their rural hinterlands, and archaeometric advances have been made in dendrochronology (tree-ring dating), iron technology, and osteology. Besides studies of town and countryside, medieval archaeology has become concerned with the sociopolitical role of churches, castles, and fortifications; investigations into trade, shipping, and numismatics; demographic patterns of medieval populations; and issues of ethnicity focusing on the Saami (Lapp) population of northern Sweden.

Urban Archaeology

The earliest phases of a few towns date to the Viking period, but the greatest development of towns was in the twelfth and thirteenth centuries. Excavation of towns with medieval remains has been necessitated by modern development in the old town centers. Few such investigations have resulted in detailed publication, but the countrywide Medieval Towns *(Medeltidsstaden)* Project, initiated in 1976, has published reports on individual towns within the boundaries of modern Sweden. The monographs in this series collected background material about historical sources and previous archaeological investigations, focusing on topographical and structural description of the layout and extent of towns from their earliest phases through later periods. Emphasis is now moving beyond descriptive groundwork toward research on topics itemized above but continues to center on occupation deposits examined by traditional archaeological methods rather than investigation of standing structures, which has been entrusted to art and architectural historians.

Masonry churches and castles are the only preserved medieval standing structures in most towns, with the exception of Stockholm and Visby. Towns were built largely of wood, and remains of these early wooden buildings are found in excavated occupation deposits. There is great interest in the conservation of well-preserved wood and its dating by dendrochronological analyses. Style and layout of the oldest wooden urban structures have Viking roots, and changes after a period of expansion c. A.D. 1200 have been traced to foreign influences. From pre-Viking through medieval times, some towns were superseded by others due to political, economic, or environmental factors, such as at Lödöse-Göteborg on the west coast and the progression of Helgö-Birka-Sigtuna-Stockholm due to land rise and shore displacement in the Mälar area. Other towns, however, including the ecclesiastical centers of Uppsala, Lund, and Skara, have remained in the same location to the present day. In the thirteenth century, towns with ties to the German Hansa, particularly Stockholm, Kalmar, Malmö, and Visby, adapted to Continental patterns.

Lund's reputation as the center of medieval archaeology studies accounts for why it is perhaps the best-studied example of a medieval town. It was founded c. 1020 on an earlier craft-production site, and the archbishopric was placed here from c. 1100. The town has remained in the same location, so occupation deposits are particularly deep, often extending below 8 m; thus, the earlier layout of medieval Lund can be studied only through excavation.

Visby is the best-preserved medieval town of Sweden, with stone fortifications and numerous church ruins. Stockholm was altered extensively in the seventeenth century but retains many standing stone structures. From 1978 to 1980, one of the most extensive archaeological excavations in Sweden was carried out within Stockholm on the island Helgeandsholmen near the Royal Palace. The excavation was necessitated by a plan to build a parking garage under the existing parliament building. Investigations revealed late twelfth-century fortifications, thirteenth-century enlargement of the ship channel, and fourteenth-century foundations of a hospital and old persons' home for the poor and the sick, Helgeandshuset (the House of the Holy Ghost). The hospital was first mentioned in a 1301 document and remained in operation until 1531, with a cemetery used through the whole period. This waterlogged site allowed good preservation of organic materials, including several boats, leather, wood, and food residues. Urban archaeology gained recognition with this extensive excavation, and the city of Stockholm procured a medieval museum within part of what had been planned as the parking garage for parliament members.

Sigtuna and Lödöse, both important for the history of Swedish numismatics, also built new museums to present excavations of their medieval origins. At Sigtuna, a precursor of Stockholm, the earliest (and only briefly active) royal mint in Sweden was discovered, dating to c. 1000. After an apparent hiatus of c. 150 years, minting was resumed at several locations, including Gamla (Old) Lödöse, where coin impressions were found in leather padding materials. Lödöse served as a port of international significance for agricultural exports in the early Medieval period, but its function as a gateway to the interior was gradually replaced by a succession of towns closer to the sea. The coastal areas were held by Norway and Denmark, and Sweden did not have direct access to the North Sea until the seventeenth century, when modern-day Göteborg was established. Lödöse shrank in size and importance; thus, its occupation layers are not as deep as those of Lund and its topography can be more easily studied. Archaeological investigation of Lödöse reflects the concerns of the Medieval Towns Project with topographical aspects of town development.

Maritime Archaeology, Markets, and Fortifications

Aspects related to urban archaeology that have not received much attention are harbors, marketplaces, and fortifications. Maritime archaeology depends upon cartographic records, place names, and anecdotal information from seamen, as well as underwater archaeology. Markets without permanent buildings often did not leave significant structural traces, hampering stratigraphic study, though artifacts and historical records offer evidence of trade. One unusually well-studied example is the herring market at Skanör in Scania. The study of defensive structures has received little concern archaeologically, though not for lack of substantial remains but due to lack of endangerment by modern development.

Rural Archaeology

While the development of urban archaeology resulted from intense rescue archaeology in cities with modern development, the archaeology of rural areas has been described as being in its infancy. With no overarching organization to compare to the Medieval Towns Project, archaeology of rural medieval Sweden has concentrated on few sites beyond research incidental to town studies. Rural settlements have been inadequately investigated, although some cemeteries have been excavated, providing material for osteological analysis and demographic estimates of populations. Rural archaeology is more variable than urban archaeology, with different subsistence strategies in various regions of the country, from the southern agricultural areas through the forests to the northern mountains. Investigations of iron-producing districts have provided information about the development of technology and transportation in the countryside.

Saami Archaeology

The study of the Saami, the indigenous people of Norrland, comprises a specific regional and ethnic category of Swedish archaeology that includes, but extends beyond, the temporal bounds of the Medieval period. The archaeology of this vast region was first studied extensively in the 1960s and 1970s, preceding the construction of hydroelectric power plants. Research has concentrated on resource utilization and the transition from a hunter-gatherer to a pastoral society, from hunting wild reindeer to herding reindeer. The rest of medieval Sweden followed a different economic model with its transition from a hierarchically structured agricultural economy to a state-controlled market economy.

There are large gaps in the archaeological data from certain periods of Saami archaeology, notably from c. A.D. 300–1000 and A.D. 1300–1500. From the intervening period, metal deposits (formerly called *sacrificial sites*) and hearths have been discovered. Artifacts recovered include organic materials such as skis, bows and arrows, and sewn boats. Both forest-zone winter sites and mountain-zone summer hunting camps have been found. The central Swedish area of contact between northern Saami people and southern Germanic people is difficult to interpret. It may reflect some assimilation of Germanic characteristics

S

into Saami culture, though there is heated debate on this issue. Finds dated to 1000–1200 from Vivallen in northwestern Härjedalen near Norway are pivotal for this discussion.

Church Archaeology

Church archaeology was identified as a specific branch of archaeology at a 1981 symposium in Århus, Denmark. Most churches that have been archaeologically investigated date from the Medieval period, so church archaeology is inseparable from medieval archaeology. The archaeology of churches in towns differs considerably from the situation in the countryside. In towns, archaeologists have excavated remains of churches in occupation layers, but in villages and rural areas, medieval churches often are still standing. These surviving structures have needed restoration and modernization, leading to investigations as historical and architectural subjects by academics from other disciplines, especially historians and art historians. This research led to the inventory series Sweden's Churches (Sveriges Kyrkor), begun in 1912 by two art historians. These surveys were based on art-historical methodologies and concerned with questions of dating and typology. The interiors and furnishings of medieval churches were described, including interior funerary monuments, altarpieces, baptismal fonts, wood and stone sculptures, mural paintings, and wooden furniture. Historical, ecclesiastical, and theological background material on saints and patrons was included.

Archaeological investigations of churches have concentrated on dating by stratigraphical and dendrochronological analyses. Dendrochronology is useful not only for timber churches but also for dating original wooden roof trusses in stone churches. Knowledge of the history of building technology allows specialists to distinguish original from replacement timbers, and more sensitive dating by this scientific method can supplement inadequate historical records pertaining to the establishment of churches. Other archaeological studies are examining ecclesiastical organization of churches and their parishes, the roles of churches in urbanization processes, and the social and economic organization of church construction (such as studies of stoneworker mobility traced through mason's marks).

Special consideration has been given to the Uppsala Cathedral and church ruins in Visby. Church archaeology also includes the study of defensive churches, such as on the Kalmar coast and the island of Öland. Recent studies of the spatial organization of monasteries and convents before the Reformation, such as the foundation at Varnhem, move beyond the inventory mentality of earlier investigations. Examination of convents is one of the few instances besides demography in which gender studies have begun to take root in Swedish medieval archaeology.

Numismatics

Coinage increases in archaeological importance for dating and economic history during the Medieval period. Hoards hidden beneath dwelling floors continue to be found, as in the preceding Viking period. A special branch of medieval numismatics related to church archaeology concerns the kyrkfynd, or church finds, composed of cumulative finds of coins found beneath church floors. The coins are assumed to have been intended as offerings but inadvertently dropped, one by one, over a long period of time. Church finds provide data about the level and frequency of coin use in the whole country, one of the few sources informative about monetary usage by the peasant or rural population. They indicate that monetization, the general use of coins for transactions throughout the population, increased beginning in the second half of the thirteenth century as a result of economic changes and increasing domination by European culture. Coins found beneath church floors differ from those found in hoards, with the former composed of lower-denomination Swedish coinage handled by peasants and the latter consisting of higher-denomination and foreign coins (especially German and English) used by merchants and the elite.

Other archaeologically significant finds include the lead and leather impressions used in cushioning the blow of striking unifaced coins called bracteates. Leather impressions from c. 1150 were excavated at Lödöse, and a lead impression from the earliest Swedish coinage was found in excavations at Sigtuna.

Prospects for Future Research

As a relatively new field of study, medieval archaeology in Sweden has blazed a trail transcending traditional disciplinary boundaries. It owes a large debt to art history and cultural history but also has attempted to distinguish itself from those disciplines. Early research in the field was represented by descriptive cataloging projects such as Medeltidsstaden and Sveriges Kyrkor. The next phase involved application of archaeological methodologies such as stratigraphic excavation and dendrochronology. Now the field is moving toward more complex interpretive methodologies, and increasing attention is being paid to questions about ethnicity and identity, power and gender relations, material culture, and lives of individuals. Not to be forgotten, however, is the pressing need to publish the enormous numbers of artifacts recovered in excavations of medieval town and fortification sites. Medieval archaeology as a discipline has come of age.

FURTHER READINGS

Ambrosiani, Björn, and Hans Andersson. Urban Archaeology in Sweden. In *European Towns: Their Archaeology and Early History*. Ed. M.W. Barley. London: Council for British Archaeology/Academic, 1977, pp. 103–126.

Andersson, Hans. Reflections on Swedish Medieval Archaeology. In *Swedish Archaeology, 1976–1980*. Ed. Åke Hyenstrand and Pontus Hellström. Stockholm: Svenska Arkeologiska Samfundet/Swedish Archaeological Society, 1983, pp. 52–60.

Andersson, Hans, Peter Carelli, and Lars Ersgård, eds. *Visions of the Past: Trends and Traditions in Swedish Medieval Archaeology*. Lund Studies in Medieval Archaeology 19. Philadelphia: Coronet, 1997.

Andrén, Anders. The Early Town in Scandinavia. In *The Birth of Europe: Archaeology and Social Development in the First Millennium A.D.* Ed. Klavs Randsborg. Analecta Romana Institutu Danici Supplementum 16. Rome: L'Erma di Bretschneider, 1989, pp. 173–177.

Arrhenius, Birgit. Knives from Eketorp: An Evidence of the Growing Influence of the Centralized Production from Medieval Town Communities. *Laborativ arkeologi* (1989) 3:97–124.

Borg, Kaj, Ulf Näsman, and Erik Wegraeus, eds. *Eketorp: Fortification and Settlement on Öland, Sweden: The Setting*. Stockholm: Almqvist and Wiksell International, 1979.

Broberg, Anders, and Kenneth Svensson. Urban and Rural Consumption Patterns in Eastern Central Sweden, A.D. 1000–1700. In *Theoretical Approaches to Artefacts, Settlement, and Society: Studies in Honour of Mats P. Malmer*. Ed. Göran Burenhult, Anders Carlsson, Åke Hyenstrand, and Torstein Sjøvold. BAR International Series 366 (ii). Oxford: British Archaeological Reports, 1987, pp. 479–488.

Carlsson, Kristina. Urban Archaeology. In *Swedish Archaeology, 1981–1985*. Ed. Anders Carlsson, David Damell, Pontus Hellström, Åke Hyenstrand, and Agneta Åkerlund. Stockholm: Svenska Arkeologiska Samfundet, 1987, pp. 141–148.

Christophersen, Axel. Raw Material, Resources, and Production Capacity in Early Medieval Comb Manufacture in Lund. *Meddelanden från Lunds Universitets Historiska Museum* (1979–1980) 3:150–165.

Cinthio, Erik. Medieval Archaeology as a Research Subject. *Meddelanden från Lunds Universitets Historiska Museum* (1962–1963):186–202.

Crumlin-Pedersen, Ole, and Birgitte Munch Thye, eds. *The Ship as Symbol in Prehistoric and Medieval Scandinavia*. Publications from the National Museum. Studies in Archaeology and History 1. Copenhagen: National Museum, 1995.

Dahlbäck, Göran, ed. *Helgeandsholmen: 1000 År i Stockholms Ström* (with English summary). Stockholm: Liber Förlag, 1982.

Ersgård, Lars, Marie Holmström, and Kristina Lamm, eds. *Rescue Research: Reflections of Society in Sweden, 700–1700 A.D.* Stockholm: Riksantikvarieämbetet, 1992.

Forsberg, Lars. Saami Archaeology in Sweden, 1985–1990: An Overview. *Current Swedish Archaeology* (1995) 3:97–104.

Högberg, U., E. Iregren, C.-H. Siven, and L. Diener. Maternal Deaths in Medieval Sweden: An Osteological and Life Table Analysis. *Journal of Biosocial Science* (1987) 19:495–503.

Hyenstrand, Åke. Iron and Iron Economy in Sweden. In *Iron and Man in Prehistoric Sweden*. Ed. Helen Clarke. Stockholm: Jernkontoret, 1979, pp. 134–156.

Jonsson, Kenneth. Numismatics. *Current Swedish Archaeology* (1995) 3:163–171.

Klackenberg, Henrik. *Monetra Nostra: Monetarisering i Medeltidens Sverige* (with English summary). Lund Studies in Medieval Archaeology 10. Stockholm: Almqvist and Wiksell International, 1992.

Lindahl, Anders. *Information through Sherds: A Case Study of the Early Glazed Earthenware from Dalby, Scania*. Lund Studies in Medieval Archaeology 3. Lund: Universitetet, Institut för Arkeologi, 1986.

Redin, Lars. Medieval Coins in Recent Archaeological Excavations in Sweden. In *Coins and Archaeology*. Ed. Helen Clarke and Erik Schia. BAR International Series 556. Oxford: British Archaeological Reports, 1989, pp. 9–14.

———. Some Remarks on Historical Archaeology in Sweden. *Current Swedish Archaeology* (1995) 3:85–95.

Sundnér, Barbro. Church Archaeology. In *Swedish Archaeology, 1981–1985*. Ed. Anders Carlsson, David Damell, Pontus Hellström, Åke Hyenstrand, and Agneta Åkerlund. Stockholm: Svenska Arkeologiska Samfundet, 1987, pp. 149–159.

S

Zachrisson, Inger. *Lapps and Scandinavians: Archaeological Finds from Northern Sweden.* Early Norrland 10. Stockholm: Kungl. Vitterhets Historie och Antikvitetsakdemien/Almqvist and Wiksell International, 1976.

———. The South Saami Culture in Archaeological Finds and West Nordic Written Sources from A.D. 800–1300. In *Social Approaches to Viking Studies.* Ed. Ross Samson. Glasgow: Cruithne, 1991, pp. 191–199.

———. A Review of Archaeological Research on Saami Prehistory in Sweden. *Current Swedish Archaeology* (1993) 1:171–182.

See also the following journals and series:

Medeltidsstaden. Rapporter (with English summaries). Stockholm: Riksantikvarieämbetet och Statens Historiska Museer, 1976–.

META. Medeltidsarkeologisk Tidskrift. Lund: Medeltidsarkeologiska Föreningen, 1979–.

Sveriges Kyrkor. Originated by Sigurd Curman and Johnny Roosval. Stockholm: Kungl. Vitterhets Historie och Antikvitetsakdemien/Almqvist and Wiksell, 1912–.

Nancy L. Wicker

SEE ALSO

Birka; Church Archaeology; Dendrochronology; Gender; Helgö; Uppsala Cathedral

T

Tephrochronology
See Farm Abandonment (Iceland).

Thetford

Thetford, now an English market town, was a place of great size and importance in the late Saxon period (850–1066). In an area of light soil at the confluence of the Little Ouse and the Thet Rivers, it sits astride the main access route into northern East Anglia, the prehistoric track known as the Icknield Way. The Little Ouse is fordable in several places at Thetford, the highest navigable point for shallow-draught boats. Recent limited archaeological excavations and chance discoveries have shown that a large middle Saxon (c. 650–850) settlement was strung out along the south bank of the river outside the northwest corner of the late Saxon town. Its extent and status are still uncertain, but coins suggest it was probably more than a mere village.

Whatever the nature of its middle Saxon predecessor, the late Saxon town grew up, sometime during the later ninth century, on a new site with such rapidity that by c. 950 it covered an area of c. 75 ha, largely on the south side of the river. The earliest mention of Thetford in the written record is in the *Anglo-Saxon Chronicle* for 870, when the Danish Viking army took winter quarters at Theodford. Whether the invaders chose a newly founded town in which to overwinter or a convenient spot next to the river crossings is uncertain, but the archaeological evidence shows that there was a booming industrial urban settlement there by c. 900. At about this time, a substantial defensive ditch and timber-reveted rampart were constructed around the town to the south of the river over more than 1.5 km. The medieval street pattern strongly suggests that the part of the town north of the river was also defended, probably at the same period.

The comparatively small area excavated in the late Saxon town south of the river, much of which was abandoned in the twelfth century, makes an assessment of the degree of planning and zoning use in the layout of the streets and areas of activity difficult. By c. 900, roads constructed of rammed flint pebbles were in use in many parts, as were timber buildings, some immediately adjacent to the road, others set back.

Manufacturing was of major importance. Pottery production was carried out on a very large scale, as was iron-working, both smelting and smithing. Evidence for copper-alloy working is widespread, less so silversmithing. Bone, antler, and horn working were major activities, as was textile production. Thetford was probably a center for the minting of "St. Edmund memorial" coins in the period c. 890–920, and there was certainly a mint there in the reign of Eadgar (959–975).

Thetford continued to expand throughout the tenth and early eleventh centuries despite being sacked twice, in 1004 and 1010. The town defenses went out of use, and several suburbs grew up. The *Domesday Book* tells us that at the time of the Norman Conquest in 1066 it was the sixth-largest town in England, with a population of about five thousand. About twelve churches were mentioned, and there were probably others. The Norman Conquest had no directly adverse effects on Thetford's fortunes. In 1071 the bishopric of East Anglia was transferred from North Elmham, and at about the same time a huge earthwork castle was thrown up by the earl of East Anglia within an Iron Age hillfort on the north bank of the river.

T

From the end of the eleventh century, Thetford began to shrink, probably because of the rise in importance of Bury St. Edmunds and Norwich and then through the foundation and rapid rise of King's Lynn. Although *Domesday* does not indicate a greatly above-normal decline in 1086 (224 out of 943 burgess tenements were empty), the bishop moved his see to the flourishing Norwich in 1094/1095. Archaeology shows that the reduction in occupation was stronger on the south side of the river. The northern area was given a boost when the newly founded Cluniac priory moved there in 1114.

Taxation records show the decline continuing in the twelfth century, and the last records of a mint are in the reign of John (1199–1215). A small castle built south of the river was briefly occupied in the 1140s. Some pre-Conquest churches on the south side survived into the Medieval period or beyond, but settlement became predominantly rural. The medieval town was of local importance only, but of sufficient significance to attract two friaries in the fourteenth century.

FURTHER READINGS

Andrews, P. *Excavations at Redcastle Furze, 1988–9.* East Anglian Archaeology 72. Dereham, Norfolk: Field Archaeology Division, Norfolk Museums Service, 1995.

Crosby, A. *A History of Thetford.* Chichester: Phillimore, 1986.

Dallas, C. *Excavations in Thetford by B.K. Davison between 1964 and 1970.* East Anglian Archaeology 62. Dereham, Norfolk: Field Archaeology Division, Norfolk Museums Service, 1993.

Davies, J.A., and T. Gregory. Excavations at Thetford Castle, 1962 and 1985–6. In *The Iron Age Forts of Norfolk,* by John A. Davies. *East Anglian Archaeology* (1992) 54:1–30. Dereham, Norfolk: Field Archaeology Division, Norfolk Museums Service.

Dunsmore, S., with D. Carr. *The Late Saxon Town of Thetford: An Archaeological and Historical Survey.* East Anglian Archaeology 4. Dereham, Norfolk: Norfolk Archaeological Unit, 1976.

Knocker, G.M. Excavations at Red Castle, Thetford. *Norfolk Archaeology* (1967) 34:119–186.

Rogerson, A., and C. Dallas. *Excavations at Thetford, 1948–59 and 1973–80.* East Anglian Archaeology 22. Dereham, Norfolk: Norfolk Archaeological Unit, 1984.

Andrew Rogerson

SEE ALSO
Norwich; Thetford-Type Ware

Thetford-Type Ware

This wheel-thrown, hard, sandy fabric, fired under reducing conditions in permanent single-flue undraught kilns, was produced in Norfolk and Suffolk between c. 850 and c. 1100 or a little later. As with other late Saxon or Saxo-Norman pottery types, dating is still rather vague, with the only closely dated pot being that containing the Morley St. Peter (Norfolk) coin hoard that was buried in c. 925.

In the later ninth and the tenth centuries, the production centers of Thetford-type ware were the large towns of Ipswich, Norwich, and Thetford, the latter giving its name to the ware because of a particularly well-preserved kiln excavated there in 1949. In the late tenth and the eleventh centuries, probably to supply a quickly expanding population, a number of kilns were established in the countryside. All the known examples are in Norfolk. Only one production site, at Grimston in the northwest, was of any size, and this was to continue as a major pottery throughout the Middle Ages. Thetford-type wares occur commonly throughout Norfolk and Suffolk and penetrate into the neighboring counties of Essex, Cambridgeshire, and Lincolnshire, where they are not easily distinguished from other Saxo-Norman gray sandy wares.

Scientific methods have failed so far to differentiate successfully among the fabrics of pots produced at the various centers, and little progress has been made in establishing a sequence of forms or fabrics throughout the period of manufacture. Some "late-looking" fabrics have been recognized, and the rather coarser and less consistently reduced fabrics produced at rural centers are distinguishable.

The characteristic form is the tallish and relatively thin-walled jar, with flat or sagging base, and a rim that is most commonly everted and hollowed internally. Jars are sometimes decorated with a horizontal band of diamond or square motifs impressed with a roller stamp or roulette on the shoulder. Bowls are less common and more varied in shape and occur more frequently in the eleventh century. The spouted pitcher is really a large jar with the addition of a spout and three handles. Storage jars are large and usually strengthened on the rim and the body with applied thumbed strips. Other forms include cresset lamps, handled, spouted, or socketed bowls, crucibles, and costrels.

FURTHER READINGS

Atkin, M., B. Ayers, and J. Jennings. Thetford-Type Ware Production in Norwich. *East Anglian Archaeology* (1983) 17:61–97.

Clarke, H. Excavations on a Kiln Site at Grimston, Pott Row, Norfolk. *Norfolk Archaeology* (1970) 35:79–95.

Dallas, C. *Excavations in Thetford by B.K. Davison between 1964 and 1970.* East Anglian Archaeology 62. Dereham, Norfolk: Field Archaeological Division, Norfolk Museums Service, 1993.

Dunning, G.C. Pottery of the Late Anglo-Saxon Period in England. *Medieval Archaeology* (1959) 3:1–78.

Hurst, J.G. The Pottery. In *The Archaeology of Anglo-Saxon England.* Ed. D.M. Wilson. London: Methuen, 1976, pp. 283–348.

McCarthy, M.R., and C.M. Brooks. *Medieval Pottery in Britain, A.D. 900–1600.* Leicester: Leicester University Press, 1988.

Rogerson, A., and N. Adams. A Saxo-Norman Kiln at Bircham. *East Anglian Archaeology* (1978) 8:33–44.

Rogerson, A., and C. Dallas. *Excavations at Thetford, 1948–59 and 1973–80.* East Anglian Archaeology 22. Dereham, Norfolk: Norfolk Archaeological Division, Norfolk Museums Service, 1984.

Smedley, N., and E.J. Owles. Some Suffolk Kilns. IV. Saxon Kilns in Cox Lane Ipswich, 1961. *Proceedings of the Suffolk Institute of Archaeology* (1963) 29:304–335.

Wade, K. Excavations at Langhale, Kirkstead. *East Anglian Archaeology* (1976) 2:101–129.

West, S.E. Excavations at Cox Lane (1958) and at the Town Defences, Shire Hall Yard, Ipswich (1959). *Proceedings of the Suffolk Institute of Archaeology* (1963) 29:233–303.

Andrew Rogerson

SEE ALSO

Ipswich; Ipswich Ware; Norwich; Thetford

Tiles

From the thirteenth century to the sixteenth, ceramic tiles were widely used to pave the floors of the most important buildings of Europe. This entry provides information on the different types of medieval floor tiles, when and where they were used, how they were made, and how their production was organized.

Types of Medieval Floor Tiles

Floor tiles are usually classified by the technique used to decorate them. As medieval tilers were very inventive, there are a wide variety of types. The main techniques are:

1. *Inlaid.* The design is carved in relief on a block of wood (the stamp). The stamp is pressed down onto a red clay quarry leaving an impression of the design. The impression is filled with white clay. The whole surface of the tile is then coated with glaze, and the tile is fired in a kiln. The glaze fires to a lighter color over the white clay than over the red clay of the quarry, giving a two-color effect.

2. *Slip Decorated.* The technique is exactly as above but the impression left by the stamp is only slight (usually less than 1 mm), and the cavity is filled with white clay that has been diluted with water (slip).

3. *Counterrelief.* The clay body is stamped with a design as described above, but the resulting cavity is not filled with white clay. The tiles may be coated with either slip and glaze or just glaze before firing.

4. *Relief.* In this case, the design stands proud of the tile base. To achieve this, the design has to be carved out of the stamp in counterrelief. Alternatively, the clay might be pressed into a mold. As above, the tiles may be coated with either slip and glaze or just glaze before firing.

5. *Mosaic.* The clay is rolled out and either coated with white clay or left bare. It is then cut into shapes using one of a number of different techniques. The tiles are glazed and fired. When laid in a pavement, light- and dark-colored tiles are alternated. Complex geometric patterns, sometimes involving a series of concentric circles, were formed using these tiles.

6. *Line Impressed.* This technique is exactly the same as counterrelief but the impressed designs are linear.

Use of Tiled Floors

Floor tiles have traditionally been dated on stylistic and, more recently, technological grounds. The difficulty of assigning dates on this basis has been highlighted by a gradual increase in the number of independently dated finds (in which the date has been determined on documentary or archaeological grounds) that have not concurred with earlier expectations. In England, for example, relief tiles from St. Albans Abbey were thought to date to the thirteenth century until a much earlier date of c.1165 was suggested on archaeological grounds.

T

While finds from the second half of the twelfth century are known from sites in England and Germany, and are very likely in France, it is from the thirteenth century that the fashion for decorative ceramic floors became widespread across much of Europe. The floors were generally reserved for buildings with important ceremonial functions, in particular the churches and chapter houses of the monasteries, royal apartments, and the private chapels of powerful members of the aristocracy.

In the fourteenth and fifteenth centuries, floor tiles continued to be used by the monasteries but were also found in parish churches and in the homes of wealthy merchants and members of the gentry. In the fifteenth century, ceramic floors were being used in the more secular buildings of monasteries, such as infirmaries and guesthouses, and in industrial buildings where there was a risk of fire. From the later fourteenth century, tiled floors were often less elaborate than earlier, with some floors made entirely of plain tiles. These were usually laid out in a checkered arrangement, like a chessboard, alternating light- and dark-colored tiles.

Manufacture of Tiles

The coarseness of the fabric used to make many medieval floor tiles suggests that little time was spent preparing the clay. Sand and other ground-up material might be added to improve its working, drying, or firing qualities, but in many cases it is likely that the raw material was used as found. The clay would either be rolled out and cut to size or shaped in molds. The sand on the base of most tiles shows that the tilers used a sandied work surface. Dimensions, both depth and the upper surface measurements of square tiles, vary considerably. Sometimes a board with nails knocked through the corners and the center would be used to hold the clay still while the tiles were cut out. The holes made by these nails are often still visible after firing, especially when a slip has not been applied. They are frequently found on late medieval plain-glazed tiles and are thought to be a manufacturing technique that originated in the Low Countries. The sides of the tiles were cut at an angle, sloping inward from top to bottom, so that they could be firmly fixed into the mortar screed. In the thirteenth and early fourteenth centuries, keys were sometimes cut into the lower surfaces of the tiles. They might be scooped out with the point of a knife or made as a series of stabbed cuts. Keying may have been intended to help the base of the tiles adhere to the mortar but would also have assisted in the drying and firing of thicker tiles.

The prepared quarries would be left to dry before decoration and glazing. Analysis suggests that the glaze contained a variety of metals, as might be expected if scrap metals were used. Intentional additions of some metals may have been made in order to produce particular colors. Additions of copper to a clear lead glaze will, for example, produce a green color, while iron will glaze yellow over a white clay and brown over a red clay.

After glazing, the tiles would be loaded into a kiln. Square tiles were stacked on edge, while mosaic shapes were supported by specially made kiln furniture. The temperature required to successfully fuse the glaze is c. 1,000°C. The body fabric of the tiles may change color during firing. Clay containing iron fires red in the presence of oxygen (said to be oxidized), but gray or black in its absence (said to be reduced). The outer surfaces of many medieval tiles are oxidized, while their centers (not reached by the oxygen) are reduced.

Recording variations in the way tiles were manufactured and decorated allows specialists to identify the products of individual industries. Comparison of these industries can then lead to broader analyses of medieval production and economic life.

Organization of Tile Production

Most work on the organization of the floor-tile industry has been done by English scholars. All known examples of early and mid-thirteenth-century kilns producing floor tiles are located in the countryside on the lands of monastic granges or other high-status sites. The kilns were quite small (1–3 m square) but substantially built, and they were constructed in order to make floor tiles for the institution on whose land they were sited. Production does not appear to have been driven by cost efficiency. Techniques were time consuming; there was much experimentation; and the quality of the end product was high. It seems likely that the means of production were provided by the consumers.

Commercial (i.e., profit-driven) production outside the monastic sphere is known from the last quarter of the thirteenth century and seems to have been carried out in a variety of circumstances. Later, in the fourteenth and fifteenth centuries, decorated tiles were often produced alongside a range of other ceramics, forming only one aspect of a more broadly based industry. These kilns were often located on the outskirts of towns. Distribution was generally fairly restricted, although longer distances were feasible when water transport was available. Late medieval plain tiles made in the Low Countries appear to have traveled farthest. They are found at many sites around the North Sea as well as in Ireland.

FURTHER READINGS

Eames, E.S. *English Medieval Tiles*. London: British Museum, 1985.

———. *Catalogue of Medieval Lead-Glazed Earthenware Tiles in the Department of Medieval and Later Antiquities, British Museum*. 3 Vols. London: British Museum, 1980.

Eames, E.S., and T. Fanning. *Irish Medieval Tiles*. Dublin: Royal Irish Academy, 1988.

Landgraf, Eleonore. *Ornamentierte Bodenfliesen des Mittelalters in Süd- und Westdeutschland, 1150–1550*. Stuttgart: Landesdenkmalamt Baden-Württemberg, 1993.

Norton, E.C. *Carreaux de pavement du moyen âge et de la Renaissance: Collections du musée Carnavalet*. Catalogues d'Art et d'Histoire de Musée Carnavalet VII. Paris: Musées, 1992.

J. Stopford

Tintagel

Tintagel, an island on the north coast of Cornwall, England, is inextricably linked with Arthurian traditions and romance. The medieval chronicler Geoffrey of Monmouth, in his *History of the Kings of Britain* (c. 1135–1138), placed King Arthur at Tintagel. No earlier Arthurian traditions or folklore exist, and *all* later references to Arthur at Tintagel rest on this. Such other traditions as exist would point more plausibly to a connection with King Mark or even Tristan and Iseult. However, the modern village of Tintagel is economically dependent upon Arthurian tourist traffic, and the Hall of Chivalry is but the most obvious manifestation of this. In the final analysis, the Arthurian connection is literary and late, not archaeological and contemporary.

Partly in reaction to the Arthurian connection, archaeological investigation in the 1930s undertaken by C.A. Ralegh Radford led to a reinterpretation of Tintagel Island as a Celtic monastery in the post-Roman period. A stone-built chapel and groups of stone-built rectangular buildings, interpreted as monastic cells, have been laid out for the public on the site. Subsequently, a prominent castle was built on the site, interpreted by Radford as the work of Earl Reginald of Cornwall c. 1141.

Dating evidence for the island is provided by pottery, including a remarkable collection of imported wares from the Mediterranean, first identified by Radford. Some have incised cross-designs; Radford interpreted them as vessels for the import of wine for Christian observances and ritual. Further work on the analysis and sourcing of this pottery has refined many of the original identifications. The vast amount of material from Tintagel (greater than that from all other sites in Britain and Ireland) has led to a reconsideration of the pottery's function by Charles Thomas. Current opinion favors a secular and economic interpretation, with Tintagel acting as the entry point for both bulk goods in amphorae and finer table wares, in exchange perhaps for raw materials such as Cornish tin.

Many more building foundations were recognized as a result of a disastrous grass fire on the site in the 1980s. This new evidence further supported Thomas's secular interpretation of the site. Small-scale investigations in the 1980s, followed by a research program led by Christopher D. Morris in the 1990s, have focused attention upon the nature and dating of the buildings on the terraces around the island. In addition to their role in trade and exchange, these structures are now interpreted as a secular citadel, perhaps seasonally occupied by the Cornish kings and princes and their retinues in the fifth and sixth centuries A.D. The castle is now reinterpreted as the work of Earl Richard in the 1230s.

Missing from the island is clear evidence of a contemporary graveyard and/or chapel. This is now provided at St. Materiana's Church on the headland opposite the island. Here Charles Thomas and Jacqueline Nowakowski have uncovered clear evidence of a sacred space with burials and ritual activities in use in the fifth and sixth centuries. This was followed by the building of a church in the late Saxon period (850–1066) and its refoundation in the Norman period (eleventh–twelfth centuries). The island and the churchyard can now be regarded as parts of one archaeological entity from the fifth century onward.

Clearly, Tintagel was a significant center of secular political and economic power in the immediately post-Roman centuries. This may explain Geoffrey of Monmouth's forging of the Arthurian connection in the twelfth century and the building of the castle in the thirteenth. The latter is then perhaps plausibly explained not in strategic terms but as a medieval "folly."

FURTHER READINGS

Thomas, Charles. *Tintagel: Arthur and Archaeology*. London: English Heritage/Batsford, 1993.

Christopher D. Morris

T

Toft

The term *toft* is thought to be of Scandinavian origin (Icelandic *topt, tuft*, meaning "a piece of ground" or "homestead"; Danish *toft*, "an enclosed homefield") and occurs as the suffix of place names in the areas of England that were most heavily influenced by Scandinavia. In the middle and later Middle Ages, it sometimes occurs in a literary context as the equivalent of *campus* (which otherwise more generally equates with "field" and often "open field") and in *Piers Plowman* (prologue, 14) as "an elevated piece of land" appropriate to the construction of a tower. The term *edor* was used in the earliest Anglo-Saxon law code (that of King Æthelberht of Kent) to define the habitative enclosure of someone of law-worthy status. Archaeological exploration of substantial buildings and associated enclosures of a comparable date (at Chalton Down, Cowdery's Down, and Thirlings, for example) suggests that this term defined a space that differed significantly as regards its use and status from the typical toft of the middle and later Middle Ages. *Toft* does, therefore, appear to be a term that is relevant only to the later period, from at earliest the ninth century but primarily to the post-Conquest period. It often occurs in Latinized form, as *tofta/-us/-um, tophtum, tufta*, etc.

In an archaeological context, the term is used quite specifically to distinguish the enclosure that contains a peasant house and farmyard from other enclosures. It is more widely known from excavations of examples laid out no earlier than the twelfth century and in occupation during the thirteenth and fourteenth centuries, when medieval population was at its height.

Such tofts are distinguished by substantial boundaries that regularly incorporate banks, walls, hedges, and ditches in various combinations, with access via one or more gates. The unusual degree of investment in the boundary is a common feature that implies an intent both to exclude and to contain, separating one parcel of private space from other adjacent examples as well as from public space, such as roadways. Such clear boundaries do not at present seem to be a characteristic of rural settlement prior to the inception of medieval villages.

Within the toft are to be found varying arrangements of buildings (of kinds detailed in the entry on Deserted Medieval Villages), generally now traceable under excavation in the form of postholes, construction trenches, padstones, or dwarf walls. Where buildings are defined primarily by individual postholes, the process of successive rebuildings over two or more centuries can render such structures very difficult to interpret. Alongside these roofed areas lies unroofed space, sections of which were often surfaced with stone and used intensively for a variety of purposes, including hard-standing for overwintering or stalling of livestock; storage of hay and other provender; timber and fuel; fowl pens; cooking fires and ovens; threshing floors; rubbish, cess-, and quarry pits; and as access ways to and from buildings and routeways.

Most excavations that have occurred on deserted or shrunken medieval villages or farmsteads have concentrated on tofts and the buildings they contain. These are, therefore, the best-researched single component in the complex suite of physical remains that variously make up the characteristic settlement forms of the medieval peasantry.

FURTHER READINGS

Astill, G., and A. Grant, eds. *The Countryside of Medieval England*. Oxford: Basil Blackwell, 1988, pp. 51–61.

N.J. Higham

SEE ALSO

Croft; Deserted Medieval Villages; Messuage

Trelleborg

See Trelleborg Fortresses.

Trelleborg Fortresses

The Trelleborg fortresses are a group of geometrically planned Viking fortresses known only in Denmark. They include Trelleborg in Sjælland, Nonnebakken in Fyn (of which very little is known), Fyrkat in northeast Jutland, and Aggersborg in northern Jutland (Fig. 1). They were built c. A.D. 980 (two of them are dated by dendrochronology), undoubtedly by King Harald Bluetooth, who died c. 987. Among his other great achievements were the conversion of Denmark, monuments at Jelling, and an extension of the Danevirke. The fortresses lasted for only a very short time and were never repaired. They are the oldest-known royal fortresses in Denmark.

The Trelleborg fortresses are constructed of timber, turf, and earth. They have the same strict overall plan to which no exact parallel is known (the fortress excavated in Trelleborg in Scania, Sweden, does not belong to this specific group). They have a circular rampart with gates at the four points of the compass; the inner area is divided into four equal parts by streets between opposite gates. the quadrants have large (c. 30-m-long) bow-sided houses

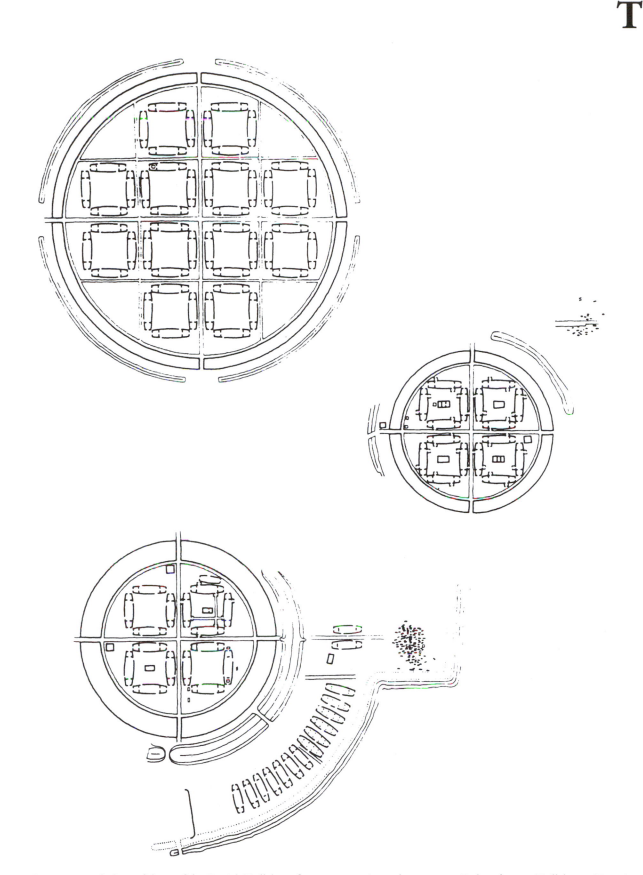

FIG. 1. Reconstructed plans of three of the Danish Trelleborg fortresses: *top,* Aggersborg; *center,* Fyrkat; *bottom:* Trelleborg. (Drawing by Holger Schmidt. Scale 1:4000.)

arranged in regular quadrangles (such a house was reconstructed in full scale at Trelleborg in 1942 and at Fyrkat in 1985, the latter taking into account research after 1942). The fortresses differed, however, in size (the inner diameter of Aggersborg being 240 m, of Trelleborg 134 m, and of Fyrkat and Nonnebakken 120 m) and in various details, and Trelleborg had an outer ward (also geometrically planned) outside the circular rampart. At Trelleborg and Fyrkat, the fortress's cemetery has been found just outside the rampart; there were graves of men, women, and children, some of them with grave goods (Fig. 2).

The fortresses are not mentioned in written sources. The interpretation of their function and purpose must be based on archaeology. The theory that they were winter camps and barracks for the armies who raided and finally conquered England under Sven Forkbeard (c. 960–1014), the son of king Harald Bluetooth, and Cnut the Great (c. 995–1035), c. A.D. 1000 has been dismissed, partly on chronological grounds. They were all situated on important inland roads and either had no access or rather difficult access to the open sea. Their main purpose was probably to control Denmark at a time of growing unrest,

although Aggersborg may well have played a role in relation to control and exploitation of the international Limfjord traffic and to Danish power in Norway. Perhaps the Trelleborg fortresses lost their role after Sven Forkbeard's successful revolt against his father c. 987.

FURTHER READINGS

Bonde, N., and K. Christensen. Trelleborgs alder: Dendrokronologisk datering (Full English translation). *Aarbøger for Nordisk Oldkyndighed og Historie* (1982): 111–152.

Christiansen, T.E. Træningslejr eller tvangsborg *Kuml* (1970):43–63. English summary.

———. Trelleborgs alder: Arkæologisk datering (Full English translation). *Aarbøger for Nordisk Oldkyndighed og Historie* (1982):84–110.

Nørlund, P. *Trelleborg.* Nordiske Fortidsminder IV: I (with English summary). København: Det kgl. nordiske Oldskriftselskab, 1948.

Olsen, O. Trelleborg-problemer: De danske vikingeborge og deres historiske baggrund (with English summary). *Scandia* (1962) 28:92–112.

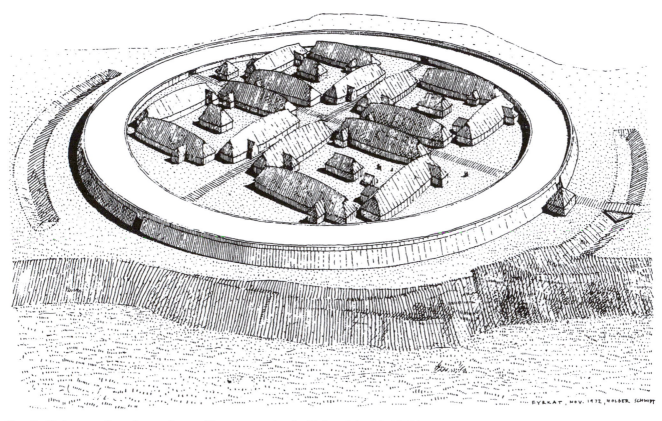

FIG. 2. Fyrkat seen from the northwest. (A reconstruction by Holger Schmidt 1972.)

———. Viking Fortresses in Denmark. *Recent Archaeological Excavations in Europe*. Ed. R. Bruce-Mitford. London: Routledge and Kegan Paul, 1975, pp. 90–110.

———. Die geometrischen dänischen Wikingerburgen. In *Burgen aus Holz und Stein: Burgenkundlisches Kolloquium in Basel 1977*. Ed. M.-L. Heyer-Boscardin. Olten und Freiburg im Breisgau: Walter-Verlag, 1979, pp. 81–94.

Olsen, O., and H. Schmidt. *Fyrkat: En jysk vikingsgeborg I: Borgen og bebyggelsen* (with English summary). København: Det kgl. nordiske Oldskriftselskab, 1977.

Roesdahl, E. *Fyrkat: En jysk vikingeborg II: Oldsagerne og gravpladsen* (with English summary). København: Det kgl. nordiske Oldskriftselskab, 1977.

———. Aggersborg in the Viking Age. In *Proceedings of the Eighth Viking Congress*. Ed. H. Bekker-Nielsen, Peter Foote, and Olaf Olsen. Odense: Odense University Press, 1981, pp. 107–122.

———. *Viking Age Denmark*. Trans. S. Margeson and K. Williams. London: British Museum Publications, 1982.

———. Vikingernes Aggersborg. In *Aggersborg gennem 1000 år* (with English summary). Ed. F. Nørgaard, Else Roesdahl, and Rour Skovmand. Herning: Poul Kristensen, 1986, pp. 53–93.

———. The Danish Geometrical Viking Fortresses and Their Context. *Anglo-Norman Studies* (1987) 9:108–126.

———. *The Vikings*. Trans. S. Margeson and K. Williams. London: Penguin, 1992.

———. Fyrkat. In *Reallexikon der Germanischen Altertumskunde*. Berlin and New York: Walter de Gruyter, in press.

Schmidt, H. The Trelleborg House Reconsidered. *Medieval Archaeology* (1973) 17:52–77.

———. *Building Customs in Viking Age Denmark*. Herning: Poul Kristensen, 1994.

Else Roesdahl

SEE ALSO
Danevirke; Jelling

Trondheim

Situated beside the Trondheim Fjord in mid-Norway, Trondheim (also formerly called Nidaros) is the northernmost of the eight medieval towns within the boundaries of modern Norway. The town expanded from a small tenth-century trading place (Norwegian *kaupang*) at the mouth of the River Nid to become Norway's ecclesiastical capital, a status arising from both its role as one of Scandinavia's major centers of pilgrimage, the shrine of St. Olaf attracting pilgrims from the mid-eleventh century onward, and the establishment here in 1152–1153 of the metropolitan see of Nidaros, the administrative center of the geographically vast Norwegian ecclesiastical province. The town's ecclesiastical associations ensured the cultural and economic basis for its status and growth, although Bergen and Oslo superseded it in economic and political importance during the thirteenth century. The town features prominently in historical sources, and, from the tenth century onward, local urban developments were closely linked with the emergence of a national monarchy, the introduction of Christianity, national unification, and the consolidation of the Church's political and economic power base.

In European terms, Trondheim was small in area and population (around three thousand inhabitants c. A.D. 1300) (Fig. 1). It ultimately comprised a dense, regulated concentration of urban tenements packed with small wooden buildings. The town's few stone buildings were its parish and monastic churches, the townscape being dominated by Nidaros Cathedral and the stone-built Archbishop's Palace to the south. Owing to the ravages of town fires, these latter comprise two of the town's few extant medieval monuments. Until recently, our understanding of Trondheim's development relied upon historical accounts and scattered archaeological finds and observations. Insight into the medieval town's complex physical and functional evolution has been enhanced greatly since the early 1970s by a wealth of archaeological data recovered during excavations conducted by the Norwegian Central Office of Historical Monuments and Sites. Good organic preservation and long-term continuity of occupation in the town center have facilitated deep stratigraphic accumulation, containing the remains of hundreds of wooden buildings and structures and thousands of artifacts associated with domestic, industrial, and commercial activities. The most important excavations have revealed a central urban quarter, an extensive metalworking quarter, the riverside waterfront, and domestic and industrial buildings in the precinct of the Archbishop's Palace. Analysis of this varied material, much of it of unique character, is yielding fresh insights into research topics of major national and international importance, such as early urbanization, spatial organization and exploitation, secular building types, ecclesiastical architecture, the development of urban-based crafts and industries, the interaction of town and hinterland, the role of major institutions in urban functions, and the character of trade and commerce.

The dynamics of Trondheim's physical, social, and economic development have emerged in a recent study of the Library Site—a large portion of a central urban quarter (see Christophersen and Nordeide 1994) (Fig. 1; Fig. 2). In a preurban stage (the tenth century up to c. 970/980), ditch-defined plots bearing scattered buildings and artifacts denote the existence around a shallow inlet of a small regulated seasonal settlement. In common with other Scandinavian kaupangs, this was a strategic center of collection, storage, and transshipment, the plots presumably being rented seasonally by maritime traders engaged in interregional commodity exchange. Unlike its royal-inspired contemporaries elsewhere, the kaupang at the mouth of the Nid was possibly established by a powerful local family of jarls (earls) as a means of controlling trade and ensuring their regional hegemony. Having usurped them, and as a step in his attempt at establishing a national monarchy, Olaf Tryggvason (c. 968–1000) in 997 shifted his powerbase away from the jarls' administrative and pagan cult center at nearby Lade and established his Court and first Christian church in their kaupang. This marked the first initiative in transforming an essentially economic center into a multifunctional urban community, as yet possibly detectable only archaeologically in a restructuring of the plot system. This second stage (c. 1000–c. 1050) sees the evolution of a true urban space, with an integrated plot, street, and wharf layout evincing increasingly intensive structural exploitation and artifacts indicative of permanent occupation and diversified trading and craft activities. Itinerant professional craftsmen, principally metalworkers producing prestige items, appear for the first time, having played no evident role in the preurban stage (unlike other kaupangs). Stage three (c. 1050–1150) is marked by dynamic expansion and increased differentiation in the building mass and activities, with specialized buildings fronting the street possibly being rented by craftsmen and traders. The wharfs were now moved from the infilled inlet to the west bank of the river, facilitating the mooring of larger vessels. Commerce—increasingly encompassing imports, such as English and Continental pottery—became the dominant urban activity, while professional craft production remained limited, satisfying the town's internal requirements. During the fourth stage (c. 1150–1325), the High Medieval town reached its maximum physical extension and exploitation. A corresponding expansion in commercial and productive activities occurred, the town functioning as the center for large-scale production and consumption of professionally produced commodities in bone, wood, metal, and textiles, for example. The increased organization, permanence, and scale of production are exemplified by the creation of an extensive metalworking quarter occupying a virgin site of c. 1 ha on the town's northern outskirts (the Mellager Site). Large-scale iron-smithing and copper-casting operations took place in workshops here from c. 1150 to c.1350. International trade expanded, the town now being clearly integrated within an extensive commercial and cultural network. It is no coincidence that this process unfolded simultaneously with the acquisition of huge economic resources by the newly established archbishopric of Nidaros. The plague epidemics of the mid-fourteenth century ended and seemingly reversed urban growth, there being a relative scarcity of late medieval remains from the town. A notable exception is the Archbishop's Palace, the administrative heart of the town's leading institution. Recent excavations within the defended precinct behind the palace's domestic and administrative buildings have revealed whole ranges of wooden functional buildings that were of central economic and political importance to the archbishopric during the turbulent decades prior to

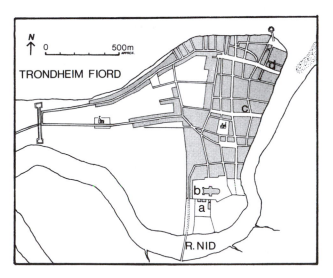

FIG. 1. The earliest existing map of Trondheim, dated 1658. The urban area (shaded) and the street pattern approximate the medieval situation. The town grew up on a peninsula formed by a meander of the River Nid where it enters the Trondheim Fjord. Extant medieval monumental buildings and major excavation sites are shown: *a,* the Archbishop's Palace; *b,* Nidaros Cathedral; *c,* the Library Site; *d,* the Mellager Site.

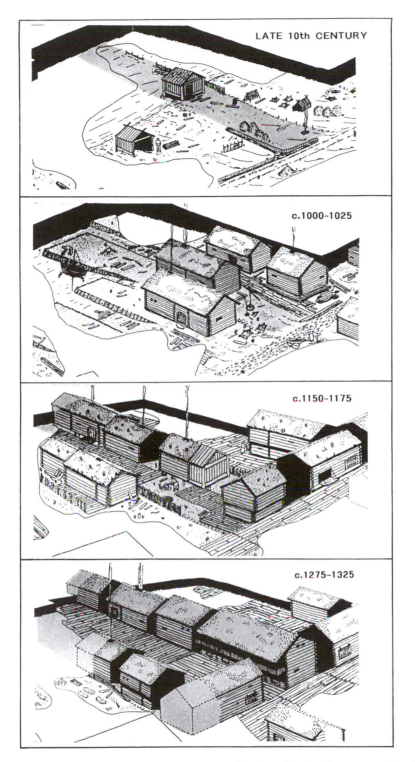

FIG. 2. Trondheim's urban development in microcosm. Reconstruction drawings showing the structural development through 300–400 years of a single urban plot (shaded) on the Library Site. In Stage 1 (top), the ditch- and fence-bounded plot is only partly exploited, a post-built building standing at the edge of the shallow inlet used as the first harbor. In Stage 2, a wattle-reveted clay terrace juts out into the silting-up inlet to form a jetty; behind it lie a timber building and an open area nearest the track. By Stage 3, the inlet is filled in and the plot almost completely occupied with timber buildings and a wooden paved passage; the buildings fronting the now wooden-paved street are possibly tradesmen's booths. In Stage 4, the plot has expanded in area and is densely built upon, with a possible two-story building nearest the street.

T

the Reformation in 1537, most notably a number of well-preserved workshops in which minting operations and arms manufacture took place.

FURTHER READINGS

Christophersen, A. Royal Authority and Early Urbanization in Trondheim during the Transition to the Historical Period. In *Archaeology and the Urban Economy: Festchrift to Asbjørn E. Herteig*. Ed. S. Myrvoll. Bergen: Arkeologiske Skrifter, Historisk Museum, Universitet i Bergen 5. 1989, pp. 91–135.

———. Dwelling Houses, Workshops, and Storehouses: Functional Aspects of the Development of Wooden Urban Buildings in Trondheim from c. A.D. 1000 to A.D. 1400. *Acta Archaeologica* (1990) 60:101–129.

Christophersen, A., and S.W. Nordeide. *Kaupangen ved Nidelva* (with English summary and illustration texts). Riksantikvarens skrifter 7. Trondheim, 1994.

Christophersen, A., E. Jondell, S.W. Nordeide, and I.W. Reed. *Excavation, Chronology and Settlement Development*. Meddelelser 17. Trondheim, 1989.

Espelund, E. The Mellager Site in Trondheim: A Complex of Metal Workshops and Its Role in Medieval Iron Metallurgy. In *Bloomery Ironmaking during 2000 Years*. Vol. 2. Ed. A. Espelund. Trondheim: Universitetet i Trondheim (NTH), 1992, pp. 93–114.

Fuglesang, S.H. *Woodcarvers: Professionals and Amateurs in Eleventh-Century Trondheim*. Occasional Paper 30. London: British Museum, 1981.

Long, C.D. Excavations in the Medieval City of Trondheim, Norway. *Medieval Archaeology* (1975a) 19:1–32.

———. Excavations in Trondheim, 1971–1974. *Zeitschrift Archäologi des Mittelalters* (1975b) Jahrgang 3: 183–207.

McLees, C. A Metal-Working Complex in the Medieval City of Trondheim, Norway. *Medieval Archaeology* (1989) 33:156–159.

———. The Late Medieval Mint Workshops at the Archbishop's Palace, Trondheim. *Antiquity* (1994) 68:264–274.

Nordeide, S.W. Activity in an Urban Community. *Acta Archaeologica* (1990) 60:130–150.

Reed, I.W. *1,000 Years of Pottery: An Analysis of Pottery, Trade, and Use*. Meddelelser 25. Trondheim, 1990.

Christopher McLees

U

Uppsala Cathedral

Uppsala is a Swedish medieval town. One of the greatest remnants from this period is the High Gothic cathedral, almost 120 m long and 50 m wide, built on top of a gravel ridge close to the south bank of the River Fyris. The building material is brick with a limestone base. The cathedral is a three-aisled basilica with single-aisled transepts and choir. The choir has a triangular east end and an ambulatory that is surrounded by five chapels. The spaces immediately to the east and west of the north transept are divided into three; their original function is uncertain. The original vestry was located between the space to the east of the north transept and the northwest chapel surrounding the ambulatory. The nave of the cathedral is lined with chapels on both sides. The two towers are built in the west end on each side of the central nave.

In the 1690s, a chapel was built between the south transept and the southwest chapel surrounding the ambulatory. In the 1890s, a restoration took place, replacing almost all of the medieval bricks in the façade of the cathedral with new ones. The stairs at each side of the two towers were remodeled.

According to written documents, the building of Uppsala Cathedral started in the 1280s. It was not consecrated until 1435, giving a construction period of almost 160 years. Archaeological examination of the walls indicates that the building of the cathedral continued from the late fourteenth century to the early sixteenth century with some breaks but with few changes from the original plan.

Archaeological excavations at Uppsala Cathedral have revealed some rune stones in the ground surface. Rune stones are sometimes found in medieval Swedish churches.

Many of them include a Christian cross. The construction of rune stones was mostly a Viking Age (c. 800–1050) custom that ceased c. 1050. Rune stones in medieval churches should be seen as technical elements of the buildings as well as a wish to preserve the symbols of ideals from an older society.

The cathedral is surrounded by a churchyard. Excavations have also revealed some graves that are older than the cathedral. However, no clear signs of an older church have been found thus far. Outside the cathedral and close to the northern entrance, a simple road and probable dwelling house have been excavated. This settlement is older than the cathedral. Further excavations are necessary to obtain an exact interpretation of the older graves and this settlement.

Just outside the northern entrance to the cathedral, parts of an old wall have been excavated. The wall is built on top of the older settlement mentioned above. The wall runs from east to west, following the line of the gravel ridge. The east and west ends of the wall have not yet been found. The wall appears to be older than the northern entrance to the cathedral. It was most likely built as a terrace wall, strengthening the slope of the ridge in preparation for the building of the cathedral. It was demolished to allow the construction of the northern entrance to the cathedral.

Today, nothing is left of the belfry. It was built to the northeast of the cathedral. Its foundation, which consisted of small boulders, has been excavated. It is difficult to determine the building material that was used in the walls of the belfry. Small pieces of brick found during excavation might have come from the walls or from the surroundings of windows or portals.

U

A brick kiln has been excavated to the south of the cathedral. The kiln was probably in use during the construction of parts of the cathedral. In the Middle Ages, the cathedral was surrounded by a large wall that was built on top of the kiln. Buildings connected with the cathedral, including the archbishop's manor to the west, were erected near and against the surrounding wall during the course of the Middle Ages. Archaeological excavations of parts of the wall and the buildings have shown that, by the end of the Middle Ages, the cathedral area had grown into a large enclosed unit, with a wall that was larger than necessary to surround the churchyard or to keep out cattle.

The increasing wealth of the Church during the Middle Ages made the construction of this complex possible. Its immense dimensions served as a symbol and mirror of the Church's political, socioeconomic, and religious power. Nowadays, some buildings to the east and northeast, parts of the archbishop's manor to the west, and the cathedral itself are all that remains of the once magnificent and wealthy ecclesiastical town in Uppsala.

FURTHER READINGS

Malm, Gunilla. Recent Excavations at Uppsala Cathedral, Sweden. *World Archaeology* (1987) 18(3):382–397.

———. Questions Concerning the Medieval Archbishop's and King's Manors in Uppsala. In *Castella Maris Baltici 1.* Ed. Knut Drake. Ekends: Archaeologia Medii Aevi Finlandiae 1, 1993, pp. 123–127.

Gunilla Malm

SEE ALSO
Sweden

Urban Archaeology

The use of documents and standing buildings for the study of Britain's medieval towns has a long history, but the systematic investigation of their buried remains is a relatively recent development. Although medieval urban sites have, on occasion, been excavated since the 1930s, the principal focus of archaeological interest in historic towns before the 1960s was the Roman period. Post-Roman deposits and structures were often removed with little or no record. Some important medieval excavations in towns such as Canterbury, Southampton, and London took place on sites cleared after wartime bomb damage, but the Winchester program of the 1960s, in which churches, dwellings, and the castle were examined, may be considered a major step forward in terms of the scale of excavation, its academic aims, and methodological approach.

In the late 1960s and early 1970s, there was a great increase in urban rescue archaeology in advance of new construction work, and most historic towns acquired a permanent, locally based archaeological team. As both the value and the vulnerability of the remains of medieval towns became apparent for the first time, their study assumed a new urgency, and new archaeological techniques were adapted to tackle their particular problems.

Methodology

As a result of the intensity of human activity that has characterized towns over the centuries, archaeological sites in urban areas are usually characterized by their depth and complexity. Below modern ground level in places like London and York there may be 5 m or more of archaeology, which consists largely of superimposed structures and hundreds, if not thousands, of deposits of refuse and building debris. In addition, the sequence of accumulation is interrupted at regular intervals by pits, ditches, and other disturbances of the ground. Another characteristic of urban sites, compared to those in rural areas, is that they produce large quantities of artifacts, including pottery, industrial waste, and building materials. Biological material, principally animal bones but also plant remains and other organic matter, may also occur in large quantities. When carefully excavated and recorded, the individual components of an urban archaeological site will allow developments, sometimes over very long periods of time, in topography, building techniques, dietary preferences, and many other aspects of life in the past to be understood.

Since the 1960s, techniques of recording urban sites have undergone continual development so that, for example, the ephemeral remains of timber structures, surviving only as postholes or the stains left by timber beams, can be readily identified. In addition, the detailed recording of all the layers on a site, rather than simply those that appear most important during excavation, can allow archaeologists, during the postexcavation analysis, to determine such things as the function of rooms and yards or the process by which a building was demolished. Computer storage of drawn and written information allows the ready recall of records during analysis.

Giving real dates to layers and structures in medieval archaeology depends, in the first instance, on the study of pottery, which occurs in large quantities on most urban sites. Detailed work relating pottery types to urban archaeological sequences has formed the fundamental basis for research in the archaeology not only of towns but of every other type of site. The principal scientific dating technique applied in medieval urban archaeology is dendrochronology, which is based on the measurement of the growth rings in ancient timber. Dendrochronology has allowed dates of great accuracy to be given to, for example, tenth-century timber buildings at York and the tenth–fourteenth-century riverfront structures in London.

Medieval sites have provided the stimulus for many areas of research on excavated material, and particular reference may be made to what is usually known as environmental archaeology. This involves examining the evidence for diet and living conditions in the past from animal bones, plant and insect remains, and other organic matter. Many aspects of the subject were pioneered at York, where the deposits of the ninth–twelfth-century town retain a high organic content. This is due to the exclusion of oxygen as a result both of rising groundwater and of the compacted nature of buried refuse tips. Preservation even extends to such microorganisms as the eggs of parasites that live in the human gut.

The study of human skeletal remains has been another important feature of medieval urban archaeology. Archaeologists and physical anthropologists have combined to develop techniques of excavation and analysis that present a dramatic picture of the medieval population not available from written sources. A number of large cemeteries, containing many hundreds of burials, have been excavated at Canterbury, Winchester, and York. Study of the bones has revealed evidence for changes in human physical stature and appearance, including a trend for skulls, which were long and narrow in the late Anglo-Saxon period (850–1066), to become short and broad after the Norman Conquest. Evidence for severe wounds and injuries and the presence of certain diseases such as rickets and arthritis can also be detected.

Archaeology and the Origins of Medieval Urbanism

One of the principal archaeological discoveries of the 1960s was, perhaps, that recognizable protourban and urban settlements existed in Anglo-Saxon times, with their origins as early as c. 700. In the absence of written sources, this had not hitherto been fully appreciated, but excavations in Southampton and subsequently Ipswich, London, and York have shown that, in the eighth–ninth centuries, there was a small group of distinctive trading settlements associated with the place-name suffix "-wic" (e.g., Eoforwic—York, Hamwic—Southampton). They were located on river estuaries; their urban character is revealed by a regular layout of streets and property divisions and the abundant archaeological evidence that a substantial proportion of the population was engaged in trade and crafts. The "wic" sites were abandoned in the second half of the ninth century, probably as a result of Viking raids, but archaeology has shown that many new towns emerged in the tenth century, some of which lay within the walls of former Roman towns and others on new sites.

The late Anglo-Saxon town that has been most extensively studied is probably London, where the steady expansion of settlement within the former Roman walled enclosure, the diverse types of timber building, and the character of the riverfront have been documented. At Winchester, the role of the Church and the Crown in an Anglo-Saxon capital has been evoked in excavations of the Old Minster on Cathedral Green. Craft activities, including the working of leather, bone, antler, and iron and other metals, have been examined in detail at 16–22 Coppergate, York, where vast quantities of artifacts and manufacturing debris were found in and around well-preserved timber buildings.

The Archaeology of the Norman and Later Medieval Town

Although only a very small proportion of Britain's medieval population were town dwellers, the eleventh–thirteenth centuries were a period of considerable urban development, with the expansion of existing towns and the foundation of new ones. This took place not only in the rich agricultural areas of the southeast, but also in the north and west of England and in Scotland and Wales.

Dating from the eleventh century onward, there are an increasing number of structures surviving above ground that may be usefully examined with archaeological techniques. These structures are primarily fortifications and churches. Most standing medieval dwellings are those of the upper classes, who could afford to build in good-quality materials. Excavation can, however, tell us about the homes of the whole of the population and chart in detail changing structural techniques.

A second source that becomes increasingly important for the study of towns from the twelfth–thirteenth centuries onward is documentary material. This provides information on property ownership and legal and commercial matters, but only limited information about

U

topography and such aspects of daily life as diet, clothing, and manufacturing techniques, which can be studied only by archaeological means.

As a result of what is now a substantial body of urban excavations, it is possible to detect elements of a common pattern in the development of medieval towns. Typically, they developed around a simple, but more or less regular, grid of streets, with their first buildings on the street frontages and yards behind them for crafts, agriculture, and refuse tipping. By the later twelfth–early thirteenth centuries, as population increased, side streets were built up, properties were subdivided, and buildings were erected on the backyards, creating a densely settled urban core.

Most towns without Roman or Anglo-Saxon walls acquired defenses after the Norman Conquest, and they form some of the most striking medieval remains surviving today. At Chester and York, for example, much of the circuit of walls still survives. Excavations have shown, however, that, as England was a relatively peaceful country, largely spared the threat of hostile foreign armies, town walls were often poorly constructed to avoid expense, and the circuits might take one hundred years or more to complete.

A feature of medieval towns founded in tenth–eleventh centuries is their large number of small churches: London had more than one hundred; Norwich and York, more than fifty. Excavated examples include St. Mary in Tanner Street and St. Pancras in Winchester, which exhibited a sequence of continual development and enlargement due to population increase and changes in ritual. In addition to churches, towns acquired, from the twelfth century onward, an increasing number of houses of religious orders, culminating in the friars who arrived in the mid-thirteenth century and moved onto any remaining vacant land. As a result of the Dissolution of Monasteries in the sixteenth century, the upstanding remains of religious houses are very scarce, but excavations have revealed the layout and form of their buildings and investigated their cemeteries and way of life.

Archaeology is able to make an important contribution to the study of the medieval urban economy. Excavation has shown, for example, how the practitioners of particular crafts congregated in specific areas. This is especially clear in respect of crafts such as the dyeing and fulling of wool, which required fixed equipment. The debris of processes such as metalworking or woodworking may also betray zones of craft specialization.

The trading contacts of medieval towns can be studied from archaeological data and in particular from pottery,

which shows how local exchange dominated most English medieval towns while a few, usually ports, grew wealthy on long-distance trade in luxury goods. In the thirteenth century, for example, the wine trade with Gascony brought great prosperity to the merchants of Southampton, which is reflected in the high-quality imported pots in their rubbish pits. The character of structures associated with marketing, storage, and transport may also be revealed in excavation. In London, the remains of timber waterfronts have been found standing several meters high on a number of sites in the city. Employed to keep the banks of the Thames sound, and preserved by refuse tipping and rising river levels, these sophisticated structures form some of the most spectacular recent discoveries made in medieval urban archaeology.

FURTHER READINGS

Ottaway, P. *Archaeology in British Towns.* London: Routledge, 1992.

Schofield, J., and R. Leech. Urban Archaeology in Britain. CBA Research Report 61. London: Council for British Archaeology, 1990.

Schofield, J., and A. Vince. *Medieval Towns.* Leicester: Leicester University Press, 1994.

There is a substantial literature relating to the archaeology of individual medieval towns. The following publication series for York and London are of particular interest:

York

Addyman, P.V., ed. *The Archaeology of York.* 19 Vols. London: Council for British Archaeology, 1976–1999, ongoing.

See in particular:

Vol. 8: *Anglo-Scandinavian York (a.d. 876–1066):*

1. Moulden, J., and D. Tweddle. 1986. Anglo-Scandinavian Settlement South-West of the Ouse.
2. Wenham, L.P., R.A. Hall, C. Briden, and D. Stocker. 1987. St. Mary Bishophill Junior and St. Mary Castlegate.
3. Addyman, P.V., and R.A. Hall. 1991. Urban Structures and Defenses, including the Lloyds Bank Excavations.

Vol. 10: *The Medieval Walled City North-East of the Ouse:*

1. Magilton, J. 1980. The Church of St. Helen-on-the Walls, Aldwark.
2. Hall, R.A., H. MacGregor, and M. Stockwell. 1988. Medieval Tenements in Aldwark and Other Sites.
3. Richards, J.D. 1993. The Bedern Foundry.

Vol. 12: *The Medieval Cemeteries:*

1. Dawes, J., and J. Magilton. 1980. The Cemetery of St. Helen-on-the Walls, Aldwark.
2. Stroud, G., and R.L. Kemp. 1993. The Cemetery at 46–54 Fishergate.
3. Lilley, J.M. 1994. The Jewish Burial Ground at Jewbury.

Vol. 15: *The Animal Bones:*

3. O'Connor, T.P. 1989. Bones from Anglo-Scandinavian Levels at 16–22 Coppergate.
4. O'Connor, T.P. 1991. Bones from 46–54 Fishergate.

Vol. 16: *The Pottery:*

5. Mainman, A.J. 1990. The Anglo-Scandinavian Pottery from 16–22 Coppergate.
6. Mainman, A.J. 1993. The Pottery from 46–54 Fishergate.

Vol. 17: *The Small Finds:*

5. Walton, P. 1989. Textiles, Cordage, and Raw Fibre from 16–22 Coppergate.
6. Ottaway, P. 1992. Anglo-Scandinavian Ironwork from 16–22 Coppergate.
7. Bayley, J. 1992. Non-Ferrous Metalworking from 16–22 Coppergate.
8. Tweddle, D. 1992. The Anglian Helmet from Coppergate.
9. Rogers, N.S.H. 1993. Anglian Finds from 46–54 Fishergate.

Vol. 18: *The Coins:*

1. Pirie, E.J.E. 1986. Post-Roman Coins from York Excavations, 1971–81.

London

London and Middlesex Archaeological Society Special Papers.

See in particular:

5. Milne, G., and C. Milne. 1982. Medieval Waterfront Development at Trig Lane, London.
11. Horsman, V., C. Milne, and G. Milne. 1988. Aspects of Saxo-Norman London 1: Building and Street Development.
12. Vince, A., ed. 1991. Aspects of Saxo-Norman London 2: Finds and Environmental Evidence.
14. Steedman, K., T. Dyson, and J. Schofield. 1992. The Bridgehead and Billingsgate to 1200.
15. Milne, G. 1992. Timber Building Techniques, c. 900–1400.

Patrick Ottaway

SEE ALSO
Chester; London

Urquhart
See Scotland: Early Royal Sites.

V

Venice

By the end of the thirteenth century, Venice was a flourishing city that had a population of more than 100,000 inhabitants. It was one of the largest cities in Europe at the time; the only places of comparable size were Milan, Florence, Naples, Palermo, and Paris. But Venice was quite different in many ways from other medieval towns in Europe. To begin with, it was a city built on water. Located in the middle of a large lagoon at the head of the Adriatic, Venice was made up of a cluster of many small islands. Building techniques were specifically adapted to the wet conditions; movement from one island to another often required the use of a boat. Moreover, Venice was unique in being a city that was not enclosed by a defensive wall. The Venetian lagoon with its ever-changing tides had served for centuries as its first line of defense. As those from Genoa were to discover to their own regret in 1379, the lagoon with its maze of marshes, mud flats, and meandering channels was no place for the uninitiated. Another way in which Venice was different was the lack of significance attached to its cathedral. Whereas it was common for the cathedral in other medieval cities to play a leading role, the one in Venice, San Pietro di Castello, was tucked away in splendid isolation on the island of Olivolo. Instead, the doge's own chapel, the Basilica of San Marco, stood out at the heart of the ceremonial, as well as the political, life in the city. Still another contrast took the form of an economy that was based primarily on other things than agriculture. Although there were some gardens, orchards, and even vineyards on the islands, the real emphasis was placed elsewhere. For example, one of the activities of economic importance throughout the Middle Ages was the production of salt at *saline* in various parts of the lagoon. Venice also came to rely heavily upon craft production and commerce. Thus, there was already a thriving glass industry in Venice by the end of the twelfth century. Due to the risks of fire, glass furnaces were banned from the city itself in 1291, and this activity shifted completely to Murano. Other important activities involved the building and maintenance of ships and the pursuit of seafaring and long-distance trade. As one index of the scale of such maritime activities, the old Arsenal (Vecchio Arsenale with its twenty-four docks) was established by the state in the twelfth century. One final way in which the city was different, when compared to other medieval towns in Europe, was the extent to which it looked to the east and specifically to Constantinople and the Byzantine world. This orientation was embodied in its early history, and it was reinforced by the major role that Venice played in the sack of Byzantium in 1204 and the economic advantages that arose from having participated in this adventure. It is, of course, well known that the art and architecture of Venice before the Renaissance often reflect the strength of its ties with Constantinople.

These few brief observations made by way of introduction are meant to convey a sense of the richness of the city's medieval history. No attempt will be made in the limited space available here to give a comprehensive account of the main events of early Venetian history or to trace the growth of the Venetian economy and the development of its early political institutions. Nor is this the place to survey the achievements in architecture and the visual arts of early medieval Venice (subjects again with an extensive literature)—a survey that would include the Basilica of San Marco, one of the great monuments of medieval Europe. Instead, the aim here is to present what

V is known about the archaeology of early Venice in a much more restricted sense of the term: the results that have been obtained from the fieldwork that archaeologists have conducted in the city and the Venetian lagoon. Urban archaeology, for reasons that we shall consider below, got off to a slow start in Venice. Indeed, prior to 1980, there was only one excavation that had made use of modern methods of recovery and documentation and that also managed to see its way into print. This was the work by a Polish mission on the island of Torcello. It is only since the mid-1980s at sites such as San Pietro di Castello, San Lorenzo, and San Francesco del Deserto that this situation has begun to change.

When viewed in retrospect, there are good reasons for the slow start. Most are connected in one way or another with the physical circumstances of the city. In the first place, the very success of Venice over the centuries has meant that space has always been in short supply. The city offers few open places where an abandoned building can simply be left on its own as a ruin in the landscape. Structures as they age have to be rebuilt from time to time; thus, the remains of an early building are incorporated into the fabric of a later one, making them no longer visible. At the same time, due to human activity and, in particular, the accumulation of fills, there has often been a marked inflation of the land surface in a given place over the centuries. At the Church of San Lorenzo, for instance, there is a difference of more than 4 m between the floor of the present church built at the end of the sixteenth century and the occupation surface dating to the seventh century A.D. Over a span of time of only about a thousand years, there has been a significant rise in the ground level at this site. One of the factors contributing to such change is subsidence, the progressive sinking of the land surface due to the subsurface geology of Venice. This phenomenon takes place at a rate estimated at c. 2 cm per century. It means that over a period of 750 years, the occupation surface at an archaeological site will find itself having a position c. 1.0 m lower in the ground than it did at the start. This explains why the well-known pavements in *opus sectile* at churches such as Santa Maria Assunta (A.D. 1008) on Torcello, San Nicolò (1050) on the Lido, SS. Maria and Donato (1141) on Murano, and the Basilica of San Marco (second half of the twelfth century) all stand today at an elevation of only c. 1.0 m above mean modern sea level. When these mosaic pavements were originally installed, they once had a position a good 1.0 m higher than they now have. There is the further implication that levels of occupation of even earlier date—for example,

those going back to the sixth and seventh centuries A.D.—should be found at elevations below sea level today. This is, in fact, just what is observed at sites such as San Lorenzo and San Pietro di Castello, where structural remains that occur *in situ* are recovered well more than 1.0 m below the mean modern sea level. Thus, the challenge of doing the archaeology of early Venice is that of working well below the ambient sea level. This is also the main reason that casual finds of buried early structures—chance discoveries made from time to time as part of the digging of foundations—have seldom been well documented in Venice. The section drawn by G. Casoni of a deeply buried wooden structure exposed at the Arsenal in 1824 is one of the few exceptions. But in most cases (see *Venezia origini* [1983], in which W. Dorigo considers many of them), the recording is not sufficient to permit unambiguous interpretation. It is only more recently that appropriate methods for working under such difficult conditions have been implemented in Venice.

There is a further complication when it comes to the study of early Venice. The kinds of evidence that are available—in terms of both quality and quantity—are often quite different for different centuries. By the time one reaches the eleventh or twelfth century, not only is there a greater opportunity to study architecture that has survived in standing form, but the historical sources are much greater in number. There are, for example, for this period administrative records by parish that allow the reconstruction of detailed patterns of land ownership for the area around Piazza San Marco. Historical documents provide a good source of information on the project to enlarge and transform the piazza initiated by Doge Sebastiani Ziani (1172–1178). In sharp contrast, if one goes back only a few centuries earlier to the period from A.D. 600 to 800, there are almost no standing remains to study (much of the earliest architecture of Venice was lost to devastating fires of 976 and 1106), and firsthand historical sources become quite rare. One of the most important of these early historical sources actually derives from archaeological work at the cathedral on Torcello at the end of the nineteenth century: the inscription on the original foundation stone dating to A.D. 639. Most of what is known about Venetian history in the seventh and eighth centuries has come down to us from chronicles written several centuries after the events. It is not always easy to assess the reliability of such later narrative accounts (with their own agenda). As the historian John Julius Norwich once remarked: "One of the most infuriating aspects of early Venetian history is the regularity with which truth and legend pursue separate courses." The situation that the archaeologist in Venice faces for these early centuries is much like the one in Rome for the Regal period, the time of the seven early kings, where again the literary tradition is of later date. In such cases, archaeology has a key role to play not only in establishing the material circumstances of life at the time, but also in determining how the later sources are to be read.

One of the vexing questions for Venice concerns whether or not the city was inhabited in Roman times. The closest well-known Roman town, Altinum, was located on the Via Annia just at the back of the lagoon (at a distance of only c. 5 km from the island of Torcello). Maritime traffic to and from Altinum would have passed through the lagoon, and settlement of one kind or another is to be expected on some of the islands in the lagoon. The famous letter by Cassiodorus to the lagoon dwellers (537/538) suggests that the habitation was quite humble in nature (houses built simply of wood) at least for the sixth century. There is now good archaeological evidence for such lagoon dwellers in the fifth century from the island of San Francesco del Deserto. It takes the form of a waterside structure made of wooden poles and even the remains of a small boat. On the nearby island of San Lorenzo di Ammiana, there may be evidence for occupation of even earlier date. On the island of Torcello, where the findings of the excavations by the Polish mission (1961–1962) and by M. Tombolani (1988) are not always in accord, there are traces of occupation that go back to at least the fifth century A.D. Within the city of Venice itself, the claim is made at San Pietro di Castello for a level of habitation that again would date to the fifth century. In short, the problem has shifted from the question of Roman presence to that of defining more clearly the exact nature of late Roman settlement in the lagoon. In light of the limited amounts of archaeological fieldwork done so far, the best position to hold is that the last word on Roman Venice is still far from having been written.

The years between Cassiodorus's letter and the movement of the ducal seat to the Realtine Islands (809–811) represent the least-well-known period of Venetian history—a time span of almost three centuries when Venice belonged to the Byzantine sphere of interest in the west. In response to the Lombard invasion of Italy in A.D. 568, the chronicles recount that many of those living in towns on the mainland sought refuge on the islands of the lagoon (Fig. 1). By 639, the same year that the Byzantine governor transferred his seat from Oderzo to Heraclea,

the situation had reached the point that the bishop of Altinum was forced to move to Torcello, where the church of Dei Genetrix was now built. Comparatively little is known about the archaeology of Heraclea, or Cittanova as it was also called. Even less is known about Malamocco, its successor as the seat of ducal power. Up until the last ten years, there was even some doubt about whether the islands making up the future city of Venice were inhabited in the sixth and seventh centuries. There is now good archaeological evidence for settlement at both San Pietro di Castello and San Lorenzo. In the case of San Lorenzo, the first phase of occupation at the site, which is dated by a series of six radiocarbon (C-14) determinations, occurs at a depth of just more than 2 m below mean modern sea level. In addition to a reed structure found *in situ,* the remains include fragments of brick, tile, and mortar, suggesting a more durable form of architecture than the one portrayed in Cassiodorus's letter to the lagoon dwellers. There is also evidence from deep borings made below the Marciana Library in 1993 that the area near the future site of Piazza San Marco was already inhabited in the eighth century A.D.

As mentioned above, the ducal seat was removed from Malamocco to the Realtine Islands (the group of islands centered on Rivoalto, the Rialto) in the early years to the ninth century (809–811). While Torcello continued to be a major trading station, a whole new course was initiated by the establishment of Civitas Rivoalti. The Rialto was now to emerge as an important marketplace, and the bishopric on Olivolo (first established in c. 775) would take its position as the new spiritual center. At still a third

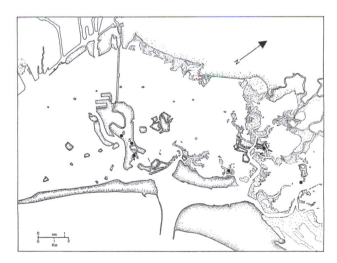

FIG. 1. Map of the Venice lagoon showing locations of the early sites.

V

place, the hub of political life in the form of the ducal palace and the Church of San Marco, the doge's own chapel, would now materialize at the head of the Grand Canal. According to tradition, the body of the evangelist was brought from Alexandria to Venice in A.D. 828. Previously, the city's patron saint had been San Teodoro, whose church was not far from the ducal palace. In the testament that Doge Giustiniano Participazio left when he died in 829, he instructed his wife to build a basilica in honor of the evangelist. If there is still active debate among architects and art historians about the size and form of the original church, or San Marco 1 as it is called by scholars (only parts of the original crypt have come down to us), there is no doubt about the importance that it rapidly assumed in the religious and ceremonial life of the city. The church standing on the site today, San Marco 3, was started by Doge Domenico Contarini in the second half of the eleventh century (Fig. 2). Of the various ninth-century churches in Venice (San Pietro on Olivolo, San Marco 1, and San Zaccaria), the one that is best known in terms of its archaeology is San Lorenzo, where one apse of the original church with its stone foundations and its field of supporting poles has been brought to light by recent excavations. On the other hand, our current knowledge of the physical remains of San Marco 1 and other buildings dating from the ninth and tenth centuries mentioned in the sources (for example, the churches of San Teodoro and San Geminiano and the ducal palace itself) is still quite limited.

After a slow start, work on the archaeology of early Venice has only begun to move forward since 1985. The reason for the slow start, as mentioned above, stems largely from the great difficulty in physical terms of doing excavation at 1–2 m below sea level. At the same time, the wet conditions account for the good state of preservation of wood and other organic materials commonly found at an early site, which enables the use of dating methods such as radiocarbon and dendrochronology and also a range of environmental studies. For the medieval archaeologist, there is the rare chance in Venice to investigate (work that has only just started) an early city that has survived under wetland conditions of preservation.

FURTHER READINGS

Ammerman, A.J., M. De Min, and R. Housley. New Evidence on the Origins of Venice. *Antiquity* (1992) 66:913–916. Evidence from San Lorenzo.

Ammerman, A.J., M. De Min, R. Housley, and C.E. McClennen. More on the Origins of Venice. *Antiquity* (1995) 69:501–510.

Blake, H., A. Bondesan, V. Favero, E. Finzi, and S. Salvatori. Cittanova Heraclia 1987: Risultati preliminari delle indagini gemorfologiche e paleogeografiche. *Quaderni di Archeologia del Veneto* (1988) 4:112–135.

Carile, A. and G. Fedalto. *Le origini di Venezia.* Bologna: Pàtron, 1978.

De Min, M. Rinvenimenti medioevali nella chiesa di S. Lorenzo: Notizie preliminari. *Venezia Arti* (1990) 4:159–166.

Demus, O. *The Church of San Marco in Venice: History, Architecture, Sculpture.* Washington, D.C.: Dumbarton Oaks, 1960.

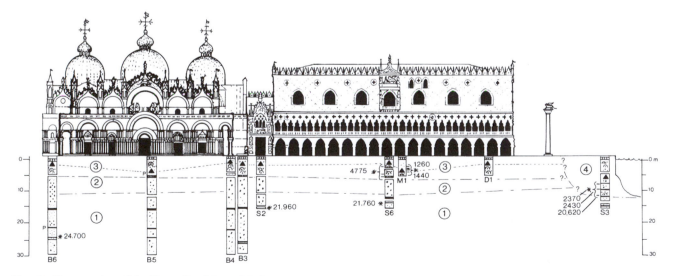

FIG. 2. Cross section of the Piazza San Marco, Venice.

Dorrigo, W. *Venezia origini: Ipotesi e richerche sulla formazione della città.* Milan: Electa, 1983.

Fedalto, G. Le origini della città di Venezia tra antiche fonti e recente storiografia. *Antichità Altoadriatiche* (1990) 36:103–127.

Fersuoch, L., E. Canal, S. Spector, and G. Zambon. Indagini archeologiche a San Lorenzo di Ammiana. *Archeologia Veneta* (1989) 12:71–96.

Leciejewicz, L., E. Tabaczynska, and S. Tabaczynski. *Torcello: Scavi, 1961–62.* Rome: Fondazione Giogio Cini, 1977.

Nicol, D.M. *Byzantium and Venice.* Cambridge: Cambridge University Press, 1988.

Norwich, J.J. *Venice: The Rise to Empire.* London: Allen Lane, 1977.

Polacco, R. *La Cattedrale di Torcello.* Treviso: Canova, 1984.

———. *San Marco: La Basilica d'Oro.* Milan: Berenice, 1991.

Tombolani, M. Saggio stratigrafico a Torcello. In *La Venezia dall' Antichita all' Alto medioevo.* Rome: Enciclopedia Italiana, 1988, pp. 205–214.

Tuzzato, S. Venezia: Gli scavi a San Pietro di Castello (Olivolo): Nota preliminare sulle campagne, 1986–89. *Quarderni di Archaeologia del Veneto* (1991) 7:92–103.

Tuzzato, S., V. Favero, and M.J. Vinals. San Pietro di Castello a Venezia: Nota preliminare dopo la campagna 1992. *Quaderni di Archeologia del Veneto* (1993) 9:72–80.

Albert J. Ammerman

SEE ALSO
Dendrochronology; Italy; Lombards

Vikings

The Vikings, or Norsemen, were a seafaring people from Scandinavia who left an indelible mark in history as the archetypical raiders from the north. They rose to prominence in northern Europe from the eighth to the eleventh centuries, and their raiding and trading voyages brought them in contact with the peoples in faraway lands, from the Kola Peninsula and Novgorod in Russia, to Istanbul, Sicily, Iceland, Greenland, and the New World.

Much if not most of the information about Vikings and their ships comes from grave mounds. Ships were used for the burial of nobles. Two of the finest Viking ships are the *Gokstad* and the *Oseberg* that were unearthed as ship burials.

Viking raids gave the Norse the reputation of fearsome warriors, but they were more than just raiders. The Norse were also brave adventurers, avid explorers, shrewd traders, talented poets, skilled shipbuilders and craftsmen, as well as successful colonists.

The Scandinavians did not call themselves Vikings. That was a name given to them by early Skaldic poets. The phrase to "go a-Viking" means to go exploring. Exploring was only a small part of Norse life. The Vikings were mostly farmers who grew oats, barley, rye, and vegetables and tended cattle, pigs, sheep, and goats, which they used for meat, wool, and dairy products. Hazelnuts and walnuts were also collected and stored for later use. Reindeer, moose, hare, bears, and other forest-dwelling creatures were taken, and game birds, whether waterfowl or land fowl, were hunted as seasonal delicacies. The Vikings were also keen fisherpeople, exploiting rich coasts and rivers, which provided plentiful cod, salmon, trout, and herring that was eaten fresh or preserved (dried, salted, or pickled). In particular, dried cod has always been a dietary staple and has traveled with the Norsemen in their voyages either as a trade item or as a source of food. Seals and whales were also part of the Norse menu, providing both food, with a high protein and fat content, and other products, such as oil, hides, and raw material for making artifacts and buildings.

The Norsemen had no centralized government or legal system. Law and order was enforced at the *Thing* meetings in which the local council met on a regular basis so that disputes and grievances could be settled in a peaceful manner. Punishments included fines and exile, while others had to perform tasks to prove their innocence, which was called *trial by ordeal.*

Local chieftains (Godi) had both secular and religious power. The chieftains had massive manor farms associated with impressive *nausts,* or boathouses, such as the site of Borg in northern Norway. The chieftains had to negotiate the alliance of local followers, but the office itself was purchased or inherited. Ritual activity before a Viking voyage or at important occasions took place at the chieftain's farm. Rituals included animal sacrifice, feasting, horse fighting, magic, and interpretation of omens. Rituals were often associated with death and the Norse belief in the afterlife, war, fertility, and success in ventures. One of the sites with evidence for ritualistic activity, such as feasting and horse fighting, was Aker, near modern Hamar in Norway. By the tenth and eleventh centuries, most of the Norse became Christian. With the conversion to Christianity, many of the traditional customs of sacrifice and

V

consumption of horsemeat were banned. The early kings used Christianity as an ideological reinforcement for their fledgling states. These kings promoted the development of ecclesiastical centers at foci of secular power such as Hamar and Nidaros, and there was a shift in power centers from the chieftain's farm to the churchyard.

During the Viking Era, a number of trade towns were developed. Kaupang, Hedeby, Birka, and Trelleborg are but a few. Upon entering the medieval era, many of these towns developed into formidable market centers due to their positioning on major trade routes. At the end of the Viking Age (c. 800–1050), the terrifying raids and invasions ceased. The Scandinavians were preoccupied with unstable local politics and disputes over rulership that forced them to abandon the "Viking way of life," but they did continue and in many instances intensified their trade ventures as merchants, inextricably linking Scandinavia with the European economic core.

FURTHER READINGS

Andersen, Per Sveaas. *Vikings of the West: The Expansion of Norway in the Middle Ages.* Sandnes: Aase Grafiske A.S., 1985.

Benedictow, Ole. Norge. In *Den nordiske Adel i Senmiddelalderen: Struktur, funktioner, og internordiske relationer.* Copenhagen: Hofbogtrykkeri, 1971, pp. 1–44.

Bigelow, Gerald F. Sandwick, Unst, and the Late Norse Shetland Economy. In *Shetland Archaeology: New Work.* Ed. Brian Smith. *Shetland in the 1970s.* Lerwick: Shetland Times, 1985, pp. 95–127.

———, ed. *The Norse of the North Atlantic.* Acta Archaeologica 61. Copenhagen: Munksgaard, 1991.

Birkely, F. *Hva vet vi om kristningen av Norge? Utforskningen av norsk kristendoms—og kirkehistorie fra 900 till 1200 tallet.* Oslo: Universitetsforlaget, 1976.

Buchholz, P. The Religious Geography of Pagan Scandinavia: A New Research Project. *Medieval Scandinavia* (1972) 5:88–91.

Christophersen, A. Drengs, Thegns, Landmen, and Kings: Some Aspects on the Forms of Social Relations in Viking Societies during the Transition to Historic Times. *MLUHM,* n.s., (1981–1982) 4.

Crawford, B.E. *Scandinavian Scotland.* Leicester: Leicester University Press, 1987.

Davidson, H.E. Human Sacrifice in the Late Pagan Period in North-Western Europe. In *The Age of Sutton Hoo: The Seventh Century in North-Western Europe.* Ed. M.O.H. Carver. Woodbridge: Boydell, 1992, pp. 331–340.

Fell, Howard B. *America B.C.: Ancient Settlers in the New World.* New York: Quadrangle/New York Times, 1976.

Hedeager, L. *Danmarks jernalder: Mellem stamme og stat.* Aarhus: Aarhus Universitetsforlag, 1990.

———. *Iron Age Societies: From Tribe to State in Northern Europe.* Oxford: Basil Blackwell, 1992a.

———. Kingdoms, Ethnicity, and Material Culture: Denmark in a European Perspective. In *The Age of Sutton Hoo: The Seventh Century in North-Western Europe.* Ed. M.O.H. Carver. Woodbridge: Boydell, 1992b, pp. 279–300.

Hernaes, Per. *De arkeologiske undersokelsene pa Aker i Vang, 1988–89: Fra Kaupang og Bygd.* Hamar: Hedmarksmuseet og Domkirkeodden, 1989.

Hines, J. The Scandinavian Character of Anglian England: An Update. In *The Age of Sutton Hoo: The Seventh Century in North-Western Europe.* Ed. M.O.H. Carver. Woodbridge: Boydell, 1992, pp. 315–329.

Hultgreen, T., O.S. Johansen, and R.W. Lie. Stiuhelleren i Rana: Dokumentasjon av korn, husdyr of sild i yngre steinalder. *Viking* (1985) 42:83–102.

Johansen, O.S. Early Farming North of the Arctic Circle. *Norwegian Archaeological Review* (1979) 12:22–32.

———. Viking Age Farms: Estimating the Number and Population Size: A Case Study from Vestvagoy. *Norwegian Archaeological Review* (1982) 15:45–69.

Jones, G. *The Norse Atlantic Saga: Being the Norse Voyages of Discovery and Settlement to Iceland, Greenland, and North America.* Oxford: Oxford University Press, 1986.

Kepler, J.S. *The Exchange of Christendom.* Leicester: Leicester University Press, 1976.

Krag, C. *Kongedomme, kirke, stat.* Oslo: Universitetsforlaget, 1983.

Lund, N., ed. *Two Voyagers at the Court of King Alfred: The Ventures of Ohthere and Wulfstan together with the Description of Northern Europe from the Old English Orosius.* Trans. C.E. Fell. With Contributory Essays by Ole Crumlin-Pedersen, P.H. Sawyer, and C.E. Fell. York: William Sessions, 1984.

Magnusson, M., and H. Palsson, trans. *The Vinland Sagas: The Norse Discovery of America: Graenlendinga Saga and Eirik's Saga.* Introduced by M. Magnusson and H. Palsson. New York: New York University Press, 1966.

Mapp, A.J. *The Golden Dragon: Alfred the Great and His Times.* Lanham: Madison Books, 1985.

Mathiasen, Per. The Disappearance of the "Vastersjofinner" from Ringvasoy: Some Problems of Terminology, Methodology, and Data in the Study of Sami History. *Acta Borealia* (1984) (1):71–84.

McGovern, Thomas H. Cows, Harp Seals, and Church Bells: Adaptation and Extinction in Norse Greenland. *Human Ecology* (1980) 8:245–275.

———. The Arctic Frontier of Norse Greenland. In *The Archaeology of Frontiers and Boundaries.* Ed. S. Green and S. Perlman. New York: Academic, 1985a, pp. 275–323.

———. Contributions to the Paleoeconomy of Norse Greenland. *Acta Archaeologica* (1985b) 54:73–122.

Morison, Samuel Eliot. *The Discovery of North America: The Northern Voyages, A.D. 500–1600.* New York: Oxford University Press, 1971.

Morris, Chris. Viking Orkney: A Survey. In *The Prehistory of Orkney.* Ed. C. Renfrew. Edinburgh: Edinburgh University Press, 1985, pp. 210–242.

Morris, Christopher, and J. Rackham, eds. *Norse and Later Settlement and Subsistence in the North Atlantic.* Glasgow: University of Glasgow Press, 1992.

Myhre, B. 1987 Chieftains' Graves and Chiefdom Territories. *Studien zur Sachsenforschung 7.*

———. Agrarian Development, Settlement History, and Social Organization in South-West Norway in the Iron Age. In *New Directions in Scandinavian Archaeology.* Ed. K. Kristiansen and C. Paludan-Muller. København: National Museum of Denmark, 1978.

———. The Royal Cemetery at Borre, Vestfold: A Norwegian Centre in a European Periphery. In *The Age of Sutton Hoo: The Seventh Century in North-Western Europe.* Ed. M.O.H. Carver. Woodbridge: Boydell, 1992, pp. 301–313.

Nordic Council of Ministers. *From Viking to Crusader: Scandinavia and Europe, A.D. 800–1200.* Uddevalla: Bohuslaningens Boktryckeri AB, 1992.

Palsson, H., and P. Edwards, eds. *Vikings in Russia: Yngvar's Saga and Eymund's Saga.* Edinburgh: Edinburgh University Press, 1989.

Perdikaris, Sophia. Status and Economy: A Zooarchaeological Perspective from the Iron Age Site of Åker, Norway. In *Chacmool Conference Proceedings.* Calgary: University of Calgary, 1993.

Poertner, Rudolf. *The Vikings: Rise and Fall of the Norse Sea Kings.* Trans. Sophie Wilkins. London: St. James, 1975.

Quinn, David B. *North America from Earliest Discovery to First Settlements: The Norse Voyages to 1612.* New York: Harper and Row, 1977.

Randsborg, K. *The Viking Age in Denmark: The Formation of a State.* London: Duckworth, 1980.

Sawyer, P.H. *The Age of the Vikings.* New York: St. Martin's, 1971.

———. *Kings and Vikings: Scandinavia and Europe, A.D. 700–1100.* London: Methuen, 1982.

———. *Vikings: Raiders from the North.* Alexandria: Time-Life Books, 1993.

Wallace, B.L. L'Anse aux Meadows: Gateway to Vinland. *Acta Archaeologica* (1991) 61:166–198.

Sophia Perdikaris

SEE ALSO

Birka; Haithabu; Pre-Viking Scandinavia; Trondheim

Visigoths

Around the beginning of the Christian era, some of the Germanic people known as Goths left their homes in Scandinavia and migrated gradually southward. They encountered little difficulty until c. A.D. 230, when they reached the River Danube. Here they were repelled by the Roman army and forced to stay north of the Danube for more than a century. During this time, they split into two groups, the Ostrogoths and the Visigoths. Since the Visigoths were then nomadic people, they left few archaeological traces. Their tombs at Petroassa on the Danube contain primarily weapons and jewelry, especially a characteristic form of brooch.

Although the Romans continued to fight the Visigoths, some Visigoths enlisted in the Roman army, which badly needed more men. By the mid-fourth century, many of the best Roman soldiers were Goths, and even ethnically Roman soldiers were buried with Visigothic brooches as a status symbol. During this period, the Visigoths converted to Arian Christianity and began to elect kings. Gradually, the Visigoths were becoming assimilated.

In 376, however, the Huns attacked the Visigoths from the northeast and forced them into a desperate effort to cross the Danube. In 378, the Visigoths finally defeated the Romans at Adrianople and entered the Roman Empire. Still dissatisfied with the treatment they received from the Romans, in 410 they sacked Rome under their king, Alaric (c. 370–410). By 418, the Romans had settled the Visigoths in southern Gaul on considerably better land and on much more favorable terms. The settlement itself seems to have been peaceful, as it left no upheaval in the archaeological record; at Marseilles and Narbonne, occupation and trading continued undisturbed.

The Visigoths stayed in southern Gaul for about a century, mingling with the considerably more numerous native population, and here they left more substantial

V

archaeological remains. At their capital, Narbonne, archaeologists have found churches and chapels. At Bordeaux, trading continued. Rich villas with mosaics were built in the countryside (e.g., Palat, near St. Emilion, and Loupian), and this seems to have been a prosperous period for the Visigoths and for southern Gaul.

However, when the Franks under Clovis (c. 466–511) defeated the Visigoths at Vouillé in 507 and drove them out of southern Gaul, the Visigoths retreated south to Spain. Since the Vandals' departure for Africa in 429, Spain had been in a state of anarchy. The Visigoths found it easy to take control. As in Gaul, they were a small minority ruling many native Hispano-Romans. By the mid-sixth century, the main focus of the Visigothic Kingdom was in Spain, while most of their territory in Gaul had been abandoned to the Franks. The Elche hoard of gold jewelry in the Byzantine style dates to this period.

The Visigoths ruled Spain c. A.D. 500–711. Much of the archaeological evidence supports the traditional view that the fall of Roman government was catastrophic for Spain and that the Visigoths did not succeed in restoring the Roman standard of living. Cities declined in size, buildings declined in quality, and the size of the population fell dramatically under Visigothic rule. At Castulo and Carmona, Visigothic burials appear well within the Roman city walls. At Tarraco, the lower town was almost abandoned. Most of the surviving population huddled behind the old Roman Republican walls of the upper town. At Cartagena, little or no fine pottery was imported after 600, probably because the Spaniards were unable to afford imported wares. Extensive surface surveys also yield almost no fine wares imported to Spain after 625. Furthermore, it appears that many Roman sites were abandoned in the fifth century and were not reoccupied in the Visigothic period. A tendency to move to easily defended locations suggests a general insecurity.

Many Roman buildings fell into disrepair during this period or were deliberately destroyed. At Tarraco, a church was built inside the ruins of the old temple of Augustus, and another was constructed in the remains of the Roman amphitheater. An old forum became a quarry and was looted for its paving stones and marble decoration. At Barcino, Roman tombstones were reused to build a church. At Toledo, a church was built inside the old Roman circus. The old Roman roads deteriorated; surveys show that Visigothic farms tended to be located along the navigable rivers rather than along roads.

However, in other ways the Visigoths were energetic and ambitious leaders. They minted good-quality gold coins (tremisses) from 507 on, though the total absence of silver and copper coins suggests that coins were not used for most retail transactions. In 483, King Euric repaired the stone bridge over the Guadaira outside Mérida (still in use today), and the state cooperated with the Church to repair the walls of the town. King Leovigild (569–586) restored the walls of Italica and also founded two new cities, Reccopolis and Victoriacum. Excavations at Reccopolis revealed a royal palace with a two-story great hall supported by massive columns and buttresses, a large church, a huge city wall, an aqueduct that supplied the city with water, and many smaller houses as well. Byzantine influence is evident in both architecture and decoration.

The Visigoths built many churches and episcopal palaces, mainly in southwestern Spain, and decorated them with sculpture and relief carvings in a variety of regional styles. Mérida, for instance, was largely rebuilt by the Visigoths. The largest of several Visigothic churches at Tarraco measured 44×20 m^2 with a very wide central nave, two aisles separated by a twin colonnade, and rich marble decoration. Because the Arabs destroyed many churches in Spain, the rural churches that survived are not the best examples of the Visigoths' work. Such churches include San Juan de Baños in Palencia, San Pedro de Balsemâo in Portugal, San Pedro de la Nave in Zamora, and Santa Comba de Bande in Orense. Foundations of Visigothic churches remain at Barcino, Tarraco, Mérida, and Toledo, and at the smaller towns of Pedrera, Segobriga, Saetabis (modern Játiva), Egara, Egitania (modern Idanha-a-Velha in Portugal), and Emporiae. All of these churches are constructed of squared stone blocks mounted drystone in the Roman fashion. Many of them were barrel vaulted with brick, which is unusual in sixth-century Europe.

While the standard of living in Spain declined following the departure of the Romans, the Visigoths did much to maintain as high a standard as was possible in the new circumstances. They compare favorably to both the Merovingians and the Vandals. Nevertheless, the arrival of the Arabs in 711 clearly marks an improvement in the Spanish situation.

FURTHER READINGS

Keay, S.J. *Roman Spain*. Berkeley: University of California Press, 1988.

King, A. *Roman Gaul and Germany*. Berkeley: University of California Press, 1990.

King, P.D. *Law and Society in the Visigothic Kingdom.* Cambridge: Cambridge University Press, 1972.

Miles, G.C. *The Coinage of the Visigoths of Spain: Leovigild to Achila II.* New York: American Numismatic Society, 1952.

Thompson, E.A. *The Goths in Spain.* Oxford: Clarendon, 1969.

Karen Carr

SEE ALSO

Spain

W

Wales: Medieval Archaeology

Medieval archaeology in Wales was firmly established just before World War II by three benchmark publications: Sir Cyril Fox, *Offa's Dyke* (1926–1934, 1955); Royal Commission on Ancient Monuments, *Anglesey Inventory* (1939); and Sir John Lloyd, *A History of Wales* (1939). These mapped out the routes of field survey and documentary inquiry, after which the study *One Hundred Years of Welsh Archaeology*, edited by V.E. Nash-Williams (1949), was pivotal in reviewing past achievements and for suggesting research agenda in the post-Roman and the post-Norman periods, though the latter review was characteristically confined to castles and abbeys.

The organization of archaeology in Wales has gradually altered since 1945. The survey body, the Royal Commission on Ancient Monuments established in 1908, has been based in Wales at Aberystwyth since 1946 and now incorporates the National Monuments Record. It has produced detailed surveys of Caernarvonshire (1956–1964), Glamorgan (1972–), and prehistoric and Roman Breconshire (1982). The executive body, the Ancient Monuments Inspectorate (also known as CADW), is now an independent section based in Cardiff under the umbrella of the Welsh Office. It has produced more than one hundred guidebooks to the scheduled monuments in its care and some research papers. It employs both archaeologists and architects. The National Museum of Wales in Cardiff has had a long and distinguished involvement in medieval archaeology, often pioneering field surveys and artifact exhibition catalogs. The senior amateur society, the Cambrian Archaeological Association, was founded in 1847 and has since published an annual journal, a variety of monographs, and conference papers; it also encourages research through regular grants and prizes. The museum and the Cambrians have a limited excavation role, though they often provide a research forum by sponsoring conferences. The University of Wales has taken the lead in Celtic archaeology, first at Cardiff, especially under Fox, Sir Mortimer Wheeler, and Leslie Alcock, and more recently at the colleges in Bangor and Lampeter. Occasionally, the National Trust and the National Parks Authorities have encouraged archaeology on their properties or within their designated areas. The main change in archaeological provision came in 1974 with the establishment of four independent trusts to conduct rescue archaeology within the areas of southeast Wales: Glamorgan/Gwent (Swansea), southwest Wales Dyfed (Carmarthen), northeast Wales: Clwyd/Powys (Welshpool), and northwest Wales: Gwynedd (Bangor). Some local museums and district councils have appointed archaeologists whose role is to survey, excavate, record, and protect. This great expansion of personnel and activities has widened field archaeology in Wales.

The post-Roman centuries have been marked by three types of study: those that sought to understand the physical legacy of Rome, those that highlighted the political divisions and various attempts to unify the country; and those that examined early Celtic Christianity. The legacy of Rome was its small towns and villas, its coastal forts, roads, and milestones. Excavations at Caerleon, Caerwent, and Usk have shown some continued occupation, with Caerwent possibly occupied as a monastic site. The excavation of the farm at Whitton near Cardiff (Jarrett and Wrathmell 1978) has not provided such clear evidence of post-Roman use as did the prewar excavation at Llantwit Major in the vale of Glamorgan. The comprehensive

W

work at Llystin southeast of Caernarfon (Hogg 1968) showed a small fort used near the end of the Roman occupation; the place name and an inscribed stone hint at continuity of site use into the post-Roman centuries. Sporadic excavation at Caer Gybi (Holyhead) has also suggested some post-Roman use. Work on Roman roads, some called "Sarn Helen," and on the burial stones beside them (such as the Bodvoc stone) has recently had a low priority, but Roman milestones, reused as burial markers, have occasionally been found and have stimulated discussion.

Research on Dark Age Wales, or preferably on the successor kingdoms, has concentrated on identifying and excavating the fortified high-status sites. Excavations by Alcock at Dinas Powys near Cardiff (Alcock 1963) and at Degannwy near Conwy (Alcock 1967) were more modest than his campaign at "Arthurian" South Cadbury in Somerset (Alcock 1972). Another "Arthurian" site, at Dinas Emrys within Snowdonia, gave ambiguous results. In all these forts and at some religious houses, the presence of imported Mediterranean wares seemed to draw the native Welsh into a wider trading network, but more work is needed. The recent excavation of a crannóg (a manmade island) in Llangorse Lake has shown an exciting range of craft and occupation debris from a ninth–tenth-century princely residence (Campbell and Lane 1989; Redknapp 1991). Fieldwork in Gwynedd has identified other "Dark Age" forts, small in area, with strong rocky defenses and difficult entrances, such as Garn Boduan and Carreg-y-llam; their farming counterparts of homesteads and fields are now being identified by Crew and Kelly. The bibliographical work of N. Edwards and A. Lane (1988) is an essential guide.

The study of major ecclesiastical sites has been hampered by their continuance in religious use. A few minor sites have been tackled: Capel Eithin on Anglesey, Llandegai near Bangor in Gwynedd, Capel Maelog near Llandrindod Wells (Britnell 1990), and Burry Holms off Gower, but most have given inconclusive results on dating. More satisfactory has been the thorough survey of early Christian memorial stones (Nash-Williams 1950); however, several new discoveries have augmented the corpus, and a new edition has been long in preparation. Edwards and Lane (1992) have provided a critical survey of early religious sites.

Relatively little evidence has emerged of Saxon and Viking raids and even less of settlements. Chronicle entries give more eloquent testimony of external pressure; archaeological evidence has been restricted to coin hoards

and isolated finds, apart from successfully identifying the Anglian *burh* (fortified town) at Rhuddlan (Manley 1987). By contrast, the Norman invasions of the period 1070–1170 irreversibly changed the political and economic landscape. Castles were erected, either at strategic locations or at the old commotal centers; new cathedrals and abbeys were built; urbanism was introduced with defended towns; and new settlers, both Norman and Fleming, were placed in nucleated villages. Pottery was introduced from midland England and soon was produced locally to serve the needs of new markets.

The most thorough excavation of a Norman timber-and-earthwork castle has been at Hen Domen near Montgomery, producing excellent evidence of many structures, tantalizing details of living standards, and clear indications of the arable fields preceding and underlying the defenses (Barker and Higham 1982, 1988, 1992). Three other early castles have been extensively sampled: Rumney (Lightfoot 1992) and Llantrithryd near Cardiff (Charlton et al. 1977) and Penmaen in Gower (Alcock 1966). The catalog prepared by A.H.A. Hogg and D.J.C. King (1963) has provided a valuable checklist. At the Norman abbeys, there has been important work at Haverfordwest and a more limited examination of Chepstow. In the latter town, there have been a number of small excavations (Shoesmith 1991), as there have been at Monmouth and Cowbridge (Robinson 1980). The only extensive urban work has been in Rhuddlan, with evidence of a Saxon Borough defense, Norman town defenses, a small church, housing, and craft workshops (Quinnell and Blockley 1994). As a by-product of the Roman excavations at Usk, the medieval structures and sequences have been recorded (Courtney 1994). Excavation on village sites has usually been limited in scope, but a few syntheses have been published (Butler 1971, 1988, 1991; Owen 1989).

The later twelfth and thirteenth centuries were marked by native Welsh resistance and renaissance. Two castles in Powys received detailed surveys (King 1974). There have been major castle excavations at Dolforwyn in Powys (Butler 1989) and Dryslwyn in Dyfed (Caple 1990). Both have been sufficiently complete to provide details of individual buildings with the sequence of their occupation and social changes. A checklist of all masonry castles in Wales has been provided by Hogg and King (1967, 1970). Prolonged excavation has occurred on three English castles: the royal one at Montgomery (Knight 1992), the baronial Laugharne (Avent 1992), and the gentry-built Penhow (Wrathmell 1990).

The Edwardian conquest (1277–1284) marked the end of an independent Welsh state, crushed by the imposition of castles and walled towns constructed with royal and baronial resources (Taylor 1973, 1977). Except at Aberystwyth, there has only been minor work on these castles, but more extensive excavation has been conducted within the walled town of Conwy (Butler 1964; Butler and Evans 1979; Kelly 1979). There have been various works of synthesis and some pioneering articles on urbanism (Griffiths 1978; Butler 1979, 1985; Soulsby 1983), but the concentration has been upon survey. There has been extensive excavation at the Greyfriars in Carmarthen (James, forthcoming) and some work on the Cistercian Abbey at Maenan, transferred from Conwy in 1283 (Butler and Evans 1980). The Cistercians have been the subject of excavation (Valle Crucis: Butler 1977; Tintern: Courtney 1989) and field survey (James 1978; Williams 1990). Church excavation has taken place on rural sites such as Highlight, Pennant Melangell (Britnell 1992), Rhosili (Davidson et al. 1987), and Llangar (Shoesmith 1980), mainly in the lowlands. Some emergency recording work has been undertaken, as on the medieval wall paintings at Llandeilo Talybont. The survey of late medieval moated homesteads (Spurgeon 1981) has emphasized their intrusive English character, as have the village excavations at Barry and Cosmeston, both in the anglicized Vale of Glamorgan. There is little to report on medieval industrial sites, apart from the survey of pottery used in Wales (Papazian and Campbell 1992), the floor tiles found in Wales (Lewis 1976), and the surviving medieval bronze vessels (Lewis 1978). Production sites are difficult to locate with certainty.

Since the end of World War II, the important work of the Royal Commission has continued in many counties, and it has published an exceptionally fine volume, *Houses of the Welsh Countryside* (Smith 1975, rev. 1988), marking the culmination of decades of study upon vernacular architecture. A new generation of national and county histories is in progress (Davies 1987; Williams 1987). Final publication of excavations lags far behind, and since 1974 there have been very few reports commensurate with the frenetic level of activity and public funding. In part this is because there has been a dichotomy between the major long-term excavations sponsored by CADW (Welsh Heritage) and the universities and, on the other hand, the myriad of minor interventions and observations undertaken by the four regional trusts. The latter are published in local journals, ephemeral news sheets, and interim reports of the respective trusts; the former excavations are usually the subject of monographs, which may be longer in gestation and even longer in production. However, there has been an expansion of museums, of local fieldwork groups, as at Monmouth, and of university students of archaeology, as at Lampeter and at Trinity College, Caermarthen. It remains to be seen whether this expansion generates greater awareness of the archaeological potential in Wales or whether the major research and record initiatives will remain with the three state-funded bodies: CADW, National Museum of Wales, and the Royal Commission on Ancient Monuments. The development of environmental research at Cardiff and Lampeter and the sponsoring of underwater research by the National Museum of Wales in Cardiff are two positive steps that offer excellent prospects for the future of study into life in medieval Wales.

FURTHER READINGS

Alcock, L. *Dinas Powys.* Cardiff: University of Wales Press, 1963.

———. Castle Tower, Penmaen. *Antiquaries Journal* (1966) 46:178–210.

———. Excavations at Degannwy Castle, 1961–6. *Archaeological Journal* (1967) 124:190–201.

———. *"By South Cadbury That Is Camelot": The Excavations of Cadbury Castle, 1966–70.* London: Thames and Hudson, 1972.

Avent, R. The Medieval Development of Laugharne Castle, Dyfed. *Chateau Gaillard* (1992) 15:7–18.

Barker, P., and R. Higham. *Hen Domen: A Timber Castle on the English-Welsh Border.* Vol. 1. London: Royal Archaeological Institute, 1982.

———. *Hen Domen: A Timber Castle on the English-Welsh Border, Excavations, 1960–88.* Worcester: Hen Domen Archaeological Project, 1988.

———. *Timber Castles.* London: Batsford, 1992.

Britnell, W.J. Capel Maelog, Llandrindod Wells, Powys: Excavations, 1984–7. *Medieval Archaeology* (1990) 34:27–96.

———. Pennant Melangell Church, Llangynog. *Archaeology in Wales* (1992) 32:67, 84.

Butler, L.A.S. Excavations in the Vicarage Garden, Conway, 1961. *Archaeologia Cambrensis* (1964) 113:97–128.

———. Medieval Settlements in Wales. In *Deserted Medieval Villages.* Ed. M.W. Beresford and J.G. Hurst. London: Lutterworth, 1971, pp. 249–276.

———. Valle Crucis Abbey: An Excavation in 1970. *Archaeologia Cambrensis* (1977) 125:80–126.

———. The Monastic City in Wales: Myth or Reality? *Bulletin of the Board of Celtic Studies* (1979) 28: 458–467.

———. Planned Anglo-Norman Towns in Wales. In *The Comparative History of Urban Origins in Non-Roman Europe.* Ed. H.B. Clarke and A. Simms. BAR International Series 255. Oxford: British Archaeological Reports, 1985, pp. 469–504.

———. Rural Building in Wales. In *The Agrarian History of England and Wales II: 1042–1350.* Ed. H.E. Hallam. Cambridge: Cambridge University Press, 1988, pp. 931–965.

———. Dolforwyn Castle, Powys: First Report, 1981–86. *Archaeologia Cambrensis* (1989) 138:78–98.

———. Rural Housing in Wales. In *The Agrarian History of England and Wales III: 1348–1500.* Ed. E. Miller. Cambridge: Cambridge University Press, 1991, pp. 891–919.

Butler, L.A.S., and D.H. Evans. The Old Vicarage, Conway: Excavations, 1963–64. *Archaeologia Cambrensis* (1979) 128:40–105.

———. The Cistercian Abbey of Aberconway. *Archaeologia Cambrensis* (1980) 129:37–63.

Campbell, E., and A. Lane. Llangorse: A Tenth-Century Royal Crannóg in Wales. *Antiquity* (1989) 63:675–681.

Caple, C. The Castle and Lifestyle of a Thirteenth-Century Independent Welsh Lord: Excavations at Dryslwyn Castle, 1980–88. *Chateau Gaillard* (1990) 14:47–59.

Charlton, D., J. Roberts, and V. Vale. *Llantrithyd: A Ringwork in South Glamorgan.* Cardiff: Cardiff Archaeological Society, 1977.

Courtney, P. Excavations on the Outer Precinct of Tintern Abbey. *Medieval Archaeology* (1989) 33:99–143.

———. *Report on the Excavations at Usk: Medieval and Later Usk.* Cardiff: University of Wales Press, 1994.

Davidson, A.F., et al. Excavations at the Sand-Covered Medieval Settlement at Rhosili, West Glamorgan. *Bulletin of the Board of Celtic Studies* (1987) 34:244–270.

Davies, R.R. *Conquest, Coexistence, and Change: Wales, 1063–1415.* Oxford: Oxford University Press, 1987.

Edwards, N., and A. Lane. *Early Medieval Settlements in Wales, A.D. 400–1100.* Bangor: University College of North Wales, 1988.

———. *The Early Church in Wales and the West.* Oxbow Monograph 16. Oxford, 1992.

Fox, C. Offa's Dyke: A Field Survey. Annual articles in *Archaeologia Cambrensis* (1926–1934).

———. *Offa's Dyke.* London: British Academy, 1955.

Griffiths, R.A., ed. *Boroughs of Medieval Wales.* Cardiff: University of Wales Press, 1978.

Hogg, A.H.A. Pen Llystin: A Roman Fort and Other Remains. *Archaeological Journal* (1968) 125:101–192.

Hogg, A.H.A., and D.J.C. King. Early Castles in Wales and the Marches. *Archaeologia Cambrensis* (1963) 112:77–144.

———. Masonry Castles in Wales and the Marches. *Archaeologia Cambrensis* (1967) 116:71–132.

———. Masonry Castles in Wales and the Marches: Additions. *Archaeologia Cambrensis* (1970) 119: 119–124.

James, T. A Survey at Whitland Abbey. *Carmarthenshire Antiquity* (1978) 14:71–77.

———. *Excavations at Carmarthen Greyfriars,* forthcoming.

Jarrett, M., and S. Wrathmell. *Whitton: An Iron Age and Roman Farmstead in South Glamorgan.* Cardiff: University of Wales Press, 1978.

Kelly, R.S. Excavations on Two Sites in Conway, 1975. *Archaeologia Cambrensis* (1979) 128:104–118.

King, D.J.C. Two Castles in Northern Powys: Dinas Bran and Caergwrle. *Archaeologia Cambrensis* (1974) 123:113–139.

Knight, J.K. Excavations at Montgomery Castle. *Archaeologia Cambrensis* (1992) 141:97–180.

Lewis, J.M. *Welsh Medieval Paving Tiles.* Cardiff: National Museum of Wales, 1976.

———. *Medieval Pottery and Metalware in Wales.* Cardiff: National Museum of Wales, 1978.

Lightfoot, K.W.B. Rumney Castle: A Ringwork and Manorial Centre in South Glamorgan. *Medieval Archaeology* (1992) 36:96–163.

Lloyd, J.E. *A History of Wales.* 3rd ed. London: Longmans, Green and Co. 1939.

Manley, J. Cledemutha: A Late Saxon Burh in North Wales. *Medieval Archaeology* (1987) 31:13–46.

Nash-Williams, V.E. *One Hundred Years of Welsh Archaeology.* Gloucester: Cambrian Archaeological Association, 1949.

———. *Early Christian Monuments in Wales.* Cardiff: University of Wales Press, 1950.

Owen, D.H., ed. *Settlement and Society in Wales.* Cardiff: University of Wales Press, 1989.

Papazian, C., and E. Campbell. Medieval Pottery and Roof Tile in Wales, A.D. 1100–1600. *Medieval and Later Pottery in Wales* (1992):1–107.

Quinnell, H., and M. Blockley. *Excavations at Rhuddlan, Clwyd, 1969–73.* CBA Research Report 95. London: Council for British Archaeology, 1994.

Redknapp, M. Llangorse Crannóg. *Archaeology in Wales* (1991) 31:38–39.

Robinson, D.M. *Cowbridge: The Archaeology and Topography of a Small Market Town in the Vale of Glamorgan.* Swansea: Glamorgan/Gwent Archaeological Trust, 1980.

———. Medieval Vernacular Buildings Below the Ground. *Glamorgan-Gwent Archaeological Trust Annual Report 1981–2:* 94–123.

Royal Commission on Ancient Monuments (RCAM). *Anglesey Inventory.* London: HMSO, 1939.

Shoesmith, R. Llangar Church. *Archaeologia Cambrensis* (1980) 129:64–123.

———. *Excavations at Chepstow, 1973–1974.* Monograph 4. Leeds: Cambrian Archaeological Association, 1991.

Smith, P. *Houses of the Welsh Countryside* London: HMSO, 1975, 1988.

Soulsby, I.N. *The Towns of Medieval Wales.* Chichester: Phillimore, 1983.

Spurgeon, C.J. Moated Sites in Wales. In *Medieval Moated Sites in North-West Europe.* Ed. F.A. Aberg and A.E. Brown. BAR International Series 121. Oxford: British Archaeological Reports, 1981, pp. 19–70.

Taylor, A.J. *The History of the King's Works in Wales, 1277–1330.* London: HMSO, 1973.

———. Castle Building in Thirteenth-Century Wales and Savoy. *Proceedings of the British Academy* (1977) 63:104–133.

Williams, D.H. *Atlas of Cistercian Lands in Wales.* Cardiff: University of Wales Press, 1990.

Williams, G. *Recovery, Reorientation, and Reformation: Wales, c. 1415–1642.* Oxford: Oxford University Press, 1987.

Wrathmell, S. Penhow Castle, Gwent: Survey and Excavation, 1976–9. *Monmouthshire Antiquary* (1990) 6:17–45.

L.A.S. Butler

SEE ALSO

Dinas Powys; Llangorse Crannóg; Wales: Medieval Settlement

Wales: Medieval Settlement

Wales is essentially a mountainous country with a substantial area above the 300-m contour. This terrain of slates and metamorphic rocks was suitable only for pastoral farming. A coastal belt varying from 32 km wide to less than 1.0 km extends around the whole of Wales from the mouth of the River Wye in the south to the Dee estuary in the north. The island of Anglesey lies within the coastal zone, which was normally devoted to arable regimes for cereal production. A middle zone on the flanks of the broad inland valleys of the east-flowing Dee, Wye, and Severn and of those rivers flowing into the seas surrounding Wales was subject to a mixed farming economy, dependent on the prevailing climate and the economic imperatives. It is this middle zone that experienced the greatest pressure for change in the period c. 400–1600. In general, the clearance of forest, the draining of marshes, the exploitation of peat beds, and the occasional cultivation of outfields were the main changes, though there are also botanical indicators of climatic amelioration between 900 and 1100 and subsequent deterioration between 1300 and 1500.

The major concerns in the study of medieval settlement have been to reconcile the evidence furnished by documents, by geography, and by archaeology. The documentary evidence for the post-Roman period is largely the information from legal codes attributed to Hywel Dda (d. c. 950). These legislate for various domestic circumstances and assign compensation within a barter economy. There is considerable emphasis on timber-building construction, on the houses of the prince's Court, and on agrarian practices, mentioning plows and widths of plow furrows. Horse rearing, cattle herds, and sheep flocks were major concerns; their meat, horns, hides, and fleece were essentials within the economy.

The geographical evidence is twofold: it is partly the use of place names to identify the date and nature of settlement; it is partly the examination of the composition and sustenance of multiple estates. The pioneering work of Glanville Jones (1972, 1989) has disentangled these relationships from clues in late medieval documents. Through discussion of soil suites and settlement siting, he has reconstructed the early medieval land conditions in the immediate post-Roman centuries. These are attractive and convincing hypotheses that still require confirmation by archaeological excavation.

The archaeological evidence has been colored by two scenarios. On the one hand, there has been a desire to confirm the theoretical model provided by the Welsh laws *(cyfraith Hywel)* and to identify the hierarchy of settlements postulated within the system of multiple estates, e.g., court *(llys)* and steward's town *(maerdref)*. On the other hand, there has been a pragmatic approach, seeking to understand the variety of visible homesteads within the post-Roman successor kingdoms in terms that make sense throughout late Celtic Iron Age in Britain before the Anglo-Saxon expansion affected the eastern borders of Wales. There has also been a need to recognize the Celtic migrations around the Irish Sea that resulted in the colonization of Brittany and the transfer of the Desi tribe from Leinster to occupy forts, or raths, in southwest Wales.

In terms of hierarchy, it seems clear that the ruling classes often lived in, or had access to, long-established hillforts or newly created craggy outposts, as at Garn Boduan, Degannwy, and Dinas Emrys. Here tribute and gift exchange stimulated the economy, smiths and bards were patronized, and religious leaders sponsored or received. There is no evidence that the Roman network of small towns or regional *oppida* continued to operate as urban centers, though a few sites, such as Caerwent and Caergybi (Holyhead), might be occupied for religious purposes. However, the continuity of villa estates into early medieval land units (mentioned in the Llancarfan and Llandaf charters) has not been proved archaeologically, though the land-utilization potential makes this an attractive possibility and would provide an efficient balance of resources (Davies 1979).

By contrast, settlement in isolated farmsteads was likely to be in rectangular or subrectangular "long huts" rather than in Romano-British round huts. These huts were ridge roofed and timber framed set on stone footings, usually with the main axis along the hill slope. Some were accompanied by walled paddocks or stockyards and contained circular pigsties with corbelled roofs. It is assumed that the pattern of small rectangular "Celtic" fields would have continued with little alteration. However, the main sustenance of the upland settlements would have been a subsistence economy based on pastoral grazing. This still needs to be confirmed more convincingly by excavation (Edwards and Lane 1988).

Although the eastern borders of Wales were subjected to Anglo-Saxon influences and occasional invasion between 800 and 1050, the physical demarcation given by Offa's Dyke (built 780–790) was generally accepted as a legal land barrier, and, apart from the *burh* (fortified town) of Cledemutha (Rhuddlan at the mouth of the River Clwyd), there was no substantial or permanent Anglo-Saxon settlement west of the dyke. Indeed, Welsh-speaking communities continued to occupy their settlements in undulating hill country around Oswestry in north Shropshire and in Archenfield of southwest Herefordshire. The Vikings raided many coastal areas and monasteries, but no certain proof of settlement has yet been found. Deposits of coin hordes and hack silver only indicate troubled conditions. The prevalence of Norse place names for peninsulas and islands does raise the problem of verbal transmission, presumably through Ireland and Viking Chester.

The major change to the character of late medieval settlement came with the Norman Conquest. This was a process extending over two centuries from 1080. The first wave of invasion effectively held the low-lying coastlands along the northern shore of the Severn estuary from the Wye at Chepstow to St. David's Head. At the same time, the eastern frontier south of the Severn at Montgomery was pushed westward to create the lordships of Builth, Brecon, and Radnor. Within these newly settled territories, the Normans created nucleated rural settlements and urban centers.

The towns were sometimes based on preexisting taxation points or monasteries, as at Carmarthen and Newport in Gwent (Soulsby 1983; Butler 1979, 1985). These towns were usually based upon a new castle, which might be named from its founding lord or from the territorial unit he controlled. The town would be laid out on a simple grid plan of streets, following as regular a pattern as the terrain allowed. Although the framework of streets and the location of churches have usually survived with little alteration, the market space has often been encroached upon, and the houses all have been replaced. The best example of urban excavation has been the work on the deserted area of the Norman town of Rhuddlan (Quinnell and Blockley 1994); this uncovered houses, smithies, and a small church. Work on Chepstow (Shoesmith 1991), Newport in Dyfed (Murphy 1994), and Usk (Courtney 1994) has explored some of the houses and burgage plots, showing evidence for traders and craftsmen but with a strong agricultural participation. All the towns had common fields surrounding them, though of widely varying extent. The introduction of coinage with mints at Cardiff, Swansea, and St. Davids was a Norman innovation, though relatively short lived as the monarchy centralized the issuing of silver pennies. The parallel introduction of pottery (Papazian and Campbell 1992) also changed the cultural patterns of the native Welsh, who then had access to a greater range of imports.

It also marked a shift from a pattern of mutual obligation based on personal service and tribute to a market economy protected by charters and reinforced by tolls and a formalized tithe system.

Excavation of castles has been discussed elsewhere, but the survey and investigation of the new Norman and Flemish settlements has been slow work (Courtney 1983; Kissock 1990). Only the excavation of the deserted village of Cosmeston near Cardiff has been on a scale that has enabled variations in the social use of space to be perceived. Elsewhere, small hamlets or individual houses have been tackled, mainly in Glamorgan (Butler 1988, 1991). No specifically Flemish settlement has been examined, though whether it would be recognizable from its constructional details or its artifactual assemblage is uncertain. In some cases, the Flemings who had retreated from the dangers of coastal inundation in eleventh-century Flanders were subjected to coastal sand-dune movement throughout the later Middle Ages. Farther east, colonization in the Wentloog levels was a phenomenon of the central Middle Ages until halted by the disastrous flood of 1610. Throughout the coastlands of south Wales and that part of the Cheshire plain that lay in northeast Wales, the incoming gentry (advenae) were defending or distinguishing their homesteads by constructing moated enclosures (Spurgeon 1981).

By contrast, those areas under Welsh rulers or under Welsh laws (The Welshry) were characterized by nonnucleated, or dispersed, settlements (Butler 1987). Either these were set in girdle fashion around the available arable land at the hillside junction, with the plowland situated below and the rough grazing above, or they were set as small hamlets (trefi) growing from an initial forest clearance or from a summer dairy farm (hafod or lluest). The most instructive of recent excavations has been at Graeanog, where four rectangular houses were set on a small terrace in the shelter of a low hill in coastal Arfon. The material culture and the radiocarbon (C-14) dating of the charcoal indicated a twelfth-century date. Different huts were used for distinct purposes—dwelling, barn, byre, and stable (Kelly 1982). Elsewhere, excavation and field survey has been small in scale, usually only a single hut excavated or a limited district surveyed (Butler 1971; Robinson 1982). The major exceptions to this have been the extensive survey work of the Royal Commission in Caernarvonshire and Glamorgan (RCAM 1964, 1982), the research program in the Moelwyns and the Rhinogs of southern Snowdonia, and the concentration upon "platform houses" in northwest Wales by C.A. Gresham (1963).

Although many surveys have given some attention to the ancillary storage building, the animal pens, and the drying kilns, they need a deeper integration with estate documents (e.g., Thomas 1970, 1975) or, in the case of the Cistercian granges, with the land charters and disputes to understand fully the farming regimes. Only Merthyrgeryn, a lowland grange of Tintern in south Wales, has had exploratory excavation to match the documentary scrutiny (Parkes and Webster 1974; Williams 1990). There is a continuing need for environmental work in the lake sediments and upland bogs to understand the vegetation patterns and changes caused by land clearance.

The conquest of northeast Wales by King Edward I (1239–1307) between 1277 and 1294 introduced a number of "bastides," or walled towns, laid out on a regular grid plan, usually located as an integral part of a castle's defenses acting as its outermost bailey (Beresford 1967). There has been some excavation in recent years, but it has usually been limited to one or two burgage plots. In Caernarvon, Conwy, and Beaumaris, a few houses still survive of late medieval date. However, the fullest information about the appearance and materials of the later medieval housing comes from the rural halls, tower houses, and chamber blocks of the incipient gentry (Smith 1975:18–139). These indicate that, apart from providing the dimensions of the houses, any excavation of low stone footings in rural locations can give little idea of the pretensions and artistic sophistication of those structures that they supported. That substantial houses could be built emphasized the accumulation of wealth based on service to the Crown and upon exploitation of the English tax system.

There were few compensating benefits for the lower classes. The search for the "peasant house" has until recently been hampered by preconceptions fostered by the eighteenth-century English gentry travelers. House-and-byre homesteads or longhouses (tai hirion) in which humans and cattle were sheltered under the same roof were recorded as a regional phenomenon in the nineteenth century. However, it is still unresolved whether these were the final primitive survivors of a once universal housing arrangement or whether there was a vernacular threshold, where the peasantry normally shared their dwellings with the animals while the gentry and yeomanry (uchelwyr) maintained a social and economic distinction, housing their animals separately. The latter class also made greater use of pigeons and fish within their diet, evidenced by dovecotes and ponds. Rabbits may also have been part of the diet, though the warrens

W

were created predominantly for the fur trade (Austin 1988:149–156).

The concentration upon the physical appearance and internal arrangements of the dwelling houses has often been at the expense of evaluating their setting, the stock processing, the mills, the craft workshops, the mineral extractions, and the field systems (Davies 1973; Jones 1973; Fleming 1987). Most of our recent knowledge has been summarized in L.A.S. Butler (1988) and D.H. Owen (1989). These general surveys will, it is hoped, provide the starting points for the next generation of archivists, economic historians, fieldworkers, and excavators to probe the gaps and question the tacit assumptions about medieval settlement in Wales.

FURTHER READINGS

Austin, D. Excavations and Survey at Bryn Cysegrfan, Llanfair Clydogau, Dyfed 1979. *Medieval Archaeology* (1988) 32:130–165.

Baker, A.R.H., and R.A. Butlin. *Studies of Field Systems in the British Isles.* Cambridge: Cambridge University Press, 1973.

Beresford, M.W. *New Towns of the Middle Ages.* London: Lutterworth, 1967.

Butler, L.A.S. Medieval Settlements in Wales. In *Deserted Medieval Villages.* Ed. M.W. Beresford and J.G. Hurst. London: Lutterworth, 1971, pp. 249–276.

———. The Monastic City in Wales: Myth or Reality? *Bulletin of the Board of Celtic Studies* (1979) 28:458–467.

———. Planned Anglo-Norman Towns in Wales. In *The Comparative History of Urban Origins in Non-Roman Europe.* Ed. H.B. Clarke and A. Simms. BAR International Series 255. Oxford: British Archaeological Reports, 1985, pp. 469–504.

———. Domestic Building in Wales and the Evidence of the Welsh Laws. *Medieval Archaeology* (1987) 31:47–58.

———. Rural Building in Wales. In *The Agrarian History of England and Wales II: 1042–1350.* Ed. H.E. Hallam. Cambridge: Cambridge University Press, 1988, pp. 931–965.

———. Rural Housing in Wales. In *The Agrarian History of England and Wales III: 1348–1500.* Ed. E. Miller. Cambridge: Cambridge University Press, 1991, pp. 891–919.

Courtney, P. The Rural Landscape of Eastern and Lower Gwent, c. A.D. 1070–1750. Ph.D. thesis, University of Wales, 1983.

———. *Medieval and Later Usk.* Cardiff: University of Wales Press, 1994.

Davies, M. Field Systems of South Wales. In *Studies of Field Systems in the British Isles.* Ed. A.R.H. Baker and R.A. Butlin. Cambridge: Cambridge University Press, 1973, pp. 480–529.

Davies, W. Roman Settlements and Post-Roman Estates in South-East Wales. In *The End of Roman Britain.* Ed. P.J. Casey. BAR British Series 71. Oxford: British Archaeological Reports, 1979, pp. 153–171.

Edwards, N., and A. Lane. *Early Medieval Settlements in Wales, A.D. 400–1100.* Bangor: University College of North Wales, 1988.

Fleming, A. Co-Axial Field Systems: Some Questions of Time and Space. *Antiquity* (1987) 61:188–202.

Gresham, C.A. The Interpretation of Settlement Patterns in North-West Wales. In *Culture and Environment.* Ed. I.L. Foster and L. Alcock. London: Routledge, Kegan Paul, 1963, pp. 263–279.

Jones, G.R.H. Post-Roman Wales. In *The Agrarian History of England and Wales I: A.D. 43–1042.* Ed. H.P.R. Finberg. Cambridge: Cambridge University Press, 1972, pp. 340–349.

———. Field Systems in North Wales. In *Studies of Field Systems in the British Isles.* Ed. A.R.H. Baker and R.A. Butlin. Cambridge: Cambridge University Press, 1973, pp. 430–479.

———. The Dark Ages. In *Settlement and Society in Wales.* Ed. D.H. Owen. Cardiff: University of Wales Press, 1989, pp. 177–197.

Kelly, R. A Medieval Farmstead at Cefn Graenog. *Bulletin of the Board of Celtic Studies* (1982) 29:859–908.

Kissock, J.A. The Origin of the Village in South Wales: A Study in Landscape Archaeology. Ph.D. thesis, Leicester University, 1990.

Murphy, K. Excavations in Three Burgage Plots in the Medieval Town of Newport, Dyfed, 1991. *Medieval Archaeology* (1994) 38:55–82.

Owen, D.H. The Middle Ages. In *Settlement and Society in Wales.* Ed. D.H. Owen. Cardiff: University of Wales Press, 1989, pp. 199–223.

———, ed. *Settlement and Society in Wales.* Cardiff: University of Wales Press, 1989.

Papazian, C., and E. Campbell. Medieval Pottery and Roof Tile in Wales, A.D. 1100–1600. *Medieval and Later Pottery in Wales* (1992):1–107.

Parkes, L.N., and P.V. Webster. Merthyrgeryn: A Grange of Tintern. *Archaeologia Cambrensis* (1974) 123:140–154.

Quinnell, H., and M. Blockley. *Excavations at Rhuddlan, Clwyd, 1969–73.* CBA Research Report 95. London: Council for British Archaeology, 1994.

Royal Commission on Ancient Monuments (RCAM). *Caernarvonshire Inventory,* 3. London: HMSO, 1964.

———. *Glamorgan Inventory,* 3, part 2. London: HMSO, 1982.

Robinson, D.M. Medieval Vernacular Buildings Below the Ground. *Glamorgan-Gwent Archaeological Trust Annual Report 1981–2:*94–123.

Shoesmith, R. *Excavations at Chepstow, 1973–1974.* Monograph 4. Leeds: Cambrian Archaeological Association, 1991.

Smith, P. *Houses of the Welsh Countryside.* London: HMSO, 1975, 1988.

Soulsby, I.N. *The Towns of Medieval Wales.* Chichester: Phillimore, 1983.

Spurgeon, C.J. Moated Sites in Wales. In *Medieval Moated Sites in North-West Europe.* Ed. F.A. Aberg and A.E. Brown. BAR International Series 121. Oxford: British Archaeological Reports, 1981, pp. 19–70.

Thomas, C. Social Organization and Rural Settlement in Medieval North Wales. *Journal of the Merionethshire Historical and Record Society* (1970) 6 (part 2):121–131.

———. Peasant Agriculture in Gwynedd. *Folk Life* (1975) 13:24–37.

Williams, D.H. *Atlas of Cistercian Lands in Wales.* Cardiff: University of Wales Press, 1990.

L.A.S. Butler

SEE ALSO
Raths; Wales: Medieval Archaeology

Warden Abbey

Warden Abbey, the premier Cistercian house in southern England and daughter house of Rievaulx, was founded by Walter Espec in 1135 in Bedfordshire on wasteland. The site has been the subject of investigation—antiquarian, amateur, and professional—since c. 1830, when an ancestor of the present owner, Samuel Whitbread, undertook wall-following and probing in the area of the church. The whole of the precinct boundary has been traced, and the complex monastic and postmonastic earthworks surveyed. They include a great dam, complexes of fishponds, industrial zones, and postmedieval gardens and ponds belonging to the Gostwick Mansion, which was built over part of the site at the Reformation. Of the claustral remains, nothing is standing above ground.

Bradford Rudge compiled the earliest drawn records in 1835. He drew a plan of most of the claustral complex that included fixed points on postmedieval masonry garden structures, which are fortunately still extant. He beautifully illustrated a range of splendid artifacts: elaborate stone bosses, superb metalwork, and unique medieval floor tiles. Investigations by the Bedford Archaeological Society in the early 1960s led to the discovery of a fine *in situ* line-impressed mosaic tile pavement within the abbey church and discovered further details of the abbey's plan.

The Bedfordshire County Archaeology Service undertook rescue excavations during the renovation of the Gostwick Mansion, elucidated more of the plan, reexcavated the tile pavement of the church, and discovered a further area of paving in what it interpreted as the abbot's lodging; this included a series of the unique tiles of the type illustrated by Rudge. The church was impressive, rivaling many cathedrals in size. The whole of the east end was rebuilt in the first quarter of the fourteenth century, and the rest refurbished on a grand scale. The works included a probable reflooring of the whole building with extremely expensive, custom-made tile paving.

The floor tiles are one of the most important aspects of Warden; more than eight thousand tiles of about five hundred designs were recovered. This expensive and rare assemblage includes two rare Cistercian tiles dating probably to the first part of the thirteenth century and paralleled at the Abbaye des Dunes, Ter Duinen, Belgium. Other types include sgraffiato tiles, two-color tiles, counterrelief, line-impressed pseudomosaic, mosaic, and line-impressed designs, and some experimental pieces. There is good evidence for proposing Warden as the major production site for line-impressed tiles, distributing designs over the East Anglian region, possibly including Ely Cathedral. It has been possible to reconstruct the designs of the two magnificent pavements, even though on one of them the surface has been almost entirely worn away, by recording glaze on the sites of the tiles. This has moved the dating of the fine mosaic in the south aisle of the church into the fourteenth century instead of the thirteenth.

The pavement in the abbot's lodging was far coarser, a pseudomosaic construction made of odds and ends left over from production of other floors. The central geometric panels were edged with a border of irregularly shaped tiles, many of which showed hand decoration. Among them were sectional tiles, segments akin to painted glass

W

window quarries, showing inscribed, multicolored pictures of animals, people, and architectural detail at various scales. Brilliant figures in red/brown, green, and yellow were depicted against a black background. The pictures include a Fall, identical to that in front of the altar in Prior Crauden's Chapel at Ely, a knight with accoutrements, heraldic lions and mythical beasts, and a horse. The backs and sides of the tiles display copious markings of Arabic numerals, Latin words and phrases, and symbols, which are a set of craftsmen's laying instructions. The pictures include a life-size effigy of an ecclesiastical figure, probably the posthumous representation of the first abbot, Simon.

The pavements are displayed in Bedford Museum.

FURTHER READINGS

Baker, Evelyn M. Un artiste majeur a l'oeuvre a Warden Abbey, Bedfordshire. *Revue de l'art* (1984) 63:77–78.

————. Craftsmanship and Design in Floors for the Wealthy: Some Implications of the Warden Abbey Pavements. In *Rotterdam Papers 4*. Ed. J.G.N. Renaud. Rotterdam: Coordinatie Commissie van Advies Inzake Archeologisch Onder Zoek Binnen het Ressort Rotterdam, 1985, pp. 5–21.

————. Images, Ceramic Floors, and Warden Abbey. *World Archaeology* (1987) 18(3):363–381.

————. The Warden Abbey Pavements: Fine Art on a Floor. In *Studies in Cistercian Art and Architecture 4*. Ed. Meredith Parsons Lillich. Cistercian Studies Series 134. Kalamazoo: Cistercian Publications, 1993, pp. 59–77.

Eames, Elizabeth E. Medieval Pseudo-Mosaic Tiles. *Journal of the British Archaeological Association* (1975) 38:81–89.

Keen, Laurence. The Fourteenth Century Tile Pavements in Prior Crauden's Chapel, and in the South Transept. *Medieval Art and Architecture at Ely Cathedral, British Archaeological Association Conference Transactions* (1979) 2:47–57.

Evelyn Baker

SEE ALSO
Tiles

Water Supply

A water supply is one of the main prerequisites for the foundation of a settlement. Different sources were used: in some cases, water was taken directly from rivers; in others, wells were used; in still others, pipe systems took the water from rivers or springs. The different systems are well known and researched in England, France, and Germany.

There are only a very few hints that water-supply systems from Roman times were still in use in the early Medieval period. Pipe systems mainly supported cloisters (e.g., St. Gallen, Christchurch at Canterbury, and Weissenburg and Lobbes in France, tenth century) as well as residences of the German emperors and castles (e.g., Harzburg, Germany).

From 1200 onward, cities were usually provided with water by a pipe system. Different materials were used for the pipes: clay, stone, wood, and metal. The connections from one pipe to another differed greatly (Fig. 1). In Germany, the construction supporting the pipes was called *Wasserkunst*. Usually, the pipes supplied wells in public places for everyone's use, as well as public and private houses which were organized in special water societies.

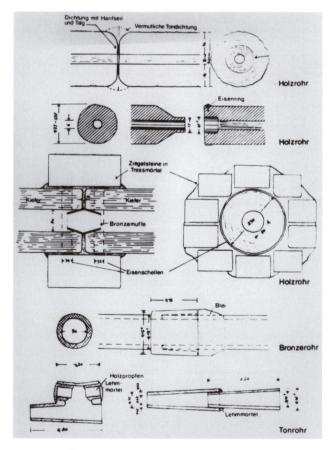

FIG. 1. Different connections between water pipes from the city of Celle, Germany (after Busch 1991).

Public wells, as well as those on private ground, continued to be used in the cities until the end of the nineteenth century, especially by the fire fighters, which were usually organized by neighborhood.

In excavations of medieval towns, wells are important for stratigraphy and for the chronology of their finds. Wells remained the main source of fresh water in the cities and rural settlements throughout the Middle Ages (Fig. 2). Their construction varied greatly. The oldest ones (dating to prehistoric times) were built of wood; later they were built of brick and, finally, of limestone or sandstone. The constructions above the wells for hoisting water ranged from simple structures to buildings in stone, which were remarkable sights on squares in the medieval towns.

Getting rid of dirty water was a great problem, especially for medieval towns. At first, sewers on private ground or channels were the only possibilities. From late medieval times onward, these systems were developed and came into use in castles and representative buildings. Underground channels led to the areas outside the castles or towns, and even rainwater was occasionally led out of the cities by these systems. Throughout the Middle Ages and up to the second half of the nineteenth century, the water supply and the sewers were a great hygienic problem and a source of many epidemic diseases.

FURTHER READINGS

Busch, R. Die Wasserversorgung des Mittelalters und der frühen Neuzeit in norddeutschen Städten. In *Stadt im Wandel.* Vol. 4. C. Meckseper. Braunschweig: Edition Cantz, Stuttgart-Bad Cannstatt, 1985, pp. 301–315.

Frontinus-Gesellschaft, ed. *Die Wasserversorgung im Mittelalter.* Geschichte der Wasserversorgung 4. Mainz: Philipp von Zabern, 1991.

R. Busch

Wat's Dyke

Behind the line of Offa's Dyke in northwestern England runs a very similar earthwork, the as yet undated Wat's Dyke. This consists of a bank and ditch, more regular in outline and more strongly sited than the longer Offa's Dyke. It runs from the coast at Basingwerk to the marches just north of the River Vrynwy (a tributary of the Severn) in the south. The line includes several defensive works, particularly the magnificent hillfort of Old Oswestry, and is altogether a more formidable obstacle. Recent work has demonstrated that it is 67 km long with no major gaps.

While it is dated by analogy to the Anglo-Saxon period, it lacks at present any context.

David Hill

SEE ALSO
Offa's Dyke

West Stow

West Stow is an early Anglo-Saxon village located near the River Lark in the northwest corner of Suffolk, England. The site is important because it was the first completely excavated Anglo-Saxon village in England. The Anglo-Saxon settlement at West Stow was discovered in 1947 during the excavation of a Romano-British pottery kiln on the site. Preliminary excavations were directed by Vera Evison between 1957 and 1961; however, the major program of excavation was undertaken by Stanley West, then county archaeologist for Suffolk, between 1965 and 1972.

Ceramic evidence suggests that West Stow was occupied from c. A.D. 420 to c. A.D. 650. Thus, the initial occupation coincided with the end of the Roman period in Britain, and the site was abandoned at the beginning of the Christian, middle Saxon period. Written sources are almost nonexistent for this period, and archaeology provides almost all our evidence for day-to-day life in pagan Saxon times. The excavations at West Stow are particularly important because they have provided detailed evidence for settlement patterns and animal-husbandry practices.

The Anglo-Saxon excavations at West Stow revealed seventy sunken-featured buildings (Grübenhäuser) clustered around seven small post-built structures termed *halls.* The sunken-featured buildings are composed of a pit, usually c. 5 m long, with one to three postholes located in the short ends of the pit. The archaeological evidence from West Stow indicates that the pits formed cellars or storage spaces under larger timber floors. These small structures might have served as workshops, sheds, or dwellings. The outlines of the larger rectangular timbered halls were revealed archaeologically by lines of postholes. A group of sunken-featured buildings clusters around each timber hall, and West has suggested that each hall cluster was occupied by a extended family group. Not more than three hall clusters appear to have been occupied at any one time, so West Stow is really more of a hamlet than a true village. Since 1974, archaeologists have attempted to reconstruct some of the buildings at

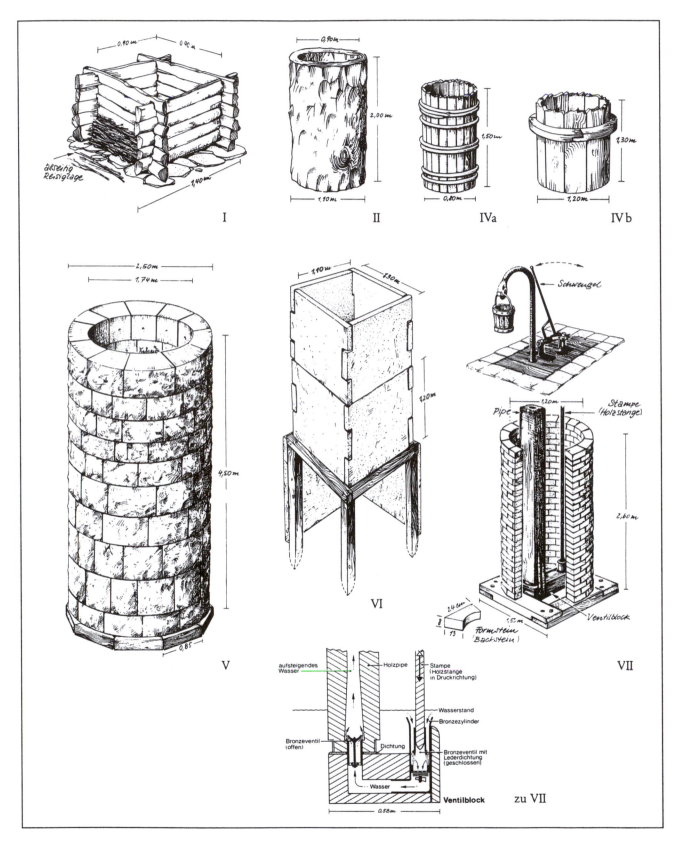

FIG. 2. Wells in the city of Braunschweig, Germany (after Rötting 1985): *I*, tenth century; *II*, thirteenth century; *IVa*, fourteenth century; *IVb*, eighteenth century; *V*, c. fifteenth century; *VI*, first half of the nineteenth century; *VII*, seventeenth century.

West Stow. Today visitors to the site can see several reconstructed sunken-featured buildings and a reconstructed hall.

The West Stow excavations also yielded an enormous faunal collection (more than 185,000 animal bones and bone fragments), which has provided unparalleled evidence for early Anglo-Saxon husbandry practices. The early Anglo-Saxon inhabitants of West Stow raised large numbers of sheep, but they also kept cattle, pigs, horses, chickens, ducks, geese, and a small number of goats. Sheep would have been particularly well suited to the relatively dry environment of the West Stow region. The denizens of West Stow supplemented their diet by hunting, fishing, and fowling. The animals they hunted include red deer, roe deer, and a range of water birds and waders, including swans and white-fronted geese. Most of the fish were perch and pike that would have been available in the River Lark. Plant remains from West Stow indicate that the site's inhabitants also raised wheat and barley. The plant and animal evidence suggests that West Stow's residents practiced a very successful, broadly based farming economy.

FURTHER READINGS

Crabtree, P.J. *West Stow, Suffolk: Early Anglo-Saxon Animal Husbandry.* East Anglian Archaeology Report 47. Ipswich: Suffolk County Planning Department, 1989.

West, S.E. *West Stow: The Anglo-Saxon Village.* East Anglian Archaeology Report 24. Ipswich: Suffolk County Planning Department, 1985.

Pam J. Crabtree

A reconstructed building in West Stow, Suffolk.

SEE ALSO
Animal Husbandry

Wharram Percy

Wharram Percy is the site of a medieval village on the chalk Wolds of Yorkshire in northeast England. A program of excavation, field survey, and documentary research began there in the early 1950s. For the next forty years, the Wharram Research Project continued to be the principal research project on English medieval rural settlement.

The prominent earthwork remains of Wharram Percy, which are now protected and maintained for the visiting public, indicate a settlement that, at its maximum size, would have contained thirty–forty peasant farmsteads. Each farmstead included a house and outbuildings within the toft (the enclosure that includes the peasant's house and farmyard) and an adjacent, enclosed croft (a small enclosed field). The rows of tenements outline an irregular triangle, the village green, crossed by hollow trackways giving access to and through the surrounding arable fields. At the northern end of the settlement, a rectilinear earthwork enclosure containing traces of large buildings has the formal characteristics of a manorial homestead. Near the southern end of the village stand the ruins of a medieval parish church that served both this and neighboring communities. Beyond the church is a late medieval fishpond, reconstituted after excavation, which was originally the pond of a water-powered cornmill. The only surviving buildings in the village area form a row of three estate-workers' cottages built c. 1850 out of a range of eighteenth-century farm buildings.

Archaeological excavations at Wharram Percy were originally carried out with the limited aim of establishing the period of depopulation. In 1952, however, there was a radical revision of research objectives. For the first time in England, there was to be a major program of excavation designed to analyze the material culture of medieval peasant farmers, redressing the balance of information that had formerly been weighted overwhelmingly toward high-status settlements—manor houses, castles, and the like. The Medieval Village Research Group was founded in that year, and it established the Wharram Project as its principal research focus. The buildings and tofts of two peasant farmsteads were examined, using open-area excavation techniques for the first time on an English medieval site.

Though the exploration of peasant culture continued for the next two decades, additional aspects of medieval

W

village life were also investigated concurrently. One of the peasant tofts proved unexpectedly to be sited on the undercroft of a twelfth-century manorial building, demonstrating significant change in the organization of the community during the thirteenth century and raising important questions about the origins and growth of the village. Similar questions were addressed in a major program of work on the medieval parish church and graveyard.

The church had remained in ecclesiastical use, serving neighboring communities, until the late 1940s. Thereafter it suffered structural decay, culminating in the partial collapse of the tower a decade later. The stabilization of the building as a ruin provided a rare opportunity to survey and record the standing structure in detail and to compare the results with evidence provided by excavation. Ultimately, the whole of the church interior was excavated, along with the sites of the aisles, chapels, and earlier chancel, which lay outside the extant walls. From its origins as a small, two-cell stone building of the late tenth or the eleventh century—possibly with a timber predecessor—the church underwent a complete rebuilding in the twelfth century, a series of expansions up to the fourteenth century, and a gradual contraction between the fourteenth and seventeenth centuries. Excavation beneath and around the building, and more extensively in the graveyard to the west and north of the church, produced the remains of nearly a thousand human skeletons, providing significant data on the medieval population of Wharram parish and on the topographical development of the churchyard itself.

During the 1970s, attention shifted from the church to the pond and dam immediately to the south. Investigation of the pond sediments was intended to recover environmental data, which are otherwise sparse on this site, as well as organic artifacts. Examination of the dam, which provided a sequence from the late Saxon period (c. 850–1066) onward, was intended to explore water utilization in an area where surface streams occur only rarely.

In the same decade, and in line with the changing emphasis of research nationally, a number of trenches were excavated across various village boundary banks in an attempt to chart the origins and growth of the medieval settlement and its ground plan, and to relate village boundaries to the wider evidence of early farming landscapes. The first model of development involved a simple outward expansion: an original Anglo-Saxon nucleus near the church and stream, with gradual expansion northward and westward onto the plateau. This was shown to be incorrect when both the initial small-scale trenches and later larger-scale excavations of boundaries and trackways indicated widespread activity in this part of the plateau in the Iron Age, Roman, and early and middle Saxon periods.

Excavation has been too limited to determine whether these discoveries signify activity focused on several distinct settlement nuclei or whether the whole of the medieval village area was occupied just as extensively in Anglo-Saxon and earlier times as it was in the twelfth and thirteenth centuries. Whatever the case, there is now some evidence to suggest that the plan of the medieval village as defined by earthwork remains was created as a deliberate act of policy in late Saxon or Norman times. Furthermore, fieldwork in the surrounding parish has demonstrated that the farming landscape was planned (or replanned) in the late Saxon period, creating a framework for open-field agriculture.

Investigations at Wharram Percy have been concerned with the decline and abandonment of the settlement, as well as with its origins and growth. Documentary evidence suggests that most of the farmsteads had been depopulated by c. 1520, though the vicarage remained, probably with at least one farmstead nearby. The site of the late medieval vicarage has been excavated, along with the adjacent remains of its seventeenth- and eighteenth-century successors. So, too, has the site of a postmedieval farmstead, shown to have been occupied in the seventeenth century and rebuilt in the late eighteenth century; it was finally abandoned c. 1850. Its courtyard-plan ranges of farm buildings have been examined, including one range that still stands, having been converted into cottages in the nineteenth century.

The program of excavations at Wharram Percy served as a barometer for the changing orientations of English medieval settlement studies over almost half a century. Yet, the amount of excavation carried out in each of the forty years spent on the site was relatively small; more than 90 percent of the settlement area remains unexcavated. The first detailed report on the work appeared in 1979, and the process of publishing continues via York University Archaeological Publications.

FURTHER READINGS

Beresford, M., and J.G. Hurst. *Wharram Percy: Deserted Medieval Village.* London: Batsford/English Heritage, 1990.

Stuart Wrathmell

Winchester
See England.

Woodland

Woodland was present in most parts of medieval Europe but to varying degrees. In Norway, Russia, Germany, Italy, and the Alps, there were (and still are) unbroken forests extending for tens of kilometers at a stretch. In Spain and Greece, woods were much more localized. In parts of England and in much of Ireland and Crete, woodland was rare and precious. There were also non-woodland trees scattered in fields and hedges. Not every settlement possessed woodland or even trees of its own.

Woodland history is based partly on written sources, but these never tell a complete story. Forest history in general can be reconstructed from palynology, although medieval pollen diagrams are often more difficult to date and interpret than those of earlier periods. Evidence from field archaeology and from the trees and plants of surviving woodlots complements the written record. The history of woodland comes from the history and archaeology of individual sites rather than from contemporary generalizations.

Medieval woodland consisted of many species of trees. It was not necessarily a survival of prehistoric wildwood. In Europe, almost any abandoned land tends to turn into woodland. Much woodland had sprung up after the end of the Roman Empire and contained Roman and earlier sites. Where woodland was extensive, especially in the early Middle Ages, it was often regarded as vacant land that could be grubbed out and made into farmland. Where woodland was scarce, it tended to become privately owned and managed; it was a major resource of some abbeys. Destruction often ended in the fourteenth century, when plague and depression halted the expansion of farming; in some regions, woodlands increased.

Especially in sparsely wooded countries such as England, woodland was actively managed and conserved. Felling of trees kept roughly in balance with their regrowth, and the woodland did not diminish. Often woods were coppiced—the trees felled on a cycle of years and allowed to grow again from the stump to provide a perpetual succession of poles and logs, used in construction, for fencing, and for domestic and industrial fuel.

The underwood produced by this process is not to be confused with timber from trees allowed to grow bigger. The choice of which species to treat as timber varied; the favorite timber of England was oak; of Spain, pine; of Tuscany, sweet-chestnut; and of Venice, larch.

Wood- and charcoal-burning industries, especially metal smelting and the making of glass, pottery, and bricks, were found all over Europe. Often there was a long-standing relationship between an industry and a particular tract of coppice woods. For centuries, the kings of England made a regular income from leasing the woods of the Forest of Dean to charcoal burners and iron smelters.

Medieval woodlots often still exist. They have their own proper names; they can be identified from documents and recognized on maps by their characteristic shapes with sinuous or zigzag outlines. They may be bounded, and sometimes subdivided, by massive banks and ditches or walls. These served to keep out animals that might eat the regrowth; they demonstrate the importance attached to woodland conservation. In England and France, woods are often separated from roads by linear clearings made to give travelers security from highwaymen. Industrial use is indicated by charcoal hearths, circular platforms typically 5–10 m across, scooped into slopes. Huge coppice stools resulting from medieval woodsmanship are still alive today in many countries.

Produce from medieval woodland sometimes survives and can be used to reconstruct the conditions in which the trees grew. In timber-framed buildings, the timbers often demonstrate a prolific production and rapid turnover of small trees. Excavations of ships and bridges also produce medieval timber. Coppice produce is found in the wattle panels of timber buildings, in excavated waterfronts and similar structures, and (in the form of charcoal) can be identified from hearths and industrial sites.

Timber in buildings can sometimes be used for dating by the science of dendrochronology, provided that at least one hundred annual rings are preserved and there is some evidence of provenance.

In other circumstances, woodland was used for pasturage, whether of cattle, sheep, or deer. Since grasses do not flourish in shade, and grazing animals tend to eat the regrowth of trees, such wood pastures often took the form of savanna, grassland with scattered trees. The trees were often pollarded or shredded—the branches regularly cropped to yield fuel or leaves for feeding animals. Pigs, ordinarily fed on rubbish, were fattened on acorns in autumn, a use of trees that diminished down the centuries

W

except in the western Mediterranean. The acorns of local species of oak were (and are) a human food in Spain; chestnuts were an important foodstuff in Italy.

Savanna has probably been underestimated because it is difficult to recognize archaeologically or in documents. The best evidence is the trees themselves. Wood pastures with living medieval trees can be seen chiefly in England and Greece, less often in France and Spain.

FURTHER READINGS

Moreno, D. *Dal documento al terreno: Storie e archeologia dei sistemi agro-silvo-pastorali.* Bologna: Il Mulino, 1990.

Rackham, O. *Trees and Woodland in the British Landscape.* 2nd ed. London: Dent, 1990.

Rackham, O., and J.A. Moody. *The Making of the Cretan Landscape.* Manchester: Manchester University Press, 1995.

Wickham, C. European Forests in the Early Middle Ages: Landscape and Land Clearance. *Settimana di studio del Centro italiano di studi sull'alto medioeva* (1989) 37:479–548.

Oliver Rackham

SEE ALSO
Dendrochronology

Worcester

Worcester lies in the English Midlands on a gravel terrace on the east bank of the River Severn, at a natural crossing point. In the Roman period, the site was occupied by a small town engaged primarily in iron smelting from the second to the fourth centuries. The settlement consisted of an enclosure with substantial earthwork defenses at the southern tip of the terrace and a simple grid of streets to the north. Late Roman inhumations in a former industrial area and widespread "dark earth" deposits mark the contraction of the occupied area; the continuity of some former urban features as later boundaries suggests a process of gradual landscape adaptation. The earthwork enclosure became the site of the new cathedral in A.D. 680, but there is also historical evidence for the survival of an active and important British church, later the parish Church of St. Helen's, just within the north gate of the enclosure.

The *burh*—the new fortified town described in a charter of c. A.D. 890—was a rectilinear defended extension or annex to the north of the old earthwork enclosure, reoc-cupying the area of the former street grid. A post-Roman, premedieval ditch and a rampart reveted with robbed Roman masonry have been excavated at a single point on the northern perimeter; these cannot be shown to have been new in the late ninth century, but they were in use in 904, when they appear as the north boundary to a block of property, or *haga,* leased by the bishop of Worcester to the Mercian royal family. The *haga* took up the entire river frontage of the new *burh* and is assumed to have been used (like similar episcopal property in London) for commerce; it may actually have predated the foundation of c. 890. The *burh* marketplace and principal street was the axial High Street. This was lined on either side by large planned rectangular plots; those on the east side backed onto a probable wall street. The core of the new town thus appears to have been another example of late Saxon (c. 850–1066) royal town planning, though on a very much smaller scale than similar ventures in Wessex.

Occupation may soon have outgrown the *burh* defenses. Further acts of town planning, perhaps under Bishop Oswald in the 960s, resulted in the leveling of the northern Roman defenses on either side of the High Street and their replacement by simple street grids. Suburban settlement in Sidbury is known at about the same time. Oswald was also responsible for the building (or rebuilding) of the Cathedral Church of St. Mary alongside the original Church of St. Peter.

Domesday Book figures suggest a possible late eleventh-century population of around two thousand. The built-up area continued to expand, and the extensive planned Foregate suburb was created on episcopal property before c. 1200. Urban growth in the eleventh–thirteenth centuries can also be measured by the colonization of minor lanes and back areas within the pre-Conquest core by dense housing on strip-type plots. The main through-street frontages were probably continuously built up long before the Norman Conquest, though a detailed chronology for this process and for the fragmentation of the identifiable large tenth-century plots is lacking.

Norman impact on the city is seen first in the construction of a motte-and-bailey castle at the expense of part of the cathedral precinct. Bishop Wulfstan's new cathedral church and cloisters were begun in 1084, and the precinct may have been substantially enlarged and replanned at this time.

Of the eleven parish churches in the city by c. 1200, and a similar number of nonparochial chapels, all but three are likely to have been of pre-Conquest origin. Hospitals were founded in the Sidbury and Foregate suburbs in the twelfth century, and friaries were attracted to peripheral intramural sites, one in the thirteenth century and a second in the mid-fourteenth. By the early twelfth century, all but the castle defenses had long been overtaken by built-up area, and the city was almost unprotected, but by c. 1200 or shortly after a new circuit of stone walls was in place.

FURTHER READINGS

Baker, N.J., H. Dalwood, R. Holt, C. Mundy, and G. Taylor. From Roman to Medieval Worcester: Development and Planning in the Anglo-Saxon City. *Antiquity* (1992) 66(250):65–74.

Barker, P.A. The Origins of Worcester. *Transactions of the Worcester Archaeological Society,* 3rd ser. (1968–1969), 2.

Bassett, S.R. Churches in Worcester before and after the Conversion of the Anglo-Saxons. *Antiquaries Journal* (1989) 69:225–256.

Carver, M.O.H., ed. Medieval Worcester. *Transactions of the Worcestershire Archaeological Society,* 3rd ser. (1980), 7.

N. J. Baker

York

See England; Urban Archaeology.

Index

C

E

Edmund, son of Aethelred II, 42
Edmund, king of Wessex, 142
edor, meaning of, 344
Edward the Confessor, 211
Edward the Elder, Saxon king
    and *Burghal Hidage*, 40
    and East Anglia, 238
    and Hyde Abbey, 170–171
    and London, 210
    and urbanism, 77
Edward I, king of England, 54, 148
    conquest of Wales, 369, 373
Edward III, king of England, 29
Edward IV, king of England, 148
Edwards, N., 368
Edwin of Northumbria, 49
Egara, 364
Egbert of Wessex, 209, 210
eggs, and chicken farming, 4, 260
Egitania, 364
Egyházy-Jurovská, B., 27
Eichstätt, 138
Eider River, 251
Eifel, 326
einkorn, 250
Eketorp, animal remains, 10
Elbe River
    and Hamburg, 154
    and Lombards, 207
    Slavic settlements, 85, 86, 89, 92
Elblag, 280
Elche hoard, 364
1155 Extent, 147
Elisenhof, wurt excavation, 140, 251
Eliska Přemyslovna, queen of Moravia, 32
Eliska Rejcka, queen of Moravia, 32
Elnone, 294
Ely Cathedral, 375, 376
Emden, wurt excavation, 140
emmer, 250
emporia, **92–97**, 364
    Dorestad, 94–95
    Fishergate, York, 98–99
    Hamwic, 95–96
    location/features of, 92, 94
    and market development, 217–219
    meaning of, 92
    Ribe, 93–94
    Types A-B-C emporia, 93
Ems, wurt excavation, 140
enamel jewelry, production of, 195, 197
Engendering Archaeology: Women and Prehistory (Gero and Spector), 129
England, **97–101**
    Anglo-Saxon archaeology, 99–101
    animal husbandry, 1–2, 4, 10
    barrows sites, 13, 14
    Boss Hall cemetery, 24–25
    Bristol, 27–29
    Burghal Hidage, 40
    burial practices, 47
    Cadbury Castle, 41–42
    castles of, 43, 44
    Chester, 53–55
    cloth production, 59, 61

coinage of, 63, 64
and Danes, 279
deserted medieval villages, 76, 77
emporia of, 93, 95–96, 98, 100
fair site, 93
fishweirs, 109–110
Glastonbury, 141–145
Grove Priory, 147–148
Hartlepool, 155–159
hedges, 159
High Medieval period, 101
Hyde Abbey, 170–171
Ipswich, 173–175
London, 208–211
medieval archaeological activities, 97–101, 353
mill sites, 223–225
Mucking, 226–228
Norman Conquest (1066), 43
Norton Priory, 236–237
Norwich, 237–238
pilgrim souvenirs, 253–254, 255
place names, 255–256
Raunds Area Project, 278–279
rescue archaeology, 280, 281
Roman sites, Anglo-Saxon terms for, 256
Roman withdrawal from, 99–100
shipbuilding, 311
Shrewsbury, 314–315
Snape cemetery, 321
Spong Hill, 324–325
survey method, 328–329
Sutton Hoo, 330–332
Thetford, 339–340
Tintagel, 343
trade with Ireland, 27, 29
Warden Abbey, 375–376
Wat's dyke, 377
West Stow, 377–378
Wharram Percy, 379–380
Worcester, 382–383
environmental archaeology, methods of, 353
environmental conditions
    and animal husbandry, 1–2, 9
    and dendrochronology, 75
    and farm abandonment, 104
environmental protection, of woodland, 170
Eoforwic, 353
Eorpeburnan, 40
epidemics
    and farm abandonment, 103
    Iceland, 103
    plague of Justinian, 270
    and water supply, 377
Epona, goddess, 225
eränkäynti (wilderness resource utilization), Finland, 106, 107
Erdmann, W., 138
erosion, and farm abandonment, 104
Erosion of History: Archaeology and Planning In Towns (Heighway), 280
Espec, Walter, 375
Essai sur l'architecture réligieuse du moyen âge (Caumont), 112
Essertines, private fortification at, 119
Essex, 209
    fishweirs of, 110
estate plans, 283

G

Winchester (*cont.*)
  royal treasury site, 196
Winchester Cathedral, Norman rebuilding of, 100
windmills, 224–225
windows, church archaeology, 57
Windsor Castle, private lodging of, 45
wine, 95, 127, 173, 354
Winiary, 259
Winkelmann, W., 140
Wirral Park, 145
Witham River, fishweirs of, 110
woad plant, dye of, 61, 83, 84
Woden, god, 256
Wollin, 139
  as emporium, 127
women
  castle-builder, 177
  childbearing and death, 46
  gender and archaeological studies, 129–130
  grave goods of, 24, 25, 38
  as jewelry-makers, 196
  life expectancy, 46, 317
  studies of skeletal remains, 317
  and yarn spinning, 61
wood, dendrochronological dating of, 69, 74–75
Wood Quay, 281
  animal remains, 10, 261
woodland, **381–382**
  coppicing, 159, 251, 381
  maintenance of, 381
  parks, 252
  pollarding, 159, 251, 381
  wood, uses of, 381
Woodnesborough, 256
wool cloth
  Bristol, 29
  dyes for, 61
  production of, 59
  yarn spinning/preparation, 60
wool production, sheep, 3, 4, 11
Wootz steel, 184
Worcester, 256, **382–383**
  churches of, 382
  Normans in, 382
  Romans in, 382
Worcestershire, 7
World War II
  destruction of Bristol, 29
  and medieval archaeology, 97–98, 111, 140, 352
  and rescue archaeology, 280
worsted yarn, 60

wrought iron, 182
Wroxeter, 256
Wulfstan, Bishop of Worcester, 382
wurts, Germany, 140, 251
Würzberg, 140
Wye River, 243, 371
Wykeham, 256

X

Xanten, 48, 138

Y

yardlands, 244
Yare River, 237
yarn, spinning/preparation of, 60–61
Yassi Ada, shipwreck at, 229
yaws, skeletal remains studies, 318
Yeavering, Venerable Bede on, 6
yellow, dye, 84
yellow fever, 270
York
  animal remains, 10
  cloth making, 61
  dye artifacts, 83, 84
  as emporium, 93, 98–99, 100
  excavations of, 98–99, 100
  Viking Age sites, 99
York Archaeological Research Center, 99
York Archaeological Trust, 98, 99
York Minster, 49
Yorkshire, 225
Yorkshire Wolds, 246
Yorvik, Viking city, 99
Yorvik Viking Center, 99

Z

Z-spinning, 61
Zadora-Rio, Elisabeth, 117, 118
Zagreb, 36
Zamora, 364
Ziani, Sebastiani, doge of Venice, 358
Zidenice, 30
Zimmermann, H.W., 138, 140
Zodan, Avar prince, 167
Zoller, D., 140
Žuran, barrows, 13